D1262116

With best wishes from the authors

The World's Columbian Commission

invites you to participate in the Ceremonies attending the Dedication of the Buildings of the World's Columbian Exposition at Jackson Park in the City of Chicago October 11th, 12th and 13th, 1892 and requests the favor of an early acceptance.

Annotated Bibliography:

World's Columbian Exposition, Chicago 1893

With Illustrations and Price Guide

—————— · ——————

Over 2700 items described

. . . BASED UPON . . .

personal visits to 27 libraries,
responses from major collectors and dealers, plus
correspondence with more than 125 other libraries and sources.

. . . ALSO CONTAINING . . .

a schematic diagram of the organization of the World's Columbian Exposition,
a detailed map of the grounds, extensive state and national
legislative information, 250 photographs of selected
items, as well as a compilation of
recent books analyzing the
1893 Fair.

. . . AIDS INCLUDE . . .

a listing of sources of
World's Columbian Exposition material,
a citation key, an exhaustive cross referenced index,
significant corrections to previous bibliographic errors and
generous space allotted for noting new items and additional information.

by

G. L. Dybwad, Ph.D.

Joy V. Bliss, M.D., J.D.

Number 318 of 1000 Copies

The Book Stops Here
Albuquerque, New Mexico
1992

DEDICATION

Dedicated to the people of Chicago and Illinois who won and lost the 1992 World's Fair commemorating 500 years in the new world since Christopher Columbus. Had they hosted the Fair, it would have been continuing proof 100 years later of the vitality, financial and administrative resourcefulness, growth potential, civic pride and spirit which they had displayed so successfully for the world in the 1890's. This reversal in regional self attitude in just 100 years will be the subject of historical, political, economic, educational and entertainment comparisons and critiques for many years.

Dybwad, G. L., and Joy V. Bliss
Annotated Bibliography: World's Columbian Exposition, Chicago 1893 : With Illustrations and Price Guide

Includes index.
1. World's Columbian Exposition, 1893.

ISBN 0-9631612-0-2 (Paper).
Library of Congress Catalog Card Number: 91-077456.

For information: The Book Stops Here, Publisher
1108 Rocky Point Court N.E., Albuquerque, NM, 87123-1952.

First Edition.

Front cover illustration: "Statue of the Republic" by Daniel French. Original in gilt at the Grand Basin.
Frontispiece illustration: Invitation to the World's Columbian Exposition opening ceremonies.
Back cover illustration: "Chicago Personified" by Thomas Nast.
Citation illustrations: Laser scanned diffusion halftones.

Printed in the United States of America by Cooper Press, Albuquerque, NM.

TABLE OF CONTENTS

INTRODUCTION

My interest in the Victorian "gay '90s" World's Columbian Exposition started as a tangent to a collecting interest in government issued postal cards. The printing, print variations, and cancellation marks of these penny postal cards were interesting. The correspondence and advertiser graphics made them unique. See *United States Postal Card Catalog #2320*. The United States government only issued a few exposition theme cards; most of the address faces were covered with a pictorial scene. The colorful lithography and design by the American Lithograph Co., New York, made the four original Columbian Exposition cards (S10 U.S. Grant, 1¢) very popular at the Fair. Many printings, ink and design variations brought the total number of U.S. Government Columbian cards to over 75. Having obtained some of these cards, my curiosity expanded to learn more about the Fair, its buildings, and the events which had generated the cards.

My search for World's Columbian Exposition (WCE) items extended to garage sales, auctions, flea markets, and antique shows. I bought a wide variety of items associated with the Fair since I found their quality, variety and nostalgia value to be high. As time went along, I concentrated on books and ephemera as they contain the most information. Period WCE books and magazines were natural collectibles for me because of my enjoyment of books and archival book repair. Buying and selling WCE books has also increased the number of knowledgeable, enthusiastic, and interesting World's Fair collectors I have met.

This bibliography started as a way of putting my WCE book collection to use; it grew into a major WCE library and private collection search. A motivating factor for starting this work was the approach of the 100th anniversary of the WCE. A few WCE collectibles books have been issued but no bibliography exists. It is primarily intended to be a reference, annotated with visual descriptions of the items. When known, prices are included. Included are WCE facts -- as well as highlights regarding the indefatigable people whose cumulative efforts ensured the WCE would remain an important event in American history.

G. L. D.

- Pricing -

Based upon condition, price variations may be large -- as it is for other collectibles. The price range listed varies as condition improves from medium condition (extensive shelf wear and rubbing; often loose or chipped bindings and pages; minor staining) to excellent condition (little noticeable shelf wear; sound binding; minor edge damage and little or no staining). If a single price is listed, it comes from a recent reference or sales catalog. In all cases, the book has all of its pages and illustrations. A book dealer will very typically buy these WCE books at 3/4 to 1/4 of the retail price; the price range given represents current auction or dealer discount prices. "Retail" price may range up to twice the values listed.

Scarcity plays an equal if not larger role than condition in determining value. Generally speaking, the non souvenir books command the highest price. Non souvenir books include reports by the states and literature handed out by the states and countries exhibiting at the Fair. Some reports, e.g., U.S. Government and religious congress records, though printed in small numbers and relatively scarce, do not command exceptional prices because of the subject matter. Limited editions, souvenir or otherwise, may have higher value. Books which exhibit fine examples of the printers' and binders' art are expected to bring elevated prices; special weight is given to books which contain colored plates. The few books which have established themselves as prime references and describers of the WCE are valuable because demand exceeds supply.

Prices will vary from those listed; for instance, an item owned or signed by a famous person will be of greater value. Regional higher prices can be expected in Chicago and Illinois, New York and California. In general, there is no price variation for the listed variants unless the binding is exceptional -- e.g., full leather.

- Content -

This bibliography is organized by subject to aid the reader in determining content. Since some items could easily fit into two or more categories, use the index to determine the location. View books issued by the WCE

Department of Publicity and Promotion are in "View Books." Guides and catalogs issued by the WCE Department of Publicity and Promotion are in "Guides." Guides to state exhibits are in "States and Cities;" guides to foreign exhibits are in "Foreign Publications."

The "General" chapter covers a variety of topics including histories, railroad publications, cookbooks, personal travel accounts, exhibit descriptions, items issued by commercial companies and pamphlets on the Sunday opening/closing debate. "General" also contains samples of some of the more interesting and high quality advertising pamphlets; they, and advertising trade cards, deserve whole volumes of their own.

A few examples of books on Christopher Columbus, issued during 1892-93, are included. Columbus items are collectible. Columbus bibliographies and compilations are available elsewhere -- e.g., the microfilm set of Library of Congress holdings.

Those magazines and newspapers located and known to have at least one article on the Fair are included (Chapter 7) as are their bound versions (Chapter 8). Since the Fair was very popular, most magazines and newspapers of the day probably contained reference to the Fair, so the list is incomplete. Some example articles have been included with selected magazines. Many professional organizations had one or more issues of their publication devoted to their presence, exhibit, or interest in the Fair. These publications are valuable sources of in depth and specific information and deserve an extended bibliography of their own.

Listed in "Recent Books" are some of the many items written about the WCE after 1901. Many are still available at reasonable cost; prices are not listed. These books and theses offer a wide spectrum of history, analysis, and critique of the Fair's and its time's impact, significance, and failings. The perspective they bring is often illuminating and generally complementary of the magic the Fair produced.

A brief list of "Unpublished Unique Works" -- diaries, scrapbooks, and miscellaneous holdings -- is included for reference purposes as well as a way to show how the Fair touched people personally. The final chapter is a listing of items from fairs "Before and After the WCE." Numerous items from the Madrid fair were displayed at the WCE.

Variants of minor and major proportions were found. They include variations in publisher, author, cover, paging, illustration, and content. We have included variants because they are important for WCE authors and researchers as content may differ in different versions of the same book.

- Book Format -

The title page title is given as completely as possible to reduce confusion on items where titles are nearly identical. Also, a complete title describes the contents for many 100 year old books.

This book is formatted leaving generous spaces between entries so that notes, prices, variants, and other new information may be added by the owner. Explanatory keys for citation format and abbreviations are found at page ix and page x.

The index is alphabetical by author, when known, and by title. Thus, entries with both are listed twice in the index. The book paragraph number, rather than its page number, is given so that the item may be found more easily in the text.

The citation model used by the Library of Congress is generally followed. Library of Congress copyright information is used for some bracketed authors' names; to locate by title, consult the index. We found some bracketed authors a hinderance to locating an item; in these cases, the "author" was moved to the annotation.

The following books were used as guides for bibliographic style when the original text was available:

Gibaldi, Joseph, and Walter S. Achtert. *MLA Handbook for Writers of Research Papers.* 3rd ed. New York: Modern Language Association of America, 1988.

Turabian, Kate L. *A Manual for Writers of Term Papers, Theses, and Dissertations.* 5th ed., rev. and exp. Chicago and London: The University of Chicago Press, 1987.

We referred to the following written source materials:

American Library Association. *The National Union Catalog : Pre-1956 Imprints.* Teikoku Gikai, Japan: James E. Allison & Co., 1973.

British Museum General Catalogue of Printed Books. London: Published by the Trustees of the British Museum, 1965.

Canadian Institute for Historical Microreproductions. *Canada, the printed record: a bibliographic register with indexes to the microfiche series of the Canadian Institute for Historical Microreproductions.* Ottawa: Canadian Institute for Historical Microreproductions, 1981-.

Dictionary catalog of the research libraries of the New York Public Library 1911-1971. N.p.: New York Public Library, printed and distributed by G. R. Hall & Co., [°1979].

Leslie, Stephen, and Sidney Lee. *Dictionary of national biography.* 21 vol. + supplements. New York: The Macmillan co., 1908.

Research Publications Temporary Reel Guide. Woodbridge, CT: Research Publications, Inc., 1989.

Taylor, Earl R., comp. *A Checklist of the Robert A. Feer collection of world fairs of North America.* Boston: Boston Public Library, 1976.

The Winterthur museum libraries collection of printed books and periodicals. Vol. 2. Wilmington, DE [and] London: Scholarly Resources Inc., [1974].

We sadly note that WCE books are becoming ever less available at libraries -- lost, stolen, badly damaged, or removed for microfilming. We wonder how many more WCE researchers will be allowed to handle the vast number of books we perused before many more must be permanently physically removed. We also note the great variation in quality of collections as a whole and in their preservation.

Correspondence solicited. Send additional WCE bibliographic and price information and corrections to: 1108 Rocky Point Ct. N.E., Albuquerque, NM 87123-1952, (505) 296-9047.

G. L. D. and J. V. B.

ACKNOWLEDGMENTS

MANY people helped provide information for this book. The authors especially thank: Dan Amato, Mrs. Charmain Andrews, Leslie K. and Beth R. Arnold, Edna A. Bliss, Marcie J. Bliss, Michael R. and Heidi Bliss, Nancy Brown, Timothy Carr, Ivana Cerna, Cathy Cherbosque, Allison Cowgill, Kathy Coyle, Thomas J. Diddle, Carole Drachler, Barbara E. Dybwad, Dan J. Dybwad, Pauline Ellingson, John Emerson, Amy J. Farnstrom, William Feis, Russ Frank, Edna F. Graham, Leo John Harris, Glenn Longacre, Yngvar Lundh, Ronald Mahoney, Andrea Mark, Elmer Martinez, Bridgett Mathews, Claire McCann, V. Eileen Mee, Steve Mobile, Larry Moeder, Gladys K. Mudgett, Rhoda S. Ratner, Al Raymond, Shizuko G. Santistevan, Dr. Stephen Sheppard, Beverly Thompson, Solveiga L. Unger, Pam Zaebst, Karen Zimmerman.

The library staff members were always helpful and we sincerely thank them. All are commended for their help and patience in making this book as complete and accurate as possible. The full list of libraries, sources contacted, and their abbreviations follows.

SOURCE ABBREVIATIONS
(Arranged alphabetically)

A:	Dan Amato, Columbus Museum, Columbus, WI
AIC:	The Art Institute of Chicago
AKLRL:	Alaska Legislative Reference Library, Juneau
AkSt:	Alaska State Library, Juneau
ALB:	State U of New York - Albany
ArkHx:	Arkansas Historical Society
ANQ:	Assemblée Nationale, Québec, PQ
AzHx:	Arizona Historical Society, Phoenix and Tuscon
*BCM:	Bowdoin College, Brunswick, ME
BM:	British Museum, London
BPL:	Boston Public Library
BU:	Boston U, Boston, MA
cat:	Auction or sales catalog
*CHx:	Chicago Historical Society Library
CoU:	Colorado U, Boulder
*CPL:	Chicago Public Library
CSA:	California State Archives, Sacramento
*csuf:	California State U - Fresno
CtHx:	The Connecticut Historical Society, Hartford
CU:	Cornell U, Ithaca, NY
CVHx:	Carson Valley Historical Society, Minden, NV
D:	Carole Drachler, private collection
DelHx:	Historical Society of Delaware, Wilmington
E:	Jim Emple, private collection
F:	Russ Frank, private collection
FSA:	Florida State Archives, Tallahassee
GDF:	Grace Dangberg Foundation, Inc., Carson City, NV
*GLD:	Gay Leon Dybwad, private collection
GPL:	Galesburg Public Library, Galesburg, IL
H:	L. John Harris, private collection
*HL:	The Huntington Library, San Marino, CA
HNO:	The Historic New Orleans Collection, New Orleans, LA
HxDC:	The Historical Society of Washington, DC
IaHx:	State Historical Society of Iowa, Des Moines/Iowa City
ICRL:	Center for Research Libraries, Chicago
IdHx:	Idaho State Historical Society, Boise
InHx:	Indiana Historical Society, Indianapolis
JHU:	Johns Hopkins U, Baltimore, MD
KsHx:	Kansas Historical Society, Topeka
*KSU:	Kansas State U, Manhattan
*KU:	Kansas U Libraries, Lawrence
KyU:	U of Kentucky
L:	Richard L'Heureux, private collection
LaMus:	State of Louisiana Office of State Museum, New Orleans
*LC:	Library of Congress
LM:	Lightner Museum, St. Augustine, FL
LMi:	Library of Michigan, Lansing
LSU:	Louisiana State U, Baton Rouge
MaHx:	Massachusetts Historical Society, Boston
*MarL:	Marshall Law School, Chicago
mcg:	McGill U - McLennan Library, Montreal, PQ.
*MnSA:	Minnesota State Archives, St. Paul
MnStL:	Minnesota State Law Library, St. Paul
MPA:	Manitoba Provincial Archives, Winnipeg, MB
MPL:	Milwaukee Public Library, Milwaukee, WI
MsA:	Mississippi Department of Archives and History, Jackson
*NA:	National Archives, Washington, DC
NAC:	National Archives of Canada, Ottawa, ON
ncsu:	North Carolina State U, Raleigh
NeHx:	Nebraska State Historical Society, Lincoln
NHHx:	New Hampshire Historical Society, Concord
NHSt:	New Hampshire State Library, Concord
NJSt:	New Jersey Department of Education, State Library, Trenton
*NL:	Newberry Library, Chicago
NLC:	National Library of Canada, Ottawa, ON
NvSt:	Nevada State Library and Archives, Carson City
nwu:	Northwestern U, Evanston, IL
*NYPL:	New York City Public Library
NYSt:	New York State Library, Albany
OC:	Oberlin College, Oberlin, OH
OhHx:	Ohio Historical Society, Columbus
OrHx:	Oregon Historical Society
OSL:	Oregon State Library, Salem
OSU:	Ohio State U, Columbus
PI:	Pratt Institute, Brooklyn
PU:	Princeton U, Princeton, NJ
R:	Al Raymond, Raymond's Antiques
RPB:	Brown U, Providence, RI
ref:	Another bibliography
RILaw:	Rhode Island State Law Library, Providence
RML:	Rand, McNally Library, Skokie, IL
RRD:	R. R. Donnelley & Sons Co., Chicago
S:	Stephen M. Sheppard, private collection
SamL:	Samford U Law Library, Birmingham, AL
SCAG:	South Carolina Attorney General's Office Library, Clinton
SCSt:	South Carolina State Library, Columbia
*SDHx:	San Diego Historical Society, San Diego, CA
SDSHx:	South Dakota State Historical Society, Pierre
*SFe:	New Mexico State Records Center & Archives - Santa Fe
*SHM:	Spanish History Museum, Albuquerque, NM
*SI:	Smithsonian Institution - American History Library
SLP:	State Library of Pennsylvania, Harrisburg
SMU:	Southern Methodist U, Dallas, TX
SSLa:	State of Louisiana, Secretary of State, Baton Rouge
SStu:	Sangamon State U, Springfield, IL
StLa:	State Library of Louisiana, Baton Rouge
SUL:	Syracuse U College of Law, Syracuse, NY
*TD:	Thomas J. Diddle, private collection
TnSt:	Tennessee State Library & Archives, Nashville
TU:	Tulane U, New Orleans, LA
*U:	Lloyd Unger, private collection
UC:	National Union Catalog
UDe:	U of Delaware, Newark
UFl:	U of Florida, Gainsville
UMC:	U of Missouri - Columbia
UMe:	U of Maine, Orono
UMi:	U of Michigan, Ann Arbor
*UMKC:	U of Missouri - Kansas City
UMSL:	U of Missouri - St. Louis
*UND:	U of North Dakota: Chester Fritz Library
UNe:	U of Nebraska, Lincoln
*UNLV:	U of Nevada - Las Vegas
*UNM:	U of New Mexico Libraries
UNR:	U of Nevada - Reno
*UoC:	U of Chicago
UOL:	U of Oklahoma Law Library, Norman
USD:	U of South Dakota, Vermillion
*USF:	U of South Florida, Tampa, FL
UTn:	U of Tennessee, Knoxville
UVa:	U of Virginia, Charlottesville
UWa:	U of Washington (state) -Seattle
UWy:	U of Wyoming, Laramie
VaHx:	Virginia Historical Society, Richmond
VtSSt:	Vermont Secretary of State
WaSt:	Washington State Library, Olympia
WiHx:	The State Historical Society of Wisconsin, Madison
*WM:	Winterthur Museum and Gardens, Winterthur, DE
WYLaw:	Wyoming State Law Library, Cheyenne
WYMus:	Wyoming State Museum, Cheyenne
Yale:	Yale U, New Haven, CT
*	WCE Maine Building, Poland Spring, ME

* Personal visits.

SOURCE ABBREVIATIONS
(Arranged alphabetically by State and Country)

Alabama: SamL
Alaska: AKLRL, AkSt
Arizona: AzHx, D
Arkansas: ArkHx
California: CSA, csuf, HL, SDHx
Canada: ANQ, mcg, MPA, NAC, NLC
Colorado: CoU
Connecticut: CtHx, YALE
Delaware: DelHx, UDe, WM
District of Columbia: HxDC, LC, NA, SI
England: BM
Florida: FSA, LM, TD, UFl, USF
Idaho: IdHx
Illinois: AIC, CHx, CPL, GPL, ICRL, MarL, NL,
    nwu, RML, RRD, SStU, UoC
Indiana: InHx
Iowa: IaHx
Kansas: KsHx, KSU, KU
Kentucky: KyU
Louisiana: HNO, LaMus, LSU, SSLa, StLa, TU
Maine: BCM, E, L, UMe
Maryland: JHU
Massachusetts: BPL, BU, MaHx
Michigan: LMi, UMi
Minnesota: H, MnSA, MnStL

Mississippi: MsA
Missouri: UMC, UMKC, UMSL
Nebraska: NeHx, UNe
Nevada: CVHx, GDF, NvSt, U, UNLV, UNR
New Hampshire: NHHx, NHSt
New Jersey: PU, NJSt
New Mexico: GLD, SFe, SHM, UNM
New York: ALB, CU, NYPL, NYSt, PI, S, SUL, R
North Carolina: F, ncsu
North Dakota: UND
Ohio: OC, OhHx, OSU
Oklahoma: UOL
Oregon: OrHx, OSL
Pennsylvania: SLP
Rhode Island: RPB, RILaw
South Carolina: SCAG, SCSt
South Dakota: SDSHx, USD
Tennessee: TnSt, UTn
Texas: SMU
Vermont: VtSSt
Virginia: UVa, VaHx
Washington: UWa, WaSt
Wisconsin: A, MPL, WiHx
Wyoming: UWy, WYLaw, WYMus

In addition to the GLD collection, materials for illustrations are provided courtesy of the following:

Art Institute of Chicago (AIC): 574
California State U - Fresno (csuf): 4, 6, 8, 450, 583, 668, 788, 866, 921, 934, 940, 952, 975, 1018, 1137,
    1171, 1612.
Chicago Public Library (CPL) Music Information Center: 1505.
Carole Drachler (D): 1199.
Kansas University (KU): 1569.
New Mexico State Records Center and Archives (SFe): 130, 142, 168, 180, 182, 185, 186, 194, 1988.
Stephen M. Sheppard (S): 28, 885, 1184, 1467, 1469, 1482, 1508, 1509, 1530, 1540, 1544, 1729, 1743.
U of Chicago (UoC): 366, 376, 569, 636, 644, 783, 871, 1668, 2003, 2290.
Karen Zimmerman (USD): 2339.

CITATION KEY

Generic Citation Example

> #. Primary Author. Secondary Author. Tertiary Author. *Title*. Place of Publication: Publisher,
> Date of Publication ᶜDate by whom; Another Place of Publication: Publisher, Date of
> Publication ᶜDate by whom.
>
> Size. Paging. Cover description. Further annotation. [Short notes about author or entry
> which are not found in the text.]
> ---- (found variant)
> ---- Also listed: (listed variant)
> * P   ☺ . (sources) $ Price range
>
> ☞ Notes about the author or entry that are not in the text of the entry, but related.

In order of appearance in the above chart:

a. Paragraph number. Unique to the item; used in the index and for cross-reference.

b. Author. The author(s) are listed in descending order. Titles and degrees, such as Rev., Capt., D.D., are omitted. Author names which appear in brackets are not found on the title page. These authors were obtained from Library of Congress copyright information or elsewhere in the item.

c. Title. The title page title is always used unless otherwise noted. If the cover title is used, the notation is "C.t." When the cover title is the same as the title page, this is noted "C.t= t.p." If the cover title is used but it is not certain whether there is a title page (e.g., missing), the notation is "title given is from cover." When the item has neither cover title nor title page, the title found above the text on the first page is used and the notation is "Caption title."

   Capitals are used when the book title has the word's first letter capitalized, the word follows a period, or the noun is known to be capitalized, e.g., "New Mexico." Lower-case is used everywhere else even though the printed title uses capital letters for entire words. "World's" and "Columbian" are always capitalized; "exposition" is capitalized when capitalized on the title page. A colon preceded and followed by a space denotes a line break; not all line breaks are shown.

d. Publication information. Location(s): publisher(s), and date(s) follow the title. Brackets denote the information is not on the title page. "Company" is consistently abbreviated in the publication data.

e. Size. In centimeters, height followed by width. Both are given when known. Expect minor variations.

f. Pagination. Includes Roman numerals, unpaged pages, leaves, and arabic paging.

g. Cover description. Given when known. Expect color variations due to aging.

h. Annotation. Content annotation is brief since the combination of the chapter heading and full title generally give an excellent idea of the content and intent of the item. Short annotation not found in the item is placed in brackets.

i. "----" denotes found as a variant with noted exceptions.

j.   "---- Also listed:" is a variant card catalog or source listing of the item. When the source information differs significantly from verified information, a "?" is appended.

k.   The last line is reserved for * (importance symbol), P (picture), source locations, and price range. A ☺ means we have seen and verified title page information and give our highest accuracy rating. If a source list is preceded by a period (.), it means we have a copy of the title page (or cover) in our files. The number of sources listed is a rough measure of the availability of the item.

l.   ☞ Parenthetical information which is not found in the citation but related to it.

————◄•►❉•◄•►————

ABBREVIATION KEY

b/w	Black and white illustrations
bldg	Building
ca.	Circa, about
chap.	Chapter
CIHM	Canadian Institute for Historical Microreproductions: Ottawa, Canada.
co.	Company
c.t.	Cover title
c.t.= t.p.	Cover title same as that given on title page
dept	Department
ed.	Edition
GPO	Government Printing Office: Washington, D.C.
hc	Hardcover
illus	Illustration(s), illustrated
l	Leaf, leaves: unpaged bound paper with print or illustration
laid in	Glued in place
n.d.	No date of publication given in book
N.p.	No place of publication given in book
no.	Number
n.p.	No publishing agency given in book
ns	New series
pub info	Publication information
os	Old series
port(s)	Portrait(s)
pt(s)	Part(s)
RPI	Research Publications, Inc. (microfilm): Woodbridge, CT, and Reading, England.
rpt.	Reprint
tipped in	Glued into place
t.p.	Title page
trans	Translation
UMI	University Microfilm International (microfilm): Ann Arbor, MI.
U	University
vol(s)	Volume(s)
wraps	Soft paper cover, wrappers: unless modified by an adjective describing the paper quality.
WCE	World's Columbian Exposition
WF	World's Fair
(xx) p.	Unpaginated counted pages of quantity xx
xx p.	Paginated with xx pages
23x12½	Height in centimeters by width in centimeters (H x W)
*	Excellent book giving much information about WCE
____: ___, ___	Publication information unknown to authors (e.g., t.p. missing)
[ ]	Information from a source other than the title page
---.	Same author as cited directly above
---. ---.	Same author(s) or same author and title as cited directly above
----	Variant item with listed exceptions.

BRIEF HISTORY OF THE COLUMBIAN EXPOSITION 1893

The Columbian Exposition was the greatest ever built. The grand design was created by the era's foremost landscape architects, including Frederick Law Olmsted, Sr., who designed Central Park in New York. The Exposition bordered Lake Michigan, about eight miles south of downtown Chicago. Lagoons, ponds, and waterways wound around all the major buildings, and Venetian gondolas and electric launches were modes of transportation. All this added to a magnificent sight.

The buildings were designed by prominent architects of the day, the most famous being Louis Sullivan. It was the opportunity for the United States to show the World how far it had come since its colonial days and to demonstrate that it was a major industrial force, able to compete on equal footing with the European powers. It took place just four years after the Paris Exposition with its dramatic centerpiece, the Eiffel Tower (984 ft. high). As a spectacular engineering achievement to rival the Eiffel tower, they built the first Ferris Wheel. It was an impressive 264 feet high, equivalent to a modern 28 story building. There were 36 cars, each holding up to 60 people for a total of 2160 at capacity. The cost of the ride was 50 cents. From the top the view was magnificent, overlooking not only the entire fair, but all of Chicago.

They built more than 200 structures. The largest was the Manufactures and Liberal Arts Building which could have easily held 14 football fields on the ground floor. At its dedication 100,000 people were seated under its roof. Inside, various manufacturers, such as Tiffany and Gorham, erected their own structures which housed their exhibits. In addition to Manufactures, there were 14 other major exhibit buildings, e.g., Agriculture, Forestry, Fisheries, Anthropological, Leather, Woman's, Government, and Administration, each filled with the latest in art and technology. Individual structures were also built for 30 states and 20 foreign countries. In the Fine Arts Building there were between 1500 and 2000 displays in the American section; foreign sections, such as England's contained 600, Germany's 900, France's 800, and Italy's 600. Two companies erected large buildings. The Krupp Building contained armaments including the largest and most powerful gun in the world. It weighed 569,513 pounds and fired a 2204 pound projectile five miles. A special railroad car was designed to carry the gun to the Fair. The Libbey Glass Company built a glass factory where glass making was demonstrated. An astounding variety of glass souvenirs were sold.

Besides the main section of the Fair, there was the Midway Plaisance, a narrow strip of land that extended about a mile to the west. In addition to the Ferris wheel on the Midway Plaisance, there was an Ice Railway where, in the middle of summer, several people could go for a ride in a sled over a controlled course. There was also a Captive Balloon which took people for rides to a height of 1492 feet in honor of Columbus. This section also contained exhibits of people from all over the world in their native dress and habitat. There was a Cairo Street, German Village, Irish village, Vienna Cafe, Lapland Village, Javanese Sea settlement, and Japanese Bazaar. Nearby was a copy of an Hawaiian Volcano, a reproduction of the homes of cliff dwellers, and, in the Middle Eastern section, where the first Egyptian belly dancing in this country took place -- quite risque at the time. The Midway Plaisance became the inspiration for Coney Island of New York and all future amusement parks.

A pier was built extending almost half a mile into Lake Michigan. On it was constructed a movable sidewalk which extended the full length of the pier making a loop at each end for a continuous ride. People could sit on benches and get a cool breeze, riding as long as they wanted for five cents. Alongside another pier to the north an exact replica of a battleship -- with real guns and rigging -- was built out of wood. Nearby was a whaling ship, a replica Viking ship, and replicas of the Santa Maria, Nina, and Pinta. All these ships could be visited. The first elevated electrical intramural railway carried people around the grounds. The Fair was known as the White City, not only because most of the major buildings were white, but because they were the first to be lit up at night by electricity.

Besides exhibits, there were about 200 different congresses and conferences such as Religion, Medicine, and Dentistry. There were athletic contests, bands and classical concerts; John Philip Sousa became popular as a result of performing here. Buffalo Bill brought his Wild West show and crowds of 18,000 people filled the grandstand.

It was an age before the automobile and the airplane. At the time people relied on the telegraph for news from far away places. The long distance telephone was demonstrated by Alexander Graham Bell for the first time between Chicago and New York.

Twenty-seven million visitors attended during the brief period of six months (May 1--Oct 30, 1893). The structures were all temporary, and, unfortunately, shortly after the Fair closed, fires destroyed most of them. Of the major structures, only the Fine Arts Building remains. It was restored with permanent material and is now the Museum of Science and Industry.

Fortunately thousands of photographs, lantern slides, stereo views, as well as extensive reproductions in books survived and permit us to recall the majesty of this spectacular event. In addition, there are extensive memorabilia and ephemera covering about 150 collecting categories.

The Columbian Exposition, like the man it commemorated, influenced the world in numerous ways. In this volume, the history of what transpired can be located. There may be few other events in history, lasting six months, that were documented so extensively. The scope of this Exposition was vast, thus this compilation helps to provide a background for further research into this interesting and important period.

Dr. Stephen Sheppard
162 West 56th Street
New York, NY 10019

Chapter 1

FICTION, POETRY, CHILDREN'S BOOKS

1. [Beidler, Jacob Hoke]. *Centripetal Chicago Centralizing Columbia.* [Mt. Pulaski, Ill?]: Beidler, 1891 [°1891 by J. H. Beidler].

   13x18. 35 *l.* Poem. Textured robin egg blue wraps, black print, string tied. CHx copy signed by author. ☺ . (CHx)

2. Boyden, Emily. *Intermittent Thoughts.* Chicago: The Union publishing co., °1897.

   15½x11. 128 p. Green cloth hc with black print. Poems, including seven on the WCE.
   (TD) $35

3. Brooks, Elbridge S. *The True story of Christopher Columbus called the great admiral.* Boston: Lathrop, Lee & Shepard Co., [°1892 by D. Lathrop Company].

   24x19. 1 *l*, 187 p. Tan cloth hc embossed in red, white and black. Children's book mostly on Christopher Columbus but small section on WCE starting at page 173.
   P↑   ☺ (GLD,S) $12 - 30

4. Burnett, Frances Hodgson. *Two Little Pilgrims' Progress : a story of the city beautiful.*   New-York: Charles Scribner's Sons, 1895 [°1895]; New York: Charles Scribner's Sons, 1897 °1895; New York: Charles Scribner's sons, 1898; London: F. Warne and co., 1896; Ann Arbor, MI: UMI [Scribner's], 1966.

Scribner's 1895: 21½x17½. 4 *l*, 191 + (16) p. of book ads. Olive cloth hc, red and dark blue print and design. First American ed.: b/w illus by Reginald B. Birch. Story appeared in *The Literette*, 1895 (#1353). Publisher's ads dated 1895-96. [Burnett authored *Little Lord Fauntleroy*, etc. She attended the Fair and enjoyed it. NL has part of the original mss.]

---- Scribner's 1895: Same paging and size. Blue cloth hc, gold and dark blue print and design (spine designs differ). Frontis: litho of young couple viewing the Fair, tissue guard.

---- Scribner's 1897: 18x12 (text). 4 *l*, 206 p., 4 *l* ads.

---- Scribner's 1898: *Two little pilgrims' progress : A Story of the City Beautiful.* 19x13½. Cloth hc depicts two cherubs playing a harp.

---- Warne 1896: 21½x17½. 215 p. Illus by R. W. Macbeth.

P↑,P↑   ☺ . (GLD,csuf,UMC,CHx,LC,NYPL,UWa,USF,OSU,NLC,UMi,NL,TD) $20 - 45

5. Burnham, Clara Louise (Root). *Sweet clover : A romance of the white city.*   Boston and New York: Houghton, Mifflin and co., 1894 [°1894 by Clara Louise Burnham]; Boston and New York: Houghton, Mifflin and co., 1895 [°1894 by Clara Louise Burnham]; Boston and New York: Houghton, Mifflin Co., 1896; Boston and New York: Houghton, Mifflin Co., 1897 [°1894 by Clara Louise Burnham]; New York: Grosset & Dunlap publishers, [°1894 by Clara Louise Burnham].

1894 Houghton: 18x12½. 2 *l*, 411, (6) p. of undated publisher's ads. Black cloth hc, silver print. Also listed without the (6) p. at end.

---- 1895 Houghton: 17½x11½. (6), 411, (1) p. Dark blue cloth hc, silver print. On copyright page: "Eleventh thousand."

---- 1897 Houghton: On copyright page: "Nineteenth thousand."

---- Grosset: 19½x12½. Published ca. 1910-11? (4), 411, (1) p. Gray cloth hc, turquoise lettering and design.

☺ . (CPL,CHx,NYPL,OSU,UMi,nwu,NYSt,NL)

6. Butterworth, Hezekiah. *Zigzag Journeys in the white city. With Visits to the Neighboring Metropolis.* Boston: Estes and Lauriat, publishers, [°1894 by Estes and Lauriat].

21½x17½. vii, (3), 12-320 p. including plates, illus. Frontis of West Lagoon, Wooded Island, and Manufacture's Bldg. Red and white cloth hc, print and Administration Bldg design in gilt. Author's Zigzag series, vol 16.

---- Also listed: viii, (19)-320 p.

---- 21½x17½. viii, 1 *l*, (11)-320 p. Same frontis, same pub info. Blue and gray cloth hc, same gilt print and design. Not identified as vol 16 of Zigzag series.

P→   ☺ . (csuf,CHx,NYPL,F,S,UoC,A,BPL,nwu) $22 - 35

☞ Butterworth spoke in the children's literary section at the World's Literary Congress held at the Art Institute. Do not confuse Hezekiah with Congressman Benjamin Butterworth.

7. Cobb, Weldon J. *A World's fair mystery.* Chicago: Melbourne publishing co., 1892 °1892 by Melbourne Publishing Co.

19x13½. 369 p. including front cover. Green glossy illus wraps, red and black print. An "American Author's Series" (pulp). Glossy illus frontis.   ☺ . (LC)

8. Crowley, Mary Catherine. *The city of wonders : a souvenir of the World's fair.* Detroit: Wm. Graham co., 1894 [ᶜ1894].

17½x13. 162 p. Brown decorative cloth hc, gold and black print. Fictional account.
P→   ⊜ . (csuf,CHx,BPL)

9. Dockarty, A. J.   (Pseud: Ebenezer Slimmens).   *Midway plaisance. The experience of an innocent boy from Vermont in the famous midway.* Chicago: Chicago World Book Co., 1894.

19½x13½. 259, (1) p., illus.   ⊜ . (CHx,BPL)

10. Earl, Fanny Kennish.   *The World's Fair : An Evening Entertainment for young people's Church and Temperance Societies.* [Lake Mills, WI: Chas. L. Hubb, Printer, ᶜ1891].

18½x12. 2 *l*, 28 p. C.t.= t.p. Poems and a juvenile, allegorical play with characters: "Uncle Sam," "Josiah Allen's Wife," "Josiah," etc.   ⊜ . (LC)

11. Edeline, Abel. *Ode a la fortune Américaine : offerte aux États-Unis a l'occasion de l'exposition de Chicago 1893.* Le Mans: Imprimerie & librairie E. Lebrault & Fils, 1894.

25x16. 12 p. Poem. LC copy signed by the author.--(LC microfilm no. 24367)   ⊜ . (LC)

12. Ferris Wheel Company. *Car No. -- : A Romance of the Ferris Wheel : The Narrative of James Black.* [Chicago: Engraved and printed by The Corbitt & Skidmore Co., ᶜ1893 by The Ferris Wheel Co.].

13½ cm diameter (circular) die cut; ribbon tied hinge. 24 p., includes Ferris port. Front and back wraps with litho illus of Ferris Wheel. Tale of James and his friend Marcy on the Wheel.   ⊜ . (H)

13. Finley, Martha. *Elsie at the World's fair.* New York: Dodd, Mead and co. Publishers, [ᶜ1894 by Dodd, Mead & co.].

18x12½. 259 p., folding frontis of bird's-eye view. Maroon cloth hc, blind stamp on front cover. Number 20 in the Elsie Dinsmore series of juvenile fiction.
⊜ . (csuf,CHx,F,TnSt,UDe,A,L)

$20 - 35

14. *5 Little Pigs.* New York: McLoughlin Bro's, ᶜ1890 by McLoughlin Bro's.

20x14. 10 linen p. Frontis of "Big pig going to market." First text page is stamped: "Children's Building : souvenir. World's fair 1893." Color illus paper covered boards. C.t. At top of cover: "Linen. Pleasewell Series."   ⊜ . (S)

15. Fuller, Henry Blake. *The Cliff-Dwellers.* New York: Harper & Bros., 1893.

Novel centering on activities of workers in a Chicago skyscraper; tangentially related to the WCE. [Do not confuse with #1007 -- the Cliff-Dwellers of the American Southwest.]   (ref)

16. Gibbs, Sarah Mather. *The World's Fair Poem : Historical-vision-of-Columbus, in 1492 : or A Bird's eye view of America in 1893.* N.p.: n.p., n.d.

   28x__. 3 *l*, typewritten unique mss found at the LC. Also LC microfilm.--(Call: 59278 PS)   (LC)

17. Hartnedy, M. M. A. *The world's fair drama. Christopher Columbus, a drama in three acts... Published and sold by The Columbus Club ... Steubenville, Ohio.* New York: P. J. Kenedy; Chicago: W. H. Sadlier, [1892].

   18½x12. 51 p. Gray wraps, black lettering. On cover: "The Catholic American play of the ..."   (csuf)

18. Holley, Marietta. (Pseud: Josiah Allen's Wife). *Samantha at the World's fair.* New York, London and Toronto: Funk & Wagnalls Co., 1893 [°1893 by Funk & Wagnalls].

   22x16½. xi, 694 p., illus. Blue cloth hc; gold, silver and black embossed illus and print. No ads after p. 694 of 1st ed. Frontis: b/w illus of 2 older folks viewing the Fair bldgs. Children's narrative account of trip to Fair; "Samantha" also went to other fairs. Common. All eds.: "(Marietta Holley)" printed below pseudonym.
   ---- 22½x16½. xi, 694 p. Half leather and half brown cloth, gilt spine print and design, top edge gilt, decorative gold floral end papers. No printing or design on covers. Salesmens' sample (#1747) refers to the binding as "Half Russia, $4.00."
   ---- Fortieth (and sixtieth) thousand printing: 694 p., 1 *l* book ads. Blue cloth hc; gold, silver and black embossed illus and print.
   ---- Fiftieth (and sixtieth) thousand printing: xi, 694 p., 1 *l* ads. Brown cloth hc with same design and print colors.
   ---- New York and London: Funk & Wagnalls co., [°1893 by Funk & Wagnalls co.]. 20x13½. 694 p. Tannish-gray cloth hc with green and black print, white illus of Administration Bldg. Number of printing is not given on t.p. (as on others above).
   P→   ☉ . (GLD,csuf,CPL,CHx,NYPL,S,E,LM,HL,NL,A,BPL,WiHx,TD,L)

Cloth: $15 - 25
Half leather: $25 - 40

19. Ingham, John Hall. *Pompeii of the west And Other Poems.* Philadelphia and London: J. B. Lippincott Co., 1903.

   20x13½. 173 p. Blue cloth hc, gold print. T.p. in red and black. "Pompeii of the west" describes loss of fairgrounds by fire but says its white vision shall be remembered.   ☉ . (LC)

20. Jenks, Tudor. *The Century World's fair book for boys and girls : being the adventures of Harry and Philip with their tutor, Mr. Douglass at the World's Columbian exposition. ...* New York: The Century Co., [°1893 by the Century Co.]; Woodbridge, CT: RPI, 1989.

24½x19. xiii, (1), 246 p. including frontis depicting "The White City," illus. Glossy paper covered boards, illus with red and black print on ocher background. Fairgrounds map on inside front cover. Very interesting and useful narrative description of the construction, bldgs and events of the WCE.

P→ ⊚ . (GLD,csuf,CHx,SI,NYPL,F,UDe,HL,UMi,UoC,A,BPL,TD) $20 - 35

21. Locke, J[ohn] S[taples]. *Little Folk's History of the United States.* Boston: De Wolfe Fiske & Co., n.d.

21x30½. 8 hard board *l* folding on linen hinges; (16) p. as each board is faced with a color litho of historical U.S. events with a printed description on the back. The last illus is President Cleveland opening the WCE and looking down onto a bird's-eye view of the grounds. C.t. The label is "1493 - The World's Columbian Exposition Chicago - 1893," but the bird's-eye view differs from the actual grounds implying a printing date of 1892. Intended as a stand up book and toy.

P↓   ⊚ . (GLD,UDe,BPL,S) $60 - 125

22. Loy, Daniel Oscar. *Poems of the white city : profusely illustrated.* Chicago: Daniel Oscar Loy, Publisher, 1893.

19½x28. 104 p., illus. Frontis of Loy. Pretty white cloth hc on beveled boards, gilt print and edges. Poetry.

⊚ . (csuf,LC,UMi)

23. Lynch, James D[aniel]. *Columbia Saluting the Nations.* [Chicago: Thayer & Jackson Stationery Co.], ᶜ1893 by the Author.

21½x10 when folded to read title; 28x21½ when unfolded and rotated 90° to read text. A poem on 7 glossy *l*, illus. Pretty light green ?silk, folding cover, gilt print. For reading, the hinge is at top (21½ cm side) and the leaves turn in note pad style. Adopted by the World's Columbian Commission as the U.S. welcome to the nations of the world.   ⊚ . (CHx,LC)

24. Monroe, Harriet. *The Columbian Ode : Designs by Will H. Bradley.* Chicago: W. Irving Way & co., 1893.

16x13. 23, (1) p. String-tied winter-white wraps, red and purple print, purple design, paper of heavy rag stock throughout, ragged edges (uncut). On cover: "Souvenir edition : The Columbian Ode." Written at the request of the Joint Committee on Ceremonies; delivered during the dedicatory ceremonies in the bldg for Manufactures and Liberal Arts. The Committee authorized Theodore Thomas, Director of Music, to request Prof. Chadwick to set the lyrics to music (see #1481). Printed at the De Vinne press. Autographed copy in GLD collection.

P↓   ⊚ . (GLD,LC,NYPL,HL,Yale,UoC,NL,nwu,RPB) $20 - 38

25. Monroe, Harriet. *Commemoration ode written by Harriet Monroe at the request of the committee on ceremonies and delivered at the dedication of the World's Columbian exposition on the four hundredth anniversary of the discovery of America.* Chicago: Printed for the author [by Rand, McNally & Co.], 1892 [ᶜ1892 by Harriet Monroe].

23x17. 2 *l*, 15 p. Deep aquamarine wraps, black print and cover design. Published in 1893 under title: "The Columbian Ode."
⊖ . (KyU,CHx,LC,NYPL,UDe,HL,UoC,NL,nwu,RPB)
---- Also in *Chicago--World's Columbian exposition, 1893. Dedicatory and opening exercises.* Chicago: 1893. p. 143-149. (RPB)

☞ Autographed copies at KyU and HL. Miss Monroe sued the *New York World* newspaper for printing part of the "Ode" prior to delivery of it at the Fair. She won $5,000 in damages.

26. [Neely, Frank Tennyson]. *Looking forward : Tennyson.* [pseud].
Chicago, New York: F. T. Neely Publisher and Wholesale Bookseller, [1889] ᶜ1889 by F. T. Neely; Chicago: [1890] ᶜ1889; Chicago, New York: F. T. Neely, Publisher and Wholesale Bookseller, [1892] ᶜ1889 by F. T. Neely; N.p.: LBS Archival Products, 1987.

1889: 19x13½. (2) p. ads, (3)-228 p. includes illus but not unpaged ports, (14) p. ads. Baby blue wraps with rust print. Neely's series, extra, vol 1, no. 7, Dec., 1889. Early pulp fiction anticipating a 1892 WF. C.t.: "Looking Forward : My Visit to the World's Fair. Tennyson. Illustrated by Baron de Grimm, ... and others."
---- 1890: 19x13½. 203 p., frontis port, illus. Neely's series vol 1, no. 9, Feb., 1890.
---- 1892: 18½x12½. 203 p., (1) p, 11 *l* ads, illus. Yellow wraps, blue design and print. Neely's popular library, no. 8, Nov. 1892. C.t.: "Looking Forward : An Imaginary Visit to the World's Fair."
---- 1987: LBS copy of 1892 ed.
⊖ . (GLD,csuf,KyU,S,RPB)   1889: $20 - 40

27. [Neely, Frank Tennyson]. *A tale of the World's fair : Giving the Experience of an Underwriter Visiting the Fair at Chicago, 1893. By Tennyson.* Chicago: F. T. Neely, ᶜ1890 by F. T. Neely.

15½x12. "Neely's Series. Vol 2. No. 15. Extra. Oct, 1890. Pulp fiction. "Imaginary description of the WCE includes tales of the people, sights, and sounds. ⊖ . (S,OC)

28. Neville, Edith. *Alice Ashland : a romance of the World's fair.* New York: Peter Fenelon Collier, Publisher, 1893.

18x11½. 216 p. Decorative wraps. At top of cover: "Vol. XL, No. 4. August 26, 1893." Pulp fiction.
P→   ⊖ . (S)

29. Peacock, Thomas Brower. *Columbian ode. An ode of greeting.* N.p.: n.p., ᶜ1892 by T. B. Peacock.

22x14½. 8 p. Printed on one side of glossy paper, black print. Caption title. Tied with gold bow through 2 punch holes at 14½ cm (top) edge. Read at the Public Press Congress, May 24, 1893.

---- A review of the poem laid in.--(HL Call: 348761).
⊜ . (LC,HL)

30. Peacock, Thomas Brower. *A Souvenir Poem and Picture: Peacock's Great International Prize Poem: The Columbian Ode ... The Portrait and History of the Beautiful Virginia Dare, the First White Girl Born in America.* N.p.: n.p., n.d.

22x14. 8 p. C.t. Read by Peacock at the Art Palace at the opening of the WF. The Board of WF Managers selected this the best submitted in the international contest. LC copy is autographed by the author for presentation to President Woodrow Wilson.   (LC)

31. *A Peep at the World's Fair.* London, Paris & New York: Raphael Tuck & Sons, n.d.

24½x18½. (25) p. Pretty hc illus of 4 doll-faced children by W & F Brundage. T.p. has full page illus. "Designed at the London Studios and Printed at the fine art works in Holland." Excellent example of Tuck quality color lithography. Children's book.
P→   ⊜ . (GLD,A,S,UDe) $60 - 120

32. Pittsinger, Eliza A. *Columbus and Isabella : A Prophecy written in Chicago 1872, and Published in San Francisco in 1893.* [San Francisco: 1893].

22x14½. (3) p. C.t. Poem. WCE souvenir.   ⊜ . (RPB)

33. [Plautus, Titus Maccius]. ... *The Latin play : the two captives of Plautus : by the students of the College of St. Francis Xavier : New York : At the World's Fair, Chicago : Music Hall : October 19th ... October 20th ...* [Chicago?: 1893].

21x15. xx, 1 *l*, 101 p., illus including frontis. Wraps. At head of title: "World's fair educational exhibit." Latin and English on opposite pages.   ⊜ . (RPB)

34. Russell, Victor. ... *The Story of Columbus.* Cincinnati, OH: The Russell printing co., ᶜ1892.

30½x25½. Multicolor illus wraps. Childrens' book. C.t. At head of title: "Victor Russell's story books." Bird's-eye of WCE grounds on back wrap.   ⊜ . (S)

35. Searles, Victor A. *The Life of Columbus In Pictures.* Boston: L. Prang & Co., ᶜ1892 by L. Prang & Co.

29x21. 15 *l* of heavy stock with color illus one side. Front hc in white cloth with black print, designs primarily in peach, yellow, tans; back cover and spine are turquoise. Illus by Searles; historical poem by Emily Shaw Forman.   ⊜ . (ref,LC) $50

36. Sergel, Annie Myers. *The Midway: A burlesque entertainment based on the famous Midway plaisance of the World's Columbian Exposition. ...* Chicago: The Dramatic Publishing Co., ᶜ1894.

22x13½. 26 p. + 3 *l* with 6 plates + 1 *l* ads. Maize wraps, brown print and design. T.p. continues: "Full directions for producing and conducting it upon the most extensive plan or on a limited scale." (LC)

37. *Short stories with a Glimpse at the Columbian Exposition.* [Grand Rapids, MI]: N. Malloy, [189-?].

13x20. (31) p. Buff wraps.   ☺ . (LMi)

38. [Stead, William Thomas]. *From the Old World to the New; or, A Christmas Story of the World's Fair, 1893. Illustrated.* London New York Melbourne: [Office Review of Reviews], 1892.

26x19. 1 *l*, 123 p. frontis, illus. Fiction. After title: "Being the Christmas number of the 'Review of Reviews.'" (See #1396 for magazine listing).   ☺ . (csuf,LC,NL)

39. [Stevens, Charles McClellan]. (pseud: "Quondam"). *The Adventures of Uncle Jeremiah and family at the Great Fair : Their Observations and Triumphs : By "Quondam" : With Sixty Illustrations.* Chicago: Laird & Lee, Publishers, 1893 [ᶜ1893 by Laird & Lee].

19½x13½. 229, (1) p. + 1 *l* ads, illus by H. Mayer. Light green glossy wraps, red and black print and design. On cover: "The Pastime series, no. 108."
---- 237, (3) p. ads, 2 *l* of plates, illus. On cover: "Century ed." otherwise same cover as above.
---- 237, (1) p., 1 *l*. Rust cloth hc, same design as in wrappers ed., but with gold lettering.
All copies have frontis of the Ferris wheel and Midway. Narrative of fictional trip to WCE, much like *Samantha*. [By 1904, 475,000 copies of this book had been sold].
P→   ☺ . (GLD,csuf,CHx,F,E,UDe,HL,UoC,NL,A,BPL,WiHx,TD,L) $15 - 30

40. Stocking, Sarah L. *Columbian Entertainments : consisting of dramas, colloquies, poems, tableaux, pantomimes : designed for the use of classes, clubs or schools.* Peoria, IL: J. W. Franks & sons, printers.and.binders, 1892.

21x15½. 210 p. Speckle dyed edges.   ☺ . (CPL)

41. Taylor, Mrs. D. C. *Halcyon Days in the Dream City.* Kankakee, IL: n.p., ᶜ1894.

18x15. 2 *l*, 5-84, (1) p. New Mexico sky blue padded cloth hc, gilt print, coated and textured white end papers. Tale of trip to WCE. (CHx,USF,S)

42. [Tower, E. M.] *Christopher Columbus Celebration Souvenir. Crank's curious composition.* Atlanta: C. P. Byrd, Printer, [1893].

16½x12. (24) p. includes illus, ports. Light blue stiff wraps, red and black print and design. C.t. The text is composed only of words beginning with the letter "c".   ☺ (CHx)

43. Van Meter, H. H. *The Vanishing Fair.* Chicago: The Literary Art Co., [°1894].

    27x22. 40 glossy p. include double frontis showing 3 panorama views, illus. Gray cloth hc, white cloth design, gold and silver design and print. Format: b/w photos and illus on versos, poems surrounded by b/w illus on rectos. T.p.: "Illustrated and Embellished by William and Charles Ottman." Subject: burning of the bldgs during the railroad strike, July, 1894.   ☉ . (CHx,LC,AIC)

44. Western, Carl T. *Adventures of Reuben and Cynthy at the World's fair, as related by themselves.* Chicago: Wellington Publishing Co., 1893.

    20½x14. 163 p., illus. Red cloth hc, black print. On cover: "New edition. Profusely illustrated. Reuben and Cynthy at the Fair."   ☉ (CHx,TD)

45. White, Annie Randall. *The Story of Columbus and the World's Columbian Exposition : embracing every historical fact and event ... Designed for Young Folks.* Chicago: A. B. Kuhlman & Co., [1892]; Chicago: Monarch Book Co., 1892; Chicago and Philadelphia: Imperial publishing co., publishers, [°1892 by Charles S. Sutphen]; Chicago, Philadelphia and Stockton, CA: Monarch Book Co. (Formerly L. P. Miller & Co.), Publishers, [°1892 by Charles S. Sutphen]; N.p.: Juvenile Book Co. (overprinted with Philadelphia: Imperial Publishing Co.), 1893 [°1892 by Charles S. Sutphen].

    25½x19½. 1 *l*, 379 p., illus, map, plates. Gray (or blue) cloth hc, gold, silver and black print and design, decorated end papers, marbled edges. Fold out frontis depicts inside of Manufacturer's Bldg where dedication ceremonies were held. T.p. in red and black.

P→   ☉ . (GLD,csuf,S,A,BPL,TD) $15 - 30

46. Woolson Spice Company. *Jeremiah Judkin's trip to the Fair : being the truthful account of a most extraordinary occurrence.* Toledo, OH: Woolson Spice Co., °1894.

    8½x15. Folded booklet parlor game. "'Uncle Jerry' with his wife and three children go to the World's Fair, and this tells what they saw."   ☉ . (BPL,TD)

47. Yandell, Enid, Jean Loughborough, and Laura Hayes. *Three girls in a flat : by Enid Yandell, of Kentucky : Jean Loughborough, of Arkansas : Laura Hayes, of Illinois.* [Chicago: Press of Knight, Leonard & Co., °1892 by Laura Hayes].

    21x15½. 154 p., illus. Blue and white cloth hc, gilt. C.t.: "Three Girls in a Flat." Illus by Helen M. Armstrong, et. al.
    ---- 2d ed.?: Yandell, Enid, and Laura Hayes. *Three girls in a flat : by Enid Yandell, of Kentucky : Laura Hayes, of Illinois.* 163, [1] p., illus. Plum cloth hc, gilt. C.t.: "Three Girls in a Flat : The Story of the Woman's Building."
        ☉ . (csuf,CHx,D)

Chapter 2

EXPOSITION PUBLICATIONS

Col. George R. Davis, Illinois Congressman who fought in the Civil War, was instrumental in securing Chicago as the site for the WCE. He was elected Director-General for the WCE by the World's Columbian Exposition Company; in this capacity, his name appears on many of the WCE official publications.

Official department publications on the location of exhibits and maps of grounds are found in the chapter entitled "Guides." Similar publications by foreign exhibitors are found in "Foreign Countries."

The World's Columbian Commission had two members from each state, territory, and the District of Columbia. The Board of Lady Managers had two members from each state, territory, and the District of Columbia with an equal number of alternates. The members of the Board of Lady Managers were appointed by the President of the United States. They served directly under the World's Columbian Commission, not the World's Columbian Exposition.

Consult the fold out wiring diagram of the WCE and the index to aid in locating items in this chapter.

48. *Brief of W. P. Black and C. B. Waite, also brief of Robert Rae, in behalf of Phoebe W. Couzins, As Secretary of the Board of Lady Managers of the World's Columbian Exposition. Prepared for the Secretary of the Treasury, June, 1891.* Chicago: Daniels, Pitkin & Hall, Printers, 1891.

23½x15. 34 p. Pea green wraps with black print. C.t.   ☺ . (CHx,UNLV)

☞ Phoebe W. Couzins, a Lady Manager from Missouri, was removed from office Sept. 3, 1891. Miscellaneous pamphlets: Official and unofficial including material on the Couzins case are located at CHx.--(CHx call: qF38MZ 1893 D3L12Z)

49. Goode, G[eorge] Brown. *First draft of A System of Classification for the World's Columbian exposition.* Washington: Gedney and Roberts, 1890; Chicago: Privately printed for the World's Columbian Commission, 1890; Woodbridge, CT: RPI, 1989.

24½x14. xv, 196 p.
---- In: *Annual Report of the Board of Regents of the Smithsonian Institution ... 1891.* (See #293).
    ☺ . (csuf,LC,NYPL,SI,OhHx)

50. Olmsted, F[rederick] L[aw], & co. *Olmsted's report on choice of site of World's Columbian exposition - Chicago 1893.* [Chicago: 1890].

27½x__. 1 *l*, 11 numbered *l*. Interleaved and mimeographed.   (OSU)
---- Rpt: Tager, Jack, and Park Dixon Goist, eds. "Report on Choice of Site of the World's Columbian Exposition." In *The Urban vision : Selected Interpretations of the Modern American City.* Homewood, IL [and] Georgetown, Ont.: The Dorsey Press, 1970. 23x15. p. 51-60.   ☺ .(USD)

☞ Do not confuse landscape architect, Frederick Law Olmsted (1822-1903), with author, Frank B. Olmstead (see #1641). Olmsted was impressed by English landscape at an early age. He helped plan Central Park in New York City and Fairmount Park, Philadelphia, site of the 1876 centennial, as well as Capitol Hill and Gallaudet College landscape in Washington, DC.

51. U.S. World's Columbian Commission and World's Columbian Exposition. Joint Board of Reference and Control. Sub-Committee. *Report of Sub-Committee of the joint Board of Reference and Control relative to the Council of Administration.* Chicago: Rand, McNally & Co., 1892.

17x11. 1 *l*, 3-8 p. Tan wraps, black print. At head of title: "World's Columbian Exposition." H. N. Higinbotham was committee chairman.
---- In a bound vol: 16½x11½. ca. 3 cm thick. "Minutes of the Meeting of the Council of Administration." Minutes are separately paginated and dated Aug. 25, 1892 to Oct. 28, 1892. An 8 p. introduction is signed in replica by Higinbotham (committee chairman), St. Clair, Stone, and Massey. "Approved by the Joint Board of Reference and Control, August 18, 1892."
⊚ . (CHx,CPL,NL)

52. U.S. World's Columbian Commission and World's Columbian Exposition. Joint Committee on Ceremonies, ed. ... *Dedicatory and Opening Ceremonies of the World's Columbian Exposition. Historical and descriptive. As authorized by the board of control* ... Chicago: published by A. L. Stone, 1893; Chicago: Stone, Kastler & Painter, 1893 [°1893 by Stone, Kastler & Painter].

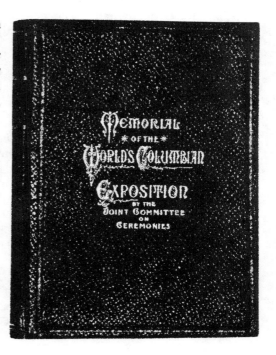

Stone: 28x20½. 320 p. Full leather hc, embossed gold lettering, decorated end papers, gilt edges, high quality paper. At top of t.p.: "Memorial Volume." C.t.: "Memorial of the World's Columbian Exposition by the Joint Committee on Ceremonies."
---- Stone, Kastler & Painter (Donohue & Henneberry Printers and Binders): 303, (1) + 8 p. of plates included in pagination. Also listed: 303, (17) p.
---- Stone, Kastler & Painter (The Henry O. Shepard Co., Printers and Binders): 320 p. Green cloth hc (or full leather), gold lettering same as Stone leather ed.
*P→   ⊚ . (GLD,csuf,CHx,NYPL,F,S,OhHx,StLa,RML,E,UDe,SLP,HL,
NYSt,Yale,UoC,NL,A,BPL,WM,AIC,BM,OC,TD,L) $35 - 65

53. U.S. World's Columbian Commission and World's Columbian Exposition. *Minutes of the Proceedings of the joint conference composed of Boards of Control of the World's Columbian Commission and of the World's Columbian Exposition, with the Representatives of the World's Fair State and Territorial Boards. Held in the city of Chicago, December 9th, 10th and 11th, 1891,* ... Chicago: Rand, McNally & Co., 1892.

22x15. 104 p. Light gray wraps, black print. Includes George R. Davis' answers to questions posed by the State and Territorial WF Boards.   ⊚ . (SFe,CHx,LC,HL,WiHx)

54. U.S. World's Columbian Commission. *Annual report, 1st. 1890.* Washington: GPO, 1891.

22½x15. 74 p.   (csuf)

55. U.S. World's Columbian Commission. Board of Directors. *The World's Columbian Exposition, jurisdiction of standing committees. Approved May 23d, 1890. Special meeting of the Board of Directors.* N.p.: n.p., [1890?].

14x22. 4 *l*. Typewritten.   (CHx)

56. U.S. World's Columbian Commission. Board of Lady Managers. *Addition Report of the Committee on Immediate Work.* N.p.: n.p., n.d.

    23½x15. 3 p. Caption title. Committee members as listed at end of report: Virginia C. Meredith, E. Nellie Beck, Rosine Ryan, Mary E. Busselle.   (NL)

57. U.S. World's Columbian Commission. Board of Lady Managers. *Address at the Dedicatory Ceremonies, October 21, 1892, by Mrs. Potter Palmer, President of the Board of Lady Managers, World's Columbian Commission.* N.p.: n.p., n.d.

    23½x15. (4) p. Caption title.   (NL)

    ☞ Mrs. Potter Palmer (Bertha Honoré) (1849-1918) was a Chicago socialite and adept organizer. She helped build her husband's, Potter Palmer (1826-1902), businesses which included the Palmer House Hotel.

58. U.S. World's Columbian Commission. Board of Lady Managers. *Address delivered by Mrs. Potter Palmer, President of the Board of Lady Managers, on the occasion of the opening of the Woman's Building, May 1, 1893.* N.p.: n.p., n.d.

    27½x20. 7 p. Plain paper wraps, black print. Photo of Palmer inside front cover.   ☉.(CHx)

59. U.S. World's Columbian Commission. Board of Lady Managers. *Addresses and Reports of Mrs. Potter Palmer : President of the Board of Lady Managers, World's Columbian Commission.* Complete ed. Chicago: Rand, McNally & Co., 1894; Woodbridge, CT: RPI, 1989.

    27½x19. 200 p. Half leather, marbled paper covered beveled boards; gold print, gilt edges. Frontis portrait of Mrs. Palmer. Lists committee meetings, letters, sales account for the Isabella (25¢) coin, attention to husband's illness, etc. [There were 40,000 Isabella coins minted, far less than the 2.5M half dollars minted.]
    ---- Glossy paper, 3/4 leather binding.
    ---- Rough paper, full leather binding.
       (UNM,CHx,NYPL,SI,RML,NL,nwu)

60. U.S. World's Columbian Commission. Board of Lady Managers. *Addresses delivered at the opening of the Woman's Building, May 1, 1893.* N.p.: n.p., [°1893].

    19½x14½. (3)-31 p. Addresses by 6 women: Mrs. Potter Palmer (same as #58), Mrs. Bedford-Fenwick, Countess of Aberdeen, Princess Mary Schahovskoy, Countess di Brazza, and Frau Professorin Kaselowsky.   (UoC,NL)

61. U.S. World's Columbian Commission. Board of Lady Managers. *Approved Official Minutes of the third session of the Board of Lady Managers : World's Columbian commission. October, 1892.* Chicago: Rand, McNally & Co, 1892.

    22½x15. 78 p. Burnt orange wraps, deep red print and design. Title varies. 1st and 2nd session minutes (Nov. 19, 1890 - Sept 9, 1891) are bound together with the act creating the commission, board by-laws, etc. and is titled: *Official Manual* (#79.)   (CHx,NL)

62. U.S. World's Columbian Commission. Board of Lady Managers. *Approved Official Minutes of the fourth session of the Board of Lady Managers : World's Columbian commission. April 26 to May 5, 1893.* Chicago: Rand, McNally & co., printers, 1893.

23x15½. 1-95 p. Burnt orange wraps, deep red print and design. This 4th session is bound together with the 5th session which has its own t.p.: *Approved Official Minutes of the fifth session ... July 7 to August 12, 1893.* Chicago: Rand, McNally & co., printers, 1893. 1-225 p.   (CHx,NL)

63. U.S. World's Columbian Commission. Board of Lady Managers. *Approved Official Minutes. Sixth session of the Board of Lady Managers of the World's Columbian Commission. October 31 to November 6, 1893.* Chicago: Rand, McNally & co., printers, 1894.

23x15. 209 p. Burnt orange wraps, deep red print and design.   ☺ . (CPL,CHx,NL)

64. U.S. World's Columbian Commission. Board of Lady Managers. *Assembly : In honor of the Judges appointed by the Board of Lady Managers of the Columbian Commission. Woman's Building : Jackson Park, Chicago : August Twenty-third 1893.* N.p.: n.p., n.d.

25x21½. Unpaged. Wraps same stock as text, black print. C.t.   ☺ . (WM)

65. U.S. World's Columbian Commission. Board of Lady Managers. *Children's Building of the World's Columbian Exposition 1893.* N.p.: n.p., n.d.

15x18. 30 *l* numbered and printed on one side only except index printed on verso of last *l*, illus, photos, floor plan. White stiff pebbled stock, green (or light blue) print, string tied. C.t. Care for the day cost 25¢ and included two meals and a bath. [This effort at the Fair got deservedly good reviews. The Children's Bldg was next to the Woman's Bldg. Do not confuse it with the Nursery Exhibit, at the end of the Midway, which was for plants, fertilizers, etc.]   ☺ . (CHx,CPL,NL)

66. U.S. World's Columbian Commission. Board of Lady Managers. Committee on Classification. *Report of the committee on classification.* N.p.: n.p., n.d.

23½x15. 6 p. Caption title. Chairman, Mrs. Sarah S. C. Angell, and other names follow final paragraph.   ☺ (NL,WM)

67. U.S. World's Columbian Commission. Board of Lady Managers. *Congresses in Woman's Building, World's Columbian Exposition. ...* N.p.: n.p., n.d.

20x15. (4) p. C.t. Title continues with committee member list. Chairman was Mary Kavanaugh (Mrs. James P.) Eagle. Pages (3-4) list the daily 11 a.m. entertainments for June 1893.   ☺ (NL,WM)

68. U.S. World's Columbian Commission. Board of Lady Managers. Cooke, Susan G. *Statement adopted by the Executive Committee of the Board of Lady Managers, and a copy of same ordered to be sent to each member of the Board of Lady Managers of the World's Columbian Commission.* N.p.: n.p., [1891?].

23½x15. 3 p. Cooke was temporary secretary to the Executive Committee at this time. Dated: Apr. 16, 1891.   ☺ (NL)

69. U.S. World's Columbian Commission. Board of Lady Managers. Cooke, Susan G. [*Statement of Work since April 15, 1891*]. [Chicago: 1891?].

23½x15. 3 p. No cover or t.p. Cooke was Secretary pro tem, replacing Phoebe Couzins. Statement dated: Chicago, Sept. 2, 1891.   ☺ (NL)

70. U.S. World's Columbian Commission. Board of Lady Managers. *Diploma of honorable mention, designers, inventors and expert artisans.* [Chicago: 1893].

31x__. 640 p. C.t. ?   (CHx-unavailable)

☞ Original award diplomas, designed by W. H. Low, are superb lithos with seal. The U.S. Bureau of Engraving issued a limited edition reproduction in 1992. The honorable mention diploma has a different design.

Award diploma: $400 - 600
Honorable Mention diploma: $100 - 250

71. U.S. World's Columbian Commission. Boards of Lady Managers. Eagle, Mary Kavanaugh Oldham, ed. *The Congress of Women : held in the woman's building, World's Columbian Exposition, Chicago, U.S.A., 1893.* ... Official ed. Chicago: Louis Benham & co., 1894 [°1894 by W. B. Conkey co.]; Chicago: W. B. Conkey Co., 1894 [°1894]; Chicago [and] Philadelphia: International publishing co, 1894 [°1894 by W. B. Conkey co.]; Chicago: H. S. Mills & co., 1894 [°1894 by W. B. Conkey co.]; Chicago [and] Philadelphia: Monarch book co. (Formerly L. P. Miller & Co.), 1894 [°1894 by W. B. Conkey co.]; New York: W. W. Wilson, 1894; Philadelphia: International Publishing Co. (consolidated with and successors to) W. W. Houston & Co. and Mammoth Publishing Co., 1895; Philadelphia: J. W. Keeler & co., 1894; N.p.: n.p., [°1894 by W. B. Conkey co.].

Benham: 26½x20½. Frontis, t.p., plates, table of contents, introduction, etc. to p. 24. Text p. 25-818 p. Gold print on dark olive hc. Also found with 824 p.
---- Conkey 1894: 27½x20½. 2 vol. Paged continuously to 824 p. Brown leather on beveled hc, gilt.
---- International, Mills, and Monarch: 26½x20½. 1 *l* (frontis), (4) p., 1 *l* port, (2) p., 1 *l* port, (2) p., 15-824 p. Plates interspersed with text are not counted in paging. Olive cloth beveled hc, gold embossed print. Also in full leather binding.
---- Also listed: W. W. Wilson: 817 p.
---- Also listed: Keeler: 26½x20½. 4 *l*, 15-824 p.
---- N.p.: 26½x20½. Rebound hc, gilt edges.
On all t.p.: "Sold only by subscription." All have frontis depicting Woman's Bldg. All are official editions.
*P→   ☺ . (GLD,csuf,KyU,CHx,NYPL,F,S,UDe,CoU,HL,UMi,NYSt,UoC,NL,A,BPL,RPB) $35 - 65

☞ Even though this is a "congress" it is not in the World's Congress chapter because it was part of the Board of Lady Manager operations of the Woman's Bldg. Do not confuse the congresses held in the Woman's Bldg (under World's Columbian Commission - Board of Lady Managers) with the

World's Congresses of Representative Women held in the Art Institute (Woman's Branch under Auxiliary).

72. U.S. World's Columbian Commission. Board of Lady Managers. Edgerton, Mrs. Rollin A., ed. ... *The Columbian Woman.* [Chicago]: n.p., °1893 by Mrs. Edgerton.

40x28. 24 p., illus, ports, on glossy sheets. Illus cover in shades of browns and beiges. Issued in honor of the WCE; has magazine quality. C.t. At head of title: "Published under the Direction of a Lady Manager." [Edgerton was a Board member from Arkansas.]   ⊚ (CHx)

73. U.S. World's Columbian Commission. Board of Lady Managers. *History of the Last Nail : Presented by Mrs. Potter Palmer ... in the Woman's Building.* [Chicago: Knight & Co. for] The World's fair souvenir nail co., 1893.

14x8½. Folded *l* making (4) p. Cream wraps, blue print and illus of sculpture with square headed nail replica. C.t. Caption title: "The Historical Souvenir of the World's Columbian Exposition. The Last Nail in the Woman's Building."   (TD)

74. U.S. World's Columbian Commission. Board of Lady Managers. *List of books sent by home and foreign committees to the library of the Woman's Building, World's Columbian Exposition, Chicago, 1893.* N.p.: n.p., n.d.

24½x16½. (2), 92 p. Orange-red wraps, maroon print and seal of the Lady Managers. Bottom of preface: "Under direction of Edith E. Clarke."
---- 26x17. 92 p. Marbled boards. CPL copy hand signed by Edith E. Clarke, director of compilers.   ⊚ . (CPL,CHx,NYPL,UNLV,NL)

75. U.S. World's Columbian Commission. Board of Lady Managers. *List of Officers, Lady Managers, and alternates of the Board of Lady Managers of the World's Columbian Commission.* Chicago: Rand, McNally & Co., 1893.

23x15. 30 p. including front cover. Powder blue wraps and text with black print. C.t.   ⊚ . (CPL,NL)

76. U.S. World's Columbian Commission. Board of Lady Managers. *Mrs. Palmer's Address to the Fortnightly Club of Chicago.* N.p.: n.p., n.d.

23x15. 8 p. To enlist the Club's interest in the work of the Board of Lady Managers and to "represent the cause and further the interests of women in connection with the Exposition."   ⊚ (NL,WM)

77. U.S. World's Columbian Commission. Board of Lady Managers. *Mrs. Palmer's remarks with reference to the Women's Building.* N.p.: n.p., n.d.

23x15. 7 p. Planning stage for space and exhibits.   ⊚ (NL)

78. U.S. World's Columbian Commission. Board of Lady Managers. ... *Names of countries represented by exhibits in the Woman's Building, and of the women representatives in the United States.* Chicago: Rand, McNally & Co., Printers, 1893.

21x15. 6 p. including front cover. Buff wraps, black print. C.t. At head of title: "World's Columbian Exposition." ☉ . (CPL)

79. U.S. World's Columbian Commission. Board of Lady Managers. *Official manual of the Board of Lady Managers of the World's Columbian commission. The Minutes of the Board ..., Including the Act of Congress, and Information ...* Chicago: Rand, McNally & co., 1891.

23x16. 334 p. Burnt orange cover, red lettering. Minutes of the Board from organization (Nov. 19, 1890) to close of 2nd session (Sept. 9, 1891). Includes articles on Alaska lady managers, badges, seal, colored people delegation, last nail in Woman's Building, and many other articles. ☉ . (KU,CHx,KyU,NL)

80. U.S. World's Columbian Commission. Board of Lady Managers. *Official minutes of the Committee on awards Certified by Virginia C. Meredith, June 27, 1896.* ____: ____, ____.

36x23. 107 p. (UC)

81. U.S. World's Columbian Commission. Board of Lady Managers. *Official Minutes of the Executive Committee Board of Lady Managers ... [1st]-7th sessions.* 3 vol. Chicago: Rand, McNally & Co., 1891-1894.

23x15. Blue wraps, dark blue print for each book. Other author: Executive Committee.
1: ... *Session April, 1891* (1st): 136, 16 p.
2: ... *Second and Third Sessions, Sept., 1891; Oct. 1892:* iv, 76 p.
3: ... *Fourth, Fifth, Sixth and Seventh Sessions, Apr. 24, May 6, October 27, 1893; May 15, 1894 ...:* iv, 128 p. (CPL,CHx,NL)

82. U.S. World's Columbian Commission. Board of Lady Managers. *Official minutes of the Executive committee. Board of lady managers of the World's Columbian Commission ... sess. 1 - April 8, 1891 -* [Chicago: 1891]-

23x__. v. Other author: Executive Committee. (UC)

83. U.S. World's Columbian Commission. Board of Lady Managers. *An Official Statement of the Action of the Executive Committee of the Board of Lady Managers in Removing from Office Miss Phoebe Couzins, Secretary of the Board of Lady Managers of the Columbian Commission. At this Session were Present Twenty-three of the Twenty-six Members Composing the Executive Committee.* N.p.: n.p., [1891?].

23½x15. 16 p. Caption title. Includes correspondence between Miss Couzins and Committee President, Bertha Palmer, regarding problems that led up to Couzins' dismissal. ☉ (NL)

84. U.S. World's Columbian Commission. Board of Lady Managers. *An Outline plan for uniform state work.* [Chicago: The Board, 1891].

23x14½. (7) p. Caption title. Suggestions and list of state items needed for displays. (UoC)

85. U.S. World's Columbian Commission. Board of Lady Managers. Palmer, Bertha. "To the Members Of the Board of Lady Managers." Letter. 16 May, 1891. New York.

3 p. printed letter urging members of the Board to commence state work in her absence. (She was in Europe until July 7th.)   ⊚ (NL)

86. U.S. World's Columbian Commission. Board of Lady Managers. *Prospectus. Board of Lady Managers of the World's Columbian Commission. Chicago, U.S.A., 1893.* [Chicago: 1893].

22½x15. 15 p. Sepia wraps, dark brown print. Machine sewn binding.   ⊚ . (SFe,NL)

87. U.S. World's Columbian Commission. Board of Lady Managers. *The Purposes of the Board of Lady Managers of the World's Columbian commission.* N.p.: n.p., n.d.

23x15½. (4) p. on glossy paper. Caption title.   ⊚ (NL)

88. U.S. World's Columbian Commission. Board of Lady Managers. *Report of Committee appointed to draft a Letter to be sent out to each Member of the Board of Lady Managers.* N.p.: n.p., n.d.

23½x15. 3 p. Caption title. Purpose: to clarify printed minutes. Names at end: Mrs. James P. [Mary Kavanaugh] Eagle, Mrs. Virginia C. Meredith, Miss Ellen A. Ford.   ⊚ (NL)

89. U.S. World's Columbian Commission. Board of Lady Managers. *Report of Mrs. Potter Palmer : President Board of Lady Managers, to the board of control of the World's Columbian Commission, and submitted to the Sub-Committee of the Committee on Appropriations of the House of Representatives, 52d Congress. Chicago, March 30, 1892.* Chicago: Rand, McNally & Co., Printers, 1892.

23x15. 1 *l*, (3)-27 p. Tables of itemized statements of expenses.   ⊚ (NL)

90. U.S. World's Columbian Commission. Board of Lady Managers. *Report of Mrs. Potter Palmer, president ... October 18, 1892.* Chicago: Rand, McNally & Co., 1892.

22 p.   (UC)

91. U.S. World's Columbian Commission. Board of Lady Managers. *Report of Mrs. Potter Palmer President, to the Board of Lady Managers of the World's Columbian commission. Fourth Session, April 26, 1893.* Chicago: Rand, McNally & Co., 1893.

23x15. 1 *l* (t.p.), (3)-11 p. Pink wraps with black print. C.t.= t.p.   ⊚ . (NL)

92. U.S. World's Columbian Commission. Board of Lady Managers. *Report of Mrs. Potter Palmer, President, to the Board of Lady Managers. September 2, 1891.* Rand, McNally & Co., 1891.

23x15. 1 *l*, (3)-32 p. Uniform light blue wraps with black print. C.t.= t.p.   ⊚ (NL,WM)

93. U.S. World's Columbian Commission. Board of Lady Managers. *Report of Mrs. Potter Palmer President, to the Executive Committee of the Board of Lady Managers of the World's Columbian commission : Seventh Session, May 15, 1894.* Chicago: Rand, McNally & Co., 1894.

23x15. 1 *l* (t.p.), (3)-30 p. Robin egg blue wraps with black print.   ⊚ . (NL)

94. U.S. World's Columbian Commission. Board of Lady Managers. *Report of the Committee on State Work.* N.p.: n.p., n.d.

23½x15. 3 p. Caption title. 1st of the 6 listed members: Miss E. Nellie Beck, Florida.   ⊘ (NL)

95. U.S. World's Columbian Commission. Board of Lady Managers. *Report of the Committee on State Work.* N.p.: n.p., n.d.

23½x15. 2 p. Caption title. 1st of the 4 listed members: Mrs. E. W. Allen.   ⊘ (NL)

96. U.S. World's Columbian Commission. Board of Lady Managers. *Report of the Executive Committee of the Board of Lady Managers of the World's Columbian commission. September 3, 1891.* Chicago: Rand, McNally & Co., 1891.

23x15. 30 p. including front cover. Plain paper wraps, black print. The greatest share of the report (p. 9-26) is devoted to chronological statements, resolutions, correspondence dealing with Phoebe Couzins' dismissal from her position as secretary of the Board.   ⊘ . (NL)

97. U.S. World's Columbian Commission. Board of Lady Managers. *Report : Of the President of the Board of Lady Managers of the World's Columbian Commission to the Executive Committee. April 8th, 1891.* [Chicago: 1891]

23x15½. 28 p. No wraps. Caption title. Attached to the report is official correspondence.   ⊘ (NL)

98. U.S. World's Columbian Commission. Board of Lady Managers. *Reports of the Committee on federal legislation of the Board of lady managers, World's Columbian Commission... October 26, 1892...[and] April 27, 1893.* Chicago: Rand, McNally, 1893.

23x__. 8 p.   (UC)

99. U.S. World's Columbian Commission. Board of Lady Managers. *Reports presented to the board of lady managers At the Session of September, 1891 from the States, Territories, District of Columbia, and City of Chicago.* N.p.: n.p., [1891?].

23½x15. 23 p. Caption title. Reports from States in alphabetical order, followed by Territories, and Chicago. ⊘ (NL,WM)

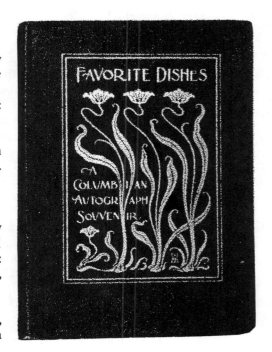

100. U.S. World's Columbian Commission. Board of Lady Managers. Shuman, Carrie V., comp. *Favorite dishes : A Columbian autograph souvenir cookery book ...* Chicago: Carrie V. Shuman [R. R. Donnelley & Sons Co., Printers], 1893 [°1893 by Carrie V. Shuman].

[Second ed.]: 22x16. 2 *l*, 221 p., illus. Orange cloth hc, gold and white design, embossed. Frontis of Bertha

Palmer. "[Second edition.]" printed on p. (4). Fine quality. Recipes from each state, signed in facsimile.

---- 1st ed.?: Same pub info and cover.

---- Limited ed. in silk cover.

P↑   ☺ (GLD,csuf,CHx,SI,NYPL,F,S,UNLV,UDe) $35 - 75

101. U.S. World's Columbian Commission. Board of Lady Managers. *The Woman's Building.* N.p.: n.p., n.d.

23x15. (4) glossy pages. Information and data prior to completion of the Woman's Building. States: "is being constructed ... at a cost of $200,000."   ☺ (NL)

102. U.S. World's Columbian Commission. Board of Lady Managers. *The Woman's building and what is to be seen in it.* N.p., n.p., n.d.

19x13. 16 p. Caption title. A description of the Woman's Building and its contents. Signed at end: Mary S[mith] Lockwood.   ☺ . (UDe)

103. U.S. World's Columbian Commission. Board of Lady Managers. *The World's Columbian exposition, Chicago.* N.p.: n.p., n.d.

23x__. 13 color plates folded in cover. C.t. Subject: Board of Lady Managers -- views.   (OC)

104. U.S. World's Columbian Commission. Board of Reference and Control. *Answer of the Board of Reference and Control of the World's Columbian Commission, to the communication from the sub-committee of the Committee on Appropriations of the House of Representatives, 52d Congress. Chicago, March 30, 1892.* Chicago: Rand, McNally & Co., printers, 1892.

23x15. 137 p. includes tables, followed by a 27 p. report of Mrs. Potter Palmer, president of the Board of Lady Managers.   (CHx)

105. U.S. World's Columbian Commission. Board of Reference and Control. *Appendix to report of Board of Reference and Control submitted to the World's Columbian Commission, at its 4th session, April first, 1891, ...* Chicago: Knight & Leonard Co., Printers, 1891.

21½x15. 44 p. Robin egg blue wraps, black print. WCC President, Thomas Wetherill Palmer, chaired.   (CHx,NL)

☞ Thomas W. Palmer (1830-1913), a senator from Michigan and Minister to Spain, was chosen for the World's Columbian Commission by President Harrison. Once on the commission, the members elected him president. After the Fair he sustained a nervous collapse requiring long rest.

106. U.S. World's Columbian Commission. Board of Reference and Control. *Appendix to report of Board of Reference and Control submitted to the World's Columbian Commission, at its fifth session September second, 1891, ...* Chicago: Knight, Leonard & Co., Printer, 1891.

21½x15. 104 p. Robin egg blue wraps, black print. Vice President McKenzie chaired.   (CHx)

107. U.S. World's Columbian Commission. Board of Reference and Control. *Appendix to report of board of reference and control submitted to the World's Columbian Commission at its sixth session, April sixth, 1892.* Chicago: Knight, Leonard & Co., Printers, 1892.

23x15. 97 p. Tan wraps, black print. C.t.= t.p. President T. W. Palmer chaired. ☻. (KyU,CHx)

108. U.S. World's Columbian Commission. Board of Reference and Control. *Appendix to report of board of reference and control submitted to the World's Columbian Commission at its seventh session October eighteenth, 1893.* Chicago: Rand, McNally & Co., Printers, 1892.

22x15. iv, 88 p. Reddish brown wraps. C.t.= t.p. ☻. (KyU)

109. U.S. World's Columbian Commission. Board of Reference and Control. *Official minutes of the Board of Reference and Control of the World's Columbian Commission, from March 24 to May 7, 1892, Inclusive.* N.p.: n.p., n.d.

23½x15½. 27 p. No wraps. Caption title. (CHx)

110. U.S. World's Columbian Commission. Board of Reference and Control. *Official minutes of the Board of Reference and Control of the World's Columbian Commission, from January 9, 1894, to January 15, 1894, Inclusive.* N.p.: n.p., n.d.

23x15. 15 p. Caption title. At the request of Commission President Palmer, the Board met in Washington, DC. Meeting was held at the Arlington Hotel. ☻.(CPL)

111. U.S. World's Columbian Commission. Bureau of Awards. Porter, Robert P. *A Plan for the organization of a bureau of awards for the World's Columbian exposition : submitted by request of the U. S. Commission.* [Washington, D. C.: Published for the World's Columbian Commission by Judd and Detweiler, 1890].

ca. 23x17. 12 p. [Name was changed from Bureau to Committee; see "Committee on Awards" for later items.] ☻.(SI,NYPL)

112. U.S. World's Columbian Commission. Commission to Europe. ... *Report of the Commission to Europe.* Chicago: Rand, McNally & Co., 1891.

23x15½. 31 p. Beige wraps, black print. C.t. At head of title: "The World's Columbian Exposition." [This commission was organized by Congressman Benjamin Butterworth, Secretary of World's Columbian Commission. It was met in London by James Dredge and later went on to other countries to gain support for the WF.] ☻.(CPL)

113. U.S. World's Columbian Commission. Committee on Awards. *Final report of executive committee of awards, World's Columbian Commission.* Washington: J. F. Sheiry, printer, 1895; Woodbridge, CT: RPI, 1989.

23½x15. 64 p.
---- In: Thacher's *Awards at the World's Columbian Exposition* #119.
(LC,SI,NYPL)

114. [U.S. World's Columbian Commission]. [Committee on Awards.] *List of Awards as copied for Mrs. Virginia C. Meredith, Chairman, Committee on Awards, Board of Lady Managers, from the official records in the office of Hon. John Boyd Thacher, Chairman, Executive Committee on Awards, Washington, D.C.* 2 vol. N.p.: n.p., n.d.

34x22. Carbon typescript. Vol 1: Domestic (list of awards by dept) is 6 cm thick. Vol 2: Foreign (list of awards alphabetically by country) is 6½ cm thick.   ☺ (CHx)

☞   Meredith, from Indiana, was the Lady Manager who certified awards. For Meredith's appointment, letters, and personal papers see InHx #2446.o.

115. U.S. World's Columbian Commission. Committee on Awards. ... *Report of the committee on awards of the World's Columbian commission. Special reports upon special subjects or groups.* 2 vol. Washington: GPO, 1901.

24x15½. 2 vol paged continuously to 1694 p., illus, many plates not included in pagination, map. Olive green cloth hc with gilt print on spine. "Limited to 3,500 copies by Act of Congress." At head of title: "World's Columbian exposition, Chicago, Ill., 1893." This copy does not have the series number on spine or document number on t.p.
---- Same title: See #279.a. (57th Cong., 1st sess. H. Doc. 510.).
      ☺ . (csuf,CHx,SI,NYPL,F,S,OSU,BU,UoC,A,BPL) $100 - 200

116. U.S. World's Columbian Commission. Committee on Awards. *Supplemental final report of the executive committee on awards of the World's Columbian Commission.* Washington: Press of Norman T. Elliot, 1896.

23½x15. 1 *l*, 6 p.
---- In: Thacher's *Awards at the World's Columbian Exposition* #119.
      (LC,NYPL)

117. U.S. World's Columbian Commission. Committee on Awards. Thacher, John Boyd. *Address of John Boyd Thacher to the American exhibitors of the World's Columbian Exposition...* N.p.: n.p., n.d.

23½x15. 16 p. Gray wraps with black print.
---- In: Thacher's *Awards at the World's Columbian Exposition* #119.
      (LC)

118. U.S. World's Columbian Commission. Committee on Awards. Thacher, John Boyd. *Awards at the World's Columbian Exposition.* Albany: 1898.

23½x15. 69 p.
---- In: Thacher's *Awards at the World's Columbian Exposition* #119.
      (LC)

119. U.S. World's Columbian Commission. Committee on Awards. Thacher, John Boyd. *Awards at the World's Columbian Exposition ... Together with an appendix in which will be found several* [3] *papers relating to the same subject.* Albany: 1898.

23½x15. A compilation of four publications including their wraps. Bound in a beautiful two-tone green tooled leather hc, gold, maroon, brown design inside and out. The LC rare book section and NYPL each have 1 of 7 presentation copies signed by Thacher. Includes: *Awards at the World's*

Columbian Exposition-- 69 p.; *Address of John Boyd Thacher to the American exhibitors of the World's Columbian Exposition*-- 16 p.; *Final report of the Executive Committee on Awards, World's Columbian Exposition*-- 64 p.; and *Supplemental Final Report of the Executive Committee on Awards of the World's Columbian Exposition*-- 6 p.   (LC,NYPL)

120. U.S. World's Columbian Commission. Committee on Classification. *Classification of the World's Columbian Exposition : Chicago, U. S. A., 1893, adopted by the World's Columbian Commission.* Chicago: Donohue & Henneberry, printers and binders, 1891; Woodbridge, CT: RPI, 1989.

   23x15. 2 *l*, 122 p., illus. Gray wraps, black print. Frontis of the Administration Bldg. C.t.= t.p.
   ⊚ . (SFe,KyU,CHx,LC,SI,NYPL,NLC,OSU,LMi,UMi,NHSt,HL,CSA,WM,WiHx,OhHx)

121. U.S. World's Columbian Commission. Committee on Classification. *Classification of the World's Columbian Exposition : Chicago, U.S.A., 1893, prepared by the Committee on Classification of the National Commission.* Pittsburgh: n.p., 1890; [Chicago: Rand, McNally & Co., 1890.]

   23x15. 93 p. Light green wraps, black print. Rand's pub info from cover.   ⊚ . (CPL,LC)

122. U.S. World's Columbian Commission. Committee on Classification. ... *Draft of a System of Classification prepared for the Committee on Classification. (Subject to revision.)* Chicago: Rand, McNally & Co., 1890; Woodbridge, CT: RPI, 1989.

   ca. 21x14. 95 p. C.t. At head of title: "World's Columbian Exposition."   ⊚ . (SI)

U.S. World's Columbian Commission. Council of Administration. See "Report of Sub-committee of the joint Board of Reference and Control" #51.

123. U.S. World's Columbian Commission. *The Official Directory of the World's Columbian Commission.* [Chicago: Press of the W.T.P.A.], n.d.

   15x12. 66 p. Dark orange slick wraps, black print and design. C.t.= t.p. [The World's Columbian Exposition (Company) issued their similar directory. See #214.]
   ---- 58 p.
   ---- 63 p. with [1891] on t.p. verso; otherwise the same.
   ⊚ . (KyU,CHx,NYPL,NL)

124. U.S. World's Columbian Commission. *The Official directory of the World's Columbian Commission : The Act of Congress, Commissioners and Alternates, with Post Office Addresses, Officers, and Committees, to July 2, 1890.* Chicago: Rand, McNally & Co., Printers, 1890; Woodbridge, CT: RPI, 1989.

   15x10. 25 p. including back cover. Covers are a uniform gray. C.t= t.p. ⊚ . (SI,OSL)

125. U.S. World's Columbian Commission. *Official manual of the World's Columbian Commission, containing the minutes and other official data of the Commission from the date of its organization, June 26, 1890, to the close of its third session, November 26, 1890, including information in reference to the Chicago directory of the World's Columbian Exposition, etc.* Chicago: Rand, McNally & Co., 1890; Woodbridge, CT: RPI, 1989.

23x15. 1 p.l, vi, 5-372 p. Green wraps with black print. Contains the "Official Minutes" for the 1st to 3rd sessions of the World's Columbian Commission.   (csuf,SI,CHx,NYPL,UMi)

126. U.S. World's Columbian Commission. *Official minutes of the Executive Committee of the World's Columbian Commission. From April 27th to October 4th, 1893, inclusive.* Chicago: Knight, Leonard & co., printers, 1893.

23x15. 96 p. Pale green wraps. C.t.   ☺ . (KyU)

127. U.S. World's Columbian Commission. *Official Minutes of the fourth session of the World's Columbian Commission held in the city of Chicago April 1st to 4th, 1891, inclusive.* Chicago: Leonard & Knight Co., 1891.

23x15½. 59 p. Tan wraps with black print.   ☺ (CHx,WM)

128. U.S. World's Columbian Commission. *Official minutes of the fifth session of the World's Columbian Commission held in the city of Chicago September 2d to 8th, 1891, inclusive.* Chicago: Knight, Leonard & co., printers, 1891.

23x15½. 110 p. Robin-egg blue wraps, black print.   ☺ . (KyU,CHx,WM)

129. U.S. World's Columbian Commission. *Official minutes of the sixth session of the World's Columbian Commission held in the city of Chicago April 6th to 11th, 1892, Inclusive.* Chicago: Knight, Leonard & Co., printers, 1892.

23x15½. 159 p. Robin-egg blue wraps, black print.
---- Also listed: v, 159 p.
   ☺ . (KyU,CHx,WM)

130. U.S. World's Columbian Commission. *Official minutes of the seventh session of the World's Columbian Commission held in the city of Chicago October 18th to 26th, 1892, inclusive.* Chicago: Knight, Leonard & Co., printers, 1892.

23x15. 259 p. Light green wraps, black print.
P→   ☺ . (SFe,WM)

131. U.S. World's Columbian Commission. *Official minutes of the eighth session of the World's Columbian Commission held in the city of Chicago April 25th to May 26th, 1893, inclusive.* Chicago: Knight, Leonard & Co., printers, 1893.

23x15½. 359 p. Pale green wraps.   ☺ . (KyU,WM)

132. U.S. World's Columbian Commission. *Official minutes of the ninth session of the World's Columbian Commission held in the city of Chicago July 1st to Sept. 11th, 1893, inclusive.* Chicago: Knight, Leonard & Co., printers, 1893.

23x15½. 547 p. Pale green wraps.   ☺ . (KyU,WM)

133. U.S. World's Columbian Commission. *Official minutes of the World's Columbian Commission. Sixth Session - Fifth Day, April 11, 1892.* N.p.: n.p., n.d.

   23x15. 10 p. No printed cover.   ☺ . (SFe)

134. U.S. World's Columbian Commission. *Official minutes of the World's Columbian Commission. Eighth Session - Twenty-fifth Day, May 26, 1893.* [Chicago]: 1893.

   8°. 5 p.   (NYPL)

135. U.S. World's Columbian Commission. *Official minutes of the World's Columbian Commission. Ninth Session - Fortieth Day, August 21, 1893.* N.p.: n.p., n.d.

   23x15. 10 p. No printed cover.   ☺ . (SFe)

136. U.S. World's Columbian Commission. *Official Minutes of the World's Columbian Commission. Tenth Session - Third Day, October 6, 1893.* N.p.: n.p., n.d.

   23x15.   (KyU)

137. U.S. World's Columbian Commission. *Official Minutes of the World's Columbian Commission. Tenth session - Fourth Day, October 7, 1893.* N.p.: n.p., n.d.   (KyU)

138. U.S. World's Columbian Commission. *Official Minutes of the World's Columbian Commission. Tenth Session - Sixth Day, October 11, 1893.* N.p.: n.p., n.d.

   23x15.   (KyU)

139. U.S. World's Columbian Commission. *Official Minutes of the World's Columbian Commission. Tenth session - Ninth Day, October 16, 1893.* N.p.: n.p., n.d.   (KyU)

140. U.S. World's Columbian Commission. *The World's Columbian Exposition : Memorial for International Arbitration. Souvenir Copy with Appendix.* N.p.: n.p., n.d.

   29x22. Note pad style with hinge 22 cm long at top), 54 *l* which are facsimiles of signatures of WCE officials from a variety of countries, 1 *l*, 15 numbered *l* have text on one side. White cloth hc, gold print, high rag watermarked leaves. T.p. printed in calligraphy in keeping with the signature facsimile format of the text.   ☺ . (LC,NYPL,mcg,BM)

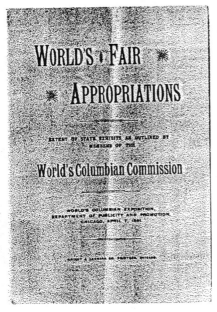

141. U.S. World's Columbian Commission. *World's Columbian exposition. Regulations governing awards.* N.p.: n.p., n.d.

28x21. (4) p. No wraps. Caption title. ☯.(WM)

142. U.S. World's Columbian Commission. *World's Fair Appropriations : Extent of state exhibits as outlined by members of the World's Columbian Commission.* ... Chicago: Knight & Leonard Co. Printers, [1891].

22½x15. 20 p. Light brown wraps, black print. C.t. Following title: "World's Columbian Exposition, Department of Publicity and Promotion, Chicago, April 7, 1891." Commission meeting in Chicago, Apr. 3rd; report issued Apr. 7, 1891.
P↑   ☯.(SFe,CPL,NYPL)

143. World's Columbian Exposition. *Annual report of the president of the World's Columbian Exposition for the year ending April 1, 1893.* Chicago: Stromberg, Allen & co., 1893.

22x14½. 31 p. including t.p. Green wraps, black print. ☯.(csuf,CHx,UoC,NL)

144. World's Columbian Exposition. *Answer of the President of the World's Columbian Exposition to questions propounded by Hon. A. M. Dockery, chairman sub-committee of the committee on appropriations, House of Representatives. Chicago, March 26, 1892.* Chicago: Rand, McNally & Co., 1892.

23x15½. 137 p. Sand wraps, black print. C.t.= t.p. WCE president was W. T. Baker. ☯.(CHx,UoC)

145. World's Columbian Exposition. Auditor's Department. ... *Classification of Accounts ... 1 September, 1891.* Chicago: Knight, Leonard & Co., Printers, 1891.

18½x11½. 32 p. Brown cloth hc, gilt lettering. C.t.= t.p. At head of title: "World's Columbian Exposition." (CHx)

146. World's Columbian Exposition. Auditor's Department. ... *Classification of Accounts ... 1st February, 1892.* Chicago: Rand, McNally & Co., Printers, 1892.

19½x13½. 47 p. White pebbled stiff wraps, black print. C.t.= t.p. At head of title: "World's Columbian Exposition." (CHx)

147. World's Columbian Exposition. Auditor's Department. ... *Classification of Accounts ... 1st July, 1892.* Chicago: Printed by the Chicago Legal News Co., 1892.

19½x13½. 54 p. White pebbled stiff wraps, black print. C.t.= t.p. At head of title: "World's Columbian Exposition." (CHx)

148. World's Columbian Exposition. Auditor's Department. ... *Classification of Accounts ... 1st January, 1893.* Chicago: Printed by the Chicago Legal News Co., 1893.

20x13½. 59 p. Rose colored wraps, black print. C.t.= t.p. At head of title: "World's Columbian Exposition." (CHx)

149. World's Columbian Exposition. Auditor's Department. ... *Report of the Auditor to the Board of Directors.* ... Chicago: P. F. Pettibone & Co., printers, [1891-1894].

Except as noted below: 21x10½ folds out to 21x30½ (two folds to make a triptych). Plain paper, black print. At head of title: "World's Columbian Exposition." C.t.= "t.p." (CHx,UoC)

The following dated issues were found at CHx:

1892:	1893:	1894:
31st July: 5 *l*	31 January: 11 p.	28 February: 2 *l*
31st October: 5 *l*	28 February: 5 *l*	31 March: 2 *l*
30th November: 5 *l*	31 March: 6 *l*	30 April: 2 *l*
31 December: 5 *l*	30 June: 6 *l*	31 May: 11 p.
	31 July: 6 *l*	30 June: 2 *l*
	31 August: 6 *l*	
	30 September: 6 *l*	
	30th November: 23x10½. 6 *l*	
	31 December: 11 p.	

150. World's Columbian Exposition. *Banquet tendered to the Foreign Commissioners to the World's Columbian Exposition by the Directors of the World's Columbian Exposition, Music Hall, Jackson Park. Wednesday, October the eleventh, eighteen hundred and ninety three. Chicago.* [Chicago: A. C. McClurg & co.], n.d.

26x20. 2 *l*, (2) p., 3 *l*. White satin flexible covers, silk inside, pink ribbon tied. Striking multicolor litho 1st *l*. Contents: grand menu, toasts, music, and list of directors of the WCE. On cover in gilt: name of invitee; e.g., "Mr. Otto Young" (a director).--(GLD)
   ⊘ (GLD) $50 - 100

151. World's Columbian Exposition. Bureau de Publicité et de Propagande. *Apres quatre siecles : "World's Fair" : La decouverte de l'Amerique sera célébrée par une Exposition Internationale a Chicago, Ill., U.S.A. : 1893.* Chicago: Bureau de Publicité et de Propagande, World's Columbian Exposition, Frantz Gindele printing co., 1891.

22x14½. 16, (4) p., illus. Dark robin egg blue with black print. C.t. Map printed on outside back cover. French version of #186.   ⊘ . (NL)

152. World's Columbian Exposition. Burnham, D[aniel] H[udson], et. al. *Final report of the Director of Works of the World's Columbian Exposition, June 1894.* 8 vol. [Chicago]: n.p., 1894; Microfiche. Andover, MA: Northeast Document Conservation Center, 1985.

55x70. 8 vol of mounted typed text, drawings, and photos (vol 8 is atlas of plans). 4 vol of mounted photos (51x64) + index to text (407 *l*; 36x__) + index to photos (62 *l*; 28x__). For recent publication, see #2330.   (AIC)

153. World's Columbian Exposition. *By-laws of the World's Columbian Exposition as revised and amended to March 13, 1891.* N.p.: n.p., n.d.

14½x9½. 13 p. No wraps. Caption title.   (csuf,CHx)

154. World's Columbian Exposition. *By-laws of the World's Columbian Exposition : As Revised and Amended to March 1, 1892.* Chicago: Rand, McNally & Co., Printers, 1892; Woodbridge, CT: RPI, 1989.

17x11. 15 p. Pale blue wraps, black print. C.t.   ⊘ . (CHx,SI)

155. World's Columbian Exposition. *By-laws of the World's exposition of 1892. Officers, standing committees and act of congress... May 12, 1890.* N.p.: n.p., 1890.

14½x9½. 25 p. Light blue wraps, black print, cloth spine.   (CHx)

156. World's Columbian Exposition. *Concession Agreements.* 7 vol. Chicago: 1891-93.

27½x21½. Each agreement separately paginated, bound in black cloth hc, gold print on spine. The numbers 1-20 are handwritten on the contracts; i.e., probably for binding. An example of a title: *Vol. 1. - Nos. 1-20. 26st August, 1891, to 15th July, 1892.* 3rd ed. [Chicago]: Auditor's office, 1893.   (CHx)

157. World's Columbian Exposition. Council of Administration. *Constitution and by-laws of the Council of Administration. Created August, 1892.* Chicago: E. J. Decker, Printer, 1892.

17x11. 16 p. Pale peach wraps, black print. C.t.= t.p.   ⊚ . (CHx)

158. World's Columbian Exposition. Council of Administration. *Minutes of the Council of Administration of the World's Columbian Exposition held ... August 25th, 1892 - Nov. 10th, 1893. ... .* Chicago: Henson Bros., 1892-93.

17½x__. 65 nos. in 7 vols.   (UoC)

159. World's Columbian Exposition. Council of Administration. *Minutes of the Meeting of the Council of Administration of the World's Columbian Exposition for the week commencing ...* Chicago: Henson Bros., 1892-93.

16½x11. 30 vol (30 booklets). All with burnt orange wraps, black print. C.t. Each contains more than one meeting, each meeting has a separate t.p.: e.g., *Minutes of the Meeting of the Council of Administration of the World's Columbian Exposition : Held in the Office of President Higinbotham, Thursday, August 25th, 1892, At 10:00 o'clock A. M.*   ⊚ . (CHx)

The ellipse in the c.t. represents the dates below:

August 22nd, 1892: 14, 6, 14 p.
August 29th, 1892: 14, 20, 4, 16, 8 p.
September 5th, 1892: 12, 12, 12, 8 p.
September 12th, 1892: 18, 11, 8, 8, 11, 12 p.
September 19th, 1892: 7, 14, 8, 9, 14, 18 p.
September 26th, 1892: 6, 16, 8, 16, 8, 7 p.
October 3rd, 1892: 15, 9, 7, 16, 3, 7 p.
October 10th, 1892: 13, 12, 7, 13, 12 + (1) p.
October 17th, 1892: 12, 7 + (1) p.
October 24th, 1892: 11, 4, 12, 8 p.
October 31st, 1892: 8, 12, 10 + (1) p.
November 7th, 1892: Variously paged.
November 14th, 1892: Variously paged.
November 21st, 1892: Variously paged.
November 28th, 1892: Variously paged.
December 5th, 1892: Variously paged.

December 12th, 1892: Variously paged.
December 19th, 1892: Variously paged.
December 26th, 1892: Variously paged.
January 2nd, 1893: Variously paged.
        1892 pub. date on cover and 1893 on t.p.
January 9th, 1893: Variously paged.
        1892 pub. date on cover and 1893 on t.p.
January 16th, 1893: Variously paged.
        1893 both on cover and t.p.
January 23rd, 1893: Variously paged.
January 30th, 1893: Variously paged.
February 6th, 1893: Variously paged.
February 13th, 1893: Variously paged.
February 27th, 1893: Variously paged.
March 6th, 1893: Variously paged.
March 12th, 1893: Variously paged.

160. World's Columbian Exposition. Departimento di Pubblicita e di Promozione. *Dopo quattro Secoli : La "World's fair" : "La scoperta del l'America : da commemorarse mediante una esposizione internazionale : Chicago, Ill., U. S. A. 1893.* Chicago: Stromberg, Allen & Co., printers, [1891].

    22x15. 16 p. Green wraps, black print. WCE plan on back wrap. C.t. Italian version of #186.
        © . (CPL)

161. World's Columbian Exposition. Department of Agriculture. ... *Department of Agriculture. Special rules and information.* N.p.: n.p., n.d.

    Folded sheet making (4) p., each page: 28x21½. No cover. At head of title: "World's Columbian Exposition." Handout to potential exhibitors. "(Signed) W. I. Buchanan, Chief, Department of Agriculture" and "(Signed) George R. Davis, Director-General" (names typed).   © . (SFe,CHx,LC,NL)

162. World's Columbian Exposition. Department of Agriculture. ... *Department of Agriculture. Special rules and information governing the exhibit of bees, honey, beeswax and bee appliances.* N.p.: n.p., n.d.

    28x22. (1) p. with b/w illus of proposed exhibit cases. At head of title: "World's Columbian Exposition."   (CHx)

163. World's Columbian Exposition. Department of Electricity. Barrett, J[ohn] P[atrick]. *Electricity at the Columbian Exposition : including an account of the exhibits in the electricity building, the power plant in machinery hall, the arc and incandescent lighting of the grounds and buildings, the transmission of power for the operation of machinery, the subway and conduits, electric launches, electric elevators, lighting of the Ferris wheel, corona lighting of the manufactures building, etc.* Chicago: R. R. Donnelley & Sons, Co., 1894 [°1894 by J. P. Barrett].

    23½x15. 2 *l*, ix-xv, 501 p., illus, port, glossy paper frontis of Barrett. Dark green cloth hc, gilt print and design. Barrett was Chief of the Dept of Electricity.
    ---- Variants: 1 to 3 *l* before ix, size to 24x16½, with and without green speckled edges.
    *   © . (PU,CPL,CHx,LC,NYPL,F,S,UTn,UMi,NYSt,UoC,NL) $45 - 80

164. World's Columbian Exposition. Department of Electricity. ... *Classification and rules department of electricity : With other information for intending Exhibitors.* [Chicago: Donohue & Henneberry], n.d.; Woodbridge, CT: RPI, 1989.

    23x15. 24 p. + large fold out plan of Electricity Building. Chartreuse wraps, black print. At head of title: WCE opening/closing dates and "World's Columbian Exposition Chicago, U.S.A. 1893." J. P. Barrett, Chief of Dept.   © . (SFe,CHx,SI,UMi,UoC,NL)

165. World's Columbian Exposition. Department of Ethnology, Archæology, History, Cartography, Latin-American Bureau, Collective and Isolated Exhibits. ... *Plan and classification department M. Ethnology, Archæology, History, Cartography, Latin-American Bureau, Collective and Isolated Exhibits.* Chicago: World's Columbian Exposition, 1892; Woodbridge, CT: RPI, 1989.

    23x14½. 27 p. + 4 tipped in fold outs in back. Sepia wraps, black print. At head of title: "World's Columbian Exposition Chicago, U.S.A. 1893." C.t.= t.p. F. W. Putnam, Chief of Dept.
    © . (SFe,KyU,CHx,SI,NYPL,S,UMi,UoC,NL,RPB,OhHx)

166. World's Columbian Exposition. Department of Ethnology, Archæology, History, Cartography, Latin-American Bureau, Collective and Isolated Exhibits. Wilson, Thomas. *Proposed classification of the section of anthropology and prehistoric archæology at the Chicago exposition, prepared, at the request of its committee, ...* N.p.: n.p., n.d.; Woodbridge, CT: RPI, 1989.

22x14. 40 p. No wraps, caption title. Thomas Wilson was curator at the United States National Museum. ☺. (LC,SI)

167. World's Columbian Exposition. Department of Fine Arts. ... *Catalogue of the United States Loan Collection (foreign masterpieces owned in the United States).* Chicago: W. B. Conkey Co. publishers to the World's Columbian Exposition, 1893; Woodbridge, CT: RPI, 1989.

ca. 21½x15. 20 p., microfilm. At head of title: "World's Columbian Exposition: Department of Fine Arts: Halsey C. Ives, chief." ☺. (SI)

168. World's Columbian Exposition. Department of Fine Arts. *Circular No. 3.* N.p.: n.p., [1892].

22x15. (8) p. No printed cover. Lists the Advisory Committees and members who juried the art to be exhibited at the WF, Dept "K", Fine Arts. Halsey C. Ives, Chief of Dept. Lithograph of "Central pavilion of fine arts building" at top of 1st p.
P→   ☺. (SFe)

169. World's Columbian Exposition. Department of Fine Arts. ... *Extracts from rules and regulations governing the administration of the department of fine arts : Approved, July 13, 1891.* Chicago: Press of W. B. Conkey Co., [1891]; Chicago: Globe Lithog. & Ptg. Co., [189-?].

22x14½. 1 *l*, (5) p. including text on inside back cover. Gray wraps, black print. Frontis has b/w illus of Art Building. At head of title: "World's Columbian Exposition Chicago, Ill., U.S.A." C.t.: "... Department of Fine Arts : General Information." ☺. (SFe,CHx,NYPL)

170. [World's Columbian Exposition]. [Department of Fine Arts]. ... *Konst-afdelningen : Allmänna Förordningar.* [Chicago: Stromberg, Allen & Co.], n.d.

22x15. 12 p. Black print on cream wraps. At head of title: "World's Columbian exposition : 1893 : Chicago, Ill., U.S.A." Trans: Dept of arts : General Regulations. Includes Dept K. Fine arts. ☺. (S)

171. World's Columbian Exposition. Department of Fish, Fisheries, Fish Products and Apparatus of Fishing. ... *Classification, Rules and General Information for Intending Exhibitors. Department of fish, fisheries, fish products and apparatus of fishing.* Chicago: Stromberg, Allen & Co., n.d.; Woodbridge, CT: RPI, 1989.

23x15. 56 p. plus 2 fold out views laid in at back cover. Patterned light green wraps with black print. At head of title: "World's Columbian Exposition Chicago, Illinois, U.S.A. 1893." Jos. Wm. Collins was Chief of the Dept. ☉. (SFe,SI,UoC)

172. World's Columbian Exposition. Department of Foreign Affairs. ... *Commissions of Foreign Countries in the United States. Corrected to April 24, 1893.* N.p.: n.p., n.d.; Woodbridge, CT: RPI, 1989.

ca. 28x17½. 8 p. Microfilm. At head of title: "World's Columbian Exposition." ☉. (SI)

173. World's Columbian Exposition. Department of Forestry. *Special Rules and Information of the Department of Forestry : World's Columbian Exposition.* N.p.: n.p., n.d.

28x22. (4) p. B/w illus on page (4). On page (3): Approved by W. I. Buchanan, Chief, Dept of Agriculture. ☉ (CHx)

174. World's Columbian Exposition. Department of Horticulture. ... *Classification and rules department of horticulture : With other information for intending Exhibitors.* [Chicago: Donohue & Henneberry, 1893]; Woodbridge, CT: RPI, 1989.

23x15. 20 p. plus a fold out plan of the fairgrounds which follows the t.p. Marine blue (or green) wraps, black print. C.t. At head of title: WCE opening/closing dates and "World's Columbian Exposition Chicago, U.S.A. 1893." J. M. Samuels, Chief of Dept. ☉. (SFe,CHx,csuf,SI,UoC,NL)

175. World's Columbian Exposition. Department of Liberal Arts. Bureau of Charities and Correction. ... *Circular no. 6. The Bureau of Charities and Correction. What it will include and instructions for preparing exhibits.* N.p.: n.p., n.d.

22x15. 19 p. No printed cover. Caption title. Nathaniel S. Rosenan, Superintendent, Bureau of Charities and Correction. At head of title: "World's Columbian exposition. Department of liberal arts." ☉. (SFe,CHx,UoC,WM)

176. World's Columbian Exposition. Department of Liberal Arts. Bureau of Charities and Correction. ... *Introduction to the English exhibits.* London: Charity Organization Society [printed by Spottiswoode and co.], [1893].

21½x14. 48 p., 8 fold. charts. Tan wraps with black print. At head of title: "The Columbian exposition 1893 : The Bureau of Charities and Correction." C.t.= t.p. ☉. (NL)

177. World's Columbian Exposition. Department of Liberal Arts. ... *Circular No. 9 : The bureau of hygiene and sanitation.* N.p.: n.p., n.d.

23x15. 14 p. No printed cover. Caption title. F. W. Brewer, Superintendent, Bureau of Hygiene and Sanitation. At head of title: "World's Columbian exposition. Department of liberal arts."
☉. (SFe,LC,NYPL,WM)

178. World's Columbian Exposition. Department of Liberal Arts. ... *Circular No. 4 : The Educational Exhibit. No. 2. Statistics by graphic methods. Wing frames; state maps.* N.p.: n.p., n.d.

22½x15. 17 p. No printed cover. Caption title. At head of title: "World's Columbian exposition. Department of liberal arts."
---- Also listed: Klemm, L[ouis] R[ichard]. ... *Display of school statistics.* *<From manuscript of Dr. L. R. Klemm; with permission of the commissioner of education.>*
            ☺ . (CHx,UoC)

179. World's Columbian Exposition. Department of Liberal Arts. ... *Circular No. 2 : The Educational Exhibit of the World's Columbian exposition.* N.p.: n.p., n.d.

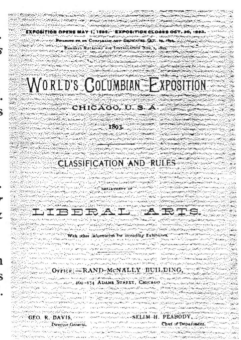

23x15. 10 p. No printed cover. Caption title. Selim H. Peabody, Chief of Dept. At head of title: "World's Columbian exposition. Department of liberal arts."
            ☺ . (SFe,CHx,SI,UoC,NL,RPB)

180. World's Columbian Exposition. Department of Liberal Arts. ... *Classification and rules department of liberal arts. : With other information for intending Exhibitors.* Chicago: [Donohue & Henneberry Printers], n.d.; Woodbridge, CT: RPI, 1989.

23x15. 31 p. + large fold out plan of Art Building laid in back. Yellow wraps, black print. At head of title: "World's Columbian Exposition Chicago, U.S.A. 1893." Selim H. Peabody, Chief of Dept.
P→   ☺ . (SFe,MaHx,NYPL,USD,UMi,UoC,NL,RPB)

181. World's Columbian Exposition. Department of Live Stock. ... *Rules, Information, and Premium List, department of live stock.* Chicago: The J. M. Jones stationery and printing co., [1891?]; Chicago: Rand, McNally & Co., Printers, [1892]; Chicago: Rand, McNally & Co., Printers, [1893?]; Woodbridge, CT: RPI [Rand 1892], 1989.

Rand [1892]: 19½x13½. 80 p. Light gray wraps, black print. Lists cash awards in each division, quarantine rules, cost of feed at WF live stock exhibit, etc. C.t. At head of title: "World's Columbian Exposition, Chicago, Illinois, U.S.A." Below title: "Revised to July 27, 1892."
---- Rand [1893?]: "Revised to June 1, 1893" printed on cover.
---- Jones: *Rules : Information and Premium List : department of Live Stock : World's Columbian Exposition : Chicago, Illinois, U.S.A. : 1893.* 16½x12. 43 p. Light green wraps, black print and design. C.t. Inside front wrap is a notice from George R. Davis dated Sept. 10, 1891. W. I. Buchanan, Chief, Dept of Agriculture.
            ☺ . (SFe,CHx,KyU,SI,F) $15 - 25

182. World's Columbian Exposition. Department of Machinery. ... *Classification and rules department of machinery : With other information for intending Exhibitors.* Chicago: Donohue & Henneberry Printers, [1892]; Woodbridge, CT: RPI, 1989.

23x15. 26 p. + large fold out plan of Machinery Hall in back. Rosy red wraps, black print. At head of title: WCE opening/closing dates and "World's Columbian Exposition Chicago, U.S.A. 1893." L. W. Robinson, U.S.N., Dept Chief.

P↑   ⊚ . (SFe,CHx,SI,NYPL,S,UMi,UoC,NL)

183. World's Columbian Exposition. Department of Manufactures.   ... *Classification and rules department of manufactures : With other information for intending Exhibitors.* [Chicago: Donohue & Henneberry, Printers], n.d.; Woodbridge, CT: RPI, 1989.

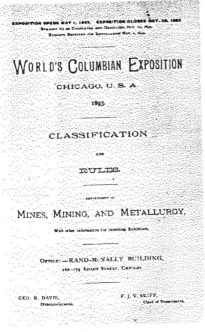

23x15. 32 p. + large fold out plan of Manufactures Building laid in back. Light gray (or rust) wraps, black print. At head of title: Opening/closing dates and "World's Columbian Exposition Chicago, U.S.A. 1893." James Allison, Dept Chief.

⊚ . (SFe,CHx,SI,NYPL,S,UMi,UoC,NL)

184. World's Columbian Exposition. Department of Manufactures. *Rules adopted by the board of judges in Department "H," Manufactures. July 21, 1893.* N.p.: n.p., n.d.

21x14½. (3) p. No wraps. Caption title.   ⊚ . (WM)

185. World's Columbian Exposition. Department of Mines, Mining, Metallurgy.   ... *Classification and rules department of Mines, Mining, and Metallurgy, With other information for intending Exhibitors.*   [Chicago: Donohue & Henneberry, 1893]; Woodbridge, CT: RPI, 1989.

23x15. 33 p. + tipped in plan of Mines Building faces title page. Very light blue (or gray or green) wraps, black print. F. J. V. Skiff, Chief of Dept. At head of title: WCE opening/closing dates and "World's Columbian Exposition, Chicago, U.S.A., 1893."

P↑   ⊚ . (SFe,CHx,SI,UMi,UoC,NL)

186. World's Columbian Exposition. Department of Publicity and Promotion. *After Four Centuries : The World's fair : The Discovery of America to be commemorated by an International Exposition : Chicago, Ill., U.S.A. 1893.* Chicago: The J. M. W. Jones Stationery and printing co., 1891; Woodbridge, CT: RPI, 1989.

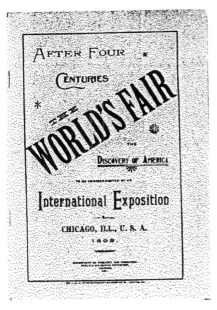

22½x15. 16 p. Light blue flecked beige wraps, black print. C.t. See several other language translations listed separately.

P→   ⊚ . (SFe,SI,NYPL,UDe,UoC,NL,WM,S)

☞ The Dept of Publicity and Promotion issued a BLIZZARD of published news and information releases. These are in ready to use newspaper column format, printed on one side, many with caption "World's Fair Notes" (in the various languages). Numerous examples found at NL and HL.--(NL call: R1832.705) and (HL call: "Ephemera file, World's Fair Chicago 1892-93)

187. World's Columbian Exposition. Department of Publicity and Promotion. Cook, Joel. *The World's fair at Chicago, described in a series of letters to "The London Times."* Chicago: Rand, McNally & Co., 1891.

    23x15½. 19 p. Yellow (or olive green) wraps, black print. C.t. Reprint of 4 articles on the WF originally published in the *London Times.* ⊚ . (SFe,CHx,SI,NYPL,USD,NHSt,UMi,UoC,NL)

188. World's Columbian Exposition. Department of Publicity and Promotion. *Depois de Quatro Seculos. "World's Fair" : a descoberta da America será celebranda por uma Exposição Internacional em Chicago, Ill., E.U.A. 1893.* Chicago: Imprensa De John Anderson publishing co., 1891.

    22x15. 16 p. Aquamarine wraps, black print, illus back wrap. C.t. Portuguese version of #186.
(CPL,UoC)

189. World's Columbian Exposition. Department of Publicity and Promotion. *Efter fire Hundred Aar. The "World's Fair" : Opdagelsen af Amerika bliver festligholdt ved En International Udstilling i Chicago, Ill., U. S. A., 1893.* Chicago: Presse- og Underretningsbureauet, World's Columbian Exposition, Skandinavens Bogtrhkkeri, 1891.

    21½x14½. 16 p. Pink wraps, black print and design. C.t. Danish version of #186. ⊚ . (UoC,NL)

190. World's Columbian Exposition. Department of Publicity and Promotion. *Efter fyra århundraden : The "World's fair" : Kommer Amerikas upptäckande : att högtidligen firas genom en Verldsutställning i Chicago, Ill., U. S. A. 1893.* Chicago: Department of Publicity and Promotion, World's Columbian exposition, Stromberg, Allen & co. printers, 1891.

    22x14½. 16 + (1) p. text on inside back cover. Chartreuse wraps, black print. WCE plan appears on outside back wrap. C.t. Swedish version of #186. ⊚ . (CPL,UoC,NL)

191. World's Columbian Exposition. Department of Publicity and Promotion. *Nach vier Jahrhunderten : Die "World's fair" : Die Entdeckung Amerika's wird durch eine Internationale Ausstellung in Chicago, Ill., U.S.A. : 1893 gefeiert werden.* Chicago: Press- und Auskunstbureau, World's Columbian Exposition, Stromberg, Allen & co., printers, 1891.

    22x15. 16 p., plates. Maize wraps, black print and design. C.t. Map printed on outside back cover. German version of #186. ⊚ . (CHx,UoC,NL)

192. World's Columbian Exposition. Department of Publicity and Promotion. *New York and the World's fair : The dinner given in the Interest of the World's Columbian Exposition by the New York Members of the National Commission, at Delmonico's, December 21, 1891.* [Chicago]: World's Columbian Exposition, Department of Publicity and Promotion, 1892.

    23½x15. 48 p. Dull green wraps, black print. C.t.= t.p. Chauncey Depew and Thos. W. Palmer, etc., were featured speakers. [The Fair directors did well to include New York in the planning of the WCE since New York had lost the bid to hold the Fair.] ⊚ . (CPL,CHx,NYPL,WM)

193. World's Columbian Exposition. Department of Publicity and Promotion. *World's Columbian Exposition ...: Its scope, present condition, purposes, and future prospects. Specially compiled for the information of the visiting members of the United States Congress, February 22, 1892.* Chicago: World's Columbian Exposition, Department of Publicity and Promotion, n.d.

17x11½. 15 p. Sepia wraps, black print. C.t. Ellipse: "Chicago, Ill., May 1 - Oct. 30, 1893." Printed by Rand, McNally & Co., 1892. ⊚ . (CPL,CHx)

194. World's Columbian Exposition. Department of Transportation. ... *Classification of department of transportation exhibits : Railways, Vessels, Vehicles. With other information for intending Exhibitors.* [Chicago: Donohue & Henneberry], n.d.; Woodbridge, CT: RPI, 1989.

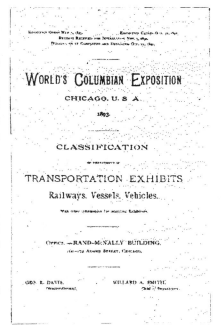

23x15. 24 p. + large fold out plan of Transportation Building and map of Jackson Park. Pale blue-gray wraps. At head of title: WCE opening/closing dates and "World's Columbian Exposition : Chicago, U.S.A. 1893." Willard A. Smith, Chief of Dept.
P→   ⊚ . (SFe,CHx,SI,NYPL,UMi,UoC,NL)

195. World's Columbian Exposition. Department of Transportation. ... *Suggestions for exhibits by railway companies.* Chicago: Published for the Department of Transportation Exhibits of the World's Columbian Exposition, [1892?].

ca. 23x15. 7 *l.* Caption title. At head of title: The World's Columbian exposition." ⊚ . (SI)

196. World's Columbian Exposition. Department of Transportation. *Testimonial : from American Exhibitors, Department of Transportation Exhibits, World's Columbian Exposition, to Willard A. Smith, Chief.* ... New York: Winchell Printing Co., 1894.

23 p., (1) plate. Proceedings of a testimonial dinner held on June 5, 1894, to honor Smith. The event included the presentation to Mr. Smith of an ornate, custom-designed silver vase. [One of the speakers was J. Elfreth Watkins, who subsequently became the Smithsonian's first curator of transportation]. ⊚ . (SI)

197. World's Columbian Exposition. Departmento de Publicidad y Promocion. *Despues de cuatro Siglos : "World's fair" : El Descubrimiento de America : Será conmemorado con una Esposicion Internacional en la ciudad de Chicago, Ill., en 1893.* Chicago: Departmento de Publicidad y Promocion, World's Columbian exposition, Stromberg, Allen & Co., printers, 1891.

22x14. 16 + (1) p. text printed on inside back cover. Dark robin egg blue wraps, black print, map printed on back cover. Spanish version of #186. ⊚ . (SFe,UoC,NL)

198. World's Columbian Exposition. *Final report of the general manager of the World's Columbian exposition, covering the post-exhibition period, October 31st, 1893, to September 1st, 1894.* N.p.: n.p., [1894].

28x__. 2 *l*, 172 numbered *l.* Type-written. Introduction signed: E. R. Graham. (AIC)

199. World's Columbian Exposition. ... *First annual report of the president. Submitted at directors' meeting, March 27, 1891. Printed for the information of stockholders and the public, by order of the board of directors. Together with a sketch of the inception and preliminary organization of the enterprise. Chicago, April 1, 1891.* Chicago: Knight and Leonard Co., Printers, [1891].

21½x15. 24 p. Light flecked gray wraps, black print. At head of title: "The World's Columbian Exposition." C.t.= t.p. [Lyman Gage was first president (1890) of the WCE.]
⊘ . (SFe,csuf,NYPL,UDe,NL,WM)

200. World's Columbian Exposition. ... *General Regulations for Exhibitors in the United States.* N.p.: n.p., n.d.

28x21½. No wraps. Caption title. At head of title: "No. 2. World's Columbian Exposition, 1893 Chicago."   ⊘ . (WM)

201. World's Columbian Exposition. Grounds and Buildings Committee. ... *Committee on grounds and buildings.* [Report]. *Chicago, August 31, 1891.* [Chicago: 1891?].

22x15. 8 p. Caption title. At head of title: "World's Columbian Exposition." Report of operations to date by E. T. Jeffery, Committee Chairman.   ⊘ . (NL)

202. World's Columbian Exposition. Grounds and Buildings Committee. *Report of operations to date, and of the organization and work done by the Supt. of Construction.* [Chicago: 1891].

8°. 8 p. No t.p.   (NYPL)

203. World's Columbian Exposition. Grounds and Buildings Committee. *Report of the grounds and building committee.* [Chicago: n.p., 1890].

21x14½. 18 p. No wraps. Caption title. Information on the choice of site (no site recommended) directed to the WCE Board of Directors and dated Sept. 8, 1890. E. T. Jeffery, et. al.   ⊘ (CHx)

204. World's Columbian Exposition. Latin-American Department. *Classification of the Latin-American Department.* Washington, D.C.: Gibson Bros., 1890.

23x__. 24 p. William Eleroy Curtis was chief of the Latin-American Department.   (UC)

205. World's Columbian Exposition. Latin-American Department. *Plan for the organization of a Latin-American department at the World's Columbian exposition ...* Washington: 1890.

10 p.   (UC)

206. World's Columbian Exposition. *List of subscribers to the World's exposition of 1892.* [Chicago: 1892].

38½x28. 76 numbered *l* with print on rectos only + 1 *l* unpaged appendix. C.t. The Exposition Company issued stock to subscribers. Subscriber listing with running totals of subscribers and monies at bottom of pages. Total: 455,709 subscribers; $4,557,090. [The stock certificates are beautiful and expensive WCE collectibles.]   (NL)

207. World's Columbian Exposition. Mechanical Department. *Operating report of the Mechanical Department, World's Columbian Exposition. May 1st to Oct. 30th, 1893.* [Chicago?]: 1893.

21x33. 104 *l.* Typewritten.   (UC)

208. World's Columbian Exposition. Mechanical Department. *Report on constructional work of the Mechanical Department, World's Columbian Exposition. October 1, 1893.* [Chicago?]: 1893.

21x33. 104 *l.* Typewritten.   (UC)

209. World's Columbian Exposition. Office of Director General. Davis, George R. ... *Remarks of Director-General Davis, May 17, 1892, : Before the World's Fair Committee of the House of Representatives. Washington, D. C.* Chicago: Rand, McNally & Co., 1892.

23x15½. 3-18 p. Gray-green wraps, black print. C.t.= t.p. At head of title: "The World's Columbian Exposition."   ☻ . (CPL,CHx)

210. World's Columbian Exposition. Office of Director General. *General regulations for foreign exhibitors at the World's Columbian exposition in Chicago : prescribed by the Director General : by authority of the World's Columbian Commission : in accordance with the Act of Congress approved April 25, 1890.* Chicago: Ruben Bros printers, for the Office of the Director General, 1891.

34½x21. 54 p. including front cover. Green wraps, black print. C.t. Lists officers and depts for exhibit.   ☻ . (LC,NYPL)

211. World's Columbian Exposition. Office of Director General. ... *Information for foreign exhibitors.* Chicago: Rand, McNally & Co., Printers, [1891?].

21x9½. 4 *l* folded twice, includes folding world map (21x27½ unfolded). Two copies found: 1) Machinery building colored rust, and 2) Machinery building colored green. C.t. On covers, both copies are dated December, 1891. Both contain general regulations and U.S. government regulations and have at head of title: "World's Columbian Exposition, Chicago, 1893." Maps of the world are colored differently in the two versions. Rust version: "Circular of Information for Foreign Exhibitors." Green version: "Official Circular of Information for Foreign Exhibitors." Card catalog may list under these titles.   ☻ . (CHx,NHSt,NL)

212. World's Columbian Exposition. [Office of Director General]. *Regolamenti generali per gli espositori esteri al "World's Columbian Exposition" in Chicago, presgritti dal direttore generale in nome della "World's Columbian Commission." in virtú della Legge del Congresso del 25 Aprile, 1890.* Chicago: Ufficio del Direttore Generale, "World's Columbian Exposition," 1891.

22x14½. 8 p. including buff wraps. Italian version of *General regulations for foreign exhibitors* (#210).
☻ . (SFe)

213. World's Columbian Exposition. Office of Director General. *The World's Columbian Exposition, Office of Director General, Chicago, May 5, 1891.* N.p.: n.p., n.d.

15x9½. 3 p. Caption title. Regulations for domestic exhibits and separate State exhibits.   (NL)

214. World's Columbian Exposition. *Official directory of the World's Columbian Exposition. Rules of order, by-laws, act of Congress, directors, officers, etc., revised July, 1891.* Chicago: Rand, McNally & Co. Printers, 1891.

17x11. 52 p. Tan wraps.

---- Title ends at "etc." (i.e., no revised date shown).
(CHx,UDe,UoC,NL)

215. World's Columbian Exposition. *Official Headquarters of the World's Columbian Exposition, Rand-McNally Building, ...* N.p.: n.p., n.d.

14½x9 (folded size), 14½x72 unfolded *l* making (16) p. each 9 cm wide. C.t. Lists WCE Board of Directors, Officers, Committee members. Message on back by Benj. Butterworth.   ⊚ . (NL)

216. World's Columbian Exposition. *Official manual of the World's Columbian Exposition : Containing list of officers of the corporation and of the World's Columbian commission, chiefs of departments, etc.; also by-laws of the corporation, acts of Congress relative to the exposition, rules of order, and other information. July 1, 1893.* Chicago: Rand, McNally & Co., Printers, 1893.

17x11. 64 p. Steel gray wraps, black print. "Compiled by the Secretary of the World's Columbian Exposition." The phone number of Gen.-Director Davis was "World's Fair 19," and Charles Yerkes was "North, 203."
---- 17x11½. 59 p. Gray wraps, black print. No date on t.p.
(CHx,Yale)

217. World's Columbian Exposition. *Report of conferences between the Board of Directors of the World's Columbian Exposition and representatives of the Labor Organizations of Chicago, Relative to the Employment of Labor.* Chicago: Wm. C. Hollister & Bros., Printers, n.d.

25x17½. 31 p. include front cover, (1) p. Gray wraps, black print. Replica signature of Lyman Gage. Labor agreements on constructing the WF grounds.   ⊚ . (CPL)

218. World's Columbian Exposition. *Report of Special Committee of Conference on Jurisdiction. Adopted by Directory of World's Columbian Exposition, November 24, 1890.* N.p.: n.p., [1890].

23x15½. 4 p. No printed covers. Caption title. The Conference created the Board of Reference and Control consisting of the president, vice chairman, and 6 members of the Commission. [The purpose of this committee was to determine powers and duties for the World's Columbian Exposition and the World's Columbian Commission bodies.]   ⊚ . (SFe)

219. World's Columbian Exposition. *Report of the Columbian Guard.* N.p.: n.p., [1894].

31½x19½. Typewritten, 94 p. + 14 typed appendices, each separately paged, [total 193 p.], illus (photos). On t.p.: "Col. Edmund Rice, U.S.A., Com." Directed to D. H. Burnham, Director of Works. Photocopy at CHx. Also listed at 33 cm. Every detail of the uniform and its cost are depicted and described. [GLD has a complete uniform as described including starched collars; in addition, it has a blackjack not described in the report.]   (CHx)

220. World's Columbian Exposition. *... Report of the director of works, October 24, 1892.* Chicago: Rand, McNally & Co., Printers, 1892.

23x15½. 17 p. Green-gray wraps, black print. C.t.= t.p. Signed by director, D. H. Burnham. At head of title: "World's Columbian Exposition." Report submitted to H. N. Higinbotham, President of the WCE.   ⊚ . (CPL,UDe)

221. World's Columbian Exposition. *Report of the President to the Board of Directors of the World's Columbian Exposition : Chicago, 1892-1893.* Chicago: Rand, McNally & Co., °1898; Chicago: [Rand, McNally & Co.], °1898; [Chicago: Rand, McNally & Co., 1898]; Woodbridge, CT: RPI, 1989.

Rand: 25x17. 497 p. including tables, fold. map (tinted) of bird's-eye view of grounds. Full leather hc, gold trim and lettered spine, gilt edges. Harlow Niles Higinbotham's report.
---- [Rand], °1898: 24½x18½. 1 *l*, 5-497 p. Half maroon leather with navy pebbled beveled board hc, navy and gilt end papers, ragged front and bottom edges, gilt top edge, large folding bird's-eye view of grounds tipped in at back cover.
---- No pub info on t.p.: 497 p.
*   ☺ . (UND,KyU,JHU,CHx,LC,SI,NYPL,F,BCM,OSU,RML,VaHx,USD,SLP,UMi,Yale,UoC,NL,BPL,RPB,WM,AIC,OC,WiHx) $50 - 100

222. World's Columbian Exposition. *Rules and regulations of the World's Columbian Exposition : operative under the Director of Works.* Chicago: Rand, McNally & Co., Printers, 1893.

28x21½. 1 *l*, 5-83 p. Morocco hc, gilt border and print. C.t: "Secretary of works, World's Columbian Exposition." ☺ . (HL)

223. World's Columbian Exposition. *Rules of the director of works for the government of the guard.* Chicago, 1893.

26, v p.   (WiHx)

224. World's Columbian Exposition. *Rules of the World's Columbian Exposition governing Rates of Entrance and Admission Fees and ...* Chicago: Rand, McNally & Co., Printers, 1893.

23x15. 26 p. Dark tan wraps, black print.   ☺ . (KyU,UDe,USD,WM,WiHx)

225. World's Columbian Exposition. *... (Supplement to Form 3. May 1, 1891.).* N.p.: n.p., 1891?.

22x15. (4) p. Wraps with sketches of Government Bldg, U.S. Coast Line Battle Ship, and Illinois State Bldg. At head of title: "World's Columbian Exposition." Subject: Changes in WCE financial arrangements and personnel.   ☺ . (WM)

226. World's Columbian Exposition. *Testimonial and resolutions unanimously adopted by the Board of Directors of the World's Columbian Exposition on the retirement of its president Lyman J. Gage.* N.p.: n.p., n.d.

36x29½. 18 *l* including port, each *l* separated by a tissue guard sheet. Half royal blue leather over blue marbled boards, same marbled design on end papers, gold designs, gold lettering on spine: "Testimonial to Lyman J. Gage." A beautiful work of art!   (CHx)

☞ A personal scrapbook (35½x26) of clippings and photographs from the Panama-California Exposition, 1915-16, compiled by Lyman Gage. Gage was President of the 1st National Bank of Chicago, Secretary of the Treasury under McKinley and T. Roosevelt, the first President of the WCE, and a resident of Pt. Loma, CA.--(SDHx call: SB 13)

227. World's Columbian Exposition. Traffic Department. *Supplement to Traffic Arrangements, Foreign Exhibits ... Domestic Exhibits ... Exhibits on Wheels, ... World's Columbian Exposition. Chicago (Jackson Park), January 4th, 1893.* N.p.: n.p., n.d.

28x21½. (3) p. No wraps. Caption title. Upper left corner of cover: "T. D. 47."   ☺ . (WM)

228. World's Columbian Exposition. Traffic Department.   ... *Traffic arrangements : General rules and regulations affecting transportation of foreign exhibits.* [Chicago]: Traffic Department, 1892.

23x15. (5)-34 p. includes map of Jackson Park frontis. 1 folding map of world tipped in ahead of back cover. Pea green wraps, black print. At head of title: "World's Columbian Exposition. 1893. Chicago, U. S. A."   ☺ . (CHx,SI,UoC,S) $20 - 40

☞ There is also a book of rules for domestic exhibitors. CHx has a copy but front cover and t.p. are missing. 23x15, tan wraps.

229. World's Columbian Exposition. Ways and Means Committee. *Bazaar of all nations. Circular.* N.p.: n.p., n.d.

17x11. (3), 4-7 p. Wraps same as text paper, black print. Caption title. C.t.: "World's Columbian Exposition 1893, Chicago, Ill., U.S.A.: Office of the Ways and Means Committee." The WCE set aside a portion of the grounds as an area to sell "relics, trinkets, and curiosities."   (CHx)

Chapter 3

FEDERAL PUBLICATIONS

An act of Congress, approved April 25, 1890, provided for the World's Columbian Exposition to celebrate the 400th anniversary of the discovery of America by Christopher Columbus. It further called for the appointment of a commission, appointed by the President of the United States, consisting of two commissioners from each State and Territory and from the District of Columbia, together with eight commissioners at large, to be designated the World's Columbian Commission. Prior to President Harrison's April 28th approval of the entire bill, the House of Representatives had voted Chicago the WCE site on the 8th ballot, February 24, 1890; the Senate followed suit. United States Government liability for the WCE was limited to $1,500,000.

Government exhibits were the responsibility of the Board of Government, Management, and Control which was composed of a representative from each executive dept, one from the Smithsonian Institution and National Museum, and one from the United States Fish Commission. These representatives were appointed by President Harrison on August 19, 1890. The Government's exhibit was to be housed in buildings erected under the authority of the Secretary of the Treasury at an aggregate cost of $400,000.

230. *Address of Special Committee on Federal Legislation of the Board of Directors to the Committee on the Columbian Exposition of the U.S. House of Representatives.* Chicago: Rand, McNally & Co., 1892.

    22x__. 6 p. (UC)

231. American Historical Association. *Annual report of the American Historical Association for the year 1894.* Washington: GPO, 1895.

    23½x15½. xii, 602 p. Navy blue cloth hc with gilt print spine. 10th annual meeting report. Chap. 24: "The existing autographs of Christopher Columbus" by William Eleroy Curtis. The 1893, 9th annual meeting was held in Chicago. Officers for 1895 included G. Brown Goode and Theodore Roosevelt. Contains a Civil War article by Rossiter Johnson.
        © (GLD) $12 - 30

232. Anderson, Alex D., Myron M. Parker, John W. Powell, Felix Agnus. *Arguments before the quadricentennial committee of the United States Senate : In support of Senate Bills Nos. 1839 and 1135, each entitled "A bill to provide for a Three Americas and World's Exposition at the National Capital [sic] in 1892," ... January 10, 1890.* Washington: GPO, 1890; [Washington, DC: Gibson bros. Printers and Bookbinders], n.d.

    GPO: 23x15. 27 p. No wraps, pulp paper. At head of title: "Three Americas exposition."
    ---- Gibson: 23x15. (4), 5-37 p., 4 *l* appendix B which is a letter from Peter C. Nains, Lieut. Colonel, Corps of Engineers and 3 plates of plans for proposed Dept of Agriculture Bldg.
        © . (CHx,NL)

233. Butterworth, Benjamin. *The World's Columbian Exposition. Speech of Hon. Benjamin Butterworth, of Ohio, In the House of Representatives, Friday, February 6, 1891.* N.p.: n.p., n.d.

    23x14½. 16 p. No printed covers. Caption title. Addressed appropriations in H. R. 13452 and championed government support and monetary aid for WCE. Butterworth was Secretary for the World's Columbian Commission. He was an author of *Columbus and Columbia* #752. © . (SFe,NL)

The *Congressional Record* is included in this section primarily to show the extended duration and the distribution of legislative activity surrounding the WCE. Page numbers are omitted. Volume numbers with publication information are given, contrary to normal citation, as an additional aid to those unacquainted with this reference.

234. *Cong. Rec.* 50th Cong., 1st sess. 1888. Vol. 19. Washington: GPO, 1888.

> 10 pts. (vols) + index vol. Half calf over marbled boards. One Senate (1165) and two House (8868, 10541) bills to hold a World's exposition in Washington. 13 petitions in favor of holding a World's exposition.   (UNM)

235. *Cong. Rec.* 51st Cong., 1st sess. 1889-90. Vol. 21. Washington: GPO, 1890.

> Six WCE bills were introduced in the Senate; 17 in the House. The House also heard petitions for the WCE site as follows: Washington (3), St. Louis (3), Chicago (26), New York (6), and a Western city (1). Four petitions for WCE Sunday closure and two petitions for Sunday opening were presented to the House. The previous *Cong. Rec.* (50th Cong., 2d sess., 1888-89) has no WCE entries.   (UNM)

> ☞   Early discussion of the WCE. The Fair at Chicago got early approval from the U.S. Government; this helped unify planning. Getting financial help was more difficult since the U.S. Government tried to keep the costs of the Fair in the private sector.

236. *Cong. Rec.* 51st Cong., 2d sess. 1890-91. Vol. 22. Washington: GPO, 1891.

> One WCE bill was introduced in the House. The House heard 31 petitions for Sunday closing and two for opening. Contains a World's Columbian Commission report (House Ex. Doc. 175) and an estimate of appropriations (House Ex. Doc. 176, 177).   (UNM)

237. *Cong. Rec.* 52d Cong., 1st sess. 1891-92. Vol. 23. Washington: GPO, 1892.

> Seven WCE bills were introduced in the Senate; 19 in the House including those for souvenir 50¢ coinage, colored race participation, free entrance to Civil War veterans, and a national bank on WCE grounds. There were 13 Joint Resolutions. Letter of Secretary of Treasury (House Ex. Doc. 161), message of President (House Ex. Doc. 142), est. of appropriations for Board of Lady Managers (House Ex. Doc. 157), est. of appropriations for Postal Service (House Ex. Doc. 246), Joint Resolution to Print World's Congress (H. Res. 131). The House heard 609 petitions for Sunday closing; 238 petitions for opening. It heard 307 petitions against liquor; no petitions for liquor.   (UNM)

238. *Cong. Rec.* 52d Cong., 2d sess. 1892-93. Vol. 24. Washington: GPO, 1893.

> Two bills were introduced in the Senate; three in the House. There were ten Joint Resolutions including a request for loan of Liberty Bell, the transfer of replica battle-ship Illinois to state of Illinois on WCE termination. Est. of appropriation expenses (H. Ex. Doc. 73), est. of appropriation expenses Board of Lady Managers (H. Ex. Doc. 74), est. of appropriation expenses to entertain guests (S. Ex. Doc. 55), est. of appropriation expenses Commission of Awards (H. Rept. Ex. Doc. 166), letter of Secretary of War on encampment at WCE (S. Ex. Doc. 24), message of President (H. Ex. Doc. 211), report on Government Exhibit (H. Ex. Doc. 1, part 9), report of Secretary of Treasury on souvenir coins (S. Ex. Doc. 29), report of Secretary of Treasury upon Sunday closing (S. Ex. Doc. 74). No petitions listed.   (UNM)

☞ The 52d Congress appropriated monies for the construction of caravel replicas of the "Niña" and "Pinta." After they were built in Spain, the caravels were slowly towed by U.S. destroyers to the U.S. and arrived at the WCE on July 7, 1893. After the Fair, all three replicas remained anchored (in pitiable condition) at the WCE site as late as February of 1897. No one could be found to accept them.

239. *Cong. Rec.* 53d Cong., 1st sess. & Special sess. of Senate. 1893. Vol. 25. Washington: GPO, 1893.

There were five Joint Resolutions.   (UNM)

240. *Cong. Rec.* 53d. Cong., 2d & 3d sess. 1894-95. Vol. 26. Washington: GPO, 1894. Vol. 27. Washington: GPO, 1895.

Of the two bills introduced in the Senate, one was transfer of certain exhibits to Columbian (Field) Museum of Chicago. Two Joint Resolutions and 15 petitions for Joint Resolutions.   (UNM)

241. *Cong. Rec.* 54th Cong., 1st sess. 1895-96. Vol. 28. Washington: GPO, 1896.

One Senate bill introduced: punishment for forging awards. Two Joint Resolutions.   (UNM)

242. *Cong. Rec.* 54th Cong., 2d sess. 1896-97. Vol. 29. Washington: GPO, 1897.

Message of President transmitting final report (H. Rept. Ex. Doc. 259), message of President transmitting report of Lady Managers at page 2525.   (UNM)

243. *Cong. Rec.* 55th Cong., 1st sess. 1897. Vol. 30. Washington: GPO, 1897.

Senate bill 764: punishment for forging awards. Message of President transmitting report of Government Exhibit (S. Doc. 73).   (UNM)

244. *Cong. Rec.* 55th Cong., 2d & 3d sess. 1897-99. Vol. 31. Washington: GPO, 1897. Vol. 32. Washington: GPO, 1899.

Report of Lady Managers at page 1918. Concurrent resolution to print report of Lady Managers (H. Res. 20).   (UNM)

245. *Cong. Rec.* 56th Cong., 1st sess. 1899-1900. Vol. 33. Washington: GPO, 1890.

Concurrent resolutions to print final report of Lady Managers and report of Awards Committee. Amendment to appropriation to print report of Awards Committee.   (UNM)

246. *Cong. Rec.* 56th Cong., 2d sess. 1900-01. Vol. 34. Washington: GPO, 1901.

Concurrent resolution in Senate to print report of Awards Committee. Several items on 1901 Pan-American Exposition at Buffalo, NY.   (UNM)

247. *Cong. Rec.* 57th Cong., 1st sess. & Special sess. of Senate. 1901-02. Vol. 35. Washington: GPO, 1902.

Last *Cong. Rec.* with WCE item: one Joint Resolution to print reports. Several items on 1901 Pan-American Exposition. [President McKinley was shot mortally on Sept. 6, 1901, at the Pan-American fair -- yet the final federal work on the WCE was just ending.]   (UNM)

248. Cregier, DeWitt C., Thos. B. Bryan, and Edward T. Jeffery. *Arguments before a special committee of the United States Senate ... in support of the application of the citizens of Chicago for the location in their city of the World's exposition of 1892. January 11, 1890.* Washington: GPO, 1890.

23x14½. 1 *l*, 3-26 p. Light blue paper wraps, black print. C.t.= t.p. Remarks by Cregier and Bryan; argument by Jeffery. They brought before the Senate the subscription list for the required $5M as an argument for Chicago's fiscal responsibility. CHx copy signed by Jeffery. [Cregier was Mayor of Chicago at the time.]   ⊚ . (CHx,NYPL,TU,NL)

249. Depew, Chauncey M[itchell], W. Bourke Cockran, Warner Miller, et. al. *Hearings before the quadro-centennial committee of the United States Senate with respect to The Commemoration of the Four-Hundredth Anniversary of the Discovery of America. Arguments ... January 11, 1890.* Washington: GPO, 1890.

23x15. 1 *l*, 3-23 p. No wraps. For other Depew items, see #762 and #794.
        ⊚ . (PU,CHx,NYPL,F,NHSt,HL,NL,BPL) $20 - 30
---- In Depew's *Orations*, ____: ____, 1896, p. 524-37.   (NHSt,NL)

250. Jones, Chas. H., and E. O. Stanard. *Reasons why The World's Fair of 1892 should be located at St. Louis. Arguments made before the Senate World's fair committee, January 8, 1890.* Washington: GPO, 1890.

23x15. 20 p. C.t. Same as #1955.   ⊚ . (NL)

Message from the President of the United States ... #273.a (51 Cong., 2d sess.); #274.g (52d Cong., 1st sess.); #275.f (52d Cong., 2d sess.).

251. Michael, W. H., ed. *The abridgment. Message from the President of the United States to the two houses of Congress at the beginning of the first session of the fifty-second Congress, with the reports of the heads of departments and selections from accompanying documents.* Washington, D.C.: GPO, 1892.

23x16. 1 *l*, 1116 p. Dark olive cloth hc. Early discussions of U.S. Government involvement in WCE.
        ⊚ (GLD) $10 - 30

252. Ray, George W. *The World's Columbian Exposition. Does it belong to the United States or to Chicago? Speech of Hon. George W. Ray, of New York, in the House of Representatives, July 18, 1892.* Washington: GPO, 1892.

22½x15. 7 p. including front cover, pulp paper. C.t. Although sad that his native state did not secure the Fair, Ray champions the U.S. government issuance of the Columbian half dollar as a U.S. government gesture backing the Fair.   ⊚ . (LC)

253. *The Reports of Committees of the House of Representatives for the First Session of the Fifty Second Congress, 1891-1892.* Washington, D.C.: GPO, 1892.   (ref) $20 - 35

254. Smithsonian Institution. *Annual report of the board of regents of the Smithsonian institution showing the operations, expenditures, and condition of the institution to July, 1890.* Washington: GPO, 1891.

23½x15. xli, 808 p. Rebound hc. Report of Secretary Langley (p. 23) contains the April 25, 1890, Act of Congress, section 16 pertaining to Government exhibits. Langley mentions concern over interference with the regular museum work schedule and damage to articles due to frequent packing for exhibitions.   ☺ . (UNM) $15 - 30

☞ Do not confuse the Smithsonian annual reports with the U.S. Museum annual reports (starting from #293) by similar title.

255. Smithsonian Institution. *Annual report of the board of regents of the Smithsonian institution, showing the operations, expenditures, and condition of the institution to July, 1891.* Washington: GPO, 1893.

23½x15. xliii, 715 p. Rebound hc. Dr. G. Brown Goode's appointment as representative of the Smithsonian Institution and the National Museum upon the Government Board of Managers and Control, and appropriations for Government exhibits (p. 20).   (UNM) $15 - 30

256. Smithsonian Institution. *Annual report of the board of regents of the Smithsonian institution, showing the operations, expenditures, and condition of the institution to July, 1892.* Washington: GPO, 1893.

23½x15½. xlix, 811 p. Black cloth hc with black print spine. Several item regarding preparation for the WCE at p. xlvii, 27, 28, and 51-55.   ☺ (GLD,UNM) $15 - 30

257. Smithsonian Institution. ... *Annual report of the board of regents of the Smithsonian institution, showing the operations, expenditures, and condition of the institution to July, 1893.* Washington: GPO, 1894.

23½x15½. xliv, 763 p. Black cloth hc. At top of t.p.: "53d Congress, 2d Session. House of Representatives. Mis.Doc.184, Part I." WCE articles: national museum-- p. 20, 36; Indian exhibits-- p. 40; World's Congress of Anthropology-- p. 604.   ☺ . (UNM,OhHx) $15 - 30

258. Smithsonian Institution. *Annual report of the board of regents of the Smithsonian institution, showing the operations, expenditures, and condition of the institution to July, 1894.* Washington: GPO, 1896.

23½x15. Rebound hc. WCE in Langley's report at p. 18. At p. 141-52: "The Henry" [unit of induction which had its name coined at the International Congress of Electricians] article rpt. from *The Atlantic Monthly* 73 (May 1894); includes some history of the Congress. Impressions of U.S. citizenry gleaned during the WCE reported (p. 159) by M. Mascart, President of French Association for the Advancement of Science.   (UNM) $15 - 30

259. Smithsonian Institution. ... *Annual report of the board of regents of the Smithsonian institution, showing the operations, expenditures, and condition of the institution for the year ending June 30, 1901.* Washington: GPO, 1902.

23½x15. lxvii, 782 p. Act of Congress authorizing printing of 3500 copies of Committee on Awards report. At top of t.p.: "57th Congress, 1st Session. House of Representatives. Doc. No. 707, Part I."

⊚ . (UNM) $15 - 30

☞   No WCE activity is indexed in the 1895-1900 and 1902-1903 annual reports.

260. Snodgrass, Henry Clay. ... *Speech of Hon. H. C. Snodgrass, of Tennessee, in the House of Representatives, March 21, 1892.* Washington: n.p., 1892.

   22x15. 15 p. At head of title: "The World's Columbian Exposition." Snodgrass spoke out against the appropriation of $5M in commemorative coins for the "Chicago show."   ⊚ . (TnSt)

261. U.S. Army. Surgeon General's Office. *Description of microscopes from the Army Medical Museum, Washington, D.C.* By John Shaw Billings. Medical Dept of the U.S. Army Exhibit at the WCE, 1893.

   8 p.   (UC)

262. U.S. Army. Surgeon General's Office. *Description of selected specimens from the Army Medical Museum, Washington, D.C.* By John Shaw Billings. Medical Dept of the U.S. Army Exhibit at the WCE, 1893.

   14 p.   (UC)

263. U.S. Army. Surgeon General's Office. Greenleaf, Charles R. ... *The personal identity of the soldier.* ... Chicago: World's Columbian exposition, 1892-93 [i.e., 1893].

   24x__. 10 p., illus. At head of title: "War department exhibit, Medical department United States Army, no. 7. NYPL film reproduction. Greenleaf was Deputy Surgeon General.   (NYPL)

264. U.S. Bureau of Education. ... *Catalog of "A. L. A." library : 5000 volumes for a popular library selected by the American library association and shown at the World's Columbian exposition.* Washington: GPO, 1893; Woodbridge, CT: RPI, 1989.

   22x14½. xx, 592 p. Tan wraps, black print. Classified by Dewey and LL Systems; contains dictionary catalogue. At top of title page: "whole number 200." At head of title: "U.S. bureau of education." Classed catalog (Dewey decimal): p. 37-144; classed catalog (Cutter expansive): p. 145-256; dictionary catalog: p. 261-582. Corrections: p. 587-92.   ⊚ . (csuf,KyU,CHx,SLS,UDe,NYSt)

   ☞ Richard Rogers Bowker (1848-1933) helped found the A. L. A. A prolific editor and publisher whose credits include *American Book Prices Current*; *Publishers Weekly*; numerous articles on the book trade, printing and social reform. He was an advocate of strong copyright laws. The R. R. Bowker, Co. was formed in 1911 and continues today; it issues ISBN numbers for new publications.

265. U.S. Bureau of Education. Eaton, John. ... *Notes on education at the Columbian exposition.* Washington: GPO, 1896.

   22½x15. p. 1015-1224, diagrams. Gray smooth wraps. C.t.= t.p. Whole Number 225. At head of title: "Reprint of chapter X of part II of the Report of the commissioner of education for 1892-93." (See report #267).   ⊚ . (NHSt,UoC)

266. U.S. Bureau of Education. ... *Education at the World's Columbian Exposition, including reports and comments ...* ____: ____, ____.

> 23x__. 2 *l*, p. 423-690. Rpt. of chapter I-VIII of pt. II of *Report of the commissioner of education for the year 1892-93* (#267). (UoC)

267. U.S. Bureau of Education. *Report of the commissioner of education for the year 1892-93. Volume 1. Containing parts I and II.* Washington: GPO, 1895.

> 23½x15½. 1224 p. Hc. "Whole Number 217." Part II is entitled: "Education and the World's Columbian exposition." Contains John Eaton's report (#265). The caption title for Eaton's report starts "Notes on education;" the index title starts "Report on education." ☺. (NHSt)

268. U.S. Commission for Fish and Fisheries. Bean, Tarleton H[offman]. ... *Report of the representative of the United States commission at the World's Columbian exposition.* Washington: GPO, 1896.

> 23x15. 1 *l*, p. 177-196, plates 1-5. Doc. 311. At head of title: "Appendix 1.--Extracted from the Report of the U.S. commissioner of fish and fisheries for 1894 ..." (see #269). (RPB)

269. U.S. Commission for Fish and Fisheries. ... *Report of the commissioner for the year ending June 30, 1894.* Washington, D.C.: GPO, 1896.

> 24x15. (i)-(v), 718 p. Black cloth hc, gilt print on spine. At head of title: "54th Congress, 1st Session.} House of Representatives. {Document No. 424. United States commission of fish and fisheries. Part XX." WCE report by Tarleton H. Bean p. 177-96 (also see #268). Detailed description of WCE Fisheries Bldg with fold out floor plans. 5 double page plates of photographs of exhibits.
>
> ☺. (GLD,UoC,RPB) $15 - 30

270. U.S. Cong. *Copies of Acts and Resolutions passed at the first session of the fifty-second Congress relating to the World's Columbian Commission and the World's Columbian Exposition.* Chicago: Knight, Leonard & Co. Printers, 1892.

> 23x15. 8 p. Plain paper with black print. C.t. Contains: Public No 202 (government exhibit, World's Columbian Commission), Public No 203 (coins minted), Public Res. No 16 (general holiday 10/21/92), Public No 198 (dedicate bldgs 10/21/92), Public No 14 (approve $30,000 for AZ Territory exhibit), Public Res. No 5 (Library of Congress may exhibit certain documents), Public No 29 (protects foreign visitors from prosecution for exhibiting wares protected by American patents and trademarks), Public No 61 (national bank on WCE grounds), Public Res. No 23 (President of U.S. may request loan of articles from Spain), Public Res. No 24 (women's inventions), Public Res. No 29 (invitation to King and Queen of Spain and Columbus' descendents), Public Res. No 30 (foreign exhibitors may bring in laborers from their respective countries to prepare exhibits). (CHx)

> The Legislative reports and documents listed below are in chronological order under the Congress and Session that created them. All are 23x14½ unless otherwise noted.

271.   **50th Cong. 1st Sess.: 1888-89**

a.   U.S. Cong. House. Foreign Affairs Committee. H. Rept. 2601. *Report ...* [on] *A bill to provide for a world's exposition at the national capitol in 1892...* N.p.: [1892?].

57 p., 1 plan.   (NYPL)

☞ See also Senate bill 1165 referred to Committee on Centennial of Constitution and Discovery of America; House report 8868 referred to Committee on Foreign Affairs (H. R. 10541 reported as substitute 5326); and House report 10541 introduced by Committee on Foreign Affairs (H. R. Report 2601) as substitute for H. R. 8868, 5326.

272.   **51st Cong. 1st Sess.: 1889-90**

a.   U.S. Cong. House. H. Rept. 37: *World's fair. Report. [To accompany bills H. R. 6883 and 6884.].* Feb. 14, 1890.

2 p. Report of the Select Committee on the World's Fair. Bills sent to this committee located the WF at St. Louis, Chicago, and New York City. The reports states it "was not practicable to present one bill covering all the localities." The committee's solution was to submit a completed bill with a blank in lieu of the location.   ⊜ . (csuf)

b.   ---. ---. House. H. Rept. 890: *World's exposition. Report. [To accompany H. R. 8393.].* Mar. 15, 1890.   ⊜ . (csuf)

21 p. Report of WCE Select Committee + 11 appendices. Improvements to H. Rept. 6883.   (CHx)

c.   ---. ---. House. Mis. Doc. 254. *[Report No. 3129.]. Columbian centennial exposition.* Sept. 19, 1890.

1 p. Report of WCE Select Committee. Resolution that a subcommittee be appointed to inquire into progress of the WF and into various Government displays.   ⊜ . (csuf)

d.   ---. ---. House. H. Rept. 3129: *Columbian centennial exposition. Report: [To accompany Mis. Doc. 254.].* Sept. 19, 1890.

2 p. Report of WCE Select Committee. Resolution that there be a subcommittee of five to inquire into progress of the WF and into various Government displays.   ⊜ . (csuf)

273.   **51st Cong. 2d Sess.: 1890-91**

a.   U.S. Cong. House. Ex. Doc. 175: *Report of the World's Columbian Commission. Message from the President of the United States, transmitting : The report of the World's Columbian Commission, with accompanying papers.* Jan. 16, 1891.

74 p. President Harrison's transmittal.   ⊜ . (csuf)

b.   ---. ---. House. Ex. Doc. 176: *Estimates of appropriations for the World's Columbian exposition. Letter from the secretary of the treasury, transmitting : A detailed estimate of appropriations submitted by the president of the World's Columbian Exposition for expenditures for the fiscal year ending June 30, 1892.* Jan. 16, 1891.

3 p.   ⊜ . (csuf)

c.   ---. ---. House. Ex. Doc. 177: *Government's exhibit at the World's Columbian exposition. Letter from the secretary of the treasury, requesting : That the sum of three hundred thousand dollars be appropriated for the Government's Exhibit at the World's Columbian Exposition for the fiscal year ending June 30, 1892.* Jan. 16, 1891.

1 p.   ⊜ . (csuf)

274.   **52d Cong. 1st Sess. 1891-92**

a.   U.S. Cong. House. Ex. Doc. 101: *World's Columbian Exposition at Chicago. Letter from the acting secretary of the treasury transmitting : Information to the House of Representatives pursuant to resolution which passed January 18, 1892.* Jan. 27, 1892.

       11 p. Reported appropriations now totalled (exclusive of the amount for the World's Congress Auxiliary) $1,085,500; also reported expenditures.   ☻.(csuf)

b.   ---. ---. House. Mis. Doc. 68: *Inquiry concerning the World's Fair. Resolution of Mr. Henderson, of Iowa.* Feb. 4, 1892.

       3 p. To insure fiscal responsibility regarding Government appropriations: recommended judicious expenditures, reports to Congress, etc.   ☻.(csuf)

c.   ---. ---. House. H. Rept. 10: *Inquiry concerning the World's fair. Report: [To accompany Mis. Doc. 68.].* Feb. 4, 1892.

       2 p. Recommend adoption of a substitute for Mr. Henderson's resolution.   ☻.(csuf)

d.   ---. ---. House. H. Rept. 236: *Detail of certain army officers. Report: [To accompany H.R. 618.].* Feb. 9, 1892.

       1 p. Regarding special duty in connection with the WCE.   ☻.(csuf)

e.   ---. ---. House. H. Rept. 423: *Ratifying as act of the legislature of Arizona. Report: [To accompany H.R. 3980.].* Feb. 23, 1892.

       1 p. Ratified the appropriation of $30,000 in aid of the AZ exhibit.   ☻.(csuf)

f.   ---. ---. Senate. S. Rept. 271. *International exposition at Chicago. [Senate Report No. 271.].* Feb. 24, 1892.

       2 p. Report of Committee on Foreign Relations regarding assurances to foreign manufactures against dishonest appropriation while showing products at the WCE.   ☻.(csuf)

g.   ---. ---. House. Ex. Doc. 142. *Columbian exposition. Message from the President of the United States, transmitting : The annual report of the World's Columbian Commission and other papers relating to the Exposition.* Feb. 25, 1892. Washington: GPO, 1892.

       92 p. Articles by President Benjamin Harrison and WCE officials. This is the 2nd annual report of the Commissioners.   ☻ (GLD,csuf) $10 - 30

h.   ---. ---. House. Ex. Doc. 153. *Government exhibit, World's Columbian exposition. Letter from the acting secretary of the treasury, requesting : That an appropriation be made for the purpose of collecting and preparing the Government exhibit for the World's Columbian Exposition under section 16 of the act of April 25, 1890.* Mar. 5, 1892.

       1 p. Request for $500,000 for the fiscal year ending June 30, 1893.   ☻.(csuf)

i.   ---. ---. House. Ex. Doc. 157. *Board of lady managers, World's Columbian exposition. Letter from the acting secretary of the treasury, transmitting : Estimates for appropriations for the board of lady managers, World's Columbian Exposition, for the fiscal year ending June 30, 1893.* Mar. 7, 1892.

       2 p. Transmitted appropriations of $120,718.   ☻.(csuf)

j.   ---. ---. House. H. Rept. 570. *Exhibition of certain books, papers, etc., from the library of Congress. Report: [To accompany H. Res. 87.].* Mar. 9, 1892.

1 p. Committee on the Columbian Exposition favored authorizing LC to exhibit and inserted that it be part of the Government exhibit.   ☻. (csuf)

k.   ---. ---. House. H. Rept. 626. *Foreign exhibitors at the World's Columbian exposition. Report: [To accompany S. 2315.].* Mar. 10, 1892.

1 p. Committee on Patents unanimously approved the bill to protect foreign exhibitors from prosecution for exhibiting wares protected by American patents and trade-marks.   ☻. (csuf)

l.   ---. ---. House. United States Territories Committee. H. Rept. 993. *Exhibit of Utah at World's Columbian exposition. Report: [To accompany H.R. 7827.].* Apr. 5, 1892. See #2081.

m.   ---. ---. House. H. Rept. 1136. *Branch national bank at World's Columbian exposition. Report: [To accompany H.R. 8001.].* Apr. 19, 1892.

1 p. Committee on Banking and Currency considered the bill to authorize a WCE National Bank and recommended its passage but requested the opinion of the Solicitor of the Treasury since, under law, no bank had the right to establish or maintain a branch at any place other than its bank office. ☻. (csuf)

n.   ---. ---. House. Committee on Appropriations. H. Rept. 1454.   ... *World's fair expenditures.* [Hearings as an] *inquiry concerning the management of the World's fair.* May 20, 1892. [Washington, GPO, 1892].

23x16. xv, 698 p., fold. map, black cloth hc, blind title on spine. Includes discussion of contracts for C. Graham and Winters Art Litho Co.
---- Serial set, no. 3047. Calf with leather labels.
     (csuf,CHx,NYPL,F,NHSt)
                                                                                    $40 - 70

o.   ---. ---. House. H. Rept. 1470. *Detail of certain officers for special duty in connection with the World's Columbian exposition. Report: [To accompany S. 866.].* May 24, 1892.

1 p. Committee on Military Affairs approved the bill authorizing the Secretary of War to detail Army officers for special duty but added no "work as a civil engineer."   ☻. (csuf)

p.   ---. ---. House. H. Rept. 1511. *Loan of certain articles for the World's Columbian exposition. Report: [To accompany H. Res. 102.].* May 27, 1892.

1 p. Select Committee on WCE amended H. Res. 102 and recommended passage.   ☻. (csuf)

q.   ---. ---. House. H. Rept. 1512. *Certain articles from the Smithsonian Institution to the World's Columbian exposition. Report: [To accompany H. Res. 106.].* May 27, 1892.

1 p. Select Committee on WCE favored passage of the bill to authorize the Secretary of the Smithsonian to send articles illustrative of the life and industries of women.   ☻. (csuf)

r.   ---. ---. House. H. Rept. 1513. *Certain models, drawings, etc., to the World's Columbian exposition. Report: [To accompany H. Res. 105.].* May 27, 1892.

1 p. Select Committee on WCE favored passage of the bill authorizing Secretary of Interior prepare and send to WCE models, drawings, etc., prepared or invented by women.   ☻. (csuf)

s. ---. ---. House. H. Rept. 1514. *Invitation to the King and Queen of Spain to participate in the World's Columbian exposition. Report: [To accompany S. R. 42.].* May 27, 1892.

1 p. WCE Select Committee recommended passage. ⊜.(csuf)

t. ---. ---. House. H. Rept. 1515. *Invitations to presidents of American republics and governors of American colonies to attend World's fair. Report: [To accompany S. Res. 41.].* May 27, 1892.

1 p. WCE Select Committee amended and recommended passage. ⊜.(csuf)

u. ---. ---. Senate. S. Res. 41. *Joint resolution extending an invitation to the presidents of the American republics and the governors of the American colonies to participate in the World's Columbian Exposition.* [Washington: GPO], 1892.

2 p.? Same title: H. Rept. 1515 and S. Rept. 372. (NYPL)

v. ---. ---. House. Ex. Doc. 246. *Postal service World's Columbian exposition. Letter from the secretary of the treasury, transmitting : An estimate of appropriations submitted by the Postmaster-General for the postal service, incident to the World's Columbian Exposition, for the fiscal years 1893 and 1894.* May 28, 1892.

2 p. Requesting $163,047.60 for postal service incident to the WCE. ⊜.(csuf)

w. ---. ---. House. H. Rept. 1660. *Four hundredth anniversary of the discovery of America. Report: [To accompany H. R. 9267.].* June 17, 1892.

7,3 p. WCE Select Committee's consideration of proposed legislation to provide necessary money to open, maintain, etc., the WCE; recommended passage. ⊜.(csuf)

x. ---. ---. Senate. Ex. Doc. 129. *Letter from the secretary of the treasury, with : A request of the Secretary of State for an additional appropriation for the Columbian Historical Exposition.* July 1, 1892.

3 p. Request for additional monies for the Madrid Exposition, fourth quarter of 1892. ⊜.(csuf)

y. ---. ---. House. H. Rept. 2091. *Dedication of buildings of the World's Columbian exposition. Report: [To accompany S. 3394.].* July 28, 1892.

2 p. WCE Select Committee recommended passage of the bill to dedicate on the accurate date of Oct. 21, 1892. Discusses the use of Gregorian calendar versus Julian calendar (in use in 1492) which placed the discovery date as Oct. 12th. During the lapse of centuries, inaccuracy based on Julius Cæsar's calendar had swelled to 9 days by the time of the discovery. ⊜.(csuf)

z. ---. ---. House. H. Rept. 2123. *Foreign exhibitors at the World's Columbian exposition. Report: [To accompany S. Res. 106.].* Aug. 4, 1892.

1 p. WCE Select Committee recommended passage of a bill allowing foreign exhibitors to bring in foreign laborers from their respective countries to prepare exhibits. Followed by S. Res. 33, approved Aug. 5, 1892 ⊜.(csuf)

275. **52nd Cong. 2d Sess.: 1892-93**

a. ---. ---. House. Ex. Doc. 73. *Appropriation for the World's Columbian commission. Letter from the secretary of the treasury, transmitting : Estimates of appropriations submitted by the President of the*

World's Columbian Commission for expenses of said Commission for the fiscal years 1893 and 1894.
Dec. 9, 1892.

4 p. Commission request for 1893: $27,999.07; for 1894: $148,185.00.   ⊚ . (csuf)

b.   U.S. Congress. House. Ex. Doc. 74. *Appropriation for board of lady managers World's Columbian exposition* [i.e., Commission]. *Letter from the secretary of the treasury, transmitting : An estimate of appropriation, submitted by the President of the World's Columbian Exposition, for expenses of the Board of Lady Managers for the fiscal year July 1, 1893.* Dec. 9, 1892.

3 p. Request for an appropriation of $93,190.   ⊚ . (csuf)

c.   ---. ---. Senate. Ex. Doc. 24. *Letter from the secretary of war, transmitting : A letter of the adjutant-general of Maryland relative to an encampment of troops at Chicago during the Columbian Exposition.*
Jan. 7, 1893.

5 p. Request for a law to provide for an encampment of 100,000 U.S. and State troops.   ⊚ . (csuf)

d.   ---. ---. Senate. Ex. Doc. 29. *Letter from the secretary of the treasury, in response : To Senate resolution of July 13, 1893, relative to the distribution of the souvenir coins of the Columbian Exposition.* Jan. 17, 1893.

3 p. Response of the Secretary to S. Res. regarding regulations and disbursement of $2,500,000 in souvenir coins conditioned upon Sunday closing.   ⊚ . (csuf)

e.   ---. ---. House. H. Rept. 2259. *North Dakota World's fair commission. Report: [To accompany S. R. 127.].* Jan. 17, 1893.

1 p. Recommended passage of a joint resolution authorizing the Smithsonian to lend the Red River cart from the National Museum to the ND exhibit.   ⊚ . (csuf)

f.   ---. ---. House. Ex. Doc. 211 ... *Message from the President of the United States, transmitting : the annual report of the World's Columbian commission and other papers relating to the exposition.* Jan. 27, 1893. Washington: GPO, 1893.

188 p. At head of caption title: "World's Columbian Exposition." Third and last WCE report from the Benjamin Harrison presidency. Congress granted $2.5M in souvenir 50¢ coins provided the Exposition gates closed on Sundays (p.15).   ⊚ (GLD,CHx,F) $15 - 30

☞ The WCE sold the coins for $5M (twice face value) to meet budgetary needs. An exception to the price was the first minted coin which was put up for public auction. The Remington typewriter company bought it for $10,000 and displayed it at their booth in the Manufactures Bldg. Later, the Fair opened on Sundays; the Commission declared it had asked for $5M and received only $2.5M and thus was not bound by the Congressional requirement. The Fair opened Sunday, May 28, 1893, closed Sunday July 23rd, and reopened August 2nd for the remainder of the Fair. Other reasons given for Sunday openings were: (1) the Fair was public education and, (2) the owners of exhibits could not be denied access to their property.

g.   ---. ---. Senate. Ex. Doc. 55. *Letter from the secretary of the treasury, transmitting : Estimate for an appropriation to enable the President to entertain certain distinguished visitors to the World's Columbian Exposition.* Feb. 9, 1893.

2 p. Request for appropriation of $25,000.   ⊚ . (csuf)

276.   **53d Cong. 1st sess & Special sess. of Senate: 1893**

a.   U.S. Cong. House. H. Rept. 108. *Amendment to act relating to admission of articles intended for the World's Columbian exposition. Report [To accompany H. Res. 22.].* Oct. 13, 1893.

1 p. Ways and Means Committee recommended foreign exhibitors pay only half of the duties then in effect. A similar concession had been granted for the 1876 Centennial in Philadelphia.   ☻ . (csuf)

277.   **53d Cong. 2d & 3d sess: 1894-95**

a.   U.S. Cong. (2d sess.) House. Ex. Doc. 165. *Administration of customs, World's Columbian exposition. Letter from the secretary of the treasury, transmitting : Report of the collector of customs, at Chicago, Ill., relating to the administration of customs affairs at the World's Columbian Exposition.* Mar. 27, 1894.

49 p. Reports of transactions and suggestions for changes in regulations based upon experience gained from the WCE.
---- Also listed: 47 p.
☻ . (csuf,CHx)

b.   ---. ---. (3d sess). House. Ex. Doc. 100. *Report of the United States commission to the Columbian Historical exposition at Madrid.* 1895.

411 p.   ☻ . (csuf)

278.   **54th Cong. 1st Sess. 1895-96**

a.   U.S. Cong. Senate. S. Rept. 394. *Report: [To accompany S. R. 78.].* Mar. 3, 1896.

2 p. Select Committee on International Expositions amended and recommended passage of the joint resolution authorizing distribution of medals and diplomas awarded by the World's Columbian Commission.   ☻ . (csuf)

279.   **57th Cong. 1st Sess. 1901-02**

a.   U.S. Cong. House. Committee on Awards. H. Doc. 510. *Report of the committee on awards of the World's Columbian commission. Special reports upon special subjects or groups.* 2 vol. Washington: GPO, 1901.

23½x15½. Full calf with red and black spine labels, gilt print. Vol I: 857 p. Vol II: iv, 859-1694 p. + many plates which are not included in pagination. At head of title: "World's Columbian exposition Chicago, Ill., 1893." On spines: Series 4373 and 4374. "Document No. 510" on t.p. At head of title: "World's Columbian exposition, Chicago, Ill., 1893." "Portraits of Columbus" and "Collective exhibit in the convent of La Rabida" by Thomas Wilson: vol 1, p. 187-200. For same title see #115.
☻ . (csuf,NHSt,BCM,BM,UTn,NHSt,UoC,NJSt) $100 - 200

280. U.S. Cong. *The statutes at large of the United States of America, from December, 1889, to March, 1891, and recent treaties, conventions, and executive proclamations.* Vol. 26. Washington: GPO, 1891; Photo reproduction. Buffalo, NY: Dennis & Co., Inc., 1968.

25x18. 1765 p. Ocher colored linen hc. T.p. reads: "As a copy of the original is practically unobtainable, this reprint is offered to enable Law Libraries to complete their set." The original Federal WCE Act: Chap. 156: "An act to provide for celebrating the four hundreth anniversary of the Discovery of America by Christopher Columbus by holding an international exhibition of arts, industries, manufactures, and the products of the soil, mine, and sea in the city of Chicago, in the State of Illinois." Approved April 25, 1890. Appropriation for the World's Columbian Commission: p. 64-65 & 965-66. WCE legislation: p. 62-65, 949, 965, & 1562.   ☺ (UNM)

☞ These Statutes are published under the direction of the Secretary of State. The 51st Cong. was the first to enact WCE legislation. *The statutes at large* vol 25 contains appropriations for the past 3 expositions but no reference to WCE.

281. U.S. Cong. *The statutes at large of the United States of America, from December, 1891, to March, 1893, and recent treaties, conventions, and executive proclamations.* Vol. 27. Washington: GPO, 1893.

28½x19½. 1178 p. Rebound hc. World's Columbian Commission statutes: p. 362, 390, & 586-87. WCE statutes: scattered from p. 7 to 757.   ☺ (UNM)

282. U.S. Cong. *The statutes at large of the United States of America, from August, 1893, to March, 1895, and recent treaties, conventions, executive proclamations.* Vol. 28. Washington: GPO, 1895.

28½x19½. 1429 p., 21 p. appendix. Rebound hc. World's Columbian Commission legislation p. 928. WCE legislation: scattered p. 1-842. World's Fair Prize Winners' Exposition: p. 8-9.   ☺ (UNM)

283. U.S. Cong. *The statutes at large of the United States of America, from December, 1895, to March, 1897, and recent treaties, conventions, executive proclamations, with an appendix containing the concurrent resolutions of the two houses of Congress.* Vol. 29. Washington: GPO, 1897.

29x20½. 1018 p. + 18 p. appendix. Rebound hc. WCE deficiency appropriations and legislation regarding distribution of medals and diplomas: p. 19-20, 270, & 466. There is no legislation pertaining to the World's Columbian Commission.   (UNM)

284. U.S. Cong. *The statutes at large of the United States of America, from March, 1897, to March, 1899, and recent treaties, conventions, executive proclamations, and the concurrent resolutions of the two houses of Congress.* Vol. 30. Washington: GPO, 1899.

28½x19½. 2026 p. Ocher linen hc. Deficiency appropriations for the WCE: p. 109 & 110.   (UNM)

285. U.S. Cong. *The statutes at large of the United States of America, from December, 1899, to March, 1901, and recent treaties, conventions, executive proclamations, and the concurrent resolutions of the two houses of Congress.* Vol. 31. Washington: GPO, 1901.

28½x20½. 2167 p. Rebound hc. A single WCE entry (p. 2007): the World's Columbian Commission reports ordered printed. The subsequent "Statutes" (57th Cong., vol 32) has no reference to the WCE.   (UNM)

286. U.S. Custom House, Chicago. *Catalogue of Unclaimed-Merchandise and Abandoned World's Fair Exhibits, to be sold pursuant to law ... Wednesday, March 7, '94.* Chicago: Jacob, Coles & Co., Printers, n.d.

24x15. (6) p. Caption title. Conditions of sale: Highest bidder, terms cash in current funds. 8 rooms of articles listed including 19 kegs of anchovies -- phew!   (CHx)

287. U.S. Department of Agriculture. Division of Entomology. *Catalogue of the exhibit of economic entomology at the World's Columbian exposition, Chicago, Ill., 1893.* Washington: GPO, 1893.

23x14½. 121 p. Gray wraps, black print. C.t.= t.p. Bugs affecting commercial plants; arsenic was a common treatment!
---- In Its Bulletin. No. 31.
⊚ . (CPL,NYPL,OSU,BM,UoC)

288. U.S. Department of Agriculture. Weather Bureau. ... *Souvenir : Weather Bureau. Explanation of weather & temperature : flags. And wind signals. Chicago, Ill., U.S.A. : 1893.* Washington, DC: __akam, n.d.

14x9. (4) p. which is a folded card. Black litho on cream stiff stock. At head of title: "World's Columbian Exposition." C.t. Red, white, and blue weather flags illus printed inside. Loose insert is a folding (29½x37 unfolded) U.S. weather map by Goes Lithographing Co., Chicago. Map printed in green and red; explanation and additional maps printed in black on reverse.
P→   ⊚ (GLD,TD) $20 - 34

289. U.S. Department of Agriculture. Wiley, Harvey Washington. *Analysis of cereals collected at the World's Columbian exposition, and comparisons with other data.* Washington: GPO, 1895.

23x__. 57 p., tables. UoC microfilm. Series: U.S. Dept of Agriculture. Division of Chemistry. Bulletin no. 45. (UoC)

290. U.S. Department of Agriculture. Willits, Edwin. "Special report of the assistant secretary of agriculture for 1893." In *Report, 1893.* Washington: GPO, 1894.

23x__. Pages 51-86. Agricultural exhibits at the WCE.   (OSU)

291. U.S. National Archives and Records Service. Helton, H. Stephen, comp. *Preliminary inventory of the records of United States participation in international conferences, commissions, and expositions (Record group 43).* Washington: 1955.

28x22. ix, 161 p. In National Archives Pub. no. 55-8 preliminary inventories, no. 76.--(NA Call: CD 3029 A21 no. 76)   (NA)

☞ This, and the next inventory, are necessary guides through the labyrinthine holdings of the National Archives government WCE documents. The WCE researcher should not neglect the National Archives. It is rich in government materials relating to the Fair including correspondence, circulars, official papers, minutes, pamphlets, reports, photographs, and awards. Perhaps most astounding for the authors is the 48 vol "Awards of the Columbian Exposition" with its shelf length of 10 feet!

292. U.S. National Archives and Records Service. Johnson, Marion M., and Mabel D. Brock, comp. *Preliminary inventory of the records of United States participation in international conferences, commissions, and expositions. Supplementary to National Archives preliminary inventory no. 76 (record group 43).* [Washington]: 1965.

28x22. 22 p. National Archives preliminary inventories, NC-95.--(NA Call: NA Box 264 VII B-1)   (NA)

293. U.S. National Museum. *Annual Report of the board of regents of the Smithsonian institution, showing the operations, expenditures, and condition of the institution for the year ending June 30, 1891. Report of the U.S. national museum.* Washington: GPO, 1892.

23½x16½. xvii, 869 p. Contains: G. Brown Goode's "First draft of a system of classification for the World's Columbian exposition." 1 *l*, 649-735 p. Also see #49. Also contains the Dept of Ethnology plan for their exhibit at p. 139, and Dept of Mammals taxidermy specimens for the WCE at p. 203.
☺ . (LC,UNM,TnSt,OSU,UoC,nwu,RPB,OC) $15 - 30

294. U.S. National Museum. *Annual report of the board of regents of the Smithsonian institution, showing the operations, expenditures, and condition of the institution for the year ending June 30, 1892. Report of the U.S. national museum.* Washington: GPO, 1893.

23½x16½. xv, 620 p. Black cloth hc, spine print only. Paragraph on which museum depts were to be represented at the WCE (p. 4).   (UNM) $15 - 30

295. U.S. National Museum. *Annual report of the board of regents of the Smithsonian institution, showing the operations, expenditures, and condition of the institution for the year ending June 30, 1893. Report of the U.S. national museum.* Washington: GPO, 1895.

23½x16½. xxi, 794 p. + many unpaginated plates. Black cloth hc, gilt print spine. Detailed description, floor plan, etc., for WCE, U.S. Government Bldg, and museum contents. G. Brown Goode, instrumental at the WCE, was the Assistant Secretary for the National Museum. Goode's report at p. 108-114; scientific dept WCE exhibits at p. 115-192; documents relating to the WCE at p. 316-323.   ☺ (GLD,UNM,JHU,LC,OhHx,OSU,UoC,RPB) $15 - 30

296. U.S. National Museum. *Annual report of the board of regents of the Smithsonian institution, showing the operations, expenditures, and condition of the institution for the year ending June 30, 1894. Report of the U.S. national museum.* Washington: GPO, 1896.

23½x16½. xxiv, 1030 p. Black cloth hc. Describes the return of WCE material to the museum and the embarrassment at having insufficient space to store or display the items (p. 21). Returned from the WCE were 1,229 boxes and packages (32 car loads); also received were 494 packages containing specimens obtained at the WCE for the museum (p. 85-86).
☺ . (ref,UNM,UoC) $15 - 30

297. U.S. National Museum. *Annual report of the board of regents of the Smithsonian Institution, showing the operations, expenditures, and condition of the institution for the year ending June 30, 1895. Report of the U.S. national museum.* Washington: GPO, 1897.

23½x16½. xx, 1080 p. Rebound hc. Received at the close of WCE but recorded in this fiscal year: mammal exhibits from the governments of Costa Rica, Ceylon, Korea, and Johore.
☺ (UNM) $15 - 30

298. U.S. National Museum. *Annual report of the board of regents of the Smithsonian institution, showing the operations, expenditures, and condition of the institution for the year ending June 30, 1901. Report of the U.S. national museum.* Washington: GPO, 1903.

23½x16½. xvi, 452 p., many unpaginated illus and photos. Green cloth hc, gilt print spine, gilt logo on center front cover. Reports donations and purchases at expositions, including the WCE, as a source of museum collections (p. 7-8). ☺ (UNM) $15 - 30

☞ No WCE activity found in annual reports of 1896-1900 and 1902-1905.

299. U.S. National Museum. Bureau of Ethnology. *Thirteenth annual report of the Bureau of Ethnology to the secretary of the Smithsonian Institution 1891-'92.* J. W. Powell, director. Washington: GPO, 1896.

28x21½. lix, 462 p. Olive cloth hc with gilt print. Tells of the staff collecting Indian artifacts for displays at the WCE. (ref) $40 - 120

☞ This is one of a large, uniform format, series on American ethnology. Undoubtedly other volumes in this time period contain articles on the WCE exhibits. Prices are high because of the information on American Indians.

300. U.S. Navy Department. Poundstone, H[omer] C., comp. *Catalogue of the Exhibit of the U.S. Navy Department : World's Columbian Exposition, 1893.* Chicago: W. B. Conkey Co. Publishers, °1893. [1893 inked over 1892]; Woodbridge, CT: RPI, 1989.

22½x14½. 233, (1) p., illus. Frontis is a folding plan of Jackson Park. Cover: color lithos of five ships under sail, tan background. C.t.: "U.S. Navy Department Exhibit. World's Columbian Exposition 1893." ☺ (LC,SI,NYPL,NYSt,NL)

301. U.S. State Department. ... *Plan and scope of the exhibit by the Department of State.* N.p.: [1892?].

Folio. 4 p. At head of title: "The World's Columbian Exposition." (NYPL)

302. U.S. Treasury Department. Customs Division. *New regulations governing the free importation of articles for exhibition at the World's Columbian exposition at Chicago under the act of Congress approved April 25, 1890.* Washington: GPO, 1891.

23½x14½. 10 p. Gray wraps with black print. C.t.= t.p. Below title: "Charles Foster, Secretary of the Treasury." ☺ . (CPL,LC,NYPL)

303. U.S. Treasury Department. Office of the Coast and Geodetic Survey. *The methods and results of the U.S. Coast and Geodetic Survey as illustrated at the World's Columbian Exposition, 1893 ...* Washington: GPO, 1893.

8°. 1 *l*, 39-98 p. (Bull. 29). (NYPL)

304. U.S. Treasury Department. Office of the Coast and Geodetic Survey. ... *The Preparation and arrangement of the exhibit of the U.S. Coast and Geodetic Survey at the World's Columbian Exposition 1893: Appendix No. 10--Report for 1893.* Washington: GPO, 1894.

24x16. Appendix No. 10   p. 425-39. At head of title: "Bibliography." Found bound with unrelated reports.   (AkSt)

References that may be of help locate additional federal government publications on the WCE:

1) Ames, John G. *Comprehensive Index to the Publications of the United States Government 1881-1893.* Vol. 2. Washington: GPO, 1905.

2) *Catalogue of the Public Documents of the 53d Congress and of all Departments of the Government of the United States for the Period From March 4, 1893 to June 30, 1895.* Washington: GPO, 1896.

3) ---. *... 54th Congress ...* [1896-97].

4) ---. *... 55th Congress ...* [1897-98].

5) *CIS US Serial Set Index : Part IV : 51st-54th Congresses : 1889-1897.* Congressional Information Service, Inc.: Washington, D.C., n.d.

6) *CIS US Serial Set Index : Part V : 55th-57th Congresses : 1897-1903.* Congressional Information Service, Inc.: Washington, D.C., n.d.

7) Kanely, Edna A., comp. *Cumulative Index to Hickcox's Monthly Catalog of United States Government Publications 1885-1894.* Vol. 1, A-F. Carrollton Press, Inc., °1891.

Chapter 4

FOREIGN COUNTRY PUBLICATIONS

Twenty four countries had buildings at the Fair; others had "Villages" on the Midway Plaisance. A total of 80 countries supplied exhibits. The various countries issued advertising literature and reports. This chapter also contains foreign country printings for the World's Congresses.

The name of the country precedes the bibliographic information to aid in locating items in this chapter. The country's name is in brackets if it is not an official publication or if that fact is unknown.

-A-

305. Argentina. Consejo Nacional de Educación. ... *Trabajos escolares : exposición de Chicago año de 1893.* Buenos Aires: Compañia Sud-Americana 'de Billetes de Banco, 1893.

  20½x15 (text). iv, 629 p. Pulp wraps and text, black print. At head of title: "Republica Argentina : Consejo nacional de educación." Trans: Scholarly works : Chicago Exposition in the year 1893. Describes school activities in Argentina.
  ---- Also listed: 622 p.
  ⊚ . (LC,NL)

306. Argentina. Decoud, Diogène. ... *Les sciences médicales dans la république Argentine.* Buenos Aires: Imprimerie Européenne, Moreno y Defensa, 1893.

  26x17. 80, CLXV p., 2 *l.* Pulp wraps and text, black print. The 165 p. are bibliography of Argentine medical papers. At head of title: "Exposition internationale de Chicago 1893." Trans: The Medical Sciences of the Argentine Republic. ⊚ . (LC,UoC)

307. Argentina. Entre Rios. Comisión á la Exposición universal de Chicago, 1893. ... *La provincia de Entre Rios : obra descriptiva : Escrita con motivo de las Exposición Universal de Chicago, bajo la dirección de la Comisión ... por decreto de fecha 10 de julio de 1892.* Paraná: Tipografia, Litografia y Encuadernación "La Velocidad," 1893.

  23½x17½. 1 *l.*, vi, 520 p., 1 *l* which is index. Flecked tan wraps, black print and small design, all edges marbled tan and beige. At head of title: "República Argentina." Trans: The Province of Entre Rios : A descriptive written report relating to the exposition, under the direction of said committee, officially dated, July 10, 1892. ⊚ . (PU,JHU,LC,NYPL,LMi,TU,UMi,UoC,NL,RPB,BM)

308. Argentina. Ministerio de justicia, culto é República Argentina. *Informe sobre la educación secundaria y normal en la República Argentina.* La Plata: Talleres de publicaciones del museo, 1893.

  25x16 (text). 332 p., plates, plans (part folding), some illus are blue-green half tone. Content: secondary education and normal schools. Spanish version of #309. ⊚ . (LC)

309. Argentina. Ministerio de justicia, culto é República Argentina. *Report upon the state of secondary and normal education in the Argentine Republic.* La Plata: Talleres de publicaciones del museo, 1893.

  25x16½. 1 *l* (t.p.), (3)-212 p., b/w illus, plans (some fold.) which are not included in paging. Gray wraps. C.t.= t.p. English version of #308. ⊚ . (UoC,NL)

310. Argentina. Olivera, Carlos. *Mision a Chicago.* Edicion oficial. La Plata: Talleres de publicaciones del museo, 1894; Woodbridge, CT: RPI, 1989.

    ca. 19x12. 91 p., microfilm. Trans: Mission to Chicago. ☺.(SI)

311. Argentina. *Pabellon argentino. 1894.* [Buenos Aires]: Waldorp & Cie, [1894].

    Trans: Argentine Pavilion.   (UC)

312. Argentina. Padilla, Tiburcio. ... *Organisation et institutions sanitaires de la république Argentine.* ... Buenos Aires: Imprenta y Casa Editora "Argos", 1893.

    20x13½. 222 p. LC microfilm. At head of title: "République Argentine Exposition Universelle de Chicago." Trans: Organizations and Institutions of Sanitation in the Argentine Republic. ☺.(LC,UoC)

313. Austria. I.R. Central Commission. *Official : special catalogue of the Austrian section of the World's Columbian exposition, Chicago 1893.* Vienna: Published by the I.R. Central Commission, printed by John Vernay, n.d.; Chicago: I.R. Central Commission, 1893.

    20x14. 112 p., 4 *l* of ads at back of book. Dark tan hc, gold lettering, black and gold design, gilt decorated end papers, red dyed edges.
    ---- Blue wraps.
         ☺. (KyU,CHx,NL)

314. Austria. K.K. Central-Commission. *Officieller bericht der K. K. Österr. central-commission für die weltausstellung in Chicago im Jahre 1893.* 4 vols. Wien: Verlag der K. K. Central-Commission, 1894-95; Woodbridge, CT: RPI, 1989.

    28x19½. Vol 1: 5 *l*, 74 p., 2 *l*, 51 p., 3 *l*, 194 p., 2 *l*, 69 p. Vol 2: 2 *l*, 135 p. + 60 fold. plates. Vol 3: 4 *l*, 69 p. + 13 fold. plates, vii, 396 p. + 11 fold. tables. Vol 4: 2 *l*, (iii)-viii, 1 *l*, 147, (1) p., 19 fold. plates, 2 *l*, (iv)-vii, 101 p., 7 fold plates. Tan paper covered boards with black print; purple cloth spines with gilt print. C.t.= t.p. ☺.(csuf,SI,BM)

315. [Austria]. Schlesinger, Robert. ... *Koch-Buch : über paprizirte Speisen : Zehnte verbesserte Auflage.* Wien: Paprika Schlesinger, n.d.

    15x11½. Buff wraps in red and green print and design. At head of title: "Gratis : Valodi magyarkirály paprika." Stamped on cover: "Paprika Schlesinger, Wien : Exposition Chicago "Old Vienna." ☺.(WM)

316. Austria. Wieser, Fr. R. v. *Die Karte des Bartolomeo Colombo über die vierte Reise des Admirals.* Innsbruck: Verlag der Wagner'schen Universitäts-Buchhandlung, 1893.

    22½x14½. 13 p. + 3 maps. Maps about Columbus' fourth voyage. ☺.(UoC)

-B-

317. Belgium. ... *Catalogue général de la section Belge \ Universal exhibition : general catalogue of the Belgian section.* [Bruxelles: Imprimerie E. Guyot], n.d.

19x13. 2 *l*, 295 p. Powder blue wraps, brown print. C.t.= t.p. Pages alternate French and English. At head of title: "Chicago 1893 : exposition universelle." ☺ . (NL)

318. Belgium. ... *Report on the laces and embroideries : addressed to Senator A. Vercruysse, President of the Belgian Commission at the Chicago Exhibition by Mademoiselle Jenny Minne-Dausaert ... member of the American jury.* Paris: Neal's Library, 1894.

22½x15. 31 p. Gray wraps, black print. C.t.= t.p. At head of title: "Chicago's Universal and International Exhibition, 1893." (CHx)

319. Brazil. Amazon. Bitancourt, Lauro B. ... *The State of Amazon : Brazil.* [Chicago: Campbell Manufacturing Co.], n.d.; Woodbridge, CT: RPI, 1989.

22x15½. 2-14, (1) p. Orange patterned wraps, black print. C.t. Bitancourt was a member of the Brazilian Commission and special commissioner of Amazon. At head of title: "Published by authority of the governor of the state." On back cover: "Chicago: Campbell Manufacturing Co."
---- (15) p. Gray wraps.
☺ . (KyU,CPL,LC,SI,NYPL,UoC,NL)

320. Brazil. Amazon. *Catalogue of woods exhibited by the State of Amazon, Brazil, at the World's Columbian Exposition, Chicago.* Chicago: John Anderson Publishing Co., 1893.

22x15. 31 p. Plain wraps. C.t. (CHx)

321. Brazil. Bahia. Vianna, Francisco Vicente, and José Carlos Ferreira. *Memoir of the State of Bahia.* Trans. Guilherme Pereira Rebello. Bahia: Printing and book-binding office of the «Diario da Bahia», 1893.

22½x14½. 4 *l*, (3)-682 p., (i)-xxvii + 6 multi-fold out tables. Green wraps, black print.
☺ . (LC,NYPL,TU)

322. Brazil. Brazilian Commission. *Catalogue of the Brazilian section at the World's Columbian Exposition. Chicago 1893.* [Chicago]: E. J. Campbell, Printer for the Brazilian Commission, 1893; Woodbridge, CT: RPI, 1989.

22x14½. 1 *l*, 145, (2) p., illus. Dull yellow wraps. Frontis of Brazilian Bldg. ☺ . (CHx,CPL,SI,UMi,NL)

323. Brazil. Ceará. *The state of Ceará : brief notes for The Exposition of Chicago.* Chicago: [E. J. Campbell], 1893; Woodbridge, CT: RPI, 1989.

ca. 22½x13½. 101 p., 10 plates, map, microfilm. T.p. states the book was authorized by the governor of Ceará, Dr. José Freire Bezerril Fontenelle.
---- 24½x16. Navy blue cloth hc, gilt print. Leaf before t.p. printed for Commissioner's signature.
☺ . (SI,NYPL,NL,F) $25 - 50

324. Brazil. *The City of Manáos and the Country of Rubber Tree : Souvenir of the Columbian Exposition Chicago, 1893.* N.p.: n.p., n.d.; Woodbridge, CT: RPI, 1989.

14½x23½. 40 *l*, plates one side (no text). Light pink wraps with black print and design. C.t. SI copy: "With Compliments from Lauro Bitancourt, Commissioner of the State of Amazon, Brazil."
---- Light green wraps with chocolate print and design.
P→ ☻ . (GLD,SI,NYPL,F,S,BPL) $16 - 30

325. Brazil. Comité Brasileiro de Senhoras. ... *Instrucçōes e regulamento geral* [sic] *norte-americano do conselho director das senhoras (Board of Lady Managers) : exhibicão de productos feminis.* Capital Federal [Rio de Janeiro]: Companhia impressora, 1892.

21x13½. 37 p. Wraps. At head of title: "Exposição universal Colombiana em Chicago ..." Brazilian Womens' Committee. Trans: Instructions and rules of the North American womens' council : exhibit of feminine products.   ☻ . (TU)

326. Brazil. Ministro da Agricultura, Commercio e Obras Publicas. Rodreigues, J. Barbosa. *Exposição sobre o estado e necissidades do Jardim botanico apresentada em 12 de Junho de 1890.* Rio de Janeiro: Typ. de G. Leuzinger & Filhos, 1893; Woodbridge, CT: RPI, 1989.

ca. 23x16. 16 p. Microfilm. Authored by the Minister of Agriculture, Commerce and Public Works. Trans: Exhibit about or status and necessity of botanical gardens, presented on June 12, 1890.   ☻ . (SI)

327. Brazil. Pará. *The state of Pará : notes for the exposition of Chicago as authorized by the governor of Pará, Brazil, Dr. Lauro Sodré.* New York: [The Knickerbocker Press, G. P. Putnam's Sons], 1893 [°1893 by Baron de Marajó]; Woodbridge, CT: RPI, 1989.

23½x15½. 4 *l*, 3-150 p., 1 *l*. 6 plates, fold. map, fold. plan. Contains four parts: 1) history, 2) physical description, 3) public instruction, 4) public revenues and commerce.
---- 23x15½. (i)-v, 2 *l*, 3-150, (1) p. Plates not included in paging. Dark gray-beige cover, black print.
☻ . (JHU,LC,SI,NYPL,TU,UMi,NYSt,UoC,NL)

328. Brazil. São Paulo. *The State of São Paulo (Brazil).* Chicago: John Anderson Publishing Co., Printers, 1893; Woodbridge, CT: RPI, 1989.

ca. 20x14. 14 p., illus. Microfilm. T.p. lists chapters I, II, III.   ☻ . (SI)

329. British Guiana. Quelch, J[ohn] J[oseph]. *Catalogue of the Exhibits of British Guiana : with notes by J. J. Quelch.* Chicago: Rand, McNally, 1893; Woodbridge, CT: RPI, 1989.

23x15½. 44 p. Brown wraps. The exhibit contained such items as convict caps made by prisoners, rums, and monkey skins.   (SI,CPL,UMi)

330. British Guiana. Rodway, James. *Hand-book of British Guiana, Prepared under the direction of the Columbian Exposition Literary Committee of the Royal Agricultural and Commercial Society.* Georgetown, British Guiana: Published by the Committee [Boston: Press of Rockwell and Churchill], 1893.

22½x16. 93 p., fold. maps, plates, 14 p. ads at end, folding map frontis. Gray wraps, black design and lettering. On verso of t.p.: The book is prepared and the engravings and plates are made by the John Andrew and son co. Boston, U.S.A." ☺ . (csuf,UDe,SLP,UoC,NL,ncsu)

331. British North Borneo. *Handbook of British North Borneo compiled from reports of the governor and officers of the residential staff in Borneo, and other sources of information of an authentic nature...* London: William Clowes & sons, Limited, 1890.

21x13½. 4 *l*, 184 p., illus, maps. Folding map of North Borneo precedes t.p. At top of cover: "The World's Columbian Exposition. Chicago, 1893." ☺ . (PU)

332. Bulgaria. *Souvenir : Bulgaria : World's Columbian exposition 1893.* [Chicago: A. L. Swift & co.], n.d.; Woodbridge, CT: RPI, 1989.

11½x15½. (4) p. Pink wraps with royal blue print and bold Bulgarian crest in red, green, and gilt; map on back wrap. History of Bulgaria. ☺ . (GLD,SI) $13 - 27

-C-

333. Canada. *The advantages of Canada for emigrants. Papers by ... and Appendices containing General Information about Canada, and a Description of the Canadian Exhibits, and the Awards they obtained, at Chicago.* London: McCorquodale & Co., Limited, 1894.

20½x13½. 40 p., illus. Pulp wraps, brown print and design, pulp paper. Papers by Lightfoot, Cavis-Brown, and Webber. C.t.= t.p. Bottom of t.p.: "Published by Authority of the Government of Canada (Department of the Interior.)" Other author: Canada High Commissioner in London. ☺ . (LC)

334. Canada. *Canadian Department of Fine Arts : World's Columbian Exposition, 1893, catalogue of paintings.* [Toronto?: n.p. (C. B. Robinson), 1893?]; Montreal: CIHM 1985.

22x__. 16 p. Microfiches from a copy at Metropolitan Toronto Library, Fine Arts Dept. (NLC)

335. Canada. *Circular to the trustees and teachers respecting the World's Columbian Exposition.* N.p.: n.p., n.d.; Montreal: CIHM, 1985.

28x22. 1 *l* (verso blank). Signed: J. Dearness, inspector. Filmed from a copy held by the D. B. Weldon Library, U of Western Ontario (Regional History Room). (NLC)

336. Canada. Executive Commissioner for Canada. *Report of the executive commissioner for Canada : to the World's Columbian exposition : Chicago, 1893 : printed by order of Parliament.* Ottawa: Printed by S. E. Dawson, printer to the Queen's most excellent majesty, 1894.

24x16. 81 p. Blue wraps. C.t.= t.p. Appeared as Paper No. 8g of Canada Parliament Sessional Papers, 1894 (*Sess. Papers* vol 27, no. 7).
---- Also listed: 2 *l*, 81 p.   ☺ . (NYPL,mcg,NAC)

337. Canada. Executive Commissioner for Canada. Saunders, William. *Report of the World's Columbian Exposition : being a statement of the progress of the work of the Canadian Section.* Ottawa: S. E. Dawson, Printer to the Queen's most excellent majesty, 1892; Ottawa: CIHM, 1981.

    21x15. 27 p. Gray wraps, black print. C.t. On cover, Saunders is listed as the "Late Executive Commissioner."   ☺ . (CPL,NYPL,mcg,NLC,WM)

338. Canada. Executive Commissioner for Canada. *Special report of the executive commissioner on awards on agricultural implements at Chicago, 1893.* Ottawa: S. E. Dawson, Printer to the Queen's most Excellent Majesty, 1894.

    24½x16. 15 p. Blue green wraps. Contains the awards reports of individual judges and complaints of irregularities by U.S. judge, A. S. Praether. See #348.   (NYPL)

339. Canada. *Exposition colombienne : bureau d'informations sic pour les canadiens-francais sous les auspices de "La Presse."* N.p.: n.p., ⸰1893; Ottawa: CIHM, 1986.

    Microfiche (8 images). Trans: Columbian exposition : Bureau of Information for French-Canadians under the auspices of "La Presse."   (mcg,NLC)

340. Canada. Geological Survey of Canada. Ferrier, Walter F[rederick]. ... *Catalogue of a stratigraphical collection of Canadian rocks : prepared for the World's Columbian exposition : Chicago, 1893.* Ottawa: Government Printing Bureau, 1893; Ottawa: CIHM, 1987; Woodbridge, CT: RPI, 1989.

    25x16½. xix, (1), 128, (2) p. Tan wraps, black print. C.t.= t.p. Ferrier was lithologist to the Survey. ☺ . (PU,LC,SI,NYPL,mcg,BCM,OSU,BM,UMi,NYSt,UoC,RPB)

341. Canada. *Guide general de la ville de Chicago et de l'Exposition colombienne de 1893.* Montreal: La société des publications françaises, 1893; Ottawa: CIHM, 1980.

    16½x13. 158 p. + ad pages. Wraps with illus of Administration Bldg. Frontis of Canadian Bldg. C.t.= t.p. In French. Trans: General Guide to Chicago and the Columbian Exposition of 1893.   (NLC)

342. Canada. ... *The map of the Rocky Mountains Park of Canada and surrounding country : and the Canadian topographical surveys : Executed by means of Photography.* Ottawa: Printed by S. E. Dawson, Printers to the Queen's Most Excellent Majesty, 1893.

    16½x12. 7 p. Light gray-blue wraps, black print. C.t.= t.p. E. Deville was Surveyor-General. WCE handout.   ☺ . (NL)

343. Canada. Nova Scotia. Education Department. ... *Education. Nova Scotia (Canada). A conspectus of the public free school system and educational institutions of the province of Nova Scotia.* Halifax: W. Macnab, 1893; Ottawa: CIHM, 1987.

    25x16. 1 *l*, 18 p. Also microfiche (15 frames). At head of title: "World's Columbian Exposition, Chicago, 1893."   (NYPL,mcg,NLC,NL)

344. Canada. Nova Scotia. Gilpin, Edwin. *Minerals of Nova Scotia.* Halifax: The commissioner of public works and mines, Queen's printer [Wm. Macnab], 1893.

22x14½. 15 p., tables. Burnt orange (or rose) wraps, black print. C.t.= t.p. "... prepared for the World's Columbian Exposition." Gilpin was Inspector of Mines.   ☻ . (LC,NYPL)

345. Canada. Ontario. Department of Agriculture. *Report of the Ontario commissioner to the World's Columbian exposition, 1893.* ... Toronto: Warwick Bros. & Rutter, printers, &c., 1894.

24½x16½. 110 p. Orange wraps. On t.p.: "Published by the Ontario Department of Agriculture" and "Printed by order of the Legislative Assembly." C.t.= t.p.   ☻ . (KyU)

346. Canada. Ontario. Education Department. May, S[amuel] Passmore. *Catalogue of school appliances : pupils' work, etc., exhibited by the education department of Ontario, Canada, at the World's Columbian exposition, Chicago, 1893.* Toronto: Printed by Warwick & sons, 1893; Ottawa: CIHM, 1986.

25x16½. (5)-68 p. Teal blue wraps, black print and design. C.t.: "The World's Columbian Exposition Chicago 1893. Catalogue of School Appliances, Pupils [sic] Work &c. Education Department, Ontario. Canada." May was director of Educational Exhibits for Ontario.
☻ . (CHx,mcg,NLC,NL)

347. Canada. Ontario. ... *Mineral Exhibit of the Province of Ontario, Descriptive Catalogue.* Toronto: Printed by Warwick and sons, 1893.

24½x16½. 64 p., catalogue. Deep teal blue wraps with black print and design. At head of title: "World's Columbian Exposition. [Chicago, Ill., May 1 to October 30, 1893.]" C.t.: "The World's Columbian Exposition Chicago 1893. Catalogue of Mineralogical Exhibits: Crown Lands Department, Ontario. Canada." "Published under the authority of N. Awrey, Commissioner for Ontario." Author David Boyle, listed on p.(3), was Superintendent of Mineral Exhibit.
P→   ☻ (GLD,CHx,UMi,BPL) $20 - 30

348. Canada. Parliament. *Sessional Papers, 1894.* Paper no. 8e, "Special reports of the Executive Commissioner on awards on agricultural implements at Chicago, 1893." See #338.   (mcg)

349. Canada. Parliament. *Sessional Papers, 1894.* Paper no. 8g, "Report of the Executive Commissioner to the World's Columbian Exposition, Chicago, 1893."   (mcg)

350. Canada. Parliament. *Sessional Papers, 1894.* Paper no. 101, "Return to an order of the House of Commons, dated the 28th May, 1894, for a detailed report showing the prizes awarded by the judges or jury at the Chicago Columbian Exposition for the work of pupils of primary and special schools of every kind and degree; and also to pupils of secondary educational institutions of each of the provinces of Canada."   (mcg)

351. Canada. Quebec. Demers, Christiane, et Jocelyn Saint-Pierre, eds. *Assemblée Nationale du Québec : Débats de l'assemblée législative : 8e législature, 3e session : 1893-94.* Québec: Journal des Débats, 1980.

24x17½. WCE legislative history on p. 101-102, 133, 249, 369.   ⊚ . (ANQ)

352. Canada. Quebec. *L'Instruction publique de la province de Québec à l'Exposition colombienne de Chicago : rapport de l'Honorable secretaire-provincial.* Quebec: C.-F. Langlois, °1895; Ottawa: CIMH, 1986.

3 microfiches (113 images). Trans: Public instruction in Quebec.   (mcg,NLC)

353. [Canada]. [Quebec]. Montreal. Bureau de commissaires d'écoles catholiques romains de Montreal. ... *Notice sur les écoles relevant du bureau des commissaires catholiques romains de la cité de Montréal [Canada].* Montreal: [Bureau des commissaires d'écoles catholiques romains de Montreal], 1893.

21½x14. 102 p., gray wraps. At head of title: "Exposition universelle de Chicago, 1893. C.t.= t.p. except at top of cover: "Hommage des Commissaires d'écoles catholiques de Montréal." French version of #354.   ⊚ . (NLC)

354. [Canada]. [Quebec]. Montreal. Catholic School Commissioners. ... *An account of the schools controlled by the Roman Catholic Board of School Commissioners of the city of Montreal (Canada).* Montreal: n.p., 1893.

22x15. 112 p. includes t.p., b/w illus, plans, tables. Light blue flecked wraps, black print and design. At head of title: "The World's Fair, Chicago, 1893." At top of front wrap: "With the compliments of the Roman Catholic school commissioners of Montreal." English version of #353.   ⊚ . (NLC,NL)

355. [Canada]. [Quebec]. Montreal. *Exhibit. Protestant schools. Montreal, Canada. Educational department. The World's Fair. Chicago, U.S.A. : 1892-93.* [Montreal: W. H. Eaton & Son, Printers], n.d.

14½x10½. 1 *l* (t.p.), (3)-17 p. Light aqua blue pebbled wraps, navy print and border. Text printed with navy ink.   ⊚ (NL)

356. Canada. Quebec. *Rapport du commissaire de la province de Quebec : à l'Exposition Colombienne de Chicago.* Montreal: Gazette Printing Co., [1894]; Ottawa: CIHM, 1986.

25x17½. 38 p. C.t. French version of #357.   ⊚ . (mcg,NLC,ANQ)

357. Canada. Quebec. *Report of the commissioner from the province of Quebec : World's Columbian Exposition : Chicago : 1st May to 31st October, 1893.* Montreal: Gazette printing co., [1894]; Ottawa: CIHM, 1896.

25x17½. 38 p. C.t. Signed and dated: John McIntosh, Jr., Commissioner, Quebec, 4th January, 1894. English version of #356.   ⊚ . (mcg,NLC,ANQ)

358. Canada. Quebec. Rouleau, Th.-G. *Notice sur l'école normale laval de Québec pour l'exposition de Chicago.* Quebec: Imprimerie L. Brousseau, 1893.

21½x13. 42 p., folding *l*. Gray wraps. NLC copy is signed by author. C.t.= t.p. Content: Review of Normal Schools in Quebec. ☺. (NLC)

359. Canada. Quebec. *Statutes of the province of Quebec, ... first session of the eighth legislature* [*1892*]. Quebec: printed by Charles François Langlois, 1892.

24½x15½ (text). Act respecting the appointment of a member of the Legislative Assembly as commissioner to the WCE. 55 Victoria, chapter 36.
---- French version exists: *Statuts de la Province de Québec, ...* 24½x15½ (text).
☺. (mcg,ANQ)

360. [Canada]. Smith, Harlan I. *Notes on Eskimo tradition.* ____: ____, ____.

Microfiches. Contents: Inuit religion and mythology. (NLC)

361. [Canada]. Richelieu & Ontario Navigation Company. *Souvenir : Canada's Cities, Lakes and Rivers : World's Columbian Exposition.* N.p.: Richelieu & Ontario Navigation Co., 1893.

22½x15. 24 p. Stapled smooth gray wraps, black print, illus of Columbus. C.t. Caption title: "Beauties of the St. Lawrence. The tourist's ideal trip ..." Same as #995. ☺. (WM) $12 - 25

362. Canada. *Statutes of Canada.* "An Act respecting the appointment of Commissioners to the World's Columbian Exposition." 56 Victoria, chapter 7. (mcg)

363. Canada. *Western Canada and its great resources : the testimony of settlers, farmer delegates and high authorities with preface and an appendix on the causes of failure and success in N.-W. farming.* Ottawa: Printed by the government printing bureau, 1893.

25x16½. 36 p. Beige stiff smooth wraps with black print and design depicting farmer gathering sheaves of grain. ☺. (WM)

364. Cape of Good Hope. *Catalogue of exhibits of the Cape of Good Hope : at the World's Columbian Exposition, Chicago, 1893.* Chicago: Rand, McNally & Co., printers, 1893; Woodbridge, CT: RPI, 1989.

19½x14. 39 p. Light green wraps. ☺. (CPL,SI)

365. Ceylon. Grinlinton, John J. *... Final report on the representation of Ceylon.* Colombo: Printed by H. C. Cottle, Acting government printer, 1895.

29½x21. 16 p. C.t. At head of title: "The World's Columbian exposition, 1893." Grinlinton, from Kentucky, was Special Commissioner for Ceylon. CPL copy signed by the author. [The commission was at St. Louis for the 1904 fair but no other fair records found.] ☺. (CPL)

366. Ceylon. *... Official handbook & catalogue of the Ceylon courts. With Map and Illustrations.* Columbo: H. C. Cottle, acting government printer, 1893.

22x14. 152 p., 8 *l* + many unpaged color plates, fold. maps. Red thin wrap over beautiful color litho stiff wraps. Frontis is b/w litho of Ceylon Court at WCE. At head of title: "World's Columbian Exposition at Chicago, 1893." C.t.: "World's Columbian Exposition Hand Book & Catalogue. Ceylon Courts."

---- 1 *l*, viii, 152 p., (1) p. + unpaged illus.

P→   ⊚ . (CPL,CHx,F,UDe,UMi,NYSt,UoC,WiHx) $25 - 45

367. Costa Rica. Calvo, J[oaquin] B[ernardo], comp. ... *The Republic of Costa Rica : some facts and figures ... Followed by an article entitled Costa Rica at the World's Columbian exposition at Chicago.* 2nd ed. Washington, D.C.: n.p., 1893; 2nd ed. Washington, D.C.: Bureau of the American Republics, 1894.

21½x15. 56 p. + plates, fold. map laid in before p. 9. C.t.= t.p. At head of title: "Bureau of the American republics, Washington, U. S. A." Contains article: "Costa Rica at the World's Fair" (in English).

⊚ . (CPL,LC,UoC,RPB)

368. Costa Rica. *Documentos de la comision oficial de la exposicion de Costa Rica en Chicago.* San José: Tipografia Nancional, 1892; Woodbridge, CT: RPI, 1989.

ca. 24x15½. 13 p. Microfilm. Trans: Documents of the official Costa Rican commission.   ⊚ . (SI)

369. Costa Rica. Guzmán, David J[oaquín], ed. *Catálogo general de los objetos que la República de Costa Rica : envía á la Exposición Universal de Chicago ...* San Jose: Tipografía Nacional, 1892; Woodbridge, CT: RPI, 1989.

24½x18. 56, (46) + 57 p. appendix with separate t.p. and title: "Estudio sobre el cultivo de algunas plantas y árboles industriales susceptibles de explotarse en la republica de Costa Rica." Tan wraps, sepia and chocolate brown print and ornate design. C.t.= t.p. Trans: General catalog of objects sent by the Republic of Costa Rica to the World's Exposition in Chicago.

---- 28x19½. 4 *l*, 56, (46), 57 p. Off-white wraps, purple print, ornate sepia border.

⊚ . (KU,CPL,CHx,SI,TU,NL,OC,WiHx)

370. Cuba. Cabrera, Raimundo. *Cartas a Govin sobre la Exposición de Chicago. Impresiones de viaje. (Segunda serie.) ... Illustrado con ocho láminas fotograbadas por Levytype C° de Filadelfia.* Habana: Tipografia de "Los Niños Huérfanos," 1893.

15x10. 202 p., 1 *l*. Shiny aquamarine (or olive) wraps, black print. Trans: Letters to Govin regarding the Exposition in Chicago. Impressions of the trip. (Second series.) Illustrated with 8 plates photoprocessed in Levytype C of Philadelphia.   ⊚ . (LC,NYPL,UoC)

371. Cuba. Pichardo, Manuel S[erafín]. *La ciudad blanca : Crónicas de la Exposición Colombina de Chicago.* Prefacio de Enrique José Varona. Habana: Biblioteca de el Figaro, 1894.

19½x12½. 2 *l*, (5)-237, (1) p. ads, tan wraps, navy blue design and print. C.t.: "La Ciudad Blanca (The White City)." T.p. in red and black. El Figaro ads both sides of back cover. Description of a trip to the WF (in Spanish). Chapter on visit to Cuba exhibits.

---- 21½x13. Tan wraps with red and black print. C.t.
⊜ . (LC,NYPL,UoC)

-D-

372. Denmark. *Bertel Thorvaldsen : the celebrated Danish sculptor : born 19th November 1770 : died 24th March 1844.* Denmark: [Centraltrykkeriet], 1893.

16½x9. 7 p. Buff wraps with tan background for black print. C.t. At bottom of cover: "The Chicago exhibition." Handout at the Denmark exhibit. ⊜ . (TD,WM) $12 - 20

373. Denmark. Danish Sloyd Association. ... *The Danish sloyd : guide to the Exposition of the Danish sloyd association.* Copenhagen: J. Jörgensen & Co. (M. A. Hannover) Printers, 1893.

18x12. viii, 47, (1) p., 2 *l.* Pale blue wraps, black print. C.t.= t.p. At head of title: "The World's Columbian exposition Chicago, U. S. A., 1893." Other author: Dansk Sløjdforening. [Danish sloyd was a method of school education separate from classroom work; what we would call vocational tech classes or "shop" today.] ⊜ . (NYPL,NL)

374. Denmark. Frederiksen, Kristine. *Amerikanske undervisnings-eksperimenter : indtryk fra Chicagoudstillingen med prøver paa elevarbejder.* Kjøbenhavn: Det Nordiske forlag, 1896.

23x14. 60, (4) p. with b/w plates both sides. 2 trifold col. plates between p. 20-21 and 50-51 are not included in paging. In Danish. Trans: American experiments in teaching : impressions from the Chicago exposition with examples of student exercises. ⊜ . (UoC)

375. Denmark. *Hans Christian Andersen : the celebrated writer of fairy tales.* Denmark: Centraltrykkeriet, 1893.

16½x9. 7 p. Plain wraps, black print on light brown background. C.t. Handout at the Denmark exhibit.
⊜ (GLD) $12 - 20

376. Denmark. Industriforeningen i Kjøbenhavn. Royal Danish Commission. *The World's Columbian Exposition : 1893 : Denmark.* [Copenhagen?: Printed by Nielsen & Lydiche], n.d.; Woodbridge, CT: RPI, 1989.

23½x16½. 163 p., double frontis of "King Christian IX and His Family," illus, errata slip at end. Gray wraps, red lettering and dark gray design. C.t.: "Denmark. The World's Columbian Exposition : Chicago, U.S.A. 1893 : Official Catalogue with illus issued by the Royal Danish Commission." The Commission was elected by Industriforeningen i Kjøbenhavn [Industrial Union in Copenhagen]. Description of Danish exhibits.
P→ ⊜ . (csuf,LC,SI,UoC,NL,WM,AIC)

377. [Denmark]. Kierulf, Marcus. *Erindringer fra en rejse til Amerika i sommeren 1893.* Odense: I kommission i den Milo'ske boghandel trykt i Milo'ske bogtrykkeri, 1894.

22x14. 88 p. Stiff wraps with no lettering or design. In Danish. Trans: Memories from a trip to America, summer 1893. ☻ . (nwu)

378. Denmark.   Udstillingskomitéen. *Officiel Beretning udgivet af den Danske Udstillingskomité ved Generalkommissæren.* Kjøbenhavn: Industriforeningen, 1895.

8°. 422 p., illus (including plans). Olive green wraps. C.t.: "The World's Columbian Exposition, Chicago, U. S. A., 1893 ... Danmark." Added t.p. in English. Trans: Official account issued by the General Commissioner of the Danish exhibition committee.   (NYPL,UDe)

-E-

379. Ecuador. "Diario de Avisos" de Guayaquil. *El Ecuador en Chicago.* New York: [A. E. Chasmar y Cía], 1894 [°1894 by W. R. Grace & Co., Agents].

32½x25½. xiv, 432, (12) p., illus. Light blue cloth hc, gilt coat of arms on front cover and gilt spine. ---- 33x25. xiv, 432, (11) p. + short page ad tipped in between (6-7) of the last (11) p. Frontis is collage of presidents of Ecuador. Black leather hc, gilt design, gilt spine print: "El Ecuador en Chicago." Decorative green and gilt end papers, all edges gilt.
    ☻ . (csuf,UoC)

380. Egypt. *A Complete "guide" to the Egyptological Exhibit in the Cairo Street Concession at the World's Columbian exposition, Chicago.* Chicago: Thayer & Jackson Stationery Co., 1893 [°1893 by A. E. Funk].

19½x13½. 176 p. Orange wraps, illus and print in black. Signed in pencil by Prof. Demetrius Masconas. His picture precedes the title page and is captioned: "Promoter and Director of the Egyptian Temple at the World's Columbian Exposition, Chicago, 1893."
P→   ☻ (GLD,UDe) $20 - 50

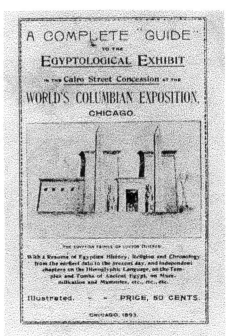

381. Egypt. De Potter, Armand. *The Egyptian Pantheon. An Explanatory Catalogue of Egyptian Antiquities. Collected and Classified with Especial Reference to the Religion and Funerary Rites of Ancient Egypt.* New York: Armand de Potter, Publisher, [°1893].

19½x13. 3 l, 44 p. Tan wraps, black print. Frontis of statue of Imhotep. Back cover shows Mercury on the globe with "de Potter European and Oriental Tours." The exhibit was in the Anthropological Bldg.   ☻ . (LC,UoC)

382. Egypt. Egypt-Chicago Exposition Co. *Street in Cairo. World's Columbian Exposition.* Chicago: Winters Art Litho Co., [°1893 by Egypt-Chicago Exposition Co.].

19½x14½. 2-15 p. C. Graham cover litho depicts Cairo Street. 8 pretty color lithos by C. Graham plus text. C.t. Caption title on p. 2: "The 'Cairo Street.' Midway Plaisance."
P↓   ☻ . (GLD,csuf,CHx,F,TD,WM) $20 - 35

383. Egypt. ... *Guide to the Egyptian temple of Luksor, (Thebes.).* N.p.: Thayer & Jackson Stationery Co., n.d.

> 20½x14. (4) p. C.t. Temple litho on front wrap. At head of title: "Chicago World's Fair."   (CHx)

384. Egypt. *Prospectus of a complete guide to the Cairo Egyptological exhibit at the World's Fair : Chicago 1893.* Cairo: Printed by Albert Hohl, n.d.

> 20x14. (7), 8-19 p. Orange wraps, black print and design, black cloth spine. C.t. Errata on inside back cover. (CHx,WM)

385. [Egypt]. *Souvenir of "Street Scene" in Cairo, Egypt : Cairo Street World's Columbian Exposition.* Chicago: Globe Litho & Printing Co., n.d.

> 15x23. (13) p. Heavy beige wraps with gold print, tied with light blue cord. Stiff stock with photos of streets of Cairo in the Midway Plaisance.   (F)

$25 - 45

-F-

386. France. Arbel, P. *Rapport sur l'exposition de Chicago concernant la métallurgie, les mines, la quincaillerie, l'arminerie, le vernerie et les industries diverses. 1893.* Saint Etienne: Théolier & Cie, 1894.

> 8°. 100 p. Trans: Report on metallurgy, mining, iron ware, etc.   (NYPL)

387. France. Bertin, L[ouis Émile]. *La marine des États-Unis.* Paris: E. Bernard et Cie, Imprimeurs-Editeurs, 1896.

> Folio: 35½x28. 2 *l*, at least 30 double (some folded again) plates including diagrams. Companion to Text. Trans: The U.S. Navy.
> Text: 27½x18. 2 *l*, 130 p. Tan-gray wraps with black print. C.t.= t.p. Describes the various U.S. WCE maritime exhibits. Companion to Folio. On cover: Bertin was "ingénieur des constructions navales ancien directeur de l'école du génie maritime directeur de matériel" [engineer of early naval construction, director of the maritime engineers school, director of supplies].
> ---- Hardcover: 26½x17½. 130 p. Vol 7 of E. Bernard's 9 part in 8 vol set (see #411).
> ☺ . (LC,HL,NLC)

388. France. Bonet-Maury, G[aston]. *Le congrès des religions : a Chicago en 1893 ...* Paris: Librairie hachette et Cie, 1895.

> 27x18. 345 p., 14 ports. Bonet-Maury was professor of protestant theology.   ☺ . (OC)

389. France. Buisson, Benjamin. *L'enseignement Primaire : aux Congrès d'éducation et a l'exposition scolaire de Chicago.* Paris: Librairie Hachette et Cie, 1896.

> 22x14. xxxiii, 260 p. Lime green smooth wraps with black print. Primary education. For two related items by G. Compayré see #402 and #403.   ☺ . (LC,NYPL,UoC)

390. France. La Cámara de Comercio de París. ... *Reseña sobre la enseñanza commercial : organizada por la cámara de comercio de París.* Paris: Imprenta y libreria central de los ferrocarriles, imprenta chaix, 1893.

27½x19. 192, (1) p. Pretty litho wraps, black and red print. At head of title: "Exposición universal de Chicago." Spanish version of #397.   ☻ . (NL)

391. France. Cercle de la librairie. Terquem, M. Émile. *Exposition de la Librairie Française : Comité 34 : Librairie impressions typographiques et lithographiques reliures, estampes géographie, cartographie, journaux.* Paris: D. Dumoulin, 1893.

25½x18½. Several contributions paged separately. First 3 sections: 1) "Exposition da la librairie Française"--8 p., 2) "Cercle de la librairie: Administration et commissions"--(9)-16 p., 3) "Catalogue des exposants Française a Chicago"--(17)-24 p. Color plates. Describes the lithography, book binding, embossing and map industry in France. This is different from #392.   (CHx)

392. France. Cercle de la librairie. Terquem, M. Émile. *Exposition de la librairie Française : Comité 34 : librairie impressions typographiques et lithographiques reliures, estampes géographie, cartographie, journaux.* N.p.: n.p., n.d.

24½x17½. 121 *l* of fancy ads for books and printing from a wide variety of European companies. Heavy bond stock, high quality printing. Lime green wraps, red print and green-gilt emblem. Different from #391.
---- [Paris: Impr. D. Dumoulin et Cie, 1893]. 121 *l*.
       ☻ . (LC,NYPL,UMi,NL,NYSt,UoC)

393. France. [Cercle de la librairie]. Terquem, [M]. Em[ile]. ... *Librairie Française : comité 34 ... Rapport.* Paris: Imprimerie Paul Schmidt, [1893].

24½x16. 12 p. Gray wraps, black print. C.t. At head of title: "Exposition internationale de Chicago : 1893." In French.   ☻ . (CHx,NYPL,NL)

394. France. Chagot, Jules, and Cº. ... *Branch of social economy : the Blanzy Colliery company : institutions for workmen.* Paris: Imprimerie F. Levé, 1893.

27½x22. 2 *l*, 85 p. Light gray wraps, black print. At head of title: "Chicago international exhibition." Social structure, finances, etc., for the Blanzy mine, France.   ☻ . (NL)

395. France. Chambre de Commerce de Paris. Lourdelet, [E.]. ... *Rapport, novembre, 1893.* Paris: Lib. imp. réunies, 1893.

8°. 2 *l*, 635 p. At head of title: "Exposition de Chicago."   (NYPL)

396. France. Chambre de Commerce de Paris. ... *Notice on the commercial instruction : organized by the Paris chamber of commerce.* Paris: Imprimerie et librairie centrales des chemins de fer Imprimerie chaix, 1893.

27½x18. 192 p., 1 *l*. Beige embossed wraps, red and black print, red, dusty blue and black design. Pretty cover. At head of title: "The Chicago World's Fair." On cover: "Commercial School. Superior

Commercial School. École des Hautes Etudes Commerciales. Free Commercial classes. (Women, Girls, Men.)" English translation of #397. ☺. (PU,LC,NLC,UMi,UoC,NL)

397. France. Chambre de Commerce de Paris. ... *Notice sur l'enseignement commercial organisé par la Chambre de Commerce de Paris.* Paris: Imprimerie chaix, 1893; Woodbridge, CT: RPI, 1989.

8°. 197 p., 9 plates, tables. C.t.: "Enseignement Commercial de la Chambre de Commerce de Paris : École commerciale. École supérieure de Commerce. École des hautes Études commerciales. Cours commerciaux gratuits. (Femmes, Jeunes Filles, Hommes)." French version of #396. ☺. (SI,NYPL,UMi)

398. France. Chiousse, Casimir. *Historique de la fédération des Sociétés Coopératives de Consommation des Employés de la Compagnie des Chemins de Fer, de Paris à Lyon : et à la Méditerranée.* Grenoble: Bureau-directeur de la fédération, n.d.

27x18½. Wraps. C.t.= t.p. Subject: History of iron worker labor unions in Paris, Lyon, and the Mediterranean. ☺. (WM)

399. France. Comité protestant français. ... *Les oeuvres du protestantisme français au XIXe siècle publiées sous la direction de Frank Puaux.* Paris: Fischbacher, 1893.

33½x__. xxxii, 480, (3) p. At head of title: "Exposition universelle de Chicago." Trans: The work of French protestants. (UoC)

400. France. Commissariat General Français. ... *Instructions pour la réexpédition des marchandises françaises exposées à Chicago.* [Chicago: Imprimerie du Courrier de Chicago, 1893?].

19x13½. 11 p. Caption title. At head of title: "Commissariat General française. Exposition internationale de Chicago." Pub info at bottom p. 11. Trans: Instruction for reshipping French exhibits at Chicago. ☺. (NL)

401. France. Commission de l'Exposition de Chicago. *Syndicat de la boulangerie de Paris : 7, quai d'anjou, 7.* Paris: n.p., 1893.

27½x17½. Wraps, border design around title. C.t.= t.p. Subject: Paris Bakers' society. ☺. (WM)

402. France. Compayré, Gabriel. *L'enseignement secondaire aux États-Unis.* Paris: Librairie Hachette et Cie, 1896.

22x14. 2 *l*, 230 p., 1 *l*. Pea green wraps, black print. Secondary education in the United States. For a related works, see Compayré (#403) and Buisson (#389). ☺. (LC,NYPL)

403. France. Compayré, Gabriel. *L'enseignement supérieur aux États-Unis.* Paris: Librairie Hachette et Cie, 1896.

22x14. 2 *l*, 360 p., 2 *l*. Pea green wraps, black print. High schools in the United States. For related works, see Compayré (#402) and Buisson (#389). ☺. (LC,NYPL,UoC)

404. [France]. Coubertin, Pierre de. *Souvenirs d'Amérique et de Grèce.* Paris: Librairie hachette et Cᶦᵉ, 1897.

> 18½x12. 3 *l*, 181, (1) p. table. Pulp pages, no illus. Dark gray-green wraps with black print. C.t.= t.p. In French.
> ---- 19x12. 2 *l*, 181 p., 1 *l*. Light blue wraps with black print on cover and spine, black design on back cover. C.t.= t.p. In French. Trans: American and Greek Souvenirs.
> ⊘ . (CHx,NL)

405. France. ... *Extrait du catalogue général de la librairie Plon : littérature -- histoire : voyages -- piété -- beaux-arts.* Paris: E. Plon, Nourrit et Cᶦᵉ, imprimeurs-éditeurs, n.d.

> 27x18½. 32 p. of illustrated book ads. Buff wraps with black print. At head of title: "Exposition universelle de Chicago : 1893." Catalogue of books available from E. Plon.
> ⊘ (GLD) $12 - 24

406. France. Grille, A[ntoine], and M. G. Lelarge. *L'Agriculture et les machines agricoles aux États-Unis.* Paris: E. Bernard et Cᶦᵉ, Imprimeurs-Editeurs, 1896.

> 26½x17½. 177 p. Vol 6 of E. Bernard's 9 part in 8 vol set (see #411). Trans: Agriculture and agricultural machinery of the U.S.   ⊘ . (NLC)

407. France. Grille, A[ntoine], and M. H. Falconnet. *Les Arts militaires aux États-Unis et a l'exposition de Chicago.* Paris: E. Bernard et Cᶦᵉ, Imprimeurs-Editeurs, 1894.

> 26½x17½. 278 p. Vol 5 of E. Bernard's 9 part in 8 vol set (see #411). Collaborateurs: MM. Métivier & Ziegler. Trans: Military art of the U.S. and of the Chicago Exposition.   ⊘ . (NLC)

408. France. Grille, A[ntoine], and M. H. Falconnet. *Les Chemins de fer a l'exposition de Chicago.* Paris: E. Bernard et Cᶦᵉ, Imprimeurs-Editeurs, 1894.

> 26½x17½. 188 p. + plates. Parts 8 (*Les Chemins*) and 9 (*Les Locomotives* by M. Grille) of 8 vol set (see #411). Trans: Railways at the Chicago Exposition.   ⊘ . (NLC)

409. France. Grille, A[ntoine], and M. H. Falconnet. *Électricité industrielle.* Paris: E. Bernard et Cᶦᵉ, Imprimeurs-Editeurs, 1894.

> 26½x17½. 250 p. Part 3 (and vol 3) of E. Bernard's 9 part in 8 vol set (see #411). Collaborateurs: MM. Desforges, Rejou, Bloxham, Bouquet. Trans: Industrial electricity.   ⊘ . (NLC)

410. France. Grille, A[ntoine], and M. H. Falconnet. *La Mécanique générale a l'exposition de Chicago : moteurs a vapeur, a gaz, a air hydraulique. Pompes grandes installations mécaniques.* Paris: E. Bernard et Cᶦᵉ, Imprimeurs-Editeurs, 1894.

> 26½x17½. 294 p. Vol 4 of a 9 part in 8 vol set (see #411). Collaborateur: M. Crépy. Trans: The machinery of the Chicago Exposition : Steam, gas and compressed air (motors/motor carriages). ⊘ . (NLC)

411. France. Grille, A[ntoine], and M. H. Falconnet. *Revue technique de l'exposition universelle de Chicago en 1893.* Paris: E. Bernard et Cᶦᵉ, Imprimeurs-Editeurs, 1894.

26½x17½. Parts 1 and 2 (also vol 1 and 2) of a 9 part in 8 vol set. Set is bound in a tortoise shell hc, dark green leather spine and gold lettering on spine. Various titles. Trans: Technical review.
Part 1: *Architecture.* 176 p. Collaborateur: M. Ch. Lebro.
Part 2: *Chaudières fixes et chaudières marines.* 174 p. Collaborateur: M. Lelarge. Trans: Regular and naval boilers.   ⊚ . (NYPL,NLC,AIC)

412. France. Gruel, Léon. ... *Catalogue des Reliures de Style et Objets artistiques en cuir ciselé.* Paris: n.p., [preface: May 1893]; Woodbridge, CT: RPI, 1989.

19½x15. 1 *l*, (1) p., xxxiii + 32 *l* of plates. Pebble textured heavy tan paper wraps with black print. At head of title: "Exposition Universelle de Chicago, 1893." French section, book dept; 32 fancy French book bindings shown in b/w photos and explained on opposite page. In French with English preface by Gruel explaining he had been invited to show his book bindings at the WCE and Em. Terquem, his agent, would be available to discuss artistic bindings. Trans: Catalog of the binding styles and art objects in tooled leather.
---- 1 *l* + (66) p. Rebound.
---- Also listed: 19x__. (36) p. plates.
⊚ . (LC,SI,BCM,BM,BU,TU,NYSt,NL,AIC,OC)

413. France. Laussedat. ... *Section française. Instruments et appareils : iconométriques et métrophotographiques : des collections du conservatorie national des arts et métiers.* Paris: Imprimerie Nationale, 1893.

25x16½. 2 *l*, 32 p., b/w illus. Drab blue fleck wraps, black print and design. At head of title: "Exposition universelle de Chicago en 1893." C.t.= t.p. Trans: Exhibit items from the museum of art and handicraft.   ⊚ . (UoC)

414. France. Lavasseur, Emile. "... Coup d'aeil sur l'ensemble de l'exposition, conférence du 21 janvier 1894." In *Annales du conserv des arts et métiers.*

8°. 31 p., 1 plan. Trans: A brief overview of the Exposition.   (NYPL)

415. France. Marteau, Charles. *Rapport sur l'industrie lainiére à l'Exposition de Chicago.* Reims: A. Marguin, printer, 1894.

8°. 75 p., 2 tables. (Sociéte industrielle de Reims. Bulletin, no. 82). Trans: Report on the wool industry.   (NYPL)

416. France. Ministère de la Guerre. ... *Service géographique de l'armée : Notice sur les objets exposés : 1893.* Paris: Imprimerie du service géographique, 1893.

24x16. 18 p. Bluish-tan wraps, black print. C.t.= t.p. Review of objects displayed by the French army.   ⊚ . (LC,WM)

417. France. Ministère des travaux publics. ... *Notices sur les appareils d'éclairage (modelès et dessins) : exposés dans le Palais de l'Électricité : par le service des phares.* Paris: Imprimerie Lahure, 1893.

24½x15½. 157 p., 8 *l* of plates. Illus, plans. Gold letters on green boards pressed in fake leather pattern. At head of title: " Exposition universelle a chicago en 1893 : république française : ministère des travaux publics." Subject: Electrical engineering.   ⊚ . (AIC)

418. France. Ministère du Commerce, de l'Industrie, des Postes et des Télégraphes. Comité des dames. Pegard, Mrs. M. *L'exposition féminine française à Chicago.* Paris: Imprimerie Nationale, 1895.

   4°. 3 *l*, 3-54 p., 1 *l*. Trans: French women at the Exposition.   (NYPL)

419. France. Ministère du Commerce, de l'Industrie, des Postes et des Télégraphes. ... *Rapports publiés sous la direction de* [M.] C[amille] *Krantz.* [*Comités 2, 5, 7-9, 12-13, 15-17, 19-38*]. 7 vol. Paris: Imprimerie Nationale, 1894-95.

   29x20. At head of title: "Exposition Internationale de Chicago en 1893." NYPL call: VC.   (NYPL)

   ☞ There were 39 comité plus two others for rules and administration. Some of these committee reports as individual publications are given below in numerical order. Camille Krantz was the Commissaire Général; Jules Roche was Le Ministre du Commerce et de l'industrie.

420. France. Ministère du Commerce, de l'Industrie, des Postes et des Télégraphes. ... *Rapports publiés sous la direction de M. Camille Krantz ... : Comité 13 : Moteurs et Générateurs -- Les Ascenseurs américains.* Paris: Imprimerie Nationale, 1894.

   28½x19½. 24 p., 1 *l*. Pale green-tan wraps, black print. C.t.= t.p. At head of title: "Exposition Internationale de Chicago en 1893." Trans: Motors and generators -- American elevators.   ☺ . (csuf)

421. France. Ministère du Commerce, de l'Industrie, des Postes et des Télégraphes. ... *Rapports publiés sous la direction de M. Camille Krantz ... : Comité 17 : Carrosserie, Harnais, Vélocipèdes et Accessoires.* Paris: Imprimerie Nationale, 1894.

   28x19. 21 p., 1 *l*. Pale green-tan wraps, black print. At head of title: "Exposition Internationale de Chicago en 1893." Trans: Carriages, harness tack, bicycles and accessories.   ☺ . (csuf)

422. France. Ministère du Commerce, de l'Industrie, des Postes et des Télégraphes. ... *Rapports publiés sous la direction de M. Camille Krantz ... : Comité 19 : Produits chimiques et pharmaceutiques, matériel de la peinture parfumerie, savonnerie.* Paris: Imprimerie Nationale, 1894.

   29x20. 282 p., 1 *l*. Pale green-tan wraps, black print. At head of title: "Exposition Internationale de Chicago en 1893." C.t.= t.p. Translates: Products from perfume and soap industry.   ☺ . (csuf)

423. France. Ministère du Commerce, de l'Industrie, des Postes et des Télégraphes. ... *Rapports publiés sous la direction de M. Camille Krantz ... : Comité 21 : Ameublement.* Paris: Imprimerie Nationale, 1894.

   29x20. 145 p., 2 *l*. Pale green-tan wraps, black print. At head of title: "Exposition Internationale de Chicago en 1893." C.t.= t.p. Trans: Furniture.   ☺ . (csuf)

424. France. Ministère du Commerce, de l'Industrie, des Postes et des Télégraphes. ... *Rapports publiés sous la direction de M. Camille Krantz ... : Comité 22 : Céramique.-- Cristaux et Verrerie.* Paris: Imprimerie Nationale, 1894.

   29x20. 35, (1) p. Pale green-tan wraps, black print. At head of title: "Exposition Internationale de Chicago en 1893." C.t.= t.p. Trans: Crystal and glassware.   ☺ . (csuf)

425. France. Ministère du Commerce, de l'Industrie, des Postes et des Télégraphes. ... *Rapports publiés sous la direction de M. Camille Krantz ... : Comité 23 : Bronzes d'art et d'ameublement.-- Bronzes d'éclairage.* Paris: Imprimerie Nationale, 1894.

29x20. 90 p., 1 *l.* Pale green-tan wraps, black print. At head of title: "Exposition Internationale de Chicago en 1893." C.t.= t.p. Trans: Bronze art for furniture and lighting. ⊚ . (csuf)

426. France. Ministère du Commerce, de l'Industrie, des Postes et des Télégraphes. ... *Rapports publiés sous la direction de M. Camille Krantz ... : Comité 24 : Bijouterie. -- Joaillerie. -- Orfèvrerie.* Paris: Imprimerie Nationale, 1894.

29x20. 205 p., 2 *l.* Pale green-tan wraps, black print. At head of title: "Exposition Internationale de Chicago en 1893." C.t.= t.p. Trans: Jewelry, goldsmithing. ⊚ . (csuf,WM)

427. France. Ministère du Commerce, de l'Industrie, des Postes et des Télégraphes. ... *Rapports publiés sous la direction de M. Camille Krantz ... : Comité 25 : Soies.-- Tissus de soie larges. -- Rubans : Fils et tissus de lin, de chanvre, de jute, de ramie et de coton : L'industrie lainière à l'Exposition de Chicago.* Paris: Imprimerie Nationale, 1894.

29x20. 86 p., 1 *l.* Pale green-tan wraps, black print. At head of title: "Exposition International de Chicago en 1893." C.t.= t.p. Trans: Silk textile industry. Ribbons, thread, and fabrics of linen, hemp, jute, and cotton. ⊚ . (csuf)

428. France. Ministère du Commerce, de l'Industrie, des Postes et des Télégraphes. ... *Rapports publiés sous la direction de M. Camille Krantz ... : Comité 26 : Accessoires du vètement. Notice sur la maison. Perrin frères & Cie, manufacture de gants a Grenoble: A messieurs les membres du jury.* [New York: L. Weiss & Co., 1893].

8°. 11 p. At head of title: "Exposition universelle de Chicago 1893." Trans: Garment accessories. Account of glove manufacture at Perrin Co., Grenoble. (NYPL)

429. France. Ministère du Commerce, de l'Industrie, des Postes et des Télégraphes. ... *Rapports publiés sous la direction de M. Camille Krantz ... : Comité 26 : Chapellerie.* Paris: Imprimerie Nationale, 1894.

27½x19. 45 p., 1 *l.* Tan-light blue wraps, black print. C.t.= t.p. At head of title: "... Exposition internationale de Chicago en 1893." Trans: Millinery. ⊚ . (LC)

430. France. Ministère du Commerce, de l'Industrie, des Postes et des Télégraphes. ... *Rapports publiés sous la direction de M. Camille Krantz ... : Comité 26 : Les Dentelles vraies.* Paris: Imprimerie Nationale, 1894.

29x20. 56 p. Pale green-tan wraps, black print. At head of title: "Exposition Internationale de Chicago en 1893." C.t.= t.p. Trans: Authentic lacework. ⊚ . (csuf)

431. France. Ministère du Commerce, de l'Industrie, des Postes et des Télégraphes. ... *Rapports publiés sous la direction de M. Camille Krantz ... : Comité 27 : Brosserie, Peignes, Maroquinerie, Articles en caoutchouc et Jouets.* Paris: Imprimerie Nationale, 1894.

29x20. 80 p. Pale green-tan wraps, black print. At head of title: "Exposition Internationale de Chicago en 1893." C.t.= t.p. Trans: Brushes, combs, articles of rubber and toys.   ⊚ . (csuf)

432. France. Ministère du Commerce, de l'Industrie, des Postes et des Télégraphes. ... *Rapports publiés sous la direction de M. Camille Krantz ... : Comité 28 : Industrie du cuir.* Paris: Imprimerie Nationale, 1894.

29x20. 83 p. + 3 fold. tables. Pale green-tan wraps, black print. At head of title: "Exposition Internationale de Chicago en 1893." C.t.= t.p. Trans: Leather industry.   ⊚ . (csuf)

433. France. Ministère du Commerce, de l'Industrie, des Postes et des Télégraphes. ... *Rapports publiés sous la direction de M. Camille Krantz ... : Comité 30 : Appareils de chauffage, Plomberie et Appareils sanitaires : Quincaillerie, Ferblanterie, Coutellerie.* Paris: Imprimerie Nationale, 1894.

28½x19½. 43 p., 1 *l*. Pale green-tan wraps, black print. At head of title: "Exposition Internationale de Chicago en 1893." C.t.= t.p. Trans: Equipment for heating, plumbing, and sanitation : iron and tinware, cutlery.   ⊚ . (csuf)

434. France. Ministère du Commerce, de l'Industrie, des Postes et des Télégraphes. ... *Rapports publiés sous la direction de M. Camille Krantz ... : Comité 31 : Électricité.* Paris: Imprimerie Nationale, 1894.

29x20. 47 p. Pale green-tan wraps, black print. At head of title: "Exposition Internationale de Chicago en 1893." C.t.= t.p. Trans: Electricity.   ⊚ . (csuf)

435. France. Ministère du Commerce de l'Industrie, des Postes et de Télégraphes. ... *Rapports publiés sous la direction de M. Camille Krantz ... Comité 34 : Imprimerie et Librairie. -- Cartographie.* Paris: Imprimerie Nationale, 1894.

29x20½. 3 *l*, (3)-164 p. Tan cover, black print and design.
French language. At head of title: "... Exposition internationale de Chicago en 1893. Rapport de M. Henri Le Soudier, librairie editeur, commissaire rapporteur." Trans: Map making.
---- Soudier's name does not appear on t.p. 28½x19. 2 *l*, 161 p., 1 *l*, tables. Greenish tan wraps, black print. C.t.= t.p.
---- Also listed: 196 p. "Cartographie Rapport de M. la Commundant G. Betfoges" from p. [167]-196.
   ⊚ . (KU,csuf,LC,NYPL,UMi,UoC,NL)

436. France. Ministère du Commerce, de l'Industrie, des Postes et des Télégraphes. ... *Rapports publiés sous la direction de M. Camille Krantz ... : Comité 36 : Génie civil -- Travaux publics -- Architecture.* Paris: Imprimerie Nationale, 1894.

29x20. 186 p., 2 *l*. Pale green-tan wraps, black print. At head of title: "Exposition Internationale de Chicago en 1893." C.t.= t.p. Trans: Civil engineers, public works, architecture.   ⊚ . (csuf)

437. France. Ministère du Commerce, de l'Industrie, des Postes et des Télégraphes. ... *Rapports publiés sous la direction de M. Camille Krantz ... : Comité 37 : Économie sociale.* Paris: Imprimerie Nationale, 1894.

29x20. 159 p., 1 *l*. Pale green-tan wraps, black print. At head of title: "Exposition Internationale de Chicago en 1893." C.t.= t.p. Trans: Social economy.   ⊚ . (csuf)

438. France. Ministère du Commerce, de l'Industrie, des Postes et des Télégraphes. ... *Rapports publiés sous la direction de M. Camille Krantz. Commissariat special des colonies de la Tunisie et de L'Algerie.* Paris: Imprimerie Nationale, 1894.

4°. 3 *l*, 1 plan, 6 *l*. Trans: Special commissioner's office of Tunisia and Algeria.   (NYPL)

439. France. Ministère du Commerce, de l'Industrie, des Postes, et des Télégraphes. ... *Rapports publiés sous la direction de M. Camille Krantz, commissaire général du gouvernement français : Congrés tenu à Chicago en 1893.* Paris: Imprimerie Nationale, 1894.

30x__. 3 *l*, 400 p. At head of title: "Exposition Internationale de Chicago en 1893 : Ministère du Commerce, de l'Industrie, des Postes, et des Télégraphes." Trans: Congress held at Chicago. (NYPL,RPB)

440. France. Ministère du Commerce, de l'Industrie, des Postes et des Télégraphes. ... *Rapports publiés sous la direction de M. Camille Krantz ... : Rapport administratif sur l'Exposition Internationale de Chicago.* Paris: Imprimerie Nationale, 1895.

28x19. liii, 278 p., 3 fold. *l*. Frontis: "Diplóme commémoratif de l'Exposition Française a Chicago." At head of title: "Exposition Internationale de Chicago en 1893." Trans: Administrative report.
   ☻ . (csuf,NYPL)

441. France. Ministère du Commerce, de l'Industrie, des Postes et des Télégraphes. Délégation ouvrière. ... *Rapports publiés sous la direction de M. Camille Krantz ... : Rapports de la délégation ouvrière a l'exposition de Chicago.* Paris: Imprimerie Nationale, 1894.

29½x20. 2 *l*, 776 p. Quarter leather with brown marbled paper boards. At head of title: "... Exposition internationale de Chicago en 1893." Krantz was commissioner general. Describes items at WCE as seen by the works delegation; includes a description of U.S. labor unions.   ☻ . (LC,NYPL)

442. France. Ministère du Commerce, de l'Industrie et des Colonies. ... *Catalogue de l'exposition historique des souvenirs franco-américains de la guerre de l'indépendance.* Paris: Imprimerie Nationale, 1893.

26x20½. 3 *l*, (3)-108 p. including facsimiles. 10 plates (3 double), tissue guards, port, plan. Gray wraps, black print. At head of title: "Exposition internationale de Chicago (1893) : Pavillon National de la république Française." On preceding half title: "French 'Commissariat général.' --1893." Souvenirs from General Washington, Benjamin Franklin, General Lafayette, and the War of Independence. Trans: An historic(al) catalog of French-American souvenirs from the War of Independence.   ☻ . (csuf,PU,CHx,NYPL,UoC,NL,RPB)

443. France. Ministère du Commerce, de l'Industrie et des Colonies. ... *Section Française : Catalogue officiel : des colonies, de l'Algérie et de la Tunisie : (French and English).* Paris: Imprimerie Nationale, 1893.

23½x15½. 2 *l*, 56 p. Gray-blue wraps with black print. C.t.= t.p. At head of title: "République Française ... Exposition Internationale de Chicago : (1893)." Trans: Official catalog of Algeria and Tunisia.   ☻ . (NL)

444. France. Ministère du Commerce, de l'Industrie et des Colonies. ... *Section Française : Catalogue officiel : (French and English).* Paris: Imprimerie Nationale, 1893; Woodbridge, CT: RPI, 1989.

24½x16. 1 *l* (t.p.), 255 p. Flecked gray-green wraps, black print and design. C.t.= t.p. Under each catalogue heading, the description is first in French and then in English. At head of title: "République Française ... Exposition Internationale de Chicago : (1893)."   ☺ . (NYPL,SI,NL)

445. France. Ministère du Commerce, de l'Industrie et des Colonies. ... *Section française. Palais des femmes. Catalogue officiel, (French and English).* Paris: Imprimerie Nationale, 1893.

25x16½. 70 p. Gray stiff wraps. At head of title: "République Française ... Exposition Internationale de Chicago. (1893)." Describes exhibit in the Woman's Bldg.   (CPL,UoC,NL)

446. France. Ministère du Commerce et de l'Industrie. ... *Conditions et prix des transports.* [Paris: Imprimerie Nationale, 1892].

21x12½. 20 p. Caption title. At head of title: "Exposition internationale de Chicago. (1893.)" Trans: Conditions and rates of transport.   ☺ . (NYPL)

447. France. Ministère du Commerce et de l'Industrie. ... *Documents officiels : règlements : comités : liste des membres des comités d'admission et d'installation.* Paris: Imprimerie Nationale, 1892.

23x14½. 131 p. Robin egg blue wraps, black print and design. At head of title: "Ministère du commerce et de l'industrie : exposition internationale de Chicago : (1893)." C.t.= t.p. Trans: Official rules, documents, committees, and members. There were 39 comités plus two for rules and administration. Impressive list of members of the extensive French committees.
---- 131, 9, (1) p. The last 10 pages are chart list of names as summary.
   ☺ . (CHx,NL)

448. France. Ministère du Commerce et de l'Industrie. ... *Règlement général.* Paris: Imprimerie Nationale, 1892.

21½x13½. 95 p. Rules for the consignment of exhibits, etc. Baby blue wraps, black print and emblem. C.t.= t.p. At head of title: "Ministère du Commerce et de l'industrie. Direction de l'enseignement industriel et commercial. Bureau de l'enseignement commercial et des expositions. Exposition Internationale de Chicago. (1893)."   ☺ . (NL)

449. France. ... *Notice sur la société générale d'éducation et d'enseignement : Autorisée le 13 Mars 1868.* Paris: Bureaux de la société générale d'éducation, 1893.

24½x16. Wraps. C.t. At head of title: "Exposition universelle de Chicago." Subject: Review of the general society of education and instruction : founded Mar. 13, 1868.   ☺ . (WM)

450. France. *Paris Chicago exhibition : 1893.* [Versailles: Imp. Cerf & Cie, 189-].

20½x14½. 122 p. Decorative wraps in colors (Imp. H. Laas, lithographer). A description of Paris with full page ads of French exhibitors.
P→   ☺ . (csuf,UDe)

451. [France]. Perrin, Jules. *Chicago et la Fête Columbienne du monde.* N.p.: n.p., [1893].

19x12½. p. (87)-105 of disbound ?magazine. On p. 105: "Jules Perrin. Chicago, 19 avril 1893." Trans: Chicago and the World's Columbian celebration.   (CHx)

452. France. ... *Section Française : beaux-arts : Catalogue officiel.* Paris: Imprimerie de l'art E. Ménard et Cie, n.d.

19x12½. 1 *l*, (3)-255 p., (1) p. table. Tan wraps with black print. At head of title: "1893 Exposition universelle de Chicago." The first *l* lists members of "Ministère de l'instruction publique des beaux-arts et des cultes." Official catalog of the beaux-art style and architecture. Trans: Fine Arts : Official catalog.   ⊚ . (NL,AIC)

453. France. ... *Section française et hellenique. Compagnie française des mines du Laurium...* Paris: 1893.

4°. 11, 4 p. At head of title: "Exposition Internationale de Chicago, 1893. Trans: Commercial French mines at Laurium. Other author: Commission, Exposition Internationale de Chicago, 1893.   (UC)

454. France. ... *Section française. Vitrines de l'imprimerie nationale (French and English).* Paris: Imprimerie Nationale, 1893.

26x17½. 23 p. French and English translation on opposite pages. Showcase of volumes exhibited by the French National Library at the WCE. At head of title: "République Française : Exposition international de Chicago (1893)." Other author: Commission, Exposition Internationale de Chicago, 1893. Trans: Showcase of National Printers works.   ⊚ . (LC,NL,WM)

455. [France]. Société centrale des architectes Français. *Supplément au Journal L'Architecture du 11 mars 1893.* Paris: Imprimerie chaix, 1893.

27x21. Wraps with French above logo and English below. Describes Society decision to exhibit at the WCE, Class 37 (Social Economy). "To be distributed to visitors."   ⊚ . (WM)

456. France. *Some words about the société de l'industrie minérale.* Saint Etienne: Imprimerie Théolier et Cie, 1893; Woodbridge, CT: RPI, 1989.

ca. 21x14. 11 p. Microfilm. At head of title: "Universal Exposition of Chicago - 1893." Trans: Society of the mineral industry.   ⊚ . (SI,WM)

457. [France]. Varigny, Henry de. *En Amérique : souvenirs de voyage et notes scientifiques ...* Paris: G. Masson, éditeur, n.d.

18x12½. 2 *l*, 300 p. Personal trip to America and the WCE. Trans: In America : souvenirs of the voyage and scientific notes.   ⊚ . (LC,NLC,TU)

-G-

458. Germany. *Amtlicher Bericht über die Weltausstellung in Chicago 1893 : erstattet vom Reichskommissar.* 2 vol. Berlin: Gedruckt in der Reichsdruckerei, 1894.

32x25½. 1263 p. Ultramarine cloth hc, gilt spine, red dyed edges, decorative end papers, glossy good quality text paper. Trans: Official report on the World's Fair made by the German commissioner. Other author: Reichskommission.   ☺ . (CHx,LC,NYPL,nwu,AIC)

459. Germany. ... *Amtlicher Katalog der Ausstellung des Deutschen Reiches.* [Berlin: Reichsdruckerei], 1893.

24x16½. 9 *l*, 256 p., 90 p. ads, maps, diagram. Dark gray-blue cloth hc, black print and design. At head of title: "Columbische Weltausstellung in Chicago." C.t.= t.p. Title trans: "Official catalogue of the exhibit of Germany." Other author: Reichskommission.
---- vii, 256 p.
---- Also listed: 7 *l*, 256 p.
    ☺ (CHx,LC,NYPL,S,NL,nwu,RPB,WiHx)

460. Germany. *Ausstellung des Deutschen Berg- und Hüttenwesens : Chicago 1893.* Berlin: Gedruckt in der Buchdruckerei W. Koebke, 1893.

22½x15½. (7)-51 p. Gray stiff wraps, black print and design. C.t.= t.p. Publisher's name is on back cover. Trans: Exhibition of German mining and metallurgy.
---- Pub info on t.p.
    ☺ . (CPL,CHx)

461. Germany. Bayerischer Kunstgewerbeverein. Gmelin, Leop[old]. *Das Deutsche Kunstgewerbe : zur Zeit der Weltausstellung in Chicago 1893 : herausgegeben vom Bayerischen Kunstgewerbe-Verein.* München: Verlag von M. Schorss, n.d.; Woodbridge, CT: RPI, 1989.

ca. 31x23. 92 p., 56 plates. Microfilm. Alternating German with English translation. English translation on t.p.: "German Artistical Handicraft at the time of the World's-Exhibition in Chicago 1893 published by the Bavarian Society of Art-Industry."   ☺ . (SL,NYPL)

462. Germany. Bayerischer Kunstgewerbeverein. ... *Verzeichniss der auf den Weltausstellung in Chicago durch den Bayer, Kunstgewerbe-verein vertretenen aussteller.* München: Ynorr & Hirth, n.d.

22x__. 16, 112 p. includes frontis, illus. At head of title: "Bayerischer kunstgewerbe-verein, München." Trans: Index to the Bavarian artistical handicraft.   (LC,NYPL)

463. Germany. Berlin, George Buss. *Beschreibung der Deutschen Pfalz und Führer durch das Deutsche Dorf \ Description of the German castle and Guide through the German village.* Berlin: Verlag Max Pasch, 1893.

25½x18 to 26x19 (overhanging pages are larger than wraps). 2 books in 1., illus. Brown parchment wraps, string tied with paper medallion dangling from strings, title in black and red German script. C.t.: "Deutsche Pfalz und deutsches Dorf (German village) : Welt-Ausstellung in Chicago, 1893." Book 1: 1 *l* (t.p.), 34 p. Book 2: 1 *l* (t.p.), 75 p.; t.p.: "Geschichte Wendelins von Langenau wie sie von ihm selbst beschrieben ... An's Licht gegeben von Heinrich Steinhausen : mit vielen schönen Bildern geziert von Wilhelm Weimar." (Steinhausen's *The history of Wendelin von Langenau.*) Both books have German and English text in parallel columns. Cover remarkably similar to #474. [Found erroneously catalogued under George Buss.]   ☺ . (CHx,UDe,SLP,NL,AIC)

464. Germany. *Bochumer verein für Bergbau & Gusstahlfabrikation.* [Berlin: C. Ringer & Shon, 1893].

34½x24½. 13 p. Silver cloth hc with beveled edges, red print, decorative end papers. On front cover: "The Columbian Exposition, Chicago 1893." Exhibit description of heavy machinery. Other author: Reichskommission. (CHx)

465. Germany. *Catalog of the Collections in the Museum of the "Wasserburg" (German village)*. N.p.: n.p. [1893].

26½x19½. 63 p. Light teal wraps with red and navy print and litho design. C.t. B/w illus and list of 2802 displayed items. ☺ . (CHx,BU,WM)

466. Germany. *... Catálogo oficial de la exposición del Imperio Alemán.* Berlin: Reichsdruckerei, 1893.

24x16½. 9 *l*, 347 p., 90 p. ads on colored paper, paging includes illus, maps, plan. Flexible red-brown cloth cover, black print. At head of title: "Exposición universal Columbina en Chicago." Official Catalog of the German Empire translated to Spanish. Other author: Reichskommission. ☺ . (LC,nwu)

467. Germany. *Catalogue of a German home and family library : a collection of the treasures of German literature : compiled and furnished by the Imperial German Commission for the Columbian exhibition (German building).* Leipzig: F. Volckmar, 1893.

19x13½. 23, (1) p. Introduction by F. Volckmar. Other author: Reichskommission. ☺ . (UDe)

468. Germany. Central-verein für das gesammte buchgewerbe. Weigel, Adolf. *Führer durch die Buchgewerbliche Kollektiv-Ausstellung des Deutschen Reiches : Chicago 1893. ...* Leipzig: Druck von Breitkopf & Härtel, 1893.

24½x16½. 1 *l*, (v)-xii, 1 *l*, 149 p. Deep copper stiff wraps, black script and design, publisher's name on back of back cover, red dyed edges, rounded corners. Subject is book industry and trade.
---- Also listed: 1 *l*, xii, 1 *l*, 149 p.
☺ . (KyU,CHx,CPL,LC,NYPL,NLC,UoC)

469. Germany. *Chicago und die Columbische Weltausstellung : 1893. Mit Zustimmung des Reichs-Kommissars : zusammengestellt.* Berlin: Walther & Apolants Verlagsbuchhandlung, Hermann Walther, 1892.

22x15½. 95 p. illus. Trans: Chicago and the WCE : compiled with the consent of the German commissioners. (WiHx)

470. [Germany]. Cornely, Eugen. *Die Welt-Ausstellung "The Worlds Columbian Exposition" in Chicago 1893.* Berlin: Verlag von Albert Goldschmidt, 1893.

17½x12. 4 *l*, (1), vi-xxxvi p., fold. map, vi p., 1 *l*, 125, (1) p., 1 *l*. Simulated wood grain paper covered boards with black print. A total of (4) p. folding maps. "Griebens Reisebücher. Band 86." Travel to the Fair. Related to #471. ☺ . (LC)

471. [Germany]. [Cornely, Eugen]. *... Von deutschen häfen über New-York nach Chicago zur weltausstellung, 1893.* Berlin: A. Goldschmidt, [1893].

17½x__. 3 *l*, (v)-xxxvi, vi p., 1 *l*, 125 p., plates, 3 fold. map, 2 fold. plan. Cornely's name is found on t.p.; t.p. follows p. xxxvi. Account of trip to WCE. Related to #470. (LC)

472. Germany. Deutsche gesellschaft für mechanik und optik, Berlin. ... *Special catalogue of the collective exhibition of scientific instruments and appliances exhibited by the Deutsche Gesellschaft für Mechanik und Optik.* Berlin: Printed by Julius Bahlke, 1893; Woodbridge, CT: RPI, 1989.

23x15½. 2 *l*, 182 p., 1 *l*. Gray wraps, black print. C.t.= t.p. At head of title: "The World's Columbian Exposition Chicago 1893: German Exhibition. Group 21." Very nice etched plates of optical apparatus. ☺. (CPL,LC,SI,OC)

473. [Germany]. *Das Deutsche haus. The German house. Am Michigan see. On Lake Michigan.* New York and Chicago: A. Wittemann, ᶜ1893.

15½x14. 10 plates on 10 *l*. C.t. Same format as *The German Village ...* (#484). (LC)

474. Germany. *Deutsche pfalz und Deutsches Dorf (German Villages) Welt-ausstellung in Chicago 1893.* [Berlin, London: Wilhelm Brene], n.d.

26x19 (overhanging pages are larger than covers). 71 p., illus. Vellum wraps, multicolor string tied, string ends in paper medallion, red and black print and design. C.t. Text in old German script and English. (CHx)

475. Germany. *Der Deutsche Tag : Chicago, 15 Juni, 1893.* Chicago: Max Stern & Co., [1893].

23x15½. (13) p. White wraps, dark green print and design. Litho of "Das deutsche Haus" at center fold. C.t. ☺. (CHx,UDe,WiHx)

476. Germany. Deutschen Landwirthschaftsrath. Mueller, Traugott. *Landwirthschaftliche Reisebeobachtungen aus Nord-Amerika. Die amerikanische Bewässerungswirthschaft.* Berlin: n.p., 1894.

26½x17½. 2 *l*, 132 p., 21 *l* plates printed on one side. Brown cloth hc, gilt print on spine only, decorative end papers, marbled edges. Describes, in German, a trip across the U.S. (including the WCE) looking at U.S. water management and irrigation methods. ☺. (LC)

477. [Germany]. Dümmler, K. *Die Ziegel- und Thonwaaren-Industrie in den Vereinigten Staaten und auf der Columbus-Weltausstellung in Chicago 1893.* Halle a.S.: Verlag von Wilhelm Knapp, 1894.

28½x20½. 3 *l*, 180 p., illus, 12 plates, diagrams. Quarter leather with brown marbled paper boards, spine stamped in gilt. Photographs by C. D. Arnold. Trans: Brick and ceramic industry. ☺. (OSU)

478. Germany. Dyck, Walther. ... *Special-Katalog der mathematischen ausstellung (gruppe X der universitäts-ausstellung).* Berlin: [Dr. Walther Dyck], 1893.

24½x16½. x, 2 *l*, (3)-115, (1) p., illus, diagrams. Tan hc, black print, gray cloth spine. C.t.= t.p. At head of title: "Deutsche Unterrichts-ausstellung in Chicago 1893." Contents: mathematical models, apparatus, and instruments. Other author: Reichskommission. ☺. (LC,SI,USD,TU,RPB)

479. Germany. Ehrenbaum, [Ernst]. *Bericht über eine Reise nach den wichtigsten Fischereiplätzen der Vereinigten Staaten und über die Fischereiabtheilung auf der Weltausstellung in Chicago im Jahre 1893.* Berlin: W. Moeser hofbuchdruckerei, [1894]; Woodbridge, CT: RPI, 1989.

25x16½. 124 p., tables. Gray wraps, black print, marbled edges. Report of a trip to the U.S. to see the fishing industries and fish displays at the WCE. In German.   ☻ . (LC,SI)

480. Germany. ... *Erinnerungsschrift des Nord-Amerikanischen Turner-Bundes Gewidmet*[?] *von dessen Vertretern bei der Weltausstellung den freunden und förderern des deutschen Turnwesens in den Vereinigten Staaten. Chicago 1893.* Chicago: Edwin Beeh, Jr., 1893.

23x15. (4)-102, 7 *l* of ads at back. Light blue wraps, black print and design. At head of title: "Gut heil." Old German script. Trans: A remembrance of the North American gym meet at the WF; for the advancement of German gymnastics in the U.S.   (CHx)

481. Germany. *Führer durch die Ausstellung der Chemischen Industrie Deutschlands auf der Columbischen Weltausstellung in Chicago 1893.* Berlin W.: Gedruckt bei Julius Sittenfeld, n.d.

22½x15. 112 p. Brown textured stiff wraps, black print. German version of #487.   ☻ . (WM)

482. Germany. ... *Führer durch die ausstellung für das höhere mädchenschulwesen und für das gesammte volksschulwesen.* Chicago: Press of Max Stern & co., [1893]; Woodbridge, CT: RPI, 1989.

21½x14½. 27 p. Rose wraps, black print. At head of title: "Deutsche Unterrichtsausstellung in Chicago 1893." C.t.= t.p. Trans: "Guide through the exhibit for high schools for girls ..."
☻ . (SI,UMi,NL,WM)

483. Germany. Gängl von Ehrenwerth, Josef. ... *Das berg- und hüttenwesen auf der Weltausstellung in Chicago, nebst mittheilungen über montanistische verhältnisse in den Vereinigten Staaten, mit besonderer berücksichtigung des eisenhüttenwesens ... Mit 11 tafeln und 98 textfiguren.* Wien: K. K. Central-commission, 1895.   (UC)

484. [Germany]. *The German Village : Das Deutsche Dorf. And German Castle. und Deutsche Pfalz. Midway Plaisance World's Fair.* New York and Chicago: A. Wittemann, publisher of American views, °1893; Woodbridge, CT: RPI, 1989.

15½x14. 10 plates, one side. Ribbon tied, comes in envelope. C.t. Similar to *Old Vienna #505.*
☻ . (SI,LC,F) $25 - 40

485. [Germany]. Götz, Hermann. *Meine Reise nach Chicago und die Kolumbische Weltausstellung.* Darmstadt: Kunstgewerblicher Verlag von Alexander Koch, 1894.

27x19. 49, (1) p., illus with plans of some bldgs. No frontis but illus on p. 1: sketch of "Deutsches Haus" with coats of arms on either side. C.t.= t.p.   ☻ . (nwu)

486. Germany. Graesel, A[rnim]. ... *Special-katalog der bibliotheks-ausstellung (gruppe IX der universitäts-ausstellung.)* Berlin: [Druck von Trowitzsch & sohn], 1893; Woodbridge, CT: RPI, 1989.

23x16. x, 44 p. Tan wraps. At head of title: "Deutsche unterrichts-ausstellung in Chicago 1893." Trans: Special catalog of the library exhibit (group IX of the university exhibit).
☻ . (PU,KyU,SI,NYPL,NL,nwu,RPB,NYSt)

487. Germany. *Guide through the exhibition of the German chemical industry. Columbian Exposition in Chicago 1893.* Berlin: Printed by Julius Sittenfeld, n.d.; Woodbridge, CT: RPI, 1989.

22½x15. v, 3 *l*, 109, (1) p., illus, plan. Brown stiff textured wraps, black print. C.t.= t.p. English version of #481. ☻ . (CPL,SI,WM)

488. [Germany]. Hofmann, Carl. *Chicago-Reise vom 5. Juli - 8. September 1893. Mitglied des kaiserlich deutschen patent-amts : herausgeber der Papier-Zeitung.* Berlin W.: Verlag der papier-zeitung, 1893.

24x16. 92 p. Brown leatherette hc, black lettering and stamped black design on front above and below author/title listing, decorative end papers. Trans: Chicago trip. Member of the royal German patent office : publisher of the "Papier" newspaper. ☻ . (nwu)

489. Germany. Imperial Insurance Department in Berlin. Zacher, [Georg], comp. *The Workmen's Insurance of the German Empire. Guide expressly prepared for the World's Exhibition in Chicago.* [Berlin and London: A. Asher & Co.], n.d.

25x16. 26 + (6) p. includes covers, tables, diagrams. Bold black and red diagonal stripe cover of same stock as text pages, black print and design, string tied. This exhibit was in Machinery Hall. English version of #508. Other author: Reichs-Versicherungsamt in Berlin. ☻ . (LC,NYPL,UoC)

490. [Germany]. Interessengemeinschaft Farbenindustrie, A.-G. *Guide to the exhibits of the Badische Anilin- & Soda-Fabrik, Ludwigshafen °/ Rhine, at Chicago, 1893.* [Ludwigshafen on the Rhine: Weiss & Hameler, 1893].

8°. 2 *l*, 24 p., 3 plates, 1 table. (NYPL,WM)

491. Germany. Jaffé, Franz. *Die Architektur der Columbischen Welt-Ausstellung zu Chicago, 1893. Nach amtlichen Quellen ...* Berlin: J. Becker, 1895.

4°. viii, 115 p. including tables, illus, plans, plates. Trans: Architecture of the WCE from official sources. (NYPL)

492. [Germany]. *John Rotzer's Gasthof zur Stadt Wien : "Old Vienna" : Charles Antosch, Manager.* N.p.: n.p., n.d.

22½x15. Unpaged. Pink stiff smooth wraps, black print and design. Contains wine list with prices, e.g., Luttenberger, 1862 at $3 a flask. ☻ . (WM)

493. Germany. *Kaiserlich deutsche reichsdruckerei auf der Columbischen weltausstellung zu Chicago : 1893.* N.p.: n.p., n.d.

35x26½. 10 *l* with text and illus of exhibit plans, one side. Light green flecked wraps, black print and design. C.t.= t.p. Trans: Imperial German printing office at the WCE. ☻ . (UoC)

494. Germany. *... Katalog der ausstellung für das höhere mädchenschulwesen und das gesammte volks-schulwesen.* Schwarze Nummern. [Chicago: Press of Max Stern & Co.], n.d.

22x15. 10 p. Gray wraps, black print. At head of title: "Deutsche unterrichts ausstellung in Chicago 1893." C.t.= t.p. Content: A reading book list for students. Other author: Reichskommission.
◎ . (NYPL,TU,NL,WM)

495. Germany. ... *Katalog der ausstellung für das höhere schulwesen. Rothe Nummern.* [Chicago: Press of Max Stern & Co., 1893]; Woodbridge, CT: RPI, 1989.

22x14½. 22 p. Gray-blue wraps, black print. At head of title: "Deutsche Unterrichtsausstellung in Chicago 1893." C.t.= t.p. High school subjects from gym, Latin, physics, decoration, etc. Other author: Reichskommission.   ◎ . (SI,UoC,NL,WM)

496. Germany. *Katalog der Deutschen Ingenieur-Ausstellung auf der Columbischen Weltausstellung in Chicago.* Berlin, J. Springer, 1893.

x, 240 p. map. Trans: Catalog of the German engineering exhibit at the WCE. Other author: Reichskommission.   (UC)

497. Germany. ... *Katalog der Universitäts-Ausstellung.*   Berlin: [Gedruckt bei L. Schumacher], 1893; Woodbridge, CT: RPI, 1989.

23x17. viii, 197 p. Gray cloth spine, light blue-gray paper covered boards, black print. At head of title: "Deutsche Unterrichts-Ausstellung in Chicago, 1893." After title: "(Unter Mitwirkung von Dr. O. Lassar bearbeitet.)" C.t.= t.p. Other author: Reichskommission.   ◎ . (SI,UoC,NL,WM)

498. Germany. *Katalog der Werke deutscher Schriftstellerinnen für die Ausstellung in Chicago.* Berlin: Berliner Buchdruckerei-Aktien Gesellschaft. 1893.

24x__. 16 p. Trans: Catalog of the works of German authors.   (UC)

499. Germany. Königlichen Bibliothek zu Berlin. *Verzeichniss der in Deutschland erschienenen wissenschaftlichen zeitschriften für die Universitäts-ausstellung in Chicago 1893 : im Auftrage des Königlich preussischen Ministeriums der Unterrichts-Angelegenheiten hrsg. von der Königlichen Bibliothek zu Berlin.* ... Berlin: Verlag von Reuther & Reichard, 1893; Woodbridge, CT: RPI, 1989.

27½x19. 2 *l*, (1)-118 p. Gray-green wraps, black print and cover border. C.t.= t.p. Trans: Index to scientific journals in Germany.   ◎ . (JHU,LC,SI,UMi,NYSt,NL)

500. Germany. *Königreich Preussen. Höhere Lehranstalten. Amtliche Nachrichten.* \ *Prussia. Secondary Instruction. Official returns.* Berlin: 1893.

13x8. Wraps with Prussian emblem and border design around title. C.t.= t.p.   ◎ . (WM)

501. Germany. *Königreich Preussen. Statistisches über Volks- und Mittelschulen. Amtliche Nachrichten.* Berlin: 1893.

13x8. Wraps with Prussian emblem and border design surrounding title. C.t.= t.p. German version of #507.   ◎ . (WM)

502. Germany. ... *Königreich Württemberg.* Chicago: Press of Max Stern & co., 1893; Woodbridge, CT: RPI, 1989.

21½x14½.   24 p.   Yellow wraps with black print.   C.t.= t.p.   At head of title: "Deutsche Unterrichtsausstellung in Chicago 1893." Lists church and state school exhibits for Württemberg.
⊚ (SI,NL,WM)

503. Germany.   Lexis, W[ilhelm Hector Richard Albrecht].   *Die Deutschen universitäten : für die universitätsausstellung in Chicago 1893 : unter mitwirkung zahlreicher universitätslehrer.* 2 vols. Berlin: Verlag von A. Asher & Co., 1893; Woodbridge, CT: RPI, 1989.

2 vol in 1. 27x21. Vol I: 2 *l*, (vii)-ix, (2) p., 1 *l*, (3)-620 p. Vol II: 2 *l*, (v)-vi, 1 *l*, 406 p. Dark green hc, gilt print on cover and spine, decorative end papers, marbled edges. Subject: German universities and colleges.
---- Vol I: "Litteratur" p. 112-14. ?
⊚ . (PU,LC,SI,NYPL,NL,RPB,OC)

504. Germany.   *List of exhibitors from Nüremberg and Fuerth* [Bavaria] *at the Columbian World's exhibition Chicago, 1893.* Nuremberg: G. P. J. Bieling-Dietz, [1893].

16°. 92 p.   (NYPL)

505. [Germany]. *Old Vienna. Alt-Wien. Midway Plaisance--World's Fair. Auf der Weltausstellung in Chicago.* New York and Chicago: A. Wittemann, publisher of American views, ᶜ1893.

15½x14. 10 *l* of cream stiff stock with illus one side. Cream wraps, red print, b/w illus of Old Vienna entrance, ribbon tied. Descriptive text inside both covers. Nice. English and German illustration subtitles. C.t.   ⊚ . (GLD,LC) $12 - 22

506. Germany. ... *Official Catalogue : Exhibition of the German Empire.* [Berlin: Reichsdruckerei, 1893]; Woodbridge, CT: RPI, 1989.

24x16. xvi, 312 p., 90 p. ads. Green stiff cloth hc, print and elaborate design in black. At head of title: "World's Columbian Exposition : Chicago : 1893." Wonderful ads on various colored papers with print in various colors, one color per page. English ed. of the Reichskommission's *Amtlicher Katalog* #459. Other author: Reichskommission.   ⊚ . (UND,CHx,SI,OSU,UoC,NL,BPL,WiHx)

507. Germany. *Prussia. Statistics of Elementary and Middle Schools. Official returns.* Berlin: 1893.

13x8. Wraps with Prussian emblem and border design surrounding title. C.t.= t.p. English version of #501.   ⊚ . (WM)

508. Germany. Reichs-Versicherungsamt in Berlin. [Imperial Insurance Department in Berlin]. Zacher, [Georg], comp. *Leitfaden zur Arbeiter-Versicherung des Deutschen Reichs. Zusammengestellt für die Weltausstellung in Chicago.* [Berlin and London: A. Asher & Co.], n.d.

25x16. 26, (6) p. German version of #489; covers have the same design and colors.   ⊚ . (LC)

509. Germany. Reuleaux, F. *Mittheilungen über die amerikanische Maschinen-Industrie : auf und ausserhalb der Kolumbischen Weltausstellung 1893.* Berlin: Druck von Leonhard Simion, 1894.

29½x23. 86 p. Tan wraps with black print. C.t. Nice b/w lithos of tool bits, lathes, pattern makers, etc. ☺. (LC)

510. Germany. *Die sächsische Textil-Industrie und ihre Bedeutung. Anhang: Verzeichniss der ausstellenden ... Industriellen.* Leipzig: 1893.

18½x13½. 88 p. German version of #511. (WM)

511. Germany. *... The Textile Industry of Saxony and its importance. Appendix: List of exhibitors interested in the Textile Industry of Saxony.* [Leipzig: Leipziger Monatschrift für Textil-Industrie (Theodor Martin's Textile Verlag), 1893].

18½x13½. 2 *l*, (5)-88 p. Two-tone green smooth wraps, black lettering and design. At head of title: "World's Columbian Exposition : Chicago 1893." C.t without "1893"= t.p. Exhibit location in Manufactures Bldg shown on outside back wrap. Contains: text descriptive of the industry, catalogue of the individual exhibitors, alphabetical list of exhibitors and numbered pages for memoranda. English version of #510. ☺ (GLD) $15 - 34

512. Germany. *Verzeichnis der seit 1850 an den Deutschen Universitäten erschienenen Doctor-Dissertationen und Habilitationsschriften aus der reinen und angewandten Mathematik. Herausgegeben auf Grund des für die Deutsche Universitäts-Ausstellung in Chicago erschienenen Verzeichnisses.* München: Kgl. Hof- und universitäts-buchdruckerei von Dr. C. Wolf & sons, 1893.

23x16. 2 *l*, 35 p. Gray wraps, black print. C.t.= t.p. Index: German doctoral math theses.
☺. (LC,UMi)

513. [Germany]. Witt, Otto N[icolaus]. *Die chemische industrie auf der Columbischen weltausstellung zu Chicago und in den Vereinigten Staaten von Nord-Amerika im jahre 1893. Bericht, dem königlich preussischen staatsminister und minister der geistlichen ...* Berlin: R. Gaertner (H. Heyfelder), 1894.

23x__. 148 p. Content: Report of chemical industry in U.S. and at the WCE. (LC,NYPL,UMi)

514. Germany. Wittmack, L[udewig]. *... Gartenbau.* Berlin: Gedruckt in der Reichsdruckerei, n.d.

32½x23. 33 glossy p., illus include photos in "Gartenbauhalle." Pale gray-green wraps, black print. Trans: Horticulture. At head of title: "Sonderabdruck aus dem Amtlichen Bericht über die Weltausstellung in Chicago 1893." ☺. (LC)

515. Germany. Wittmack, L[udewig]. *... Landwirthschaftliche Erzeugnisse.* Berlin: Gedruckt in der Reichsdruckerei, n.d.

32½x23. 28 glossy p., illus at p. 27 is "Ausstellung der deutschen Kaliwerke." Pale gray-green wraps, black print. C.t. German script text on agricultural production. At head of title: "Sonderabdruck aus dem Amtlichen Bericht über die Weltausstellung in Chicago 1893." ☺. (LC)

516. Germany. Wohltmann, F[erdinand]. *Landwirthschaftliche reisestudien über Chicago und Nord-Amerika.* Breslau: Schlettersche Buchhandlung, 1894.

    23x17. 4 *l*, 440 p. Green cloth over beveled board hc with white print. All edges dyed red. Old German script.   (CHx)

517. Granada. *Clasificacion de los productos destinados á la exposicion Colombina de 1893 en Chicago.* Managua: Tipografía Nacional, n.d.

    24½x17. xviii, (1) p. Light gray wraps, illus of la Rabida on back cover. Cover: "Antonio Salaverri commisionado especial." Cover shows litho: "carabela de Colón" (caravel of Columbus). "Granada-1892." Trans: Classification of the products destined for the Columbian exposition."   ⊚ . (CPL)

518. Great Britain. [McCormick, Robert]. *The future trade relations between Great Britain and the United States, and the World's Columbian Exposition to be held at Chicago in 1893.* London: Printed by W S. Trounce, 1892.

    25x16½. 48 p. includes covers. Plain paper wraps, black print. C.t. McCormick's name on preface. Speech of Robert McCormick, official representative in Great Britain of the WCE, and several reprints of articles which appeared in newspapers and magazines of the day.   ⊚ . (LC,NL)

519. Great Britain. Royal Commission for the Chicago Exhibition, 1893. *Baroness Burdett-Coutts; A sketch of the public life and work prepared for the Lady Managers of the World's Columbian Exposition by command of Her Royal Highness, Princess Mary Adelaide, Duchess of Teck.* Chicago: A. C. McClurg and Co., 1893.

    16x10½. 204 p., frontis (port). Green cloth hc, gold print. Duchess Teck was Princess of Great Britain and Ireland.   (UND,UoC,NL)

520. Great Britain. Royal Commission for the Chicago Exhibition, 1893. Burdett-Coutts, ed. *Woman's mission: a series of congress papers on the philanthropic work of women, by eminent writers.* London: S. Low, Marston & Co., 1893.

    8°. xxiv, 485 p.   (NYPL)

521. Great Britain. Royal Commission for the Chicago Exhibition, 1893. ... *Handbook of Regulations and general information. May, 1893.* London: William Clowes and Sons, Limited, 1893; Woodbridge, CT: RPI, 1989.

    18½x12½. 228 p. + fold. frontis of bird's-eye view of grounds. Bright blue (or pale blue) stiff wraps, black print. 2 other unpaged fold. maps. Paged ads from 179-228. At head of title: "Royal Commission for the Chicago Exhibition, 1893." On cover: "Final edition." C.t.= t.p. [The Royal Commission has been active in every WF since the first in London (1851).]   ⊚ . (CPL,SI,UoC,NL)

522. Great Britain. Royal Commission for the Chicago Exhibition, 1893. ... *Official catalogue of the British section.* London: William Clowes & Sons, Limited, 1893; Woodbridge, CT: RPI, 1989.

    1st ed.: 18x12. Fold. map ahead of t.p., xlii, 544 p. + xcii of interspersed ads, frontis (plan). Light blue stiff wraps, deep royal blue print and design. C.t.= t.p. At head of title: "Royal Commission for the Chicago Exhibition, 1893." At top of t.p.: "[under revision.] On cover: "Presentation copy." Pears soap ad on outside back cover.

---- 1st ed. [under revision]: xlii, 544, + cix p. interspersed ads.

---- 1st ed.: xlii, 536 p.

---- 2nd ed.: 18½x11. xlii, 542 p. + ads at beginning and end. Dark blue with black leather spine.

---- 2nd ed.: xlii, 534 p.

         ☺ . (CHx,LC,SI,NYPL,NLC,OSU,PU,UDe,SLP,NHSt,HL,NYSt,UoC,NL,nwu,RPB,WiHx)

523. **Great Britain. Royal Commission for the Chicago Exhibition, 1893.** Pascoe, Charles Eyre. *An Illustrated Souvenir of Victoria House : The Head-Quarters of the Royal Commission for Great Britain at the World's Columbian Exposition, Chicago, 1893.* London: Johnstone, Norman & Co., n.d.; Woodbridge, CT: RPI, 1989.

14½x11½. 58 p. on stiff, coated stock, illus. Tan wraps, brown print and design. Frontis of the Queen. Pascoe was editor of "London of To-Day." ☺ . (CPL,CHx,SLS,UMi,AIC)

☞ The Victoria House's 30 rooms were designed and built in England at the request of Queen Victoria, who asked that the various rooms duplicate the ornate English walnut carvings, curved stairways and other interior designs found in certain English palaces which she admired. After meeting with the Queen's approval, it was dismantled and shipped to Chicago.

After the Fair, Victoria House was purchased by J. C. Rogers, a Wamego, KS, banker. It was torn down, and stored in Kansas City, where storage costs accumulated. At the WCE, Colonel Daniel Burns Dyer (1849-1912) exhibited his American Indian artifacts, winning prizes. He visited Victoria House and decided that if he ever built a home he wanted some of the interior designs he saw there. He learned the stored bldg was being offered for sale and purchased it. He combined Victoria House with parts of bldgs from the St. Louis 1904 Fair and, in 1907, built his mansion, "Idlewild," on a 40 acre bluff overlooking Kansas City, Independence, Clay County, and the Missouri and Blue Rivers. In 1920, Dyer's heirs sold to B. P. Bagby who planned to convert the home into a motion picture studio (one picture was produced -- "Jesse James Under the Black Flag"). Bagby met with financial reverses and forfeited to the heirs in 1922. For 12 years it was the G. Wilse Robinson Sanitarium. From 1935 it was unoccupied, deteriorated, purchased by the Sheffield steel Corp. in 1939 and demolished by them the following year. [From various K.C. newspapers: 1906, 1923, 1939, 1971.]

524. **Great Britain. Women's Department.** ... *Loan Collection of Portraits. Detailed catalogue.* Bristol: H. Hill, Printer and Stationer, n.d.

18½x12½. 31 p. Plain paper wraps, black print and design. C.t. At head of title: "Chicago - Women's Department." Catalog of ports of eminent British women. [Note: spelling is women's rather than woman's.] (CHx)

525. **Greece.** *Catalogue of casts exhibited by the Greek government at the World's Columbian exposition in Chicago.* Athens: S. C. Vlastos, 1893.

20 p. (OC)

526. **[Greece].** Graf, Theodor. *Catalogue of the Theodor Graf collection of unique ancient Greek portraits : 2000 years old : recently discovered and now on view in Old Vienna, Midway Plaisance : at the World's Columbian Exposition Chicago.* N.p.: n.p., [1893?]; Woodbridge, CT: RPI, 1989.

23x15. 49 p. (include 35 plates). "Catalogue by F. H. Richter and F. von Ostini." Graf lived in Greece and collected artifacts from the Greek classical period.

---- Bound with: Ebers, Georg [Moritz]. *The Hellenic portraits from the Fayum : at present in the collection of Herr Graf : with some remarks on other works of this class at Berlin and elsewhere.* New York: D. Appleton and Co., 1893 [°1893 by D. Appleton and Co.]. 19x13. 110 p., frontis, illus, plates.
  ⊚ . (PU,SI,mcg,UDe)

527. Greece. *Greece. Official catalogue World's Columbian Exposition, Chicago. 1893.* Chicago: Knight, Leonard & Co., [1893].

  19x13½. 24 p. Dark tan wraps, black print. C.t.= t.p.   ⊚ . (CPL)

528. Guadeloupe (West Indies). Guesde, L[ouis Athanase-Mathieu]. ... *Guadeloupe (West Indies).* Guadeloupe: Basse-terre Government printing office, 1892; Woodbridge, CT: RPI, 1989.

  ca. 17x9½. 15 p. Microfilm. At head of title: "World's Columbian exposition 1893."   ⊚ . (SI,NYPL)

529. Guatemala. Comisión de Guatemala. Guzmán, Gustavo E. *Informe relativo á los Trabajos de la Comisión de Guatemala para la exposición de Chicago ... 1893.* Guatemala: Encuadernación y Tipografía Nacional, 1893.

  24x17. 9 p. Trans: Informative report of the work of the Guatemalan Commission for the Chicago Exposition.   ⊚ . (CPL)

-H-

530. Haiti. Commission de l'Exposition haïtienne. ... *Haïti a l'exposition colombienne de Chicago : avec une liste de ses produits exposés et des notices de M. Dulciné Jean-Louis...* Port-au-Prince: Imprimerie Vᵛᵉ J. Chevet, 1893.

  24x16. 2 *l*, 112 p., errata slip laid in after p. 112. Blue wraps, black print. At head of title: "Bibliothèque Haitienne Robert Gentil & Henri Chauvet." M. Dulciné Jean-Louis was vice president of the Commission. Trans: Haiti at the Columbian Exposition of Chicago : with a list of displayed products and the notices of M. Dulciné Jean-Louis.   ⊚ . (CPL)

531. Haiti. Douglass, Frederick. *Lecture on Haiti : The Haitian Pavilion Dedication Ceremonies Delivered at the World's Fair, in Jackson Park, Chicago, Jan. 2d, 1893.* N.p.: n.p., n.d.

  22½x14½. 57 p. Douglass was Ex-Minister to Haiti. LC microfilm.   ⊚ . (LC)

532. [Holland]. *Catalogue of the Paintings from the Holland Section of Fine Arts at the World's Columbian exposition : Chicago, Ill. : to be sold by auction ... March 29th and 30th ... Fifth Avenue Art Galleries ...* [New York: John C. Rankin Co.], 1894.

  22x14. 43, (1) p., 15 *l* of b/w plates of paintings. Green textured wraps with black print. C.t.: "Paintings In Oil and Water Color Contributed by Holland To the World's Columbian Exposition."
  ⊚ . (NYSt,WM)

533. Hungary. Ottlik, Iván. *Úti levelek Amerikából, irta Ottlik Iván ...* Budapest: [Franklin-Társulat], 1894.

8°. 87 p. Rpt.: Budapesti Szemle, 1894. (NYPL)

-I-

534. India. Office of Inspector-General of Forests. ... *Hand-book to accompany the collection of exhibits furnished by the forest department of the government of India.* Calcutta: Office of the superintendent of government printing, India, 1893; Woodbridge, CT: RPI, 1989.

24½x15½. 34, xvii, (1) p. Green wraps with black print. C.t.= t.p. At head of title: "Chicago exhibition, 1893." ⊚ . (CPL,SI)

535. Ireland. Irish Industries Association. *Guide to the Irish Industrial Village and Blarney Castle, the exhibit of The Irish Industries Association at the World's Columbian exposition, Chicago.* N.p.: Irish Village Book Store [Rand, McNally & Co., Printers], 1893 [°1893].

21½x15½. (10), 11-67, (1) p. Light lime green wraps with black print and design. The (10) pages are ads plus a bird's-eye view of the Irish Industrial Village in Midway Plaisance and its floor plan. T.p. is found on page (8). ⊚ . (LC)

536. Ireland. Irish Industries Association. *The Irish Village of the Irish Industries Association.* N.p.: n.p., °1893 by the Irish Industries Association.

20x15. 2-14, (1) p. Includes 6 color lithos by C. Graham. Front and back wraps have decorative tan borders around Graham color lithos, white and chocolate print. Caption title.
⊚ (GLD) $15 - 32

537. Ireland. Johnson, Edmond. *Description and history of Irish antique art metal work : Fac-simile reproductions of which have been specially manufactured for exhibition at Chicago.* Dublin: Printed by Sealy, Bryers and Walker, 1893; Woodbridge, CT: RPI, 1989.

ca. 18x12. 108 p. Microfilm. ⊚ . (SI)

538. [Italy]. Brazza, Cora A[nn] Slocomb di. *A guide to Old and New Lace in Italy: Exhibited at Chicago in 1893.* Chicago: W. B. Conkey Co., °1893 by Cora A. Slocomb di Brazza; Venezia: F. Ongania, 1893; Woodbridge, CT: RPI [Conkey], 1989.

21½x15. 1 *l*, 2 folding facsimiles with text across two open pages -- "Libro di Lorieri" and "Serenissma Signora," 186 p., frontis, illus t.p., ports. Microfilm.
Author's name may be listed: Contessa Cora Ann (Slocomb) di Brazzà Savorgnan.
---- 22½x16. White cloth hc with red print and dark green design, red dyed edges.
⊚ . (SI,LC,S,ucsu,HL,TU,NYSt,UoC,AIC,F) $25 - 50

539. Italy. Candiani, Ettore. *L'industria chimica : all'esposizione di Chicago.* Milano: Ulrico Hoepli, 1895.

23x16. 6 *l*, (3)-121, (1) p. index. Red leather over thick boards, gilt print and design, all edges gilt, decorative end papers. No frontis, t.p. in red and black. Beautiful binding. ⊚ . (UoC)

540. Italy. Capacci, Celso. ... *L'esposizione ed i congressi di Chicago (Ill. U.S.A.) : nel 1893.* Firenze: Tipografia di G. Carnesecchi e figli, 1894.

24½x16½. 84, (1) p. At head of title: Collegio degli architetti ed ingegneri di firenze."   ☉ . (UoC)

541. Italy. ... *Catalogo Ufficiale delle sezioni Italiane.* Chicago: Max Stern & Co., Printers, [1893].

22x14½. 68 p., rust wraps, black print. Bird's-eye view of grounds printed on back cover. At head of title: "Regno D'italia. Regio Commissariato Generale all' Esposizione Internazionale Colombiana di Chicago." Official catalog of the Italian section.   ☉ . (KyU,UMi,NL)

542. [Italy]. *Catalogue of U. Hoepli's publications : 1872-1893.* Milan: n.p., n.d.

23x12½. Ornate border surrounds cover title. C.t.= t.p. except at top of cover: "World's Columbian exposition : Chicago 1893."   ☉ . (WM)

543. Italy. *Educational publications in Italy, notes by Piero Barbera.* Florence: Barbera, 1893.

14 p.   (UC)

-J-

544. Jamaica. Ward, C[harles] J., comp. *World's Fair. Jamaica at Chicago. An account descriptive of the colony of Jamaica, with historical and other appendices.* New York: Wm. J. Pell, Printer, 1893 [°1893 by Charles J. Ward].

25½x18. 95, (1) p., illus, fold. map. Royal blue cloth hc, decorative end papers, cover has Jamaican coat of arms and lettering in gilt. Diminutive c.t.: "Jamaica at the Columbian exposition 1893." No frontis. Description of Jamaica for free distribution at WCE. Lt. Col. Ward was honorary commissioner for Jamaica. Similar to #545.

☉ . (GLD,csuf,CHx,NYPL,OSU,CoU,HL,TU,UMi,NYSt,NL,nwu,UDe,RPB,OC,TD) $20 - 40

545. Jamaica. Ward, C[harles] J., comp. *World's Fair. Jamaica at Chicago. An Account Descriptive of the Colony of Jamaica, With Historical and Other Appendices.* New York: Wm. J. Pell, Printer, [1893].

17x25. 63 p., (1) p., pale green wraps. Similar to #544.   ☉ . (KyU,LC)

When known, Romanized Japanese authors are given in annotation. Card catalogs may list them as primary authors; we found this confusing since this information is not on the title pages. Personal Japanese names are given Oriental style: last name first without comma.

---

546. Japan. *Advertisements of The Japanese Representations in The World's Columbian Exposition. 1893.* N.p.: n.p., n.d.

25½x17. 14 *l* of ads (in English) and includes 3 folding colored block prints -- plate one of which shows the Hō-ō-den Japanese Pavilion on the Wooded Island. At head of title in Kanji translates: The Japanese exhibition. C.t. Wraps are block printed in tan and shaded blue with black print. Last *l* is title in Japanese. Last 11 *l* in typical Japanese folded fashion.   ☉ . (NYPL,NL)

547. [Japan]. [*Bankoku Shukyo Taikai. Reports of the World's Congress of Religions, translated into Japanese by Ohara, Kakichi*]. [Osaka: Kanagawa, 1893].

19x11½. 102 p. In Japanese characters. 4 reports. Other author: World's Parliament of Religions.
⊚ . (OC)

548. Japan. Batchelor, John. *An itinerary of Hokkaido, Japan.* ... Tokyo: Printed at the Tokyo Tsukiji type foundry, 1893.

19½x13. 1 *l*, ii, 28 p. + folding view litho of harbor and town of Hakodate, + (2) p. summary and (10) p. ads. Color block print illus on front and back of folded front cover, string tied. Presented by the Hakodate Chamber of Commerce.
⊚ . (GLD,CHx,S) $20 - 50

549. [Japan]. [Beikoku Daihakurankai Nihon Fujinkai]. [*Nihon no fujin.* \ Japanese women]. N.p.: n.p., [28 years after Meiji -- i.e., 1895].

23x__. 4, 226 p., 10 *l* plates, illus. Romanized Japanese cover title. Author trans: Great American Exhibition of the Japanese Women's Association.   (LC)

550. Japan. *A brief description of the pictures of Japanese hunting exhibited in the World's Columbian Exposition.* N.p.: Agricultural Bureau of the Department of Agriculture and Commerce, 1893.

22x15. 4 p. Light tan wraps only slightly heavier stock than text, black print. C.t. Contents: "Japanese Hawking." Author: Dept of Agriculture and Commerce, Agricultural Bureau. / [Nōshōmushō. Nōmukyoku].   ⊚ . (LC)

551. Japan. *A brief description of the taxidermic specimens of Ohiki, Shamo and Chabo. Exhibited in the World's Columbian Exposition.* N.p.: Agricultural Bureau of the Department of Agriculture and Commerce, 1893.

22x15. 2 p. Wraps same as text, black print. C.t. Ohiki is Japanese Long-tailed fowl, Shamo is Malay or Siamese game, and Chabo is Japanese Bantam (pure breed is kept only in Japan). Author: Dept of Agriculture and Commerce, Agricultural Bureau. \ [Nōshōmushō. Nōmukyoku].   ⊚ . (LC)

552. Japan. Brinkley, F[rank]. *Artistic Japan at Chicago: a description of Japanese works of art sent to the World's fair: works in metal, glyptic works, textile fabrics, lacquer, enamel, pictures, porcelains.* Yokohoma: Printed at the "Japan mail" office, n.d.

26x18½. 33 p. Faded green wraps with fine line border and print in black. C.t.
---- Also listed: 28x__. 26 p.
⊚ . (CHx,NYPL,OC,AIC)

553. Japan. *Catalogue of objects exhibited at the World's Columbian exposition : Chicago, U.S.A., 1893.* Tokyo: Department of Education, 1893.

21½x15. 2 *l*, 112, (1) p., illus not counted in pagination. Buff stiff wraps with black print. C.t.= t.p. The English title is on the first *l*; in Japanese fashion, the Japanese title is at the end -- (1) p. Author: The Dept of Education. \ [Mombushō]. ⊚ . (KyU,LC,NYPL,UMi,TU,UoC,WiHx)

554. Japan. Central Meteorological Observatory of Japan, Tokio. *Explanatory notes on the exhibits to the World's Columbian exposition at Chicago, U.S.A., 1893.* Tokio: [1893?].

22½x__. (1), 14, (1) p.   (NYPL,UoC)

555. Japan. Central Meteorological Observatory of Japan, Tokio. *Organization of the meteorological system in Japan.* Tokio: 1893.

4°. Folio.   (NYPL)

556. Japan. *Chambers of Commerce in the Empire of Japan.* Tokyo: M. Onuki for the Bureau of Commerce and Industry, Dept. of Agriculture and Commerce, 1893.

22x__. 1, 22 p. Author: The Dept of Agriculture and Commerce, Bureau of Commerce and Industry. \ [Nōshōmushō. Shōkōkyoku].   (UC)

557. Japan. *A Description of bees, honey, beeswax and bee appliances exhibited in the World's Columbian Exposition.* N.p.: Agriculture Bureau, Department of Agriculture and Commerce, 1893.

22x15. 4 p. Light tan wraps only slightly heavier stock than text, black print. 2½ p. list of plants from which bees collect honey. Author: The Dept of Agriculture and Commerce, Bureau of Agriculture. \ [Nōshōmushō. Nōmukyoku].   (LC)

558. Japan. *Descriptive catalogue of exhibits relating to the fisheries of Japan at the World's Columbian Exposition held at Chicago, Ill., U.S.A., from Bureau of Agriculture, Dept. of Agriculture and Commerce, Imperial Japanese Government.* Tokio: n.p., 1893; Woodbridge, CT: RPI, 1989.

22x__. ii, 38 p. Microfilm. Author: Dept of Agriculture and Commerce, Agricultural Bureau. \ [Nōshōmushō. Nōmukyoku].   (LC,SI)

559. Japan. *A descriptive catalogue of Japanese forage plants exhibited in the World's Columbian exposition.* [Tokyo]: Agricultural Bureau, Department of Agriculture and Commerce, 1893.

23x16. 1 *l*, 24 p. Gray-green wraps, black print. C.t.= t.p. In English. Author: Dept of Agriculture and Commerce, Agricultural Bureau. \ [Nōshōmushō. Nōmukyoku].   ☻ (LC,NL)

560. Japan. *A descriptive catalogue of Japanese wild birds, useful and injurious, exhibited in the World's Columbian exposition.* [Tokyo?]: Agricultural Bureau of the Department of Agriculture and Commerce, 1893; Woodbridge, CT: RPI, 1989.

ca. 21½x14. 32 p. C.t. Author: Dept of Agriculture and Commerce, Agricultural Bureau. \ [Nōshōmushō. Nōmukyoku].   ☻ . (UWa,SI)

561. Japan. ... *A descriptive catalogue of the agricultural products, exhibited in the World's Columbian exposition.* Tokio: Printed by Seishibun-sha, 1893.

21x14. ii, 115 p. Green-gray wraps, black print. At head of title: "Japan. Agricultural bureau, department of agriculture and commerce." C.t.= t.p. Author: Dept of Agriculture and Commerce, Agricultural Bureau. \ [Nōshōmushō. Nōmukyoku].   ⊚ . (KyU,PU,JHU,LC,NYPL,TU,UoC,NL)

562. Japan. *Details of the industrial specimens exposed at the World's Columbian Exposition by the Bureau of Commerce and Industry, Department of Agriculture and Commerce, Japan.* Tokyo: Printed by M. Onuki, 1893.

22x14. 2 *l*, 21 p. Beige wraps. Author: Dept of Agriculture and Commerce, Bureau of Commerce and Industry. \ [Nōshōmushō. Shōkōkyoku].
---- 26x16½.
⊚ . (csuf,KyU,LC,NYPL,NL)

563. Japan. *Details of the weights and measures exposed at the World's Columbian Exposition.* Tokyo: Printed by M. Onuki, 1803 [1893 printed on cover].

22x13. (2), 9 p. Wraps. Author: Dept of Agriculture and Commerce, Bureau of Commerce and Industry. \ [Nōshōmushō. Shōkōkyoku].   ⊚ . (LC,NYPL,USD,NL)

564. Japan. *Explanation of the Japanese Lady's Boudoir, with the articles therein, exhibited in the Woman's Building of the World's Columbian exposition, ...* Chicago: Privately printed by A. C. McClurg & Co. for The Japanese Ladies' Committee, Tokio, n.d.; Woodbridge, CT: RPI, 1989.

21x16. 16 p. (include t.p.), 4 diagrams. Tan heavy rag wraps, black print. C.t.= t.p.   ⊚ . (SI,NL)

565. Japan. *General view of commerce & industry in the empire of Japan. Published by the bureau of commerce and industry, department of agriculture and commerce, Japan.* Tōkyō: Printed by M. Onuki, 1893.

19x13. 2 *l*, ii, 492 p. include fold. map, fold. plans. Author: Dept of Agriculture and Commerce, Bureau of Commerce and Industry. \ [Nōshōmushō. Shōkōkyoku].   ⊚ . (UDe)

566. [Japan]. Hasegawa Takejiro. *Exhibition of figures representing life in old and new Japan.* [Tokio: T. Hasegawa, 1892].

18½x__. 13 double *l* folded Chinese style. Caption title. C.t.: "Japan old & new." "Collection of life-like figures ... specially designed for the World's fair, with the object of illustrating various episodes in the history of Japan."   (NYPL)

567. [Japan]. Hayashi Tadamasa. *Twelve bronze falcons exhibited at the World's Columbian exposition : Chicago 1893.* Tokyo: n.p., 1893.

28x20. 2 *l*, ix, 14 plates. Artist: Chokichi Suzuki; exhibitor and designer: Hayashi. Includes remarks of daily papers of Japan (ix p.) and inserted newspaper clipping. Cover illus of Japanese falconers.
---- 8 *l* includes t.p., 14 plates.
⊚ . (PU,NYPL)

568. Japan. *The History of Japan : compiled and translated by the department of education : Japan : for the World's Columbian exposition : Chicago, U. S. A., 1893.* Tokyo: Imperial Japanese commission, [1893].

23½x15½. 364 p., plates (5 colored).   ⊚ . (AIC)

569. Japan. *History of the Empire of Japan. Compiled and Translated
for the Imperial Japanese commission of the World's Columbian
exposition, Chicago, U.S.A., 1893.* [Trans. Captain F.
Brinkley]. Tokyo: Dai Nippon Tosho Kabushiki Kwaisha, by
order of the Department of Education [Printed at the "Japan
mail" office, Yokohama, 1893].

23½x15½. 2 *l*, vi, vi, 428, (1) p.   Last p. in Japanese
characters. Tipped in rice paper illus (some double; some in
color), many double plates not included in pagination. 38
plates. Author: Dept of Education. \ [Mombushō].
---- Also listed: A revised ed. issued later by the Japan
Education Dept: *Japan, from the Japanese government history.*
---- [Printed at the Shueisha lot branch office: Tokyo].
23x15½. 2 *l*, vi, vi, 426 p., 1 *l*. 35 plates (5 colored), fold.
map, 2 fold plans. T.p. print variation. Hc with beige
background, gilt cloud design.
---- Also listed: Without 2 *l*.
P→   ⊚ . (KyU,PU,LC,NYPL,BU,UTn,Yale,UMi,UoC,nwu,OC)

570. Japan. *Imperial geological survey of Japan, with a catalogue of articles exhibited by the Geological survey at
the World's Columbian exposition.* Tokyo: Published by the Imperial Geological Survey of Japan,
Department of Agriculture and Commerce, 1893; Woodbridge, CT: RPI, 1989.

24½x16½. 49, (1) p. + 3 *l* maps printed on recto only (stiffer stock than text pages). Wraps same
stock as text, black print. Author: Geological Survey Research Section. \ [Chishitsu. Chōsajo].
---- Also listed: 1 *l*, 49 p., 1 *l*.
---- 24½x17. 17 p. Brown wraps, black print.
        (LC,CPL,SI,UoC)

571. Japan. *Japanese Woman's Commission for the World's Columbian Exposition.* Chicago: W. B. Conkey co.,
Printers and Binders, n.d.

20½x15. 1 *l* (t.p.), 3-7 p. Off-white high rag content wraps, sepia print and design. C.t.= t.p.
Contents: organization of the Japanese women, exhibits, articles to be exhibited, etc. The Commission
held its 1st meeting in Tokyo, May 13, 1892.   ⊚ . (NL)

572. Japan. Japanese Woman's Commission. *Japanese Women.* Chicago: Privately printed by A. C. McClurg
& Co., for the Japanese Woman's Commission for the World's Columbian exposition, [1893?].

20½x15. 3 *l*, 3-159 p., b/w illus, sample of musical scores.
---- 22½x14. 1 *l*, (1)-159 p. Off-white wraps of same stock as text pages, black print. C.t. Preface
dated 1893.
        ⊚ . (UNLV,UMi,UoC,NL,RPB)

573. [Japan]. Kubota Beisen. *Kakuryu sekai hakuran-kai bijitsu-hin gafu.* [World's Columbian Exposition; a
collection of art objects copied by Beisen Kubota]. [Tokyo: Okura Shoten, 1893-94].

3 vol in portfolio. (UoC)

574. Japan. Kyoto Exhibitors' Association. *Kyoto. Compliments of Kyoto Exhibitors' Association.* N.p.: n.p., n.d.

23½x16. 41 double *l*, folded in oriental style. C.t. Cover illus of spring blossoms. Prepared for the WCE, Japanese section. ---- Also listed: 38 double *l*.
P→   ◎ . (PU,AIC)

575. Japan. Okakura Kakudzo. *The Hō-ō-den : (Phoenix hall) : an illustrated description of the buildings erected by the Japanese government at the World's Columbian exposition, Jackson Park, Chicago.* Tokyō: K. Ogawa, publisher [Chicago: W. B. Conkey Co., printers and binders], 1893 ᶜ1893 by C. D. Arnold.

23x15½. 40 p., 2 *l*, illus, map. Tan background cover with very pretty multicolor -- rose, blue, peach, lime green, beige, browns -- litho wraps, floral and bird design. C.t.: "Illustrated Description of the Hō-ō-den (Phoenix Hall) at the World's Columbian exposition."
◎ . (CPL,LC,UDe,UoC,NL,AIC)

576. Japan. *Outlines of the Modern Education in Japan.* Tokyo: Dept. of Education, 1893.

23x__. 218 p. Author: Dept of Education. \ [Mombushō]. (UC)

577. Japan. Takahashi Nobusada, ed. ... *Descriptive notes on silks and cocoons exhibited in the World's Columbian exposition.* Tokyo: Printed at the Tokyo Tsukiji type foundry, 1893.

26½x20. 1 *l*, 20 p. Tan wraps same stock as text pages, black print. C.t. At head of title: "Japan." Other author: [Dept of Agriculture and Commerce, Agricultural Bureau. \ Nōshōmushō. Nōmukyoku].
◎ . (LC)

578. Java. *The Javanese Theater, Java Village, Midway Plaisance. World's Columbian Exposition, Chicago, 1893. Containing also a Short Description of Java : The People, Languages, Customs Food, Products, Etc.* N.p.: Java Chicago Exhibition Syndicate, n.d.

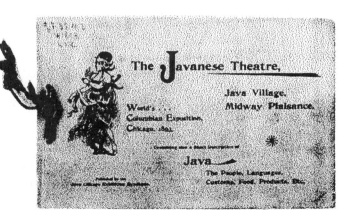

13x20. (24) p. Off-white (or peach or silver-gray) heavy paper wraps tied with cord, black lettering and design of dancing native. B/w photos of Java Village and Theater with complete description. C.t.
P→   ◎ . (GLD,F,UDe,CHx)

$20 - 35

579. Java. *The Javanese Theater, the Java Village, Midway Plaisance: World's Columbian Exposition, Chicago, 1893.* [Chicago]: Java Chicago Exhibition Syndicate, [ca. 1893].

20½x14. 3 p. Above title: "The Java Village."
(R,csuf)

$16 - 35

-L-

580. Liberia. *Liberia 1847-1893. Catalogue of the Liberian exhibit classified by tribes.* N.p.: n.p., n.d.

23x15. 32 p., illus. White stiff wraps with black print. Liberian flag on front in red, white, and blue. Liberian president's residence on back. C.t.; second title starts p. 15. Inside front cover: "Government of the republic of Liberia." (List of statesmen). First page: "Liberian commissioners to World's Columbian exposition at Chicago, Ill., U.S.A., 1893." ☺. (CPL)

-M-

581. Mexico. *Boletín de la exposición Mexicana en la internacional de Chicago.* Mexico: Oficina tip. de la secretaría de fomento, 1892.

22½x16½. 912 p., xii. Quarter leather spine with gilt print, paper covered marbled boards. Description of the Mexico exhibits at the WCE. Last 12 pages are the index. Subject: Bulletin of the Mexican exhibit. ☺. (NYPL)

582. Mexico. *Boletín de la exposición Mexicana en la internacional de Chicago.* Mexico: Oficina tip. de la secretaría de fomento, 1892; Woodbridge, CT: RPI, 1989.

8°. 80 p. Microfilm. C.t.= t.p. On cover: "numero 1." Item from bound compilation (#581). Subject: Bulletin of the Mexican exhibit. ☺. (SI,NYPL)

583. Mexico. Caballero, Manuel. *Mexico en Chicago : 1893.* [Chicago: Knight, Leonard & Co., ᶜ1893 by Knight, Leonard & Co.].

25x30. 304, (2) p., illus. Quarter red morocco over orange-red silk, gilt on spine, t.p. lithographed in colors. Text in English and Spanish. First p. of each chapter has background design in a color.
---- Also listed: 463 p. total including plates.
P→   (csuf,NYPL)

584. Mexico. Comisión Geográfico Exploradora. Díaz, Agustín. ... *Comisión geográfico-exploradora de la República Mexicana. Catálogo de los objetos que componen el contingente de la Comisión, precedido de algunas notas sobre su organización y trabajos.* Xalapa-Enriquez: Tipografia de la Comisión Geográfico-exploradora, 1893; Woodbridge, CT: RPI, 1989.

26½x22. 24 p. + 43 plates one side only. Includes maps, plans, tables, diagrams in colors black, red, and green. Dark tan wraps, black print. C.t.= t.p. At head of title: "Exposición internacional Colombina de Chicago en 1893." Agustín Díaz was engineering director. Trans: Geographical exploration commission of Mexico. Catalog of the objects which compose the divisions of the commission, with annotations about the organization and its works. ☺. (PU,LC,SI,TU,WiHx)

585. Mexico. Comisión Mexicana en la Exposicion de Chicago. *Reglamento ecónomic para la Comisión Mexicana en la Exposición Columbina de Chicago.* Mexico [City]: Oficina Tip. de la Secretaria de Fomento, 1893.

22x15. 16 p. Gray-blue wraps with black print. Trans: Economic rules. . (CPL)

586. Mexico. Junta local del Distrito Federal. ... *Explicación de las cuatro reconstrucciones histórico-arqueológicas de las Ciudad de México, en el año de 1519. .... Explanation of the four historical and archeological reconstructions of the City of Mexico, in the year 1519.* Mexico: Imprenta de Aguilar e Hijos, 1893.

15x10½. 15 p. Blue-gray wraps. Spanish and English on opposite pages. At head of title: "Junta local del distrito federal para la exposicion de Chicago: Mexico." ☺. (CPL,NL,WiHx)

587. Mexico. Martínez Baca, Francisco, y Manuel Vergara. *Estudios de Antropologia Criminal : Memoria que por disposicion del superior gobierno del estado de Puebla, presentan, para concurrir á la Exposición International de Chicago.* Puebla: Imprenta, litografia y encuadernacion de Benjamin Lara, 1892.

22½x16. xii, 123 p., 10 *l* of large fold. tables, illus. Quarter leather with mottled paper covered boards. Trans: Studies of criminal anthropology : Memorial for the disposition of a superior government of the state of Puebla, presented to the international exposition for concurrence. ☺.(LC)

588. Mexico. Ministerio de fomento, colonización é industria. ... *Catalogo de las principales obras impresas en la Oficina tipografica de dicha secretaria y que se remiten á la exposición international de Chicago.* México: Oficina tip. de la Secretaria de fomento, 1893.

22½x__. 30 p. Trans: Catalog of the principal books printed by the official printer in the office of said secretary which are forwarded to the international exposition in Chicago. (LC)

589. Mexico. Paz, Ireneo. ... *Correspondencias de Ireneo Paz.* Mexico: "La Patria," 1894.

16°. 120 p. C.t. At head of title: "La exposición International de Chicago." Trans: Writings of Ireneo Paz. (NYPL)

590. [Mexico]. *Premios concedidos a los expositores Mexicanos en la Exposición universal Colombina.* Tipográfica de la Secretaria de Fomento, 1894.

30x__. 47 p. Trans: Awards conferred upon the Mexican exhibitors to the WCE. (UC)

591. Mexico. *Sinopsis de los trabajos desempeñados por la Junta directiva de señoras México correspondiente de la de la exposicion universal de Chicago y por las de los estados y territorios de la república Mexicana.* México: Ofician tipográfica de la secretaría de fomento, 1894.

32x24. 12 p. Other author: Junta directiva de señoras de Mexico correspondiente de la de la Exposición de Chicago. Trans: Synopsis of financial affairs. By Mexican committee of lady managers and Mexican states and territories. ☺. (nwu)

592. Mexico. [Vigil, José María], comp. *Poetisas Mexicanas. Siglos XVI, XVII, XVIII y XIX. Antología formada por encargo de la junta de señoras : correspondiente de la de la [sic] exposición de Chicago.* México: Oficina tip. de la secretaría de fomento, 1893.

32x22. xxxiii, 362 p., ports. Trans: Women Mexican Poets. 16th to 19th century. Anthology formulated by the committee of ladies corresponding with the Exposition in Chicago. Preface by José Mariá Vigil, named in annotation. For 1977 reprint, see #2410. ☺. (LC,BU,UoC,nwu)

593. Monaco. Mackie, A. *Monaco at the World's Columbian Exposition : Chicago, 1893.* [Chicago: 1893].

23½x15½. 23 p. Wraps: cream top half, bottom half red, black print. C.t.= t.p. Mackie was commissioner for Monaco and member of the board of judges. Visitors' handout. Albert I was Prince of Monaco. ☺. (CPL,NYPL,NL)

-N-

594. New South Wales. ... *Catalogue of New South Wales Exhibits. Department of Woman's Work.* Sydney: Charles Potter, Government Printer, 1893.

24½x15½. Pages 717-42, teal blue wraps, black print. C.t. At head of title: "World's Columbian Exposition, Chicago, 1893." (CHx)

595. New South Wales. New South Wales Commissioners. Brewer, F. C. ... *The drama and music in New South Wales.* Sydney: Charles Potter, government printer, 1892; Woodbridge, CT: RPI, 1989.

ca. 23x14½. 95 p. Microfilm. At head of title: "Published by Authority of the New South Wales Commissioners for the World's Columbian Exposition, Chicago, 1893." ☺. (SI)

596. New South Wales. New South Wales Commissioners. ... *Catalogue of New South Wales exhibits. Department A. Agriculture, food and its accessories, machinery and appliances.* Sydney: Charles Potter, Government Printer, 1893; Woodbridge, CT: RPI, 1989.

23½x13½. 138 p. Teal blue wraps, black print. At head of title: "World's Columbian Exposition, Chicago, 1893." C.t.= t.p. Detailed account of wools, grasses, etc., by exhibiter and by district. ☺. (ALB,CPL,SI,NYPL)

597. New South Wales. New South Wales Commissioners. ... *Catalogue of New South Wales Exhibits. Department E. Mines, mining, and metallurgy.* Sydney: Charles Potter, Government Printer, 1893; Woodbridge, CT: RPI, 1989.

24½x15½. Pages 216-369, tables, index. Pink wraps. At head of title: "World's Columbian Exposition, Chicago, 1893." C.t. ☺. (SI,NYPL)

598. New South Wales. New South Wales Commissioners. ... *Catalogue of New South Wales Exhibits. Department G. Transportation, railways, vessels, vehicles.* Sydney: Charles Potter, government printer, 1893; Woodbridge, CT: RPI, 1989.

> Pages 386-403. Microfilm. (SI)

599. New South Wales. New South Wales Commissioners. *Catalogue of New South Wales exhibits. Department L. Liberal arts, education, literature, engineering, public works, music and drama.* Sydney: C. Potter, printer, 1893.

> 8°. Pages 443-642. (NYPL)

600. New South Wales. New South Wales Commissioners. ... *Catalogue of New South Wales Exhibits. Department N. Forestry.* Sydney: Charles Potter, Government Printer, 1893.

> 24½x16. p. 678-714. Bright green wraps, black print. Describes large display of woods, gums, baskets, etc. At head of title: "World's Columbian Exposition, Chicago, 1893." ☉. (NYPL)

601. New South Wales. New South Wales Commissioners ... *Catalogue of the exhibits in the New South Wales courts.* Sydney: Charles Potter, government printer, 1893; Woodbridge, CT: RPI, 1989.

> 25x16. viii, 782 p. Red pebbled cloth hc, no printing on cover. At head of title: "World's Columbian Exposition, Chicago, 1893." ☉. (UND,LC,SI,UoC,NL,nwu,WiHx)

602. New South Wales. New South Wales Commissioners. Coghlan, T. A. ... *Sheep and wool in New South Wales, with history and growth of the pastoral industry of the colony as regards both these items of production.* Sydney: Charles Potter, government printer, 1893.

> 21½x14. 23 p., many tables, frontis: black and red bar graph. Pink wraps, black print and design. At head of title: "Published by Authority of the New South Wales Commissioners for the World's Columbian Exposition, Chicago, 1893." C.t.= t.p. Coghlan was government statistician. ☉. (LC,NL)

603. New South Wales. New South Wales Commissioners. Cohen, Philip. ... *The marine fish and fisheries of New South Wales, past and present, in their commercial aspect.* Sydney: Charles Potter, government printer, 1892; Woodbridge, CT: RPI, 1989.

> ca. 24x15. 30 p., fold. map. Microfilm. At head of title: "Published by Authority of the New South Wales Commissioners for the World's Columbian Exposition, Chicago, 1893." ☉. (SI)

604. New South Wales. New South Wales Commissioners. Department of Mines. ... *Extracts from the annual report of the under secretary for mines ... for the year 1892.* Sydney: Charles Potter, government printer, 1893; Woodbridge, CT: RPI, 1989.

> ca. 22½x14. 85 p., tables. Microfilm. At head of title: "Published by Authority of the New South Wales Commissioners for the World's Columbian Exposition, Chicago, 1893." ☉. (SI)

605. New South Wales. New South Wales Commissioners. Fraser, John. ... *The Aborigines of New South Wales.* Sydney: Charles Potter, government printer, 1892; Woodbridge, CT: RPI, 1989.

ca. 22½x14. 102 p., illus, tables, maps. Microfilm. At head of title: "Published by Authority of the New South Wales Commissioners for the World's Columbian Exposition, Chicago, 1893." ☉ . (SI,UDe,OC)

606. New South Wales. New South Wales Commissioners. Gill, William Wyatt. ... *The South Pacific and New Guinea : past and present; with notes on the Hervey group, an illustrative song and various myths.* Sydney: Charles Potter, government printer, 1892; Woodbridge, CT: RPI, 1989.

ca. 23x14½. 38 p. Microfilm. At head of title: "Published by Authority of the New South Wales Commissioners for the World's Columbian Exposition, Chicago, 1893." ☉ . (SI,OC)

607. New South Wales. New South Wales Commissioners. [Greville, Edward], comp. ... *New South Wales: statistics, history, and resources.* [Sydney: Yearbook of Australia Publishing Co., ltd.], n.d.; Woodbridge, CT: RPI, 1989.

22x14. 160 p. Green wraps, black print and design, large fold. map of New South Wales tipped in behind front cover, tables. At head of title: "Published by Authority of the Commissioners for New South Wales." Below title: "Compiled by the Editor [Edward Greville] of 'The Year Book of Australia' for circulation by the executive commissioner for New South Wales at the World's Columbian Exposition, Chicago, 1893." ☉ . (KyU,LC,SI,NYPL,USD,SLP,UoC,NL,nwu)

608. New South Wales. New South Wales Commissioners. Hanson, William. ... *Geographical encyclopædia of New South Wales, including the counties, towns, and villages, within the colony, with ... map, and diagram of light-houses on the coast.* Sydney: Charles Potter, government printer, 1892; Woodbridge, CT: RPI, 1989.

24x15. Fold. map, 4 *l*, 462 p., 5 *l*. Front color map shows the location of coastal light houses. At head of title: "Published by Authority of the Government of New South Wales for the World's Columbian Exposition, Chicago, 1893." A <u>complete</u> work on New South Wales! ☉ . (LC,SI,SLP,NL)

609. New South Wales. New South Wales Commissioners. Hyman, Coleman P. ... *An Account of the Coins, Coinages, and Currency of Australasia.* Sydney: Charles Potter, government printer, 1893.

24x__. 2 *l*, (vii)-viii, (2), 159 p. facsimiles. At head of title: Published by Authority of the New South Wales Commissioners for the World's Columbian Exposition, Chicago, 1893." ☉ . (SLP)

610. New South Wales. New South Wales Commissioners. Hyman, Coleman P., exhibitor. ... *Catalogue of Coins, Coinages, and Currency of Australasia, with specimens of medals.* Sydney: Charles Potter, government printer, ᶜ1893; Woodbridge, CT: RPI, 1989.

24½x15½. 1 *l*, 17 p. Sea foam green wraps, black print. C.t.= t.p. At head of title: "Published by Authority of the New South Wales Commissioners for the World's Columbian Exposition, Chicago, 1893." ☉ . (LC,SI)

611. New South Wales. New South Wales Commissioners. Miller, George. ... *The Prison system of New South Wales.* Sydney: Charles Potter, government printer, 1893; Woodbridge, CT: RPI, 1989.

ca. 23½x15. 4 p. Microfilm. At head of title: "Published by Authority of the New South Wales Commissioners for the World's Columbian Exposition, Chicago, 1893." ☉ . (SI)

612. New South Wales. New South Wales Commissioners. ... *New South Wales wool exhibits arranged according to wool districts.* Sydney: Charles Potter, Government Printer, 1893; Woodbridge, CT: RPI, 1989.

    ca. 23½x15. 19 p. Microfilm. At head of title: "Published by Authority of the New South Wales Commissioners for the World's Columbian Exposition, Chicago, 1893." Also ahead of title: "World's Columbian Exposition, Chicago, 1893." ⊜ . (SI)

613. New South Wales. New South Wales Commissioners. Ogilby, J. Douglas. ... *Edible Fishes and Crustaceans of New South Wales.* Sydney: Charles Potter, government printer, 1893; Woodbridge, CT: RPI, 1989.

    ca. 24½x15. 212 p., (51 plates). Microfilm. At head of title: "Published by Authority of the New South Wales Commissioners for the World's Columbian Exposition, Chicago, 1893." ⊜ . (SI,UMi)

614. New South Wales. New South Wales Commissioners. O'Sullivan, E[dwin] W[illiam], comp. ... *Social, industrial, political, and co-operative associations, Etc., in New South Wales, Australia.* Sydney: Charles Potter, Government Printers, 1892 ['1892]; Woodbridge, CT: RPI, 1989.

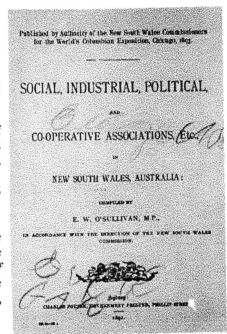

    24½x15. iv, 24 p. Light blue wraps, black print. At head of title: "Published by Authority of the New South Wales Commissioners for the World's Columbian Exposition, Chicago, 1893."

P→   ⊜ . (GLD,csuf,SI,NYPL) $15 - 35

615. New South Wales. New South Wales Commissioners. *Pamphlets issued by the New South Wales Commissioners for the World's Columbian exposition, Chicago, 1893, for the Information of Visitors to the Exhibition, the American Public, and others interested.* 2 vol. Sydney: Charles Potter, government printer, 1893.

    The 2 vols have identical t.p. and are compilations of pamphlets issued separately and given out at the Fair.
    Vol I: 22½x14½. Separately paged, many with fold. maps, ca. 5 cm thick.
    Vol II: 22½x14½. Separately paged, many with fold. maps, ca. 9 cm thick. ⊜ . (LC,UoC)

616. New South Wales. New South Wales Commissioners. Pulsford, Edward. ... *The rise, progress, and present position of trade and commerce in New South Wales.* Sydney: Charles Potter, government printer, 1892.

    ca. 23½x13½. 51 p. Microfilm. At head of title: "Published by Authority of the New South Wales Commissioners for the World's Columbian Exposition, Chicago, 1893." ⊜ . (SI)

617. New South Wales. New South Wales Commissioners. Russell, H. C. ... *Physical geography and climate of New South Wales.* 2nd ed. Sydney: Charles Potter, government printer, 1892; Woodbridge, CT: RPI, 1989.

ca. 24x14. 35 p., tables, charts, maps. Microfilm. At head of title: "Published by Authority of the New South Wales Commissioners for the World's Columbian Exposition, Chicago, 1893." ☻ . (SI)

618. New South Wales. New South Wales Commissioners. Thompson, Lindsay G. ... *History of the fisheries of New South Wales : with a sketch of the laws by which they have been regulated ...* Sydney: Charles Potter government printer, 1893; Woodbridge, CT: RPI, 1989.

ca. 23½x14½. 126 p., illus, tables, color maps. Microfilm. At head of title: "Published by Authority of the New South Wales Commissioners for the World's Columbian Exposition, Chicago, 1893." ☻ . (SI,UMi,OC)

619. New South Wales. New South Wales Commissioners. Tregarthen, Greville. ... *A sketch of the progress and resources of New South Wales.* Sydney: Charles Potter government printer, 1893; Woodbridge, CT: RPI, 1989.

ca. 23½x15. 47 p., tables, (10) charts. Microfilm. At head of title: "Published by Authority of the New South Wales Commissioners for the World's Columbian Exposition, Chicago, 1893." ☻ . (SI)

620. New South Wales. New South Wales Commissioners. Warren, W[illiam] H[enry]. ... *Australian timbers.* Sydney: Charles Potter, government printer, 1892.

24x14½. 3 *l*, 67 p. includes tables, frontis (fold. map), 44 (i.e. 45) plates (36 folding). At head of title: "Published by authority of the New South Wales Commissioners for the World's Columbian Exposition, Chicago, 1893." ☻ . (LC,OSU,UTn,UMi,NYSt)

621. New South Wales. ... *Report of the Executive Commissioner for New South Wales to the World's Columbian Exposition, Chicago, 1893. Presented to Parliament by Command.* Sydney: Charles Potter, government printer, 1894.

33x21½. iv, 671 p., 120 *l*, 1 map. Gray paper covered hc, black print. At top of title page: "1894. (Second session.) New South Wales." Other author: Executive Commissioner to the World's Columbian Exposition. ☻ . (UoC,NHSt)

622. Norway. Andersen, Magnus. *Vikingefærden : en illustreret beskrivelse af "Vikings" reise i 1893.* Kristiania: Eget forlag [self published], 1895.

22x14½. 1 *l*, 480 p., xxix, 1 *l*. Pretty multicolor litho wraps with the Norwegian Viking ship replica sailing into harbor. The replica was sailed to the WCE. Detailed account of its construction for the WF; a reminder that the Vikings landed in America <u>before</u> Columbus? The replica arrived in Chicago on July 12, 1893, was sunk in a Chicago storm on Sept. 5, 1894, after the Fair, raised, and then given to the Field Museum in Chicago. For other Andersen entries, see #1024, #1542, #2313, and #2415. Trans: Viking travels : an illustrated account of the "Viking" trip in 1893.
---- Also listed: 1 *l*, 496, xxix, (2) p.
☻ . (CHx,LC,UoC)

623. Norway. Anderssen, Joh[anne]s. *Stipendie-reise til verdensudstillingen i Chikago 1893 : indberetning til den kongelige norske regjerings departement for det indre.* Christiania og Kjøbenhavn: Alb. Cammermeyers forlag, n.d.

21½x14½. vii, 127 p., illus, port, table. No frontis but port of Anderssen before p. 1. Black cloth hc. In Norwegian. Trans: Fellowship trip to the WCE : A report to the Royal Norwegian Dept of the Interior. ☻ . (nwu)

624. Norway. *Catalogue of the Exhibit of Norway at the World's Columbian Exposition, Chicago, 1893.* Chicago: John Anderson Publishing Co., 1893; Woodbridge, CT: RPI, 1989.

22½x15½. 1 *l*, (5)-84 p., illus. Sand wraps. First *l* is a frontis illus of the Norway Pavilion, patterned after a 12th century Stavkirke (stave church). The Norwegian Women's Rights Association had an exhibit in the Woman's Bldg.
☻ . (KyU,CHx,SI,NL)

☞ The Norway Bldg was built in Trondheim, Norway, for the WCE. After the Fair, it was moved to Blue Mounds, Wisconsin, where it is currently a part of the "Little Norway" outdoor museum. It looks today as it did 100 years ago; some refurbishing will take place in preparation for its centennial. A book is being written on the history of the Norway Bldg (see #2322). P→

-P-

625. Paraguay. Comision Central. Aceval, Benjamin. *República del Paraguay : Apuntes geograficos e historicos.* Asuncion: Imp. de La Democracia, 1893.

25½x17½. 62 p. includes folded tables. Salmon wraps with black print, string sewn. C.t.= t.p. Aceval was president of Paraguay's WCE commission. Trans: Republic of Paraguay : Geographical and historical notes. Lists climate, products, product value, etc.
---- 25½x16½. 45 p. + 3 folded tables.
☻ . (LC,NYPL,UoC)

626. Peru. Ministerio de Gobierno y poliofa. *Reglas, datos y lista de premios para la seccion de ganila? en pie la Exposicion Universal Columbiana en Chicago, Illinois, Estados Unidos de America, 1893.* Lima: Imp. del Estado, 1892.

4°. 24 p., 1 *l*. Rules, regulations and awards for the section. (NYPL)

627. Portugal. Society of Portuguese Civil Engineers. ... *Portugal : contribution of the society of Portuguese civil engineers : [Associação dos Engenheiros civis portuguezes] : descriptive catalogue of the collection of albuns* [sic]*, memoirs and designs exhibited.* Lisbon: National printing office, 1893; Woodbridge, CT: RPI, 1989.

25½x16½. (2), 187 p. At head of title: "World's Columbian exposition: Engineering congress at Chicago : 1893." ☻ . (SI,NYPL,UoC)

628. Puerto Rico. Valle, José G. Del. *Puerto-Rico. Chicago. Trabajos descriptivos y de investigaciones criticas.* N.p.: n.p., 1895.

19x13½. xi, 1 *l*, (15)-233 p., 4 *l*. Pale light green textured wraps, black and red print, pulp pages. Describes: Chicago, the WCE, and Puerto Rico's exhibits. Preface: Don Alejandro Onfiesta. Trans: Descriptive works and critiques. ☺ . (LC,NYSt)

-R-

> For Russian citations, if the title page is in Cyrillic, the format is as follows: Cyrillic [Romanized Russian (if title found catalogued as such) \ English translation]. This sequence holds for author, title, and publication information.

629. Russia. ... *Account of the ore deposits, lead, zinc, silver, gold, manganese, bismuth, iron, at the estate Nagolchik owned by Glebov, A. engineer in the Taganrog region, province of the don Cossacks, Russia. With explanatory drawings.* S.- Petersburg: Tipografia P. P. Soikin, 1893.

24½x__. 27 p., 2 folding diagrams. (UC)

630. Russia. ... *Catalogue of exhibits of the Imperial Russian state paper manufactury.* St.-Petersburg: Printed at the Imperial State Paper Manufactory, 1893; Woodbridge, CT: RPI, 1989.

22½x15½. 18 p. Gray wraps, dark brown print. C.t.= t.p. At head of title: "World's Columbian Fair, Chicago 1893." ☺ . (ALB,CPL,SI,F,NL,WM) $20 - 30

631. Russia. ... *СИБИРЬ И ВЕЛИКАЯ СИБИРСКАЯ ЖЕЛѢЗНАЯ ДОРОГА* [Siberia and the Great Siberian Railway]. С.-Петербургъ: Типографія И. А. Ефрона [Published by I. A. Yefron], 1896.

26½x18. (4) p. ads, 1 *l*, (6) p., (v)-viii table of contents, 283 p., folding map tipped in following p. 283, (20) p. ads. Light rose wraps, black print and small design. At head of title translates: Ministry of Finance : Dept of Trade and Manufactures. UoC: Bound for preservation with spine title: Russia Department Torgovli i Manufaktur 1896. ☺ . (UoC)

632. Russia. ... *Статисстическій обзоръ желѣзныхъ дорогъ и внутрен-нихъ водныхъ путей,* ... [Statistical Survey of Railways and Water Ways in Russia]. ___: [Statistics Department of Ministry of Information], 189_.

8°. 98 p., map. At head of title (in Cyrillic) trans: World's Columbian Exposition 1893 in Chicago. (BM)

633. Russia. Department of Trade and Manufactures Ministry of Finance. *The industries of Russia : ... for the World's Columbian exposition at Chicago.* Ed. of the English translation John Martin Crawford. 5 vol. St Petersburg: [Trenke & Fusnot, printers (and others)], 1893; Woodbridge, CT: RPI, 1989.

5 vol in 4: 26½x16½. Maps (part fold., part color) diagrams, facsimiles. The ellipse in the title stands for each of the titles of the 5 vols:
Vol I and II: *Manufactures and trade* ... liv, fold. color map, 576 p.
Vol III: *Agriculture and forestry* ... (published by the Department of Agriculture). xxxii, 487 p.
Vol IV: *Mining and metallurgy* ... ix, 97 p.

Vol V: *Siberia and the great Siberian railway* ... xii, 265 p. Color map of Russia showing the Siberian RR tipped in at back cover.

---- 24x17. 5 vol in 3. Half red leather with marbled paper covered boards, peach end papers. Vols I and II printed by Trenke & Fusnot; vols III and IV printed by W. Kirschbaum; vol V printed by E. A. Evdokimov. Vols IV and V bound together but have separate t.p.

---- 25½x18. 5 vol in 3 (Vols I/II; Vols III/IV, Vol V). Red cloth hc with black print and straight line border design, gilt lettering on spine, speckled edges. At head of c.t.: "World's Columbian Exposition 1893 at Chicago." Vol I: XV, LIV, 280 p.; vol II: (2), I-II, 281-576 p.; vol III: (I)-XXXII, 487 p. + (1) p. errata; vol IV: (I)-IX, 97 p. + (1) p. errata; vol V: (I)-XII, 265 p.

⊗ . (UWa,SI,NYPL,BCM,OSU,UDe,UMi,OC)

634. Russia. Депавтамента Торговли и Мануфактуръ Министерства Финансовъ [Department torgovli i manufaktur ministerstvo finansov \ Department of Trade and Manufacture of the Ministry of Finances]. ... *ФАБРИЧНО-ЗАВОДСКАЯ ПРОМЫШЛЕННОСТЬ: и ТОРГОВЛЯ РОССІИ.* ... [Fabrichno-zavodskaia promyshlennost' i torqovlia Rossii. \ Industry and Commerce of Russia]. 2 vol. С.-Петербургъ [St. Petersburg]: Типографія В. С. БалаЩева и В. Ф. Демакова [Published by V. S. Balashev and V. F. Demakov], 1893.

26x18½. 2 *l*, 60, 334 p.; 351 p. Folding colored map. Half leather, gilt print, speckled edges. At head of title translates: World's Columbian Exposition 1893 at Chicago.   ⊗ . (PU,UoC)

635. Russia. *Detailed list of articles exposed by the St. Petersburg Metallic Works at the World's Columbian Exposition in 1893 at Chikago, U. S. A.* S.-Petersburg: n.p., 1893.

23x16. (9) p. with 1 plate + 5 p. plates. Tan wraps, black design, brown and black print. B/w boiler illus on back cover. C.t.: "St. Petersburg Metallic Works. At the World's Columbian Exposition at Chicago. 1893." In English.   ⊗ . (LC)

636. Russia. Высочайше учрежденной Коммиссіи по участію Россіи [General'nyi kommisar russkago otdiela vsemïrnoï Kolumbovoi vsytavki v Chicago. \ Imperial Russian Commission for the Participation of Russia]. ... *УКАЗАТЕЛЬ : РУССКАГО ОТДѢЛА.* ... [Ukazatel' Russkago otdiela \ Catalogue of the Russian section]. С.-Петербургъ [St. Petersburg]: Типографія Е. Евдокимова [Tipographia E. Evodokimova \ Published by Y. Yevdokimov], 1893.

26½x18. (iii)-xii, 578 p. Russian language version of #638. Full cover color litho tipped on hc as in English language version, cloth spine, marbled edges. At head of title: "ВСЕМІРНАЯ КОЛУМБОВА ВЫСТАВКА : 1893 : ГОДА : ВЪ ЧИКАГО." [Vsemirnaia kolumbova vystavka 1893 goda v Chikago. \ World's Columbian Exposition : 1893 : in Chicago.]

P→   ⊗ . (LC,UoC,NL)

637. Russia. Глуховского, П. И. [Glukhovskoj, P. I.]. ... *ОТЧЕТЪ : ГЕНЕРАЛЬНАГО КОММИСАРА РУССКАГО ОТДѢЛА : ВСЕМІРНОЙ КОЛУМБОВОЙ ВЫСТАВКЙ ВЪ ЧИКАГО* [Otchet : General'nago kommisara Russkogo otdela Vsemirnoi kolumbovoi vystavki v Chikago \ Report : of the

commissioner general of the Russian section at the World's Columbian Exposition in Chicago]. С.-Петербургъ [S.-Petersburg]: Типографія В. Киршбаума [Tipografiia V. Kirshbauma \ Published by V. Kirshbaum], 1895; Woodbridge, CT: RPI, 1989.

28½x20½. 2 *l*, ii, 210 p. + many unpaged plates with tissue guards. At head of title (Romanized): "Ego Vysokoprevoskhoditel'stvu gospodinu Ministru finansov Tainomu sovietniku S.IU. Vitte." Found in card catalogs under "Ministerstvo finansov."
---- 29½x22. Beautiful blind stamped calf on heavy boards, gilt edges, heavy satin end papers. Best of the printers' and binders' art!
⊚ . (LC,CHx,SI,UMi,UoC,AIC)

638. Russia. Imperial Russian Commission for the participation of Russia. ... *Catalogue of the Russian section.* S.-Petersburg: [For the Commission by I. Libermann and P. Soikin], 1893.

26x18. xv, 572 p. Tan (or blue-gray) cloth spine over tan paper hc, black print on spine. Beautiful multicolor litho tipped-in on front cover. In English by I. Libermann and P. Soikin, printers. At head of title: "World's Columbian exposition : 1893 : Chicago." Contents: list of the Imperial Commission, Ladies Committee, and delegates; comparison of Russian and foreign money and measures and lists of Russian exhibitors and exhibits. Card catalog author: General'nyi kommisar russkago otdiela vsemïrnoï Kolumbovoi vsytavki v Chicago. English version of #636.
P→ ⊚ . (GLD,KU,UND,KyU,csuf,UNe,CHx,NYPL,F, $40 - 80
S,TnSt,BCM,OSU,LMi,USD,UTn,UMi,NYSt,RPB,nwu)

639. Russia. Ismailoff, Theo[dore]. ... *Russian Horses.* Chicago: [Regan printing house], 1893; Woodbridge, CT: RPI, 1989.

19x13½. (2)-29 p. Rust wraps, black print. At head of title: "World's Columbian exposition." C.t.= t.p. Contains condensed catalog of the Russian horse barn at the WCE. ⊚ . (CHx,SI,BU,S)

640. Russia. Kirpichev, V. L. ... ____. [... *Otchet o komandirovkie v Sievernuiu Ameriku* \ Report on a Business Trip to North America]. S.-Peterburg: [Izd. Departamenta torgovli i manufaktur Ministerstva finansov \ Published by Department of Trade and Manufactures of the Ministry of Finances], 1895.

25x__. 69 p., 8 *l* of plates, illus. C.t. At head of title (Romanized): "Vsemirnaia Kolumbova vystavka v Chikago" \ World's Columbian Exposition at Chicago. (LC,UDe)

641. Russia. Kovalevsky, V. I., ed. Сельское и лѣсное хозяйство Россіи. Съ приложеніемъ *47 картъ и діаграммъ* [Agriculture and Forestry of Russia. With 47 Maps and Diagrams]. ____: [Department of Agriculture Ministry of State Property], 189_.

8°. ii, xxvi, 647 p. (BM)

642. Russia. Леонардъ, Н. [Leonard, N.]. *Въ Чикаго : НА ВЫСТАВКУ!* ... [V Chikago : na vystavku! \ In Chicago to the Exposition!] С.-Петербургъ [S.-Petersburg]: Типографія С. Ф. Яздовскаго и К° [Published by S. F. Yazdovskij], 1893.

18x11. 96 p., map of Chicago, (I)-III, (1) p. Star and stripe design on back cover. Bold cover title: "Въ Чикаго НА ВЫСТАЬКУ! 1893 г. С.П.Б." [In Chicago to the Exposition! 1893, S. P. B.]. ☻ . (LC)

643. Russia. Manufactures of Ivanovo-Voznesensk. Bocharoff, Alexis [Nazarovich]. ... *Russia : City of Ivanovo-Voznesensk, in the government of Vladimir. Information about its Locality and Industries.* Chicago: [P. F. Pettibone], 1893; Woodbridge, CT: RPI, 1989.

30x21. 16 p. including t.p. Tan wraps with navy print and design, text print and illus in navy ink. At head of title: "World's Columbian Exposition of 1893, in Chicago." ☻ . (SI,NL)

644. Russia. Meck, A. K. Von. ... *The Imperial society for promoting Russian commercial shipping : short historical sketch.* Moscow: Printing offices O. Herbeck and Lashkewitch, Znamensky & C°, 1893 [°1893].

30x23. 48 p. + 1 fold. table and 1 fold. color map, multicolor litho stiff wraps. C.t.= t.p. At head of title: "The World's Columbian Exposition in Chicago. Russia's Section." English text. Cyrillic title on back cover. Meck was member of the Council to promote shipping and Director of the Moscow-Kazan Railway Company.

P→   ☻ . (UoC)

645. Russia. Мельникова, Н. П. [Melnikov, N. P.]. ... *ДВА НОВЫХЪ РАСТЕНІЯ : для культуры въ россіи : (Панъ-корнъ и Пинодъ)* [Two new plants for Russia: Popcorn and Peanuts]. Одесса [Odessa]: Типографія "Одесскихъ Новостей" [Typographia Odesskichi Novosteii \ Published by Odesskie Novosti], 1893; Woodbridge, CT: RPI, 1989.

ca. 22½x15. 16 p., illus. Microfilm. Cyrillic at head of title translates to: World's Fair at Chicago, 1893. ☻ . (SI)

646. Russia. Мельникова, Н. П. [Melnikov, N. P.]. *Чудеса : Высмаьки Въ Чикаго* [Wonders of the Exposition in Chicago]. Одесса [Odessa]: Типографія "Одесскихъ Новостей" [Published by Odesskie Novosti], 1893; Woodbridge, CT: RPI, 1989.

ca. 22½x15. 70, 96 p. including illus. In Russian.   ☻ . (SI)

647. Russia. [Ministerstvo narodnogo prosvieshcheniia]. *The Russian Ministry of public education at the World's Columbian exposition - Report and Catalogue.* St. Petersburg: [Impr. Trenké et Fusnot], 1893.

24x16½. 2 *l*, 64 p. Dark gold hc with maroon spine, multicolor design on cover. Detailed report of public education in Russia. No photos or drawings. (LC,F)

$25 - 40

648. Russia. [Ministerstvo Putei Soobsheheniya. Otdyel Statistiki i Kartografii.] ... *Statistical survey of railways and internal water ways* ... St. Petersburg: 1893.

4°. 32+ p. (incomplete). At head of title: "World's Columbian Exposition, Chicago, 1893. Russia. Ministry of Ways of Communication, Statistical Section." Appended to this survey is a list of the Statistical Section presented at the WCE.   (NYPL,UMi)

649. Russia. Р., Е. [R., Е.]. *ЧИКАГО.* ... [Chicago. ...]. ___: Типо-Литографія В. А. Вацлика [Typo-Lithography V. A. Vaclik], 1893.

15½x11. 133, (3) p. of ads at back. Maize wraps. On cover below title translates: An illustrated guide to the WCE with detailed reports about transportation on railroad and on ocean liners with indication of fare prices. Detailed description of travel and of the city of Chicago and the exposition.   ⊚ . (CHx)

650. Russia. *The petroleum industry of Baku and Nobel Brothers petroleum production company. June, 1893.* St. Petersburg: Trenké & Fusnot, 1893.

25½x__. 20 p., 3 charts laid in, map laid in.   (ALB)

651. Russia. Плискаго, Н. [Pliskij, Nikolai]. *Подробный Путеводитель : на Всемірную Колумбову Выставку : въ Чикаго 1893 года.* ... [Podrobnyi putevoditel' : na Vsemirnuiu Kolumbovu vystavku : v Chikago 1893 goda : s prilozheniem anglo-russkikh razgovorov spetsial'no sostavlennykh dlia lits neznaiushchikh angliiskago iazyka, s kartoiu puti. \ A Detailed Guide of the World's Columbian Exposition in Chicago, 1893]. С.-Петербургъ [S.-Petersburg]: n.p. [Tipo-lit. "Stefanov i Kachka"], 1893.

17½x12½. 173 p. Light green flecked wraps, black print and design. Pages run: (1)-32, 49-64, 49-125, 2 *l*, (I)-III, 1-32, 5 , (I)-III, 1 fold out *l*. In Russian.   ⊚ . (LC)

652. Russia. *Russie : bureau des dames institué par ordre de s. m. l'impératrice. Section de Moscou. Sous le patronage de s. i. madame la G-de duchess Élisabeth. L'oeuvre de la femme a Moscou.* Moscou: Imprimerie de A. Mamontoff & C°, 1893.

22x14½. 2 *l*, 1-122 p. Light blue flecked wraps, black print. C.t.= t.p. In French. Trans: Russia: Bureau of women founded by order of Empress S. M. Moscow section. Under the patronage of ... duchess Elizabeth. The works (complete works) of the women of Moscow.   ⊚ . (NL)

653. Russia. *St. Olga Hospital for Children, Moscow.* Moscow, И.Н. Кушнеревъ [I. N. Kishnerev], 1893.

26x__. 8 p. T.p. and c.t. in English, Russian, French, and German. At head of title: "1893." (ALB)

654. Russia. ... *A short historical sketch of the labours of the Imperial Russian Technical Society, from its foundation to Jan. 1st. 1893.* St. Petersburgh: Printed by R. Golicke, 1893.

24x16. 40 p. of pulp. Pale olive wraps with black print. C.t. Describes (in English) the organization in 1866, and its involvement with schools. At head of title: "World's Columbian exposition Chicago 1893."   ⊚ . (LC)

655. Russia. War Department. ... *Sketch of the articles exposed by the War Department at the World's Columbian exposition of 1893 at Chicago.* St.-Petersburg: Military Typography (in the building of the General Staff), 1893.

> 25x17. (2), 54 p. Wraps, black lettering. At head of title: "World's Columbian Exposition of 1893 at Chicago, U.S.A. Russia. War Department." May be listed under author: Voennoe Ministerstvo (War Dept). ☻ . (csuf,WM)

-S-

656. Siam. Mayer, Frederic. *The Siamese Exhibits at the World's Columbian Exposition : Chicago 1893.* [Chicago: 1893]; Woodbridge, CT: RPI, 1989.

> 19½x13½. 16 p. Yellowish beige wraps. C.t. Mayer was a member of the Board of Judges at the WCE. ☻ . (KyU,SI,NL,WM)

657. Siam. *Royal Siamese Commission to the World's Columbian Exposition Chicago 1893.* N.p.: n.p., n.d.

> 20x13½. 16 p. Caption title. ☻ . (CPL)

658. South Africa. *Orange Free State (republic.) South Africa.* Chicago: Rand, McNally & Co., Printers, 1893; Woodbridge, CT: RPI, 1989.

> ca. 21x14. 15 p. Microfilm. T.p. also lists index. ☻ . (SI,S,WM)

659. Spain. *Antologia de poetas hispano-americanos.* Madrid: Est. Tip de los Sucs. de Rivadeneyra, 1893.

> Published by the Royal Spanish Academy with an introduction by Marcelino Menédez y Pelayo. Trans: Anthology of Spanish-American poets. (ref)

660. Spain. Aramburu, Fernando. *Apuntes administrativos para el informe de la Comisión Militar sobre la Exposición Universal de 1893 en Chicago...* Madrid: Cuerpo administrativo del ejercito, 1894.

> 8°. 218 p. including diagrams, illus, tables. On cover: "Exposición Universal de Chicago. Material administrativo-militar..." Subject: Military Committee memorandum. (NYPL)

661. Spain. Comisión general de España. ... *Adición al catálogo de la sección Española comprende las islas de Cuba, Puerto Rico y Filipinas.* Madrid: Imprenta de Ricardo Rojas, 1894.

> 24½x17. 124 p. Tan-gray wraps, red and black print. C.t.= t.p. At head of title: "Exposición universal de Chicago de 1893." Trans: Additions to the catalog of the Spanish section including the islands of Cuba, Puerto Rico and the Philippines. ☻ . (CPL)

662. Spain. Comisión general de España. ... *Catálogo de la Sección Española.* Madrid: Imprenta de Ricardo Rojas, 1893.

> 23x17. 1 *l* (t.p.), (v)-xiii, 1053 p., 1 *l*, pulp paper. Tan wraps with red and black print. T.p. in red and black print. At head of title: "Exposición Universal de Chicago de 1893." C.t. Trans: Catalog of the Spanish section. ☻ . (LC,NL)

663. Spain. Comisión general de España. *Relación de los expositores Españoles premiados en la exposición universal de Chicago de 1893.* Madrid: Imprenta de Ricardo Rojas, 1894.

23x16. xv, 818 p., (1) p. corrections. Tan wraps, red and black print. C.t.= t.p. Trans: Account of Spanish exhibitor awards. ☺. (LC,NYPL)

664. Spain. Comisionados del gobierno Español. Faura, Federico, y José Algué. ... *La meteorología en la exposición Colombina de Chicago (1893) : Memoria.* ... Barcelona: Imprenta de Henrich y Compañia en comandita, 1894.

30½x22. 116 p., 1 *l*. Describes the Congress of Meteorology apparatus and instrument exhibits. At head of title: "Observatorio meteorológico de Manila: Dirigido por los PP. de la Compañia de Jesús." Trans: Meteorology at the Columbian exposition of Chicago : Report. ☺. (LC,UMi)

665. Spain. *IV Centenario del descubrimiento de América. Congreso Literario Hispano-Americano.* Madrid: Ext. Tip. de Ricardo Fe, 1893.

Organized by the Association of Spanish writers and artists, and initiated by its president, Señor D. Gaspar Núñez de Arce (from Oct. 31 to Nov. 10, 1892). Trans: The 4th century of the discovery of America. Spanish-American Literary Congress. (ref)

666. Spain. Puig y Valls, Rafael. *Exposición Universal de Chicago : (notas científicas) : Memoria publicada por acuerdo de la Diputación provincial de Barcelona.* Barcelona: Tipografía de la Casa provincial de Caridad, 1896.

ca. 23x16. 274 p., tables. Microfilm. Wraps. C.t. Trans: Scientific notes. Results of the memorial publication of the specially deputized committee of the Province of Barcelona. ☺. (SI)

667. Spain. Puig y Valls, Rafael. ... *Memoria sobre la expositión Colombina de Chicago : desde el punto de vista industrial y commercial.* Barcelona: Tipografia Española, 1895.

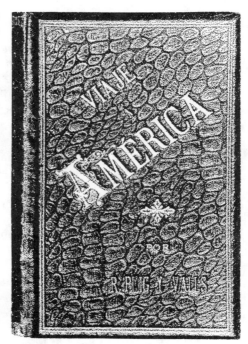

21x13½. 253, (1) p., fold. plan, tables (part fold.). Vellum wraps. At head of title: "Fomento del trabajo nacional." "Tirada especial de 30 ejemplares. Ejemplar numbero 29..." ☺. (CHx,UoC)
---- 24 *l* typescript trans of p. 1-29 and 151-52 by Margaret Scriven. "Memorial on the Chicago Columbian Exposition from an industrial and commercial point of view."--(CHx call: qF38MZ 1893 B1P96a)

668. Spain. Puig y Valls, Rafael. *Viaje á América : Estados Unidos, Exposición Universal de Chicago, México, Cuba y Puerto Rico.* Barcelona: Tipolitografía de Luis Tasso, 1894.

18½x13. 2 vols in 1. 235, (3,2) p., 262 p., 1 *l*, illus. Purple textured cloth hc on beveled boards, gilt, fancy red and gold edge design. Vol 1, p. 43-201: "Chicago and the World's Columbian Exposition." Pretty. Trans: Trip to America : United States, World's exposition in Chicago, Mexico, Cuba and Puerto Rico.

P↑   ◎ . (csuf,CHx)

---- 4 *l* typewritten translation of chapter entitled "Opening of the Exposition," vol 1, p. 77-81. Trans. by Margaret Scriven, 1955.--(CHx call: qE168 P95a)

669. Sweden. Bohlin, K. J. *Genom den stora västern. Minnen från Världsutställningen i Chicago, Klippbärgen, mormonernas Zion, Stillahafskusten och Yellowstoneparken.* Stockholm: K. J. Bohlins Förlag, [1893].

19x13½. 216 p. including frontis of canyon in Sweden, illus. Pretty orange/blue/green/gold and black cover on blue-green cloth, gold print. Personal account of trip to the U.S. including a stay at the Fair. Trans: Memories from the World's Fair in Chicago, mother's mother to zion (means they may have come from Sweden when they came to Chicago), Atlantic Ocean and Yellowstone Park.
◎ . (CHx,LC,NL,WiHx)

670. Sweden. The General Export Association of Sweden. Tesch, Wilhelm, ed. *Catalogue of Swedish Exports.* Stockholm: Royal printing office, P.A. Norstedt & söner, 1892; Woodbridge, CT: RPI, 1989.

ca. 22½x15. vi, 219 p. Microfilm. Tesch was managing director of the association. ◎ . (SI)

671. [Sweden]. Gullberg, Gustaf. *Boken om Chicago : Snabbmålningar från en resa till verldsutställningen 1893.* Stockholm: Fr. Hellbergs Förlag, 1893.

17x11. 1 *l*, (3)-194 p., 1 *l*. Rebound hc. Trans: Book about Chicago : Sketches and pictures from a trip to the World's Fair in 1893. ◎ . (LC,UoC)

672. Sweden. ... *Iron- & Steel Manufactures.* Falun: Falu nya boktr.-aktiebolag, 1892; Woodbridge, CT: RPI, 1989.

ca. 21x13½. 19 p. Microfilm. At head of title: "Stora Kopparbergs Bergslags Aktiebolag: Falun, Sweden. Telegraph Address: Bergslaget, Falun." ◎ . (SI)

673. Sweden. Leijonhufvud, Sigrid, och Sigrid Brithelli. *Kvinnan inom Svenska litteraturen : intell år 1893 en bibliografi utarbetad med anledning af världsutställningen i Chicago.* Stockholm: Kungl. boktryckeriet. P. A. Norstedt & söner, 1893.

21x13½. 198 p. Tan smooth thin wraps, black print. C.t. In Swedish. Trans: Women in Swedish literature; bibliography to 1893 compiled on the occasion of the WCE. ◎ . (NL)

674. Sweden. *Öfversigt af den Svenska kvinnans sociala ställning : utgifven i anledning af verldsutställningen i Chicago : år 1893.* Stockholm: Tryckt hos A. L. Normans boktryckeri - aktiebolag, 1892; New Haven, CT: RPI, 1977.

26½x21. 26 p. Olive green wraps, black print, design in green and maize. Trans: Swedish women's social display which was at the World's Fair. C.t.: "Den Svenska kvinnans sociala stallning." Bound with the English trans (#678), which is an additional 30 p. ◎ . (KU,USF,UNLV,NL)

675. Sweden. *Reports from the Swedish ladies' committee to the World's Columbian exposition at Chicago 1893.* Stockholm: Printed by Central-tryckeriet, 1893; Woodbridge, CT: RPI, 1989.

20½x14. 56, 72, 42, 16 p. The four items bound together are: I. Education; II. Philanthropy; III. Literature and art; IV. The public service, trade and business. ⊚ . (SI,NYPL,UNLV,UDe,UoC)

676. Sweden. The Royal Swedish Commission. Posse, Nils. *Columbian Collection of Essays on Swedish gymnastics.* Boston: Posse Gymnasium, 1896 [°1893].

23x15. 47 p. Gray green wraps, dark green print. C.t.= t.p. Posse was Swedish Commissioner to the WCE, and honorary V.P. to the World's Congress on Physical Education. ⊚ . (csuf)

677. Sweden. The Royal Swedish Commission. *Swedish catalogue.* 2 vol. [Stockholm: Press of Ivar Hæggström, 1893].

Vol I. *Swedish catalogue I. Exhibits. World's Columbian Exposition : 1893. Chicago.*

22x14. xvii, 62 p. Gray wraps, black print and design.

Vol II. *Swedish catalogue II. Statistics. By Dr. S. A. Löfström, Actuary of the Royal Swedish Statistical Central Bureau. World's Columbian exposition : 1893. Chicago.*

22x14. xiii, 240 p. Gray wraps, black print and design.

---- 2 vol in 1. [Stockholm: Press of Ivar Hæggström, 1893]. 21½x13. xvii, 62 p.; xiii, 240 p. Brown cloth hc, gilt. T.p. for vol II states simply: "Statistics." ⊚ . (KyU,csuf,CHx,NYPL,NLC,UoC,NL,WM)

678. Sweden. *The social condition of the Swedish woman. Prepared with a design to the World's Columbian exposition : A.D. 1893.* Stockholm: Printed by A. L Normans boktryckeri - aktiebolag, 1893; New Haven, CT: RPI, 1977.

26½x21. 30 p. Found bound with its English trans (#674). Has its own t.p. ⊚ . (KU,UNLV,NL,WM)

679. Switzerland. Blom, [O.]. *Die Installationen der verschiedenen Länder und das Kunstgewerbe an der Weltausstellung in Chicago.* Bern: F. Haller & Co., 1894.

8°. 35 p. Berichte der schweizerischen Delegierten. (NYPL)

680. Switzerland. Boos-Jegher, [Edward]. *Die Thätighert der Frau in Amerika.* Bern: Muhel A. Büchler, 1894.

8°. 68 p. Berichte der schweizerischen Delegierten zur Weltausstellung in Chicago, 1893. (NYPL)

681. Switzerland. Escher, [R.]., and [A.] Unitlenmier-Shetty. *Mitteilungen aus dem Gebiete des Maschinenwesens.* Bern: F. Hatler & Co., 1894.

8°. 40 p. Berichte der schweizerischen Delegierten zur Weltausstellung in Chicago, 1893. Subject: Information on machinery systems. (NYPL)

682. Switzerland. Geneva. *Notice on Geneva : Watches : Jewelry : Enamels : Musical Boxes : etc. etc.* [Geneva: Haussmann & Lips, 1892?].

15x11. 64 p., illus. Light blue wraps with picture of pine trees, lake, and Geneva in the distance. Lettering and design in black. ☺. (CHx,WM)

683. Switzerland. Genoud, [S.]. *Les metiers et l'industrie domestique à l'Exposition de Chicago et aux Etats Unis.* Fribourg: Imprimerie Galley, 1894.

8°. 28 p. Subject: Handicrafts and domestic industry at the WCE and in the U.S. (NYPL)

684. Switzerland. Hourick, [C.]. *Rapport concernant la petite núcanique et ses applications à la fabrication de l'hurlagerie aux Etats-Unis d'Amerique ...* Chaux-le-Fonds: Imprimerie R. Haefeli & Cie, 1894.

8°. 72 p. Subject: clocks and watches. (NYPL)

685. Switzerland. Hunziker, O[tto]. *Das Schweizerische Schulwesen. Geschichtliche Entwicklung und gegenwärtige Verhältnisse.* Chicago: n.p., 1893; Woodbridge, CT: RPI, 1989.

ca. 23x15½. 46 p. Microfilm. Subject: Swiss school system. Historical development and present circumstances. ☺. (SI,NL)

686. Switzerland. Hunziker, O[tto]. ... *Das Schweizerische Schulwesen. Herausgegeben aus Auftrag des Schweizerischen Departement des Innern anlässlich der Weltausstellung in Chicago 1893.* N.p.: n.p., n.d.

22½x15. (4), 111, (1) p. corrigendum. Light blue flecked wraps, black print and border. Large 1888-91 map tipped in between p. 80-81. Many tables. At head of title: "Union der schweizerischen permanenten Schulausstellungen." Subject: Swiss school system. Presented by order of the Swiss Dept of the Interior on the occasion of the WCE. ☺. (NL)

687. Switzerland. Landolt, J. F. ... *Der Schulunterricht in den Vereinigten Staaten von Amerika.* Bern: Haller'sche Buchdruckerei Fritz Haller & Co., 1895.

23x15½. 44 p. Wraps. C.t.= t.p. At head of title: "Weltausstellung in Chicago, 1893 : Berichte der schweizerischen Delegierten." Subject: School instruction in the U.S.A. ☺. (BPL)

688. Switzerland. Lunge. ... *Die chemische Industrie und die chemisch-technischen Hochschulen in Nord-Amerika.* Bern: Buchdruckerei Michel & Büchler, 1894.

23x15½. 22 p. Wraps. At head of title: "Weltausstellung in Chicago, 1893. Berichte der schweizerischen Delegierten." Dr. Lunge was "Professor am Eldg. Polytechnikum in Zürich." Subject: Chemical industry and trade schools in North America. ☺. (BPL)

689. Switzerland. Meyer, H. ... *Die Amerikanische Seidenindustrie und die Seidenindustrie an der Weltausstellung in Chicago 1893.* Bern: Buchdruckerei Michel & Büchler, 1894.

23x16. 72 p., illus of machines in text. Green wraps with black print and small design border. At head of title: "Weltausstellung in Chicago, 1893. Berichte der schweizerischen Delegierten." C.t.= t.p. Content: Silk manufacture and trade in America and at the WCE. ☺. (NYPL,nwu)

690. Switzerland. Meyer-Baeschlin, and [J.] Leponi. *Architektur, Bruhonstrulitionen und Baueinrichlung in nordamerikanischen Städten.* Bern: F. Haller & Co., 1894.

8°. 44 p. Berichte der schweizerischen Delegierten zur Weltausstellung in Chicago, 1893. Subject: Architecture and the construction industry in North American cities. (NYPL)

691. Switzerland. Meyer-Zschöhbe, [J. L.]. *Die Holzindustrie in Chicago in Beziehung auf Stil, Bearbeitung, Werkzeug, Material und Arbeitsverhältnisse zur Zeit der Weltausstellung in Chicago.* Bern: Michel & Büchler, 1894.

8°. 68 p. Berichte der schweizerischen Delegierten. Subject: The wood industry in Chicago in relation to style, use, tools, materials and facilities. (NYPL)

692. Switzerland. Moss, [H.]. *Die Landwirtsshaft der Vereinigten Staaten von Amerika in ihrem Lande und an der Weltausstellung in Chicago.* Bern: F. Haller & Co., 1894.

8°. 1 *l*, 180 p., 1 *l*. Berichte der schweizerischen Delegierten. Subject: Agriculture in the U.S., its territories and the WCE. (NYPL,BPL)

693. Switzerland. Ritter, Wilhelm. ... *Der brückenbau in den Vereinigten Staaten Americkas. Mit 12 tafeln und 60 textfiguren ...* Bern: F. Haller & Co., 1894; Zürich: A. Raustein, 1895.

23x__. 66 p. illus, plates. At head of title: "Weltausstellung in Chicago, 1893. Berichte der schweizerischen Delegierten." Subject: U.S. bridge construction. (UMi,Yale,RPB)

694. Switzerland. Schmidlin, U. *Das Technische und kommerzielle Bildungswesen in den Vereinigten Staaten Nord-Amerikas.* Bern: Haller'sche Buchdruckerei Fritz Haller & Co., 1894.

23x15½. 49 p. Wraps. C.t.= t.p. At head of title: "Weltausstellung in Chicago, 1893 : Berichte der schweizerischen Delegierten." Subject: Technical and commercial organizations in the U.S. (NYPL,BPL)

695. Switzerland. Schweitzer, [T. O.]. *Die Baumwolle nebst Notizen über deren Kultur und Vërarbeitung in Amerika.* Bern: F. Haller & Co., 1894.

8°. 79 p. Berichte der schweizerischen Delegierten zur Weltausstellung in Chicago, 1893. Subject: Cotton cultivation and processing in America. (NYPL)

696. Switzerland. Schweitzer, [T. O.]. *Kurze Notizen und Betrachtungen über das amerikanische Verkehrswesen.* Bern: F. Haller & Co., 1894.

8°. 39 p. Berichte der schweizerischen Delegierten zur Weltausstellung in Chicago, 1893. Subject: American trade methods. (NYPL,BPL)

697. Switzerland. ... *Switzerland : Official Catalogue of Swiss exhibitors.* N.p.: n.p., n.d

20½x14. 20 p. Gray wraps, black print and design. C.t.= t.p. At head of title: "World's Columbian Exposition 1893 Chicago, Ill."

---- Chaux-de-fonds: Imp. Sauser & Hæ feli, n.d. (2)-20 p. Tan wraps with pale green and black print and design, litho of Daniel Jeanrichard on back cover.
           ◎ . (CPL,CHx,NL,WM)

-T-

698. Trinidad. Trinidad Court of the World's Fair. Clark, Henry James. *"Ïëre," the land of the humming bird, being a sketch of the Island of Trinidad.* Port-of-Spain: Printed at the government printing office, 1893.

21x15½. 3 *l*, 96 p., xxxi, 12 *l* ads, illus, tables. Pale lime wraps, green print and design. C.t.= t.p. Frontis of "Port-of-Spain from the Harbour." xxxi are tables and statistics.
---- Also listed: 2 *l*, 96 p., xxxi.
           ◎ . (LC,UoC,nwu)

699. Turkey. *Souvenir Programme : Turkish Theater : Midway Plaisance : World's Fair, Chicago.* [Chicago: The American Engraving Co., 1893?].

18½x12½. (20) p. including decorative coated wraps, illus, part color. On cover: "Price 10 Cents" and "Pierre Antonius & Co. Managers." C.t.   ◎ . (GLD,csuf,KyU,CHx,F) $25 - 45

-U-

700. Uruguay. Castro, Juan José. *Estudio sobre los ferrocarriles sudamericanos y las grandes líneas internationales publicado bajo los auspicios del Ministerio de fomento de la República O. del Uruguay y enviado á la exposición universal de Chicago.* Montevideo: Imprenta á vapor de la Nación, 1893.

25½x18½. 1 *l*, (5)-651 p., 1 *l* including tables, plates, maps of Uruguay back cover pocket. Spanish version of #701.   ◎ (KU,nwu)

701. Uruguay. Castro, Juan José. *Treatise on the South American railways and the great international lines : published under the auspices of the Ministry of foment of the Oriental republic of Uruguay and sent to the World's exhibition at Chicago.* Montevideo: La Nación steam printing office, 1893.

26½x18. 1 *l* (t.p.), (5)-601 p., 15 numbered diagrams between p. 127 and (129) are not included in pagination. Tan wraps, black print and design. Describes the railroads of Uruguay, Argentine Republic, United States of Brazil, and the republics of Chile, Paraguay, Bolivia and Perú. English version of #700.
---- Also listed: 601 p., 15 plates (2 fold.).
           ◎ . (PU,LC,OSU,USD,ncsu,UMi,UoC,NL,RPB,OC)

702. Uruguay. Comisión del IV Centenario. *Montevideo-Colon : Numero unico: Publicado por la Comisión del iv Centenario del Descubrimiento de América.* Montevideo: Imprento "el siglo ilustrado"; Litografia, fototipia y fotograbado de la escuela nacional de artes y oficios, 1892.

45x32. 126 p., viii, illus, glossy leaves. Very elaborate Columbian memorial folio. Trans: Only number authorized by the 4th century commission of the discovery of America.   ◎ . (LC)

703. Uruguay. Dirección General de Instrucción Pública / Department of Public Schools. *La Instrucción Pública del Uruguay en la exposición Columbina de Chicago / The Public Schools of Uruguay at the Chicago Columbian World's Fair.* Montevideo: Dornaleche y Reyes, printers, 1893; Woodbridge, CT: RPI, 1989.

15½x10. 109 p. includes front cover. Pale blue-green wraps with blue print, pulp pages. Dual language; Spanish and English on alternate pages.
---- Also listed: 111 p.
   © . (SI,NYPL,BM)

704. Uruguay. *1492 á Colon el Circulo de Bellas Artes.* Uruguay: Enrique Rubiños, n.d.

38½x27. 2 *l*, 73 p., 2 *l*, illus, facsimiles, unpaged plates. Tan stiff wraps in charcoal, off-red, and gilt print. Columbus memorial in Spanish. Trans: A brochure of fine arts commemorating Columbus 1492. [Oct. 12, 1893, Columbus Day, was fittingly "Italian Day" at the WCE.] (LC)

705. Uruguay. Peña, Carlos Maria de, and Honore Roustan. *The Oriental Republic of Uruguay at the World's Columbian Exhibition, Chicago, 1893. Geography, rural industries, commerce, general statistics.* Trans. into English by J. J. Rethore. Montevideo: n.p., 1893; Woodbridge, CT: RPI, 1989.

25x17. 54 p., folding colored map. Orange stiff wraps with black print.   © . (csuf,CHx,SI)

-V-

706. Venezuela. ... *Los Estados Unidos de Venezuela en 1893.* Nueva York: Pub. de órden del Gobierno de Venezuela, [1893].

21½x14. 158, (1) p. of index, folding map tipped in behind front cover. Dusty green wraps with black print and design. Frontis: "Edificio de Venezuela en Jackson Park." At head of title: "Exposicion Universal Colombina de Chicago." C.t.= t.p. Essays by Arístides Rojas. Spanish version of #707. Other author: Ministerio de Relaciones Exteriores.   © . (LC,NYPL,TU,UMi)

707. Venezuela. ... *The United States of Venezuela in 1893.* New York: Published by order of the Government of Venezuela [printed by the Caxton Press], [1893]; Woodbridge, CT: RPI, 1989.

21½x14. Folding map, frontis of Venezuela Bldg, 74 p., 2 *l*, 77-149 p., 1 *l*. Two folded color crest plates between pages 108-109. Gray wraps with black print. At head of title: "World's Columbian exposition at Chicago." Historical objects of Venezuela at the WCE; essays by Arístides Rojas at pages (76)-149. English version of #706. Other author: Ministerio de Relaciones Exteriores.
---- Also listed: 22½x__. 154 p.
---- 21½x14½. 74 p., 1 *l*. Without Rojas' essays.
  © . (GLD,SI,NYPL,OSU,LMi,TU,UMi,LSU,UoC,BPL,nwu,RPB,OC) $20 - 38

708. Venezuela. Rojas, Arístides. *Objetos historicos de Venezuela en la exposicion de Chicago : Estudios acerca de ellos.* ... Edicion oficial. Caracas: Imprenta y litografia nacional, 1893.

30½x21. vi, 70 p., 1 *l*. Manila wraps with black print. Venezuela history through the WCE. Trans: Studies about historical objects of Venezuela in the exposition at Chicago.   © . (LC,NYPL,UoC,NL)

Chapter 5

GENERAL

This chapter covers a variety of topics including histories, railroad publications, cookbooks, personal travel accounts, exhibit descriptions, items issued by commercial companies and pamphlets on the Sunday opening/closing debate. Also included are some of the more interesting and high quality advertising pamphlets as samples.

709. Abbot, Willis John. *Carter Henry Harrison : A Memoir.* New York: Dodd, Mead & co., 1895.

> 23x16. 4 *l*, 254 p. + unpaged illus. Navy blue cloth hc, gilt print spine. 1st *l* is frontis of Harrision. Mayor Harrison of Chicago was shot dead at his home by a former city employee after a day at the Fair. ☻ . (BCM)

710. *Acme : The Perfection of all Plastering Material. Acme Cement Plaster : Not a Patent but Nature's Own Mixture.* [Salina, KS?: Acme Cement Plaster Co.?, 1893?]; (Chicago: Palm, Knott & Co., Printers).

> 12½x19. 32 p., illus. Khaki wraps, black print. C.t. This interesting advertising item explains the use of Acme Cement for exterior and interior finishing work on 6 main WCE bldgs. The Acme Co. exhibit was in the Mines and Mining Bldg. Lithos of WCE and other prominent bldgs plastered with Acme material. ☻ . (KU,NL)

711. Adams, Myron. *Open the gates : a discourse delivered by Rev. Myron Adams, Pastor of a Congregational church, May 28, 1893.* Rochester, NY: Milton H. Smith, Publisher, 1893.

> 23x15½. 14, (1) p. On printed wraps: "Open the gates of the Columbian Exposition on Sunday : price 10 cents." ☻ . (UDe,BPL)

712. Adler, Felix. *The Sabbath and the World's fair : lecture delivered by Prof. Felix Adler, before the Society for ethical culture, at Chickering hall, January 29, 1893.* New York: Leimairer & Bro., 1893.

> 20x__. 16 p. (NYPL)

713. *Albany Business College and School of Shorthand, Typewriting, and Telegraphy.* N.p.: n.p, n.d.

> 17x22½. 144 p. Two color cloth hc with embossed print. Replica of official ribbon issued by the WCE at front hinge. Inside book is replica of the College's WCE award certificate designed by Low. ☻ . (S)

714. *All the World at the Fair : Being Representatives of Thirty-seven Nationalities in Gala Costume.* London: Hare & Co. Ltd., [1893].

> 15½x12½. 34 p. Color plates of people in native costumes. Color process: "Chromotypography." ☻ . (S)

715. American Bell Telephone Co. *Exhibit of The American Bell Telephone Co. : electricity building : Columbian exposition : Chicago : 1893.* [Boston: Alfred Mudge & son, printers], n.d.

24½x17. (1)-(10), 11-37 p. Steel gray wraps, black print. Text and illus in navy ink. Two fold. maps of AT&T lines tipped in ahead of back wrap.   ☺ . (NL)

716. *The American Farmers' almanac for 1892 : A compilation of useful ...*   Chicago: Reuben H. Donnelley, publisher, ᶜ1891.

18½x13½. 96 p. including front wrap. Light tan wraps, print and illus in black and gold. Text has information and full page illustrations on the WCE. Top of front cover: "World's Fair Edition."
   ☺ (GLD) $10 - 22

717. *The American Farmers' almanac for 1893. A compilation of useful ...*   Chicago: Reuben H. Donnelley, publisher, ᶜ1892.

18½x13½. 80 p. Wraps.   ☺ . (A) $10 - 22

718. American Jersey Cattle Club. *The Jersey herd at the World's Columbian Exposition, Chicago, 1893. Report of Valancey E. Fuller, superintendent of the herd.*   New York: published by the club, 1894.

23½x17½. 54 p., 1 *l.* Wraps. C.t.   ☺ . (csuf)

719. American Philatelic Association. *American Philatelic Association's exhibit of Postage Stamps at the World's Columbian exposition, Chicago, 1893.*   Birmingham, CT: Press of D. H. Bacon & Co., n.d.

23½x15. 4 *l.* Light green wraps, black print. Print of U.S. Government Bldg on back cover. Information regarding the exhibit and the APA organization.
   ☺ (F,TD) $20 - 45

720. American Philatelic Association. *Catalogue of the American Philatelic Association's loan exhibit of postage stamps to the United States Post Office Department at the World's Columbian Exposition, Chicago, 1893.*   Birmingham, CT: D. H. Bacon & Co., Printers, 1893.

23x15. 68 p. Gray wraps, black and brown print and border. The exhibit was in the Government Bldg which is depicted on the back cover. On cover: "Official catalogue."
---- Dark green cloth hc, gilt print.
   (CHx,F,Yale,TD)   Wraps: $25 - 45
                                                                                              Bound: $65

721. *The American Republic : Discovery--Settlement--Wars--Independence--Constitution--Dissension--Secession Peace. 1492--400 years--1892. Official maps in colors of every state and territory in the Union, showing all railroads, post offices, etc, etc. Also historical and geographical description of each state and territory, with ... and Grand Panorama Main Buildings, World's Columbian exposition.*   Chicago: John W. Iliff & Co., [ᶜ1892 by John W. Iliff]; Woodbridge, CT: RPI, 1989.

37½x30. 100 p., illus. Black print and design on gray hc. For related Iliff item see #811.
---- Compliments of Hermance & co. Fine Shoes, Rockford, IL.
   ☺ . (CHx,SLA,TD)

722. *Art and Decoration in Tissue Paper : Illustrating the many Artistic Uses of Dennison's Crêpe and Tissue Paper ...* Boston, New York, Philadelphia, Chicago, Cincinnati and St. Louis: Dennison Mfg. Co., n.d.

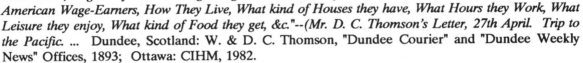

22x15. 1 *l*, 78 p. Glossy wraps illus and printed in black and half tones. Tipped in examples of ca.100 different colors of crepe and tissue paper made by Dennison. Description of napkins on (p. 75): "World's Fair Napkins: printed in different colors: size 16 x 20 [inches], per 100, 60¢." This period craft booklet and catalogue was published ca.1892-93. The authors have the Dennison "Map of Jackson Park" napkin in which the Pier off the Peristyle is "T" form. It turned out to be "I" form in 1893.

P→   ☺ (GLD) $10 - 30

723. *Artisan expedition to the World's fair, Chicago, organized by the Dundee Courier and the Dundee Weekly News. A tour of observation, to get "Information Regarding the Conditions of the American Wage-Earners, How They Live, What kind of Houses they have, What Hours they Work, What Leisure they enjoy, What kind of Food they get, &c."--(Mr. D. C. Thomson's Letter, 27th April. Trip to the Pacific. ...* Dundee, Scotland: W. & D. C. Thomson, "Dundee Courier" and "Dundee Weekly News" Offices, 1893; Ottawa: CIHM, 1982.

24½x15½. viii, 168 p.; (2), 70 p.; 12 p.; illus ports. Bound in burgundy leather, gold print. C.t.: "British artisan expedition to America." Contents: articles from the 2 newspapers published in book form. A book of reference as to the conditions of wage-earners in North America. WCE in Part I, p. 36-48; part II, p. 4-9.   ☺ . (mcg,NLC,HL)

724. Associated Manufacturers of the United States of America. ... *Tin and terne plate exhibit at the World's Columbian Exposition, Chicago, 1893.* N.p.: Press of Tin and Terne, [1893?].

19½x13½. 15, (1) p. Wraps. At head of title: "Associated Manufactures of the United States of America." C.t. On cover: John Jarrett, Secretary. Exhibit was in the South Gallery - Mining Bldg. ["Terne" is a tin/lead alloy used for protective plating.]   ☺ . (csuf)

725. ... *The Audubon : World's Columbian Exposition : Woodlawn Park : Chicago.* [Chicago: The Henry O. Shepard co., printers and binders], n.d.

15½x23. (20) p. on glossy stock includes 4 plates of WF bldgs and 3 floor plans. Elegant pale green wraps with embossed gilt lettering, string tied. Map on inside back wrap shows the location of the Audubon Hotel near the Midway Plaisance. At head of title: "1893." Hotel was to open May 1, 1893. $3.00 per day for 2 people (exclusive of food).

☺ (GLD) $15 - 32

726. *Autographs of prominent men and women.* Chicago: Richmond and Stone, [1893].

13x17. 113 p. Tan wraps, red string tied, green glitter print. Glossy leaves with facsimiles of autographs, a number being associated with the Fair. C.t.= t.p. (CHx)

727. Bailey, L[iberty] H[yde]. *Annuals of Horticulture In North America for the year 1889 : A Witness of Passing Events and a Record of Progress.* New York: Rural Publishing Co., 1890 °1889. ☉ . (LC)

728. Bailey, L[iberty] H[yde]. *Annuals of Horticulture In North America for the year 1893 : A Witness of Passing Events and a Record of Progress : comprising an account of the horticulture of the Columbian Exposition.* New York: Orange Judd Co., 1894 [°1894 by Orange Judd Co.]; Woodbridge, CT: RPI, 1989.

19x13½. 179, (1), 4 p. Dark green cloth hc, blind stamp, gilt spine print, decorative end papers. Describes landscape gardening on the Fair grounds. The plants were labeled in various ways, nearly all of which faded, broke, killed the plant, etc.
---- 17½x12. vii, 179 p., (1) p., illus.
---- 18½x12½. vii, (1), 179, (2), 2-4 p. The final 6 pages are publishers' ads.
☉ . (CPL,LC,SI,OSU,UTn)

729. Baker, J. C. "Marine Department of Exhibits at the World's Columbian Exposition." *Beeson's inland marine guide.* 5th ed. Detroit MI: Harvey C. Beeson, 1892.

24x17. Guide is 200 p. Tan-yellow litho cover with dark red borders around the print and a black spine. The article is on p. 108; illus of the Transportation Exhibit Bldg on p. 109. Baker was Supt., Marine Division of the WCE. ☉ . (MPL)

730. Baldwin Locomotive Works. ... *Exhibit of locomotives by the Baldwin Locomotive Works, Burnham, Williams & Co., Proprietors, Philadelphia, Pa., U.S.A.* Philadelphia: [J. B. Lippincott, °1893].

28x20. 78 p., (1) p., illus. Red cloth hc, gilt print, decorative floral end papers. Frontis of interior of Works. Illus of locomotives displayed. At head of title: "The World's Columbian Exposition, Chicago, Illinois, May--October, 1893." A list of agencies is also found on t.p. ☉ . (CPL,NYPL,HL)

731. Baltimore and Ohio Railroad. *B & O at the World's Fair : A Souvenir With Sylvan Scene Illustrations Along the Line.* Baltimore: Passenger Department. Baltimore and Ohio Railroad, n.d.

28x18½. 3 *l*, 96 p., 3 *l*. White and green cloth hc, gold and silver embossed lily and B & O logo design. Frontis of Administration Bldg. Intended to list ads on the 6 *l*, each entitled "Sylvan Scenes Advertisements." Contains lithographs of WCE bldgs and routes. Spine: "Sylvan scenes."
P→ ☉ (GLD,NYPL,VaHx)

$25 -40

732. Baltimore and Ohio Railroad. Phelps, Henry P. *The World's fair via Baltimore & Ohio R.R. : the sightseeing route to Chicago : through the greatest cities, over the grandest mountains, where railway travel reaches the sublime.* Baltimore: Passenger Department, Baltimore & Ohio R.R., 1893.

17½x21. 92, (2) p. (2) p. are maps. Multicolor wraps with design of Grand Basin and Administration Bldg. Narrative of sight seeing trip from East Coast to Fair grounds. Includes detail of B & O Fair exhibit. ☻. (Sl,F,S,OC,TD) $30 - 55

733. Bancroft, Hubert Howe. *The Book of the Fair : an Historical and Descriptive presentation of the World's Science, Art, and Industry, as viewed through the Columbian Exposition at Chicago in 1893...* 25 pts. bound in 2, 3, 4, or 5 vols. Chicago and San Francisco: The Bancroft Co., 1893 [°1893 by Hubert H. Bancroft]; Chicago and San Francisco: The Bancroft co., publishers, 1895 [°1895 by Hubert H. Bancroft].

Bound: 40½x32. 1 *l*, 1000 p., paged continuously. Various hc bindings: full leather, half leather, cloth, etc.

---- 1893: Found complete in 1, 2, 3, 4, or 5 vols. Heavily illustrated, detailed, written by noted historian of the time. High quality stiff glossy paper. Edges found gilt; also red dyed. T.p. found in red and black print; also black print. [The first parts of this book were printed at the Fair on a Michle Press, located at section 34, column Q-33, Machinery Hall.] Excellent reference on the WCE.
---- 1895: 41½x31. 2 vol. Leather with gilt print and design. Bancroft's signature replica on cover. Vol I: 508 p.
---- Also listed: 1895 Bound. 41x__. 3 vol. Sub-title varies.
---- Also listed: 1893 Subscription set: 45x__. ? 25 subscription parts issued.
*P→ ☻. (GLD,UMKC,CPL,NYPL,F,S,OhHx,TnSt,nwu,BU,ncsu,UTn,NHSt,HL,Yale,TU,UMi,NYSt,UoC,LSU,CoU,A, BPL,UDe,E,RPB,AIC,OC,WM,WiHx,TD,L) $125 - 250

734. ---. ---. Author's edition. 10 vol. Chicago and San Francisco: The Bancroft co., publishers, 1893 [°1893 by Hubert H. Bancroft]; Chicago and San Francisco: The Bancroft co., publishers, 1895.

1893: 57x43½. Author's ed.: a limited 10 vol ed. of 150 signed copies. Proof plates; made from first impression.
---- Also listed: 1895. 57x__. 10 vol.
(CHx,NYPL,UoC) Complete set: $2000 - 3500

735. ---. ---. Columbian edition. 10 parts. Chicago and San Francisco: The Bancroft Co., 1893.

48x37. Paginated continuously, illus, 100 colored plates. Limited ed. 10 color plates per part; descriptive letter-press. Olive cloth hc folios, brown print on each section.
☻ (KyU,CHx,NYPL,OSU,UoC,BPL,TD) Complete set: $700 - 1800

736. ---. ---. Edition de Luxe. 10 vol. Chicago and San Francisco: The Bancroft co., publishers, 1893 [°1893 by Hubert H. Bancroft].

56½x43. White cloth spine and corners, red cloth hc, gilt design in upper left corner is vol number in script, all edges gilt. Paged continuously; e.g., vol one: 2 *l*, 3-100 p. Limited to 400; UoC has no. 9. (UoC,A,AIC) Complete set: $500 - 1000

737. ---. ---. Fin de Siecle edition. 10 vols. Chicago and San Francisco: The Bancroft Co., 1893 [°1893 by Hubert H. Bancroft].

56½x44. 1 *l*, 1000 p. Brown linen spine and tan linen on hard boards with a plain paper dust jackets. T.p. in red and black print. Limited ed. of 950 copies. Contents same as #733. InHx has no. 9; BPL no. 23; GLD no. 126; nwu no. 798.

☺ (GLD,NYPL,InHx,UoC,BPL,nwu,GPL)   Complete set: $300 - 700

738. ---. ---. Imperial edition. 10 vols. Chicago and San Francisco: The Bancroft Co., 1895.

40½x30½. Green cloth hc, dark blue print, gilt edges. Limited to 1,000 copies. TD has no. 107; E no. 115.   (E,TD)

739. ---. ---. Rpt. of 1895. 2 vol. New York: Bounty Books - Crown Publishers, Inc., [1973?].

28½x21½. 1000 p. Smaller than the original.
*   ☺ . (UND,LM,E,NL,TD)

740. [Banks, Charles Eugene]. *The artistic Guide to Chicago and the World's Columbian exposition. : illustrated.* [Chicago]: Columbian Art Co., 1892 [°1891 by R [sic] S. Peale co.]; Chicago: R. S. Peale Co., 1892 [°1891]; Chicago, Philadelphia, Stockton, CA: Monarch Book Co., 1892 [°1891 by R. S. Peale Co.].

Columbian Art: 23x16½. 1 *l*, 421 p. Gray cloth hc with gold and black embossed design on front and back cover, decorative end papers. Four fold. b/w frontis is bird's-eye view of Chicago shoreline. See Banks (#741); it has the same contents but different color and design of cover. Banks' name does not appear on the t.p. of the gray edition. Common.
---- Columbian Art: Same except has ads front: (4) p., and back: (5) p.
---- Peale: 1 *l* frontis, 421 + (4) p.
*P→   ☺ . (GLD,csuf,CHx,NYPL,E,TnSt,HL,NYSt,UoC, $18 - 34
                 A,BPL,nwu,RPB,OC,L)

741. Banks, Charles Eugene. *The artistic Guide to Chicago and the World's Columbian exposition by Charles Eugene Banks : illustrated.* [Chicago]: R. S. Peale co., 1893 °1893; N.p.: Columbian Art Co., 1893 [°1893 by R. S. Peale co.].

23x16½. 1 *l*, 418 p. Brown hc, gold and black print and design, pulp paper pages, decorative end papers four fold. frontis is bird's-eye view of Chicago shoreline. Brown cover books have same contents as gray (#740) by the same title but do list Banks as author on t.p.
---- Also listed: 419 p. including plates, ports, plan. Folding frontis.
P↓   ☺ . (GLD,CHx,D,nwu,UTn,NL,OC,TD) $18 - 34

742. Barton, George. *Columbus the Catholic--a comprehensive story of the discovery.* Baltimore: J. Murphy and Co., 1893.

19x__. xiii, 143 p., frontis, plates, ports. "Catholics at the World's Fair," by J. L. Spalding: p. 120-28; "Columbus at Chicago," by E. T. Lauder: p. 129-43. (LC)

743. Bashford, J. W. *The Lord's Day and the World's Fair. A sermon preached by J. W. Bashford, President of the Ohio Wesleyan University, before the Students and Citizens of Delaware, Ohio, October 9, 1892.* [Delaware, OH: F. T. Evans printing and publishing house, 1892].

23½x13. 20 p. Wraps. On t.p.: "Published by request."
⊚ . (OhHx)

744. Bather, F[rancis] A. "Natural Science at the Chicago Exhibition." Rpt. from *Natural Science* 3 (1893). London: Rath, Henderson & Co., 1893; Woodbridge, CT: RPI, 1989.

23½x15. p. 336-343. Microfilm. ⊚ . (SI)

745. Belfast and Northern Counties Railway Company. *Irish scenery at the World's Columbian exposition, Chicago, 1893, transportation department.* N.p.: n.p., n.d., Woodbridge, CT: RPI, 1989.

ca. 27x21. 4 p. ad. Microfilm. Caption title. Exhibit was in the Transportation Bldg. ⊚ . (SI)

746. Berger, Georges. "Suggestions for the Next World's Fair." ____: ____, [1890?].

24x16½. 7 p. Bound article (?rpt.). Suggestions from the Director-General of the 1889 Paris Exhibition on how to make the upcoming WCE a success. (S)

747. *The biographical dictionary and portrait gallery of representative men of Chicago and the World's Columbian exposition. With illustrations on steel.* Chicago and New York: American biographical publishing co. [Press of Knight, Leonard & co.], 1892.

29x23½. 4 *l*, (5)-806, (2) p. including ports. with tissue guards. Frontis: Gunther port. of Columbus. Full black leather beveled hc, gilt cover border and spine lettering, gilt edges, decorative end papers. Includes biographies of Burnham, Gage, Bonney, W. T. Baker, Geo. R. Davis, Chauncey Depew, Potter Palmer, Thomas W. Palmer, and many other WCE notables.

⊚ (GLD,AIC) $100 - 200

748. *The biographical dictionary and portrait gallery of representative men of Chicago, Iowa and the World's Columbian exposition. With illustrations on steel.* Chicago and New York: American biographical publishing co., 1893.

29x23½. 744 p. Rebound, gilt edges, ca. 6½ cm thick. ⊚ . (LC)

749. *The biographical dictionary and portrait gallery of representative men of Chicago, Minnesota cities and the World's Columbian exposition. With illustrations on steel.* Chicago and New York: American biographical publishing co., 1892.

ca. 29x24. 1033 p., 2 *l.* Rebound, gilt edges, ca. 10 cm thick. ☻ . (LC)

750. *The biographical dictionary and portrait gallery of representative men of Chicago, St. Louis : and the World's Columbian exposition.* Chicago and New York: American biographical publishing co. [Press of Knight, Leonard & co.], 1893.

29½x23½. 1 *l* (frontis), 725 p. Frontis: Gunther port of Columbus. Black leather beveled hc, gilt design and spine print, gilt edges. ☻ (WM)

751. *The biographical dictionary and portrait gallery of representative men of Chicago, Wisconsin and the World's Columbian exposition. With illustrations on steel.* Chicago and New York: American biographical publishing co., 1892; Chicago and New York: American biographical publishing co., 1895.

1892 ed.: 913 p.
---- 1895 ed.: ca. 29x24. 609 p., iv. Rebound, gilt edges, ca. 8 cm thick.
☻ . (LC,S)

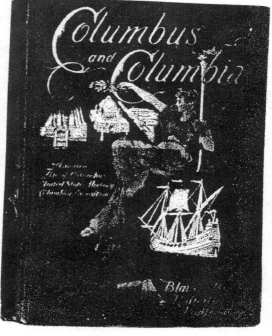

752. Blaine, James G[illespie], J[ames] W[illiam] Buel, John Clark Ridpath, and Benj[amin] Butterworth. *Columbus and Columbia : A Pictorial History of the Man and the Nation : embracing a review of our country's progress, ... Four Books in One Volume.* Boston: Desmond Publishing co., [1892]; Charleston: Martin Hoyt, ᶜ1892; Chicago: The Pontiac Publishing Co., [1892]; Cincinnati: Caïe, Montgomery & Moore, ᶜ1892; Denver [and] Philadelphia: World publishing co., [ᶜ1892 by H. S. Smith]; New York: Hunt & Eaton, 1892; Philadelphia: Historical Publishing Co., [ᶜ1892 by H. S. Smith]; Richmond, VA: B. F. Johnson & Co., [ᶜ1892]; Seattle: Dominion Publishing Co., [ᶜ1892].

Historical Pub, World Pub: 26½x20½. 2 *l*, xvi, (8) plates, 1 *l*, 832 p. Turquoise blue cloth hc, gold, silver, and black lettering; illus end papers, t.p. in red and black. Chromolitho plates, including a 3 page fold out of fairgrounds facing p. 781 and fold out Chicago map facing p. 823. WCE description by Hon. Benj. Butterworth, Secretary Columbian Commission. C.t.: "Columbus and Columbia." Common but useful. Also published in 1894 under title: *Pictorial History of the United States* (#753).
---- Historical Pub: Maroon hc, gilt print, no design.
---- Hunt & Eaton, B. F. Johnson, and Caïe. 2 *l*, 832 p. All with turquoise blue hc described above.
---- B. F. Johnson. Listed at (17)-832 p., 12 p. color plates.
---- Pontiac. Listed at (15)-832.

P↑,P→   ☻ . (GLD,csuf,UWa,NYPL,S,ncsu,NYSt,LSU,A,BPL,OC,WiHx,TD,L) $10 - 35

753. Blaine, James G[illespie], J[ames] W[illiam] Buel, John C[lark] Ridpath, and Benjamin Butterworth. *Pictorial History of the United States.* Philadelphia: Historical Publishing Co., 1894.

> 1 *l*, 17-832 p., colored frontis, illus including ports. Also published under title: *Columbus and Columbia* (#752). (LC)

754. Blanc, Marie Thérèse (de Solms). *The condition of woman in the United States. A Traveller's Notes.* Trans. Abby Langdon Alger. Boston: Roberts Brothers, 1895 [°1895 by Roberts Brothers].

> 18x13. 4 *l*, (7)-285 p., front. (port of Blanc). Light blue (or brown) cloth hc, gilt print. Discusses WCE, women's colleges, clubs, prisons, negresses, etc. ⊚ (CHx,HL)

755. Blanchard, Rufus. *The World's Fair Agitator : an illustrated history of Chicago and environs, with a biographical sketch of Christopher Columbus.* Chicago: Fred Limouze & co., publishers [Press of The Chicago Publication Co.], 1890.

> 30x23½. 8 *l* ads, 236 p. text, 14 *l* ads. Columbus illus on front cover. In upper right corner of t.p.: "Souvenir of the World's fair. The Carbolic Smoke Ball Co." ⊚ . (CHx,S,NL)

756. Böettcher, Karl. *Chicago! Weltausstellungs-Briefe.* Leipzig: W. Friedrich, 1893.

> 16°. xii, 190 p. Translates to "World's Fair Letter." (NYPL)

757. *Boston, New York, Chicago : relay : April, 30 May, 1, 2, 3. 1893.* N.p.: n.p., n.d.

> 13½x8½. 22 p. C.t. Rest of print after c.t.: "Under the auspices of the New York Recorder, Boston Post, Chicago Herald. 1,241 Miles in 90 Hours. Carrying a Message on Bicycles from Governor Russell, of Mass., to Governor Altgeld, of Illinois." ⊚ . (S)

758. Bowes, Ella E. (Lane). "Ancient religions, games and folk-lore." [Chicago: 1893].

> 33x__. 64 *l* (typescript). Describes WCE exhibits in these categories. CHx call: qF38MZ 1893 N1B7. (CHx)

759. Boyd, James P. *Columbia: From Discovery in 1492 to the World's Columbian Exposition 1892.* Philadelphia and Chicago: J. H. Moore & Co., [°1893 by Jas. P. Boyd].

> 23½x17. 768 p. Leather hc. (E,TD)

760. Brand, James. *The Sabbath and the World's fair.* N.p.: 1892?

> 15½x9. 16 p. Caption title. Brand was a doctor of divinity, Oberlin, OH, and president of the Oberlin "Rest Day League." At bottom p. 16: *Advance,* July 7, 1892. ⊚ . (OC)

761. *Brandreth Columbian ABC for The Little Ones.* [New York?]: n.p., °1893.

18½x13. 18 p., illus. Color wraps illus: doll faced child peering through torn picture of fairgrounds. Issued to advertise Allcock's Porous Plasters and Brandreth's pills. On back wrap: Allen Clark, Ph. G., Prescription Druggist, Chelsea, Mass.   ⊚ . (UDe,TD)

762. Brewer, David J., ed. ... *The World's Best Orations : from the earliest period to the present time.* 10 vol. St. Louis [and] Chicago: Ferd. P. Kaiser, 1899.

25½x18. 10 vol paged continuously. Vol 5: 1623-2028; contains Chauncey Depew's Columbian oration at p. 1769-82 (see #826). At head of title: "Official edition."   ⊚ . (NHSt)

763. Brooklyn Eagle. Chicago Bureau. *World* [sic] *Columbian Exposition.* 4th ed. [Chicago]: n.p., 1893.

15x__. 56 p., fold. colored map. C.t. Pub under "Chicago Bureau of the Brooklyn daily eagle."   (LC)

764. Brooks Locomotive Works. ... *Exhibit of Locomotives : made by Brooks locomotive works, Dunkirk, N. Y. : U. S. A.* N.p.: n.p., n.d.

17x25½. (27) p. Maroon cloth with gold letters. At head of title: "World's Columbian exposition. Chicago, 1893." C.t.: "Brooks Locomotive Works. Dunkirk, N.Y. : U.S.A. ..."
---- Same title. Buffalo, NY: Matthews-Northrup Co., [1893]. 17x26. viii, 481-489 p., 9 *l* plates (i.e., 26 p.). At head of title: "World's Columbian Exposition, Chicago, Ill., Chicago, 1893." ?
    ⊚ . (CPL,UMi,NYSt)

765. [Brown, Arthur]. *The dream of Chicago Cregier's Clean City : or, A Full Account of the World's Fair at Chicago, U. S. A.* Chicago: n.p., 1889 [°1889 by A. Brown].

14½x15. 87 p. Tan wraps, blue-black print. At end of Preface: "Chicago, Aug. 11, 1889." On cover: "price, Ten Cents." DeWitt C. Cregier was mayor of Chicago at this early date of WCE activity. For more on Cregier see #248.   ⊚ . (LC)

766. [Buck, Lillie (West) Brown]. (Pseud: Amy Leslie). *Amy Leslie at the fair : containing sixty special illustrations.* Chicago: W. B. Conkey Co. publishers, 1893 [°1893].

20½x14. 263 p., illus. Cream cloth hc, gold print. Frontis shows Buck with inscribed star: "Chicago Daily News reporter." [From 1889, Buck was dramatic critic for the newspaper].
---- Autographed ed. of 200 copies. BPL no. 36; NYPL no. 200.
    ⊚ . (csuf,KyU,CHx,LC,NYPL,HL,BPL)

767. *Buffalo Bill's Wild West and Congress of Rough Riders of the World : Col. W. F. Cody. Chicago, Ill - 1893.* Chicago: The Blakely Printing Co., [1893].

24x18½. 64 p., illus. Colorful litho wraps by "Goes Litho. Co. Chicago." Contains programme, port of Annie Oakley.   ⊚ . (CPL)

768. Burnham, Daniel Hudson, and Francis Davis Millet. ... *The book of the builders : being the chronicle of the origins and plan of the world's fair; of the architecture of the buildings and landscapes; of the work of construction; of the decorations and embellishments, and of the operation.* Chicago, IL and Springfield, OH: Columbian Memorial Publication Society, 1894.

42x31 (wraps); 38½x30½ (text). (1)-47 p., 24 *l*, 2 *l*. Orange wraps, red print and design, fine color illus. At head of title: "World's Columbian Exposition." On cover: "The Columbian serial." Issued biweekly to total (at least) 6 pts. Sold by subscription for later binding.
---- Micropublished as no. 247 on Reel 17, in "American Architectural Books," based on the Henry-Russell Hitchcock bibliography of the same title. New Haven, CT: RPI, 1972.
＊　　　◎ . (UNM,CHx,BPL,AIC,WiHx)

☞ E. D. Weary. 53x__. (1) p., 24 *l* of plates, color illus in portfolio. Reproductions of paintings by various artists originally made for publication by Daniel H. Burnham (1846-1912) and Francis Davis Millet's *World's Columbian Exposition : the book of the builders.* Only 6 pts. had been published by the Columbian Memorial Publication Society when the enterprise failed. The left over color prints were sold to Edwin D. Weary.--(UoC computer information.)

☞ The unified architecture of the Fair, set amongst waterways and park-like settings, made the WCE a model for emulation. The Library of Congress (Jefferson Bldg) was the first government bldg beneficiary.

769. Burrell, David James. "A plea for sabbath rest at the Columbian Fair." Collegiate Church. Chicago?, 10 July, 1892.

18½x12½. Pages (21)-36. Caption title. Sermon preached by Dr. Burrell.　　(CHx)

770. *The Business college exhibit at the World's fair.* [New York: Press of J. J. Little & Co., 1892.]

19x__. 32 p., plates ports, plan, illus t.p.　　(UC)

771. Cameron, William E[velyn], ed. *History of the World's Columbian Exposition.* 2nd ed. Chicago: Columbian History Co., 1893 [ᶜ1893 by the Columbian History Co. (Printed by the Foster Press)]; 2nd ed. Chicago: Columbian History Co., 1894.

1893: 48½x32½. 356 p., (6) p., illus includes ports. Full green leather hc with gilt spine print and design, gilt edges, glossy text paper.
---- 1893: Half leather, gilt print and design.
---- 1893 Subscription set: 48½x32 (text). 4 parts. E.g.: vol 1: (1)-82 p.; vol 4: 271-356 + (6) p. Green wraps, black print.
---- 1894 Subscription set: "Columbian historical series."
---- Also listed: Chicago: Foster press, ᶜ1892. ? 48x31. Unpaged. Folio.
　　　◎ . (GLD,UNe,CHx,S,NHHx,RML,HL,NL,A,BPL,E,RPB,AIC,CoU,TD)　　　　　$40 - 100

772. Cameron, William E[velyn]. *The World's Fair, being a pictorial history of The Columbian Exposition : containing a complete history of the world-renowned exposition at Chicago; ...* Boston: M. J. Monahan, [1893]; Chicago: Chicago Publication & Lithograph Co., [ᶜ1893]; Chicago: J. R. Jones Publishing Co., 1893; Chicago: A. B. Kuhlman & Co., 1893; Philadelphia: National Publishing Co., [ᶜ1893]; Philadelphia & Chicago: S. I. Bell & co., [ᶜ1893 by J. R. Jones]; Philadelphia Boston New York Chicago: Home Library publishing co., [ᶜ1893 by J. R. Jones]; Philadelphia and Chicago: J. H. Moore & Co., [ᶜ1893 by J. R. Jones]; Newark, OH: Allison publishing co., [ᶜ1893 by J. R. Jones]; Reading, PA: J. I. Mattes, 1893 [ᶜ1893 by J. R. Jones]; [N.p.: 1893]; Woodbridge, CT: RPI [Chicago Publication & Lithograph], 1989.

Introduction by Thomas W. Palmer; chapter on the Woman's Dept by Frances E. Willard. On the 1 *l* before text: "Presented to ___ by ___" in beautiful gilt, black, white, and red print.

---- Bell: 27x20. 816 p. Blue hc with gilt print and design of Statue of the Republic holding banner "World Columbian Exposition 1893."
---- Chicago Pub. & Litho.: 25½x19½. 2 *l*, 3-854 p. + 18 glossy *l*. Rebound, all edges gilt.
---- Chicago Pub. & Litho.: Listed at 919 p.
---- Home Library: 26x19. 919 p.
---- Jones Pub.: Listed at 854 p. illus.
---- Mattes: 26½x20. 1 *l*, 816 p. + 18 glossy *l* with illus both sides, t.p. in red and black. Full morocco hc, elaborate blind stamp design, gold embossed print "World's Columbian Exposition."
---- Moore: 3 *l*, 816 p. Brown leather, gilt.
---- National Pub.: 26½x20. 3 *l*, 919, (1) p. ads. Blue cloth hc with gilt, silver, and red lettering and design (includes statue of the Republic), decorative end papers, marbled edges. T.p. in red and black.
---- N.p.: Listed at 816 p.

    *   ☺ . (GLD,csuf,CHx,SI,NYPL,WyMus,LM,HL,A,BPL,NAC,WiHx) $20 - 40

773. Campbell, James B. *Campbell's Illustrated History of the World's Columbian exposition. In Two Volumes. Compiled as the Exposition progressed from the Official Reports, and most profusely Illustrated with Copperplate Engravings.* 2 vols. Boston: Ed. Gately & Co., 1894 [°1894 by James B. Campbell]; Chicago: J. B. Campbell, 1894; Chicago: N. Juul & Co., 1894; Philadelphia: Sessler & Dungan, 1894 [°1894 by James B. Campbell]; Woodbridge, CT: RPI [Campbell], 1989.

Campbell: 39½x28½. xvi, (1) p., 18-640 p. Paged continuously, illus including ports. Full brown leather hc, gold print and design. Compiled from Campbell's *World's Columbian Exposition Illustrated* (magazine). "The Prize History."
---- Gately: 39x28. 360 p. each vol. Dark gold cloth hc, black print and design (or brown hc, gilt print and design).
---- Juul: Lettered on cover: "The Prize History."
---- Sessler: 40x28½. 640 p., illus. Brown cloth hc, black and gilt design and lettering.

    *   ☺ . (csuf,KyU,CHx,SI,F,NHHx,NL,A,S,TD) $100 - 225

774. Campbell, J[ames] B. *Official List of state boards : World's Columbian Exposition.* Chicago: J. B. Campbell, publisher World's Columbian Exposition Illustrated, °1892.

18x10. 16 p. including both covers. Cream wraps and text, black print.   ☺ . (CPL)

775. *Canadian Pacific Railway at the World's fair : Chicago : 1893 : Transportation building.* [Chicago?: The Company, 1893].

21x13. 1 sheet 21x105 folded to 21x13, illus. C.t. Broad ornate border surrounds c.t.   ☺ . (UDe)

776. *The Canadian Pacific : the new highway to the Orient : across the Mountains, Prairies and Rivers of Canada.* ____ : ____, 189_.

26½x19½. 48 p. Buff wraps with green-blue print and railroad trestle over mountain stream illus. C.t. Caption title: "The Canadian Pacific Railway."   . (WM)

777. Carson, Hampton L[awrence]. *Oration delivered at the Invitation of the City of Chicago and of the World's Fair Commission, On the 4th Day of July, 1893, in Jackson Park, Chicago.* Philadelphia: Allen, Lane & Scott's printing house, 1893.

25x17½. 18 p.   ☺ . (VaHx)

778. *Catalogue of model of St. Peter's at Rome : located southwest of Ferris wheel, midway plaisance, World's Columbian Exposition* ... Chicago: J. B. Campbell, n.d.

19½x13. 16 p. White glossy wraps with black print and b/w illus of St. Peter's model. C.t. Cover states: "Admission, 25 Cents. Catalogue, 10 Cents." [After the WCE, the model was moved to Logerot Garden in New York City. A catalog was issued for NYC display.--(S)]

P↓   ☺ . (GLD,NL) $13 - 26

779. *Catalogue of Singer Sewing Machines : for family use.* [New York: Strauss & Klee Press, 1893].

18½x12½. 32 p. includes 9 color lithographic plates. Machine stitched stiff wraps with glossy color lithograph, map on back cover. [Singer had a strong presence at the Fair and issued colorful high quality publication items.]

P↑   ☺ (GLD,F,NHHx) $20 - 35

780. *Catalogue of the Exhibit of the papal Josephinum college of the Holy Congregation of the Propagation of Faith. Columbus, Ohio. World's Columbian Exposition. Chicago, 1893. Department: liberal arts.* [Columbus, OH?: 1893?].

22x15½. 15 p., illus. Wraps. Catalogued under: Pontifical College, Worthington, OH.   ☺ . (WiHx)

781. Catholic Educational Exhibit. *Catalogue : Catholic Educational Exhibit : with supplementary list of errors and omissions, also List of Awards Decreed by the World's Fair, World's Columbian Exposition, Chicago, 1893. Southeast Gallery, Section 1, Manufactures and Liberal Arts Building.* Chicago: Rokker-O'Donnell Printing Co., Printers and Binders, [1894].

21½x14½. 5 *l*, 5-327, (44) p., plates, ports, diagram. Rust wraps. Title from cover.   ☺ . (CPL,Chx)

782. Catholic Educational Exhibit. *Catalogue : Catholic Educational Exhibit : World's Columbian Exposition, Chicago, 1893. Southeast Gallery, Section 1, Manufactures and Liberal Arts Building.* Chicago: La Monte-O'Donnell Co., printers, 1893.

21½x15. 300 p. + (4) p. ads on rose pulp paper. Peach wraps with black print and small cover illus of Columbus landing. C.t.= t.p. Glossy double page ports of members of the exhibit committee and a double page diagram of the exhibit. ⊚ . (NYPL,NL)

783. Catholic Educational Exhibit. *The Catholic educational exhibit at the World's Columbian Exposition, Chicago, 1893. Illustrative and Descriptive. Edited by a well known Catholic writer, under the special supervision of the Rev. Brother Maurelian ...* Chicago: J. S. Hyland and Co. Publishers, 1896 ᶜ1894.

42x32½. (1)-(3), 4-259 p., including t.p. Letter and photo of Pope Leo XIII on p. (2)-(3), illus. Pebbled brown cloth hc, gilt lettering and design, all edges gilt. ---- Half leather over dark green pebbled cloth hc, gilt print and design, decorative green and gold end papers, all edges gilt.
P→ ⊚ . (csuf,CPL,CHx,UoC,WiHx)

784. Catholic Educational Exhibit. *... Circular of information and directions : May 1, 1893.* Chicago: [Donohue & Henneberry, Prs., engrs. and binders], [1892?].

19½x13. 24 p. Peachy tan wraps, black print and illus of Columbus. At head of title: "Catholic educational exhibit. World's Columbian Exposition, Chicago, 1893." Signed Spalding and Maurelian on p. 24: May 1, 1892. ⊚ (NL)

785. Catholic Educational Exhibit. *Final report. Catholic educational exhibit, World's Columbian Exposition, Chicago, 1893, by Brother Maurelian ... to Right Reverend J. L. Spalding ...* [Chicago]: 1893.

23x15. 202 p. includes frontis, illus, plates, ports. White wraps with black print and design.
(NYPL,F) $20 - 35

786. [Catholic Education Exhibit]. *Souvenir. Catholic Education Day : World's Columbian Exposition : Festival Hall, Jackson Park : Chicago, 1893.* Chicago: Donohue & Henneberry, printers and binders, [1893?].

21½x15. 1 *l*, 3-42 p. Beige wraps, black print and Columbus illus. C.t.= t.p. (NL)

787. Catlin, George L. *Switzerland. The St. Gothard Railway.* Zurich: Printed by art institute Orell Fussli, 1893.

18½x12½. Illus wraps. C.t.: "Over the Alps via the St. Gothard Railway." ⊚ . (WM)

788. The Chicago Daily News Company. *The Chicago Record's History of The World's Fair. Copiously illustrated.* [Chicago]: The Chicago Daily News Co., 1893 ᶜ1893 by the Chicago Daily News Co.; Woodbridge, CT: RPI, 1989.

21x14½. 256 p., illus. Blue printed tan wraps. C.t.= t.p. On cover: "The Chicago quarterly of the Chicago Record and The Chicago Daily News ... Vol. 1, No. 1. October, 1893."
---- Also listed: WiHx microfilm.
P↑   ☺ . (csuf,CHx,SI,UoC,NL,OC,WiHx,TD)

789. The Chicago Daily News Company. *The Daily News Almanac and Political Register for 1893.* Ninth year. Chicago: Chicago Daily News Co., 1893.

20x14½. 424 p. Bright blue cloth hc, gold print, red dyed edges. Expanded section on WCE.
---- Eighth year: 20x14½. 404 p. Same except "... Register for 1892."
(CHx)

790. Chicago, Milwaukee & St. Paul Railway Co. *How to See the World's Fair in Six Days, Three Days, or in One Day.* Chicago: Rand, McNally & Co., n.d.

16½x10. 11 p. Off-white wraps with black print and red litho of Administration Bldg. Map on back cover. Bird's-eye view inside front cover.
P→   ☺ (GLD,WM) $12 - 26

791. *Chicago of To-day. The metropolis of the West. The Nation's choice for the World's Columbian exposition. Handsomely illustrated. 1892.* Chicago: Acme publishing and engraving co., [°1891 by the Acme Publishing and Engraving Co.].

25½x19. xv, (1), 33-248 p. Multicolor litho wraps. WCE text and bldg lithos, list of Chicago businesses.   ☺ . (UoC)

792. *Christopher Columbus almanac for the year 1892.* Boston: The Oak Grove form co., [1892].

24½x16½. (24) p. Buff wraps with pretty gilt design and print. Columbus information, calendars, and many ads.
P→   ☺ (GLD) $12 - 24

793. Clarke, Edith E. *Woman in Literature at the Fair, from the Standpoint of a Librarian and Cataloger.* Chicago: n.p., [1894?].

19½x11½. 1 *l* (t.p.), 10 p. On t.p. it states Clarke was from Newberry Library and "Paper read before the Chicago Library Club : January, 1894." (NL)

794. Clemens, Will M., ed. *The Depew story book.* London [and] New York: F. Tennyson Neely, publisher, [1898].

19x14. 206 p. Hc. Contains Depew's "Columbian Oration." Also see #826. [Clemens was a relative of Mark Twain.] ☉ . (S)

795. *Columbian bazaar : given under the auspices of the Friday club ...* [Chicago: Metcalf stationery co. (late Cobbs library co.), 1892?].

21x17½. (36) p. Elegant white slick wraps with gilt lettering. Fine lithos and ornate printing of ads for multinational sale items. C.t.: "The Columbian Bazaar : December 7th & 8th : 1892 ... Price 25 cents." Includes ad for *Fame's Tributes* [sic] *to Children* (#871) by Miss M. S. Hill, president of the Friday Club.
P→   ☉ (GLD) $20 - 38

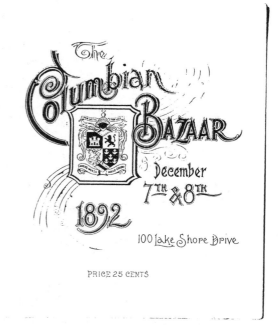

796. *Columbian Day.   October 21, 1892.   The Official Programme : as arranged and adopted by the superintendents of education in accordance with the plan of "The Youth's Companion" to provide for a uniform observance of the celebration of Columbus day. ____ : ____, 189_.*

42x27½. Litho: "Landing of Columbus on San Salvador" plus ads on cover.   . (WM)

797. *Columbian Exhibit : New York Condensed Milk Company.* New York: Albertype Co., [°1892].

20x15. (56) p. String tied glossy light yellow wraps lithographed and printed in black. Opens in vertical note pad orientation, 15 cm wide at top. An exhibit handout along with advertising cards all in a manilla envelope with black print. C.t.
P→   ☉ (GLD,S,BPL,TD) $20 - 40

798. *The Columbian Exposition and World's fair illustrated : descriptive : historical : statistical.* Philadelphia and Chicago: The Columbian Engraving and Publishing Co., [°1893].

35½x28½. xxxvi, 432 p. of illus (includes ports, plans). Brown leather hc with ornate gold print and engraved border. Contents: Federal legislation, proclamation, information plus WCE description. ☉ . (CHx,LC)

799. *Columbian exposition Dedication Ceremonies memorial : a graphic description of the ceremonies at Chicago, October, 1892 : the 400th anniversary of the discovery of America. ...* Chicago: Metropolitan Art Engraving and Publishing Co., 1893 [°1892 by Frederick J. Prior].

34½x26. 4 *l*, 648 p., glossy paper. 1st *l* is Moro port of Columbus frontis. Brown cloth beveled hc, gilt print and black border design, all edges gilt, decorative end papers. Sections on the life of Columbus; beginnings of WCE, dedication ceremonies, the work between dedication and opening, opening ceremonies, Exposition bldgs, state bldgs, Midway Plaisance, a history of Chicago, and portrait gallery. An excellent book on the history of WCE and photos of its participants. Author listed: [Prior, Frederick John], ed. and comp.

* ☺ . (GLD,CHx,LC,NYPL,nwu,UoC,AIC) $50 - 175

800. Columbian Exposition International Exhibit and Information Company. *Columbian Exposition International Exhibit and Information Co. Exhibit department for the benefit of exhibitors at the World's fair to be held at Chicago, Illinois, U. S. A., 1893.* Chicago: R. R. Donnelley & sons, Co., ᶜ1891.

15x__. 16 p. At head of title: "Columbian exposition international exhibit and information co.."
---- Also listed: French (or German) text. 15x__. 8 p. C.t.
(LC)

801. Columbian Exposition International Exhibit and Information Company. *Columbian Exposition International Exhibit and Information Co. : for the especial benefit and convenience of Visitors to the World's Fair : 1893.* [Chicago: Columbian Exposition International Exhibit and Information Co.], ᶜ1891.

17x11½. 16 p., illus. C.t.: "Columbian Exposition : International Exhibit and Information Company. 1893 : Information department." On front end paper: "Notice." Also printed in French. ☺ . (LC)

802. ... *Columbian Globe Calendar. A souvenir.* Gouverneur, NY: n.p., ᶜ1892 by J. C. Lee.

24x15. 24 p. Hinged at top (15 cm edge) with rings in 2 punch holes. Port on cover. At head of title: "1492. 1893." A souvenir calendar with 401 couplets on alternate pages from calendar pages. ☺ . (S)

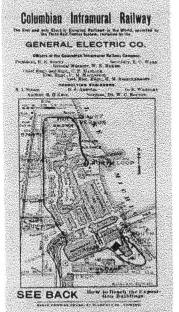

803. *Columbian Intramural Railway : the First and only Electric Elevated Railroad in the World, operated by the Third Rail Trolley System, installed by the General Electric Co.* Chicago: Regan printing house, [1893?].

17½x9. 2 *l*, map. Buff paper ad leaflet for the French Bakery. Caption title. The unique 13 mile railway circled the grounds for the convenience of fair visitors. The route around the grounds is shown in red on the map on front; the fare at the Fair was 10¢. The French Bakery was located next to the Wind Mills Exhibit and gave a free railway ride in exchange for the ad leaflet and a 30¢ purchase at the bakery. 30¢ was a lot since coffee, cakes, milk, and waffles were 5¢ each and ham sandwiches were 10¢.

P→ ☺ (GLD,csuf,TD) $12 - 20

804. *The Columbian Jubilee; or four centuries of Catholicity in America, being a historical and biographical retrospect from the landing of Christopher Columbus to the Chicago Catholic Congress of 1893.* 2 vol. Chicago: J. S. Hyland, 1892.

25x__. (UC)

805. Columbian Movable Sidewalk Company. *The movable sidewalk or multiple speed railway.* [Chicago: 1893].

17½x13½. 16 p. Tan-yellow wraps, dark blue print and cover illus. C.t. Also on cover: "World's Columbian Exposition Souvenir." Text in blue print. The movable sidewalk had a low speed outer track and a higher speed inner track with seats. It was located on the Pier jutting into Lake Michigan past the Peristyle. (CHx)

806. *The Columbian Recipes : a publication of the Methodist Cook-Book : As Revised by the Ladies of the Main Street M. E. Church, Akron, Ohio. Edition of 1893.* Akron, OH: Capron & Curtice, prompt printers, 1893.

23x16. 152 p. Burgundy hc, gilt print. T.p. verso: illus of Main Street M. E. Church. ☻.(KSU)

807. *Columbian souvenir institute Note Book.* Chicago: W. M. Welch & Co., °1897 by W. M. Welch & Co.

22½x13½. 72 p. Blue print and photo illus on tan wraps. ☻.(A)

808. *The Columbian World's Fair Atlas : containing complete illustrations of the World's fair grounds and buildings, general illustrations of the public buildings, parks, monuments, street scenes, etc., of Chicago, and maps of every state and territory in the United States and Canada, and General Maps of the World.* Chicago: The Columbian World's Fair Atlas Co., n.d.; Spokane: J. F. Adams, n.d.; Brooklyn: Bourke & Ryan, n.d.

Columbian World's Fair Atlas Co.: 35½x29. (2) p. ads + 192 p. + (2) p. ads, (book starts with t.p. at fifth p.). Black cloth hc, all edges marbled. Color maps, ads, b/w lithographs of WCE bldgs, data, bird's-eye view, etc.
---- Published for any merchant: Blakeslee Dry Goods Emporium, New York; Forbes & Co., Beatrice, NE, 190 p. + (4) p. ads; H. C. Kariher, Champaign, IL; T. H. O'Brien, dry goods, Fon Du Lac, WI; John Onken & Bros., Champaign, IL; Geo. W. Wells, Attica, NY, 194 p. includes last 2 p. ads; Woods Brothers, Unadilla, NY, 194 p. includes last 2 p. ads.
☻ (GLD,csuf,ncsu,NYSt,A,BPL,WM) $25 - 45

809. *Columbian World's Fair : souvenir diary.* N.p.: n.p., n.d.

13x6. Gilt print on red cover. After c.t.: "Compliments Brand Stove Co. Milwaukee, ... Chicago, ..." Diary for 1893; two days per page. ☻.(A)

810. *Columbia's Calendar for 1893 : 12 designs in color by Walter Crane.* Boston: L. Prang & Co., 1893.

29½x23. 14 *l*. Red and blue print and design on heavy white smooth stock wraps. 12 *l* are wonderful color lithographs by Walter H. Crane, English illustrator, each with a month of the year 1893. Opens upward, string tied at top (23 cm wide). Typical of quality Prang art work. December shows Republic holding a plan of the WCE. See #815 for another Crane item.
☻ (GLD) $50 -120

811. *Columbus Memorial: 1492 - 400 years - 1892 : discovery, settlement, wars, independence, constitution, dissensions, secession, peace. ...* N.p.: n.p, [°1892 by John W. Iliff].

37x29. 22 *l*, illus. Tan wraps with dark blue (or black) print. Large lithos of bldgs, maps. Historical tribute to the New World. For related Iliff item see #721.

⊚ (GLD,CPL,CHx,NYPL,S,BPL) $25 - 42

812. Colville, W[illiam] J[uvenal]. *World's fair text book of Mental Therapeutics, comprising twelve lessons delivered at the Health College ...* 7th ed. Chicago: Donohue & Henneberry, printers and binders, ᶜ1893; 16th ed. Chicago: The Educator publishing co., [ᶜ1893 by W. J. Colville].

7th ed.: 19½x12½. 139 p., (1) p., 4 *l*. The only connection with the WCE is the title. [The main interest in this spiritualism book is that was a bequest to LC rare books from the Harry Houdini estate, April, 1927.]
---- Sixteenth ed.: 19½x13½. 139, (1) p., 5 *l*. Maroon stiff wraps embossed in checker-board pattern, gilt print.

⊚ (GLD,LC) $18 - 40

813. Cook, Thomas & Son, London. *The World's Fair at Chicago, 1893. Information for Travelers.* London New York Chicago: Thos. Cook & Son, n.d.

21½x14. 2 *l*, (7)-94 p. White stiff wraps with lithos, print, and design in shades of green, also gilt design on front cover. On back cover: "Designed & Printed by Blades East & Blades London." "1893" on front cover.

P→   ⊚ (GLD,CHx,LC,SI,S,NL,TD) $20 - 35

814. Cook, Tho[ma]s & Sons, New York. *Programme of Cook's Tours to the World's Columbian Exposition, Chicago, 1893...* New York: Thos. Cook & Son, [1893].

11½x15. 32 p., illus. Decorative wraps.   ⊚ . (csuf,BPL,WM)

815. Crane, Walter. *Columbia's Courtship: a picture history of the United States in twelve emblematic designs in color with accompanying verses.* Boston: L. Prang & Co, n.d. copyrighted by Prang & Co.

27x23. 14 *l*. Full page color plates and poetry. Also see Crane #810.   ⊚ .(S)

816. *Crystal Water Palace. World's Columbian Exposition, Chicago, 1893. Foot of Van Buren Street.* [Chicago: Rand, McNally & Co.], n.d.

22x13. (4) p. C.t. Cover has illus of the proposed (never realized) domed bldg with amphitheater, roof gardens, and restaurants. The title comes from the 150 foot high glass dome which was to be bathed in water from a fountain atop the structure. It was to have been on the pier where the World's Fair Steamship Co. delivered Fair visitors to Van Buren Street. Designed with a Moveable Sidewalk (see #805).   ⊚ .(CHx,NL)

817. Cunard Steamship Company. *The Cunard line and : The World's Fair, Chicago, 1893.* London: Printed and Published for The Cunard Steamship Co., Limited, by The Electrotype co., 1893.

15x25. 82 p., 26 *l* of plates include some colored illus, folded maps, plans. Hc. WCE: pages 71-81 include text, plates, and illus. ☺ . (UDe,USD,NYSt)

818. Cunard Steamship Company. "The Cunard Royal mail twin-screw steamers 'Campania' and 'Lucania' and the World's Columbian Exposition, 1893." Rpt. from *Engineering*. London: Offices of Engineering, [1893?].

36x__. 134 p. illus, 13 plates. (OSU)

819. Curtis, William Eleroy. *Christopher Columbus : his portraits and his monuments : a descriptive catalogue ... part II.* Chicago: The W. H. Lowdermilk Co., 1893.

21x14½. 72 p., illus, port. C.t.: "Souvenir of La Rabida. World's Columbian Exposition [pt. 2]." Part 1 is titled: ... *The Relics of Columbus* (#820).
---- Also listed: Parts 1 and 2 bound together. ?
☺ . (KyU,NYPL,UMi,Yale,UDe,RPB,BM)

820. Curtis, William Eleroy. ... *The Relics of Columbus : an Illustrated Description of the Historical Collection in the Monastery of La Rabida.* Washington, D.C.: The William H. Lowdermilk co., Publishers [Chicago: W. B. Conkey co., printers and binders], [ᶜ1893 by William E. Curtis].

22x14½. 224 p., pulp paper. Red-brown wraps with black design and print. At head of title: "Souvenir of La Rabida : World's Columbian exposition." This book is pt 1 of 2 pts. Pt 2 is #819. List of 1,067 Columbus relics located at La Rabida Monastery in Spain. LC has original manuscript.
---- 216 p. Purple cloth hc with gilt print.
☺ . (GLD,csuf,LC,NYPL,F,S,UDe,HL,UoC,RPB,BM,OC,TD) $20 - 35

☞ Curtis wrote for the *Chicago Record* for many years, directed the Bureau of American Republics, and was Chief of the Latin-American Bureau, WCE. Another Curtis writing can be found in the *Report ... to the Columbian Historical Exposition at Madrid* #2456.

821. Curtis, W. W., comp. *First edition of World's fair Blue Book : as presented at the great Columbian exposition, holden at Chicago, A. D. 1893, representing financially : America's Most Eminent Business Men.* Boston: n.p., ᶜ1893 [ᶜ1893 by W. W. Curtis].

16x12. 183 p. Prussian blue cloth hc with bold gilt print. C.t.: "World's fair Blue Book." Lists names, addresses, products, and services of subscriber companies.
---- 353 p. Same cover and c.t.
---- 15½x12. 607 p. plus a 3 p. list of bank presidents. Same cover and c.t. Text states: "business cards of a limited number of the most eminent business men."
☺ . (GLD,LC,UoC,BPL) $20 - 38

822. Cutler, H[arry] G[ardner]. *The World's fair : its meaning and scope : Its Old-World Friends, Their Countries, Customs and Religions : what they will exhibit. The United States at the Fair. The city and the site. The colossal structures.* San Francisco: The King publishing co. [and] Chicago: Star Publishing Co., 1891 [ᶜ1891 by Star publishing co.]; Rev. ed. Chicago: Chicago publishing co., 1893 [ᶜ1892 by Star Publishing Co.]; Rev. ed. Chicago: Star publishing co., 1892 [ᶜ1892 by Star publishing co.]; Rev. ed.: San Francisco: The King Publishing Co. [and] Chicago: Star Publishing Co., n.d.

1891: 25½x19. 1 *l* (frontis), viii, 9-640 p. Frontis: b/w litho of sleeping woman dreaming of the Fair, 4 color plates. Brown cloth hc, gold and black print and design, decorative end papers, marbled edges. Early description of WCE including many bldg plans and ideas that never matured. On t.p.: "Illustrated."

---- Rev. ed. Chicago: Star publishing co., 1892 [ᶜ 1892 by Star publishing co.]. 26x18½. viii, 9-602 p. including illus, ports, colored frontis, plates (3 color). Brown hc gold print and design. On t.p.: "Profusely illustrated."

---- Rev. ed. San Francisco: The King Publishing Co. [and] Chicago: Star Publishing Co., n.d. 26x18½. viii, 9-602 p., illus, chromolitho frontis of Micronesian weapons; same cover. On t.p.: "Profusely illustrated."

P→   ☺ . (GLD,csuf,CHx,LC,NYPL,F,S,E,OSL,HL,NYSt,LSU,A,TD) $22 - 36

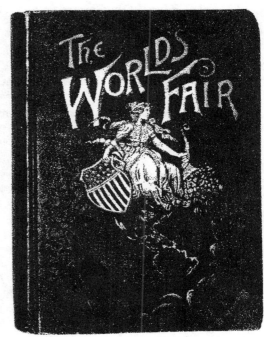

823. Dean, C. *The World's fair city and her enterprising sons.* [Chicago]: United Publishing Co., 1892 [ᶜ1892].

21½x16½. 512 p., plates. Frontis: bird's-eye view. Green decorative cloth hc with gilt, silver, and black print and design. Goethe quote on t.p.   ☺ . (csuf,AIC,WiHx)

824. Dean, Teresa [H]. *White city chips.* Chicago: Warren Publishing Co, 1895 [ᶜ1895].

20x13½. x, 425 p., illus, frontis (port), originally published in the *Chicago Daily Inter Ocean*, 1893. On t.p.: "'An I should live a thousand years I never should forget it.'"   ☺ . (CPL,CHx,LC,UoC,NL,BPL,TD)

825. Deere & Company. *History and description of the Columbian peace plow, by a member of the Columbian liberty bell executive committee.* Moline, IL: Deere & Co., [1893].

23x__. 14 p.   (WiHx-missing)

826. Depew, Chauncey Mitchell. *The Columbian oration : delivered at the dedication ceremonies of the World's fair at Chicago, October 21, 1892, ...* [New York: Edwin C. Lockwood, state printer, 1892?].

23x15. 24 p. Buff stiff wraps, black print. C.t.= t.p. Stamped at top of cover: "Compliments of Chauncey M. Depew" [signature replica]. [Depew (1834-1928) was a famed lawyer, orator on widely varied topics, and president of the New York Central and Hudson River Railroad.]

---- In: Brewer, David J., ed. *The World's Best Orations* (see #762). Vol 5; p. 1769-82.

---- In: Clemens, Will M. *The Depew story book* (see #794).

   ☺ . (PU,CHx,NYPL,F,NHSt,HL,NL,BPL) $20 - 30

827. Dernburg, Friedrich. *Aus der Weissen Stadt. Spaziergänge in der Chicagoer Weltausstellung und weitere Fahrten.* Berlin: Verlag von Julius Springer, 1893.

Hardbound: 21½x14. 3 *l*, 218 p. Maroon cloth hc, gilt print on spine, decorative end papers, speckled edges. Old German script. Translates: "From the White City. Special trip to the Chicago World's Fair and other Travels." Personal account.

---- Softbound: 20x13. Same paging. Beige wraps with navy print, navy and hunter green design, plain edges. Old German script. C.t.= t.p.

     ⊘ . (CHx,NL)

828. ... *Descriptive Souvenir of the Columbian Liberty Bell and silver model of U.S. Treasury Building.* Chicago: W. B. Conkey Co., publishers to the World's Columbian Exposition, [°1893].

11x17. 20 numbered *l* with print on rectos only, 1 unnumbered *l* at end with photo of Liberty Bell. White glossy wraps, black and red print and seal. At head of title: World's Columbian Exposition 1893." ⊘ . (LC)

☞ The Columbian Liberty Bell was first rung on the Anniversary of California's admission to the Union -- Sept. 9, 1893 -- one stroke for each of the states and territories of the U.S., and five strokes for the nations. *Columbian Liberty Bell Committee. Circular Letter, No. 13.* Dated Nov. 22, 1893.-- (WM call: T500 C6 M6 no. 5).

829. Dewar, Thomas R[obert]. *A ramble round the globe.* London: Chatto and Windus, 1894.

19½x14. 3 *l*, vii-xv, 316 p., 4 + 32 p. list of books, illus, frontis has a port of Dewar with a tissue guard sheet. Teal blue cloth hc, color illus on front cover (ship) and spine (train), gilt print on spine, decorative end papers, t.p. in black and red. ⊘ (CHx)

830. Dorr, R[obert] E. A. *The Columbian Exposition : a visit to the World's Fair, Chicago, illustrated by Sixty-one Photographic Lantern Slides, accompanied with an Original Descriptive Lecture.* New York: T. H. McAllister, Manufacturing Optician, °1893.

23x15. 34 p., 1 *l*. Tan wraps, black print. 61 stereo slides shown; back cover litho of audience viewing the show projected on a screen. Long list of WF slides available for purchase at $45/100. At top of t.p.: "McAllister's series of 'Lantern Lectures.'" ⊘ . (LC)

831. Dredge, James. *Chicago and Her Exposition of 1893. A Stereopticon Lecture : Recently Delivered Before the London Polytechic Institute.* ... [American ed.] Chicago: H. V. Holmes, 1892.

22x14½. 1 *l*, 59 (i.e., 61 p.) includes illus, plates, double map, frontis (port of Dredge). Red wraps, black print. C.t.: "American edition ... The World's Columbian Exposition and the city of Chicago viewed from the English standpoint." ⊘ . (LC,UoC)

832. Dredge, James. *A record of the transportation exhibits at the World's Columbian exposition of 1893.* London: Offices of "Engineering" [and] New York: John Wiley & sons, 1894; Woodbridge, CT: RPI, 1989.

37½x29½. lii, 779 p. but many blank pages counted in the pagination and some numbers are skipped entirely, illus, 192 plates. On t.p.: "Engineering series" and "Partly reprinted from *'Engineering.'"* Wonderful lithos of various train/passenger cars. LC copy: "This volume is dedicated to the President of the United States, Mr. Grover Cleveland, as a Souvenir of the first of May, eighteen hundred and ninety-three." ⊘ . (csuf,CHx,LC,SI,NYPL,UDe,HL)

833. Eastland, Clara F. *World's Fair Souvenir : Dedicated To the Loyal Sons and Daughters of America.* [Chicago?: 1893?]

14x21. (22) p. Ribbon tied wraps with scalloped edges. C.t. ☻ . (BPL)

834. Eggleston, R[ichard] Beverly [sic Beverley]. *Four days at Chicago : Descriptive and Historical.* Richmond, VA: Whittet & Shepperson, Printers, 1901.

19½x13½. 61 p. Pink wraps, black print. Eggleston was pastor of the Third Presbyterian Church in Richmond. An account of the WCE. ☻ . (CHx,NYPL,VaHx,UVa)

835. Elliott, Maud Howe, ed. *Art and handicraft in the Woman's Building of the World's Columbian exposition Chicago, 1893.* Official ed. Chicago and New York: Rand, McNally & Co., 1894 [°1894 by Rand, McNally & Co, °1893 by Boussod, Valadon & Co.]; Paris and New York: Goupil & Co., Boussod, Valadon & Co., Successors, 1893 [°1893 by Boussod, Valadon & Co.]; Woodbridge, CT: RPI [Goupil], 1989.

Goupil 1893 (Cover design 1): 24½x18. 5 *l*, 287 p., illus, color lithograph is 1st *l* and reads "Art and Handicraft in the Women's Building" which is the cover for the wraps edition. Frontis of Woman's Bldg. Beautiful ocher cloth beveled hc, gold and silver print and arabesque design, gilt edges. Bottom of spine reads: "Rand, Mc.Nally [sic] and Company Publishers Chicago." C.t.: "Official edition : Illustrated art and handicraft in the woman's building."
---- Goupil 1893: Same cover design 1. Navy blue background. Rand NOT printed on spine or t.p.
*P→ Design 1: $40 - 70

---- Goupil 1893 (Cover design 2): 24½x17½. 4 *l*, 287 p. Frontis of Women's Bldg. Lacks color litho of cover design 1. Yellow-tan linen hc (not beveled) with brown, green and gold lettering, chocolate brown design with lilies, yellow stained top edge. C.t.: "Art and handicraft. Illustrated designs for the needle, brush and pen." Rand printed on spine.
---- Rand 1894 (Cover design 2): 24½x17½. 320 p. Woman's bldg frontis. Goupil cover design 2 except brown and gold (no green) lettering. Rand printed on spine.
*P→ Design 2: $25 - 50

---- Softbound: 287 p. Wraps with the same color litho for cover as the 1st *l* of "Goupil cover design 1." Has "Official edition" at the top and pub info outside the image at the bottom.
---- Softbound: 320 p. Wraps same as softbound above except without "Official edition" at the top and with ornamentation (not pub info) outside the image at the bottom.
* ☻ . (GLD,csuf,CHx,SI,NYPL,USF,F,S,TnSt,NLC,RML,UDe,UTn,CoU,HL,UMi,UoC,NL,BPL,nwu,RPB,AIC,WM,TD)

---- Presentation copy: From Rand, McNally & Co. to Mrs. Potter Palmer. White leather hc with silver edging, engraving of Woman's Bldg on front cover. (CHx)

☞ Maud was wife of English painter John Elliott and daughter of Samuel Gridley Howe. John Elliott painted a mural in Mrs. Potter Palmer's home. Maud wrote several books -- chiefly on women. Her mother, Julia Ward Howe, was very active at the WCE.

836. Ellis, John, ed. *Chicago and the World's Columbian Exposition : with a portrait gallery of eminent citizens : in City and State.* Chicago: Trans-continental Art Publishing co. (Printed by the Blakely printing co.), 1895 [°1893 by The Trans-continental art publishing co.].

38x29½. 691 p. illus, ports, glossy paper text. At head of title: "1492 Quadri-centennial memorial volume 1893." Title in red and black.   ☺ . (CPL,CHx,NL,nwu,AIC)

837. *Erie lines : Columbian Exposition.* New York: ____ co., 189_.

23x11. Folded time-table and large folding bird's-eye of the WCE. Pale green wraps, red and black print and logo.

(TD) $100

838. Evans, Frederick W. *The World's Fair! Shall it be Closed one Day in the week to please a certain sect.* Pittsfield, Mass.: Press Eagle Publishing Co., 1891.

11½x8½. 5 p. Tan wraps, black print. Argues for opening on Sunday to ensure minimum losses to the exhibitors and maximum information to patrons in this age of reason. C.t.   ☺ . (NL)

839. *Excelsior Diary : Columbian Edition : 1893.* N.p.: n.p., n.d.

12½x7½. Leather pocket diary. Gilt print on maroon leather. See #2445.a for another edition. ---- Gilt print on light orange brown cloth hc, gilt edges.
☺ . (A,TD)   Blank: $20 - 36

840. *Facts on Cut Glass.* Toledo, OH: B. F. Wade Co, n.d.

16½x12. 42 p. ad book about Libbey Glass and the Libbey exhibit at the WF. Pale blue wraps, red print. Given as compliments of M. W. Belveridge.   (S,TD)

841. Farmer, Lydia Hoyt, ed. *The National Exposition souvenir : what America owes to women.* Buffalo Chicago New York: Charles Wells Moulton, 1893.

23x17. 504 p. Ivory cloth hc with gilt print and woman's port. Frontis of Martha Washington.
☺ . (BPL,S)

842. Felts, W[illia]m B. *The scheme of Queen Isabella's Theatre. A Private Enterprise for The Columbian World's Fair.* N.p.: n.p., [°1891].

25x19½. (22) p. Pink wraps, black print. C.t. Wm. B. Felts autographed the LC copy. Felts was "Supervisor General, Russell Springs, Kansas."   ☺ . (LC,TU)

843. Ferris Wheel Company. *A brief history of the invention and construction of The Ferris Wheel : together with a Short Biography of George W. G. Ferris, Esq.* N.p.: Ferris Wheel Co. [Chicago: Winters Art Litho co.], °1893 by the Ferris Wheel co.

19½x14½. (9) p., color illus, port. Caption title. C.t.: "The Ferris Wheel : Souvenir." The first Ferris wheel was invented and constructed for exhibition at the WCE. For more on the Ferris wheel, see #1018.

⊘ . (KyU,R,CHx,CVHx) $25 - 45

☞ George Washington Gale Ferris came from the Gale family which founded Galesburg, IL. He was an engineer on the Dangberg Ranch in Carson Valley, NV, and tended the numerous irrigation wheels on the ranch. From these wheels he got the idea for the heroic WCE ride he built. He was sued for patent infringement (Garden city Observation Wheel Co. v. The Ferris Wheel Co.) and won. Ferris died of typhoid fever on Nov. 22, 1896, at the age of 37; his obituary was on the front page of the *New York Times*. The Ferris wheel was exhibited at the 1904 St. Louis World's Fair.

844. Field Columbian Museum. *Annual report of the director to the board of trustees for the year 1894-95.* Report Series. Publication 6. Vol. 1, No. 1. Chicago: Oct. 1895.

23½x15. 2 *l*, 5-79 p. Gray-green pulp wraps, black print. List of donor of WCE exposition stock p. 67-79.
---- In: *Publications of the Field Columbian Museum : report series : Volume I.* Chicago: 1894-1900.
⊘ . (NL)

845. Field Columbian Museum. Curtis, William Eleroy. *The Authentic Letters of Columbus.* Publication 1. [Historical series]. Vol. 1, No. 2. Chicago: May, 1895.

24x15½. 2 *l*, 95-200, (1) p. Pea green pulp wraps. Frontis: "Facsimile of autographic statement of gold brought by Columbus from America." The original Columbus documents described were exhibited at the WCE and photographed; the negatives were presented to the Field Museum and the illus in this bulletin were made from them (p. 98). T.p. lists Curtis as the Honorary Curator, Dept of Columbus Memorial. [A typewritten note, signed by Skiff and dated Sept. 5, 1911, is tipped into the NL copy and states nos. 1 and 2 of Vol I, Historical Series, were all that had been issued of the series.] ⊘ . (NL)

846. Field Columbian Museum. *An historical and descriptive account of the Field Columbian museum.* Pub. 1. [Historical series]. Vol. I, No. 1. Chicago: Dec., 1894.

24x15½. 1 *l*, (3)-(6), 7-91 p. Pea green pulp wraps. Green-tone frontis of Field Columbian Museum. A red and black map of Jackson Park is on p. 91. F. J. V. Skiff was museum director. Account of articles donated to the museum by various WCE exhibitors. ⊘ . (NL,BPL)

847. Field, Kate. *The drama of glass.* N.p.: Published by the Libbey Glass Co., n.d. [references in text imply published on or after 1896].

17x11. 47 p., illus. Frontis port of Kate Field. Paper covered hc is designed with gold decorations and two shades of green. Written to describe the Toledo, Ohio, Libbey Exhibit at WCE.

[Kate Field spoke at the World's Press Congress and the World's Literary Congress at the Art Institute.]
P↑   ☺ . (GLD,F,TD,S) $25 - 60

848. Field (Marshall) & Company. *World's Columbian Exposition souvenir and kid glove price list.* Chicago: [1893].

13x__. (24) p., illus.   (CHx)

849. Fletcher, Banister. [*Report on the Columbian Exposition at Chicago 1893*]. N.p.: n.p., 1893.

Microfilm. Title from microfilm box. London: Microfilm Systems Limited, [1988?].   (AIC)

850. Fryer, John. *An illustrated account of the World's Columbian exposition at Chicago, 1893.* Rpt. from *Chinese Scientific and Industrial Magazine.* [1893?].

28x18. 30 *l* rice paper folded Chinese style to make (60) p. String tied yellow-tan wraps. Tipped in c.t. in English; Chinese text and Chinese title on last p. Illus of WF bldgs.   ☺ . (NL)

851. *Gasmotoren-Fabrik Deutz in Köln-Deutz. Actien-Gesellschaft, Capital 6 Millionen Mark. 140 Medaillen, Ehrenpreise, Ehrendiplome.* N.p.: n.p., n.d.

18½x15. 37 p. Wraps. Frontis of the factory. Exhibitor at WCE. In German. Ad for "Otto-Motor" on back cover.   ☺ . (A)

852. Gentzke, M. O. *Das Carlsbad von Amerika : oder die heissen Quellen in Hot Springs : in den Black Hills dem wunderschönen Gebirge in Süd-Dakota. Heilkraft der Bäder. World's fair edition.* West Point, Nebr.: Nebraska Volksblatt und Cuming Advertiser, n.d.

20x13½. 1 *l*, 30 p. Pinkish tan wraps with black print. Old German script. Illus outside back wrap: "Minnekahta Block, Hot Springs, S. Dak."   ☺ . (NL)

853. German Kali-Works. *Potash : origin, trade and its use in agriculture.* [Berlin: Printed by H. S. Hermann], n.d.

24½x16. 19, (1) p., include tables and illus. White smooth wraps with striking red, navy blue, and gilt print and blue design. Between "Potash" and "origin": "Columbian Exposition Chicago : German Kali-Works : Leopoldshall Stassfurt." C.t. In English.
P→   ☺ . (GLD,UDe,WM,TD) $18 - 36

854. Godoy, José F. *La Ciudad de Chicago y la Exposición universal de 1893.* Chicago--San Francisco: Compañia publicista pan-American, [°1892].

40½x29½. 7 *l*, 163 p.,(1) p., 4 *l* ads, includes fold. map. Paper covered boards, with b/w litho of Machinery Hall, glossy leaves. Fine illus and lithos of Chicago and WCE sights.   ☻ . (LC)

855. Gordon, H. Panmure. *The land of the almighty dollar.* London and New York: Frederick Warne & co., [1892?].

21x15. Frontis (port of Gordon), tissue guard, 3 *l*, 215, (1) p. Olive green cloth beveled hc, gilt print; red, white, blue and silver design. WCE: p. (193)-200. Preface dated June 1892.   (csuf)

856. *The Gospel according to Saint John: translated out of the original Greek; ...* Souvenir ed. New York: American Bible Society, 1893.

12x8. 48 p. Blind stamped maroon paper covered boards. C.t.: "Columbian Exposition : Holy Scripture : Souvenir Edition."   ☻ . (E,S,TD)

857. Grand Trunk Railway. *How to visit the World's Fair at Chicago, May to October, 1893.* [Buffalo, NY: 1893].

23x__. Folder, map.   (CHx)

858. Grand Trunk Railway. ... *Pen and Sunlight Sketches of scenery reached by the Grand Trunk Railway and connections including Niagara Falls, Thousand Islands ...* Columbian ed. N.p.: Grand Trunk Railway co., 1893.

31x23½. 108 p. At head of title: "'The tourist route of America.'" Compliments of the Passenger Dept.   ☻ . (S)

859. *The graphic history of the fair : containing a sketch of international expositions, a review of the events leading to the discovery of America, and a history of the World's Columbian exposition : held ... May 1 to October 31, 1893. ...* Chicago: G. P. Engelhard & Co., 1894; Chicago: The Graphic co., [°1894 by The Graphic Co.]; 2d and rev. ed. Chicago: G. P. Engelhard & co., 1895 [°1895 by G. P. Engelhard & Co].

Engelhard: 41x28½. 239, (1) p., illus. Maroon cloth hc with gilt design.
---- Graphic: Same size and paging. Black cloth hc, silver print and design; also red print and design on green cloth hc.
---- Engelhard: 2nd and rev. ed., 1895. 40x27½. 240 p. Dark maroon with black spine.
   ☻ . (GLD,csuf,CHx,S,OhHx,UoC,A,AIC,OC,WiHx) $50 - 125

860. *The Great School Exhibits. Liberal arts department, World's fair.* Milwaukee, WI: Wm. Geo. Bruce, Publisher, °1894.

11½x18½. 50 *l.*   ☻ . (WiHx)

861. Green, Mary E[lizabeth]. *Food Products of the World.* Chicago: The Hotel World, 1895.

20x__. v, 1 *l*, [vii]-xi, 249, vii p., illus. The subject matter of this book was originally published in a series of magazine articles begun just after the close of the WCE. (preface). On t.p.: "Ed. and illus by Grace Green Bohn."   (UWa,LC,UoC)

862. *Hagenbeck's Arena and World's Museum : Midway Plaisance : World's Columbian Exposition.* [Chicago?]: Mark L. Stone, [1893].

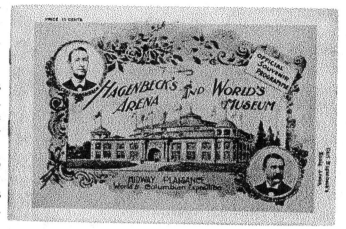

16½x23. (4) p., illus. Decorative wraps printed in black on green (or pink). C.t. "Official souvenir programme." The programme states: "Smoking positively prohibited."
P→　　⊚ (GLD,csuf,BPL,WM,TD)　　$18 - 36

☞ Carl Hagenbeck (1844-1913) took his trained animal show all over the world. The Arena was located near the entrance to the Midway next to the railroad tracks.

863. *Handbook of General Information for university men visiting Chicago.* Chicago: Wm. Johnston Printing Co., 1893.

14x9½. Stapled wraps. C.t.= t.p.　⊚ . (WM)

864. Hartzell, Josiah. *Life of Columbus.* Akron, OH: Aultman, Miller & co. (printed by The Matthews-Northrup co.), [1893].

20½x13½. 32 p. Light brown wraps with red "1892." Illus of Santa Maria making landfall; caption: "The moment of Triumph!" with "T," "M," and "T" in red. Souvenir of the WCE compliments of Aultman, Miller & Co., manufacturers of Buckeye Harvesting Machines.　⊚ . (OhHx,BPL)

865. Hartzler, H[enry] B. *Moody in Chicago : or the World's fair gospel campaign : an account of six months' evangelistic work in the city of Chicago and vicinity during the time of the World's Columbian exposition, conducted by Dwight L. Moody and his associates.* New York Chicago Toronto: Fleming H. Revell Co., [°1894].

19½x13½. 255 p. Dark blue (or dark red) cloth hc, gold print on spine only.
⊚ . (LC,F,UoC,NL)　　$20 - 35

866. Hawthorne, Hildegarde. *The fairest of the fair.* Philadelphia: Henry Altemus, 1894.

15½x11. Frontis of The Grand Basin + 1 *l*, 293 p., plates. Silver decoration, gilt lettering and design, top edge gilt.
P→　　⊚ (csuf,LC)

867. Hawthorne, Julian. *Humors of the Fair.* Chicago: E. A. Weeks & Co., °1893 by E. A. Weeks & Co.

19x13. Pulp frontis of "Hildegarde," 1 glossy plate with b/w illus both sides, (3)-205 p., (2) p. ads, illus. White glossy wraps, black and red print. On t.p.: "The Marguerite Series No.12. Sept. 15th 1893. Plates printed on both sides. 1st plate precedes t.p. Issued Semi Monthly." "This volume is meant to serve as an antidote to the various guide books ... [a] sustained effort has been made to divest its pages of anything that could be construed as Useful Information." Illus by Will. E. Chapin. ☺!

---- *Humors of the fair.* Same pub info. Same frontis; no glossy plate, (5), 9-205 p. Rose tinged glossy wraps with sepia print and 2 b/w illus of people.

☺ . (csuf,CHx,NYPL,S,HL,UoC,NL,Yale,WiHx,TD) $45

868. *The Hercules blue book No. 1.* Supplementary Issue March 1, 1893. Aurora, IL: Hercules Ice Machine Co., [ᶜ1891 by the Hercules Iron Works].

23½x15½. 72 p. with (27) p. testimonials in back. Bright royal blue cloth hc, gold lettering and design. Describes Hercules' ice machines, locations installed at WCE, including the ill fated cold storage pavilion illus p.8. Supplement at p. 69. [The pavilion burned to the ground on July 10, 1893, killing 17 people.]

P→   ☺ . (GLD) $20 - 45

869. Heron, Addie E. *Dainty Work for Pleasure and Profit.* Chicago: Thompson and Thompson, 1893; 3rd ed. Chicago: Thompson and Thompson, 1904.

1893: 24x18. 444 p. Red-brown cloth hc; gilt lettering. How to book on darning, crocheting, embroidering and other craft work. Preface dedicates book to Mrs. Potter Palmer.

---- 1904: 24x19. 458 p. Dark brown cloth hc.

☺ . (S)

870. Hill, Josephine D. *A souvenir of World's Fair Women and wives of prominent officials connected with the World's Columbian Exposition.* Chicago: The Blocher Co., 1892 ᶜ1892 by Josephine D. Hill.

20½x15. 63 *l*, port. White cloth hc, gold print, glossy leaves. Description of each woman next to her port.

---- Same size, 64 *l*. Dark green cloth hc with gilt c.t.: "Souvenir. World's Fair Women." Format: port on verso with biographical material on facing recto followed by blank *l*.

☺ . (CHx,LC,NYPL)

871. [Hill, Martha S.], ed. *Fame's tribute to children : being a collection of autograph sentiments contributed by famous men and women for this volume. Done in fac-simile and published for the benefit of the Children's home, of the World's Columbian exposition : Chicago 1893.* Chicago: A. C. McClurg and co., 1892; 2nd ed. Chicago: [Hayes and Co.], [ᶜ1892 by Hayes and co.].

McClurg 1st ed.: 26x20½. 149 p. of facsimiles. White cloth hc with gilt print.

---- Hayes 2nd ed.: 26x20½. 6 *l*, 15-101 p., 1 *l*, includes facsimiles of autographs and music. Red (or olive) cloth spine over decorated two-tone green (or gilt decorative) paper covered boards. Title vignette. Gilt c.t.: "Fame's Tribute to Children." On cover: "Presented by Chicago Great Western Ry. 'The Maple Leaf Route.'" Routes to Chicago appear on the back cover in gilt. Explanatory note by Martha S. Hill.

---- Hayes 2nd ed.: Also listed. Part I: 84 p. Part II: 101 p. Both in one vol.

P↑　　⊚ . (JHU,UWa,CHx,NYPL,S,UDe,UMi,UoC,BPL,nwu,RPB,OC,TD,RPB)　　　　1st ed: $75

872. Hill, Thomas E[die]. *Hill's album of Biography and Art : Containing Portraits and Pen-Sketches of Many Persons who have been and are ...* World's Fair ed. Chicago: Danks & Co. Publishers, 1892 [ᶜ1891 by Danks & Co.].

27½x23. 590 p., 1 *l* (ad). Brown cloth hc printed and designed in black and gold, red stained edges. WCE section from page 564 to the end.

⊚ (GLD,S,E)　　　　$10 - 25

873. *History of Chicago and Souvenir of the Liquor Interest : The Nation's Choice for the Great Columbian Exposition, 1893: Illustrated.* Chicago: Belgravia Publishing Co., ᶜ1891.

27x20. (7), 34-256 p., (6) p. ads, illus. Color litho paper covered boards, dark green cloth spine. Wonderful ads. C.t.: "History of Chicago. Souvenir of the Liquor Interest."　⊚ . (CPL)

874. *History of the Great Lakes Illustrated.* 2 vol. Chicago: J. H. Beers & Co., 1899.

28x22½. Vol 1: xvi, 10 *l* maps, 928 p. Vol 2: 3 *l*, 1108 p. Gilt edges. Vol 2, chap. 41, gives a brief account of ships at the WCE.　(CHx)

875. *History of the World's Columbian Exposition : Chicago : 1492-1892.* Chicago: World's Columbian Exposition History PubL. Co., [1892-].

48x31½. Subscription set 20 nos., many photos, illus, glossy sheets. Tan wraps. Some issues with multicolor lithograph covers; some monochromatic. Ads at back of issues. C.t.

---- Also listed: 48x__. 20 (i.e. 21) nos. (2), 326, (16) p. color illus in portfolio.

---- Bound: 2nd ed. ᶜ1893 by the Columbian History Co. 47½x32½. 362 p. Brown leather hc.

⊚ . (CHx,UoC,A,RPB,L)

876. Hitchcock, [James] Ripley [Wellman], ed. *The art of the world : illustrated in the painting, statuary and architecture of the World's Columbian Exposition. ...* Artists' Facsimile Japan ed. New York: D. Appleton, [1893].

50x39. Maroon with gold and gray hc. 3 vol. Vols 1-2, some plates preceded by guard sheet with descriptive letterpress; [vol 3] entirely matted colored plates. Limited to 150 copies: UWa has no. 7; NYPL has no. 61 in original 10 parts.　(UWa,NYPL)

☞ Hitchcock was a prolific art critic, author and editor; literary advisor of D. Appleton & Co. 1890-1902. He championed international copyright. Hitchcock also published numerous items for the St. Louis 1904 Fair.

877. ---. ---. Edition de Luxe. 10 vols. New York: D. Appleton and Co., 1893 [°1893 by D. Appleton].

49x38. Unpaginated, one of 1,000 copies. Blue cloth spine on gray paper covered boards, lettering in gold. Columbus design front cover in black. Color lithographs and fine b/w engravings. C.t.: "The Art of the World." Text by Burnham, Ives, Handy, Roger-Balla, Yriarte, H. Ward, H. Vos. [Excellent examples of printer and binder's art. Broken sets are valuable here because of the large and excellent illustrations.] ☉ (GLD,S,BPL) Set: $250 - 500

878. ---. ---. Grand (Columbian) Edition de Luxe. 10 vols. New York: D. Appleton and Co., 1893 [°1893 by D. Appleton].

49½x38½. Half leather and coarse mottled light brown cloth hc, gilt print, blind stamp design of Columbus, t.p. in red and black. Limited to 500 copies: BPL has no. 150; UoC no. 185. (UoC,BPL)

879. ---. ---. Imperial India Edition. New York: D. Appleton and Co., 1894 [°1893 by D. Appleton].

6 vol set. Two tone maroon cloth hc, part floral blind stamped. Vols 1-5 are "Art of the World." Vol 6 is "History" (#881). Limited to 1000 copies. (TD,AIC)

880. ---. ---. Subscription (standard) Edition. 30 parts. New York: D. Appleton and Co., 1893 [°1893 by D. Appleton]; New York: D. Appleton and Co., 1894; New York: D. Appleton and Co., 1895 [°1893, 1894 by D. Appleton and co.].

42½x32½. Unpaginated, same contents as Edition de Luxe (#878) except small borders on each page.
---- 1893: Subscription set: Heavy gray paper wraps, gold and deep blue lettering and designs, loose pages. Ad on back of wraps states each part will cost $1.
---- Also, editions printed in 1894, 1895, and 1896. Bound as 1, 2, or 5 vols.
---- 1894: 2 vol. Brown cloth hc, gold lettering and design.
---- 1895: 1 vol. 1 *l* (t.p.), (v)-x, 1 matted colored plate, 95, (1) p., 1 *l*, 1 plate with guard, i-xlvii, (1) p., many matted plates, some colored. Full heavy leather hc, some blind-stamp print, some gilt print, decorative end papers, all edges gilt. C.t.: "The art of the world."
---- 1895: 2 vol. Full two tone morocco hc, gold lettering. C.t.: "The Art of the World."
P→ ☉ (GLD,KU,UMC,csuf,CHx,NYPL,S,NLC,BCM,UTn,UMi,NYSt,UoC,NL,BPL,A,AIC,WiHx,TD) 30 parts: $200 - 400

881. Hitchcock, [James] Ripley [Wellman], ed. *The story of the exposition : illustrated in its history, architecture, and art*. New York: D. Appleton and Co., 1895 [°1893, 1894 by D. Appleton and Co.].

43x33. iv, lxxxiv p., illus, plates (1 color), color plan. Two tone maroon cloth hc, part floral blind stamped. C.t.: "The art of the world. History." A vol with its own t.p. from a 6 vol set entitled "The art of the world" (#879). Fine engraved lithos of major WCE bldgs.
☉ . (WiHx,TD) $65 - 120

882. Hollingsworth, Adelaide. *The Columbian Cook Book. Toilet, Household, Medical, and Cooking Recipes, Flowers and Their Culture ... Embracing all the points necessary for successful housekeeping.* [Chicago]: Columbia Publishing Co., n.d.

25x20. 3 *l*, 9-792 p., frontis with bird's-eye view of WCE, illus. Dark blue cloth hc, brown lettering and design, decorative end papers. Port of Mrs. Potter Palmer between p. 22 and 23. C.t.: "Columbia cookbook." ◎ (CHx)

883. Holt, Ben. *Good style, small expense; or, we'll never go there any more.* New York: for the trade [press, of J. J. Little & Co.], 1894.

12°. viii, (9)-197 p. Account of a visit to the WCE. (LC)

884. *Home Almanac : A souvenir : 1893.* New York: Home Insurance Co. for the Vermont Record Newspaper, 1893.

23½x17. 32 p. Color lithographed wraps. Facts and lithographs from the WF.
P↓ ◎ (GLD,S,TD) $14 - 26

 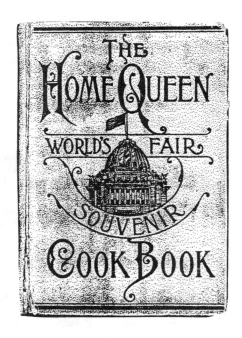

885. *The "Home Queen" World's Fair souvenir Cook Book, Two Thousand Valuable Recipes : on Cookery and Household Economy, Menus, Table Etiquette, Toilet, Etc. Contributed by over two hundred World's fair lady managers, wives of governors and other ladies of position and influence.* Chicago: John F. Waite publishing co., [ᶜ1893 by Geo. F. Cram. ᶜ1894 by JNO F. Waite. ᶜ1895 by JNO F. Waite]; New York and Chicago: Geo. F. Cram, 1893.

24x15½. 608 p., 2 *l* plates, illus, ports. White oil cloth hc, black printing, marbled edges. Frontis of Juliet Corson, founder of Cooking Schools in America.
P↑ ◎ . (LC,S,A)

886. *Homes for visitors to the World's fair. A list of families in Chicago who will accommodate visitors during the period of the World's Columbian exposition : also a list of the hotels in the city.* ... Chicago: Poole Bros., Publishers, 1893 ᶜ1892 by Poole Bros.; Revised ed. Chicago: Poole Bros., Publishers, 1893 ᶜ1893 by Poole Bros.

ᶜ1892: 24½x20. 3 *l*, (2), (9)-63 p., b/w illus, maps. Tan wraps, chocolate print. Chicago double map 1st 2 *l*, other maps interspersed. C.t.: "Homes for Visitors To The World's Fair." On cover: "Price 50 cents."
---- ᶜ1893: Revised ed. 25x19½. (3), 8-58 p., 3 *l*, illus, maps. Chicago fold out map in front is sectioned and labeled to correspond with list of family/hotel names. Same c.t. and price.
    ☺ . (GLD,CHx) $18 - 38

887. Houghton, Mifflin and Company. *Descriptive list of the five hundred and forty eight books published by Houghton, Mifflin and company and exhibited in the model library of the American Library Association at the Chicago exposition of 1893.* Boston and New York: Houghton, Mifflin and co., 1894.

22½x14. (2), (1)-78 p. Gray-green pulp wraps, black print and Riverside Press seal. Catalog of this publisher's books which are in the A.L.A. Library plus an index of authors. ☺ . (NL)

888. Houghton, Mifflin and Company. *Four old portraits of Columbus with a fac-simile of his manuscript and his coat of arms : together with a list of books on Columbus, the discovery of America, and other topics allied thereto : Houghton, Mifflin and company of Boston, New York, and Chicago : Manufacturers' Building : Department of Liberal Arts, Section E : World's Columbian Exposition : Chicago.* [Boston: Houghton, Mifflin and co., 1893].

21½x14. (12) p. includes illus, ports. Front wrap has design of globe with interlocking "C"s. C.t.
    ☺ . (UDe)

889. *Illustrations of the different languages and dialects in which the Holy Bible in whole or in part has been printed and circulated by the American Bible Society and the British and Foreign Bible Society. Souvenir edition. Columbian exposition 1893.* [New York]: American Bible Society, n.d.

17x11½. 64 p. polyglot of John 3:16 in 242 languages and dialects. Colorful wraps have dark maroon background with pink, peach, and green lettering. B/w illus on inside of both wraps.
    ☺ . (GLD,csuf,S,NL,A,BPL) $12 - 26

890. International Linguistics Institute of Chicago. *The World's Columbian Exposition Phrasebook. In Thirty languages.* Composed and issued under the auspices of the author.

12x16½. 3 *l*, (ix)-xx, 202 p.   (LC)

891. Jay, John. *The national responsibility for an international exposition : a letter to The Honourable Chauncey M. Depew* ... New York: Dodd, Mead & co., 1889.

22½x14½. 15 p. Wraps same stock as text. Cover states Jay was late minister to Vienna. ☺ . (csuf,NYPL)

892. Jefferis, B. G., and J. L. Nichols. *Search lights on health : Light on Dark Corners. A complete sexual science* ... 9th ed. Naperville, IL: J. L. Nichols, 1895 [ᶜ1894 by J. L Nichols].

18x12½. 2 *l*, 472 p. Black blind stamped cloth hc, gilt print spine. Two lithographs of WCE. Advice to maiden, wife, and mother. Standard home medical advisor for marriage. Curiosity.

⊚ (GLD) $5 - 10

893. Jensen, E. S. & Company. *What is the proper housing for an Exposition in 1893?* Chicago: Shea Smith & Co., printers, 1890.

17½x11½. (3)-35 p. Pink glossy wraps, black print. C.t.= t.p. Tissue paper diagram of proposed temporary tent-like dormitory bldg tipped in at center fold.   ⊚ . (CHx,UDe)

894. *John Brown souvenir : (1893) of the (1893) : World's Columbian exposition.* N.p.: n.p., [°1893 by Alexander M. Ross].

23x11½. (2) p. card. Vignette litho of John Brown, "liberator of Kansas and martyr of Virginia," plus text on front; facsimile of Brown's last written words on back.   ⊚ . (LC)

895. Johnson, [Edwin] Rossiter, ed. *A history of the World's Columbian exposition : held in Chicago in 1893 : by authority of the board of directors.* 4 vols. New York: D. Appleton and co., 1897-98 [°1897 by D. Appleton and co.].

29½x22. xiii, 512 p.; 526 p.; 530 p.; and 528 p., illus, ports. Half morocco with marble paper covered boards, gilt spines, marbled end papers match covers. Frontis (ports) for vols 1 to 4 respectively: Harlow N. Higinbotham, Thomas W. Palmer, Geo. R. Davis, and Bertha Palmer.

*   ⊚ . (csuf,KyU,CHx,SI,NYPL,USF,F,OSU,UFl,SLP,CoU,UMi,NYSt,UoC,NL,nwu,AIC,BM,OC,WiHx) $200 - 350

☞ Johnson (1840-1931) was a prolific writer on the Civil War, Spanish-American War, and the First World War, plus he wrote poems, children's stories and other histories. This is a major reference on the WCE as is Hubert Howe Bancroft.

896. Johnson, William Fletcher, and John Habberton. *"My Country, 'Tis of Thee!" : or, The United States of America; Past, Present and Future. A Philosophic View of American History and of Our Present Status, to be Seen in the Columbian exhibition.* ... Philadelphia [and] Chicago: International publishing co., 1892 [°1892 by B. W. Urian]; Philadelphia [and] Chicago: International publishing co., 1893 [°1892].

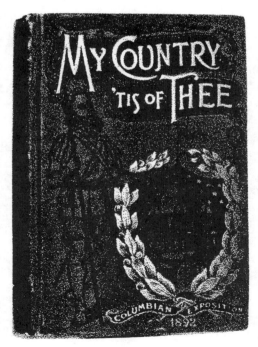

1892: 21½x15. 3 *l*, 611 p. Brown cloth hc, gilt and black lettering and design, decorative floral end papers. WCE is described in chapters 4 & 5. Two page bird's-eye view frontis (2 *l*). Biographical sketches by John Habberton.
---- 1893: Half morocco over blue cloth boards, gilt lettered spine.
---- 1893: Blue cloth hc.
P→   ⊚ . (GLD,csuf,S,E,BPL,A,TD) $15 - 25

897. [Keeler, Ezra W.] *America focalized at the Columbian World's Fair : Chicago 1893 : ocean to ocean in miniature.* N.p.: n.p., °1891 by E. W. Keeler.

19x12. 8 p. + unpaged illus, black printed paper covered boards (back cover marbled), maroon cloth spine. Proposed bldg and exhibit for California showing America in miniature (never materialized). Elaborate plan for street and rail transportation to the exhibit. Fold. litho of exhibit front and back.
⊛ . (LC)

898. K[elly], M[ichael] J[ames]. ... *"San Salvador:" A Story of Columbus and His Discoveries and a short account of the Mound Builders, Visits of Norsemen, Modern Discovery and the World's Columbian exposition.* Chicago: American Popular Publication Co., [°1892].

16x12. 1 *l*, 121 p. Lemon wraps, black print, frontis of Columbus. At head of title: "American Popular Publications. No. 1." and "1492--1892." ⊛ . (LC)

899. Kelsey, D. M. *Columbus and the New World Heros of discovery and conquest, embracing the lives, voyages and explorations of* [list of navigators] *with introduction by Hon. Geo. R. Davis, director-general World's Columbian Exposition.* St. Louis and Philadelphia: Scammell & Co., publishers, 1892.

22½x17. 3 *l*, ix-xxiv, 25-679 + (1) p. Rebound hc. 2 *l* map of the world between x and xi. T.p. states: "200 engravings." Frontis litho: "Columbus Before Isabella and the Council." ⊛ . (LC)

900. Kinney, Henry C. *Why the Columbian Exposition Should be Opened on Sunday. A Religio-Social Study.* Chicago: Rand, McNally & Co., printers 1892 [°1892 by Rev. Henry C. Kinney].

23x15. 2 *l*, 5-57 p. of pulp paper. Tan wraps with black print. Booklet is divided into "The Civil Sunday" and "The Religious Sunday." Errata slip before t.p. Kinney was "missionary of the P.E.C. at the stock yards, Chicago." ⊛ (CHx,NYPL,NL)

901. Kirkland, Joseph. *The Story of Chicago.* 2 vol. Chicago: Dibble publishing co., 1892-94 [°1892 by Dibble publishing co.].

27½x20. Vol 1: 3 *l*, xii-xxiii, 488 p., frontis, illus includes ports, maps, facsimiles. Frontis is a photo of the Robert Cavelier bronze monument; tissue guard. 2 page map between p. (16)-17 is not included in paging. WCE: vol 1, p. 418-436; vol 2, p. 17-252. Vol 2: "By Joseph Kirkland and Caroline Kirkland." Pub. after J. Kirkland's death.
---- 2nd ed.: Vol 1: 1 *l* frontis of LaSalle statue, (iii)-xxiii, 490 p.
⊛ . (CHx,LC,OSU,SLP,UoC,NL,nwu,RPB,WiHx)

902. Klein, Fred., Company. *Unsere Weltausstellung : Eine Beschreibung der Columbischen Weltausstellung in Chicago, 1893.* ... In 36 Lieferungen. Chicago: Druck und Verlag der Fred Klein co., 1894 [°1894 by Fred. Klein co.].

45x32. 568 p. (4 vol paged continuously), glossy text sheets. On cover: "German historical series, bd. 1, no. 1-36."
---- 40½x29. 568 p., illus (including facsimiles). Half black crushed morocco over purple pebbled cloth, top edge gilt. Bound from 36 subscription issues.
---- In 1 vol. Burgundy pebbled hc, gilt lettered c.t.: "Unsere Weltausstellung." Special binding by C. R. Troost.
---- In 2 vol. 44½x32. 568 p. Quarter leather over navy blue cloth beveled hc, elaborate silver print and design, marbled edges, decorative end papers. On t.p.: "In 18 Doppel-Lieferungen." C.t.: "Unsere Weltausstellung : Chicago, 1893."
⊛ (GLD,csuf,CHx,LC,SLP,HL,UoC,nwu,WiHx) $70 - 150

903. [Koenig, Albert]. *Are You Going to the World's Columbian Exposition at Chicago in 1893? Call or address World's Columbian Exposition Transportation Co. of Pittsburgh, PA.* Pittsburgh: Nicholson, printer, n.d.

15½x12. 15 p. Blue-green wraps with black print and border. ⊘ . (CHx)

904. Krupp Pavilion. *Cast-steel works of Fried. Krupp : Essen, Germany : Articles Exhibited in the Krupp Pavilion at the World's Columbian Exposition.* [Chicago: Rand, McNally & Co., ᶜ1892]?

18x12 (folded). Twice folded leaf (18x48) making (8) p. Shows etching of pavilion, floor plan of pavilion, location and names of steel forging, casting, etc. exhibits in the pavilion and map of location on grounds (on the Lake shore) next to the Leather exhibit bldg. [The Pavilion was a $1.5M replica of the Krupp home, "Villa Hügel."]
P→   ⊘ (GLD,CHx,NL) $12 - 25

905. *The Krupp Pavilion. Der Krupp Pavillon. World's Columbian Exposition, Chicago, 1893.* New York [and] Chicago: Published and copyrighted by A. Wittemann, 1893.

15½x13½. 10 *l*, illus. C.t. Cover vignette of Krupp Bldg. Ribbon tied. Captions in German and English.   ⊘ . (UDe)

906. Krupp Pavilion. *Exhibition Catalogue of the Cast Steel Works of Fried. Krupp : Essen on the Ruhr (Rhenish Prussia). World's Columbian Exposition : 1893 : Chicago.* [Berlin: Otto V. Holten, n.d.].

17½x12. 210, (2) p., 2 *l*, III-XI p., 3 *l* plans. Text, illus and tables. Stiff wraps, red and black print with gilt litho of factory on steel gray background (front); plain red (back). Red dyed edges, rounded corners.
---- Same but without 3 *l* plans.
         ⊘ (GLD,NYPL,S,HL) $22 - 40

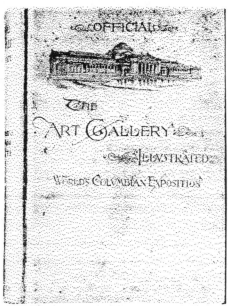

907. Kurtz, Charles M., ed. *Official : illustrations (three hundred and thirty-six engravings) from the art gallery of the World's Columbian exposition.* 1st ed. Philadelphia: George Barrie, [ᶜ1893 by George Barrie].

21½x15. 383 p. include frontis (2 p. plan), plates, plans. White smooth cloth hc with gold embossed lettering and design front and back, red stained edges. C.t.: "Official : The Art Gallery Illustrated : World's Columbian Exposition."
---- Other bindings found: 1) half leather over marbled boards, red stained edges; 2) solid brown hc without print; 3) gray wraps with black print, edges not stained.
      P→   ⊘ . (GLD,csuf,KyU,CHx,NYPL,F,S,OhHx,OSU,NLC,E,UDe,BU,UTn,CoU,HL,UMi,NYSt,Yale,UoC,NL,A,BPL,RPB,AIC,OC,WM,TD) $20 - 40

908. Landis, Jacob F. *The World's fair recipe book.   Containing over 500 practical and economical recipes.* Philadelphia: Jacob F. Landis, °1893.

    16x12. 118 p. Sepia wraps, black print. Ferris wheel litho on front cover. C.t.

    ◎ . (GLD,LC) $10 - 30

909. Lantz, D[aniel] O. *Six months in the Reformed Tabernacle.* Chicago: D. O. Lantz, [1893].

    24x15½. Illus wraps with vignettes of Administration Bldg and Tabernacles. 111, (1) p., illus, ports. Cover: "World's Fair Souvenir : six Months in the reformed Tabernacle." RPB copy cover inscribed: "Mary C. Fisher, Penn Hall, Pa. Nov. 30, 1893."   ◎ . (RPB)

910. Leffingwell, William Bruce. *Pussy Wants A Corner : in this book, which reviews the delights of the World's fair and contains a series of articles depicting the pleasures of field sports.* N.p.: n.p., °1894 by E. S. Rice, Chicago.

    23½x17. 96 p., illus, includes paged ads interspersed. Very pretty blue-gray wraps, gold design work and litho of child and cat. Not for kids! Ads are for gun powder manufacturers, shotgun shooting rules in back. Illus of state bldgs with explanatory text. [Meaning of title not discernible from the text.] ◎ . (LC,CHx)

911. Lehigh University. *Catalog of Articles in the exhibit of the Lehigh University, at the World's Columbian Exposition, 1893.* [Prepared by Mansfield Merriman]. Rpt. South Bethlehem, PA: n.p., 1893.

    23x15. 22 p. Greenish tan wraps with black print. C.t. List of 502 exhibit items in the Manufactures Bldg. Below title: "Reprinted from *The Lehigh Quarterly*."

    ◎ . (GLD,CPL) $18 - 36

912. *Libbey Glass Company : World's Fair 1893.* Chicago: The Foster Press, n.d.

    11½x16. (16) p. Glossy wraps printed and illustrated in blue and red. Describes and shows the Libbey Glass Factory Bldg on the Midway. It also shows the spun glass dress woven for Princess Eulalia of Spain. C.t.

    P→   ◎ . (GLD,S,A,TD) $12 - 30

913. Libby Prison War Museum Association. *Libby prison war museum catalogue and program...* Chicago: Libby Prison War Museum Association, [189-].

    23x15½. (40) p., illus (includes ports, facsimiles). Pink wraps, blue lettering and design. C.t. Ad matter interspersed. This infamous confederate prison was moved to Chicago as a display.

    (ALB,F,TD) $20 - 30

914. *The Liberty Bell. Independence Hall. Philadelphia. 1893.* Philadelphia: Press of Allen, Lane & Scott, n.d.

23x15. 31 p. Yellow wraps. At head of title: "World's fair souvenir." ☻. (KyU)

915. Lipscomb, Dabney. *James D. Lynch : Poet-Laureate of the World's Columbian Exposition ...* Rpt. [N.p.: 1900?].

24½x15½. Wraps. (127)-137, (2) p. Title given is from cover. On cover: "Reprinted from Publications of The Mississippi Historical Society -- Vol. III." ☻. (RPB)

916. Long, J[ohn] H[arper]. *Chemical notes from the Columbian Exposition.* Easton, PA: Chemical Pub. Co., 1893.

8°. 10 p. Pre-print: *Jour. of the Amer. Chemical Soc.* vol 15, no. 3. (NYPL)

917. Lönnkvist, Fred. ... *De Hem vi lemnade och De Hem vi funno. Det pittoreska Sverige och det pittoreska Amerika.* ... Minneapolis, MN: I. M. Ayer Publishing Co., 1893.

28x21. 509 p. Illus dark tan cloth hc with green and gilt print. At head of title: "Att? minneswerk ofver Sverige och Amerika." Illus history of the U.S., including the WCE, in Swedish. (TD)

918. Lord's Day Alliance of the United States. *Brief In Favor of Keeping the World's Fair Closed on Sunday. Before the Committee of the United States Senate and House of Representatives : Washington, April, 1892...* [New York: Mail and Express Print, 1892.

24x16½. 20 p. Caption title. Signed by E. F. Shepard, President American Sabbath Union. Other author: [Shepard, Elliott Fitch]. ☻. (NYPL,OhHx)

919. Lossing, Benson J. *The progress of Four Hundred Years in the great republic of the west.* ... New York: Gay Brothers & co., 1892 [°1892 by Gay Brothers & co.].

24x18½. 1 *l*, xxvii, 1 *l*, iv, 1 *l*, cxxxvi, 6 pl, 2 *l*, 35-536 p. The 136 p. in front are about the WCE. Olive green cloth hc, black and gold print and designs, decorated end papers, red splatter edges. Steel engraved frontis of Columbus; fold out bird's-eye view of WCE (first *l*).
☻ (GLD,S,TD) $15 - 30

920. Mabie, Hamilton W. *Footprints of four centuries : The story of the American people comprising the important events, episodes, and incidents ...* Philadelphia: W. W. Houston & Co., 1894 [°1894 by W. E. Scull]; Philadelphia and Chicago: International Publishing Co., [°1894 and °1897 by W. E. Scull].

Houston: 26½x21. xxvii, (1) p., 1 *l*, 21-851 p. Gray-blue cloth hc, design and print in gold and black, t.p. printed in red and black. WCE from p. 710. At top of t.p.: "A topical history of the United States."
---- International: 26x20. 2 *l*, xxvii, (1) p., 1 *l*, 21-856 p., same binding. WCE from p. 711. First *l* is color frontis of Washington meeting Rochambeau.
☻ (GLD) $12 - 32

921. Magee, Thomas. *The Alphabet and Language : Immortality of the Big Trees : Wealth and Poverty of the Chicago Exposition : Three Essays.* San Francisco: William Doxey, 1895.

19½x12. 109 p. Dark green cloth hc, blind stamped design, gilt print. Autographed copy at csuf.
P↓ ⊜ . (csuf,HL,NL)

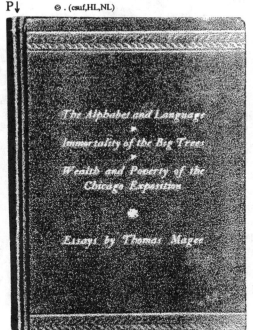

922. Mattill, H[enry], comp. *Life of Christopher Columbus. The discovery of America and early settlements.*
World's Fair ed. Cleveland, OH: Lauer & Mattill, n.d. [copyright by Lauer & Mattill].

1st ed.: 20½x16. (2) + 7-331 p. Black (or brown) cloth hc, silver lettering and design on globe. T.p. is fifth page, no leaves or frontis. WCE from 310-331. C.t.: 1492 World's Fair edition life of Columbus 1893."
---- 2nd ed.: 20½x15. (2) + 7-332 p., bird's-eye view of the Exposition on p. 332, dark green cloth hc, pulp pages. WCE from 310-332. LC copyright stamp: 1893.
P↑ ⊜ . (GLD,LC,A,S) $12 - 25

923. McClure, J[ames] B[aird]. *The World's Columbian exposition : complete with illustrations and descriptions of the public, state, foreign, and other prominent buildings on the fairgrounds, together with ...* Chicago: Rhodes & McClure, pub. co., 1893.

19x13. (14-23), 25-466, (2) p., illus. Brown cloth hc, gold print, decorative end papers. Frontis is Moro's port of Columbus. C.t.: "The World's Columbian Exposition Complete : Illustrated." ⊜ . (CPL,S)

924. McDowell, William O., comp. *Liberty primer. Giving the dates of the anniversaries commemorated by the ringing of the Columbian liberty bell. ...* N.p.: n.p., ᶜ1894 by William O. McDowell.

23½x15½. 100 p. Pale green smooth wraps, black print. Bell was first rung Sept. 11, 1893, for the meeting of World's Congress of Religions. The Bell was controversial since it was made up of melted artifacts; many thought the artifacts more valuable than the resulting Bell. Small souvenir bells were made for sale. ⊜ . (UoC)

925. McKee, Oliver. *U.S. "Snap Shots" : An Independent, National, and Memorial Encyclopedia. ...* World's Fair ed. N.p.: n.p., n.d

21x15. 565 p. Red cloth hc, gold embossed c.t. and crossed flags emblem. Nice color lithographs of the main WCE bldgs. Presidential nominee biographies for up coming elections: Benjamin Harrison

and Whitelaw Reid (Republican), Grover Cleveland and Gen. Adlai Stevenson (Democratic), Gen. James Weaver (Populist), and Gen. John Bidwell and Cranfill (Prohibitionist).
P→ ☺ . (GLD,S,TD) $10 - 25

926. Melville, Geo[rge] W[allace]. *Grand panoramic view of Chicago : overlooking the business portion of the city, Lake Michigan and the World's Fair ... : also, sketch of Chicago from 1812, the large buildings of today, comparative heights of the tall structures, church spires, railway depots, etc. and the principal buildings of World's Columbian Exposition, 1893.* Chicago: Engraved and published by Geo. W. Melville, °1893.

23x__. (8) p. includes illus. Folded panoramic view tipped in at back cover. Brochure of the Cincinnati, Hamilton and Dayton Railroad Company. (CoU-missing)

927. Merck, E. ... *Catalogue of the exhibitions of \Katalog der ausstellungen von\ : E. Merck Darmstadt. ...* Chicago: n.p., 1893; Woodbridge, CT: RPI, 1989.

24x17. 63 p. At head of title: "World's Columbian Exposition." Beige wrap gives both English and German. Below title: "I. Special exhibition\Besondere ausstellung \ in 'Merck Building' opposite the\gegenüber dem \ 'Illinois State Building.' II. Collective exhibition in the German section, department of chemical industry\Collectiv ausstellung in der deutschen abtheilung, section für chemie." Ad material. ☺ . (KyU,SI,WM)

928. Merrill, J. S. *Art clippings From the Pen of Walter Cranston Larned and other critics at the fair.* [Chicago]: n.p., °1893 by J. S. Merrill; Woodbridge, CT: RPI, 1989.

19½x13. Vol 1: "Architecture and sculpture" is 34, (1) p. Wraps. C.t.: "Art at the White City." Vol 2 is listed at (30) p. ☺ . (SI,NL)

929. Midland Railway Company. *The Midland Railway of England.* [Derby, Eng.: Pemrose & Sons, Printers, 1893].

16x12½. 1 *l*, 47, (2) p. + tipped in color fold. map. 1 *l* is frontis of Midland Grand Hotel and Railway Station, London. On cover: "Visitors' Souvenir of the World's Fair, Chicago." On t.p.: Geo. H. Turner, General Manager."
---- Also listed: 50 p.
☺ . (CHx,BPL,WM,TD) $45

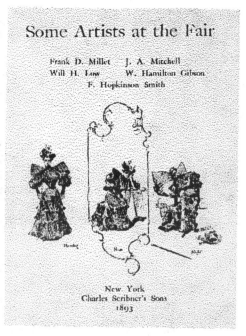

930. Millet, Frank D., J. A. Mitchell, Will H. Low, W. Hamilton Gibson, and F. Hopkinson Smith. *Some artists at the Fair ...* New York: Charles Scribner's Sons, 1893 [°1893 by Charles Scribner's sons].

24x16. xi, 123 p., (1) p. Gray cloth dust jacket on stiff wraps, jacket printed in sepia and dark blue. Frontis by F. Hopkinson Smith of Court of Honor looking towards Administration Bldg. Good quality paper and binding. C.t.= t.p. Ellipse represents the authors' names.

*P↑   ☺ . (GLD,csuf,CHx,LC,SI,S,OSU,UDe,SLP,HL,TU,NYSt,NL,BPL,nwu,AIC,BM,OC,WM,WiHx) $20 - 40

931. Mills, James P., ed. *Voices of the people in petition and remonstrance against Sunday opening of the World's Columbian Exposition in 1893.* Chicago: American Sabbath Union (Woman's Temperance Publishing Association), 1891.

17x12½. 3 *l*, (7)-204, (4) p. 1st *l* title. Stapled pulp booklet issued without printed wraps.   ☺ . (HL)

932. Monroe, Harriet. *John Wellborn Root : a study of his life and work.* Boston and New York: Houghton, Mifflin & Co., 1896.

24½x18½. xii, 291 p., illus, plates. Green polished cloth hc, gilt, frontis of Root. Fine craftsmanship. ---- Brown polished cloth hc, gilt top edge, gilt print.
     ☺ . (csuf,CHx)

☞ Root (1850-1891) was Chicago architect, partner to D. H. Burnham, who helped promote and shape the WCE grounds and style. He died on Jan. 15, 1891, before the Fair opened. Burnham appointed Charles B. Atwood to succeed Root.

933. Morgan, Geo. H. *Annual Statement of the trade and commerce of St. Louis, for the Year 1892, ...* World's Fair ed. St. Louis: R. P. Studley & Co., 1893.

23x15. 257 p. Tan wraps with black lithographic front cover print and design. Curiosity.
     ☺ (GLD) $5 - 15

934. Morgan, Horace H[ills]. *The Historical World's Columbian Exposition and Chicago Guide: authentic and reliable instructor for visitors to the exposition and the most profitable companion for the sight-seer who has to stay at home. ... Illustrated from official drawings.* St. Louis: James H. Mason & Co., 1892 [°1892 by J. L. Hebert]; St. Louis and San Francisco: The Pacific Publishing Co., 1892 [°1892 by J. L. Hebert]; Woodbridge, CT: RPI [Pacific], 1989.

Mason: 24x16½. 480 p. Dark blue cloth hc, red and gold print and design, marbled edges.
---- Pacific: 24x16½. 1 *l*, 416 p. include frontis. Light blue hc, red, black, and gold print and design. T.p. in black and red print. C.t.: "The World's Columbian Exposition : and Chicago guide : Illustrated."
---- Pacific: Half leather over green boards with gilt print, only design being a small bust of Columbus. C.t.: The World's Columbian Exposition : 1893."
Many lithographs, some in color, scattered throughout. Fold out bird's-eye views: 1) bldgs and fairgrounds in color, 2) City of Chicago in sepia tone.

P→   ☺ . (csuf,CHx,LC,SI,S,LM,NHSt,UMi,UoC,A,ncsu,BPL,OC) $20 - 45

935. Morgan, Horace H[ills]. *The historical World's Columbian Exposition : Chicago and St. Louis, the carnival city of the world. Authentic and reliable instructor for visitors to the exposition and the most profitable companion for the sight-seer who has to stay at home. Trustworthy accounts of the exhibits. ... Illustrated from official drawings.* Indianapolis: Ward Publishing Co., [°1892 by J. L. Herbert].

23x15½. 480 p., illus, maps. Light blue cloth hc, red and gold print. T.p. variant of #936. ☺ . (NHSt,L)

936. Morgan, Horace H[ills]. *The historical World's Columbian Exposition and guide to Chicago and St. Louis, the carnival city of the world. ...* St. Louis and San Francisco: The Pacific publishing co., 1893.

23x16. (2), 480 p. plus plates (some folded, some color). Hc. The t.p. is the same as Morgan #935 except for the added words "and guide to" on this t.p. ☺ . (BPL)

937. Morse, W. F. *The disposal of the garbage and waste of the World's Columbian Exposition ...* Brooklyn, NY: [1893].

8°. 16 p. Rpt: *The Sanitarian*, Dec. 1893. (NYPL)

938. The Mosely Folding Bath Tub Company. *The "Mosely" folding bath tub, Self-Heating, Using Gas or Gasoline.* Chicago: n.p., [1893].

22x14½. 16 p. No printed wraps. Wonderful etched illus of various models. Testimonials. Catalogue no. 5, March 15, 1893. Stamped on cover: "World's fair exhibit, Man'f'g Bld'g Sec. "N" Ground floor." (CHx)

939. Moses. [John, and Joseph] Kirkland. *... History of Chicago : Illinois.* 2 vol. Chicago & New York: Munsell & Co., Publishers, 1895 [°1895 by the Munsell publishing co.].

28½x24½. Vol 1: xii, (3)-785, xxxvii, (1) p. Vol 2: xi, 777, xxxii p. Found with and without gilt edges, hc, t.p. in red and black. At head of title: "Aboriginal to metropolitan." ☺ . (CHx,UoC,HL)

940. Moses, John, and Paul Selby. *The white city. The Historical, Biographical and Philanthropical Record of Illinois, to which is added a sketch of the District of Columbia, the presidents of the United States, and Illinois at the World's Columbian exposition. Classified and illustrated.* Chicago: Chicago World Book Co., 1893; Ottawa: CIHM, 1981; Woodbridge, CT: RPI, 1989.

26½x20. 3 pts. in 1 vol. 170, (4), 132, (4), 166 p., frontis of Chas. E. Davis holding a copy of the book, illus. Maroon cloth hc, black and gold lettering and design. Part III is on WCE. Elaborate paged ads. See #1055.
---- Also listed: 24x__.

P→   ☺ . (csuf,PU,CHx,SI,NYPL,TnSt,NLC,LMi,SDSHx,CoU,NHSt,HL,NYSt,UoC,NL,A,BPL,nwu,AIC,WiHx)

941. Murphy, Richard M. *Columbus. A Stereoptican Lecture Written in Exploitation of the World's Fair, At Chicago, 1893.* [Chicago: n.p., 1893].

14x21. Typewritten (carbon), 72 p. numbered one side + (1) p. Cardboard covers, string tied. Pauses are noted in lecture for accompanying named pictures. Murphy was secretary of the WCE Dept of Publicity and Promotion.   (CHx)

942. Muybridge, Eadweard. *Descriptive zoopraxography : or the science of animal locomotion made popular by Eadweard Muybridge.* [Philadelphia]: U of Pennsylvania, 1893.

21x__. 1 vol with various paging, illus. Content: "animal locomotion" -- an electro-photographic investigation [precursor to motion pictures]. Published as a memento of a series of lectures given by Muybridge, at Zoopraxographical Hall on the Midway Plaisance, under the auspices of the U.S., Government Board of Education. [Muybridge is well known for being the first to understand how a horse runs.]   (Yale)

943. *National religious liberty association. Sunday and the World's Fair.* N.p.: [Religious Liberty Association], 1892?.

20½x12½. (2) p.? Caption title.   ☺ . (WiHx)

944. Naylor, Robert Anderton. *Across the Atlantic.* Westminster, Eng.: The Roxburghe Press, n.d.

24x18½. xii, 305 p. Brown cloth hc, gilt print. This personal account of a trip to the U.S. includes "Chicago" (chapter 4) and "The World's Fair" (chapter 5).
---- 24x18. xii, 305 p. Dark olive cloth hc, gilt print on cover and spine, fore and foot edges ragged, top edge gilt.
      ☺ . (CHx,HL,NL)

945. Neal, Juana A. "Mrs. Juana Neal's plan for a permanent Woman's building as a monument to the women of U.S." N.p.: n.p., n.d.

28x21½. (5) p., 11 *l*, stapled at top (21½ cm edge), folded once. Turquoise back paper. First (5) p. in blue paper are printed reproductions of letters of support. Last 11 *l* are typed letter on manila paper proposing that several permanent structures be built on the grounds to replace those lost in the fire of early 1894. Signed by Mrs. Neal at top of 1st *l*.--(CHx call: qF38JD N25).   (CHx)

946. *New Hampshire Grange excursion to the World's fair at Chicago on October 3-13, 1893.* [Concord: Printed by Republican Press Association], n.d.

20x15. 11 p. including front cover, glossy leaves. C.t. Lists participants and highlights of trip. On cover: "Compliments of the Independent Statesman."   ☺ . (LC)

947. *The New Testament of our Lord and Saviour Jesus Christ: ...* New York: The American Bible society, 1892.

12½x8½. Gilt print and design on black leather. C.t.: "Columbian exposition : New Testament : souvenir edition."   ☺ . (A)

948. *New Year's greeting and welcome to Chicago and the World's Columbian exposition : 1893.* Chicago: Chandler & co., n.d.

15½x9. 20 p. Gray wraps with black and red lettering. Illus of Columbus on front wrap and his landing on back wrap. ⊚ . (CHx)

949. Noble, Frederic Perry. "Africa at the Columbian exposition." *Our Day* Nov. 1892: rpt.

23x15. 17 p. No printed cover. Caption title. Argues for African participation at WCE. After author's name: "Newberry Library, Chicago." [Noble (1863-1945) was assistant librarian at the NL and secretary of the Chicago congress on Africa at the WCE. The World's Congress Auxiliary subsequently did have a division of African Ethnology (see #2164).] ⊚ . (SFe,CHx,NYPL)

950. Normandie, James De. *Sunday and the Columbian Fair : a sermon preached to the First Church, Roxbury, Boston : July 24, 1892.* Boston: Damrell & Upham, 1892.

19½x12½. 14 p. Pale green wraps, black print. ⊚ . (NL)

951. Northrop, Henry Davenport. *Four Centuries of Progress : or Panorama of American History from the Discovery of the American Continent to the Present Time : containing ... A Magnificent Description of the Columbian Exposition.* Philadelphia & Chicago: International publishing co., [°1893].

26½x20½. xxiv, (17)-923 p., (1) p. ad. Illus, maps. T.p. in red and blue. Antique blue cloth hc, black and gilt print and design, decorative end papers, marbled edges. (NYPL,GLD) $24 - 42

952. Northrop, Henry Davenport. *Pictorial history of the World's Columbian Exposition : being a complete account of the great celebration of the four-hundredth anniversary of the discovery of America by Columbus. Containing a complete history of the World's fair; ... Embellished with Hundreds of Beautiful Engravings.* Bridgeport, CT: Union Book Co., [1893]; New York: W. J. Holland, [°1893 by Henry Davenport Northrop]; ____: Imperial Publishing Co., [1893].

Union: 23½x17. 1 *l*, xxii, (15)-736 p., illus, plates, t.p. in black and red. Turquoise cloth hc, red and gold lettering and design, marbled edges. First *l* is colored "Presented to __ by __" leaf. Back cover has blind stamp design of front cover.
---- Holland: Red leather embossed hc. C.t.: "History of the World's Fair.
P→ ⊚ . (csuf,S,D,BPL)

953. Northrop, Henry Davenport. *Story of the new world. Being a complete History of the United States from the Discovery of the American Continent to the Present Time, ... Magnificent Columbian Edition. Embellished with nearly 500 superb engravings.* Philadelphia [and] Chicago: Elliott and Beezley, 1892 [°1892 by J. R. Jones].

26½x19. 918 p. Hc. T.p. in red and black. ⊚ . (E,S)

954. Northrop, H[enry] D[avenport]. *The World's fair as seen in One Hundred Days. Containing a complete history of the World's Columbian exposition; captivating descriptions ... Embellished with Hundreds of Beautiful Engravings.* Cincinnati, Chicago & Kansas City: Standard publishing co., [°1893 by Henry Davenport Northrop]; Philadelphia: Ariel Book Co., [°1893 by Henry Davenport Northrop]; Philadelphia: Lyceum publishing co., [°1893 by Henry Davenport Northrop]; Philadelphia: National Publishing Co., °1893; Chicago: Rowe, [°1893 by Henry Davenport Northrop]; N.p.: n.p., [1893]; Woodbridge, CT: RPI [Ariel], 1989.

National: 23½x16½. xxii, 736 p. Blue cloth hc with gold and silver embossed title, marbled edges. Chapter on the Woman's Dept by Mrs. Nancy H. Banks. Cover states: "By Henry Davenport Northrop and Mrs. Nancy Huston Banks : With an Introduction by Mrs. Potter Palmer." Book is an historical sketch of Chicago and the Fair.
---- National: Listed at 720 p.
---- Ariel: xxii, 736 p. Blue cloth hc printed in red, white, and blue.
---- Lyceum: Blue cloth hc, title embossed in red, white and blue, marbled edges.
---- Rowe: Presentation page, 1 *l*, iii-xxii (with interspersed unpaged plates not counted in pagination), 17-736 p. (with interspersed unpaged plated not counted in pagination). Turquoise hc, chocolate and silver embossed title.
---- Standard Pub: Listed at xxii, 736 p., 14 *l* plates.

☺ . (GLD,CHx,SLF,S,BU,UoC,CoU,A,TD,WiHx) $20 - 35

955. *The North-Western Line : Columbian Daily Record. With compliments of the passenger department.* [Buffalo, NY: The Matthews-Northrup co., °1893].

14½x7. (88)p. 1893 calendar/diary (7 days per page), North-Western Line ads, color WF map, and illus. Brown stiff wraps, tan print, red and black logo. C.t.

☺ (GLD,TD)   Blank: $16 - 30

956. Norton, C[harles] B[enjamin]. *World's fairs from London 1851 to Chicago 1893 : illustrated with views and portraits in the Maas arttype.* Chicago: Milton Weston co., 1890 [°1890 by C. B. Norton].

25x17½. 93 p. + large number unpaged plates, frontis of Columbus. Red-brown wraps with black print and design, folding map in back. Bottom of t.p.: "Published for the World's Columbian Exposition, 1893." The Maas Arttype was a litho method. Early description of Chicago, U.S. Commission, WCE Company and empty site. For similar title see #1076.   ☺ . (LC,BCM,NL,HL)

957. Ober, Frederick A[lbion]. *In the wake of Columbus : adventures of the special commissioner sent by the World's Columbian exposition to the West Indies : ... With above two hundred illustrations from photographs by the Author, and sketches by H. R. Blaney.* Boston: D. Lothrop co., 1893; Microfiche. Chicago: Library Resources, Inc., 1970.

22½x14. (16), 515, (9) p. including frontis, illus, plates, maps.
---- Also listed: 8 *l*, 515, (8) p.
☺ . (CHx,NvSt,BPL,S)

☞ Ober (1849-1913), a Smithsonian ornithologist, supervised the WCE ornithology exhibits. In 1891, he was appointed to explore the various Columbus landing sites and collect artifacts. He authored many books.

958. Oberlin Rest Day League. *Sunday closing of the World's fair : Oberlin Rest Day League.* Oberlin, OH: 1892.

21x14. (3) p. No wraps. Caption title. Dated March 1, 1892. "Under the auspices of the American Sabbath Union." ⊚ . (OC)

959. *Official Hand-Book Retail Furniture Dealers Association of Chicago.* N.p.: n.p., 1892.

30½x24. Dark red cloth cover. Ad book with list of members. Contains full page pictures of the WF bldgs. (S)

960. *Official Souvenir Programme: Dedicatory Ceremonies World's Columbian Exposition Chicago: October 20th 21st & 22nd 1892.* [Chicago: 1892].

25½x18½. (32) p. plus fold out tinted bird's-eye view facing back cover. Handsome yellow, red, and black illus front wrap showing the Administration Bldg, World's Columbian Commission seal, etc. C.t.

P→   ⊚ . (GLD,OhHx,UoC,NL,A,WM,TD) $20 - 40

961. O'Neil, J. S. *The Columbian Celebration, the part taken by the congregation of St. Louis Bertrand.* Louisville: n.p., 1892.

12°. (UC)

962. ... *Panorama of the Swiss Alps. (Bernese Oberland). Explanatory notice followed by a : Description of Switzerland.* Geneva: Imprimerie Suisse, 1893.

18x12. 64 p. + color fold out map before back wrap. Very light greenish tan wraps, black print and litho of boy and goats on Alpine pasture. At head of title: "The World's Columbian Exhibition: Chicago U.S.A. 1893."
⊚ . (GLD,A) $15 - 32

963. *Panorama of the Swiss Alps. Midway Plaisance.* N.p.: n.p., n.d.

19x13; folds out to 19x49½. Hand out for the Swiss Alps exhibit; shows panorama and has text explanations. ⊚ (GLD) $15 - 32

964. Parloa, Maria. *Choice Receipts.* Dorchester, MA: Walter Baker & co., 1893 ᶜ1892 by Walter Baker & Co.

15x9. 31, (1) p. Tan smooth wraps with black, red, and blue print; color lithos front and back. All recipes are for Baker's chocolate deserts. C.t.: "Choice Receipts By Miss Parloa : specially prepared for the Walter Baker & Cᵒˢ Exhibit at the World's Columbian Exposition 1893." [Baker's pavilion was on the water front next to the Liberal Arts Bldg.]
⊚ (GLD) $12 - 25

965. Peattie, Elia W. *Our Land of Liberty : or The wonderful story of America containing the romantic incidents of history ...* Chicago and Philadelphia: International Publishing Co., 1895 [ᶜ1895 by Robert O. Law].

23½x19. 3 *l*, (7)-800 p. Light brown cloth hc, embossed black and silver print, red stained edges. First *l* is frontis of G. Washington. Same spine design as *History of World's Fair*, Mammoth Publishing Co. which sold out to International. Contents different. Chapter CXI is the WCE chapter.

P→   ☺ (GLD) $15 - 30

966. Pennsylvania Railroad Company. *Catalogue of the exhibit of the Pennsylvania Railroad Company at the World's Columbian Exposition : Chicago 1893.* N.p.: n.p., n.d.; Woodbridge, CT: RPI, 1989.

Large Format: 31x25. 12 *l*, 7-158 p., 12 *l* facsimiles, frontis, plates. On cover: "Under the direction of Theo. N. Ely ... [and] J. Elfreth Watkins ..."
---- Small Format: Same title. 23½x18. 5 *l*, 7-158 p., frontis (2 photos) of Pennsylvania Railroad Bldg and the Pennsylvania Railroad exhibit. Pea green wraps, gilt lettering, red emblem. C.t.= t.p.
      ☺ . (PU,UWa,LC,CPL,CHx,SI,NYPL,S,BCM,UTn,SLP,UMi,CoU,NYSt,NL)

967. Pennsylvania Railroad Company. *Chemin de fer Pennsylvanie (Pennsylvania Railroad) : à l'exposition Colombienne : suivi de notes descriptives des villes de New-York, Philadelphie, Washington, Chicago, et d'un guide complet des emplacements et des palais de l'exposition : avec artes et illustrations.* Philadelphie: Cie. Chemin de Fer Pennsylvanie, 1892 [°1892 by La Compagne du chemin de fer Pennsylvanie].

19½x15½. 1 *l* frontis of Statue of Liberty, 117 p., illus, fold. maps (6 color maps not included in paging). Tan wraps, red and silver print; French coat of arms. Guide for French visitors by rail to the Fair. French version of #971.   ☺ . (CHx,NYPL,NLC)

968. Pennsylvania Railroad Company. *El Ferrocarril de Pennsylvania y la Exposición Colombina, con notas descriptivas de las ciudades de New York, Philadelphia, Washington, Chicago, y una descripción completa de los Terrenos y Edificios de la Exposición, Con Mapas é Ilustraciones.* Philadelphia: Compañia del Ferrocarril de Pennsylvania, 1892 [°1892 por la compañia del ferrocarril de Pennsylvania].

19½x15½. 1 *l*, 139 p., also 2 fold map. Pea green wraps, gilt print. 1 *l* is frontis of Statue of Liberty. Cover in English. Spanish version of #971.   ☺ . (NL)

969. Pennsylvania Railroad Company. *Ferrovia Pensilvania (Pennsylvania railroad) guida alla Esposizione Colombiana : con note descrittive delle città di New York, Philadelphia, Washington, Chicago. Ed una completa descrizione dei Terreni e degli Edifizii della Esposizione, Con Carte Geografiche ed Illustrazioni.* Filadelfia: Ferrovia della Compagnia Pensilvania, 1892 [°1892 by Compagnia della Ferrovia Pensilvania].

19½x16. 1 *l* frontis of Statue of Liberty, (1)-117 p., 6 maps tipped in (some fold.), many b/w illus. Italian version of #971.   ☺ . (NYPL,UoC)

970. Pennsylvania Railroad Company. *Mit der Pennsylvania eisenbahn zur Columbian Welt-Ausstellung, nebst beschreibenden bemerkungen ueber die stædte : New York, Philadelphia, Washington, Chicago, sowie einer ausführlichen beschreibung des ausstelllungs-platzes* [sic] *und der gebäude, Mit Karten und Illustrationen.* Philadelphia: Pennsylvania Eisenbahn-Gesellschaft, 1892.

19½x15½. 129 p. German version of #971. ☺.(NYSt)

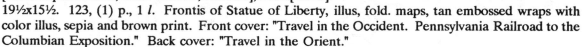

971. Pennsylvania Railroad Company. *Pennsylvania Railroad to the Columbian Exposition, with descriptive notes of the cities of New York, Philadelphia, Washington, Chicago, and a complete description of the Exposition Grounds and Buildings, With Maps and Illustrations.* Philadelphia: Pennsylvania Railroad Co., 1892 [°1892 by the Pennsylvania Railroad co.; Woodbridge, CT: RPI, 1989.

19½x15½. 1 *l*, 110 p., 6 fold out maps. Gray wraps, gold print front and back. 1 *l* frontis of Statue of Liberty. Describes route to the Fair on the Pennsylvania Railroad and sights at the Fair.
---- 2nd ed.: *Pennsylvania railroad to the Columbian Exposition, with descriptive notes of the cities of New York, Philadelphia, Baltimore, Washington, Chicago, ...* [Philadelphia: Allen, Lane & Scott, Printers], 1893 [°1893].
19½x15½. 123, (1) p., 1 *l*. Frontis of Statue of Liberty, illus, fold. maps, tan embossed wraps with color illus, sepia and brown print. Front cover: "Travel in the Occident. Pennsylvania Railroad to the Columbian Exposition." Back cover: "Travel in the Orient."
P→   ☺.(GLD,JHU,LC,SI,NYPL,S) $15 - 32

972. Pennsylvania Railroad Company. *Pennsylvania R. R. : Pennsylvania Railroad Exhibit : World's Columbian Exposition : information for visitors of a general and special interest.* Phila[delphia]: Allen, Lane & Scott, Prs., [1893].

18x9 folded; 36x54 unfolded. Unfolded: tables, illus, and text printed one side in blue; full size plan of WF grounds by Rand, McNally in black, red, and yellow on other side. C.t. (when folded).
P→   ☺(GLD,TD) $12 - 26

973. Perry, William Stevens. *America, The Study of Nations: Her Religious Destiny. The Columbian Sermon : delivered in S. Paul's Cathedral, Buffalo, New York, ...* Davenport, Iowa: Edward Borcherdt, printer, 1893.

24½x15½. 22 p. Light green wraps printed in black. A sermon about Columbus. ☺.(UoC)

974. *Philadelphia Record Almanac : 1893.* [Philadelphia]: The Record Publishing Co., n.d.

20½x15½. 96 p. Frontis is Lotto port of Columbus. Buff wraps, black print and ornate borders; back wrap litho of Record Bldg. Typical almanac text with interspersed plates of WCE bldgs.
☺(GLD) $10 - 20

975. *Picturesque Chicago and Guide to the World's Fair. Profusely illustrated.* Baltimore: R. H. Woodward and co., 1892 [°1892].

23½x16½. xiii, (2), 304 p., includes frontis, illus. Red cloth hc with black design and gold lettering. See #994 for a later version.

P↓ ☺ . (csuf,CHx,NYPL,NYSt,BPL,OC,AIC)

976. Pierce, James Wilson. ... *Photographic history of the World's fair and sketch of the city of Chicago. Also, a guide to the World's fair and Chicago.* ... Baltimore: R. H. Woodward and co., 1893 [°1893 by R. H. Woodward and co.]; N.p.: Lennox Publishing Co., 1893; Woodbridge, CT: RPI [Woodward], 1989.

Woodward: 23½x17. 1 *l* frontis of Administration Bldg, xiv, 1 *l*, 493 p. Red cloth hc with gold and black letters and design. At head of title: "Authentic edition."
---- Woodward: Same except frontis incorrectly titled "The Government building."
---- Lennox: 23x17. xvi, 493 p. Red leather, gilt edges. At head of title: "Authentic edition."
*P↑ ☺ . (GLD,csuf,CHx,SI,S,D,E,UDe,ncsu,CoU,UMi,NYSt,A,L) $20 - 40

977. Pinchot, Gifford. *Biltmore forest : the property of Mr. George W. Vanderbilt : an account of its treatment, and the results of the first year's work.* Chicago: n.p., 1893.

12½x18. 49 p., frontis of workers clearing forest and underbrush. Brown wraps. [Pinchot used this booklet for the WCE forestry exhibit; no mention of WCE. The Biltmore estate was completed in 1895.]
☺ . (CPL,TU,NYSt,BPL)

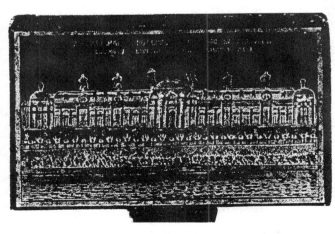

978. [Pocket Slate]. (paper souvenir).

11x7. 3 *l*. The covers are gold embossed black paper covered hc. The 3 *l* are black paper covered hard board "slates." A loop is provided for small pencil. Embossed cover design is printed:

"Agricultural Building, Columbian Exposition." Not a "book," but look for written comments on the Fair on the slates which would make it unique.

P↑   ⊜ . (GLD)   Blank: $15 - 30

979. Ponce de Leon, Nestor. *The Columbus gallery : The "discoverer of the new world" as represented in portraits, monuments, statues, medals and painting. Historical description.* New York: N. Ponce de Leon, 1893 [°1893 by N. Ponce de Leon].

29x20½. 4 *l*, 178 p. Gray (or maroon) cloth hc, embossed design and gold print. Columbus art from the Madrid Exhibition and medals struck for the WCE. Pretty.

P→   ⊜ (GLD,S,A) $25 - 60

980. [Pope, Albert Augustus] *A Memorial to Congress on the subject of a comprehensive exhibit of roads, their construction and maintenance, at the World's Columbian Exposition.* [Boston]: n.p., [1892].

22½x14½. 110 p. Tan wraps, black print. Introductory letter by Albert A. Pope, Boston, MA., July 6, 1892.   ⊜ . (SFe,NYPL,UMi,OC)

981. [Pope, Albert Augustus]. *A Memorial to Congress on the subject of A Road Department at Washington, D.C. : and a comprehensive exhibit of roads, their construction and maintenance at the World's Columbian Exposition.* Boston: Albert A. Pope, 1893; Woodbridge, CT: RPI, 1989.

ca. 21½x13½. 96 p. Microfilm. C.t.= t.p.   ⊜ . (SI,NYPL)

982. Pope, Albert A[ugustus]. *The movement for better roads : An address by Col. Albert A. Pope ... before the Board of Trade at Hartford, Conn., February 11, 1890. An open letter to the people of the United States. Relating to a department of road construction and maintenance at the World's Columbian exposition. Width of tires. Extracts from recent special consular reports on streets and highways in foreign countries.* Boston: Pope Manufacturing Co., 1892.

21x__. 31 p. Microfilm.   (UoC)

983. *The Popular Atlas of the world.* Philadelphia [and] Springfield, OH: Published by Mast, Crowell and Kirkpatrick, °1892.

35½x28½. 208 p. Red brown embossed hc, gold lettering. Chapter on upcoming World's Fair. T.p. illus of the Capitol, at Washington, DC.   ⊜ . (S)

984. Porter, Mrs. M. E. *The New World's Fair Cook Book and Housekeeper's Companion ...* Boston: B. B. Russell, [1891]; Philadelphia: John E. Potter & Co., 1891.

Russell: 20½x14. 485 p. Striking black wavy line pattern on olive green paper covered hc, red lettering and design. Recipes, household and baby hints, etc. Early pub. for the recently announced (and assumed 1892) Columbian fair; no WF content other than title.

---- Potter & Co.: 20½x14. 474 p.

$30 - 50

⊘ . (S,R)

985. Pratt Institute, Brooklyn. *Exhibit of the Women Graduates and Pupils of Pratt Institute ... Columbian Exposition : 1893.* [Brooklyn, NY: 1893].

14½x10. 16 p. ⊘ . (NYPL,PI)

986. *Proceedings of the Convention of Southern Governors, held in the city of Richmond, Virginia, on April 12th and 13th, 1893. With papers prepared by the governors of Arkansas, Alabama, South Carolina and Virginia, in regard to the physical resources of their respective states.* Richmond: C. N. Williams, printer, 1893.

22x14½. 82 p. include plates. Page 4-5: "Resolved ... that these papers be prepared ... [and] published in pamphlet form for distribution at the World's Fair at Chicago." Title on front wrap: "Handbook of Arkansas, Alabama, South Carolina, Virginia." ⊘ . (UDe)

987. *The Publishers' and Other Book Exhibits at the World's Columbian Exposition.* New York: Office of the Publishers' Weekly, 1893.

16x11. 1 *l* map, frontis (plan showing location of publishing exhibits), 74 p., 11 *l* book ads. Beige wraps, black print. "Compiled from issues of the Publishers' Weekly." Found with author: [Growoll, Aldolf]. [Richard R. Bowker was editor. The Bowker Co. now issues ISBN numbers to book publishers.] ⊘ . (OSU,NYSt,NL,WiHx)

988. Queen Isabella Association. *Letters of Commendation of the work of the Queen Isabella Association.* ____: The Association, 18__.

Published letters from prelates of the U.S. approving the plan adopted by the Association. The Association was organized on Aug. 17, 1889, for the purpose of honoring Queen Isabella by erecting a statue to Isabella of Castile to be unveiled at the WCE. [Miscellaneous Association pamphlets.--(CHx call no. F38MZ W1893 L1W).] (CHx)

989. Ralph, Julian. *Harper's Chicago and the World's fair : the chapters on the exposition being collated from official sources and approved by the department of publicity and promotion of the World's Columbian exposition.* New York: Harper & brothers, 1892; New York: Harper & brothers publishers, 1893 [°1892 by Harper & Brothers]; Woodbridge, CT: RPI, 1989.

Harper 1893: 21x15. 2 *l*, v-xi, 1 *l*, 244, (4), (10) p. ads + many unpaginated photos. Frontis of Grand Court. Sepia cloth hc, gold lettering and olive green design on spine and front cover. Assemblage of *Harper's Weekly* information in true book form. Very useful.

*P→ ⊘ . (GLD,csuf,CHx,SI,NYPL,VaHx,BU,SLP,HL,NYSt,UoC,NL,BPL,AIC,CoU,WiHx,TD)

$20 - 40

990. *Raymond's Vacation Excursions : California, the Pacific Northwest, Alaska : and the World's Columbian exposition. Four spring tours Leaving New York April 24 and May 24, 1893.* New York: Raymond & Whitcomb (American printing & engraving co.), n.d.

11x14. 208 p. Tan and gray glossy wraps with black print and lithos. C.t.
⊗ (GLD,AkHx) $14 - 28

991. *Raymond's Vacation Excursions : trips to the World's Columbian Exposition, Leaving Boston between April 28 and October 21, 1893, and tours beyond Chicago.* Boston: Raymond & Whitcomb (American printing & engraving), [1893].

11x14. 111, (1) p., illus + map. Title from cover. T.p.: "The World's Columbian Exposition to be held in Chicago from May 1st to October 30th, 1893. A series of 116 tours from Boston in special vestibuled trains ... the Raymond & Whitcomb Grand..." ⊗ . (BPL) $14 - 28
---- Also available: "Souvenir List of Members of the Columbian Exposition Party, Raymond's Vacation Excursions ... May 27, 1893." 9x15½. 4 *l*. Wraps.   ⊗ (GLD,WM) $12 - 22

992. Reddall, Henry. *Columbus the Navigator: The Story of His Life and Work.* New York: Empire pub. co., [°1892].

20x__. 285 p. includes illus, port, map. frontis.   (cat,LC) $15

993. *Reisenotizen eines Chicagoreisenden. Für Freunde als Manuskript gedruckt.* Lahr: Druck von Moritz Schauenburg, 1893.

16x11. 1 *l* (t.p.), 188 p. Dark olive wraps, black script title plus small design on back wrap. Trip account which includes WCE.
⊗ . (NL)

994. Religious Herald. *Picturesque Chicago and guide to the World's fair : issued by The Religious Herald, and presented to its subscribers as a souvenir of fifty years publication of the paper. Profusely illustrated.* Hartford: D. S. Moseley, 1893.

23½x14½. 7 *l*, v-xiii, 1 *l*, 334 p., illus, maps. Red cloth hc, black and gilt print and design. C.t.: "Picturesque Chicago and Guide to the World's Fair. For earlier edition see #975.
---- Also listed: xiii, 334 p.

⊗ . (PU,NYPL,BCM,UMi,NYSt,HL,UoC,RPB,OC)

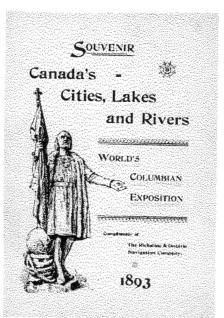

995. Richelieu & Ontario Navigation Company. *Souvenir : Canada's Cities, Lakes and Rivers : World's Columbian Exposition ... 1893.* N.p.: Desbarats Co., Engravers and printers, entered according to Act of Parliament of Canada in the year 1893.

23x15½. 24 p. White smooth wraps, dark green print and design of Columbus statue with flag. C.t. Same as #361.
P→   ⊗ . (GLD,WM) $12 - 25

996. Rogers Locomotive Company. ... *Exhibit of locomotives made by Rogers Locomotive Company. Paterson, New Jersey U. S. A.* N.p.: n.p., n.d.; Woodbridge, CT: RPI, 1989.

    ca. 16x26. 20 p., illus. Microfilm. At head of title: "World's Columbian Exposition Chicago, 1893."
    ⊚ . (SI)

997. Roltair, Henry. *Creation : the formation of the earth and its inhabitants : evolved for the benefit of all people who visit the World's fair.* N.p.: n.p., n.d.

    15x23. Illus and cover print on muted red background. C.t.: "Roltair's Creation;" cover illus of never realized GRAND exhibit intending to show man's entire history.   ⊚ . (KyU,LC)

998. [Romeike, Henry], comp. *300 reasons why Chicago should have the World's Fair.* New York: Henry Romeike, ᶜ1889.

    17x12. 113 p., 1 *l.* Red textured wraps, black print. C.t.= t.p. Not what it seems; a <u>sarcastic</u>, joke filled <u>jib</u> from New York <u>against</u> Chicago hosting the WF.   (CHx,LC,NYPL)

999. *Ropp's Commercial Calculator World's Fair Edition.* ____: C. Ropp, n.d.

    16½x10. 144 p. Contains tables, calculation, and a section on the Fair.   (S)

1000. Rorer, Sarah T[yson]. *Recipes used in Illinois Corn Exhibit : Model Kitchen : Woman's Building : Columbian Exposition Chicago 1893...* [Philadelphia: Printed by George H. Buchanan and Co., ᶜ1893 by Mrs. S. T. Rorer].

    14½x9. 15, (1) p. Tan wraps with green and chocolate print and design. C.t. On cover: "Under the auspices of Illinois Women's Exposition Board." [Mrs. Rorer, author of numerous cookbooks, also wrote a souvenir cookbook for the 1904 St. Louis Fair.]
    P→   ⊚ (GLD,LC) $15 - 30

1001. [Ryan, Carroll]. *Chicago the magnificent. The empire city of the west. A Souvenir of the World's Fair. Its Phenomenal Rise. Its Present Marvelous Status. Its Future Greatness.* New York and Montreal: John P. Williams, [ᶜ1892].

    13½x20½. 64 p. Tan wraps, black print. C.t.= t.p., no illus.   ⊚ . (LC)

1002. S., J. F. *A trip across the Atlantic, a tour in the States, and a visit to the World's fair.* Southampton, [England]: Printed at the "Southampton Times" Steam Printing Works, 1893.

    18½x11½. 123 p. LC microfilm.   ⊚ . (LC)

1003. Sala, George Augustus, Bret Harte, Joseph Hatton, and Geo. R. Sims. *Sunlight.* Britain: Sunlight Soap, Lever Brothers Ltd., n.d.

16x12½. 32 p. Tan wraps, brown print. Short stories. A handout at the Fair.

P→   ⊚ (GLD) $20 - 30

1004. ... *Shakespeare Boiled Down : Containing the Story of all of Shakespeares* [sic] *Days carefully condensed.* N.p.: The New Home Sewing Machine Co., ᶜ1890.

23x15½. 64 p. At head of title: "Souvenir World's Fair : May 1st to Nov 1st 1893." C.t. Yellow wraps, ornate black litho cover design and print.   ⊚ . (S)

1005. Sheldon, [J. D.] & Co. *American products : illustrated Columbian Exposition : successful and enterprising manufactures & distributors.* New York: J. D. Sheldon & Co., 1894.

ob. 16°. 111 p.   (NYPL)

1006. Smith Exploring Company, H. Jay. *Catalogue of collections of Weapons, Implements, Utensils and mummified bodies of the Cliff Dwellers : also Fac-Simile Reproduction of the Canons of Colorado and Utah, Where They Were Found : cliff dwellers' exhibit : World's Columbian Exposition Chicago.* [Chicago: La Monte, O'Donnell & Co., Printers and Binders, 1893]; Woodbridge, CT: RPI, 1989.

23x15½. 24 p., b/w illus. Gray wraps, black print and illus of explorer climbing cliff face. Descriptions of the Pueblo Indians of the American Southwest.   ⊚ . (CHx,SI,BPL,WM,TD) $15 - 30

1007. Smith Exploring Company, H. Jay. *The Cliff Dwellers : The H. Jay Smith Exploring Company : World's Columbian Exposition : 1893.* [Chicago: La Monte-O'Donnell Co., Printers, 1893?].

23½x15½. 19, (1) p., b/w illus. Sand wraps, black lettering. C.t. Illus include Indian pueblo ruins, pottery, and weaving.   ⊚ . (GLD,csuf,NYPL,UDe,R) $20 - 35

1008. Smith, Frank H., comp. *Art History : Midway Plaisance and World's Columbian Exposition : fully illustrated.* Chicago: The Foster press, ᶜ1893.

27x20. (106) p., illus, ports. Brown paper covered boards with gold print; illus of Ferris wheel in gold on back cover. Small t.p. illus depicts ringing bell.
---- "(second edition)" printed below the words "... fully illustrated." Same pub info. Small t.p. illus depicts sun at horizon shining through foliage.
  ⊚ . (CHx,UDe,WM)

1009. Snider, Denton J[aques]. *World's Fair Studies.* Chicago: Sigma publishing co., [ᶜ1895].

19x13½. 383, (1) p. Description of the Fair starts with the Ferris wheel. Includes philosophical musings of the Fair and its events.
---- Also listed: 21x__.
  ⊚ . (csuf,CHx,LC,nwu,SLP,OC,WiHx)

1010. Snider, Denton J[aques]. *World's Fair Studies : number one : the four domes.* Chicago: Chicago Kindergarten College, n.d.; Woodbridge, CT: RPI, 1989.

18x12½. 30 p. Description of the WCE domed bldgs.   ⊚ . (CHx,SI,NL)

Snider's book above and the following four entries have identical pub info. All wraps are greenish tan with rust print and a small design. All are the same size.

1011. ---. *World's Fair Studies : number two : the organization of the fair.* 30 + (2) p. book ads. Study of the actual results of WCE planning.   ⊚ . (CHx,SI,NL)

1012. ---. *World's Fair Studies : number three : state buildings - colonial.* 32 p.   ⊚ . (CHx,SI,NL)

1013. ---. *World's Fair Studies : number four : state buildings - from east to west.* 31 + (1) p.   ⊚ . (CHx,SI,NL)

1014. ---. *World's Fair Studies : number five : the Greek columns at the fair.* 31 p.   ⊚ . (CHx,SI,NL)

1015. Snider, Denton J[aques]. *World's fair studies : The Plaisance--First Series, ...* Chicago: Chicago Kindergarten College, n.d.

17½x12½. 64 p. Tan wraps with brown print. Contents: "I) The Plaisance in General, II) Arabia, ..., III) Animal, ...".   ⊚ . (CHx)

1016. ---. *World's fair studies : The Plaisance--Second Series, ...* Chicago: Chicago Kindergarten College, n.d.

17½x12½. 64 p. Tan wraps with brown print. Contents: " I) The Street in Cairo, II) Savage Life, III) Ethnic Summary."   ⊚ . (CHx)

1017. *Something of Interest to All : The South-Land.* ____ : ____, 189_.

17x12½. Wraps. Caption title: "The New South. Its agricultural, mineral, manufacturing And commercial Advantages : set forth to the world. The Governors of the Southern States Co-operating in Building up the South."   . (WM)

1018. *Souvenir of a ride on The Ferris Wheel at the World's Fair Chicago.* Chicago: The American Engraving Co., ⁰1893.

15x23½. (16) p. illus of and from the Ferris wheel (from various stops on the ride). Decorated smooth coated wraps, printed in light blue, gold, and red. C.t. 1st p. is of George W. Ferris.
---- 1 *l*, (16) p. where the *l* is an ad for American Engraving Co., otherwise the same.
For a brief history of the wheel, see #843.
P→   ⊚ . (csuf,CHx,LC,F,HL,GPL,L)

$40 - 65

☞ Ride certificates were issued; e.g., a certificate certifying that Eva K. Dangberg (see #2377), niece of Ferris, took 64 rides in the Ferris Wheel.--(CVHx call: 5-G-70). The first wedding on the Ferris Wheel was at (high) noon atop the wheel on Oct. 24, 1893.

1019. *Souvenir of gallery exhibiters, Electrical Building, Worlds* [sic] *fair.* Chicago: Columbian Engraving Co., [ca.1893]; Chicago: Smith and Colbert, 1893; Woodbridge, CT: RPI, 1989.

8x13. 16 *l*, mostly illus. Decorative wraps. Distributed by the gallery exhibitors.   (csuf,SI)

1020. ... *A Souvenir of the Four Hundreth Anniversary of the Landing of Columbus. The story of Columbus. His voyages and discovery. The Columbian Exposition, its inception, development and history.* N.p.: n.p., n.d.

23x17½. 3 *l*, cxxxv, (1) p. includes fold. bird's-eye view of grounds and Columbus frontis. Orange patterned wraps, black and red print and design, marbled edges. At head of title: "1492-1892."
☺ . (LC,NYPL)

1021. *Souvenir of the World's Fair and Chicago.* Chicago: Columbian Souvenir Publishing Co., 1892 copyrighted by Mrs. Emma T. Whitney.

15½x__. 24 *l*, illus, fold. map, ports. Green wraps, design in black, gold lettering.   (csuf)

1022. Spalding, J. L. *The Catholic Educational Exhibit in the Columbian exposition.* Rpt. from *The Catholic World.* July, 1892. [Chicago]: Donohue & Henneberry, Printers and Binders, n.d.

23½x15. 8 p. Peach wraps, black. "Birdseye [sic] view of World's Columbian Exposition" on outside back wrap.   ☺ . (NL)

1023. Stead, William T[homas]. *If Christ came to Chicago! A Plea for the Union of All Who Love in the Service of All Who Suffer.* Chicago: Laird & Lee, Publishers, 1894 °1894 by Wm T. Stead.

19x13½. 472 p. Pulp pages. Several reprints of this work exist.   ☺ . (UoC)

1024. Stenholt, L[ars] A. *Moderne Vikinger. Historisk Skildring af Kapt. Magnus Andersens fredelige Vikingefoerd.* Minneapolis: Waldm, Kriedt Publishing Co., 1894 [°1893 by Waldm, Kriedt].

19½x13½. 100 p. in Norwegian. Pale blue wraps, black print, pulp leaves. A brief history and biography of Magnus Andersen and his Viking ship replica sailed from Christiania to the WCE. For books by Andersen, see #622 and #2313.   ☺ . (LC,WiHx)

1025. Stevens, Mrs. Mark. *A lecture on What You Missed in not visiting the World's fair.* N.p.: n.p., [applied for °1895].

23½x15½. 31 p. Text and wraps of same paper. C.t. [The authors ask: "Who was Mrs. Stevens?"]
☺ . (LC)

1026. Stevens, Mrs. Mark. *Six months at the World's fair : a little here and a little there of the great white city--the World's fair.* [Detroit]: The Detroit free press printing co., 1895 °1895 by Mrs. Mark Stevens.

23x15. 382 p., frontis (port of Mrs. Stevens), plates. Burgundy (or brown) cloth hc with gold print. Personal description of the WCE.   ⊚ . (CHx,HL,UMi,S)

1027. *The Story of Chicago : Told in Pictures. From the Log Cabin to the World's Fair. A souvenir.* Chicago: F. P. Kenkel, Publisher, 1893 [°1893 by F. P. Kenkel].

27x20. ca. 75 p. Gold on tan wraps. C.t.: "From the Log Cabin to the World's Fair. Chicago : Souvenir." ⊚ . (A)

1028. *The Story of Columbus.* New York: Edward Brandus & Co., Publishers, °1893.

15½x22. 32 *l*, glossy pages, text and illus one side. White smooth string tied wraps with red print; red, blue, yellow, and black crest. T.p. illus of the Monastery of La Rabida. C.t.: "Christopher Columbus." Also on cover: "Souvenir, World's Columbian exposition. Chicago. 1893. Bought on the Fair Grounds." ⊚ . (GLD,NL,BPL,HL) $10 - 26

1029. *The Story of Columbus and the World's Columbian Exposition. By special authors : profusely illustrated.* Detroit and Windsor, Ont.: F. B. Dickerson co., 1892 [°1892 by F. B. Dickerson Co.].

22x16½. xvi, 17-485. Gray cloth hc with map of World on front cover in brown, black, and gold. Frontis of "Columbus' first sight of land." ⊚ . (CPL,S,OC,TD)

1030. *Story of Pullman.* N.p.: n.p., n.d.; Woodbridge, CT: RPI, 1989.

30 p., (13) p. of plates (1 fold out): illus, port, photos. A description of the growth of the Pullman Palace Car co., the town of Pullman, IL, and the Pullman exhibition train, displayed at the exposition. [The violent rail strikes of 1894 caused Pullman to fear for his life.]   (SI)

1031. Straus, Michael. *Modern art creations : A collection of artotype reproductions of noted paintings and sculpture by artists of all nations, with critical and descriptive text.* Chicago: Rand, McNally & Co., [°1894].

37½x32. 479 p., glossy leaves. Format: art reproductions on rectos, text on opposite verso.
---- Also listed: 39x__. 470 p.
        ⊚ . (LC,NYPL,AIC)

1032. Studebaker Bros. Manufacturing Co. *The Studebaker aluminum wagon, exhibited at the World's Columbian Exposition, Jackson Park, Chicago, 1893.* [South Bend, IN?]: n.p., [1893].

12x22. 5 *l* include glossy wraps and one color litho of wagon. Red string tied, dark blue and red print cover, print on one side of leaves.   (CHx)

☞ Clem Studebaker, President of the Board of World's Fair Managers of Indiana, was active in promoting Indiana and transportation at the WF.

1033. Sylvestre, Henri, Jr. *The marvels in art of the fin de siècle : containing the most notable paintings of to-day selected from the modern masterpieces of the great World's Columbian exhibition : one hundred large plates photogravures also one hundred typogravures.* Philadelphia: The Gebbie publishing co., limited, publishers, [°1893].

Subscription set ("no subscription for less than complete set") totaling 25 pts; $2.00 each pt. Intended to be bound in 2 vol: Vol I -- Typogravures; Vol II -- Photogravures. Text by Sylvestre. 19th and 20th century paintings. 106 plates (6 color mounted). Best of printers' art!
---- 2 vol. 52x36½.
---- 4 vol. 45x32. 50 *l* each vol; 25 lithographs facing 25 explanatory pages with a tissue guard between. Flexible black leather covers, gold print and design, gilt edges.
---- Deluxe ed.: 52x__. 10 pts. Each pt. contains 10 photogravures, 10 typogravures, and 1 color plate. Limited to 1000 copies. AIC has no. 14.
---- Imperial ed.: 10 vol in portfolios. 52x37. 119 mounted plates (19 of the original 100 plates are duplicated -- 9 colored, 10 satin).
---- Limited ed.: 2 vol in 1. 50½x35.
---- Special ed.: 2 vol. 48½x33½. Unpaginated. At top of cover: "Special edition." Marbled edges.
          ☺ . (UND,JHU,LC,S,nwu,RPB,AIC)

1034. Telang, Purushotam Rao. *A World's Fair Souvenir : Impressions of the World's fair and America in general.* San Francisco: Pacific Press Publishing Co., 1893.

23x15. 1 *l*, 3-39 p., frontis port of Telang. Gray wraps, black print. On t.p.: Telang is described as a "High Caste Brahmin, of Bombay, India." Descriptions of scenes and exhibits as seen through the author's eyes. ☺ (CHx)

1035. Thiergarten, Ferdinand. *Von Karlsruhe nach Chicago. Reiseskizzen und Plaudereien von der Weltausstellung.* Karlsruhe: F. Thiergarten, 1894.

Folio. 144 p., frontis (port), illus (facsimiles), map, plates. Trip to the WCE. (NYPL)

1036. Tiffany & Co. *Catalogue of Tiffany & Co's Exhibit.* New York: Tiffany & Co., 1893; Woodbridge, CT: RPI, 1989.

13½x9½. 112 p. Dark green stiff wraps, silver-green print and design. (CHx,SI,NYSt,NL)

1037. Tiffany & Co. *Diamond cutting as shown in the Mines and mining building, World's Columbian Exposition, Chicago, 1893, by Tiffany & co.* New York: Tiffany & Co.,[1893?].

13x__. 7, (1) p. (UC)

1038. Tiffany & Co. *A Glimpse of the Tiffany Exhibit at the World's Columbian Exposition, Chicago ...* ___: ___, ___; Woodbridge, CT: RPI, 1989.

24x17. 1 *l*, 14 p. Blue wraps, gold print and design. Caption title same as c.t. Rpt. "from the August number of Godey's Magazine. 1893." (CHx,SI)

1039. Tiffany Glass & Decorating Company. *A synopsis of the exhibit of the Tiffany Glass and Decorating company in the American section of the Manufactures and Liberal Arts Building at the World's Fair, ...* New York: Tiffany Glass & Decorating Co., °1893.

24x17. 3-32 glossy p. Light tan wraps, black print. Text and photos of Tiffany's glass work.   (CHx)

1040. Towne, E. C., A. J. Canfield, and George J. Hagar, eds. *Rays of Light from all Lands. The Bibles and beliefs of Mankind : Scriptures, Faiths and Systems of Every Age, Race and Nation : A Complete Story of all churches and communions : notable utterances by foremost representatives of all faiths.* New York: Gay Brothers & Co., [°1895].

25x18. 1 *l*, xxx, 7-866 p. Olive green cloth hc, gold and black print and design. C.t.: "Rays of Light from all Lands." Summary of Bonney's Parliament from p. 691 to end.   ☻ . (LC)

1041. Townsend, Grace. *The New Columbian White House Cookery : containing toilet, medical, and cooking receipts, comprehending economical and practical information ... superbly illustrated.* Chicago, Philadelphia, and Stockton, CA: Monarch Book Co. (Formerly L. P. Miller & Co.), [1893].

25½x18½. 527 p. Deep slate blue cover, black lettering and design. Cook book plus household and etiquette hints. See #1770 for what appears to be the same pub by a different author.   ☻ . (S)

1042. Truman, Ben[jamin] C[ummings]. *History of the World's Fair : being a Complete and Authentic Description of the Columbian Exposition From Its Inception.* Augusta, ME: T. H. Bodge & Co., 1893; Chicago [and] Philadelphia: Mammoth publishing co., [°1893 by Ben C. Truman]; Philadelphia: J. W. Keeler & Co., [1893]; Philadelphia: H. W. Kelly, 1893; Philadelphia: Keystone Publishing Co., [°1893 by Ben C. Truman]; Philadelphia: Mammoth publishing co., [°1893 by Ben C. Truman]; Philadelphia: Standard Publishing Co., 1893; Philadelphia: Syndicate Publishing Co., 1___; Philadelphia: John C. Winston, 1893; Philadelphia [and] Port Byron, IL: C. R. Parish & Co., [°1893 by Ben C. Truman]; [n.p., n.p., °1893]; Ottawa: CIHM, 1985.

Mammoth (Philadelphia): 26½x20½. 610 p. includes 17 plates. Light blue cloth hc, decorated embossed spine and cover in brown, gold, and black. Many contributors such as Mrs. Potter Palmer, Moses P. Handy, D. Burnham, etc. Frontis is early bird's-eye view drawing of the grounds. A common and useful book covering all aspects of the WCE. Many variants found, including page variation.
---- Mammoth (Chicago and Philadelphia): 27x20. 610 p. Gold print on navy blue hc. Lacks illus cover of other printings. Title variant: ... *being a complete description of the World's Columbian Exposition ...*
*P→   ☻ . (GLD,csuf,CHx,NYPL,UNLV,F,NLC,ANQ,BCM,E,WyMus,UMi,A,BPL,NJSt,WiHx,TD,L) $20 - 40

---- Reprint ed.: ... *being a Complete and Authentic Description ...* Rpt. New York: Arno Press, 1976.

26x19. 610 p., 11 *l* of plates. Gold on blue cloth hc. Rpt. of 1893 ed. published by H. W. Kelly, Philadelphia, from a copy in the NYPL. Part of set: "America in Two Centuries."
---- Also listed: Rpt. edition of 1893 ed. which was published by Mammoth, Philadelphia.
   ☻ . (UMKC,UNe,OSU,UNR,ncsu,TU,UoC,NL,A,RPB,AIC,BM,WiHx)

1043. Twain, Mark. No book.

Mark Twain went to the Fair, got sick, went home, and did not write about the Fair -- a pity.

1044. Union Pacific. ... *Sights and scenes in Idaho and Montana for tourists.*   Omaha, NE: Passenger Department Union Pacific System [Knight, Leonard & Co., Printers], n.d.

21½x10. Wraps with mountain scene illus. At head of title: "Fifth edition" surrounds Union Pacific logo. C.t.: "Idaho and Montana : Sights and Scenes for the Tourist."   ⊚ . (WM)

1045. University of Chicago. University Extension Division. Taft, Lorado. *Syllabus of a course of six lecture-studies : The art of the World's Columbian exposition.* Chicago, Boston, New York, and London: The U Press of Chicago, D. C. Heath & Co., [°1893 by the U of Chicago].

19½x13½. (1)-(3), 4-23 p. Wraps same stock as text pages, black print. C.t. At upper left corner of cover: "Lecture-study department: No.24.-Price, 15 Cts." [Taft was responsible for several of the sculptures and decorations about the WCE grounds.]   ⊚ (NL,WM)

1046. Wabash Railroad. *The Wabash line : the banner route to Chicago : The World's Columbian Exposition.* St. Louis: Passenger Department of the Wabash R.R., Poole Bros., Chicago, °1892 by F. Chandler.

14x22½. 28 *l*. Tan stiff wraps, multicolor litho front and back. Tinted illus of bldgs on rectos; text on opposite facing verso. Very pretty ad item. C.t. Also on front cover: "Compliments Passenger Department Wabash Railroad." Title on 2nd leaf (t.p. ?): "Souvenir edition: The World's Columbian Exposition Chicago" flanked by "1492 1893."   ⊚ . (LC,S,TD)

1047. Walton, William. ... *Art and Architecture.* Columbus edition. Philadelphia: George Barrie, [°1893-95].

Subscription set: 49½x36. 30 parts, each with light blue hc, gold print and design. At head of title: "World's Columbian Exposition: MDCCCXCIII."
---- Subscription set: 43½x30½. 30 pts. Gray wraps, gold and blue print.
---- Bound: 48x37. Leather hc, gold print and design.
---- Bound: 43x31. 3 vol. On cover: "Official Illustrated Publication." Gilt edges.
---- Bound: 43x__. 3 vol in 2. On cover: "Official Illustrated Publication." Vol 1 is "The Architecture plus "The Art" pt. 1. Vol 2 is "The Art" pt. 2.
---- Also listed: A limited "Columbus edition." 57x__. 11 vol. Different ed. ? SLP has no. 846.
(KU,UMC,csuf,KyU,CPL,CHx,NYPL,S,mcg,NLC,ANQ,nwu,HL,TU,NYSt,UoC,NL,BPL,SLP,AIC,OC,WM,WiHx)

1048. ---. ---. Edition de Luxe. 11 parts. Philadelphia: G. Barrie, [°1893-95].

48x33½. 11 parts bound in 3 vols. Limited to 1000 copies. At head of title: "Official Illustrated Publication. World's Columbian Exposition MDCCCXCIII." CHx has copy no. 122.   (CHx,S)

1049. ---. ---. Edition of the Republic. 11 parts. Philadelphia: George Barrie, [°1893-95].

57x40½. Limited to 100 copies. Each part paginated. Folding hard board covers in white shiny paper and half red leather with red ribbon tied corners. At head of title: "Official Illustrated Publication. World's Columbian Exposition: MDCCCXCIII." Front cover has design of Republic statue in Grand Basin in gold. Each part has an inner stiff paper cover covered in white textured paper and embossed with Republic statue design. Each part contains matted color lithographs. Each has loose leaf pages on high rag content paper. Tissue guards front each b/w or color lithograph. Subscriber's name printed on a separate leaf in part 1. Each part was shipped in a well crafted heavy cardboard box: 58½x41½, 3 cm thick. Box covered with white textured cloth; a gray and red address label tipped in. The inside of the box is felt lined throughout. The best of the printers' art!

⊚ (GLD,csuf,NYPL,S,RPB)   Complete set: $700 - 2,000

1050. Ward, Artemas, comp. *Columbus Outdone : an exact narrative of the voyage of The Yankee Skipper, Capt. Wm. A. Andrews, In the Boat "Sapolio."* New York: Enoch Morgan's Sons Co.?, 1893.

20x14. 198 p. Cloth hc depicts 14 foot "Sapolio" on its voyage from Atlantic City to Spain. "World's Fair souvenir edition" on cover. Frontis port of Andrews.

1051. Wellesley College. *World's Columbian Exposition 1893 : Wellesley college : Wellesley, Mass.* Albany, NY: Printed by Amasa? J. Parker, receiver of Weed, Parsons & Co., n.d.

13x8. 43, (1) p., illus, glossy pages. Frontis: Farnsworth Art Bldg. Description of campus bldgs, activities, etc.   ⊚ . (NL,BPL)

1052. Wells, Fargo and Company. *Catalogue : Wells, Fargo and Company : historical exhibit, etc. : at the 1893 World's Columbian exposition : Chicago, Illinois, U.S.A. and across the seas.* San Francisco: H. S. Crocker, Co., n.d.

19½x13½. 32 p. Turquoise (or light beige) wraps, black print. 173 numbered paragraphs of information. The last p. lists robberies for 14 years ending Nov., 1884. Text on both sides of front and back covers. C.t.

⊚ . (KU,ALB,F,UDe,HL,TD) $20 - 35

1053. Wells, Ida B., ed. *The Reason Why the Colored American is not in the World's Columbian Exposition. The Afro-American's contribution to Columbian literature ...* Chicago: Ida B. Wells, 1893.

18x12½. 81, (1) p., illus. C.t.
---- Also listed: 20x__. 2 *l*, 81 p. illus.

(R,CHx,Yale,nwu,BPL) $20 - 40

1054. Wheeler, George Montague. *A universal World's exhibit.* Washington, D.C.: Judd & Detweiler, printers, 1890 [°1890 by George M. Wheeler].

23½x14½. 6 p. includes pulp front cover, black print. Early proposal for permanent (unrealized) exhibit. Large fold. circular ground plan with the various depts in concentric rings expanding away from the center which was to be the central power station. Each ring divided into quadrants, each with a triumphal arch (4 total) in the distal ring. C.t. At head of title: "Confidential." Wheeler was Major, Corps of Engineers, U.S. Army, (Retired).
---- NL copy: tipped in hand written letter from Wheeler to Wm. E. Poole requesting Poole to comment on the pamphlet and exhibit.
⊚ . (LC,NL)

1055. *The white city : the Historical, Biographical, and Philanthropical Record of Virginia and West Virginia and their state exhibits at the World's Columbian exposition : classified and illustrated.* [Chicago]: Chicago World Book co., 1893.

27x19. 1 *l* (t.p.), v-viii, (24) p. text and illus, (3) p., followed by variously pagination to include other states. Text is 3½ cm thick. Burgundy and black cloth hc with gilt print, illus of Columbus. C.t.: "The White City : New York." Strange book: has "New York" printed on cover, "Virginia and West Virginia" on t.p., plus, includes many other states. No index or table of contents. May be promotional copy? See #940 for similar format by Chicago World Book Co. ⊜ . (UoC,S,RPB)

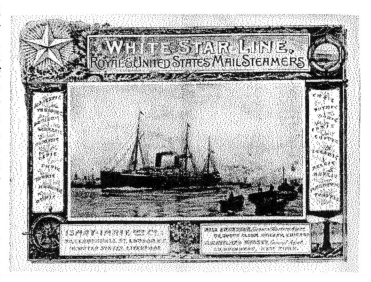

1056. *White Star Line of Steamships : A Résumé of Twenty Years Progress :...* [London and Liverpool: Ismay-Imrie & Co., 1893].

21½x28. (24) p., glossy pages. White stiff wraps printed and illus in dark brown. Handout at WCE. The White Star Line bldg was next to Horticulture Hall.
P↑   ⊜ (GLD,WM) $15 - 30

1057. White, Trumbull, and Wm. Igleheart. *The World's Columbian Exposition, Chicago, 1893. A Complete History of the Enterprise; a Full Description of the Buildings and Exhibits in all Departments; and a Short Account of Previous Expositions, ... fully illustrated : with half-tone and wood engravings and pen drawings by the best artists.* Boston: Gately & O'Gorman, [°1893 by J. W. Ziegler]; Boston: Standard Silverware Co., [°1893 by J. W. Ziegler]; Charleston, SC: Martin & Hoyt co., [°1893]; Chicago: J. S. Ziegler & Co., [°1893]; Philadelphia: Elliott & Beezley, [°1893]; Philadelphia: Charles Foster pub. co., °1893; Philadelphia: Historical Publishing Co., 1893; Philadelphia: W. W. Houston and Co., 1893; Philadelphia [and] Chicago: International publishing co., [°1893 by Trumbull White]; Philadelphia [and] Chicago: International Publishing Co., [°1893 by J. W. Ziegler]; Philadelphia: J. C. McCurdy & Co. Ltd., [°1893 by J. W. Ziegler]; Philadelphia and Chicago: Monarch book co. (Successors to and formerly L. P. Miller & Co.), [°1893 by J. W. Ziegler]; Philadelphia and Chicago: J. H. Moore & Co., [°1893 by J. W.

Ziegler]; Philadelphia and St. Louis: P. W. Ziegler & co., [°1893 by Trumbull White]; Philadelphia and St. Louis: P. W. Ziegler & co., [°1893 by J. W. Ziegler]; N.p.: n.p., [°1893 by J. W. Ziegler].

24½x18½. 1 *l* is frontis of Administration Bldg. Red and black printed t.p. Introduction by George R. Davis. C.t. on all: "Worlds [sic] Columbian Exposition 1893." Common but useful. Covers: 1)

Light blue cloth hc, attractive gold, brown, blue, and black print and design, decorative end papers; 2) Brown leather hc, gilt lettering; 3) Red leather hc, blind stamped design, gilt lettering; 4) Morocco hc, gilt print, all edges gilt.

---- 1 *l*, 628 p. publishers: Foster, Gately, Monarch, Standard, J. S. Ziegler, P. W. Ziegler.

---- 1 *l*, 640 p. publishers: Elliott, Historical, International, Martin, McCurdy, Moore, P. W. Ziegler, and n.p.

*P↑   ⊚ . (GLD,csuf,UND,KyU,CHx,NYPL,S,E,BCM,OhHx,UDe,USD,WyMus,HL,UMi,SLP,UoC,NL,A,BPL,AIC,OC,GPL,TD) $12 - 28

☞ White was World's Fair Correspondent; Igleheart was World's Fair Editor of the *Chicago Record.*

1058. Whitney, Emma T. *Souvenir of World's Fair and Chicago.* Chicago: Columbian souvenir publishing co., 1892 copyrighted by Mrs. Emma T. Whitney.

15½x12. 23 *l*. Pea green wraps.   ⊚ (CHx)

1059. Wilberforce, Archibald, ed. *Capitols of the Globe.* New York: Peter Fenelton Collier, 1893.

34½x27½. 586 p. Red cloth hc, black and gilt print, embossed design. Content: 10 p. on the WCE prior to its opening.   (S)

1060. Wilkie, Franc B. *A life of Christopher Columbus.* Chicago New York: F. T. Neely, Publisher, [°1893 by F. T. Neely].

15x10. vi, 7-184 p., 4 *l* ads. Light tan wraps, blue print and decoration. Vol III. No. 7 of "Neely's Popular Library." The series also contains Neely's *Looking Forward* (#26).

P→   ⊚ (GLD) $10 - 20

1061. *Windsor Castle at Chicago, To which is added The Home of Sunlight Soap.* England: Press of Lever Brothers, Limited, n.d.; Woodbridge, CT: RPI, 1989.

15x12. 31 p., (1) p., illus. Gray-blue textured wraps, black print. Lever Brothers sponsored the large model of Windsor Castle at the Fair (illus p. 3). Description of Sunlight Soap factory in England by George Augustus Sala. (Also see Sala, #1003.)   ⊚ (GLD,SI,F,S,UDe,TD) $16 - 26

1062. Wisthaler, Johanna S[ara]. *By Water to the Columbian Exposition.* Schenectady, NY: [Ernst Knauer], 1894 [°1894].

23x15½. 131, (1) p. includes plate frontis, fold. plate, fold. map. Decorative end papers, errata at end. "Revised" bird's-eye view of exposition grounds. On t.p.: "'Travel is the great source of true wisdom.' -- Beaconsfield."   ⊚ . (LC,S,NYSt)

1063. *Wonderful Chicago and the World's fair, historical and picturesque, early days ... modern Chicago ... religious Chicago ... and the principal attractions of the World's Columbian exposition.* Chicago: George W. Melville, [°1892 by George W. Melville]; Woodbridge, CT: RPI, 1989.

24½x34. (136) p., illus, maps. Red cloth hc, gilt and black print and design, light gold decorated end papers. Bold gilt c.t.: "Wonderful Chicago and The World's Fair. Illustrated and Published by, George W. Melville Chicago." Many lithos, photos, and ads. Descriptions and illus of Chicago, Chicago history, and the WCE including biographies of the mayors of Chicago to 1893.
---- 24½x34. 4 l, (112) p. + 5 l accordion fold Grand Panoramic View of Chicago tipped in ahead of p. (19). Green cloth hc with gilt and black print, red dyed edges. T.p. in red and black.
---- 24½x34. (126) p. Silver cloth hc with gilt print.
---- Also listed: (114) p., illus, ports, map. Microfilm.
         ☻. (GLD,CHx,SLS,A) $25 - 42

1064. ... *The World Almanac.* New York: The Press Publishing Co., 1893 copyrighted by The Press Publishing Co.

19x13. 464 p. At head of title: "1893." Contains a map and brief information on the upcoming Fair. Cover illus of the World newspaper bldg in New York City.   ☻. (S)

1065. *The World's carriage building center : Cincinnati, Ohio, U. S. A.* Cincinnati: Press of Robert Clarke & Co., 1893 [°1893 by E. W. Hedges].

18½x12½. 4 l, vii-viii, 9-73, (1) p. Frontis is a collage of 7 carriage factories. Two-tone gray cloth hc, gilt print and design on cover and spine. "Souvenir of the World's Columbian Exposition, for visitors interested in Carriage building." Attractive book.   ☻. (LC,OhHx,UDe,UMi,A)

1066. *World's Columbian Exposition souvenir : containing a story of Christopher Columbus and his discoveries : a treatise on Illinois and Chicago : also the Columbian exposition : personal memoirs of leading citizens of Illinois : illustrated with steel engravings.* Chicago: North American Engraving and Publishing Co., 1895.

1895: 30x24. 3 l, (2), (5)-279 p., frontis of Columbus, 6 plates, 36 ports protected by tissue guards. Hc, all edges gilt. C.t.: "Illinois in the Columbian year"; binder's subtitle: "Contemporary biography of Illinois." Nice.
---- Chicago: North American Engraving and Publishing Co., 1892.
---- *World's Columbian Exposition souvenir : containing a story of Christopher Columbus and his discoveries, a treatise on Illinois, Chicago and the Columbian exposition : Personal Memoirs of leading citizens of Illinois : illustrated with steel engravings.* 1894. 30½x24. (5)-77 p., ports with tissue guards. Green flexible cloth stiff cover, black print. No edges gilt. C.t.: "World's Columbian Exposition Souvenir." Apparently a salesmen's sample but has no subscription forms.
       ☻. (csuf,CHx,NL)

1067. *The World's Columbian exposition to be held at Chicago in 1893.* N.p.: n.p., n.d.

17x11. 36 p. + 1 fold out map. Tan wraps with black print. Nine flowers in center of front wrap. C.t. On cover: "Compliments of The Columbia Transit Co. of Atlanta and Chicago."   ☻. (CHx)

1068. *The World's Fair and the Journey Thereto, by We Four.* N.p.: n.p., [1893].

23x15. 35 p., (3 photoplates). Brown hc with gold print. C.t.: "Trip of We Four." Photos of each traveler tipped in on front end paper with words "We Four." A diary account of 4 Philadelphians (Chas. and John Vanfleet, Wm. and Chas. Ambler) who made the B & O railroad trip to Chicago, Sat. Oct 21 to Tues. Oct 31st, 1893 (last 10 days of the Fair). (UMKC)

1069. *The World's Fair closed on Sunday! Enlightened America ruled by beer, bishops, and bribery. The people ask knowledge, they are given rum and religion.* [Chicago: 1893]; [New York: The Truth Seeker, 1892].

19x12. 8 p. including wraps. Wraps with cartoon on front are same stock as text, black print. Argument for WF Sunday opening based upon educational benefits.   ⊘ . (CHx,NYPL)

1070. *World's Fair Excursions. Special features of the "New England grocer's" plan. A simple, Business-Like Arrangement, which all can Understand. Payments can be made in cash or installments.* Boston: Benjamin Johnson, manager, Grocers' exchange, [1893].

24½x15½. 26 p., port, illus, map. Front wrap included in pagination; illus of Administration Bldg. Ad.   ⊘ . (CHx,BPL,WM)

1071. *The World's Fair from the Electric Launches on the Lagoons ... ____*: Electric Launch and Navigation Co., n.d.

19x15. Folded white *l* making (4) p. Caption title. Blue print and small design of launch.   (TD)

1072. The World's Fair Hotel and Boarding Bureau. ... *World's Columbian Exposition Souvenir hand-book.* Chicago: Chicago hand-book co., n.d.

8½x16. 48 p. + map before back wrap. Lime green wraps with black lettering and design. C.t. At head of title: "Compliments of World's Fair Hotel and Boarding Bureau for Kentucky and West Virginia. General Office, Huntington, West Virginia." B/w illus of WCE bldgs and Bureau hotels.   ⊘ (GLD) $14 - 28

1073. *The World's Fair Illustrated : containing a brief account of the life of Christopher Columbus and the important events with which he was connected, copies of the famous paintings in which he is represented, and a concise history of the United States together with portraits of the most prominent ... officials,...* Chicago: Lanward Publishing Co., [1892].

25½x34½. (128) p. Fancy blue on white lithographed heavy wraps, blue cloth spine. Many interesting period ads. C.t.: "The World's Fair 1893: Compliments of West Shore Railroad."
---- Also listed: 76 p.
P→   ⊘ . (GLD,UC)

$25 - 40

1074. *The World's Fair. In Commemoration of the World's Columbian Exposition Chicago 1893.* Boston: A. Shuman & Co., 1893.

60x46. 4 p., illus Elaborate black print and design. C.t. Large newspaper format commemorating the opening of the WF, May 1893. Perhaps a supplement or mail out since both c0opies were heavily folded into quarter size in exactly the same place.
   ⊘ . (GLD,SI,BPL) $15 - 35

1075. *The World's Fair Steamship Company : time table of steamship Christopher Columbus.* N.p.: n.p., n.d.

> 14x8. Single white stiff card, blue print and litho of the whaleback. Round trip was 25 cents.
> (TD)
> $40

1076. *World's Fairs from London 1851 to Chicago 1893 : (copyrighted) : illustrated with views and portraits and Containing Authentic and Official Information of the World's Columbian Exposition, 1893 and all Previous World's Fairs.* Chicago: Midway Publishing co., 1892; Woodbridge, CT: RPI, 1989.

> 26x17. 3 *l*, 82 p., frontis, illus, ports, plans. LC lists author: [Miles, George S.] ed. See C. B. Norton #956.
> ---- Also listed: 25x__. 82 p., (46) p. of plates (some folded), (26) p. of ads. 15 *l*, each describing a single WCE bldg, inserted in pocket.
> ☺ . (LC,SI,NYPL,nwu,AIC)

1077. Young, William Euclid. *How to celebrate the Four Hundreth Anniversary of the discovery of America.* N.p.: n.p., [1886?].

> 23½x15. Earth brown wraps, black print. Caption title. C.t.: "The World's fair for 1892." ☺ . (S)

1078. Zimmermann, G. H. *Vierhundert Jahre Amerikanischer Geschichte. ...* [Four Hundred Years of American History]. Milwaukee: Verlag von Geo. Brumder, 1893.

> 22x16. 1 *l*, xi, 736 p. Red cloth hc, black and silver print and design, decorated end papers, 1st *l* is frontis of U.S. Capitol. Old German language script. Last section is illus description of WCE.
> P→ ☺ . (GLD)
> $10 - 25

Chapter 6

GUIDES

1079. *The ABC guide of Chicago and the World's Columbian exposition. Replies to questions asked every day by the guests and citizens of the World's fair city. Fully illustrated. Suggestions to sightseers : practical information for practical people.* [Chicago: Nickel Publishing Co., °1893].

16x12½. 128 p., illus maps. Wraps. C.t. ☺.(BPL)

1080. *The American-Hispano Pocket Guide of the World's Fair : 1893 : Guia de Bolsillo Hispano-Americana Para La Exposicion Colombina.* New York: n.p., [1893?]; New York: Haurie-Emes, publisher, [1893?]; Woodbridge, CT: RPI, 1989.

16½x11½. (32) p. catalog of Knox Hats, (9-20), 21-138 p., (20) p. ads and poetry. Fold out map of grounds tipped in before p. 21, fold out map of Chicago downtown tipped in before p. 55. Title is on p. (9). Gray cloth hc, black embossed lettering. Interesting guide book and advertising item. Dual language. C.t.= t.p.
---- Same guide without (32) p. catalog.
Both versions have "E. M. Knox, publisher, ... N.Y." on cover.
P→ ☺ (GLD,csuf,CHx,SI,NYPL,S,TnSt,UDe,HL,TU,UMi,UoC,A,RPB,WiHx,TD) $15 - 30

1081. *Authentic guide to Chicago and the World's Columbian exposition.* Chicago: Merchant's World's fair bureau of information co. [The H. Sellschopp printing and publishing co.], 1893.

16½x12. 216 p., illus, fold. map. Tan wraps with navy blue print, design and fountain scene litho. C.t.= t.p. ☺.(LC,OC)

1082. *Birds-eye* [sic] *view of the World's Columbian Exposition 1893.* Chicago: Knight, Leonard & co., printers, [1893?]; Chicago: A. Teese & Co., [1893?].

Knight: 17x10. (1) plate (fold.), map. Wraps. C.t. Plate measures 31x65½. ☺.(BPL)

1083. Bloom, Sol, comp. *Bloom's directory to Chicago and the World's Columbian Exposition : A Complete and Reliable Book of Reference for Tourists and Strangers Visiting the Great City ...* Chicago: Frank's Bros., 1893; Chicago: Siegel, Cooper & co., [1893].

Siegel: 23x16. 56 p. with fold out map after last page. White glossy wraps, black and tinted cover illus both sides. Siegel, Cooper & Co. was a large dept store at the corner of State and Van Buren, Chicago.
---- Frank's. 23x16. 56 p.
P→ ☺.(GLD,CHx,S) $20 - 35

1084. Bowes, Edwin N[athan]. *Guide and illustrated hand-book of the World's Columbian Exposition.* Chicago: Edwin N. Bowes, [°1892].

18x11½. (59) p. + 2 maps. Bright red smooth wraps, black print and design of Columbus (front) and South Lagoon (back). C.t.
---- 72 p. + (1) folding map of Jackson Park.
          ⊚ . (CHx,LC)

1085. *The buildings of the World's Fair, with map of the grounds. A useful souvenir. ...* Chicago: A. R. Montgomery: [1893].

71½x53½ folds to 18x11½. Large map and illus. C.t. Also on cover: "For the use of the originals of the engravings in this work we are indebted to the courtesy of the publishers of The Graphic, Chicago." Grounds map by John J. Flinn. (NYPL)

1086. *Catalogue collection of the Byzantine paintings from Saint Bontiface's College : Rome, Italy. Loaned by Brother Maurelian to the "Field Columbian Museum" ...* Chicago: Rokker-O'Donnell Printing Co., [1893?].

23x15. 16 p. Light blue wraps printed in dark blue. C.t.
P→   ⊚ (GLD) $15 - 35

1087. *Chicago and its environs. A complete guide to the city and the World's fair.* Columbian ed. Chicago: F. P. Kenkel (L. Schick), 1893 [°1893 by F. P. Kenkel].con

18x13. 4 *l*, (5)-523, 48, 16 *l*, + fold. color map laid in at back cover. Red cloth flexible cover, gold print. 13 p. guide to the Fair and grounds. Ads and illus.
P→   ⊚ (GLD) $15 - 30

1088. *Chicago and the World's Columbian Exposition : 1893.* Chicago: ____ Midway Publishing Co., n.d.

25½x10½. Folder of one large leaf to make 8 p. When fully open, maps of Jackson Park and Chicago + "correct central view World's Columbian Exposition" are seen across the front pages. Information on verso: Chicago in general, WCE, state and territory appropriations, WCE bldgs, and general information on the Board of Lady Managers, Auxiliary, Midway Plaisance, medical bureau, restaurants, etc. Gray stiff wraps, black print. C.t. LC author: [Miles, George S.].   ⊚ . (LC)

1089. *Chicago and World's Fair guide.* [Chicago]: n.p., [1893?].

14½x9. (48) p. Chartreuse wraps, black print. C.t. Facts about the Fair, city attractions, local ads, etc. "Compliments of the Cosmopolitan Hotel."
P→   ⊗ (GLD,S) $15 - 25

1090. *Chicago Checker-Board guide : World's Fair Edition : illustrated : Containing a Miniature Reproduction of the Business Portion of Chicago in the shape of a Checker-Board : Compiled especially for the Visitor of a few days or weeks.* Chicago: A. H. Pokorny & co., [1893?].

16½x12. (3)-64 p., 1 *l* of plates : illus, fold. map. Frontis: Policeman's memorial monument (Haymarket Square). On printed wraps: "Compliments of Fuller & Fuller co., importers and wholesale druggists." ⊗ . (UDe,BPL)

1091. Chicago Cottage Organ Co. *Map and Pocket Guide of Chicago.* Chicago: Arney & Stoner Advertising Agency, ᶜ1893.

14x7½. (12) p. Cream wraps same stock as text, black print. Ad for the Company's "Conover" Pianos on back wrap. Contains Chicago and WF facts; double map at centerfold.
⊗ (GLD) $8 - 16

1092. Chicago Herald. ... *Condensed guide to the World's fair. What to see and how to see it...* Chicago: Chicago Herald, 1893.

28x22½. 31, (1) p., illus, maps. Brown wraps with black lettering and illus of the Herald Bldg. At head of title: "The Chicago Herald : Chicago, Tuesday, July 25, 1893." C.t. ⊗ . (OhHx,UDe)

1093. Chicago Jewelers Association. ... *Columbian Souvenir : Visitors Directory : With Compliments of the Chicago Jewelers association.* [Chicago: 1893?].

17x26. (48) p. (includes front and back wraps), illus, ports, maps. C.t. At head of title: "1492 : 1893." Cover litho by Orcutt Co., Chicago. ⊗ . (BPL)

1094. *Chicago's Souvenir. What to See and How to See it.* [Chicago]: Chicago Souvenir Co., ᶜ1893.

20x13½. 63, (1) p., illus, map. C.t. Cover illus: Grant Statue in Lincoln Park. ⊗ . (NYPL,BPL)

1095. *Conkey's complete guide to the World's Columbian Exposition : May 1 to October 30, 1893, containing description and location of ... buildings; ... map, ... together with general information concerning the fair. ...* Chicago: W. B. Conkey co., 1893 [ᶜ1893]; Woodbridge, CT: RPI, 1989.

19½x13½. 211, (1) p., illus, plan. Decorative wraps.
---- 222 p. includes index starting at p. 212.
⊗ . (R,csuf,CHx,ALB,SI,S,TU) $15 - 30

1096. *Directory to the World's fair exhibits and exhibitors. A Handy Volume of General Information on the World's Columbian Exposition. Five Thousand Exhibits Indexed and Located. ...* Chicago: Wellington Publishing Co., 1893. (Copyright by Richard R. Murphy).

15x7. 178 p., fold. map of grounds at back cover. Blood red slick wraps with black print.   ⊚ (CHx)

1097. Dredge, James. *The Columbian exposition of 1893: what to see and how to get there.* London: The Polytechnic, 1892; Woodbridge, CT: RPI, 1989.

22x15½. 60 p., illus, maps. Dark red wraps with black print. On t.p.: "Part I.--The City of Chicago and her exposition of 1893." and "Part II.-- The Polytechnic cheap trips to Chicago." ⊚ . (CHx,SI)

1098. *The economizer : how and where to find the Gems of the Fair : with diagrams Locating the Exhibits of the World's Columbian Exposition.* Chicago: Rand, McNally & co., publishers, 1893 [ᶜ1893 by Rand, McNally & Co.]; Woodbridge, CT: RPI, 1989.

17x9½. 68 p., (11) p. for "Memoranda" + (1) p. ads. Maps, plans. Turquoise wraps with blue print. ⊚ . (csuf,SI,NYPL,S,E,UDe,UoC,NL,WM)

1099. *The English-German Guide to the City of Chicago and The World's Columbian Exposition.* Chicago, New York: Universe Publishing co., ᶜ1892.

19x13½. 2 *l*, 5-151 p., (11) p. ads. Flexible cloth cover in deep blue-green, gilt print and design. Ads inside front cover and both sides of back cover. Port of T. W. Palmer faces copyright page. On t.p.: "Price 25¢." C.t.= t.p. Each page is divided into 2 columns -- one English, one German (old script). ⊚ (CHx)

1100. *Facts about the World's fair.* Hudson, NY: C. H. Evans & Sons, [ᶜ1893 by S. C. Patterson].

13½x8½. (8) p. Attractive pale blue wraps with gilt print and red globe. C.t. Simple guide plus ad for Evans' ale. ⊚ (GLD,WiHx,TD,HL)

1101. *Facts of interest and Guide to the World's Fair.* Bridgeport, CT: Stewart and Rockefeller Pub'g. Co., [ᶜ1893].

26½x18½. 6 *l*, illus. Gray wraps, black print and design. C.t. Intended as an ad guide (blank spaces are left between text and illus for ad insertion. Cover litho of Columbus and the Government Bldg. LC copyright stamp: 1893. ⊚ . (LC)

1102. Flinn, John J[oseph], comp. *The best things to be seen at the World's fair : published by authority of the exposition management.* Chicago: The Columbian Guide co., [ᶜ by The World's Columbian exposition (LC copyright stamp, 1893)].

21x14½. 3 *l*, 9-182, (10) p., includes frontis (Grand Basin and "Court of Honor"), illus, plates, plans. Turquoise cloth flexible cover with black print and gilt design of the Statue of the Republic. Unpaginated pages in back are for visitor memoranda.
---- 22x15. 4 *l*, (7)-183, (9) p. Dark green cloth flexible cover.
---- 22x14½. 1 *l*, 10 p., 2 *l*, (11)-182, (10) p.
⊚ . (GLD,csuf,UWa,LC,SI,NYPL,E,D,BPL,A,OC,OhHx) $16 - 34

1103. Flinn, John J[oseph]. *Chicago : The Marvelous City of the West. A history, an encyclopedia, and a guide. 1891. Illustrated.* Chicago: Flinn & Sheppard, [°1890 by John J. Flinn].

17x13½. 3 *l*, xix, 1 *l*, 17-543 p. illus, maps (1 fold. in pocket), pulp paper. Red cloth hc with black and gold lettering. Frontis of barren Jackson Park, scene of forthcoming WCE. C.t.: "The standard guide to Chicago for the year 1891." Part 4: "The World's Columbian Exposition." ⊗ . (OhHx,NL,RPB,AIC,WiHx)

1104. Flinn, John J[oseph]. *Chicago : The Marvelous City of the West. A history, an encyclopedia, and a guide. Second edition. Illustrated. 1892.* Chicago: Mercantile Pub. and Adv. Co., 1892; Chicago: National Book and Picture Co., 1893; Chicago: The Standard Guide Co., n.d. [copyrighted by John J. Flinn].

Standard: 17x13½. viii, 1 *l*, xvii, (1) p., 1 *l*, 17-632 p., xxxii of ads at back. Has: frontis, plates, map in back pocket. Marbled edges. C.t.: "The standard guide to Chicago for the year 1892." Part 1: "Chicago as it was." Part 2: "Chicago as it is." Part 3: "The encyclopedia." Part 4: "The World's Columbian Exposition." Part 5: The guide."
---- Mercantile: 20x14½. xvii, (xviii), 5 *l*, (i)-xvii, (1) p., 1 *l*, 17-632 with many uncounted leaves of plates interspersed, 3, iv-xxxii follow text. Red cloth hc, gilt and black print and design, all edges marbled. Ads on inside front and back covers. Frontis. C.t.: "The Standard Guide to Chicago for the Year 1892."
---- 10 *l*, xvii, (1) p., 1 *l*, 17-632 p., (iii)-xxxii ads in back.
---- 584 p.
---- National: (5), 632, xxxii p.
⊗ . (PU,CHx,CHx,S,NLC,NL,WiHx)

1105. Flinn, John J[oseph]. *Ein führen über den Welt-Ausstellungsplatz und durch die Gebäulichseiten nebst offiziellem Adress-Buch mit Karte und Illustrationen.* Chicago: The Standard Guide Co., °1892.

22x15. (7)-38 p., tipped in map of bldgs and grounds at front cover, frontis. Rose wraps with black print.   (CHx)

1106. Flinn, John J[oseph]. *Guide Général de l'Exposition Universelle et annuaire officiel illustré.* [Chicago: Donohue & Henneberry, printers and binders, 1892]. (as shown on copyright page).

22x14½. (7)-39 + (1) p., illus. Orange wraps with black print. Colored map of bldgs and grounds tipped in at front cover.   (CHx)

1107. Flinn, John J[oseph]. *Guide to the World's fair grounds and buildings and official directory with map and illustrations.* October ed. Chicago: The Standard Guide co., [°1892 by Flinn and Sheppard].

23x15. 40 p., frontis of Administration Bldg, fold out color map tipped in ahead of back cover. Apple green wraps. C.t.= t.p. except only cover bears the words "October edition."
---- As an advertising issue: N.p.: n.p., [°1892 by Flinn & Sheppard]. Cover: "Complimentary to the users of S. S. Sleeper & Co.'s best of all Mocha and Java Coffees (two pound cans only.) Boston." "Edition" not stated.
⊗ . (KyU,NL,E)

1108. Flinn, John J[oseph]. *Guide to the World's fair grounds, buildings and attractions. Illustrated. Divided into seven principal groups and routes. A handy reference book for everybody.* Chicago: The Standard Guide Co., [°1893 by The Standard Guide Co.].

22x15. 67 p., illus color and folding map. Green decorative covers, black lettering and litho of Administration Bldg. ☺ . (csuf,CHx,S,UDe,AIC,L)

1109. Flinn, John J[oseph], comp. *Hand-book of the World's Columbian Exposition : illustrated : compiled from official sources.* Chicago: The Standard guide co., [°1892]; Woodbridge, CT: RPI, 1989.

14½x11. 9 *l* including frontis, ix, (9), 17-350 p., 1 *l*. Red dyed edges. Color litho frontis: "The Lagoon and Surroundings."
---- 2nd ed.: 350 p., (44) plates, (12) p. ads. Microfilm.
☺ . (CHx,LC,SI,S,UDe,UoC)

1110. Flinn, John J[oseph], comp. *Official Guide to Midway Plaisance : otherwise known as "The Highway Through The Nations"* ... Chicago (WCE Administration Building): The Columbian Guide Co., 1893.

19½x13½. 48 p. Tan wraps, illus and print in black. Lists 63 exhibits, e.g., the 1/15 scale Eifel Tower, captive balloon, and Tree of Wonder. Bird's-eye of Midway on back wrap.
P→   ☺ (GLD,LC,S,WM,TD)

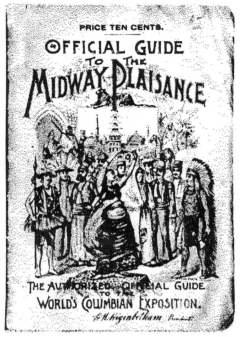

$15 - 30

1111. Flinn, John J., comp. *Official guide to the World's Columbian Exposition in the city of Chicago, state of Illinois, May 1 to October 26, 1893, by authority of the United States of America.* ... Chicago: Columbian Guide co., [°1893 by The World's Columbian Exposition]; Woodbridge, CT: RPI [hand book ed.], 1989.

Hand book ed.: 19x12½. 192 p., (2) p. Maroon coated wraps, gold print, frontis of Viking ship. Black (or maroon) coated wraps, gold print, frontis of Columbus sighting America. The last (2) p. are for visitor notes. Look for entries -- these are a real find and make the book more valuable, e.g., a copy with personal notes at KU.
---- Souvenir ed.: 19x12½. 301 p., frontis of Columbus sighting America. Flexible blue cloth covers printed in black, labeled "Popular Edition." Also found with red cloth hc, gilt print, top edge gilt.
---- Midway Plaisance ed.: 19x12½. 301 p. Stiff cloth -- red coated leatherette texture.
*P→   ☺ . (GLD,KU,csuf,CHx,LC,SI,NYPL,F,S,OhHx,TnSt,D,OSL,E,UDe,USD,SLP, CoU, NHSt, HL,
        TU,UMi,UoC,NL,BPL,RPB,WM,AIC,OC,WiHx,L)

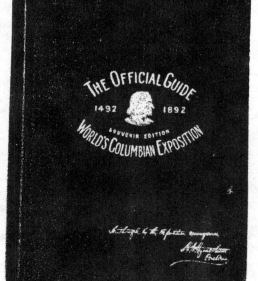

$10 - 45

1112. Flinn, John J[oseph]. *Offizieller Führer durch den Columbischen Welt-Ausstellungs - Platz und die Gebäulichseiten.* Chicago: The Columbian Guide Co., n.d. [° by the World's Columbian Exposition].

19½x13. 72 p. Robin egg blue wraps, black print and illus of the German Bldg. Map of grounds at front. Frontis of Machinery Hall. Flinn's official guide. At upper left of cover: "German edition." ⊜ (GLD,CHx) $15 - 28

1113. [Fulton, Albert Watson]. *What will it cost me to see the World's fair? Some Timely Suggestions to Intending Visitors.* Chicago: Donohue & Henneberry, 1893 [°1893 by Albert W. Fulton].

16½x11½. 32 p. Glossy paper covered boards, red and black print, pulp pages. Bottom of t.p. reads: "By a Chicago newspaper reporter : 1893." ⊜ . (LC)

1114. ... *Godey's Illustrated Souvenir Guide to Chicago, World's fair and New York.* ... [Chicago and New York: E. Lockwood & Co., °1893].

19½x13½. 108, 64 p. guide to N.Y. City, (2) p. maps, (7) p. color lithos of bldgs, other unpaged b/w lithos and ads. Beautiful multicolor litho front and back stiff wraps; maroon, green, and ocher color spine reads: "Godey's Souvenir Guide." At head of title: "English edition." ⊜ . (CHx,LC)

1115. Goldman, Henry. *World's Fair Guide for office men : Classification, Location and Description of exhibits of Special Interest to Office Men.* ... Chicago: The Office Men's Record Co. Publishers, 1893 °1893 by The Office Men's Record Co.

14x8. 42, (6) p., illus. Selects from the WCE those items of "special interest to office men," including office machines, inks, labels, letter files, pens, scales, etc. ⊜ . (CHx,SI)

1116. ... *Guia Ilustrada de Godey para Nueva York, la exposicion universal Colombina y Chicago.* ... New York: E. Lockwood & Co., unicos agentes de The international publishing co., n.d.

20x13½. 57, (3) p. Color litho wraps same as English version above. C.t.: "World's Fair Chicago." At head of title: "Edición Española." Back cover has color border which surrounds an ad for Roke & Bro. done in navy ink. Spanish version of Godey's Guide (#1114). ⊜ . (NYPL)

1117. *Guide book to the Joss House : Temple of China : Chinese Theater, Tea Garden, Cafe and Chinese Bazaar.* N.p.: [Wah Mee Exposition Co., 1893?].

23x15. (8) p. including wraps, black print. Frontis: Temple on the Midway. Back wrap: cafe menu. ⊜ (GLD,WM) $15 - 30

1118. *Guide to Chicago : valuable and reliable information carefully compiled for the benefit of visitors.* Chicago: Pictorial Printing Co., [1892?].

9½x7. 20 p. Red wraps, black print. C.t.: "Guide to Chicago : issued to the drug trade. Compliments of Pictorial Printing Co." ⊜ . (A)

1119. *A guide to the Columbian World's Fair : Chicago, Illinois.* Rev. ed. Chicago: Knight, Leonard & Co., publishers, 1892 [°1892].

21½x14½. 62 p. + large fold out bird's-eye litho of grounds. Light gray wraps, red and black print and design. Compiled by the publishers. ⊜ . (CHx,LC,NL)

1120. *Guide to the Exhibits of American Wool Manufactures, including hosiery and knit goods, groups 103 and 104, World's Columbian exposition, Chicago, Illinois, U.S.A. : 1893. Department of manufactures, section P.* Boston: Press of Rockwell and Churchill, 1893.

> 23x15. 34 p., folding diagram. Black print on tan wraps. C.t.= t.p. ☺. (HL,A)

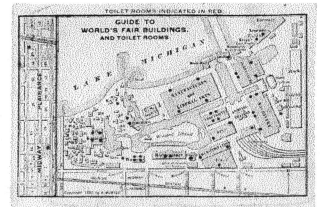

1121. *Guide to the Field Museum : With Diagrams and Descriptions.* Chicago: [P. F. Pettibone & Co., Printers], 1894 [°1894 by the Field Columbian Museum].

> 19x12½. 248 p. Gray wraps with black print.
> ---- Other copies: 2nd ed.-- 263 p.; 4th ed. (1896)-- 267 p.; 5th ed. (1897-98)-- 277 p.
> P→ ☺ (GLD,S) $20 - 40

> ☞ The museum, which was named after Chicago benefactor Marshall Field, contained artifacts and displays from WCE. Museum was the permanent Fine Arts Bldg at the WCE -- now the Museum of Science and Industry.

1122. *Guide to World's fair buildings. And toilet rooms.* [Chicago]: A. Hunter, °1893.

> 10½x15. Paper covered cardboard, black print both sides, red over printing on front side. In red at head of title: "Toilet Rooms Indicated in Red." Map of grounds on front uses red dots to show their locations. Stamped on front: "Hunter & Raymond Price 5 cts." Two ads on back.
> P→ ☺ (GLD) $12 - 25

> ☞ About 1,500 free toilets were provided by the Bureau of Public Comfort at their bldg north of the Woman's Bldg and elsewhere on the grounds. In addition, sumptuous private concession toilets, such as Hunter & Raymond's, provided elegant surroundings for the more discriminating visitor. The admission price for all private rest rooms was 5¢.

1123. Hamilton, W. E., comp. *The Time-Saver. A book which Names and Locates : 5,000 Things 5,000 : at the World's Fair that visitors should not fail to see.* Chicago: W. E. Hamilton [The Cushing Printing Co., 1893], [°1893 by W. E. Hamilton]; Woodbridge, CT: RPI, 1989.

> 15½x9. 111 p., plans. Lime green wraps with black print. The Hamilton telephone number (2574) is printed on the cover, as is "Price 25 cents." C.t.= t.p.
> P↓ ☺. (GLD,CHx,LC,SI,NYPL,F,E,LMi,UDe,NL,OC,WM,WiHx,TD,OhHx) $14 - 26

1124. *Handy pocket guide to the World's fair and city of Chicago : free sights and useful information.* [Chicago?: 1893?].

12½x8½. (4) p., map. Caption title. Below title: "Presented with Compliments of the Eminent Specialists : Dr. Hathaway & co." ⊜ . (BPL)

1125. Hill, Tho[ma]s E[die]. ... *Hill's guide to Chicago and the World's Fair : the great exposition fully described ... at a glance : 33 Maps, 248 Pages, 413 Illustrations.* Chicago: Laird & Lee, Publishers, 1893 ᶜ1892 [and] ᶜ1893 by Laird & Lee.

19½x11½. 248 p. At head of title: "New edition, complete." Same frontis as Hill guide #1126. ⊜ . (S)

1126. Hill, Thomas E[die]. ... *Hill's souvenir guide to Chicago and the World's fair.* Chicago: Laird & Lee, Publishers, 1892 ᶜ1892 by Laird & Lee; Chicago: Laird & Lee, 1893 ᶜ1892 by Laird & Lee.

1892: 20x11. 232 p., maps, illus, tables. Frontis is bird's-eye view and 3 caravels. Flexible cloth cover, rounded corners, with (or without) gilt edges. At head of title: "Thorough, accurate, reliable." Same Hill who published *Hill's Album* #872.
⊜ . (CHx,LC,NYPL,S,UDe,A,WiHx)

1127. ... *Hotel Endeavor on the beach at World's fair : for all Christian people.* Chicago: International Christian Endeavor Y.M.C.A. and Sunday-school Headquarters at Chicago during World's Columbian exposition, n.d.

15½x9. (3)-14 p. Tan wraps with black print. C.t. Hotel with its wooded central courtyard was located south of the Fair at 75th and Lake Michigan. ⊜ (HL)

1128. Hull, Paul. *Illustrated World's fair guide : containing map of the exposition grounds and buildings : illustrations and descriptions of all the principal buildings, and General Directory of the Exposition ...* [Chicago?: 1893?].

22x15. 24 p., illus, map. Gray wraps, black lettering. C.t. (no t.p.). ⊜ . (csuf,CHx,WiHx)

1129. Igleheart, William. *A "Fair" companion : giving daily programs for visits to the World's Fair of from one day to a week, various plans to suit the time and tastes of a visitor, ...* Chicago: Poole Bros., publishers, 1893.

24x18½ (also 26½x20). 64 p., illus, map at last 2 p. Light tan wraps with black print. With and without: "Compliments of Marshall Field & Co., Chicago" at head of title.
⊜ . (csuf,CHx)

1130. *Illustrated guide to the World's fair and Chicago : being a complete directory and guide to the World's fair grounds and buildings ...* Chicago: Chicago Herald, ᶜ1893 by The Blakely Printing Co.; Chicago: J. H. Walker, 1893; Cincinnati: The

Bradford Belting Co., °1893 by The Blakely Printing Co.; Detroit, MI: Hunter, Glenn & Hunter, 1893; Philadelphia: John Wanamaker, [1893]; Quebec, Can.: Frank Carrel Publisher, °1893 by The Blakely Printing Co.

Herald & Bradford: 19x13½. (80) p. [partial pagination to p. 27], illus, fold. map. Color lithographed wraps. T.p.: "The Matter Contained in This Guide is Authentic : Paul Hull [signature replica] : Department of Publicity and Promotion, World's Columbian Exposition."
---- Published under a variety of business names. On the back of back cover: e.g., "Compliments of The Bradford Belting Co." or "Compliments of the Hercules Powder Co."
---- Carrel: C.t.: "For World's fair take Grand Trunk Ry : Illustrated guide to the World's fair : Chicago and Quebec : 4 Trains Daily, G. T. R. to Chicago."
P↑   ☉ . (GLD,csuf,KyU,F,ANQ,TD) $15 - 30

1131. *The International guide to the World's Columbian Exposition to be held at Chicago, U.S.A., May to October, 1893, containing information to visitors from all parts of the World: ...* London: The International guide syndicate, [1892].

21½x14. 192 p., illus. White wraps, white print with black outline. Statue of Liberty with flags is at center of front wrap; 4 circles with persons representing Europe, America, Africa, and Asia are at corners.   ☉ . (CHx)

1132. International Linguistics Institute. *Linguistic guide in Thirty Foreign Languages. Containing over 10,000 Words and Phrases in European, Asiatic and Latin-American Languages. Basic Language--English.* New York: Linguistic Guide publishing co., °1892.

12x16½ (text). xx, 202 p.   ☉ . (LC)

1133. [Kaine, John Langdon]. *... The Best Things to See and How to Find Them : With blank pages and wide margins for memoranda and with routes for visits of from one to twelve days.* Chicago: The White City Publishing Co., °1893; Woodbridge, CT: RPI, 1989.

14x11. 127 p. includes front *l*: "Memoranda." Red and yellow stiff wraps, red and yellow lettering, map on back cover. No illus. At head of title: "Pocket guide and note book of the World's fair." Author's name on cover.
---- 3rd ed. 17x11. 125 p., (3) p.
P→   ☉ . (GLD,csuf,CHx,LC,Sl,NYPL,S,BPL,TD) $12 - 25

1134. Kenny, D[aniel] J. *Illustrated guide to Cincinnati and The World's Columbian Exposition. Authentic and reliable instructor for visitors to the exposition, and the most profitable companion for the sight-seer who has to stay at home ...* Cincinnati: Robert Clarke & Co. [and] St. Louis and San Francisco: The Pacific publishing co., 1893 [°1893 By Pacific Publishing Co.].

23½x16½. 432 p., 8 color plates, illus. Brown and gold hc with black and gold lettering and illus. Color presentation plate of Ledge & Davis Machine Tool Co., Cincinnati.   ☉ . (NYPL,OhHx,BPL)

1135. Marquis, A[lbert]. N. & Company. *A. N. Marquis & Co.'s Ready Reference Guide to Chicago and the World's Columbian Exposition. What to see and how to see it ...* Chicago: A. N. Marquis & Co., 1893 ℅1893.

17x11½. 4 *l*, 294 p., 1 *l* + fold. map laid in at back cover. Red cloth hc, gold print. Same as #1145. (CHx)

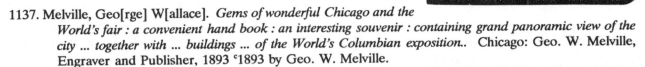

1136. *The Matthews-Northrup adequate travel-atlas of the United States.* Buffalo, NY: Matthews-Northrup Co., [℅1893 by the Matthews-Northrup Co.].

18½x12½. 244 p. Red cloth covered thin hc, black and silver print. Front illus end paper has WCE scenes. Chicago section has WCE grounds map, information, etc.

P→ ⊚ (GLD) $10 - 20

1137. Melville, Geo[rge] W[allace]. *Gems of wonderful Chicago and the World's fair : a convenient hand book : an interesting souvenir : containing grand panoramic view of the city ... together with ... buildings ... of the World's Columbian exposition..* Chicago: Geo. W. Melville, Engraver and Publisher, 1893 ℅1893 by Geo. W. Melville.

23½x14½. 87, (1) p., illus, fold. map. Red cloth, silver and gold lettering, silver design.

P→ ⊚ . (csuf,CHx,S,SLP,BPL,UDe)

1138. *Methodist Headquarters at Chicago : during the Columbian Exposition : Hotel Epworth at Jackson Park : the site of the World's fair ...* [Chicago: Epworth World's fair ass'n.], n.d.

15½x9. 14 p. Blue smooth wraps with black print. C.t. ⊚ (HL)

1139. *The Moorish palace and its startling wonders. The chief attraction of Midway Plaisance ...* Chicago: [Metcalf Stationery Co.], n.d.

23x15. 15, (1) p. Lavender wraps, black design and lettering. C.t.= t.p. At head of title: "World's Columbian Exposition 1893." Laid in is a broadside announcing the Palace. Contents: descriptions of individual exhibits in the Palace which represent things found in Germany, Italy, France, etc.
---- Covers printed in different font style.

P↓ ⊚ . (GLD,csuf,CHx,F,NL,WM) $22 - 38

1140. Moran, George E., comp. *Moran's Dictionary of Chicago and its vicinity, with Map of Chicago and Its Environs. An Alphabetically Arranged Dictionary, Comprising all of the Interests that Contribute to Chicago's Greatness.* Chicago: George E. Moran, publisher and proprietor, 1893.

17x12½. (16), 326 p., illus, map. Frontis is a port of Moran. Ads: (16) p. + p. 279-326 and interspersed. ⊚ . (UDe)

1141. Murphy, Richard J., comp. *Authentic visitors' guide to the World's Columbian Exposition and Chicago. May 1 to October 30, 1893. Dedicatory Ceremonies, October 20, 21, 22, 1892. Condensed information compiled from official sources. Revised to date.* Chicago-New York: The Union News co., [°1892]; Woodbridge, CT: RPI, 1989.

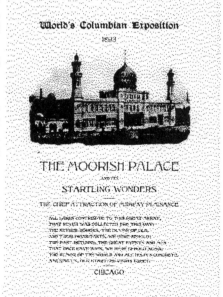

Hard cover: 17x11½. (4) p. ads, 67 p. text, (8) p. ads. Burgundy red hc, beveled boards, gilt print. Also 2 tipped in fold out maps of grounds and Chicago (new city limits). Unpaged are ads and empty visitor memoranda pages. Found with and without "by Richard J. Murphy" on t.p.
---- Hard cover: (3) p. ads, 67 p. text, (9) p. ads. Hc.
---- Soft cover: (2) p. maps, 65 p. text, (2) p. memoranda, (3) p. maps. Red stiff wraps, black print. Maps printed on inside of front and back wraps.
---- Soft cover: (4) p. ads, 65 p. text, (8) p. ads, (3) p. memoranda and maps. Wraps.
⊚ . (GLD,KU,PU,UNe,R,csuf,KyU,CHx,LC,SI,NYPL,S,HL,UoC,OC,WiHx,TD) $20 - 34

1142. [Musket, Robert]. *Chicago : yesterday and to-day : A Guide to the Garden City and the Columbian exposition.* [Chicago: Donohue & Henneberry, °1893 by R. Musket.]

19x13½. 48 p. Pale blue wraps, black print. The last chap. (XI) describes the WCE.   ⊚ . (LC)

1143. Otis Brothers & Co. *Diagrams of World's Fair Buildings showing location of exhibits, Chicago, 1893.* [Chicago: Rand, McNally & Co., Printers], °1893 by Rand, McNally & Co.

15x11. 31, (1) p. Gray (or red) wraps with rounded corners, black print. Diagrams are yellow and black with red print. Gives locations of Otis elevators on the WCE grounds. Cover: "Compliments of Otis Brothers & Co. New York, Hale Elevator Co. Chicago," etc. Issued for advertising purposes. Same as #1153.   ⊚ . (GLD,CPL,LC,HL) $14 - 26

1144. Parker, M[artha] [J]. *How to See the World's Fair With Little Money : Giving a brief description of some of the most interesting things to be seen at the World's Columbian Exposition in Chicago, and how to see them with the least possible expense : 1893.* Chicago: M. Parker, Publisher, [°1893].

19½x14. 14 p., 1 l. Gray-green wraps, black print. C.t. 1 l lists local hotels and room rates.   ⊚ . (LC)

1145. *The People's Ready Reference Guide to Chicago and the World's Columbian Exposition. What to See and How to See it. Every Question Answered. Illustrations. Maps. Diagrams.* Chicago: World's Columbian bureau of information, °1893 by A. N. Marquis & Co.

18x11½. 294 p., illus. Also issued for advertising purposes; see #1135.   ⊚ . (CHx)

1146. *Pictorial Guide to Chicago and the World's Columbian exposition : with maps and plans.* Chicago and New York: Rand, McNally & Co., Publishers, 1893 [°1893 by Rand, McNally & Co., Chicago].

16½x11. 125, (3) p. for memoranda, tipped in map of Chicago between memoranda pages. Gray-green wraps with black print and illus. C.t.: "Pictorial Guide to Chicago and World's Fair." On cover: "Presented by the Jos. Schlitz Brewing Co. : Milwaukee." Schlitz ad on back cover.
---- Issued by the Svenska Tribunen (#1164).
---- Also listed: Ad piece for the Royal Insurance Company of Liverpool. 125 p.
         ☺ . (NL,WiHx)

1147. *Plan of World's Columbian Exposition and Handy Map of Chicago.* 1893. Chicago: Rand, McNally & Co., printers, [°1893].

14½x10. Single large folded color map of WCE. Red stiff wraps printed and illus in black. C.t. Compliments of Henry R. Worthington, New York.
         ☺ (GLD,TD) $15 - 25

1148. ["Plans of building and map of Jackson Park."]. Chicago: 1893.

42x__. Map 45x49. 10 plates. 11 sheets; no t.p.; no cover.--
(RPB call: RAvgC W 89)   ☺ (RPB)

1149. ... *Pocket Record Book : alphabetically arranged and illustrated With Cuts, Map and Plans of all the Principal Buildings : the greatest time-saver.* Chicago: Dibble publishing co., 1893; Woodbridge, CT: RPI, 1989.

17x11. (64) p., with map, illus. Light red wraps, black print and illus of Administration Bldg, rounded corners. At head of title: "The World's Columbian exposition."
         ☺ . (cat,CHx,SI) $20

1150. *Rand, McNally & co.'s a week at the fair : illustrating the exhibits and wonders of the World's Columbian Exposition : with special descriptive articles by Mrs. Potter Palmer,* [and others] ... Chicago: Rand, McNally & Co., Publishers, 1893 [°1893 by Rand, McNally & Co.].

[These are enlarged editions of *Rand, McNally & Co.'s handbook* (#1155) which is abridged.]
---- Softbound: 23x15. 268 p., illus, fold. map. Color lithographed wraps, printed spine, colorful fold out map precedes p. 13. Excellent descriptions, ads, etc.
*P↑ $25 - 35

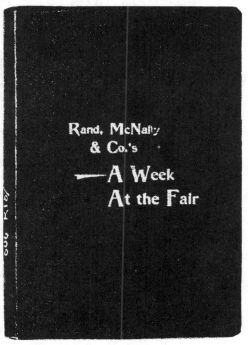

---- Clothbound: 23x16. 268 p. Red cloth flexible cover with gold embossed title, color fold out map precedes p. 13. Title on fifth page. Ads not the same as in softbound version. C.t.= t.p.
*P→   ☺ . (GLD,csuf,CHx,NYPL,F,S,E,OhHx,nwu,RML,NHSt,TU, $25 - 45
            NYSt,NL,BPL,A,AIC,OC)

1151. *Rand, McNally & Co.'s advance guide to the World's Columbian Exposition.* Chicago and New York: Rand, McNally & Co., Publishers, 1893 ᶜ1893 by Rand, McNally & Co.

19½x13½. 64 p. not including large fold. map of Chicago and WCE tipped in before back cover. Sandstone wraps, red and black print, litho of Columbus standing in New World. Inside both covers are small maps of grounds and Midway Plaisance. ☺ . (LC,NYPL)

1152. *Rand, McNally & Co.'s bird's-eye views and guide to Chicago : indispensable to every visitor. Containing innumerable details ...* Chicago and New York: Rand, McNally & co., 1893 [ᶜ1893 by Rand, McNally & Co., Chicago].

19x13. 320 p. Flexible morocco with gilt edges; also bound in cloth or paper covers. Fold out map. Special section on WCE p. 302-306.
☺ . (GLD,NL)

$20 - 35

1153. *Rand, McNally & Co.'s Diagrams of the World's Fair Buildings showing Location of Exhibits.* Chicago: Rand, McNally & Co., ᶜ1893; Woodbridge, CT: RPI, 1989.

14½x11. 31 p., illus, plans, map. Light khaki wraps with black print. Fore edge corners rounded. Also issued for advertising purposes (see #1143). ☺ . (SLS,HL,BPL,OC,OhHx)

1154. [*Rand, McNally & Co.'s*] *guide to Chicago and the World's Columbian Exposition. What to see and how to see it.* Chicago and New York: Rand, McNally & co., 1893.

18*x*__. 216, (3) p., illus, fold. map. This and other editions of the guide were issued with different t.p. and covers for distribution by business firms. Firm's name may appear at head of title: e.g., CHx,BPL copies: Sykes & Street's (in place of Rand, McNally & Co.'s, see #1156). (CHx,S,BPL)

1155. *Rand, McNally & Co.'s handbook of the World's Columbian Exposition : with Special Descriptive Articles by Mrs. Potter Palmer* [and others] : *also maps, plans, and illustrations.* Chicago: Rand, McNally & Co., Publishers, 1893 [ᶜ1893 by Rand, McNally & Co.]; Woodbridge, CT: RPI, 1989.

Softbound: 18½x13. 2 *l*, 5-224 p. include illus, maps, ads. Decorative off-white wraps with black and red lettering depict Sullivan's entrance to the Transportation Bldg. C.t.: "Rand, McNally & Co.'s Hand Book of The World's Columbian Exposition." On cover: "Globe library.-- Vol. 1. No. 180. May 2, 1893." Abridged version of *A week at the fair* #1150.
---- Clothbound: 19½x14. 1 *l*, 5-224. Red cloth flexible cover, gilt print, marbled edges. C.t.: "Rand, McNally & Co.'s Handbook to the World's Columbian Exposition."
P→   ☺ . (GLD,csuf,KyU,CHx,SL,PU,NYPL,S,E,TnSt,RML,OSU, $25 - 40
           UDe,UMi,UoC,NL,BPL,AIC,OC,WiHx,TD,OhHx)

1156. *Rand, McNally & Co.'s handy Guide to Chicago and World's Columbian Exposition. Illustrated. What to See and How to See It.* Chicago and New York: Rand, McNally & Co., Publishers, 1892; Chicago and New York: Rand, McNally & Co., Publishers, 1893; Woodbridge, CT: RPI [Rand 1893], 1989.

1892: 18(17)x__. 220 p. illus (including port), fold. map. Other editions were issued with different t.p. and cover, for distribution by various business firms, see #1154.

---- 1893: 17x11. 215 p. + (29) p. index, ads, and fold. map. Tan wraps with red and blue print. With and without fore edge corners rounded. Frontis of Masonic Temple in Chicago.

---- 215 p., (1) p., 1 *l*, fold. map.
　　　　　　◎ . (GLD,KyU,CHx,LC,SI,NYPL,S,RML,UDe,UoC)　　　　**$12 - 26**

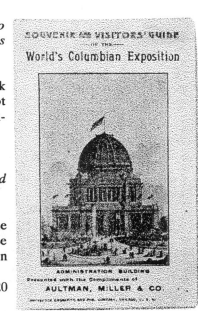

1157. *Save time, money and fatigue.* The World's fair and Chicago, in 3, 6 or 10 days. By a Chicago Reporter.　Chicago: John A. Nichol & co., ᶜ1893.

21½x14½. 48 p. Lilac wraps with red and gold print.　◎ . (CHx)

1158. *A Scamper Through the States : being An Illustrated Guide to the World's fair of 1893.* (To which is added an Account of the Columbian Exposition by James Dredge...).　London: Office of "Polytechnic Magazine," [ca.1893].

ca. 22x15. 120 p., illus, frontis of the U.S. government "Illinois battleship" exhibit.　◎ . (csuf,BM,WM)

1159. Schuh, C[harles] G., ed. *Deutsch-Englisches Hand-Buch über Chicago und die Welt-Ausstellung : Für unsere deutschen Freunde und das Publikum überhaupt.*　N.p.: n.p., ᶜ1893 by C. G. Schuh.

23½x15. 35 p. includes front cover and ads. Green wraps, black print. Folding bird's-eye view tipped in before back cover (not included in paging). C.t. Text is all German (i.e., not Deutsch-Englisches).　◎ . (CHx,LC)

1160. *Souvenir and Visitor's Guide To The World's Columbian Exposition and Chicago.*　Chicago: Vandercook Engraving and Pub. Co., n.d.

11x7. (23) accordion folding p. Printed in dark blue on stiff blue wraps. C.t. Bldg views and WCE facts and locations. Three different cover designs found. "Compliments of [the advertiser]" on cover.

P↑,P→,P↓　◎ (GLD,UDe,BPL,TD)　　　　**$10 - 20**

1161. *Souvenir of the World's Columbian Exposition : Chicago, 1893 : Compliments of Mandel Brothers : Chicago.*　Chicago: Mandel Brothers, [1893].

10½x21. (32) p. + fold out street map. Cloth spine, light tan wraps, green (or navy) print and design which includes bust of Columbus and Grand Basin by Manz & Co. C.t. Chicago guide map and street index.　◎ . (CHx,S,TD)　　　　**$10 - 22**

1162. [Stone, Herbert Stuart]. *Chicago and The World's Fair : a popular guide : illustrated.*　Chicago: 1893 [ᶜ1892 by Herbert S. Stone].

16x11½. (3), iv, 64 p. Terra cotta colored wraps, black print. Frontis litho of "the street of Cairo." At top of cover: "112th thousand." C.t. is not the same as t.p.

---- 14½x11. (8), iv, 64, (4) p. ads. Same frontis as above. Robin egg blue wraps, black print. On cover: "Published by the Plymouth Rock Pants co. of Boston."

⊚ . (NL,HL)

1163. [Stone, Herbert Stuart]. *The Terra Cotta Guide : Chicago and the World's fair.* ... Chicago: Stone & Kimball, 1893 [°1892 by H. S. Stone. °1893 by Stone & Kimball].

14½x11. (2) p. map frontis, 105, (3) p., illus. Terra cotta colored wraps, black print. At top of cover: "117th thousand." C.t.= t.p.

⊚ . (CHx,LC,NL)

1164. *Svenska Tribunens : pictorial guide to Chicago and the World's Columbian exposition : with maps and plans.* Chicago: Svenska Tribunen, 1893 [°1893 by Rand, McNally & Co.].

17x11. 125, (3) p. + folding map laid in between memoranda pages. Light gray wraps with black print, cover illus of Swedish Pavilion. See #1146.

⊚ (GLD) $20 - 32

1165. *Tillotson's pocket atlas and guide of Chicago 1893 : Presenting in plat form the blocks, streets, alleys, street numbers, street car lines, railroads, elevated roads and location of depots ... World's Columbian Exposition Buildings, Etc., Etc.* Chicago: The City Atlas & Guide Co., °1893.

18½x11. 7 *l*, xviii, 162 p., 15 *l*, maps, illus. Gray wraps, black print. Frontis: General Index.   ⊚ . (CPL)

1166. *A True Guide Through The World's Fair Grounds.* Chicago: Globe lithographing and printing Co., n.d.

15x9. 2 *l*, folding ad card with detailed map of grounds inside; blue, red, and black print. C.t.

⊚ (GLD,TD) $10 - 20

1167. [Vernon, Samuel E.]. *The Columbian Souvenir Note Book : For tourists and those wishing to make notes on the exhibits seen in each building, with illustration of all the principal buildings and description of the same interleaved between each 8 sheets of paper.* N.p.: n.p., [°1889].

21½x12. Red paper covered stiff cardboard wraps, black print, olive cloth spine, red dyed edges. For reading, it opens like note pad (12 cm hinge at top). Ruled leaves like "Big Chief" school tablet plus interspersed leaves depicting WCE bldgs with explanation paragraph. "Price 25 cents."   ⊚ . (LC)

1168. *A vest pocket directory of the Leading Business Houses of Chicago, with Guide to the City and World's Fair Grounds, containing views, maps, and a great deal of useful information.* [Chicago]: J. H. Groene & co., Publishers, °1893.

15x7. 95 p., illus, maps include one folding. Dark blue flexible cloth cover, gilt print, rounded corners. Paging includes 17 p. of "Memorandum" blanks. C.t.: "Directory guide of Chicago and the World's Columbian Exposition."   ⊚ . (CHx,NL,BPL)

1169. [Vynne, Harold Richard]. *Chicago by Day and Night. The pleasure seeker's guide to the Paris of America.*
... Chicago: Thomson and Zimmerman, 1892 [°1892 by Thomson and Zimmerman].

19x12½. 2 *l*, (5)-281, (2) p. ads. 7 plates interspersed (not counted in paging), frontis of Lillian
Russell. Glossy plain paper wraps, red and black print, illus of period woman on cover. T.p.
continues: "300 pages. 59 illustrations. Published for the trade." Description, social life, customs,
amusements of Chicago. ☻ . (LC,CHx,TnSt,NL,HL)

1170. Wade, Stuart C[harles], and Walter S. Wrenn, comp. *"The nut shell" : The ideal pocket guide to the
World's fair and what to see there. Every important exhibit or sight accurately located with ground plans.*
Chicago: [Wholesale Agency], 1893 [°1893 by J. A. Burton]; Chicago: The Merchant's World's Fair
Bureau of Information Co., 1893; Woodbridge, CT: RPI [Merchant's], 1989.

Merchant's: 17x10½. 191, (1) p. Brown wraps, black design and print. On cover: "price 25 cts."
Wade was literary editor and Wrenn was assistant guide compiler for Rand, McNally & Co.
---- Wholesale: Same size, wraps, price. 192, (8) p. illus,
fold. map, plans. Bottom front wrap: "Wholesale
Agency."
    ☻ . (CPL,CHx,SI,UDe,BPL)

1171. *A week in Chicago : containing Descriptions of all Points of
Interest, including Parks, Boulevards, Prominent Buildings,
... also The World's Columbian Exposition, with full
directions for reaching them.* ... Chicago and New York:
Rand, McNally & Co., 1892 [°1887 and °1892].

27½x20. vi ads, 88, vii-l ads, (2) p. maps, illus, also ads
inside front and back covers. Decorative peach wraps
with navy and sea foam green background designs, black
print, b/w front cover lithos of the Administration Bldg
and the landing of Columbus. Ad for Oaklawn on back
cover. C.t.: "A Week in Chicago with Views and Plans of
the World's Columbian Exposition." LC and UDe list
[Heckel, George Baugh] as author.
P→   ☻ . (csuf,LC,UDe)

1172. *What to see and how to find it : Gems of the Fair : also a complete illustrated Guide to Chicago and the
Exposition : 10,000 facts Concerning Objects of Interest; also a Complete list of pictures receiving medals
in the Fine Arts Department : Compiled by Press Representatives of the Fair : save time and money.*
[Chicago]: World's Fair & Chicago Guide Co., n.d.

20x14. Various paging (paging starts and stops + many unpaginated pages). Yellow slick wraps, red
and black print. C.t. Illus of each State's bldg.
    ☻ . (CHx,SI,UoC) $ 15 - 30

1173. World's Columbian Exposition. Bureau of the American Republics. Curtis, William Eleroy. ...
*Illustrated and Descriptive Catalogue of the exhibit of the Bureau of the American Republics : East gallery,
U. S. Government building.* Chicago: W. B. Conkey co., Publishers to the World's Columbian
Exposition, 1893; Woodbridge, CT: RPI, 1989.

22½x14. 245 p. includes illus, ports. At head of title: "World's Columbian Exposition." Also on t.p.: "East Gallery, U. S. Government Building." Same cover format as: *Condensed Official Catalogue* (#1175) and *Official Catalogue* (#1176). ☻ . (SI,UDe)

1174. World's Columbian Exposition. Department of Publicity and Promotion. *Condensed catalogue of Interesting Exhibits with their locations in the World's Columbian Exposition : also Complete Plans and Diagrams of all exhibit buildings.* Chicago: W. B. Conkey Co. Publishers to the World's Columbian Exposition, 1893 [°1893 by W. B. Conkey co.].

22½x15. 152 p. Black on orange wraps, WCE seal. This publication and #396 are different. Moses P. Handy's name is not on t.p. On cover: "Condensed official catalogue of World's Columbian exposition." ☻ . (LC,NYPL,A)

1175. World's Columbian Exposition. Department of Publicity and Promotion. *Condensed official catalogue of interesting exhibits with their locations in the World's Columbian Exposition : also complete plans and diagrams of all exhibit buildings with map. Edited by the department of publicity and promotion : M. P. Handy, Chief.* Chicago: W. B. Conkey Co., Publishers to the World's Columbian Exposition, 1893 [°1893 by the World's Columbian Exposition].

22½x15. 154 p. includes frontis of Administration Bldg. Red wraps with gilt globe-seal and black print; fold. map tipped in after front wrap. Found with and without original price ("25 cents") on front wrap covered by blank red paper label. C.t.: "Condensed official catalogue of World's Columbian exposition : interesting exhibits and where to find them : plans and diagrams of exhibit buildings." (not the same as t.p.). This publication is different from #1174.
---- 22½x15. 162 p. Red wraps, black print, gilt globe-seal. An additional six pages are: "Interesting exhibits in Department K.-- Fine Arts" after p. 110. An additional 2 pages are blank but counted in paging and follow p. 129. C.t.= t.p.
P→   ☻ (GLD,CHx,LC,NYPL,F,S,UDe)

$20 - 40

1176. World's Columbian Exposition. Department of Publicity and Promotion. *Official Catalogue.* Ed. by the Department of Publicity and Promotion. M. P. Handy, Chief. Chicago: W. B. Conkey Co. for the Department of Publicity and Promotion, 1893.

22x17. Brown (or orange) cloth (or full leather) hc, gilt, all edges stained red, fore edge notched alphabetically. C.t. Fold. map of the grounds tipped in after front cover.
---- Maximum: 19 parts ("18 vol") in 1 vol.
---- 14 individual dept catalogs in 1 vol (lacks Dept C). Separately paged sections total 926 p.
---- Also listed: 12 pts. in 1 vol; 13 pts. in 1 vol; 14 pts. in 2 vol.
---- Softbound: Orange-brown wraps, black print. C.t.: "Official Catalogue of exhibits : World's Columbian Exposition : Department, agriculture : horticulture : fish and fisheries : mines and mining : machinery : transportation : manufactures : electricity : liberal arts : ethnology, archaeology : woman's building. Price $1.00"
     *   (csuf,CHx,KyU,NYPL,PU,F,OSL,UDe,USD,UoC,NL,RPB,WM,OC,WiHx)

Bound: $100 - 250

Individual booklets were issued by the Department of Publicity and Promotion for the various depts. There are 19 parts in the largest of the bound books directly above. In this section, the individual issues are arranged numerically by "part" as found in the 19 part bound volume (#1176). Be careful, though; the individual version may differ from its counterpart in the bound version. Also, several individual booklets were revised/reissued, and some were issued to cover more than one part. Where a title page lists more than one part, the booklets may be found below under the first "part" given on the title page. Individual booklets were handy take along versions of the entire bound book.

Each booklet: $15 - 40

Pt. 1. Department A.: Agriculture building and dairy building

1177. World's Columbian Exposition. Department of Publicity and Promotion. ... *Official Catalogue : Part I. Agriculture building and dairy building : Department A. Agriculture : food and its accessories : machinery and appliances : W. I. Buchanan, Chief : Edited by The Department of Publicity and Promotion : M. P. Handy, Chief.* Chicago: W. B. Conkey co., Publishers to the World's Columbian Exposition, 1893; Woodbridge, CT: RPI, 1989.

21½x15. 327 p. Light pink wraps, black print, WCE globe-seal at lower left. Illus of wheat heads and threshing scene. At head of title: "World's Columbian Exposition : 1893." C.t.: "Revised edition. Official catalogue of exhibits. World's Columbian Exposition : Department A. Agricultural Building : Price 45 cents." ☉ . (SI,WM)

Pt. 2. Department B: Horticulture building, Wooded Island, lawns and Midway plaisance nursery

1178. ---. ---. ... *Official Catalogue. Part II. Horticulture building : wooded island, lawns and midway plaisance nursery : Department B. Horticulture : viticulture, pomology, floriculture, etc. J. M. Samuels, Chief : Edited by The Department of Publicity and Promotion : M. P. Handy, Chief.* Chicago: W. B. Conkey, co., Publishers to the World's Columbian Exposition, 1893; Woodbridge, CT: RPI, 1989.

20x14. 119 p. Light purple wraps, black print, WCE globe-seal at lower left; cover illus includes Horticulture Bldg and maiden draped with flowers. At head of title: "World's Columbian Exposition : 1893." C.t.: "Revised edition. Official catalogue of Exhibits. World's Columbian Exposition : Department B : Horticulture Building : Price, 20 Cents." ☉ . (SI,WM)

Pt. 3. Department C: Live stock exhibits

1179. ---. ---. ... *Official Catalogue : part III. Live Stock Exhibits. Department C.--live stock. ... Division A.-- cattle, ... Division B.--Horses, ... Edited by the Department of Live Stock. Department of Publicity and Promotion, M. P. Handy, Chief.* Chicago: W. B. Conkey co., Publishers to the World's Columbian Exposition, 1893; Woodbridge, CT: RPI, 1989.

20½x14. 99, 99 p. At head of title: "World's Columbian Exposition : 1893." C.t.: "Revised edition. Official Catalogue of exhibits : World's Columbian Exposition : Department C. Live stock : Price 20 Cents." WCE globe-seal at lower left cover. ☉ . (SI)

Pt. 4. Department D: Fisheries building and aquaria

1180. ---. ---. ... *Official Catalogue : part IV. Fisheries Building and Aquaria : Department D. Fish, Fisheries, Fish Products and Apparatus of Fishing : J. W. Collins, Chief. Edited by The Department of Publicity and Promotion, M. P. Handy, Chief.* Chicago: W. B. Conkey co., Publishers to the World's Columbian Exposition, 1893.

21½x15. 36 p. Wraps without usual WCE globe-seal; no cover illus. Frontis illus of Fish and Fisheries Bldg. At head of title: "World's Columbian Exposition, 1893." C.t.: "Official Catalogue of exhibits. World's Columbian Exposition : Departments D and F. Fish, Fisheries and Machinery : parts IV and VI. Price, 10 cents." ☉.(S)

1181. ---. ---. ... *Official catalogue : part IV. Fisheries Building and Aquaria : Department D. Fish, fisheries, Fish Products and Apparatus of Fishing : J. W. Collins, Chief : Edited by The Department of Publicity and Promotion : M. P. Handy, Chief.* Chicago: W. B. Conkey co., Publishers to the World's Columbian Exposition, 1893; Woodbridge, CT: RPI, 1989.

21½x15. 28 p. At head of title: World's Columbian Exposition : 1893." C.t.: "Revised edition. Official catalogue of Exhibits. World's Columbian Exposition : Department D. Fish & Fisheries : Price. 10 cents." WCE globe without underlying seal at lower left cover; cover illus of men in dory pulling in fishnet. ☉.(SI)

Pt. 5. Department E: Mines and mining building

1182. ---. ---. ... *Official Catalogue : part V. Mines and Mining Building : Department E. Mines mining and metallurgy: F. J. V. Skiff, Chief : Edited by The Department of Publicity and Promotion : M. P. Handy, Chief.* Chicago: W. B. Conkey co., Publishers to the World's Columbian Exposition, 1893 [°1893 by The World's Columbian Exposition].

21½x15. 94 p. Orange-red wraps, black print. Lacks WCE globe-seal; no cover illus. At head of title: "World's Columbian Exposition : 1893." C.t.: "Official Catalogue of exhibits. World's Columbian Exposition : Department E. Mines and Mining Building : part V. Price, 15 cents." (A)

1183. ---. ---. ... *Official catalogue : part V. Mines and Mining Building : Department E. Mines : mining and metallurgy : F. J. V. Skiff, Chief : Edited by The Department of Publicity and Promotion : M. P. Handy, Chief.* Chicago: W. B. Conkey co., Publishers to the World's Columbian Exposition, 1893; Woodbridge, CT: RPI, 1989.

21½x15. 198 p. At head of title: "World's Columbian Exposition : 1893." C.t.: "Revised edition. Official Catalogue of Exhibits. World's Columbian Exposition : Department E. Mines and mining building : Price, 25 cents." WCE globe-seal lower left cover; cover illus of miner with tool. ☉.(SI)

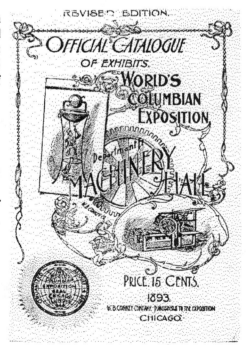

Pt. 6. Department F: Machinery hall and machinery annexes

1184. ---. ---. ... *Official catalogue : part VI. Machinery Hall and Machinery Annexes : Department F. Machinery : L. W. Robinson, U.S.N., Chief : Edited by The Department of Publicity and Promotion : M. P. Handy, Chief.* Chicago: W. B. Conkey co., Publishers to the World's Columbian Exposition, 1893; Woodbridge, CT: RPI, 1989.

21½x15. 51 p. At head of title: "World's Columbian Exposition : 1893." C.t.: "Revised edition. Official Catalogue of exhibits. World's Columbian Exposition : Department F. Machinery Hall : Price. 15 Cents." WCE globe and seal lower left cover. Cover design includes cog wheel and printing press.

---- 48 p.

P↑   ☻ . (SLS)

Pt. 7. Department G: Transportation exhibits building, annex special buildings and the lagoon

1185. ---. ---. ... *Official catalogue : part VII. Transportation exhibits building, annex, special buildings and the lagoon : Department G. Transportation Exhibits : railways, vessels, vehicles : Williard A. Smith, Chief : Edited by The Department of Publicity and Promotion : M. P. Handy, Chief.* Chicago: W. B. Conkey co., Publishers to the World's Columbian Exposition, 1893; Woodbridge, CT: RPI, 1989.

21½x15. 63 p.: illus, map. At head of title: "World's Columbian Exposition : 1893." C.t.: "Revised edition. Official catalogue of exhibits. World's Columbian Exposition : Department G. Transportation Building : Price, 15 cents." WCE globe-seal at lower left cover; cover illus are vignettes of modes of transportation.   (SI,UoC,RPB)

Pt. 8. Department H: Manufactures and liberal arts building, leather and shoe trades building, merchant tailors building

1186. ---. ---. ... *Official catalogue : part VIII. Manufactures and Liberal Arts Building : Leather and Shoe Building : Department H. Manufactures : James Allison, Chief : Edited by The Department of Publicity and Promotion : M. P. Handy, Chief.* Chicago: W. B. Conkey co., Publishers, 1893 [°1893 by World's Columbian Exposition].

21½x15. 144 p. Orange-red wraps, black print, WCE globe-seal middle left cover; no other cover design. At head of title: "World's Columbian Exposition : 1893." C.t.: "Official Catalogue of exhibits. World's Columbian Exposition : Department H. Manufactures and Liberal Arts Building. Shoe and Leather Building. Part VIII. Price, 25 cents." ☻ . (A)

1187. ---. ---. ... *Official catalogue : part VIII. Manufactures and Liberal Arts Building : Leather and Shoe Building : Department H. Manufactures : James Allison, Chief : Edited by The Department of Publicity and Promotion : M. P. Handy, Chief.* Chicago: W. B. Conkey co., Publishers, 1893 [°1893 by World's Columbian Exposition].

21½x15. 97 p. Frontis: Manufactures and Liberal Arts Bldg. Map of Chicago and WCE ground plans. Light green wraps with red WCE globe-seal. At head of title: "World's Columbian Exposition : 1893." Rev. ed. ☻ . (OhHx)

1188. ---. ---. ... *Official Catalogue. Part VIII. Manufactures and Liberal Arts Building. Leather and Shoe building. Department H. Manufactures. James Allison, Chief. Edited by the Department of Publicity and Promotion. M. P. Handy, Chief.* Chicago: W. B. Conkey Co., 1893.

21x15. 265, (3) p., 2 *l* of plates. Frontis, map. At head of title: "World's Columbian Exposition : 1893." Revised ed.   (BPL)

1189. ---. ---. ... *Official Catalogue of exhibits. World's Columbian Exposition : Departments H & L. Manufactures and Liberal Arts Building. Leather and shoe trades building. Merchant tailors building.* Chicago: W. B. Conkey Co., Publishers to the exposition, 1893.

21½x15. Pale pea green wraps, black print. C.t. At head of c.t.: "Revised edition." Bottom of cover: "Price 50 cents." Each of the 2 pts. has its own t.p. Pt. 8: (Manufactures and Liberal Arts Building : Leather and Shoe Building : Department H. Manufactures)--265 p. Pt. 11: Dept L--97 p. At head of each t.p. title: "World's Columbian Exposition : 1893." ☻ . (WM)

1190. ---. ---. *Official Catalogue of exhibits : World's Columbian Exposition: Departments H, L, & M. Manufactures and Liberal Arts Building. Leather and Shoe Trades Building, and Anthropological Building. Parts VIII, XI, and XII.* Chicago: W. B. Conkey co., 1893.

21x15. Red seal, orange-red wraps, black print. C.t. Frontis is illus of Manufactures and Liberal Arts Bldg. Each of the 3 pts. has its own t.p. Pt. 8: (Manufactures and Liberal Arts Building : Leather and Shoe Building : Department H. Manufactures)--145 p. Pt. 11: (Manufactures and Liberal Arts Building and Anthropological Building : Department L)--72 p. Pt. 12: (Anthropological Building : Midway Plaisance and Isolated Exhibits : Department M. Ethnology)--28 p. At head of all t.p. titles: "World's Columbian Exposition : 1893." P→ ☺.(GLD) $15 - 30

Pt. 9. Department J: Electricity building

1191. ---. ---. ... *Official catalogue : part IX. Electricity building : Department J : electricity and electrical appliances : J. P. Barrett, Chief : J. A. Hornsby, Assistant Chief : Edited by The Department of Publicity and Promotion : M. P. Handy, Chief.* Chicago: W. B. Conkey co., Publishers to the World's Columbian Exposition, 1893.

21½x15. 42 p. Lavender wraps, black print, red WCE globe-seal lower left. At head of title: "World's Columbian Exposition : 1893." C.t.: "Official catalogue of exhibits. World's Columbian exposition : Department J. Electricity building : Price, 10 cents." Same cover illus as revised edition (#1192).

1192. ---. ---. ... *Official catalogue : part IX. Electricity building : Department J : electricity and electrical appliances : J. P. Barrett, Chief : J. A. Hornsby, Assistant Chief : Edited by The Department of Publicity and Promotion : M. P. Handy, Chief.* Chicago: W. B. Conkey co., Publishers to the World's Columbian Exposition, 1893; Woodbridge, CT: RPI, 1989.

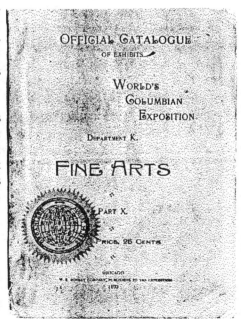

21½x15. 42 p., illus, map. At head of title: "World's Columbian Exposition : 1893." C.t.: "Revised edition. Official catalogue of exhibits. World's Columbian exposition : Department J. Electricity building : Price, 10 cents." Light colored WCE globe and seal lower left cover. Cover illus include Ben Franklin and electrical apparatus. ☺.(SI,OhHx,UoC)

Pt. 10. Department K: Fine arts

1193. ---. ---. ... *Official catalogue : part X. Art galleries and annexes : Department K. Fine arts : Painting, Sculpture, Architecture, Decoration : Halsey C. Ives, Chief : Edited by The Department of Publicity and Promotion : M. P. Handy, Chief.* Chicago: W. B. Conkey, co., 1893 [°1893 by World's Columbian Exposition]; Woodbridge, CT: RPI, 1989.

21½x15½. 1 *l*, 141 p., (8) p. for memoranda. 1 *l* is frontis illus of Art Palace. At head of title: World's Columbian Exposition : 1893." Orange-red wraps, black print, red WCE globe-seal; no other

cover illus. C.t.: "Official Catalogue of exhibits : World's Columbian Exposition : Department K. Fine Arts : Part X. Price, 25 Cents."
P↑   ☺ . (GLD,NYPL,S,SI,AIC,WiHx) $15 - 30

1194. ---. ---. ... *Official Catalogue. Part X. Department K. Fine Arts : Halsey C. Ives, Chief. Edited by The Department of Publicity and Promotion, M. P. Handy, Chief.* Chicago: W. B. Conkey, publishers to the World's Columbian exposition, 1893 [°1893 by The World's Columbian exposition].

21½x15. 196 p. + (16) p. for "Memoranda." Frontis illus of Art Palace. Black on orange-red wraps, WCE globe-seal. Allegorical sculpture illustrated on front wrap. At head of title: "World's Columbian Exposition, 1893." C.t.: "Official Catalogue of exhibits : World's Columbian Exposition : Department K : Fine Arts: Price, 35 cents."
☺ . (CPL,NYPL,TnSt,JHU,PU,UWy,WyMus,NHSt,MaHx,LaMus,UoC,NL,BPL,A,AIC,TD,HL,WiHx)

1195. ---. ---. ... *Revised catalogue : Department of Fine Arts : with index of exhibitors : for this catalogue, the pictures are numbered consecutively, as they appear on the gallery walls : department of publicity and promotion : Moses P. Handy, chief.* Chicago: W. B. Conkey co., publishers to the exposition, 1893; Woodbridge, CT: RPI, 1989.

22½x15½. 506 p. Orange-red wraps, illus, frontis, plates, ports. At head of title: "World's Columbian exposition : official publications."
---- Pebbled leather, gilt print, edges gilt. Autographed by W. E. Conkey for Mr. George Schneider, Oct. 27, 1893. [Schneider was Director of Ways and Means for the WCE.]
☺ . (ALB,CHx,SI,NYPL,HL,Yale,UoC,AIC,WiHx)

Pt. 11. Department L: Manufactures and liberal arts building

1196. ---. ---. ... *Official catalogue : part XI. Manufactures and liberal arts building : Department L--Liberal Arts : education, literature, medicine, surgery and dentistry, hygiene and sanitation, physical apparatus, photography, constructive architecture, commerce, religious organization, charities and corrections, music. Selim H. Peabody, Chief. Edited by the department of publicity and promotion. M. P. Handy, Chief.* Chicago: W. B. Conkey co., 1893 [°1893 by The World's Columbian Exposition].

21½x15½. 1 *l* frontis of Manufactures and Liberal Arts Bldg, (4), 107 p. Folding map of Chicago and fairgrounds laid in after front cover. Light green smooth wraps with black print and red seal. At head of title: "World's Columbian Exposition : 1893." On cover: "Revised Edition." "Price, 15 cents."
P→   ☺ . (GLD,WM) $16 - 32

Pt. 12. Department M: Anthropological building, Midway plaisance and isolated exhibits

1197. ---. ---. ... *Official catalogue : part XII. Anthropological building : midway plaisance and isolated exhibits : Department M. Ethnology : Archæology, Physical Anthropology, History, Natural History, Isolated and Collective Exhibits. F. W. Putnam, Chief : Edited by The Department of Publicity and Promotion : M. P. Handy, Chief.* Chicago: W. B. Conkey co., Publishers to the World's Columbian Exposition, 1893; Woodbridge, CT: RPI, 1989.

20½x14½. 1 *l*, 90 p., 1 map. At head of title: "World's Columbian Exposition : 1893." C.t.: "Revised Edition. Official Catalogue of exhibits and descriptive catalogue : World's Columbian Exposition : Department M. Anthropological Building : Midway Plaisance and Isolated Exhibits. Price, 15 cents." WCE globe-seal left center of cover; no other cover design. ☉. (SI,NYPL,BPL,WiHx)

Pt. 13. Department N: Forestry building

1198. ---. ---. ... *Official catalogue : part XIII. Forestry building : Department N. Forestry and forest products : W. I Buchanan, Chief : Edited by The Department of Publicity and Promotion : M. P. Handy, Chief.* Chicago: W. B. Conkey co., Publishers to the World's Columbian Exposition, 1893; Woodbridge, CT: RPI, 1989.

21½x15. 39 p. illus, map. At head of title: World's Columbian Exposition : 1893." C.t.: "Revised Edition. Official catalogue of exhibits : World's Columbian Exposition : Department N. Forestry Building : price, 10 cents." WCE globe without underlying seal at middle left cover; no other cover design. ☉. (SI)

Pt. 14. Woman's building

1199. ---. ---. ... *Official catalogue : part XIV. Woman's building : Mrs. Bertha H. Palmer, President Board of Lady Managers. Edited by The Department of Publicity and Promotion : M. P. Handy, Chief.* Chicago: W. B. Conkey co., Publishers to the World's Columbian Exposition, 1893; Woodbridge, CT: RPI, 1989.

21½x15. 141 p., may be followed by (3) p. for memoranda. Frontis is a litho of the Woman's Bldg. Blue (or royal blue) wraps, black print, WCE globe-seal. At head of title: "World's Columbian Exposition : 1893." C.t.: "Revised Edition. Official Catalogue of exhibits. World's Columbian Exposition : Woman's Building : Mrs. Potter Palmer : President Board of Lady Managers." Original price (15 cents) blackened; "Price, 25 cents" at bottom front wrap. P→   ☉. (SI,D)

Pt. 15. Leather and shoe trades building (See #1190)

Pt. 16. United States Government building

1200. ---. ---. ... *Official catalogue : United States Government Building : part XVI. Board of control and management. Edwin Willits, Dept. of Agriculture, Chairman. ... Edited by The Department of Publicity and Promotion, M. P. Handy, Chief.* W. B. Conkey co., Publisher to the World's Columbian Exposition, 1893.

21½x15. 156 p. Buff wraps, black print, red WCE globe-seal at upper left corner. At head of title: "World's Columbian Exposition : 1893." C.t.: "Official Catalogue of Exhibits : World's Columbian exposition : United States Government Building : part XVI. Price, 25 Cents." ☉. (WM)

1201. ---. ---. ... *Official catalogue : United States Government Building : part XVI. Board of control and management. Edwin Willits, Dept. of Agriculture, Chairman. ... Edited by The Department of Publicity and Promotion, M. P. Handy, Chief.* Chicago: W. B. Conkey co., Publishers to the World's Columbian Exposition, 1893; Woodbridge, CT: RPI, 1989.

21½x15. 177 p. includes illus, plans, map. At head of title: "World's Columbian Exposition : 1893." C.t.: "Official Catalogue of Exhibits. World's Columbian Exposition : U.S. Government Building : price, 25 cents." WCE globe-seal on lower left corner of front wrap. Frontis and cover illus of Government Bldg. ☉ . (SI,UoC,S)

Pt. 17. Group 176. Isolated exhibits, Midway plaisance

1202. ---. ---. ... *Official Catalogue : 1893 : of exhibits on the Midway Plaisance : Department M--Ethnology. Isolated exhibits, midway plaisance. John Bidlake, Superintendent. Group 176. F. W. Putnam, Chief. Edited by The Department of Publicity and Promotion, M. P. Handy, Chief.* Chicago: W. B. Conkey co., Publishers to the World's Columbian Exposition, 1893.

21½x15. 22 p. White cover, black print, red WCE globe-seal. At head of title: "World's Columbian Exposition." C.t.: "Official Catalogue of exhibits on the Midway Plaisance. World's Columbian Exposition : Department M--Ethnology : Group 176." On cover: "Price, 10 cents." Lists 41 exhibits. ☉ . (S,UoC,CHx,WM) $20 - 35

1203. ---. ---. ... *Official Catalogue : 1893 : of exhibits on the Midway Plaisance : isolated exhibits, midway plaisance. Group 176. Edited by The Department of Publicity and Promotion, M. P. Handy, Chief.* Chicago: W. B. Conkey Co., Publishers to the World's Columbian Exposition, 1893 [°1893 by the World's Columbian exposition]; Woodbridge, CT: RPI, 1989.

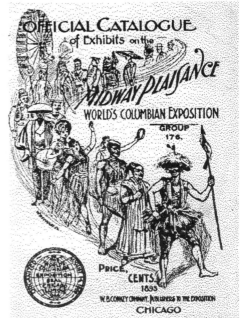

21½x15. 3 *l*, (5)-35 p. Map of Midway Plaisance on 1st *l*, followed by double map of main grounds. Orange-red wraps with red WCE globe-seal and black print. "Price, 10 cents." List of 41 numbered and 8 unnumbered exhibits. At head of title: "World's Columbian Exposition." Cover litho: parade of foreign peoples from the Midway.
 ☉ . (GLD,CHx,ALB,A,F,TD) $20 - 35

1204. ---. ---. ... *Official Catalogue : part XVII. 1893 : of exhibits on the Midway Plaisance : isolated exhibits, midway plaisance. Group 176. Edited by The Department of Publicity and Promotion, M. P. Handy, Chief.* Chicago: W. B. Conkey co., Publishers to the World's Columbian Exposition, 1893 [°1893 by the World's Columbian Exposition]; Woodbridge, CT: RPI, 1989.

21½x15. 36 p. Cream wraps, black print and WCE globe without underlying seal. General index inside front cover. At head of title: "World's Columbian Exposition." On cover: "Price, 5 cents." Map of Midway Plaisance on p. (1); double map of main grounds on p. (2)-(3). List of 41 numbered and 10 separately numbered exhibits -- e.g. "No. 1 A." Cover litho: parade of foreign peoples from the Midway.
---- Orange-red wraps, black print and WCE seal. 36 p. On cover: "Price, 5 cents." Info. from cover; t.p. info. unknown.
---- Orange-red wraps, black print and WCE seal. 36 p. On cover: "Price, 10 cents." Info. from cover; t.p. info. unknown.

P↑   ⊚ . (GLD,CHx,SI,TD) $20 - 35

Pt. 18. Department G: Collective exhibits of the Krupp cast-steel works, Essen, Germany

1205. ---. ---. ... *Official Catalogue of collective exhibits of the Krupp cast-steel works : Essen, Germany.*
Department G. Part XVIII. Edited by the department of publicity and promotion : M. P. Handy, Chief.
Chicago: W. B. Conkey co., publishers to the World's Columbian exposition, 1893; Woodbridge, CT:
RPI, 1989.

21½x15. 11 p., illus, plans, map. Baby blue front wrap, black print, red WCE globe-seal lower left
corner. At head of title: "World's Columbian Exposition : 1893." C.t. is found on front wrap: "Official
Catalogue of the Collective Exhibits of Krupp Cast Steel works : Department G. Price 10 Cents."
Giant Krupp field gun illus on front wrap. This Krupp catalog is the first of a 2 part booklet; the
second pt. is #1206.   ⊚ . (GLD,SI,WM)   Both parts: $15 - 30

Pt. 19. Department M: Exhibits of the Columbus caravels (Santa Maria, Nina and Pinta)

1206. ---. ---. ... *Official Catalogue : exhibits of the Columbus Caravels (Santa Maria, Nina and Pinta,) : part*
XIX. Department M. Edited by the department of publicity and promotion, M. P. Handy, Chief. W. B.
Conkey co., Publishers to the World's Columbian Exposition, 1893.

21½x15½. (13)-16 p. This is the second part of a 2 part booklet (see #1205 for the 1st part). C.t.
is found on back wrap: "Official catalogue of exhibits of the Columbus Caravels : Santa Maria : Niña
and Pinta : 1893 : Department M." Baby blue back wrap, black print, no WCE seal. Illus of the 3
caravels.   ⊚ . (GLD,SI,WM)   Both parts: $15 - 30

End of Official Catalog section.

1207. World's Columbian Exposition. Department of Publicity and Promotions. *The official directory of the*
World's Columbian Exposition : May 1st to October 30th, 1893. A reference book of exhibitors and
exhibits; of the officers and members of the World's Columbian commission, ... Copiously illustrated. Ed.
Moses P. Handy, Chief. Chicago: W. B. Conkey Co., Publishers, 1893 [°1892 by W. B. Conkey];
Woodbridge, CT: RPI, 1989.

26x18½. viii includes frontis of the Administration Bldg, 1 *l*, 1120 p., plates, illus, plans (1 fold. of
grounds before back cover). Blue cloth hc, gold and black print, marbled edges. The BEST -- a must
for the collector and student of WCE. [Conkey Co. became a subsidiary of Rand, McNally Co.].
---- (iii)-viii, 1120 p.
*P↓   ⊚ . (GLD,csuf,CHx,LC,SI,NYPL,F,S,OhHx,OSU,nwu,PU,RML,UDe,UTn,NHSt,UMi,NYSt,UoC,NL,BPL,A,RPB,WM,OC) $100 - 250

1208. World's Columbian Exposition. Department of Publicity and Promotion. *Official guide to the grounds*
and buildings of the World's Columbian Exposition during construction. Chicago: World's Columbian
Exposition, Department of Publicity and Promotion (Rand, McNally & Co., Printers), 1892;
Woodbridge, CT: RPI, 1989.

19½x13. 40 p. with illus + fold. map. Light green wraps with black print and litho of Columbus
statue. On cover: "Preliminary." Moses P. Handy, Chief.
---- Another ed.: On cover: "During construction." On t.p.: "July 1892." Same pub info.
---- Another ed.: On t.p.: "During construction" and "October, 1892." Same pub info. 20x13½. 40
p. + laid in fold. map in back. Light green wraps, black print and litho.
      ⊚ . (GLD,csuf,CHx,LC,SI,S,CoU,UoC,NL,UDe,WM,AIC,WM,OhHx) $12 - 25

1209. World's Columbian Exposition. Department of Publicity and Promotion. *Plans and diagrams of all exhibit buildings in the World's Columbian exposition : compiled from the official catalogues showing the location of exhibits.* Ed. M. P. Handy, Chief. Chicago: W. B. Conkey Co., 1893.

21½x14½. 52 p., plans, fold. maps, illus. Red wraps, gold seal, black print. "15 cents." ☻.(LC)

1210. *The World's Columbian Exposition Hand Book : souvenir : illustrated. Description of the buildings, Statistics, Interesting Items, General Information.* Chicago: Chicago Hand Book co., ℅1892.

8½x15. Unpaginated, illus. Light gray wraps with dark and light blue print, sunburst design in gold and blue. ☻.(CHₓ,LC)

1211. *The World's fair manual, Containing Full Descriptions and Elegant Cuts of the Exposition Buildings, ...* Akron, OH: W. F. Manual Co., ℅1892.

13½x6½. (3)-89, (6) p. Golden brown textured wraps, black print. Reads like note pad; 6½ cm wide stapled hinge at top. ☻(GLD) $12 - 25

1212. *The World's Fair Maps and Guide.* Chicago: Wm. P. Kimball & Co., n.d.

15½x9. 23, (1) p. + a folded map before first p. and after last p. Light pea green smooth wraps, black print and design. C.t. ☻.(WM,HL)

1213. *The World's Fair : some of its principal sights and exhibits.* New York: Columbia novelty publishing co., ℅1892.

21x__. 31 p., illus. (LC)

1214. World's Fair Tourists Accommodation Association, Chicago. *The World's fair tourist.* Chicago: World's Fair Tourists Accommodation Association, 1892.

21 p. (UC)

1215. *The Worlds* [sic] *Fair Visitor. A compendium of information for those intending to visit the World's Columbian exposition. To be held in the City of Chicago, 1893.* Chicago: [Titman & Son, printers for] The World's Fair Visitors' Association, [℅1891].

19½x13½. (24) p. Salmon wraps with black print.
---- 15 p., illus.
          ☻.(CHₓ,LC)

Chapter 7

MAGAZINES, NEWSPAPERS AND PERIODICALS

> Format: **Volume . Number (Year): Pages.** Number or issue month added when considered helpful.

1216. *Actualidades* [Spain]. Primer semestre (1893).

> Reparaz, G. "España en la Exposición de Chicago." Primer semestre (1893): 51-59. Politics, arts, literature, monuments, bibliography, photographs and biographies, music, scenes, notes of society, critiques, fashions. Imp. de la "Revista de Navegación y Comercio." [Magazine of Navigation and Commerce]. In Spanish.

1217. *Adventist Heritage.* 2 (1975).

1218. *Age of Discovery : a theme catalog : 1992 World's Fair.* 1 (1985).

> 27x21. 105 p. Gray slick wraps, blue and white print and design. On cover: "April 1985. First Edition. Volume One." Published by the Chicago World's Fair--1992 Authority, ᶜ1985. The 1992 Authority presented this edition "to stimulate expanded public discussion and comment about what ... the 1992 World's Fair should encompass."

1219. *Age of Steel.* 73 (1893).

1220. *American Anthropologist.* os 6 (1893).

1221. *American Antiquarian.* 15 (1893).

> Deans, James. "Totem posts at the World's Fair." 15 (1893): 281-6.

1222. *American Architect.* 28 (1890), 32 (1891), 36 (1892), 37 (1892), 38 (1893), 39 (1893), 42 (1893).

1223. *American Architect and building news.* (1893).

1224. *American Collector.* 7 (1938).

1225. *American Heritage.* 6 (1955), 11 (1960).

> Lynes, Russell. "Chateau builder to Fifth Avenue: Richard Morris Hunt gave "The 400" the architecture it liked : costly imitations of European grandeur." 6 (Feb. 1955): 20-25. Illus.
> Hirschl, Jessie Heckman. "The Great White City [World's Columbian Exposition, 1893.]" 11.6 (June? 1960): 8+. Illus.

1226. *American Historical Review.* 82 (1977).

> Hines, Thomas S. David F. Burg, "Chicago's White City of 1893." 82 (1977): 194-95.

1227. *American Institute of Mine Engineering Transactions.* 22 (1894), 23 (1894).

1228. *American Manufacturer.* (1893).

1229. *American Music.* 3 (1985), 4 (1986).

1230. *American Philatelist.* 93 (1979), 94 (1980), 98 (1984).

WCE articles found: 93.11 (1979): 994-1006, 94.8 (1980): 713-26, 98.9 (1984): 895-99.

1231. *American Scholar.* 4 (1935).

1232. *American Scientist.* 54 (1966).

1233. *American Studies.* 8 (___).

Massa, Ann. "Black women in the 'White City.'" 8.3 (___): 319-37.

1234. *Americana.* New York: American Heritage. 7 (1979).

Fauster, Carl U. "1893 Mementos of the Fair." May/June (1979): 56-58. Illus.

1235. *Anchor News.* July/Oct. (1892).

Valli, Isacco A. *The Columbus Disaster.* July/Oct. (1892): 76-84. The whaleback, "Christopher Columbus." WCE p. 77. For more on the whaleback, see #1320 and #1360.

1236. *Annales du Conserv. des arts et Metiers.* 25 (1894).

1237. *Antiques Journal.* Westfield, NY. 12 (1957).

Schrader, Isabel G. "Spoons of the World's Columbian Exposition -- 1893." 12 (Apr. 1957): 36-37.

1238. *Architectural Record.* 3 (1893), 4 (1895), 33 (1913).
*

1239. *Architectural Review.* 2 (1893), 3 (1895), 162 (1977).

1240. *Architecture and Building.* 15 (1891), 16 (1892), 18 (1893), 19 (1893).

1241. *Archives of the International Folk-Lore Association.* 1 (1898). See International folk-lore congress.

1242. *Arena.* 7 (1892-93), 11 (1894), 16 (1896).

1243. *Arizona and the West.* Autumn (1893).

"Arizona goes to the fair, World's Columbian Exposition 1893." Autumn (1893): 261.

1244. *Arizona Enterprise* [Florence, AZ]. 28 Dec. 1893.

"The World's Fair: final report of Arizona commissioners and their stewardship." 28 Dec. 1893.

1245. *Arizona Gazette* [Phoenix, AZ]. 1 Aug. 1893.

Special World's Fair edition. 1 Aug. 1893.

1246. *Art Amateur.* 29 (1893).

1247. *Art Journal.* (1893).

"Chicago and the Columbian Exposition." p. i-xxxii, illus. (1893)

1248. *Art Quarterly.* 16 (1953).

1249. *Arte moderno y contemporáneo.* (1952).

> Fernández, Justino. "El monumento a Colón." (1952): 243-45.

1250. *Atlantic Monthly.* 70 (189_), 71 (1893).

1251. *Ave Maria : A magazine devoted to the honor of the Blessed Virgin.* Notre Dame, IN., copyright Rev. D. E. Hudson. 37 (1 July 1893).

> Cary, Emma F. "The Elevation of Womanhood through Veneration of the Blessed Virgin." (Paper read before the Women's Congress.) 37 (1 July 1893).

1252. *B & O Field.* Baltimore, MD. (Mar. 1893).

1253. *Black Diamond.* (1893). Subject: Mining.

1254. *Boston Herald.*

1255. *Bryant Post* [Bryant, SD]. (21 Aug. 1893).

1256. *Bulletin of Atlanta University.* No. 48 (1893).

> No. 48 is the "Exposition Number," July 1893.

1257. *Business Education.* 1 (1892).

1258. *California History.* 61 (1982).

1259. *California's Monthly Worlds* [sic] *Fair Magazine.* San Francisco: B. Fehnemann, Publisher. 1 (1891-92).

> 23x14½. Tan wraps, black print and logo which includes CA seal. No. 1-2 (May and June, 1891) title as above; No. 3 (Jan. 1892) adds "Authorized official organ" at head of title; No. 4-8 (Feb.-June 1892) in addition add officers of CA World's Fair Commission at head of title.

1260. *Canadian Gazette.*

> NAC has copies from 1893-1903 in record group 76, vol 42, file 979, part 1. Microfilm reel no. C-4703.

1261. *Catholic World.* (1892).

> Spalding, J. L. "The Catholic Educational Exhibit in the Columbian Exposition." July (1892).

1262. *Centenario, El* [Madrid]. t. II (1892).

> Alcalá Galliano, José. "La Exposición Universal Colombina de Chicago." t. II (1892): 352-70.

1263. *Century Magazine.* ns 17, 22 (1892), 23 (1892-93), 24 (1893).

> Old series vol no. also printed on t.p.
> P→ $12 - 26

1264. *Chautauquan.* 16 (1892), 17 (1893).

1265. *Chicago.* 26 (1977), __ (1982).

> Heise, Kenan. "Chicago's Personal Past: New York's white city." 26 (Mar. 1977): 90-94. Illus.
> Duis, Perry R., and Glen E. Holt. "Checking in at the fair : The hotel boom of the 1893 Columbian Exposition left a legacy to be learned from." __ (July 1983): 84-86.

1266. *Chicago Commerce.* 19 (1923).

> 19 (1923): Several articles celebrate the 30th anniversary of the WCE and its effect on Chicago.

1267. *Chicago Evening Post.*

> ---- Also listed: Chicago Evening Post Souvenir.

1268. *Chicago Herald.*

1269. *Chicago History.* [Chicago Historical Society]. os 3 (1953), os 8 (1968), ns 3 (1974), ns 4 (1975), ns 6 (1977), ns 9 (1980), ns 12 (1983), ns 14 (1985).

> Angle, Paul McClelland. "The World's Columbian Exposition: a nostalgic exhibit." os 3 (Spring 1953): 193-215.
> Angle, Paul McClelland. "The Columbus caravels." os 8 (Fall 1968): 257-69.
> Dornfeld, A. A. "The 'Viking' in Lincoln Park." ns 3 (Fall 1974): 111-116. Article on the Viking Ship and the 3 caravels from Spain.
> Riedy, James L. "Sculpture at the Columbian Exposition." 4 (Summer 1975): 99-107.
> Weimann, Jeanne Madeline. "A temple to women's genius: the Women's Building of 1893." ns 6 (Spring 1977): 23-33.
> Barnes, Sisley. "George Ferris' Wheel : The Great Attraction of the Midway Plaisance." ns 6 (Fall 1977): 177-82.
> Osterbrock, Donald E. "America's first world astronomy meeting : Chicago 1893." ns 9 (Fall 1980): 178-85.
> Nagel, Paul Chester. "Twice to the fair." ns 14 (Spring 1985): 4-19.

1270. *Chicago Post.*

1271. *Chicago Record.* [Wm. Igleheart was World's Fair Editor.]

1272. *Chicago Tribune.* 16 Feb. 1896, 11 Sept. 1966.

> "Gondolas of the Fair - their present quarters and their probable destiny." 16 Feb. 1896: 25.
> "Cleaning Bares Rare Photo." 11 Sept. 1966: 2 (section 10). Photo found showed the 1895 Ferris Wheel reassembly at Clark and Wrightwood in Chicago.

1273. *Chinese Scientific and Industrial Magazine.* [1893?]. See #850.

1274. *Clarion-Ledger* [Jackson, MS]. Newspaper. 18 July 1893.

> Coverage of the Mississippi exhibit. 18 July 1893. Rpt. in the *Daily Clarion.* 31 Dec. 1937, centennial ed.

1275. *Columbian Bulletin American Business Colleges.* July (1893).

> Below title: "Manufactures Building, Exposition Grounds, Chicago, USA, July, 1893."

1276. *Columbian Exposition Herald : Marion County Number.* Marion County, OH. June 1893.

56x38½. 4 p. Newspaper format. Caption title. "Price three cents."

1277. *Construction Moderne, La.* 6 (1891).

1278. *Contemporary Review.* 65 (1894).

1279. *Coronet.*

    Boswell, Charles, and Lewis Thompson. "Big Wheel From Chicago." (George Ferris.) p. 126.

1280. *Cosmopolitan.* [monthly]. New York. John Brisben Walker, ed. 8 (1889), 12 (?), 15 (1893), 16 (1893-94).

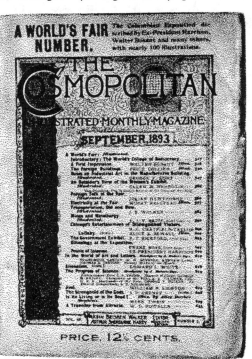

25x18.
Astor, William Waldorf. "New York's candidacy for the World's Fair of 1892. A reply to Senator Farwell, of Illinois." 8 (Dec. 1889): (165?)-167.
15.1-2 (May-June 1893).
15.5 (Sept. 1893): At top of cover: "A World's Fair Number. The Columbian Exposition described by Ex-President Harrison, Walter Besant and many others, with nearly 100 illustrations."
16.1 (Nov. 1893).
16.2 (Dec. 1893): At top of cover: "After the World's Fair, with nearly 200 illustrations." Many fine and descriptive WCE articles.
16.3-4 and 16.6 (Jan.-Feb, Apr. 1894).
*P→ $10 - 28

1281. *Daily Citizen* [Albuquerque, NM]. Newspaper. 9 Apr. 1892

1282. *Daily Columbian.*

    * The official bulletin of the WCE. [UoC has 158 numbers. Complete set. ?]

1283. *Daily Presto.*

    Put out by Presto Music as a daily music news item during the Fair.

1284. *Demorest's Family Magazine.* April and Nov., 1892; June and Sept. 1893.

    Exposition number. June 1893. ©1893 by W. Jennings Demorest. 28x21. Cover peppered with illus of various WCE bldgs.

1285. *Des Moines Leader* [Des Moines, IA]. Newspaper.

1286. *Dial.* 13 (1892), 14 (1893), 15 (1893).

1287. *Discovery Five Hundred.* Joseph M. Laufer, ed. U.S. National Alliance for the quincentennial.

    28x21. Newsletter. Controversial U.S. Government promotion of the Quincentennial.

1288. *... Dry Goods Economist.* Extra No. 2564½. New York, Chicago: The Textile Publishing Co., Sept. 1893.

36½x27. 3-202 p., ads as end papers front and back covers. Burgundy cloth hc, beveled boards, large colored lithos with gilt borders glued to outside of both covers. C.t. At head of title: "1893 Special Exposition Number of the ..." Very attractive.

1289. *Electrical Engineer* [London weekly]. ns 12 (1893).

1290. *Electrical Engineering* [An illustrated monthly magazine]. Chicago: Fred De Land, [°1893 by Electrical Engineering Publishing Co.]. 2 (1893).

23x15½. WCE addressed in "Editor's Outlook." 2 (1893): 288-99.
Title varies (*Electrical Engineering and Telephone Magazine*; listed in Union List of Serials under *Telephone Magazine.*). See #1432 for Vol 1: *World's Fair Electrical Engineering.*

1291. *Electrical World.* (1893).

1292. *Engineering : An Illustrated Weekly Journal.* [London]: Offices for Advertisements and Publication, ____. (1893).

21 Apr. 1893: "The Cunard Royal mail twin-screw steamers 'Campania' and 'Lucania' and the World's Columbian Exposition, 1893." (Also reprinted).

1293. *Engineering Magazine.* 2 (1891), 5 (1893), 6 (1894).

6.4 (Jan. 1894): Souvenir number. 24x17. Gray wraps. "C.t.": "The World's Fair in Retrospect: A souvenir number of the Engineering Magazine specially designed to indicate the practical value of the World's Columbian Exposition to the science and industry of the time." Many articles separately paginated, several pages of photos before and following the articles.

1294. *Engineering News.* (1893).

1295. *Engineering Record.* Oct. 21, 28, and Nov. 4 (1893).

1296. *Exposition Echo.* 1 (1893).

An advertising newspaper. $15 - 30

1297. *Exposition Graphic.* 1 (1891-93).

A quarterly edition of the Graphic. Vol 1, no. 1 was Oct.-Dec., 1891. 40½x28. 48 p. Printed in English, German, French, and Spanish. Lavishly illustrated.
Vol 1, No. 3 contains practically all the illustrations of *The Graphic* Dedication Number.
---- 2nd revised English ed.
P→

1298. *Fair News.* Sarasota, FL: World's Fair Collectors' Society.

Emple, Jim. "Columbian Exposition Buildings Then and Now." 22 (Nov. 1990): 14-15.
---. "I lost my teeth at the Columbian Exposition." 23 (July 1991): 3.
Schneider, Bill. "Norway Building from 1893 Expo." 22 (Nov. 1990): 3.

Per Year: $15

1299. *Five Hundred: Official Publication of the Christopher Columbus Quincentenary Jubilee Commission.* Coral Gables, FL: Quintis Communications Group, 1989-. 1 (1989). 28x__.

1300. *Florida Historical Quarterly.* Florida Historical Society.

    22½x14.
    Kerber, Stephen. "Florida and the World's Columbian Exposition of 1893." (July 1987): 25-.

1301. *Florida Home Seeker.* Avon Park, FL. July and Aug. (1893).

    40x29. Newspaper format. $60 - 100

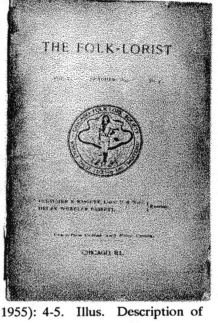

1302. *Folk-Lorist.* 1 (1893).

    The Folk-Lore Society held their first Congress at the WCE July 11-16, 1893.
    P→ $12 - 26

1303. *Forum.* 8 (___), 14 (1892-93), 16 (1893), 18 (1894).

1304. *Frank Leslie's Illustrated Weekly.* 77 (1893).
    * $18 - 40

1305. *Frank Leslie's Popular Monthly.* 36 (?).

1306. *Germania Club News.* 15 (1955).

    Reichert, William. "Earth and fire! - our picture." 15 (Mar. 1955): 4-5. Illus. Description of porcelain painting originally exhibited at WCE.

1307. *Godey's.* 126 (1893).
    P→ $15 - 32

1308. *Golden Era.* 42 (1893). $20 - 40

1309. *Graphic.* Chicago.

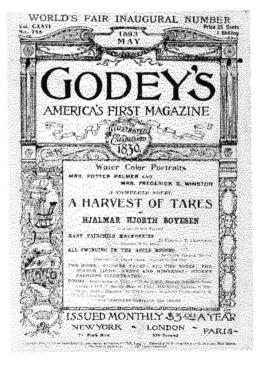

    40x28½. "An Illustrated Weekly Newspaper." Title varies: *Graphic News, Illustrated Graphic News, Chicago Illustrated Graphic News.* Vol designations vary. Printed weekly on glossy leaves in English, German, French, and Spanish.
    ---- Dec. 10, 1892 (Vol 7, No. 24): Sculpture number.
    ---- Spain at the Columbian Exposition (España en la Exposición Colombina) featured in the Oct. 12, 1893, Spanish edition. 40x28½. 24 p. includes illus, port, facsimiles. A special number of the Graphic.
    ---- Germany at the Columbian exposition featured in the Sept. 23, 1893 issue.

1310. *Habana Literaria, La.* 2 (1891).

    A. Z. "La mujer [woman] en la Exposición de Chicago." 2.6 (1891): 133-35.

1311. *Halligan's Illustrated World's Fair.* See #1324.

1312. *Hartford Courant.*

1313. *Harper's Monthly*. 84 (1891-92), 85 (1892), 86 (1892-93), 87 (1893). $10 - 20

1314. *Harper's Weekly : A Journal of Civilization*. 33 (1889), 34 (1890), 35 (1891), 36 (1892), 37 (1893), 38 (1894), 39 (1895).

> 36.1838 (12 Mar. 1892).
> 36.1871 (29 Oct. 1892): On cover, "Dedication of the buildings of the World's Columbian Exposition."
> 37.1890 (11 Mar. 1893), 37.1891 (18 Mar. 1893), 37.1894 (8 Apr. 1893), 37.1899 (13 May 1893), 37.1924 (4 Nov. 1893).
> P→ $16 - 34

1315. *Harper's Young People*. 13 (1892), 14 (1892-93).

> C.t.: "Reunion souvenir number." Tan wraps with green design and brown print. Handout at the WCE. 14 (1893): (617)-48.
> P↓ $12 - 26

1316. *Hayes Historical Journal*. Fremont, OH: Hayes Historical Society. 1 (1977).

> Andrews, William D. "Women and the fairs of 1876 and 1893." 1 (Spring 1977): 173-84.

1317. *Heating and Ventilation*. (1893).

1318. *Helicon nine : a journal of women's arts and letters*. 1 (1979).

> Paine, Judith. "Sophia Hayden and the Woman's Building." 1 (Fall/Winter 1979): 28-37.
> Webster, Sally. "Mary Cassatt's allegory of modern woman." 1 (Fall/Winter 1979): 38-47.

1319. *Heresies*. 1 (1978), 2 (1979).

1320. *Historical Messenger*. Milwaukee County Historical Society. 10 (____).

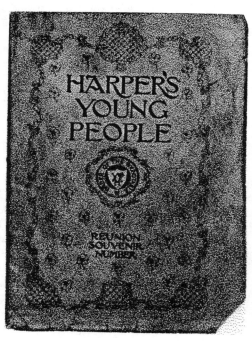

> 10.4: An illus source of information about the "Christopher Columbus," whaleback built for the WCE passenger service between Jackson Park and Chicago city center. For more on the whaleback, see #1235 and #1360.

1321. *Homiletic Review*. (May, 1893).

1322. *Illinois Quarterly*. 37 (1974).

1323. *Illustrated American*. New York: Illustrated American Publishing Co. 13(1893), 14 (1893).

> Columbian Exposition Number (May-Nov. 1893). Independent 80 p. special number. 31x23½. Green and red print on cream stiff wraps. C.t.: "The World's Fair or, Columbian Exposition." "Compiled under the direction of Maurice M. Minton."

P→ $16 - 30

1324. *Illustrated World's Fair : devoted to the World's fair, art and scientific literature.* Chicago: Illustrated World's Fair Publishing Co., 1890-93. 1, 2, 3 (1892), 4 (1893), 5.

40x27½. Jewell N. Halligan, general manager. Popularly known as: "Halligan's Illustrated World's Fair" because the cover title of the bound vol reads: "Halligan's Illustrated World's Fair: A Pictorial and Literary History of the World's Columbian Exposition." Title varies: 1890-Apr. 1893 as *The Illustrated World's Fair*; May-Nov. 1893 as *Halligan's Illustrated World's Fair*. The Nov. 1892, issue states the magazine will be known as "The Illustrated World" after Dec. 1893. No more published?
---- June, 1893: "Special holiday issue." Cover is peppered with ports and contains a fac-simile of a portion of the cover for a bound vol.
---- Great Britain ed. At bottom of cover: "Edited for Great Britain and the Colonies published by Sampson Low, Marston & Co. ... London." 40x27½. 5 vol, 30 pts. Title varies as indicated for U.S. edition above. Month and vol number do not always correlate with U.S. edition.
*P→ $16 - 40

1325. *India Rubber World.* 8 (1893). $10 - 20

1326. *Indianapolis Freeman.*

1327. *Industrial Chicago.* Goodspeed publishing co. 4 (1894).

"The World's Columbian exposition." 4 (1894): 327-45.

1328. *Inland Architect.* 17 (1891), 21 (1893), 22 (1893).

Olmsted, Frederick Law. "The landscape architecture of the World's Columbian Exposition." 22 (Sept. 1893): 18-21.

1329. *Inter Ocean : illustrated supplement.* Chicago: 1893.

44½x29½. Illustrated supplement of the *Chicago Daily.* Issued Sundays; also issued Wednesdays during the WCE. The front and back covers are in color and many of them illustrate WCE events: e.g., on 2 Aug. 1893 the Michigan State Bldg was depicted. An example of early coloration by machine for newspapers.
*P↓ $14 - 36

1330. *International Journal of Women's Studies.* 5 (1982).

1331. *Iowa State Register* [Des Moines, IA]. Newspaper.

1332. *Irrigator.* DeLand, FL. Aug. 1893.

1333. *Journal of American Culture.* 1 (1978).

1334. *Journal of American Folk-Lore.* Boston and New York: Published for The American Folk-Lore Society by Houghton, Mifflin and co., 1894 [°1894 by The American Folk-Lore Society]. 7 (1894).

Hale, Horatio Emmons. "The fall of Hochelaga, a study of popular tradition." 7 (Jan.-Mar. 1894): 1-14. For rpt. see #2175.
Culin, Stewart. "Retrospect of the folk-lore of the Columbian Exposition." 7 (Jan.-Mar. 1894): 51-59. For rpt. see #2198.

1335. *Journal of American Studies.* 8 (1974).

1336. *Journal of Popular Culture.* 6 (1973).

1337. *Journal of the American Chemical Society.* 15 (1893?).

Long, J[ohn] H[arper]. "Chemical notes from the Columbian Exposition." 15.5. See #916.

1338. *Journal of the Franklin Institute.* 133 (1892).

1339. *Journal of the Illinois State Historical Society.* 17 (1924), 18 (1925), 27 (1934), 59 (1966), 65 (1972), 76 (1983).

"Fine Arts Building Chicago, World's Fair Saved." 17 (1924): 279.
"German building, Jackson Park, Chicago." 18 (1925): 461-64.
Neufeld, Maurice. "The White City. The Beginnings of a Planned Civilization in America." 27 (Apr. 1934): 71-93.
Wilson, Robert E. "The Infanta at the Fair." 59 (1966): 252-71.

1340. *Journal of the Society of Arts : and Official Organ of the Royal Commission for the Chicago Exhibition, 1893.* Published every Friday. London: Published for the Society by George Bell and Sons. 40 (1891), 41 (1892). $8 - 20

22½x16½. Gray wraps. Samples of articles:
"Chicago Exhibition, 1893: Meeting of the Royal Commission.-- Applications for Space in the British Section." 40 (20 Nov. 1891): 6.
"Chicago Exhibition, 1893: Meeting of the Royal Commission. Executive Committee." 41 (2 Dec. 1892): 37.
"Germany and Russia at the Chicago Exhibition." 41 (2 Dec. 1892): 54.

1341. *Judge.* 16 (1889), 17 (1890), 21 (1891), 22 (1892), 24 (to June 1893), 25 (from July 1893).

Color cartoons from early battles over the site of the WCE (vol 16) to other problem areas during the Fair -- e.g., Sunday opening/closing. $10 - 28

1342. *Judge's Library.* No. 52
     P↑ $10 - 28

1343. *Kanhistique.* 4 (1979).

     Rozar, Lily-B. "History carved in wood." 4 (Apr. 1979): 4.

1344. *Kansas Magazine.* (1942).

     Beals, Carleton. "Kansas at the World's Fair." (1942): 19-24.

1345. *Kansas State Board of Agriculture Monthly Report.* (1891).

     [Address sent out by Bureau of Promotion, proposing plan for state of Kansas to make an exhibit.] (Apr. 1891): 11.

1346. *Keystone: The Organ of the Retail Jewelry Trade.* 14 (1893).

     14.5 (May 1893): WCE issue.
     P→ $25 - 55

$16 - 32

1347. *Ladies' Home Journal.* 10 (1893).

$10 - 22

1348. *Ladies' World.* 14 (1893).

1349. *Legal News* [Chicago]. (1893).

1350. *Lehigh Quarterly.* Lehigh U., Bethlehem, PA.

1351. *Lewiston* [Maine] *Journal.* (1921).

     "Many 'Springs' of Historical Interest in Maine Building at Poland Springs." 28 Jan. 1921, Magazine section: 1-2.

1352. *Life.* 18.451 (Aug. 1891): (87)-96.

1353. *Literette* [Chicago]. (1895).

     Burnett, Frances Hodgson. "Two little pilgrims progress; a story of the City Beautiful." No. 1 (1895): 1-12. 24x31½.

1354. *Magazine of American History.* 24 (1890), 26 (1891).

1355. *Marine Review.* 7 (1893).

     13x9½. 18 p., 1 *l.* Light blue wraps printed in black. At head of title: "Miniature World's fair edition." Shows nice litho of the WF passenger ship "Christopher Columbus." 7.19 (1893). For more ship information, see #1360.
     P→

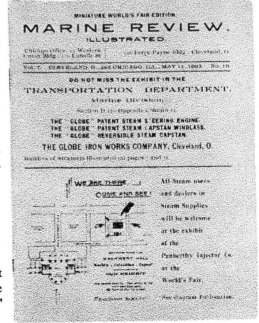

$18 - 36

1356. *Master Mechanic.* (1893).

1357. *Message and Deaconess World*. Oak Park, IL. (Sept. 1893).

1358. *Mid-America*. 63 (1981).

1359. *Midland Monthly*. No. 1 (1894), No. 3 (1894).

1360. *Milwaukee Reader*. [Milwaukee Public Library monthly.] 48 (1990).

> Christopher Columbus whaleback photographs with captions. 48 (July/Aug. 1990): (2)-(3). For more on the "Christopher Columbus," see #1235 and #1320.

> ☞ The 362 foot long "Christopher Columbus" (Off. No. 126952) whaleback was built by S. F. Hodge & Co. for the World's Fair Steam Ship Co. in 1893. She was the only passenger whaleback ever built. Her first job was to ferry passengers from the WCE to the Van Buren St. pier, Chicago. She had but one accident (1917) and was scraped in the summer of 1936. Ship information and data record is located in The Herman G. Runge Collection at the MPL.

1361. *Monthly Bulletin, Bureau of American Republics*. Feb. (1894).

1362. *Munsey's*. 8 (1893).

> Handy, Mrs. M. P. "The women of the World's Fair city." 8 (1983): March. 24½x__. 7 p. article, ports.

1363. *Nacional, El* [Mexico]. 16 Mar. 1958.

> Monterde, Francisco. "Una antología conmemorativa. IV Centenario del descubrimiento." March 16, 1958: 2.

1364. *Nation*. 57 (1893).

1365. *National Eclectic Medical Association Trans*. 21 (1894).

1366. *National Stenographer*. 4 (1893).

> Contains a section in each number on the "Congress of Stenographers." No. 7, 8, and 9 contain: "Official Report of the Proceedings of the World's Congress of Stenographers." No. 10 and 11 are "World's Souvenir Numbers."

1367. *Natural Science*. 3 (1893).

> Bather, F[rancis] A. "Natural Science at the Chicago Exhibition." Nov., No. 21.

1368. *New England Magazine*. __ (1894), 14 (1896).

> Mattocks, Charles P. "Maine at the World's Fair." __ (May 1894): 295-305.

1369. *New York Age*.

1370. *New York Recorder*. (1893).

> Color print WCE views inserted as supplements.

1371. *New York Times.*

Even a brief review of article titles reveals a RICH fabric of: <u>success</u> (e.g., "American [Art] Exhibit Praised by Mr. Tarbell), <u>ideas</u> (e.g., "California's Supplemental World's Fair Proposed"), <u>problems</u> ("Cholera: National Quarantine; Director Davis's Reports to Council of Administration"), <u>dissention</u> (e.g., "National Commission Adopts Investigating Committee's Report Suggesting Resignation [of T. Thomas, Musical Director]," "Photographing Privileges; Rules; Amateur's Complaints," "Methodist Church Refuses to Make Exhibit," and "Lady Managers' Board Quarrels Denounced by Mrs. Palmer"), <u>controversy</u> (e.g., "Canadian Parliament Debate; Motions to Close Exhibit" and "American Sabbath Union Appeal Against Sunday Opening"), and <u>the unusual</u> (e.g., "Old Time's Distillery Seized by Internal Revenue Officers" and "Elephant to be Constructed by Syndicate").

Source: *The New York Times Index : for the published news of 1890-1893 : the master key to the news.* Prior series. Vol. 6. New York & London: Reprinted for The New York Times co. by R. R. Bowker co., [°1966]. [As an additional aid, consult the 1894-98 index.]

1372. *Newspaper Library.* 4 (1892).

4 (Jan. 1892): "Holiday Number : 1492 1892." 23½x31½. Black on white wraps. Cover has Yanez port of Columbus.

1373. *Nineteenth Century.* 31 (1892).

1374. *North American Review.* 149(1889), 150 (1890), 154 (1892), 155 (1892), 156 (1893), 157 (1893).

149 (1889). Hawley (senator) describes fairs and suggests New York would be a good location for an 1892 fair.

1375. *Northern Christian Advocate.* 53 (1893).

1376. *Our Day.* 10 (1892), 12 (1893).

1377. *Outlook.* 48 (1893).

1378. *Pacific Banner.* Winthrop Centre, NE. (May 1893).

1379. *Palimpsest.* 6 (1925).

1380. *Partido Liberal, El* [Mexico]. 13 Sept. 1893.

Quesada, Gonzalo de. "En la Exposición de Chicago. La mujer [woman] de México." Sept. 13, 1893: 1-2.

1381. *Pencilpoints.* 19 (1938).

1382. *Peterson's Magazine.* ns 1 (1892), 2 (1893).

The os stopped with vol 100 -- their 50 year anniversary. $10 - 30

1383. *Philadelphia Inquirer.*

Art Supplement with color illus.

1384. *Phylon.* 26 (1965).

1385. *Popular Science Monthly.* 43 (1893), 44 (1893-94). $8 - 16

1386. *Power.* (1893).

1387. *Public Opinion.* 17.

1388. *Puck.* 26 (to 5 Mar. 1890), 27 (from 12 Mar. 1890), 30 (Sept.-Oct. 1891), 30 (Jan. 1892), 32 (1892), 33 (1893).

At the Fair this was printed as *World's Fair Puck* (see #1435).

1389. *Quaker City Philatelist : A monthly Journal for Stamp Collectors.* Philadelphia: Quaker City Philatelic publishing co. 8.96 (1893): (142)-158.

24½x17½. Buff wraps, black print. $45

1390. *Quarterly Review.* 177 (1893).

1391. *Railroad Gazette.* (1893).

1392. *Ram's Horn: a religious weekly.* Chicago: F. L. Chapman & Co., [1893].

"A directory of valuable information about the World's Columbian Exposition." 14 p., 1 plan, 1 plate.

1393. *Records of the Columbia Historical Society of Washington, D.C.* 37-38 (1937), 46-47 (1947).

Moore, Charles. "Personalities in Washington Architecture." 37-38 (1937).
Caemmerer, H. Paul. "Charles Moore and the Plan of Washington." 46-47 (1947). With the construction of the Library of Congress, Washington, DC, was the first beneficiary of architectural success of the WCE (p. 241). [Olmsted planned the grounds area.]

1394. *Religious Liberty Library.* [Monthly]. Battle Creek, MI Chicago New York Oakland, CA: International Liberty Association. No. 6 (Mar. 1893).

Jones, Alonzo T[révier]. "The captivity of the republic : a report of Hearing by House Committee on Columbian Exposition, January 10-13, 1893 : and the present status and effect of the legislation on Sunday closing of the World's fair." Religious liberty library no. 6, (Mar. 1893). 19½x13½. (2), 3-126 p. Gray wraps, black print.

1395. *Rensselaer Polytechnic Institute's Alumni Bulletin.* Spring (1981).

Cover and lead article: "The Year of the Ferris Wheel." [Ferris was an 1880 civil engineering graduate of the Institute. List of 1880 graduates.--(CVHx 5-G-72)]

1396. *Review of Reviews.* 6 (1892), 7 (1893), 8 (1893), 9 (1894).

6 (1892): [124]-142 -- "The Christmas number." Contains William Thomas Stead's "From the Old World to the New, or A Christmas Story of the World's Fair, 1893." (See #38 for the book.)
7 (June 1893): "Art at the Columbian exposition" and other articles.
8? (July 1893): "An Englishman's Impressions at the Fair" by Stead.
8? (Sept. 1893): "Engineer Ferris and his Wheel" by J. P. Barrett.

1397. *Revue d'Art Canadienne* [Canadian Art Review]. 5 (1978-79).

1398. *San Francisco Chronicle.* "California at the World's Fair."

21x14½. 2 *l*, illus. Reduced facsimile of the front pages of the *Chronicle* for May (1), 2, 18, and April 30, 1893. $15 - 26

1399. *Sanitarian*. Dec. (1893).

Morse, W. F. "The disposal of the garbage and waste of the World's Columbian Exposition." Dec. 1893.

1400. *Scientific American*. 62 (1890), 63 (1891), 69 (1893), 70 (1894), 71 (1894), 75 (1896).

Cover and article featuring the Ferris Wheel. (July. 1893)
"Fate of the World's Fair Buildings." (Oct. 1896): 267. $10 - 40

1401. *Scientific American Supplement*. 36 (1893). $10 - 40

1402. *Scribner's Magazine* [monthly]. 12 (1892), 13 (1893), 14 (1893), 24 (1898).

"Exhibition Number", May 1893. Label added on front cover. For handout at the Scribner's Exhibit. Dark and medium brown print on tan paper covers.
*P→ $15 - 28

1403. *Sea and Shade*. New York. Dec. (1893).

1404. *Seaboard: Illustrated Marine Weekly*. New York. (28 Sept. 1893).

1405. *Shekel*. Margate, FL: American Israel Numismatic Association. 24 (1991)

Lewi, Isidor. "Yom Kippur on the Midway." Jewish influence in the Turkish Village; Palestine was a part of the Turkish Empire. 24.3 (1991): 25-27.

1406. *Smithsonian*. July (1983): 2-.

July (1983): 2-. Article on G. W. G. Ferris.

1407. *South Dakota Educator*. 5 (1892).

5 (Oct. 1892): 1-17. At bottom of cover: World's Columbian Exposition. "Official program the national public school celebration of Columbus day, Oct, 21, 1892." p. 13-17. Harry L. Brass, ed. Mitchell, SD: The Educator School Blank co. 4500 copies printed.

1408. *St. Nicholas*. 20 (1892-93).

Jenks, Tudor. "World's fair palaces." 20.2: 519.
Bates, Clara Doty. "The Childrens Building of the Columbian Exposition." July 1893: 714-15.
* $12 - 26

1409. *Street Railway Gazette*. (1893).

1410. *Studio*. 6 (1891).

1411. *Sunshine and Silver.* Tuscon, AZ. (1893).

> For special World's fair editions, see *Arizona* #1779. $15 - 40

1412. *Swedish pioneer historical quarterly.* 7 (1956).

> Boethius, Gerda. "Anders Zorn, the artist, in Chicago." 7 (1956): 3-10.

1413. *To-Day's Events.* [A daily publication]. Chicago: Stewart & Co., 1893.

> 31x23½. Various leaves per issue. Salmon pulp, illus, ads. Caption title. Example: "Chicago, Wednesday, Sept. 13, 1893. Price, 1 cent." 4 *l.* Gives daily information on WF concerts, events, etc.
> ---- Oct. 13th. Minnesota Day. 3 *l.*

1414. *Topeka Daily Capital* [Kansas]. 17 Mar. 1891.

> "The people loyal, Kansas will have an exhibit at the World's fair." 17 Mar. 1891.

1415. *Tribune Monthly* [Chicago Tribune]. 5 (1893).

> 24½x16½. 58 p. includes front cover. Cream wrap, black print, same paper as text. No. 9. Sept. 1893 issue devoted to "Art and Architecture at the World's Fair."
> ---- 26x17. Pea green wraps, black print and design.

1416. *UBC Engineer* [U of British Columbia, Vancouver]. 5 (1965).

> Meehan, Pat. "The big wheel." [Ferris wheel of the World's Columbian Exposition, 1893]. 5 (1965): 29-33.

1417. *Union Signal and World's Fair White Ribbon.* Temperance newspaper. 19 (1893). $12 - 22

1418. *United States trade mark association bulletin.* New York. 5 (1893).

> "Trade Marks at the World's Columbian Exposition." 5.1 (July 1893).

1419. *University of Chicago Magazine.* July-Oct. (1970), Mar.-? (1971).

> July-Oct. 1970: Memory album of pictures from the UoC archives with follow-up in Mar.-? 1971.

1420. *Utah World's Fair Advocate.* 1 (1892).

> On cover: "Authorized official organ Utah World's Fair Commission." For same, see # 2085.

1421. *Weekly World's Fair Electrical Industries* [Chicago]. (7 Sept. 1893).

1422. *Western Electrician.* (1893).

1423. *Western Pennsylvania historical magazine.* 17 (1934).

1424. *Wisconsin Magazine of History.* 67 (1984).

> Cassell, Frank A., and Marguerite E. Cassell. "Wisconsin at the World's Columbian Exposition of 1893." 67.4 (Summer 1984): 243-62. Excellent account from 1893 WI reports of the organization, politics, finances, etc., of the State and its people at the WCE.

1425. *Woman suffrage leaflet.* [Bi-monthly]. Boston, MA. 6 (1893).

> Young, Virginia D. "The star in the west." 6.1 (Jan. 1893). 25x15½. 4 p. Young was the only lady member of the South Carolina Press Association.

1426. *Woman's Home Missions.* Delaware, OH. Sept. (1893).

1427. *Woman's Tribune.* Washington, DC. (1893).

> 1 Apr., 7 July, 19 Aug., 26 Aug., 2 Sept. 1893

1428. *World.* New York. (Columbian Exposition Edition -- 17 May 1891).

1429. *World's Columbian Exposition Illustrated : devoted to the interests of the Columbian Exposition, art and literature.* [Monthly]. Chicago: J. B. Campbell [etc], 1891-94 [copyrighted by James B. Campbell. [Monthly] 1, 2, 3 (Feb. 1891 - Feb. 1894).

> 39x27. Vol 1: Feb. 1891-Feb. 1892, vol 2: Mar. 1892-Feb 1893, vol 3: Mar. 1893-Feb 1894.
> To clarify continuation issues: There were 5 vols total.
> Vol 4 (June 1894 to Apr. 1895) continued as "Campbell's Illustrated Monthly." Confusing -- since it was advertised to be continued as "Campbell's Columbian Journal" (on Columbus' hat of May 1893 issue cover).
> Vol 5 (Oct. 20, 1895 - Jan. 11, 1896) continued as "Campbell's Illustrated Weekly."
> *P→   Each $16 - 40

1430. *World's Columbian magazine : Weekly.* Chicago: Press of Knight & Leonard co., ᶜ1890 by F. L. Dana.

> 26x17½. Vol I, no. I. states the magazine was to have been printed weekly in English and Spanish. It contains an article by Dana proposing a "Columbian Social Court" for the WCE. Each issue to contain a ballot to be filled out for the subscriber's choice of a society lady to named one of the "Queens of Society" for the court. Wraps have litho of woman with eagle and star head dress.

1431. *World's Fair.* 1 (1981) to present.   Per year: $30

> Corte Madera, CA: World's Fair, Inc., 1981-. Quarterly. 1.1 issued Feb. 1981.

1432. *World's Fair Electrical Engineering.* Chicago: Fred DeLand. 1 (1893).

> 1.1-5: 452 p., ix-xii, paged continuously, devoted entirely to the WCE. Many illus and diagrams. Special number of, and continued as, *Electrical Engineering* #1290.

1433. *World's Fair Illustrator.* Keene, NH: L. E. Mason. 1 (n.d.).

> 1.1: 46x31. 8 p. Litho of Administration Bldg on front cover.

1434. *World's Fair News.* 1 (1893). $15 - 30

1435. *World's Fair Puck.* Chicago: Puck Building, Jackson Park, °1893 by Keppler & Schwarzmann. 1.1-26 (1893).

29x23½. 2-310 p. Weekly with just 26 issues. No. 1-26: May 1 - Oct. 30, 1893. C.t. The color cartoons are fun and attractive. Each: $25 - 50

1436. *Yankee Doodle at the fair : an historical and artistique memorial, 1893.* Philadelphia: G. Barrie, °1894. 1 (1894).

45x__. Serial with very colorful cover lithos. 1.1 issued Jan. 1894.

1437. *Yerkes Observatory.* Bull. no. 1.

Hale, G. "Organization of the Yerkes Observatory." [Yerkes, Chicago businessman and benefactor, had the new telescope set up at the WCE. It currently is located at Lake Geneva, WI.]

1438. *Young Crusader.* Chicago. Aug. (1893).

1439. *Youth's Companion.* 66 (Jan.-June 1893), 67th year (July-Dec. 1893), 68th year (Jan.-Dec. 1894). Boston.

41½x29½. Ads, articles, illus, fiction, etc., on WCE throughout. Often with pretty multicolor covers. WF "extra number" issued May 4, 1893, after the opening. 36 p., illus.
*P→ $10 - 26

1440. *Youth's Companion New England Edition.*

Same vol designations as *Youth's Companion* above. 41½x29½. Yellow covers with black print.
*

$5 - 16

As an aid to finding further items in this category, consult:

1) Cushing, Helen Grant, and Adah V. Morris. *Nineteenth Century Readers' Guide to Periodical Literature 1890-1899.* 2 vol. New York: The H. W. Wilson Co., 1944. Vol. 1, A-K.

2) Fletcher, William I., and Franklin O. Poole. *Poole's Index to Periodical Literature Supplement 1892-96.* Boston and New York: Houghton, Mifflin and Co. (The Riverside Press), 1897.

3) Titus, Edna Brown, ed. *Union list of serials in libraries of the United States and Canada : third edition ...* New York: The H. W. Wilson co., 1965.

Chapter 8

MAGAZINES - BOUND

1441. *The American Architect and building news.* Boston: Ticknor & co., 35-36 (Jan.-June 1892), 41-42 (July-Dec. 1893).

   33x24. Vol 35: viii, 208 p. and vol 36: viii, 204 p. Also ca. 400 *l* of plates one side -- many of the WCE building and grounds. Red cloth hc, blind stamp, gilt spine.
   ---- Vol. 41: viii, 200 p. and vol 42: viii, 160 p. Also ca. 400 *l* of plates one side -- many of the WCE buildings and grounds. Same binding.
   ☺ (GLD)   Each: $50 - 150

1442. *The Century : illustrated monthly magazine.* New York [and] London: The Century co. (De Vinne Press), [° by The Century Co]. n.s. 22 (May - Oct. 1892), 23 (Nov. 1892 - Apr. 1893), 24 (May - Oct. 1893).

   25x18½. ca.950 p. each. Vol 22, p. 87 contains a reprint of the large format Bird's-Eye View of the WCE by Graham. Many other WCE articles. Various bindings.
   ☺ . (GLD,F,S,A) $15 - 30

1443. *The Cosmopolitan : a monthly illustrated magazine.* New York. 15 (May - Oct. 1893). John Brisben Walker, ed.

   24x18. 768 p. Half leather, marbled edges. Vol 15 has the full issue on the WCE ("World's Fair Number," Sept. 1893) but many editorials and articles are scattered throughout.
   ---- Sept. 1893 (No. 5): Tan wraps with red and dark blue print.
   ---- Sept. 1893 (No. 5): Black cloth hc. Also found in half leather.
   *   (GLD)   Volume 15: $20 - 40
                                                                  Sept. 1893 Issue (No. 5): $15 - 30

1444. *The Cosmopolitan : a monthly illustrated magazine.* New York: 16 (Nov. 1893 - Apr. 1894). John Brisben Walker, ed.

   24x18. 768 p. Vol 16 has the full issue "After the World's Fair" (Dec. 1893) but other articles are scattered throughout.
   ---- Dec. 1893 (No. 2): Tan wraps with red and dark blue print.
   *   ☺ (GLD,S,A)   Volume 16: $20 - 40
                                                                  Dec. 1893 Issue (No. 2): $15 - 30

1445. *The Cosmopolitan : a monthly illustrated magazine.* New York: 1893.

   25x__. 2 numbers in 1 vol: Sept. and Dec. 1893.   (AIC)

1446. *Daily Pioneer Press.* Minneapolis-St. Paul: ____, ____. (April 1893).

   59½x44½. Bound newspapers. Tan cloth hc vol. Contains an abundance of Fair articles.   (S)

1447. *Electrical Engineering.* Chicago: Fred DeLand, 1893.

   Bound vol I: Jan. to June, 1893. Bound vol II: July to Dec., 1893. Many technical articles on the Fair.
   . (LC)

1448. *Engineering : An Illustrated Weekly Journal.* W. H. Maw and J. Dredge, eds. London?: Offices for Advertisements and Publication, ____.

   35x26½ (all issues). (July to Dec. 1890). 776 p.   (S)

35x26½ (all issues). (July to Dec. 1890). 776 p.   (S)

---. ---. (Jan. to June 1891). 774 p.   (S)
---. ---. (July to Dec. 1891). 770 p.   (S)
---. ---. (Jan. to June 1892). 796 p.   (S)
---. ---. (July to Dec. 1892). 806 p.   (S)

---. ---. (Jan. to June 1893). 918 p.   (S)
---. ---. (July to Dec. 1893). 836 p.   (S)
---. ---. (Jan. to June 1894). 862 p.   (S)

1449. *The Graphic : An Illustrated Weekly Newspaper.* Chicago: The Graphic co. 8 (1893), 9 (1893), 10 (1894).

41x29. Vols paged continuously; one vol every 6 months.
---- Red cloth hc: Jan. to June, 1893, and July to Dec., 1893.--(CHx call: F38AP G76 folio)
---- Black cloth spine over marbled paper boards: July 1, 1893, to Jan. 4, 1894.
       ◎ (GLD,CHx)   Per volume: $100 - 200

1450. *Harper's New Monthly Magazine.* European ed. London: James Osgood, 1892. 23 (Dec. 1891 - May 1892).

Early WCE articles.   ◎ (GLD) $15 - 35

1451. *Harper's New Monthly Magazine.* New York: Harper & Bros. Publishers, 1892. 85 (June to Nov. 1892).

25x18. 972 p. Half leather and marbled hc.
---- Vol 86: (Dec. 1892 - May 1893): 25 x 18, 980 p.
       ◎ (GLD)   Each: $15 - 35

1452. *Harper's Weekly : A Journal of Civilization.* New York: ᶜ1893 by Harper & Brothers.

40½x30½. 52 issues from 1893 bound together. 1264 p. Filled with numerous great WCE articles and lithos.   (S)

1453. *Harper's Young People.* New York: Harper & Bros., 1892. 13 (May - Oct. 1892).

28½x21 (text). Weekly magazine for young people. Various articles on WCE.
       ◎ (GLD) $20 - 40

1454. *Harper's Young People.* New York: Harper & Bros., 1893. 14 (Nov. 1892 - Oct. 1893).

29x22. 904 p. Dark green cloth hc; red, black, and gold embossed print and design.
P→   ◎ (GLD) $25 - 45

1455. *The Illustrated American.* New York: Illustrated American Publishing Co., 14 (July - Dec. 1893).

32x25½. 776 p. Many articles and illustrations of the Fair throughout. Ad announces the upcoming special Columbian Exposition Number. For individual issues see #1323.
       ◎ (GLD) $30 - 50

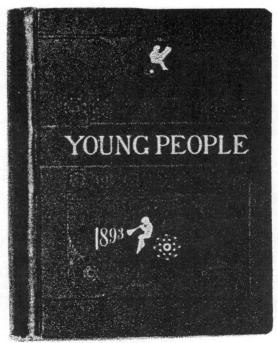

1456. *The Illustrated World's Fair : devoted to the World's fair, art and scientific literature.*   Chicago: The Illustrated World's Fair Publishing Co., 1890-93. Ed. John McGovern.

40x28. Monthly. Copyrighted by general manager, Jewell N. Halligan. C.t.: "Halligan's Illustrated World's Fair : A Pictorial and Literary History of the World's Columbian Exposition." Halligan's Exposition office was in the Northwest Pavilion of the Administration Bldg.
---- Bound: 39½x28. 4 vol in 2. Half leather and brown cloth hc. Vol 1: 404 p., vol 2: 331 p.
---- Bound: 4 vol in 2.
---- Bound: 5 vol in 12. 40x__.
---- Bound: 5 vol in 1.
---- Bound: 4 vol.
Title varies: Nov.1890-Apr.1893: "The Illustrated World's fair." May-Nov. 1893: "Halligan's illustrated World's fair." See also #1324.
* ☻ (LC,CHx,F,S,OSU,nwu)   Each: $125 - 175

1457. *Popular Science Monthly.* New York: D. Appleton and Co., 43 (May - Oct. 1893), 44 (Nov. 1893 - Apr. 1894). William Jay Youmans, ed.

23½x16½. Vol 43: 864 p.; vol 44: 873 p. Black cloth hc, decorative end papers. Several science articles on WCE in each vol.
☻ (GLD)   Each volume: $10 - 30

1458. *St. Nicholas.* New York: Century Co., 1893. 20 (Nov. 1892 - Apr. 1893). Mary Mapes Dodge, ed.

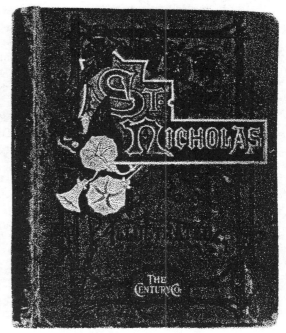

24½x19½. 960 p. Ocher cloth hc, gold and black letters and design, decorative end papers. Popular children's and young folk's magazine. Mary Mapes Dodge authored *Hans Brinker of the Silver Skates.*
*P→   ☻ (GLD) $20 - 45

1459. *Scientific American.* [Weekly]. New York: Munn & Co. 69 (1893), 70 (1894), 71 (1894).

Vol 69: July 1 - Dec. 31, 1893.   (GPL)
Vol 70 and 71: 41½x30. 2 vol in 1. Each vol is paged continuously. Half black leather over black paper covered boards, gilt spine print. Jan. - Dec. 1894.   (TD)   52 issues: $200

1460. *Scientific American Supplement.* New York: Munn & Co., 1893. 36 (July - Dec. 1893).

41½x30. 428 p. starting at p. 14,584. Black cloth hc, gold letters. Detailed articles on technology at the Fair including the "Movable Sidewalk" at the Pier (5¢ a ride); see also #805. Wonderful etched illus.
☻ (GLD) $90 - 150

1461. *Scribner's Magazine.* New York: Charles Scribner's Sons, 1893. 12 (July - Dec. 1892), 14 (July - Dec. 1893).

Vol 12: 24x18. 792 p.; vol 14: 24x18. 792 p. Various colored cloth bindings, gold print.
☻ (GLD) $20 - 35

1462. *World's Columbian Exposition Illustrated : devoted to the interests of the Columbian Exposition, art and literature.* Chicago: James B. Campbell, 1891-94 [copyrighted by James B. Campbell ᶜ1891, ᶜ1892, or ᶜ1893].

38½x28. 36 issues (1 issue per month from Feb. 1891 to Feb. 1894 except no issue for Sept. 1891).
Vol I, no. 1-12 (Feb. 1891 - Feb. 1892): 332 p. total.
Vol II, no. 1-12 (Mar. 1892 - Feb. 1893): 292 p. total.
Vol III, no. 1-12 (Mar. 1893 - Feb. 1894): 348 p. total.
Found bound as 1, 2, 3 or 6 hc books. Various bindings include full leather, half leather, and cloth; with gilt, red dyed, or marbled edges. Title given is caption title which appears at the start of each issue. The wraps of each issue were often beautifully colored; these wraps are frequently missing in the bound books. The 1st book of the various bindings by Campbell may have t.p.: *Volume I. Containing First Twelve* [or Six] *Numbers of The World's Columbian Exposition Illustrated. (February 1891 to February 1892.) The complete volumes will be an authentic Illustrated Encyclopedia of the Worlds* [sic] *Columbian exposition.* Book c.t. such as: *World's Columbian Exposition Illustrated 1492-1892.* Excellent reference as it shows the early construction as well as the final results. For help clarifying continuation issues, see #1429.

*P→ ☺ . (GLD,CHx,LC,NYPL,F,S,   6 issue bound vol: $25 - 50
      OSU,UoC,NL,E,A)   12 issue bound vol: $40 - 80
                            Complete set: $120 - 225

1463. *World's Fair Puck.* Chicago: Keppler & Schwarzmann, 1893, [°1893].

Bound: May 1 (No. 1) to Oct. 30 (No. 26), 1893. 29x23½. 2-310 p. illus (partly colored). An illustrated weekly with just 26 issues. Black half leather over textured cloth hc, all edges marbled, gilt print on spine: "Puck. 1893." On cover: "Puck Building : Jackson Park, Chicago. 10¢." Color political cartoons and lampoons.
---- Bound May 1 to Oct. 30, 1893. 24x23½. Maroon half leather over marbled boards. Decorative end papers same as marbled boards, gilt top edge and spine print.
---- 29x23½. Full brown leather, gilt print.
       ☺ (CHx,LC,HL,NL,S)

1464. *Yankee Doodle at the fair : an historical and artistique memorial, 1893.* Philadelphia: G. Barrie, [°1896].

Vol 1 (no. 1-12): 45x__. 236 p., illus (part color), ports. Vol 1, no. 1 is dated Jan. 1894.   (LC)

1465. *Youth's Companion.* Boston: Perry Mason & Co. 66 (Jan. - Dec. 1893).

40½x29. 672 p. includes the "New England Supplement." Half leather and marbled boards, speckled edges. "Extra Number" issue with color lithographed covers.
      ☺ (GLD,A,TD)   Bound volume: $50 - 100
                               WCE "Extra Number" with covers: $15 - 30

Chapter 9

MUSIC

Dedicated to Mr. Ron Mahoney, Head of Special Collections, California State University - Fresno, who suggested this chapter, and to Dr. Stephen Sheppard who contributed heavily to it from his collection.

Music may also be found in World's Congresses, e.g., under Department of Music and International Eisteddvodd; and in Exposition Publications under Board of Lady Managers which had its own musical programs in the Woman's Building.

1466. *America's National Songs ... : Revised and enlarged.* Philadelphia: Current Publishing Co., 1894.

    20½x14. (16) p. Tan wraps printed in brown. Booklet of patriotic songs. Top of front cover: "Columbian Edition."
    ---- Blue wraps. Different litho.
    P→   ◎ (GLD,S,TD) $10 - 15

1467. Arnold, Ion. *Conover March.* Chicago: Chicago Cottage Organ Co., copyrighted n.d.

    34½x26. 4 *l.* Black lettering and design on beige wraps. Following c.t.: "Dedicated to the officials of the World's Columbian exposition." [Named for Cottage Organ Company's Conover Pianos.]
    P↓   ◎ . (csuf,S,TD) $50

1468. *The Auditorium.* Chicago: Knight, Leonard & Co., n.d.

    19x13. (4) p. "programme for the stage production of Imre Kiralfy's 'America,' Saturday, April 22d, 1893," at the Auditorium. See Kiralfy #1506. Front cover has Auditorium lithograph.
    P↓   ◎ . (GLD,WM) $10 - 20

1469. Baldanza, E. *Grand International World's fair waltz for piano.* Chicago: Published for the Author by The S. Brainard's Sons Co., 1893.

    36x27½. 8 p. Black lettering and design on beige wraps.
    P↓   ◎ . (S) $50

1470. Bilhorn, P. P. *... Bilhorn's Male Chorus : No. 1. Pocket edition.* Chicago: Bilhorn bros., Publishers, n.d.

    14½x10½. (111) p. (96 selections). Black (or teal blue with teal and gilt decorative end papers) hc with silver print. Red dyed edges, rounded corners. At head of title: "Columbian Issue : 1893." T.p. lists morocco, gilt edges as another binding.   ◎ . (GLD,S) $20 - 40

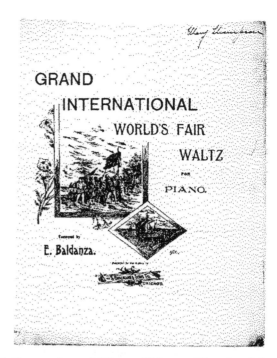

1471. Blanchard, Rufus. *Columbian Memorial Songs, Historical Geography and Maps.* Chicago: Blanchard & Co., 1892.

17½x12. 125 p., frontis, illus, plates, ports. Words, no music. LC microfilm. ⊚ . (CHx,LC,UDe,NL,RPB)

1472. Bloss, Bernhard. *The World's fair grand march.* Chicago: National Music Co., °1889 by National music co.

35½x26½. 4 l. Two "seals" on cover: "1892 World's Exposition Chicago." [Do not confuse with sheet music by Crist #1487.]
⊚ . (csuf,S,TD) $50

1473. Boyden, Emily M. (Blakeslee). *Christo Columbo in Perspective.* Chicago: Emily M. Boyden, °1891.

36x28. 2 *l.* White wraps, black print. After title: "Words and music by Emily M. Boyden." C.t.: "1492--1892. Christo Columbo In Perspective. (Pindaric ode.)" ⊚ . (CHx)

1474. Boyden, Emily M. *World's fair march 1892! For children.* Chicago: Emily M. Boyden, °1889.

36x28. 2 *l.* White wraps, black print. ⊚ . (CHx)

1475. Brainard, Chas. S. *Sounds from St. John.* Chicago: The S. Brainard's Sons Co., n.d.

12½x9. Cream wraps with red print on green tinted landscape background (litho by Orcutt Co.). 12 samples of Brainard music including WF selections. Verso of front wrap: "World's fair greeting!" C.t.
⊚ . (GLD,S) $8 - 18

1476. Brooke, T. P. *Columbian Guards March. Op. 204.* Philadelphia: Harry Coleman, °1893.

34½x27. 5 p. including b/w litho on cream color front cover. On cover: "Dedicated to Col. Rice and The Columbian Guard. The Musical Hit of the World's Fair." Front cover depicts the colonel and the Administration Bldg. ☻ . (CPL,F,S,TD) $30 - 65

1477. Bryant, Francis [J]. *Christofo Columbo (Christopher Columbus) : a Historical Subject Written up To Suit the Times.* New York: M. Witmark & Sons, ᶜ1893 by M. Witmark & Sons.

35x27½. 6 p. Blue lettering and illus on beige wraps. At head of c.t.: "The Hit of the Day! Sung by Leading Comedians." At bottom of 1st p.: "Secure the World's Fair Novelty and Historical Song Sensation ..." ☻ . (S) $50

1478. *Cairo Street Waltz.* Chicago: Signor Guglielmo Ricci, ᶜ1893.

33½x25½. 4 p. not including the covers which are 2 cm wider than the sheets of music. Beautiful color litho cover of Cairo street scene. ☻ . (CHx)

1479. Cappy, J. W. *The Wreck of Battle Creek : On Oct. 20th 1893.* Grand Rapids, MI?: n.p., ᶜ1894 by H. V. Appley.

35½x27½. 8 p. Black print and design on beige wraps. Song about train wreck of people who visited the Fair. ☻ . (S) $50

1480. Chadwick, G[eorge] W[hitefield]. *Columbia : an ode for the dedication of The Columbian Exposition at Chicago, 1892.* N.p.: n.p., 1892-1907.

46x__. Score (103) p. Choruses, Secular (Mixed voices, 8 pts.) with orchestra. (LC)

1481. Chadwick, G[eorge] W[hitefield], and Harriet Monroe. *Ode for the opening of the World's Fair : Held at Chicago, 1892.* Cincinnati: Published by The John Church Co., ᶜ1892 by The John Church Co.

28½x20½. 56 p. Sepia wraps, black print. LC has a signed mss. Music by Chadwick; poem by Harriet Monroe. ☻ . (CPL,CHx,UoC,NL,S)

1482. *Choice vocal and instrumental Gems.* Chicago: Geo. F. Rosche & Co., ᶜ1893 by Geo. F. Rosche.

35½x26½. 4 p. Black print and litho of Administration Bldg on beige wrap.
P→ ☻ . (S) $50

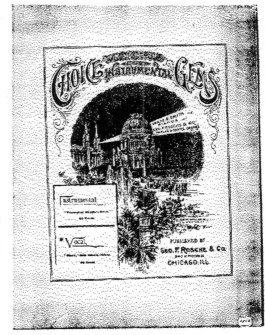

1483. Coles, Abraham. *National hymns used at the meeting of the Columbian Liberty Bell Committee held in Independence Hall, in Philadelphia, Pennsylvania, June 7th, 1893.* Philadelphia: n.p., 1893.

(10) p. [Coles, a religious writer and philosopher, died in 1891.]   (UC)

1484. *Columbian Music Festival May 4, 5, 6 and 7th under the direction of John Philip Sousa.* ____: ____, 1893.

ca. 25x24. Two performances daily at the Mechanics Bldg, 1893.
(GLD) $18 - 35

1485. *Columbus grand march.* Chicago: Gage-Downs Co., n.d.

35½x27½. p. 99-101 (i.e., 3 p.). Black print on cream paper. Composed by Geo. Maywood.   ☺ (TD)

1486. *Concert given in honor of Their Royal Highnesses, The Infanta Eulalia and the Infante Antonio, of Spain.* ... Chicago: S. D. Childs & Co., [1893].

16½x14. 4 p. "programme." Buff stiff paper cover tied with yellow and red rope strings. Caption title. Engraved front covers design printed in brown. The musical director was Theodore Thomas; held in Festival Hall, June 10, 1893. [Thomas was director of music for the Bureau of Music. He formed the World's Columbian Orchestra. A grand array of serious concerts gave way to free and more popular band concerts, like those by John Philip Sousa. Thomas left his post on Aug. 12, 1893.]
☺ . (GLD,TD) $12 - 25

1487. Crist, D. W. *World's Fair Grand March.* Moultrie, OH: D. W. Crist, 1893.

35x27½. 4 *l.* Blue print on cover, red design, and port of Crist. Sheet music. Below title: "For the Piano or Cabinet Organ." Do not confuse with Bloss (#1472).
P→   ☺ (GLD) $30 - 50

1488. *Death in the Flames : or The Terrible World's Fair Calamity.* Chicago: National Music Co., ᶜ1893.

36x26½. 3 *l.* White cover, chocolate print and design. Words by Arthur J. Lamb; music arranged by Otto Mueller. Design shows the Cold Storage Bldg in flames.
☺ . (CHx,S) $60

1489. DeMoss Family. *The Columbian souvenir songs ...* DeMoss Springs, OR: DeMoss Music Publishers, n.d.

30x22½. 161, (1) p. Music to p. 160; index p. 161. T.p. continues: "Composed and sung by the DeMoss family, lyric bards: Official Song-Writers of the World's Columbian Exposition, Chicago, U.S.A., 1893." ☺ . (csuf)

1490. Drayton, Frank. *Columbus, or; World's fair Grand March.* Chicago: National Music Co., ᶜ1892.

35½x26½. 3 *l.* At top of cover: "1492 1892." Fancy design border surrounds c.t.   ☺ . (csuf)

1491. Dreshfield, C. *World's fair waltzes.* New York: Richard A. Saalfield, ᶜ1891 by Richard A. Saalfield.

34½x26½. 6 p. Black print and border design on beige wraps. C.t.

☻ . (S) $50

1492. ...*The Dudley Buck Glee Club of Colorado : The World's Fair 1893.* [Pueblo, CO: Chieftain Job Rooms], n.d.

16½x26. (8) p. Green wraps, black print and design. C.t. At head of title: "Souvenir Program." Repertoire list of the chorus and Colorado ads.
P→   ☻ (GLD) $14 - 32

1493. Everett Piano Co. *World's fair musical souvenir presented by the Everett Piano Co. Boston, Mass.* Chicago-Cincinnati: The John Church Co., n.d.

24½x17. 1 *l*, 66 p. Tan smooth wraps, brown print and design of the Peristyle and statue of the Republic, center printed in light blue. 22 musical numbers. C.t.= t.p.
P→   ☻ (GLD) $15 - 26

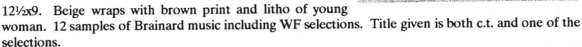

1494. Eversole, R. M. *Columbus Military Schottisch.* Chicago: The S. Brainard's Sons Co., ᶜ1893 by The S. Brainard's Sons Co.

35½x26. 8 p. Beige wrap with rose print and green litho design of Columbus' landing.

☻ . (S) $50

1495. Ferber, Richard. *My Love's Dear Eyes : or Beauty's Eyes.* Chicago: The S. Brainard's Sons Co., n.d.

12½x9. Beige wraps with brown print and litho of young woman. 12 samples of Brainard music including WF selections. Title given is both c.t. and one of the selections.

☻ . (GLD,S) $8 - 18

1496. Glass, T., and G. W. Morse. *Lincoln Park.* Chicago: G. W. Morse, ᶜ1893.

33x25. 5 p. including b/w front cover showing two monuments in the park. On cover after title: "A Solo and Chorus." Words by Morse; music by Glass.   ☻ . (CPL)

1497. Glazounow, Alexander. *Triumphal March : on the occasion of the World's Columbian Exposition in Chicago : 1893 : Composed for grand orchestra with chorus (ad libitum) : op. 40.* Leipzig: M. P. Belaieff (printed by C. G. Röder), 1893.

33x26. 35 p. Litho cover: ornate black print and Columbus design; remainder of design gilt and blue. C.t. ☺ . (NL)

1498. Glück, Adelaide Marcelia. *World's Columbian Exposition Waltz.* Chicago: A. M. Glück & Co., ᶜ1892.

33x26½. 8 p. including front cover. Color litho of gondola and Administration Bldg in the moonlight. Piano solo. At top of front cover: "By Special Permission Respectfully Dedicated to Mrs. Potter Palmer." On cover: "Expressly Composed for the Grand Opening of the World's Fair Chicago." ---- 35½x27½. (3)-8 p. Blue hc with gold print on spine: "World's Columbian Exposition Waltz. Mrs. Potter Palmer." Color lithos on front and back covers. At top of sheet music cover: "Compliments of the Columbian Woolen Mills ... by special permission Respectfully Dedicated to Mrs. Potter Palmer." Mills ad inside front cover. Bound with Nov. 1, 1935 ads from *The Engineer* p. 17-48.
 ☺ . (CHx,NL,S) $100

1499. *The Hand that Holds the Bread: Progress and Protest in the Gilded Age; Songs from the Civil War to the Columbian Exposition.* New World Records NW 267, ᶜ1978.

31⅓x31⅓. Sound Recording. Tan cover, black ink. 1 disc. 33⅓ rpm stereo, 12 inch. Cincinnati Singers; Earl Rivers, director. Recorded at Corbett Auditorium, U of Cincinnati. Protest songs. Extensive comments on the songs and period by William Brooks. 8 p.   (UMKC,NvSt,AkHx)

1500. Henninges, R. E. ... *Fair Columbia.* Chicago: The Brainard's Sons Co., [ᶜ1891].

35½x27½. 8 p. Blue, rose, and black print and design. At head of c.t.: Dedicated to the World's Columbian Exposition. At Chicago, 1893. A National Hymn."
 ☺ . (S) $50

1501. Herman, Andrew. *Columbian Exposition Waltz, op. 230.* New York: Carl Fischer, ᶜ1893.

36x27½. 5 l. Color litho cover of south lagoon and Machinery Hall. At top of cover: "To Thomas W. Palmer President of the World's Columbian Exposition." ☺ . (csuf)

1502. *Hitchcock's Musical, Pictorial and Descriptive Souvenir of the World's Columbian Exposition in celebration of the discovery of America.* New York: Benjamin W. Hitchcock, Publisher, ᶜ1892; Chicago: National Music Co., n.d.

30½x24. 80 p. White smooth wraps, multicolor litho. C.t.= t.p. Music and text about the WCE, Columbus, etc. ☺ . (CPL,BPL,RPB)

1503. Holst, Eduard. *World's Columbian Exposition March.* Milwaukee: Wm. Rohlfing & Sons, ᶜ1892 by Wm. Rohlfing & Sons.

34½x27. 10 p. plus covers. Multicolor litho of bird's-eye view on front wrap. Red title lettering on black background. Cover described directly below follows front wrap of this version.
---- 34½x27. Same pub info, title, and music except "1893 Welt-Ausstellungs Marsch" below English title. No bird's-eye illus on cover. Gold and black lettering on bright green background.
 ☺ . (S)   ca. $120

1504. Holst, Edward. *Echoes from the White City.* Chicago: The S. Brainard's Sons Co., °1893 by The S. Brainard's Sons Co.

35½x26½. 12 p. Waltz. At top of cover: "Dedicated to H. N. Higginbotham [sic], Esq. : President World's Columbian Exposition." Montage of fairgrounds views in brown ink, green partial border.
⊚ . (S) $50

1505. [Innes, Frederick N.] *Libretto of "War and Peace," words and music with "Day at the World's Fair" synopsis.* Brooklyn, NY: Rich G. Hollaman, Publisher, n.d.

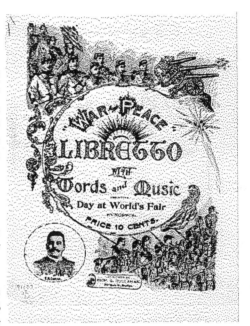

30x23½ (cover). Gray wraps, blue print and design of soldiers and canon circling title, inset of Innes. C.t.: "War and Peace Libretto with Words and Music including Day at World's Fair." Program of Innes' concert at the Fair is the "synopsis." First *l* of the synopsis is a programme description only (no music). Part I: Morning; Part II: Noon and Night.
P→   ⊚ . (CPL)

1506. Kiralfy, Imre. *Imre Kiralfy's grand historical spectacle : America : in four acts, and seventeen scenes.* [Chicago?]: °1893 by Imre Kiralfy.

22x14½. 36 p. Beautiful multicolor litho wraps; George Washington port surrounded by wreath of names of 13 original states and locations of battles of Revolutionary War. Color prints of scenes; one opens up. Abbey, Schoeffel & Grau, proprietors and managers; music by Angelo Venanzi. Written for production at the Auditorium in Chicago during the period of the WCE.
---- Later cover. Rarer. C.t.: "Imre Kiralfy's Gorgeous Spectacle : America : as produced at the Chicago Auditorium 281 times and witnessed by 1.200.000 people : Under the exclusive Direction and Ownership of Abbey, Schoeffel & Grau." Upper left hand corner port of Columbus.
⊚ . (OhHx,BPL,S,WM,TD,L)

Regular cover: $60
Later cover: $75

☞ Examples of Kiralfy's pre-WCE productions: 1) *Columbus and the Discovery of America.* °1892 by J. A. Bailey. Produced in connection with the Barnum & Bailey Greatest Show on Earth. 23x15½. Color litho cover of Columbus landing scene.--(S). 2) *The "Santa Maria," "Nina" and "Pinta" on the unknown seas.* °1891 by Imre Kiralfy. 36x26½. (8) p. Cover lithos of landing of Columbus and the three caravels at sea.--(BPL).

1507. Koelling, Carl. *World's Columbian Exposition Waltz.* Chicago: Clayton F. Summy [and] London: Weekes & co., [°1893].

35½x27. 12 p. All black design and print on beige wraps. C.t. At top of cover: "Respectfully dedicated to Mr. Theodore Thomas, played by the Thomas Orchestra, at the World's Columbian Exposition Concerts." ⊚ . (S) $75
---- Flyer. 18x12½. Folded leaf making (4) p. Litho on cover is miniaturized version of above. Brown print. ⊚ (GLD) $6 -12

1508. Lampard, G. R. *Columbian Exposition March.* Boston: White-Smith Music Publishing Co., [°1891].

35½x26½. 6 p. Green print and design on beige wrap. At top of cover: "To W. W. Kimball Co., Chicago, Ill." P→ ☺.(S) $50 - 60

1509. Lawrence, Frank W. *The Columbian World's Fair Grand March.* East Orange, NJ: Lawrence Brothers, °1893 by F. W. Lawrence.

28x34½. 8 p. Black print and litho of Administration Bldg, Lawrence port, and representation of female Republic with shield and eagle. Below illus: "As played at the 'World's fair.'" P↓ ☺.(S) $50

1510. Little, C. E. *Chicago World's Exposition grand march.* Chicago: The Chicago Music Co., [°1890 by C. E. Little].

36x27. (2)-6 p. does not include wraps. White wraps with bold red, white, and blue stars and stripes shield. WCE bird's-eye view in blue. ☺ (GLD) $30 - 50

1511. Luders, Gustav. *An Afternoon in Midway Plaisance.* Chicago: Henry Detmer Music House, °1893.

36x27½. 12 p. including covers. Multicolor litho cover showing the Midway and Ferris wheel. Below title: "Going to the Fair by Train." ☺.(CHx)

1512. Mathewson, Lillian Beatrice. *Columbian Polka.* Detroit?: n.p., °1893 by Lillian B. Mathewson.

32½x26. 8 p. C.t. Black lettering on beige cover. At head of title: "Dedicated by permission to Mrs. Potter Palmer. President Board of Lady Managers of the World's Columbian Exposition." ☺.(S) $50

1513. May, William. *World's fair galop.* Chicago: National Music co., °1889 by National Music Co.

35½x26½. 6 p. Black lettering and design on beige wraps. ☺.(S) $40

1514. Maywood, Geo. *World's Exposition March.* Chicago: The S. Brainard's Sons co., °1889 by The S. Brainard's Sons Co.

33½x25. 6 p. Red lettering on beige wraps. ⊚ . (S) $50

1515. Mirault, A. ... *Columbus Grand March : written in commemoration of the World's fair.* Boston: Miles and Thompson, ᶜ1892 by A. Mirault.

35x27. Black print on beige wraps. C.t. At head of title: "Respectfully dedicated to Mrs. Potter Palmer, ..." ⊚ . (S)

1516. Melarmet, D. *Columbus. Festival Cantata.* ____ : ____, 1892.

Soprano, alto, tenor, base soli; men's chorus and orchestra. German words by Wm. Keilmann; English translation by E. Buck. (ref)

1517. Mockaye, Steele. *The Great Discovery, or the World Finder.*

A (grand) play in 6 acts about Columbus. [Mockaye was to present this spectacle in the Spectatorium being built just north of Jackson Park near the lake. The costs rose so high that work was stopped and the shell sold to scrap in the hard times of 1893.]

1518. Moelling, Theo. *Columbia Fair : Grand March.* Chicago: The Thompson Music Co., ᶜ1892.

33x26. 7 p. including glossy front cover which has b/w bird's-eye view litho in center. At top of cover: "Dedicated to Mrs. Frederick Leser." ⊚ . (CPL)

1519. *National convention of women's Amateur Musical Clubs : held in Recital Hall - Music Building, World's Columbian exposition.* Chicago: Stromberg, Allen & Co., 1893.

18½x14. 104 p. Deep blue cloth spine and glossy white paper covered boards, blue print. Mrs. Theodore Thomas was chairman of the "Committee on Representation of Women's Amateur Musical Clubs, World's Columbian Exposition, 1893." ⊚ . (CH₃,LC)

1520. *"Old Vienna." Musical Programme. "Alt Wien."* Chicago: Gindele Printing Co., n.d.

21½x12½. (4) p. programme for Saturday, Sept. 16th, 1893, in Old Vienna on the Midway. The performance included the "Columbian March" by conductor C. M. Ziehrer (see #1562). C.t.
P→   ⊚ (GLD,WM) $12 - 25

"OLD VIENNA."
MUSICAL PROGRAMME.

Court Director, C. M. ZIEHRER.

"ALT WIEN."

1521. Ortenstein, Louis. *On the Midway or the Jolly Bum.* Chicago: S. Brainard's Sons Co., 1893.

35½x27½. 5 p. Off-white wraps, black print and design of characters from the Midway.
(F) $45 - 65

1522. Paine, John Knowles. *Columbus March and Hymn.* Boston [and] London: Oliver Ditson co., [ᶜ1892 by Oliver Ditson Co.].

27x18. 9 p. including front wrap. C.t. Ornate black print on buff. Title: "Columbus Hymn." At top of cover: "Chorus edition of the hymn." Cover: "Written by official invitation for the Opening Ceremonies ..." ☺ . (NL)

1523. Philadelphia. Catholic Columbian Celebration, 1892. *Selection of Patriotic and Popular Songs to be Sung by Two Thousand Girls of the Catholic Schools of New York City, on the Occasion of the School and College Parade, Columbian Celebration, October 10th, 1892.* New York, J. H. Tinsley, Printer, 1892?.

14 p.   (UC)

1524. Pratt, S. G. *A Columbian Festival Allegory.* ____: ____, 1892.

Opera.   (ref)

1525. Presto Music Times. *Musical instruments at the World's Columbian Exposition. A review of musical instruments, publications and musical instrument supplies of all kinds exhibited at the World's Columbian exposition ...* Ed. and comp. by the Editorial Staff of The Presto, Frank D. Abbott, managing editor. Chicago: Printed and Published by The Presto Co., ᶜ1895.

27x19½. 310 p., xvi, p. 327 and p. 328, illus fold. plate. Paper covered card wrappers, black design and lettering. T.p. states this work was originally issued in leather, cloth, boards, and paper covers. Excellent description of the music exhibits and musicians at the Fair. [A notable absence was that of Steinway & Sons which refused to exhibit. Music section was "Section I" in the Liberal Arts Bldg.] NL presentation signed by Abbott.
*   ☺ . (csuf,LC,NYPL,NL)

1526. Reed (A.) & Sons, Chicago. *Concerning the official report to the German government upon the musical instrument exhibit at the World's Columbian Exposition, 1893. The Reed system of piano construction ...* [Chicago: 1895].

22x__. (6) p.   (CHx)

1527. *Samples of latest music. Try them on your piano.* Chicago: S. Brainard's Sons Co., [1893?].

18½x13. (14) p. Black print on beige wraps; design is cover of #1532. Samples of Brainard's music including WF selections.   ☺ . (S) $20

1528. Schlathoelter, L. *Columbus March.* St. Louis: Bollman Bros. Music Co. for the author, ᶜ1892.

34½x26½. Tan wraps with black ink. Sheet music.   (UMKC)

1529. Schleiffarth, Geo. *In Cairo Street.* Chicago: The S. Brainard's Sons Co., ᶜ1893.

33x26. 8 p. including glossy front cover. On cover after title: "A characteristic Fantasie for Piano" and "Dedicated to Geo. C. Prussing, Esq., President, And the Managers of Cairo Street."   ☺ . (CPL)

1530. Schleiffarth, Geo. ... *Shoninger Grand March.* Chicago: B. Shoninger Co., ᶜ1890 by the B. Shoninger co.

35½x28. (3)-5 p. plus wraps. Off-white wraps, black print, design with upright piano. C.t. At head of title: "Souvenir of the World's Columbian Exposition. 1893." P→ ☺ . (GLD,F,A,S) $20 - 40

1531. Schleiffarth, Geo. *The Song of the Ferris Wheel.* Chicago: The Chicago Music Co., [1893] copyrighted by The Ferris Wheel Co.

36x28. 6 p. Brown litho of Ferris Wheel on green background; beige border. Publication data on mustard yellow background. Words by M. A. Sturgis; dedicated to Margaret A. Ferris.
☺ . (S) $50

1532. Schleiffarth, Geo. *A trip through the Midway Plaisance : Grand Medley.* Chicago: The S. Brainard's Sons Co., ᶜ1893.

33½x25½. 10 p. including glossy dark buff front cover with dark gray-green and red print. At top of front cover: "Chicago World's Fair 1893." ☺ . (CPL)

1533. Schleiffarth, Geo., and Arthur J. Lamb. *The World's Fair Grenadiers : Marching Song and Drill.* Chicago: National Music Co., ᶜ1893.

35½x26½. 8 p. C.t. Black print and design on beige background. "Duet ad libitum."
☺ . (S) $50

1534. Scobey, Z. D. *World's Columbian Exposition Songs. Inscribed to the Nations.* N.p.: n.p., n.d.

20x13. 4 *l* includes cover, pulp paper. Words for songs, no musical scores. C.t. ☺ . (NYPL)

1535. Sousa, John Philip. *The Liberty Bell march.* [Cincinnati, New York, London]: The John Church Co., ᶜ1893.

35½x27½. Beige wraps, black print; illus of Sousa and Liberty Bell. Score title. ☺ . (S)

1536. Steinert, M[orris]. *Catalogue of the M. Steinert collection of keyed and stringed instruments exhibited as a loan collection at the World's Columbian Exposition by its proprietor M. Steinert ... International Exposition for Music and Theater, Vienna, 1892.* [New Haven, CT: Press of Tuttle, Morehouse & Taylor, 1893].

23x14. 2 *l*, (3)-30 p. includes frontis of M. Steinert. (LC,CHx,NYPL,BM)

1537. Tomlins, William L[awrence], arr. *Children's Souvenir Song Book.* London and New York: Novello, Ewer & co., [°1893 by Novello, Ewer & Co.].

26x20. 116 p. Pretty gray wraps with red and black print, gilt design. [Tomlins was choral director of the WCE.] ☻ . (ref,NL,S) $15 - 35

1538. *Try these pieces on your piano. Ferris Wheel March by Geo. Maywood.* Baltimore, MD: Chas. M. Stieff, [1893].

18½x13. (16) p. including covers. Pulp paper. Excerpts from S. Brainard's sheet music includes "On The Midway." Back cover gives Stieff piano exhibit location in Liberal Arts. C.t. Litho of Ferris Wheel and "compliments of Chas. M. Stieff" on cover. On verso of front cover: "World's fair greeting! From the S. Brainard's sons co. ..."
P↓   ☻ . (GLD,RPB) $10 - 20

1539. *Try this new music on your piano. Select samples of the Latest Music.* Baltimore, MD: Chas. M. Stieff, [1893].

18½x13. (16) p. including covers. Pulp paper. S. Brainard's song excerpts include "The Viking March" (#1542) and "Blacktown and the Fair." With compliments of Chas. M. Stieff on front cover. On verso of front cover: "World's fair greeting! From the S. Brainard's sons co. ..." Stieff ad on back cover.
P↑   ☻ (GLD) $10 - 20

1540. Valisi, G. *Chicago Day Waltz.* Chicago: Valisi Bros. Publishers, °1893.

35½x27½. 4 *l.* Fine color Orcutt Co. litho cover of the Grand Basin and Administration Bldg. On cover: "Chicago Day Waltz : October 9th 1893." Dedicated to Lena Burton Clarke, chairman, Committee on Music, Board of Lady Managers.
P↑   ☻ . (GLD,CHx,csuf,F,S) $35 - 60

1541. Valisi, G. *The Ferris Wheel Waltz.* Chicago: Valisi & Giorgi, ᶜ1893.

> 36x28. 4 *l.* Tan wraps, color tinted litho of Ferris wheel on Midway Plaisance on front cover. Words by Harry C. Clyde; music by G. Valisi. C.t.: "The Ferris Wheel Souvenir. World's Fair 1893. Waltz-Polka."
> ⊚ . (CHx,CPL,csuf,F,NL,A,S) $50 - 80

1542. Verner, M. C. *The Viking March (Captain Andersens Viking Ship from Norway to the World's Fair).* Chicago: S. Brainard's Sons Co., 1893.

> 30½x23½. 3 p. Light green wraps, blue print and a design of the Viking ship at the Fair. For Andersen's book, see #622. (F) $25 - 50

1543. Viets, S. L. *Polka de la Plaisance.* Chicago: National Music Co., ᶜ1893.

> 34x26. 2 *l*?, lacking unknown leaves. Top cover printed in turquoise. Litho of Ferris wheel. Cover illus is same as #1544. ⊚ . (csuf)

1544. Viets, S. L. *Schottische de la Plaisance.* Chicago: National Music Co., ᶜ1893.

> 35x26½. 8 p. Black print and litho of Ferris wheel and Plaisance. Cover illus is same as #1543.
> P→ ⊚ . (S) $50

1545. Vogel, Victor. *Chicago : World's Exposition : Grand March.* Chicago: National Music Co., n.d.; Chicago [and] New York: National Music co., n.d.; N.p.: F. S. Chandler & Co., ᶜ1890.

> Chandler: 34x25½. 3 *l.* Dark cover: black and chocolate brown print and design on brown background.
> ---- Chicago [and] New York: National. 35½x26½. Dark cover as above.
> ---- Chicago: National. 35½x26½. Light cover: black print and design on beige background (or on pink background with beige border).
> All front covers depict "Uncle Sam" and globe flanked by "1492" and "1893." Composed by Vogel; arr. by J. E. Hartel.
> ⊚ . (CHx,CPL,csuf,S) $50

1546. Walsh, Robt. F. ... *In Chicago.* New York: Richard A. Saalfield, ᶜ1892 by R. A. Saalfield.

> 34½x26½. 6 p. Yellow and blue design, blue lettering on beige wraps. At head of title: "The Hit of the Season : Descriptive Topical Song."
> ⊚ . (S) $50

1547. *Wiener Musik : erinnerung an old Vienna in Chicago.* Wien: Verlag der old Vienna co. druck von R. V. Waldheim, 1893.

19x12½. 39 p. Gray stiff smooth wraps with black print and litho of church labeled "Stefansthurm." C.t.= t.p.   ☉ . (WM)

1548. World's Columbian Exposition. Bureau of Music. *Music for the inaugaral* [sic] *exercises of the Columbian exposition.* ... [Chicago]: Published for the Music Bureau, [1892].

27x19½. 30 p. Black print on white wraps. Contents: "The Star Spangled Banner," "The Hallelujah Chorus," "The Heavens are Telling," "The Heavens Resound," "My Country 'Tis of Thee." ---- Also listed: 26x__. 30, 56 p.
☉ . (CHx,A)

1549. World's Columbian Exposition. Bureau of Music. *The Official programmes of exposition concerts. May-October, 1893.* 2 vols. Chicago:[1893].

22½x16. 2 vol unpaged; each vol 5½ cm thick. Half leather with maroon pebbled cloth hc, decorative end papers. Binder's title: "World's Fair Program." No t.p.; title from spine; first *l* is description of the contents and purpose of the 2 vols. Reproductions of concert programs.
☉ . (CHx,LC,NL)

1550. World's Columbian Exposition. Bureau of Music. [*Programmes of concerts.*] *Festival Hall series, no. 1-27 (May 22- Aug. 5, 1893).* Chicago, 1893.

23x15. 27 nos. in 1 vol. Conductor, Theodore Thomas. "Director at piano, Arthur Mees." Binder's title: "Arthur Mees Program. v. 6."

---- Each no. was issued separately; e.g., *Festival Hall : Organ Recital No. 2 by George E. Whiting.* Tuesday, August 1, 1893. 2 *l.*
(UC,S)   Individual issues: $20 - 40

1551. World's Columbian Exposition. Bureau of Music. [*Programmes of concerts.*] *Music Hall series, no. 1-36 (May 2 - Aug. 4, 1893).* Chicago, 1893.

22½x15. 53 nos. in 1 vol. Conductor, Theodore Thomas. "Director at piano, Arthur Mees." Binder's title: "Arthur Mees programs. v. 7."

---- Each no. was issued separately; e.g. *Music Hall series no. 30 : Concert of American Music.* July 7. Folded to make 2 *l* of 22½x15. Program printed on cover and both sides of 2nd *l*. High rag content paper.
---- *Music Hall Series No. 36. The exposition orchestra of 114.* August 4. 2 *l.*
(UC,NL,S,TD)

1552. World's Columbian Exposition. Bureau of Music. [*Programmes of concerts.*] *Popular orchestral series, no. 1-53 (May 3 - Aug. 11, 1893).* Chicago: 1893.

8°. 53 nos. in 1 vol. Conductor, Theodore Thomas. "Director at piano, Arthur Mees." Binder's title: "Arthur Mees programs. v. 8."   (UC)

1553. World's Columbian Exposition. Bureau of Music. *World's Columbian Exposition Musical Hall Series, Nos. 38 and 39 : Stoughton Musical Society of Stoughton, Mass. : Monday, August, 14 and 15 3 o'clock.* ____ : ____, 18__.

22½x15½. (4) p. ⊚ (GLD) $14 - 32

1554. *World's fair ballad collection.* Boston: Oliver Ditson Co., 1892.

33x26. 144 p. 38 ballads. Various bindings: wraps, boards, cloth. Front cover illus of Administration Bldg. Selections are not about the WCE. (E,TD)

1555. *The World's fair collection of patriotic songs and airs of different nations : vocal and instrumental music.* Boston: Oliver Ditson Co., ᶜ1893 by Oliver Ditson co.

26x18. 91 p. Decorative wraps with flags of 14 nations in color.
. (csuf,BPL,S) $100

1556.a. *World's Fair Dance Music Collection.* Boston: [Oliver Ditson Co.], ᶜ1892 by Oliver Ditson Co.

33x26½. 144 p. Green cloth beveled hc, black print, gilt design, gilt edges. 36 dances. C.t.: "World's Fair Dance Collection."
---- Green paper covered boards with illus of Administration Bldg.
---- Also listed: With wraps.
⊚ . (GLD,NL,S) $20 - 50

1556.b. *The World's fair Grand March.* New York: Benjamin W. Hitchcock [and] Chicago: National music co., [ᶜ1890 by Hitchcock and McCargo Publishing Co.].

35½x27½. 3-5 p. not including covers. Buff wraps with black print and Victorian musical arabesque design. Composed by Alberto Himan. Early piece which assumed an 1892 fair.
⊚ (GLD) $20 - 45

1557. *World's Fair march Collection.* Boston: [Oliver Ditson Co.], ᶜ1892 by Oliver Ditson Co.

33x26½. 144 p. Light brown cloth, gilt design, black lettering, beveled edges. Piano scores. Contains 39 marches, none of which relates specifically to the WCE.
---- Tan wraps, blue print with light purple illus of Administration Bldg.
---- Also listed: With boards.
⊚ . (csuf,S) $50

1558. *World's Fair Music Collections.* Boston: O. Ditson Co., n.d.

12x8½. (8) p. including wraps. Buff wraps same as text. Prospectus for Ditson World's Fair music books -- e.g., # 1559. Front wrap litho of Administration Bldg.
⊚ (GLD) $6 - 14

1559. *World's fair piano-music collection.* Boston: O. Ditson Co., 1892.

33x26. 144 p. The cover illus features the Maryland State Bldg. 31 compositions.
---- Same except dark green cloth beveled hc, black and gold embossed print. Cover illus features Delaware State Bldg.
---- Listed with various bindings: wraps, boards, cloth.

(UC,F) $50 - 75

1560. *World's fair song and chorus collection.*   Boston: Oliver Ditson Co., ᶜ1892.

> 33x26½. 144 p. 44 selections, colored t.p. Various bindings. Each song catalogued separately; none of the selections appear to be directly related to the WCE.   (UC,RPB)

1561. *The World's fair songster, a collection of songs and quartettes.*   Chicago: The S. Brainard's Sons Co., ᶜ1892.

> 23x__. 32 p. "Price 10 cents."   (UC,ref)

1562. Ziehrer, C. M. *Columbian March.* *Op. 502.* Chicago: The S. Brainard's Sons Co., ᶜ1893 by Marcus Braun.

> 32½x26. 8 p. Orange print, slate blue illus on front wrap. At head of title: "Respectfully Dedicated to His Excellency, Grover Cleveland. President of the United States." (See also #1520).
>
> ☺ . (S) $50

Chapter 10

VIEW BOOKS

View books contain mostly illustrations -- generally of buildings or scenes on the fairgrounds. Inexpensive and rapid reproduction of photographic images using half-tones had recently been perfected so views were popular and the number of view books issued large. View books were a common item of the day as a means of vicarious travel, as they still are today. Because of the scenic content, their general format was oblong, as in a landscape. Issues ranged from small free advertising booklets to grand folio productions with excellent printing quality.

View books are confusing because of the multiple titles used for same or similar photo sets, the many subscription editions, the similarity in titles for books that are actually different, and the multiple publishers who issued the same book in several locations. Care should be exercised to assure proper identification.

Included here are art reproduction books in the oblong view book format.

1563. *An accurate and authentic World's fair album, containing all the principal buildings.* Chicago: The Unique parlor game co., [°1892].

    25½x30. 12 plates. C.t.   (LC)

1564. [The Allgeier Company]. *Book of World's fair photographs.* [Chicago: The Allgeier co., °1893].

    23x28. 65 photos in portfolio.   (LC)

1565. American Biscuit and Manufacturing Co. *The World's Fair reproduced with a Camera for the Customers of the American Biscuit and Manufacturing Co. ...* Chicago: Globe Litho & Print Co., n.d.

    12½x17. 1 *l*, (4) p. text, 69 *l* b/w views one side. Maize wraps, brown print, blue design. C.t. Top of cover: "Omaha, Neb." in blue.
P→   ⊚ (GLD,CHx) $14 - 26

1566. *Ansichten der Weltausstellung und Midway Plaisance.* Chicago: W. B. Conkey Co., Verleger, 1894 [°1894 by W. B. Conkey co.].

    14½x17. 1 *l*, (3) of port, (189) p. of illus. Half leather over light green cloth hc, silver and red print. The subscription set labeled "Franklin series." German version of *Views of the World's Fair* (#1689) by W. B. Conkey, Co.   ⊚ . (LC,A)

1567. *Architects* [sic] *Sketch of the World's Fair To be held at Chicago : 1893.* Germany: n.p., n.d.

    16x12½. (2), 12 *l* of plates (continuous strip 138 cm folded to form 12 *l*; several open to reveal panoramic view). Hc with rounded edges, floral and swallow design. C.t.   ⊚ . (UDe,AIC)

1568. *Art and Artists of All Nations : a collection of the famous paintings of the world : embracing over four hundred photographic reproductions of great modern masterpieces : including ... art from the principal public galleries, famous private collections, and studios of eminent artists, and one hundred of the most notable paintings at the World's Columbian exposition ... with an introduction by General Lew Wallace ... all painting approved by a committee of selection consisting of Will Carleton ... Henri Giudicelli ... Angelo del Nero ...* Boston: Bay state co. publishers, 1905 [°1894].

28x37. 400 p. illus. Rebound. Edited under the supervision of John Clark Ridpath. The introduction is identical with that of *Famous paintings of the World* (#1609), also published under the title *Gems of Modern Art* (#1615). ☻. (NYPL,OSU)

1569. *Art and Artists of All Nations : Over Four Hundred Photographic Reproductions of Great Paintings embracing masterpieces of modern ... art : Including About One Hundred of the Greatest Paintings Exhibited in the Department of Fine Arts at the World's Columbian Exposition : description of each painting prepared expressly for this work by well-known writers and art critics, among whom are commissioners of fine arts at the World's Columbian exposition : Angelo Del Nero ... Henri Giudicelli ... J. W. Beck ...* Chicago: C. W. Slauson pub. co., 1896; New York: Arkell Weekly Co., 1894; New York: Arkell Weekly Co., 1895; New York: Knight & Brown, 1900 [°1894]; New York: Knight & Brown, 1902 [°1894 by Bryan, Taylor and Co.].

Knight & Brown (1900 and 1902): 28½x37. 400 p. Burgundy leather hc, gilt lettering and design, gilt edges. Format: photo with caption below each.
---- Arkell (1895): 28½x36. Listed with 400 p. and with 400, 16 p.
---- Slauson: 28x36. 400 p.
All edited by John Clark Ridpath.
P→ (KU,NYPL,LC,OhHx,HL,AIC,TD)

1570. *Art and artists of all nations : over four hundred photographic reproductions of great paintings embracing masterpieces of modern ... art : including more than One Hundred and Forty of the Greatest Paintings Exhibited in the Department of Fine Arts at the World's Columbian Exposition : descriptions of each painting prepared expressly for this work by well-known writers and art critics, among whom are commissioners of fine arts at the World's Columbian exposition : Angelo Del Nero ... Henri Giudicelli ... J. W. Beck ...* New York: Bryan, Taylor & Co. [press of J. J. Little & Co.], 1894 °1894.

28x36. 400 p. Brown cloth hc, gilt print. John Clark Ridpath is named in the list of contributors but not as editor.
---- Also listed: Same pub info. Title variant: *... over four hundred celebrated paintings ...*
☻. (LC,ANQ,L)

1571. *Art Folio of World's Columbian Exposition.* Chicago: Rand, McNally & Co., °1892.

27x32. 14 views in portfolio. No t.p. Other author: Rand, McNally & Co. ☻ (CHx,LC,SLP,TD)
---- (LC one-of-a-kind): 29½x25. (2) p. bird's-eye view folded at front + 13 *l.* No t.p. WCE lithos on fine rice paper attached to rectos only, heavy stock, embossed borders around lithos, caption printed below each litho. Each p. bears LC copyright stamp: "Aug 19, 1892." LC call T500.A2 R172.

1572. *Art Gems From the World's Columbian Exposition.* [Chicago]: Chicago Herald, 1893-94.

22x28½. (Gem series; no. 1,2,3.). 3 portfolios of plates; each portfolio contains 12 prints by the Orcutt Co. Subscription ed.; at lower left cover: "Published monthly by the Chicago Herald." Beige wraps with brown tone litho of the Art Bldg; pale green, rust and black print and design. C.t.

⊜ . (GLD,PU,A,AIC)   Each no.: $14 - 22

1573. *Art souvenir : World's Columbian Exposition and views of Chicago.* Chicago: Photo-Mezzo Art Co., ᶜ1892 by R. A. Wallace.

16½x25. 16 *l.* Turquoise wraps, dark blue print and design. Glossy white leaves, black litho on tan background on each verso; explanatory text on facing recto. Part? of a subscription set. ⊜ . (LC)

1574. *Art treasures from the World's fair : Reproductions of the Famous Statuary That Adorned the Buildings : to which are added many of the famous paintings exhibited in the art palace.* Chicago, New York, London, Paris, Berlin: The Werner Co., 1895 [ᶜ1894 by the Werner Co.].

29x35. 4 *l*, (13)-171 p. 1st *l* frontis of artists. T.p. in red and black. Green cloth hc, dark green embossed design and print. Photos with captions one side, pagination is odd number only.

⊜ (GLD,LC,WiHx,TD) $20 - 40

1575. *Beautiful scenes of the White City : a portfolio of original copper-plate half-tone engravings of the World's fair ... A comprehensive review of the ... Midway Plaisance ...* Art Portfolio Series. Chicago: Laird & Lee, 1894.

Subscription set: 28x34. 17 parts. (16) p. per part, illus with descriptive text. C.t.
---- Bound: Farewell ed. Chicago: Laird & Lee, ᶜ1894; New York and Chicago: George F. Cram, ᶜ1894; Woodbridge, CT: RPI, 1989. 27½x32. 1 *l*, (240) p.

(UNe,CHx,LC,SI,NYPL,NYSt,OC,TD)

1576. Belden, Franklin Edson. *Pictorial Wonderland : of Painting and Sculpture From the World's Great Galleries and Famous Private Collections: embracing the Masterpieces of Artists and Sculptors of All Nationalities, medieval and modern, including choice selections from the World's Columbian exhibit ...* Chicago: The Werner Co., 1893 [ᶜ1893 by Franklin Edson Belden].

21½x28. xiii, 504 p. Silver print on black hc. C.t.: "Pictorial Wonderland of Paintings and Sculpture."

⊜ . (A)

1577. *Berühmte Kunstwerke. Eine Sammlung von Lichtdrucken der hervorragendsten Bilder und Statuen aller Kunstrichtungen und aller Nationen mit beschreibendem und fritischem Terte.* Chicago: Rand, McNally & Co., 1895 [ᶜ1894]; Chicago: North American publishing co., [ᶜ1895].

28½x35. 244 p., glossy leaves, reproductions both side. Gilt edges. Reproduction of art in Art Palace. German version of Rand, McNally & Co.'s *Famous Art Reproduced* #1608.   ⊜ . (LC)

1578. Bucklen, H. E. & Co. *Souvenir portfolio of the World's Columbian Exposition.* Chicago: H. E. Bucklen & Co., n.d.

19½x26½. 16 p. C. Graham color illus. Wraps. Contents: Dr. Kings's discoveries, cures, etc.

$15 - 30

1579. Buel, J[ames W[illiam]. ... *The Magic City : a massive portfolio of Original Photographic Views of the Great World's Fair ...* St. Louis [and] Philadelphia: Historical Publishing Co., 1894 [°1893 by H. S. Smith]; St. Louis [and] Philadelphia: Historical Publishing Co., 1894 [°1894 by H. S. Smith]; Woodbridge, CT: RPI, 1981; Woodbridge, CT: RPI, 1989.

29x34½. (292) p. Embossed brown cloth hc loose leaf folder which holds all of the 18 subscription issues -- each held by a string down the fold of the issue signature, gold lettering on front cover. Photos and captions both sides of each leaf. At head of title: "Historical fine art series." Descriptive letterpress.
---- Bound: 29x34½. (292) p. Half leather beveled hc with brown cloth, gilt design and lettering.
---- Bound: Same except beautiful bright red blind stamped cloth hc, gilt print.
---- Bound: Maroon linen, gilt and blind stamped on spine and front cover.
---- Subscription set: 28½x35. (292) p. total. Drab olive-tan wraps, black print. Historical fine arts series. Vol I, No. 1, is dated Jan. 15, 1894. That cover states: "Published Weekly." C.t.: "The Magic City : a portfolio of original photographic views of the great World's fair." Cover of the 1st issue found with and without "From the Book Department of John Wanamaker, Philadelphia," in the lower left corner.

* ☺ . (GLD,csuf,PU,ALB,SI,NYPL,OhHx,NLC,E,D,nwu,LM,UDe,BU,ncsu,NHSt,HL,TU,   Bound: $16 - 35
UMi,NYSt,A,BPL,RPB,OC,WM,WiHx,L)   Subscription set with wraps: $25 - 60

---- Rpt. ed.: David Manning White, ed. New York: Arno Press, A New York Time Co., 1974 [°1894]. 26x31. 290 p. Cloth hc. A book in a set entitled *Popular Culture in America: 1800-1925.*
(UNe,RML,UDe,UMi,BU,AIC,OC,WiHx)

1580. *Buildings and art at the World's fair : containing view of grounds, ... : supplemented with a collection of artotypes of the most famous paintings and statuary exhibited at the World's fair, Chicago, 1893.* Chicago: Rand, McNally Co., 1894 [°1894 by Rand, McNally & Co.].

28x34. 1 *l*, 244 p. Gilt lettering on green and maroon hc, edges gilt. Earlier ed. published in 1894 under the titles: *World's Columbian Exposition Reproduced*, Rand, McNally & Co. (#1719); and *World's Fair Album*, J. Waite (#1722).
---- Also listed: 28x35. (256), 244 p. plates.
---- Also listed: 28x34. 1 *l*, (228), 5-239 p. of illus, 241-244 p.
☺ . (KyU,CHx,LC,RML,A,RPB,WiHx)

1581. *The Buildings of the World's Columbian Exposition.* Published by authority. New York: New York Photogravure Co., 1892; New York, Chicago, London, Paris, Washington: Brentano, °1892.

Brentano: 26½x32. 3 *l*, 12 pl. with tissue guards. Sepia half tone lithos. Paper covered hc, beveled edges. Litho on cover is in shades of browns, tans, black cloth spine, brown end papers.
(PU,NYPL,LC,S,UMi,BPL,AIC,TD) $30 - 65
---- [New York Photogravure co., 1892]. 26x34. 12 plates. C.t. Stiff stock light tan wraps, print and design in shades of browns and tans, no text other than captions for illus. Bound with example of subscription page: "Rand, McNally & Co.'s World's Columbian Exposition Reproduced." LC one-of-a-kind. ?

1582. *Chicago Album.* [Portland, ME: Chisholm Bros.], n.d.

15½x25. 28 *l* of folding plates accordion style. Printed in Germany? Lithographed violet brown on cream, green cloth hc, gold and black design, gold lettering. C.t. One of the <u>many</u> "Chisholm" accordion style folding productions. Common. ☺ . (ᴄᴀᴜf) $8 - 18

1583. *Chicago (album of buildings and scenes in Chicago at time of World's Fair).* N.p.: n.p., n.d.

   1 vol, unpaged. No t.p. Photography copyrighted by S. L. Stein Pub. Co. SLP call: 606 C43123.   (SLP)

1584. *Chicago and the World's Columbian Exposition. Photo-Gravures from Recent Negatives by the Albertype Company.* New York: The Albertype Co., ᶜ1893 by A. Wittemann.

   20x25. 1 *l*, 16 plates on one side of 16 heavy stock sheets, some photos tinted green. Embossed maize stiff wraps, decorative gilt and black end papers. Other Wittemann Albertypes: #1585, #1650, #1670, #1671, #1674, #1695, #1717, #1726.   (CHₓ,LC,NYPL)

1585. *Chicago and the World's fair. Photo-gravures.* New York: The Albertype Co., ᶜ1893 by A. Wittemann.

   31 plates, (1 fold.).   (OhHₓ)

1586. *Chicago Cottage Organ Co. World's Fair Souvenir.* [Chicago]: J. D. Jones, ᶜ1891.

   16x25. 126 *l* printed both sides, ads scattered throughout. Pebble textured deep burgundy wraps, black print.   (CPL,CHₓ) $20 - 30

1587. Chicago Herald and Examiner. *Photographs of the World's Columbian Exposition by W. H. Jackson.* Chicago: n.d.

   49 plates in a portfolio.   (UC)

1588. *Chicago illustrated.* [Chicago: R. F. Griffis, 1892].

   19½x18½. (48) p., illus. String tied wraps depict woman with "I will" on breastplate.   . (BPL)

   ☞ The robust woman was known as "Chicago Personified" (or "Miss Chicago" ?), and was created by Thomas Nast, artist, for WCE promotional purposes. Her image appears on numerous publications; a variety of statues were also created.   P→

1589. Chicago Times. *The Magic city, the Chicago Times World's fair views.* ____: ____, 1__.

   29x__. 125 p.   (CHₓ)

1590. *Chicago Times portfolio of the Midway types.* Chicago: American Eng[raving] co., ᶜ1893.

20x28. 12 pts. in 1 vol, illus. 240 plates on 120 *l*. C.t. Also issued as: *Midway types*; *Portfolio of Midway types*; and *World's Columbian exposition of Midway types*.
(CHx,S,UDe,UoC)

1591. *The Chicago Tribune art supplements in two parts : World's Columbian Exposition.* Chicago: Winters Art Litho Co., n.d.

22x30. 2 parts; 11 *l* each of color lithographs by C. Graham. C.t. Stiff wraps are string tied, color lithographed, paper covered linen. The front cover reads "Part One" or "Part Two." Each plate copyrighted by The Winters Art Litho. Co., Chicago.
P→　　⊚ . (GLD,CPL,CHx,UoC,NL,A,BPL,AIC,WiHx)　　　　Each Part: $20 - 45

1592. *The Chicago Tribune. From Peristyle to Plaisance. Illustrated in Colors by C. Graham. With a Short History of the World's Columbian Exposition, Chicago, 1893.* Chicago: Winters Art Litho Co., ᶜ1893 by The Chicago Tribune.

20x30. 19x29½ (text). Found in 5 pts. Many pretty color lithos by Graham. C.t.= t.p. For related item see #1614.　⊚ . (CHx,NL)

1593. *Chicago Tribune Glimpses of the World's Fair : A Selection of Gems of the White City Seen Through the Tribune's Camera : Main Exhibition Buildings, Grounds, All Foreign Buildings, All State and Territorial Buildings, Statuary, Lagoons, and The Midway Plaisance.* Chicago: Laird & Lee, 1893 [ᶜ1893 by Laird & Lee].

12½x17. (194) p. [1 *l* t.p., 96 *l* with 192 b/w photos]. Same gray wraps printed in red, gray, and black as listed for *Glimpses ... Through a Camera* (#1618). Nearly the same photo set but arranged in different order; same c.t. except this book has above c.t.: "Chicago Tribune Souvenir" in red print. Found with and without the copyright information on the t.p.
---- Also listed: (188) p. of illus.
P→　　⊚ . (GLD,JHU,CHx,NL,A,BPL,GPL,TD)　　　　$12 - 25

1594. *The City of Palaces. A Magnificient Showing of the Wonders of the World's Fair ... the Columbian Exposition again ...* Chicago: W. B. Conkey Co., 1894; Chicago: W. B. Conkey Co., 1895.

28½x34. (160) p. Known by other titles: *Wonders of the World's Fair*, W. B. Conkey Co. (#1698); *Glories of the World's Fair*, "The Fair" of Chicago (#1619); *The Great White City*, The Syndicate Trading Co. (#1622).
(UMC,csuf,CHx,NYPL,S,E,BPL,TD)　　　　$18 - 35

1595. *Columbian Album : Containing Photographic Views of Buildings and Points of Interest about the Grounds of the World's Columbian Exposition.* Chicago and New York: Rand, McNally & co., Publishers, °1893 by Rand, McNally & Co.

22½x28½. (16) p. per part, illus both sides. Tan wraps, black print. "Illustrated Series". Published weekly from Nov. 6, 1893 - Feb. 5, 1894. 14 (15?) part subscription set. "Part Eight," for example, is found in the upper left hand corner of cover. Wraps c.t. Subscription set for *The Columbian exposition album* (#1596). ☺ . (LC,NYPL,NHSt,BPL,UDe)

1596. *The Columbian exposition album : Containing Views of the Grounds, Main and State Buildings, Statuary, Architectural Details, Interiors, Midway Plaisance Scenes, and other Interesting Objects which had place at the World's Columbian Exposition : Chicago, 1893.* Chicago and New York: Rand, McNally & co., Publishers, [°1893 by Rand, McNally & Co.]; Woodbridge, CT: RPI, 1989.

23½x29½. 2 *l*, (220) p., illus both sides. Dark green cloth on beveled boards with gilt print and 2 small designs, decorated end papers, gilt edges. 2 *l* are t.p. and preface.
---- Variant paging: 2 *l* plus (192) or (200) or (220).
---- Variant covers: Beveled cloth hc with gilt print and small design in: 1) dark maroon, 2) dark green, 3) red, 4) red and blue. Non-beveled gilt stamped leather hc in burgundy and brown.
---- Variant sizes: 23x29½ to 25½x28½.
---- 23x28½. Gilt on maroon hc with c.t.: "The Morning Advertiser's Souvenir of The World's Fair."
---- Other editions published 1893-94 with varying titles: *Columbian Exposition Photographed, Columbian Album, The World's fair album,* and *Das Columbische Weltausstellungs-Album.* Some partial editions.
P↓   ☺ . (GLD,csuf,CHx,LC,SI,NYPL,F,OhHx,OSU,MPL,LM,RML,E,SDSHx,LMi,UWy,UMi,NL,A,BPL,AIC,OC,WM,WiHx,TD) $20 - 35

1597. *Columbian exposition and Chicago's Wonders : with Visitors' Guide To theatres panoramas ... : with Indexed Map To streets hotels ... : World's fair buildings : lithographic and photographic views.* Chicago: Exposition Guide Co., °1893 by Joseph N. Parker.

14½x20. 45 p. (i.e., 47; there are two different p. 45 with p. 46 between them), colored illus which are reproductions of water color pictures around WCE grounds and bldgs (costs noted). Deep burgundy covers with gilt print and a gilt illus of Chicago Masonic Temple on back cover. C.t.
---- Bright turquoise wraps. At head of each numbered page: "Columbian visitors' guide."
P↑   ☺ . (GLD,LC,A) $12 - 25

1598. *Columbian Exposition Photographed : consisting of Views of the Buildings, Interiors, Statuary, The Midway Plaisance, Etc.* Chicago and New York: Rand, McNally & Co., Publishers, °1893.

23½x29. Unpaged (8 *l*/part). Light green wraps, black print. Subscription set of at least 19 parts. "Part Thirteen," for example, is found in upper left hand corner of front cover. The back of part 18 lists photos in extra number, 19. C.t.   ☻ . (LC,NYPL)

1599. *The Columbian gallery : a portfolio of photographs from the World's fair : including the chief palaces, interiors, statuary, architectural and scenic groups, characters, typical exhibits, and marvels of the midway plaisance. ...* Chicago: The Werner co., [°1894]; Woodbridge, CT: RPI, 1989.

28x34. (4), (230), 10 p. Paging consists of: (4) p. which are t.p., copyright p., and 2 p. introduction; (230) p. of photos; 10 p. text on the Midway Plaisance. Brown cloth hc, silver print and leaf design. From an exposed spine it appears to be made up of (4) p. plus 15 parts of 16 p. per part. For probable subscription set, see #1656.
---- Light brown hc, chocolate print and design.
---- (256) p. Blue cloth hc decorated with darker and lighter shades of blue and gold lettering. Two muses on the cover, one with a camera on tripod, the other standing in front of the fair bldgs. Contains a 10p. section on the Midway Plaisance. Verbiage and drawings -- not photos -- reprinted from the *Illustrated American*.
---- Spine title: "World's fair views."
---- 28½x36. 16 numbers in hc, bound with wraps. Part 1: (18) p. includes (2) p. t.p. and verso for *The Columbian gallery*; parts 2-15: (16) p. each; part 16: (20) p. C.t.: "The Philadelphia Inquirer : Stoddard art series." °1894.
---- Also listed: Werner, 1893. ?
    ☻ . (UND,UMKC,KyU,CHx,SI,NYPL,F,S,OhHx,TnSt,NLC,U,UMi,NYSt,HL,UoC,NL,A,BPL,nwu,WM,AIC,OC,TD) $20 - 30

1600. *The Columbian Portfolio of photographs of the World's fair.* N.p.: n.p., n.d.; [Cincinnati: The Jones Bros. Pub. Co., °1893]. LC copyright stamp: Feb 5, 1894.

32x23. (48) p. Red cloth hc portfolio with flaps, gilt print and design. C.t. 24 loose sepia plates (22½x30½) one side with description on reverse. Note: cover and plate orientation are different.
    ☻ . (GLD,csuf,KyU,LC,NYPL,S,OhHx,nwu,NeHx,UMi,NYSt,BPL,TD) $12 - 24

1601. *The Columbian Souvenir Album : A Memento of the World's Fair.* Boston: The Art Souvenir Co., [°1892 by E. E. Gay.]

14x21½. 52 *l*. White and blue (or all white) cloth hc, gold print and design, gilt edges. Glossy paper with 50 *l* photos one side.
P→   ☻ . (GLD,LC,NYPL,E,BPL,TD) $15 - 25

1602. *Die Columbische gallerie. Ein portfolio photographischer ansichten der Weltausstellung, umfassend die hervorragendsten Palaste, inneren Ausstattungen, Sculpturen, architectonische und scenische Gruppen, Charactere, typische Gegenstände und die erstaunlichen Sehenswürdigkeiten der Midway Plaisance, nebst treffenden getreuen Beschreibungen zu jeder Abbildung.* Chicago: Werner Co., [1894].

28x33. 1 (unpaged) vol of illus. 129 *l*. German version of *The Columbian gallery* (#1599).

1603. *Das Columbische Weltausstellungs-album : Enthaltend Abbildungen des Platzes, der Haupt- und Staats-Gebäude, Statuen, architektonische Details, innere Ansichten, Scenen der Midway Plaisance und andere interessante Gegenstände, dargestellt auf der Columbischen Weltausstellungen, Chicago, 1893.* Chicago und New York: Rand, McNally & Co., Verleger, [ᶜ1893]; Milwaukee, WI: Germania Pub. Co., [1894 ᶜ1893].

20x30. 2 *l*, 108 *l* of plates both sides of glossy sheets. Dark green cloth on beveled boards, gilt print and 2 small cover designs, decorative gilt end papers, all edges gilt. Captions in old German script. C.t.: "Die Illustrirte Welt-Ausstellung Chicago, 1893." German version of *Columbian Exposition Album.* (#1596).
---- Also listed: Rand. 23x29. ca. 125 p.
---- Also listed: Rand. 2 *l*, (220) p. of illus.
           ☺ . (CHx,LC,UoC)

1604. Crane, W[alter] H. ... *Midway Plaisance : sketches by W. H. Crane.* [Chicago: The Orcutt Co., 1893].

21½x29½. 14 *l* of very colorful plates. Decorative gray stiff wraps, tie. C.t. On some copies at head of title: "Printed at the World's Columbian Exposition." ☺ . (csuf,CHx,S,UDe,TD)

☞ Walter H. Crane was a noted English illustrator; do not confuse with William Hunter Crane, born the same year, who was confidant of T. Roosevelt.

1605. *The dream city : A Portfolio of Photographic Views of the World's Columbian Exposition.* ... St. Louis: N. D. Thompson Publishing co., 1893-94 [ᶜ1893 by N. D. Thompson Publishing co.]; Woodbridge, CT: RPI, 1989.

Subscription set: 27½x35. 272 photos on 138 glossy *l*. 8 *l* per issue except no. 1 which has 10 *l* (1 *l* t.p., 1 *l* introduction, 8 *l* illus). Light blue gray decorative paper cover; at top: "Educational Art Series." Weekly subscription of 17 issues (Nov. 9, 1893 to Feb. 29, 1894); meant to be bound, hence various bindings.
---- Bound: Variety of covers, including different color cloths and leather. Cover decoration and title vary also. Found with c.t.: 1) "The Dream City," and 2) "The Dream City : Illustrated World's Columbian Exposition." The bound version is much more prevalent than the complete set of subscription issues. Common but useful.
---- Folio boxes: 1) green box; 2) gilt print and light blue vines on light brown tie folio cover box. Both with c.t.: "The Dream City."
---- Loose binder vol: Blue-black cloth hc loose leaf binder with each subscription section held in place with a metal bar. Cover reads: "The Boston Post World's Fair Art Series."
*   ☺ (GLD,UWa,CHx,SI,NYPL,F,NLC,OSU,StLa,nwu,E,LM,UDe,USD,ncsu,LaMus,SLP,   Bound: $15 - 30
             NHSt,HL,TU,UMi,NYSt,UoC,NL,A,BPL,RPB,WM,AIC,OC,WiHx,TD,L)   Subscription set: $25 - 60

1606. *1893 : Worlds* [sic] *Columbian Exposition.* N.p.: n.p., n.d.

13x20. 27 p. Wraps: orange print on green background with light orange borders at top and bottom edges, rose color burst design left upper corner with "1893." C.t. Examples of contents: Electrical Bldg p. 2 with description p. 3; Machinery Hall p. 27 with description p. 26. ☺ . (A,TD)

1607. *The Exposition publishing company's art folio (No. 1) : of the World's Columbian Exposition : illustrations from authentic and official sources ...* Chicago: The Exposition publishing co., [1892].

19½x26½. 1st ("Grounds and Principal Buildings") in a planned series of 4 issues. Red, white, and blue stars and stripes ribbon binds celluloid flexible wraps; black litho.   (S)

1608. *Famous Art Reproduced : being a collection of artotype engravings of noted modern paintings and sculptures of all schools and from all nations, with descriptive and critical text.* Chicago: Rand, McNally & Co., 1895 ᶜ1894 [and] ᶜ1895.

28½x34½. 244 p., illus. LC microfilm. LC lists author as Rand, McNally & Co.   (LC)

1609. *Famous paintings of the World : a collection of photographic reproductions of great modern masterpieces embracing three hundred and twenty of the finest specimens of ... art, from the principal public galleries, famous private collections, and studios of eminent artists including one hundred of the most notable paintings at the World's Columbian exposition exemplifying the most attractive, interesting, pure and inspiring qualities of contemporaneous art : with an introduction by General Lew Wallace ... : All pictures approved by a committee of selection, consisting of Will Carlton ... Horace Bradley ... Angelo Del Nero : under the editorial supervision of John Clark Ridpath ...* New York: Fine Art Publishing Co., 1894 [ᶜ1894]; New York: Fine Art Publishing Co., 1895.

1894: 28x35½. 4 *l*, 323 p. Pinkish tan wraps, black print, glossy pages with illus both sides, marbled edges. "Fine Art Series" on top of each wrap. The illustrated wraps from each of the 20 weekly subscription issues were designed by Dan Beard. Those paintings depicted which were exhibited at the WCE are so marked beneath the lower right corner of the picture.
---- 1894: Wraps included in the bound vol.
---- 1895: 28x36. 5 *l*, 5-323 p. Also published with title: *Gems of Modern Art* (see #1615).
⊚ (GLD,LC,NYPL,HL,TU,RPB,OC)   Subscription set: $25 - 50

1610. *Fine arts at the World's Columbian exposition : being a collection of artotypes of the most famous paintings and statuary exhibited at the World's Fair, Chicago, 1893.* Chicago: Rand, McNally & Co., 1894 [ᶜ1894 by Rand, McNally & Co.]; Cincinnati: Turner, Looker Co., 1895 [ᶜ1894].

28x34 to 29x35½. 244 p. Format: photos both sides with caption below each. Found with cloth (blue or half beige and half turquoise) and half morocco hc. Gilt print, with and without beveled boards, with and without gilt edges. Cover titles: 1) "Famous Art Reproduced" and 2) "Fine Arts at the World's Columbian Exposition."
---- Bound: Listed with 160 p. Partial subscription set. ?
---- Subscription set: "University series." 10 parts.
⊚ . (GLD,CHx,LC,S,E,RML,A,AIC,WiHx) $22 - 42

1611. Flower, Henry E. *Glimpses of the World's Fair : an interesting collection of instantaneous views of the grounds, buildings and accessories of the World's Columbian exposition. From recent photographs.* Philadelphia: Engraved and Printed by the Levytype Co. for Henry E. Flower, [ᶜ1893].

11½x14½. 1 *l*, 31 *l* of plates (b/w photos on one side of glossy sheets with location caption below photo, no other text). Tan stiff wraps, fine black print and design.   ⊚ . (LC,S)

1612. *Fotografiska vyer af Verldsutställningen och Midway Plaisance : ...* Chicago: Svenska Tribunen, [1894]; Chicago: Swedish Book Co., [ᶜ1894].

15½x25. 1 *l*, 226 p., color frontis. Red cloth hc, gold lettering, silver and black design. Swedish Book Co.: C.t.= t.p. T.p. in red and black. Swedish version of #1647.

P→   ☺ . (csuf,CPL,LC,CoU,nwu)

1613. *Fotografiske Billeder af Verdensudstillingen og Midway Plaisance. Hovedbygninger, Portaler, Udenlandske, Stats- og Territorial-Bygninger, ...* Chicago: N. Juul & Co., 1894.

16x24. 226 p. colored frontis, illus, ports. Translates: Photographic Pictures of the World's exposition and Midway Plaisance. Official bldgs, ornamental gate-way, foreign, state and territorial bldgs, etc. Danish version of #1647.   ☺ . (LC)

1614. *From Peristyle to Plaisance: or The White City Picturesque : painted in water colors by C. Graham. Together with a Brief Illustrated History of the World's Columbian Exposition : Chicago, 1893.* [Chicago: Winters Art Litho Co., 1893].

23x30½. (62) p. text plus 38 plates with one double size bird's-eye view color illus by Charles Graham and text on WF. Brown leather over brown cloth hc. For related item see Chicago Tribune (#1592). ---- Subscription set: Pictorial Art Series. 22x30. 8 nos. in vol 1. Published weekly from Mar. 19 to Apr. 7, 1894. C.t.: World's Fair in Water Colors : From Peristyle to Plaisance : Illustrated in colors by C. Graham. Also Embracing Reproductions in Fac-Simile Colors of the Prize Paintings of the Art Gallery : With a Short History of the World's Columbian Exposition." At bottom of front wrap: "Published by The Winters Art Litho Co., Chicago, Ills., and Springfield, Ohio."
☺ . (GLD,BPL,S) $60 - 120

1615. *Gems of Modern Art : A collection of photographic reproductions of great modern paintings : embracing more than three hundred and forty of the finest specimens of art, from the principal public galleries, famous private collections, and studios of eminent artists in Europe and America including nearly one hundred of the most notable paintings at the World's Columbian exposition with an introduction by General Lew Wallace ... : descriptions of paintings by Will Carlton ... John Clark Ridpath ... Angelo Del Nero ...* New York: Bryan, Taylor & Co., 1894 [°1894].

27½x36. 6 *l*, 5-324 p., frontis of "The Hungry Quartet" (4 cats). Rebound hc. Format: a vertical or horizontal b/w photo each page with caption beneath. Also published under the title: *Famous Painting of the World* (#1609). Same introduction as in *Art and Artists of All Nations* (#1568).   ☺ (LC)

1616. *Gems of the World's fair and Midway Plaisance : With Accurate and Valuable Descriptions of Each, forming a Complete Panorama of the Most Magnificent Exhibition of Ancient or Modern Times, the whole comprising the World's fair in picture and story.* Philadelphia: Historical publishing co., [°1894].

28½x34½. (146) p., illus, port.   ☺ . (BPL)

1617. *Gems of the World's fair. Over 200 photographic views. A collection of Famous Scenes from the World's Columbian Exposition, from Instantaneous Photographs, ...* Springfield, OH: Mast, Crowell & Kirkpatrick, 1893 [°1893 by Mast, Crowell & Kirkpatrick].

12½x17½. (1) p., 262 p. (chiefly plates). Yellow wraps, red lettering. "Farm and Fireside Library. November, 1893. ... Double Number 105."
---- "Subscription double number 105": Same pub info. 26½x34. 30 *l* with photos + 6 *l* paged 19-21 carrying descriptions of photos. Rose pulp wraps, black print. Note the size differences. ?
☺ . (csuf,LC,A)

1618. *Glimpses of the World's Fair : A Selection of Gems of the White City seen Through a Camera : Main Exhibition Buildings, Grounds, All Foreign Buildings, All State and Territorial Buildings, Statuary, Lagoons and The Midway Plaisance.* Chicago: Laird & Lee, 1893 [ᶜ1893 by Laird & Lee]; Chicago: A. H. Abbott & Co. (tipped in sticker on title page), n.d.

Laird & Lee: 13x18. 1 *l* (t.p.) + 191 b/w photos on 96 *l*. Chocolate brown cloth hc, gilt print and design. On verso of t.p.: "All pictures in this book were taken with a No. 4 Kodak ..."
---- Laird & Lee: Blue (or light red) cloth hc with gilt print and design.
---- Abbott: 13x18. 1 *l* (t.p.) + 192 b/w photos on 96 *l*. Blue cloth hc with gold lettering and design. Neither Cramer plate nor Kodak message appear on verso of t.p. Order of photos is different from Laird version; photo quality is poorer than Laird version.
---- Laird & Lee (softbound): 12½x17½. 1 *l* (t.p.) + 190 b/w photos on 95 *l*, bound with illus. Gray (or yellow) wraps printed in red, gray, and black. On t.p. verso: "All the engravings in this book were made from negatives on the celebrated Cramer plates ..."
---- Also listed: Laird and Lee, 1890. ?
---- Also listed: 7th ed.
---- 12½x17½. At top of cover: "Tenth Edition : 150th Thousand."
---- German ed. See *Moment-Aufnahmen* #1635.
P↓,P↓   ☺ . (GLD,csuf,ALB,CHx,NYPL,UNLV,WyMus,UMi,NHSt,HL,E,UoC,A,BPL,RPB,AIC,OC,WiHx,TD) $12 - 25

1619. *The Glories of the World's Fair : only the most magnificent views.* Chicago: Published by The Fair, [1894].

28x34. Brown pulp wrap, black print. 10 pt. subscription set [ᶜ1894 by W. B. Conkey Co.]. C.t. See *The City of Palaces* #1594.   (LC,CHx)

1620. *The Government collection of original views of the World's Columbian Exposition secured by the official government photographer for preservation in the Archives at Washington. ...* Introduction by Halsey C. Ives. Special limited ed. deLuxe from the Original Plates. Chicago: Preston Publishing Co., 1895; Woodbridge, CT: RPI, 1989.

27½x33½. 3 *l*, (272) p. of illus.   ☺ . (UMKC,CHx,LC,SI)

1621. Graham, C. *The World's Fair in Water Colors.* Philadelphia: Sessler and Dungan Publishers, n.d.; Springfield, OH: Mast, Crowell & Kirkpatrick, ᶜ1893 by Mast, Crowell & Kirkpatrick.

30½x24. Folding folio with blue cloth spine and corners. Paper covered hc with decorative embossed pattern, gold print. Contains 23 loose color lithographs by Graham and a (4) p. description of the WCE and the lithographs. These are held in the folio by three light blue folding cloth flaps. [CHx has several of the original Graham watercolor paintings of the Fair.] Note: #1614 subscription set by the same title has a different publisher.

         ☺ . (GLD,csuf,UNe,NYPL,BPL,TD) $40 - 85

1622. *The Great White City: A Picture Gallery of the World's Fair and Midway Plaisance.* N.p.: Syndicate trading co., n.d. [LC copyright stamp: Apr 10, 1894].

27½x33½. Subscription set of 10 parts, 8 *l* per part. Burnt orange wraps. C.t.   (LC,S,BPL)

1623. Halligan, Jewell N. *Halligan's illustrated world. A portfolio of photographic views of the World's Columbian Exposition carefully selected by Halligan's Illustrated World's Fair ... with an introductory article and descriptions by John McGovern, Editor.* London, New York, Chicago, Paris, Berlin: The Jewell N. Halligan co., publishers, 1894 [ᶜ1894 by Jewell N. Halligan]; Woodbridge, CT: RPI, 1989.

Bound: 28x40. (320) p. text and illus both sides. Half leather over navy blue cloth beveled hc, gilt print and Halligan's logo, marbled edges. C.t.: "Halligan's Illustrated World's Fair : a Pictorial Literary History of the World's Columbian Exposition : portfolio edition."
---- Also listed: 8, (320) p.
---- Subscription ed.: 26½x40. World's Fair Series. 20 pts; (16) p. published weekly. "Published in the English, French, German and Spanish languages."

         ☺ . (GLD,PU,UNe,SI,NYPL,USD,TU,UMi,NL,A,nwu,AIC,OC,WiHx)   Bound: $50 - 125

1624. *Halligan's Illustrierte Welt. Photographische Ansichten der Columbischen Weltausstellung : Sorgfählt von Halligan's Illustrated World's Fair ... Mit Einführung und Beschreibungen von dem Redakteur: John McGovern, ...* Chicago. New York. Berlin. London. Paris: The Jewell N. Halligan co., 1894.

Bound: 26½x40. ca. (324) p., illus, plates. Brown leather hc, gold lettering, gilt edges. In German. Front cover: "Ansichten der Columbischen Welt-Ausstellung." Format: a picture on each side of leaf with caption to the side. Content: preparation, construction, and final results of WCE bldgs and exhibits.
---- Subscription set: 27x39½. 20 parts. Wraps with black print.

         ☺ . (UMKC,csuf,CPL)

1625. *The illustrated World's Columbian Exposition souvenir.* New York: Commercial Travelers Home Association of America, [1892].

25½x30½. 14 *l*, plates, b/w lithographs on one side. Tan string tied stiff wraps, red and black print and design. C.t.
---- 13 *l* of plates. Light green stiff covers.
P→   ☺ (GLD,S) $15 - 30

1626. *In Remembrance of the World's Columbian Exposition, Chicago.* [Chicago and Frankfurt a/M.: American Souvenir & Advertising Co., Hergert & Frey], n.d.

16x24½. Plates folding accordion style to form 21 *l*, the 1st attached to cover. Plate captions in English, German, French, and Spanish. Gray-brown lithographs on coated paper; red cloth hc, gold lettering and design. C.t. Same format as Chisholm Bros. (#?). Found with various covers. Common.

---- Also: *In Remembrance \ Zum Andenken \ En memorie \ of the World's Columbian Exposition.* 16x24½. Hc. C.t. [New York and Boston: American Souvenir & Advertising Co., Hergert & Frey, 1893]. 1 sheet fold. to 14 plates. "Made in Germany."

---- 13x15½. Plates on strip 12x168 folded to form 12 leaves.

◎ . (KU,csuf,CHx,NYPL,S,HL,A,BPL,nwu,L) $8 - 18

1627. [Jackson, William Henry]. *Jackson's Famous Pictures of the World's Fair.* *"The White Flower of Perfect Architecture."* [Chicago: The White City Art Co., 1895].

Bound (vertical): 45x36. 4 *l*, 80 plates with full page photos on one side, heavy stock with tissue guard between each leaf.

---- Bound (oblong): 36x46. Same plates but in different order.

---- Subscription set: Chicago: The White City Art co., [1895]. 45x36½. Beige wraps with navy print. On cover: "Educational Fine Art Series." Vol IV, Serial No. 7-12, May-Dec. 1895. C.t.: "Jackson's famous pictures." Each folio in the series contains 12 plates, 30½x35½; full set contains 80. 7 numbers of 12 plates per number with the exception of no. 7 which has 8 plates plus text.

◎ . (csuf,CHx,NYPL,nwu,UMi,UoC,AIC,RRD,WiHx,TD)

☞ Jackson, a prolific writer and photographer of the Rocky Mountains, lived to be 99.

1628. [Jackson, William Henry]. *The White City : (As it Was).* Chicago and Denver: The White City Art Co., ᶜ1894.

Bound: 35½x45½. 8 *l* includes t.p. are interspersed with 80 *l* of plates. All are printed one side, heavy stock. Heavily embossed full leather hc, bold gilt letters, gilt edges. All photos by W. H. Jackson; descriptive text by Stanley Wood. T.p. in red and black. Caption title on first page of text: "The White City : (As it Was) : the story of the World's Columbian Exposition." Printed by The Lakeside Press, R. R. Donnelley & sons, co. Fine craftsmanship.

---- Half leather over marbled paper covered boards, gilt print.

---- Also listed: 35x47. (9) p., 80 plates.

---- Subscription set: 36x48. 20 pts. "Educational Fine Art Series." Vol I, ser. 1-20. Some subscription pts. have a theme printed on wraps, e.g., Part 11: "Electric Number"; Part 15: "Agricultural Number."

---- Also listed: Subscription set: 39x57. (2)-4, (5) *l*, 80 plates. 20 pts. "Educational Fine Art Series." Vol I, ser. 1-20.

---- Also listed: Subscription set: Educational Fine Art Series. Vol IV. 1895. ?

---- Another ed. was published with title: *Jackson's famous pictures of the World's fair* (#1627). Note difference in orientation.

◎ . (GLD,csuf,PU,JHU,CHx,LC,NYPL,S,OhHx,OSU,nwu,TU,UMi,NYSt,NL,RPB,AIC,OC,RRD,WiHx)   Bound: $45 - 75

1629. [Jackson, William Henry]. *The White City (as it was) : the story of the World's Columbian exposition illustrated by a series of eighty perfect pictures by W. H. Jackson.* Directors Edition. Chicago: The White City Art co., Publishers, 1894 [ᶜ1894 by The White City Art co.].

35x44½. 1 *l* frontis, 1 *l* t.p., (1) p. preface, (81) p. of plates, (1), (1)-5 p. Frontis illus of statue of Columbus. White cloth hc, bold gilt script c.t.: "The White City." Tissue page tipped in ahead of frontis states in red print: "Directors Edition. Number ___ : Limited to 2,000 copies." CHx has no. 289, GLD no. 301.

◎ (GLD,UMSL,CHx) $100 - 250

1630. Martin, J. F. *Martin's World's fair album-atlas and family souvenir.* ... Chicago: National Book & Picture Co., 1893 [°1892 by J. F. Martin]; Chicago: C. Ropp & Sons, [°1892 by J. F. Martin]; Chicago: P. W. Rowe, 1894 [°1892 by J. F. Martin].

Ropp [°1892]: 20x28. (306) p. Red cloth beveled hc with gilt print; embossed design in gilt and black; decorative end papers, all edges gilt (or dark green beveled hc with gilt print, embossed design in gilt and black, decorative end papers, all edges speckled; or brown linen hc stamped in gilt and black).

---- Ropp [°1892]: 20x29. (288) p. Red cloth. Page variant of above entry.

---- National: 20x28. (288) p. illus includes ports and colored maps. Gilt print on brown cloth hc (or gilt print, black and gilt design on gray cloth hc).

---- Rowe: 20x26½. (284) p. Green cloth hc, gilt print, gilt edge.

P→ ◎ . (GLD,csuf,CHx,LC,NYPL,S,UDe,SLP,HL,UMi,UoC,A,BPL,OC,WiHx,TD) $15 - 30

1631. Massey, W[alter] E[dward] H[art]. *The World's fair through a camera : and how I made my pictures.* Toronto: W. Briggs; Montreal: C. W. Coates; Halifax: S. F. Huestis, 1894; Ottawa: CIHM, 1985.

13x__. 12 p., 40 *l* of plates. Microfiche (49 frames). Filmed from a copy held by the Metropolitan Toronto Library, Fine Arts Dept. Introduction by W. H. Withrow. (mcg,NLC)

1632. *Memories of the fair from note book and camera : a concise pictorial and descriptive history of the World's Columbian exposition.* 5 vol. Chicago: Premium art co., °1894.

27½x35. Illus, ports. (LC)

1633. *The Midway plaisance of the World's Fair.* New York and Chicago: A. Wittemann (The Albertype co.), °1892 by A. Wittemann; New York and Chicago: A. Wittemann (The Albertype co.), °1893 by A. Wittemann.

°1892: 11x18. 13 *l*, 12 being photo-gravures one side. Red stiff wraps, wood-grain pattern, embossed gold letters.

---- °1893: Red smooth stiff wraps, embossed gilt letters, string tied. Very attractive.

◎ (GLD,S,TD) $10 - 22

1634. *Midway Types : A Book of Illustrated Lessons About : The People of the Midway Plaisance : World's fair 1893.* Chicago: The American Engraving Co., 1894 °1894 by The American Engraving Co.

20x28. (226?) p., illus. Black cloth hc, gilt print, red dyed edges.
---- Found with c.t.: "World's Fair 1893 : Types & Scenes from the Midway Plaisance." (226) p. Gilt print on red cloth hc.
---- 19½x27½. 116 *l*, plates. Brown cloth hc, gilt lettering and design.
---- Also issued as: *Chicago Times portfolio of the Midway Types*; *Portfolio of Midway types*; and *World's Columbian exposition portfolio of Midway types*.
⊘ . (csuf,CPL,CHx,S,UoC,NL,A)

1635. *Moment-Aufnahmen der Weltausstellung : Eine Auswahl der Schönsten Ansichten der Weissen Stadt : ...* Chicago: Laird & Lee, Herausgeber, ᶜ1893 by Laird & Lee.

13x18. 97 *l*. German version of *Glimpses of the World's Fair* #1618.
⊘ . (csuf,nwu,TD) $25

1636. *Monarch Book Company's Illustrated World's fair memorial souvenir ...* Chicago Philadelphia Stockton: Monarch Book Co., n.d.

18x25. 16 *l*. (CHx)

1637. *Neely's photographs : Chicago Minneapolis St. Paul.* New York-Chicago-London: F. T. Neely, [ca. 1895].

14½x21. (160) p. of plates on 80 *l*. Dull red cloth hc with silver and black print and design. C.t. Whale back boat, "Columbus," shown as well as Art Institute and Auditorium on Michigan Ave. Curiosity showing Neely items printed after the Fair. ⊘ (GLD) $5 - 15

1638. *Official Photographs of the World's fair and Midway Plaisance with Accurate and Valuable Descriptions of Each ... the whole comprising the World's fair in picture and story.* Philadelphia: World's Fair Art Co., [ᶜ1894 by the World's Fair Art Co.].

28½x34½. (144) p., photographs and captions on both sides. Green cloth (or tan-orange) hc, print and design in black. C.t.: "Gems of the World's Fair and Midway Plaisance." Perhaps related to salesmen's sample #1746 (same c.t. and size).
P→ ⊘ (GLD,L) $20 - 30

1639. *Official portfolio of the World's Columbian Exposition. Illustrated from water colour drawings, by Charles Graham. ...* [Chicago: Winters Art Litho. Co., ᶜ1892]; Chicago: Winters Art Lithographing Co., 1893.

9x13. (30) p. String tied light green wraps, black print, Columbus vignette in gold frame, red ribbon. Color centerfold bird's-eye view of WCE grounds. C.t.: "Portfolio : World's Fair. Chicago, 1893."
⊘ . (OhHx,TD)

1640. *Ohio State Journal Portfolio : Midway types.* Chicago: The American Eng. Co. Publishers and Printers, ᶜ1893 by The American Eng Co.

20½x28. ca. 208 p. Yellow-green wraps with black print and ethnic figures in each letter of the word "types." Same as #1655. ☺.(OhHx)

1641. Olmstead, F[rank] B. *The World's Fair Album : and Reliable Guide to the City of Chicago : constituting A Valuable Souvenir of the Exposition : And a Trusty Companion to the Stranger.* Chicago: The World's Exposition Guide Co., °1891 by F. B. Olmstead.

10x20. 16 *l.* Off-white wraps, dusty blue print and design which includes litho of Agricultural Bldg. Frontis is WCE bird's-eye view litho in dusty blue. Attached to inside back cover is a detailed Chicago street map. Back cover: "Compliments of the World's Exposition Guide Company,..."
---- Off-white wraps, brown print and design which includes Administration Bldg. Brown bird's eye. Black cloth spine. Lacks "compliments" on back wrap.
☺.(CHx,LC,TD) $12 - 25

1642. Orcutt Company. *Authentic portfolio of the World's Columbian exposition : illustrations from water color drawings by our special artists.* Chicago: The Orcutt Co., n.d.

19x26½. (28) p. Nice color lithos on buff stock. Color litho cover of boating couple on Lagoon in front of the Art Bldg. C.t.: "World's Fair Portfolio." Cover placard: "The Orcutt Comp'y : Leading Lithographers : Chicago."
---- Same except cover placard: "Published by Siegel, Cooper & Co : Chicago."
☺.(CHx,TD)

1643. *Oriental and occidental northern and southern portrait types of the midway plaisance : a collection of Photographs of Individual Types of various nations from all parts of the World ...* St. Louis: N. D. Thompson Publishing Co., 1894 [°1894 by N. D. Thompson Publishing Co.; Woodbridge, CT: RPI, 1989.

39x31½. 82 *l.* Embossed maroon cloth hc, gold lettering, decorated end papers. Photos one side of 80 glossy *l* with short explanation below each. Introduction by F. W. Putnam, Chief, Ethnology Dept.
---- Brown leather, gilt print, all edges gilt.
---- Subscription set: Each weekly issue has gray wraps, black print; 8 photos each. On cover: "Educational Art Series" and "Portrait Types of the Midway Plaisance."
P→ ☺ (GLD,csuf,CHx,SI,NYPL,S,nwu,LM,TU,UoC,NL,BPL,AIC,OC,TD)

Bound: $40 - 75
Ten part subscription set: $50 - 100

1644. Peterson, O. M. *Verdensudstillingen og Verdensudstillings-Staden: Souvenir i tegninger med text til "Skandinavens" holdere for 1893.* Chicago: John Anderson Publishing Co., [°1893].

24x32. 64 p., illus. Blue cloth hc, black and gold print. Brown printed text, lithos of bldgs and Chicago sights. C.t.: Skandinavens Udstillings Souvenir" in bold old Swedish script. ☺.(LC,A)

1645. *The Photographic Panorama of the World's Fair : being a magnificent collection of photographic views of the World's Columbian Exposition and the Midway Plaisance : forming a Pictorial History of the Greatest Achievements of the Age ...* Springfield, OH: Mast, Crowell & Kirkpatrick, °1894.

28x34½. 20 + (116) p., single picture with description on each page. This is the format of J. W. Buel's *The Magic City* (#1579). In fact, the exact title and copyright pages from Buel's book is found in the middle of this book. The green linen hc is printed in black: "Chicago. The Magic City. 1893."
---- 20, 20, 20, 20, (96) p. chiefly illus. Morocco. The last 96 p. relate to the San Francisco Midwinter Fair. Gilt c.t.: "Chicago and San Francisco Expositions."
---- 20 p. bound with *Scenes and gems of art from every land* (#1665).
---- 27x35. 4 vol. Farm and fireside library, Jan. 1894.
      ☺ (GLD,csuf,CHx,UDe) $15 - 25

1646. *Photographic views of the World's Columbian Exposition.* Chicago: Stone, Kastler & Painter, 1894.

27x19. 1 vol, illus, ports. Contents: pt 1: The main bldgs; pt 2: State and foreign bldgs; pt 3: General views; pt 4: Midway and general views; pt 5: General views.
---- Issued as separate sections. Example: *Part 2.--State and Foreign Buildings. Photographic views of the World's Columbian Exposition.* 27½x19½. Wraps. On front wrap: "The engravings within are selections from the official memorial of the World's Columbian exposition, edited by the Joint Committee on Ceremonies ... It contains 400 views and portraits. ..." Available bindings: silk cloth and full morocco.
      ☺ . (CHx,BPL)

1647. *The Photographic World's Fair and Midway Plaisance : the main buildings, the entrances, the foreign, state and territorial buildings ...* Chicago: W. B. Conkey Co., 1894; Chicago [and] Philadelphia: Monarch Book Co. (formerly L. P. Miller & co.), 1894; Chicago: John W. Iliff & Co., 1894; Woodbridge, CT: RPI, 1989.

Conkey: 16x24. 4 p. text, 5-226 p. of illus. Green cloth beveled hc; silver, gold, and black embossed cover design.   ☺ . (UND,LC,SI,CHx,S,NYSt,TD)

1648. *Photographien der Welt-Ausstellung und Midway Plaisance.* ____: ____, 18__.

15½x24. 226 p. German version of #1647.   (A)

1649. *Photographs of the World's fair : an elaborate collection of photographs of the buildings, grounds, and exhibits of the World's Columbian Exposition : with a special description of the famous midway plaisance.* Boston: E. Gately & Co., [1894]; Chicago: Werner Co., [°1894 by The Werner Co.]; Cleveland: N. G. Hamilton Pub. Co., [1894]; New York: J. A. Hill & Co., °1894; Woodbridge, CT: RPI [Werner], 1989.

Werner: 29x33. 351 p. chiefly plates, numbered on rectos only; but blank versos counted in pagination. Photos one side with brief explanation beneath. "Sold only by subscription." C.t.: "Photographs of the World's Fair." Full leather embossed hc, gilt lettering, gilt edges.
---- Werner: Brown (or olive) cloth hc, dark chocolate print.
---- Werner: 29x35½. 1 *l*, (4), 13-351 p. (table of contents from 13-16 p.; plates from 17-351). Chocolate brown cloth hc, gilt and black print, gilt, black, and silver design.
---- Gately: 29x35. (7)-16 p., 17-351 plates.
---- Hill: Same as Werner.
---- Hamilton: 29x34. 351 p. illus.

---- 28½x34½. C.t. only (no t.p.), 252 p. Dark blue cloth hc, gold embossed print. Photos copyrighted by Werner.

☺ . (UND,KU,csuf,CHx,SI,NYPL,F,S,nwu,OhHx,LMi,UMi,UoC,NL,A,E,WiHx,TD) $25 - 40

1650. *Photo-gravures : of : The World's Columbian Exposition.* New York: The Albertype Co., °1893 by A. Wittemann.

11x18½. 13 *l.* Embossed caramel (or red) smooth wraps, string tied. (CHx,BPL,UDe,TD)

1651. *Pictorial album and history : World's fair and midway.* [Chicago: Harry T. Smith & Co. (Printed by the Foster Press)], n.d. [copyrighted by Harry T. Smith & Co.].

20½x28. (287) p., illus (includes ports). Black cloth hc, embossed design and gold print, glossy leaves. This view book is useful in that it depicts group photos of grounds staff showing their various types of uniforms: admissions, band members, Columbian guards, etc. C.t.= t.p.
---- Also listed: (288) p.

☺ . (CHx,NYPL,F,S,UoC,CoU,WiHx) $35 - 70

1652. *Picturesque World's Fair. An Elaborate Collection of Colored Views. ...* Chicago: W. B. Conkey Co., [°1894 by W. B. Conkey Co.]; Woodbridge, CT: RPI, 1989.

Subscription set: 27½x34. 16 subscription sections; issued weekly Feb. 10-May 26, 1894. Full set is 256 p., chiefly color illus. Glossy wraps, brown and blue lettering and design. On covers: "Fine art series." Colored/tinted photo reproductions. "Published with the Endorsement and Approval of George R. Davis, Director-General" (frontis port). C.t.= t.p.
---- Bound: 27x33½. Green (or brown) cloth hc, silver lettering. C.t.: "The City of Palaces."
---- Partial sets found bound: (160 or 176 or 240 p.).

P→ ☺ . (GLD,csuf,UNe,CHx,SI,NYPL,S,UoC,NL,BPL,A,AIC,BM,GPL,WiHx,TD,L)

Bound: $30 - 50
Subscription set with covers: $40 - 70

1653. *Populäre Sammlung von Ansichten der Winters Kunst-Lithograph Compagnie von der Columbischen Welt-Ausstellung.* German ed. Chicago: Die Winters Kunst-Lithograph Compagnie, °1891 by the Winters Art Lithographic Co.

16x24. 16 *l* of cream stock, 8 color lithos by C. Graham. Gray wraps with blue, black, and dark gray print and design. C.t.: "Portfolio: Worlds [sic] Columbian Exposition 1893." German version of *Winters Art* (#1697). ☺ .(CPL)

1654. *Portfolio of "Edition de Luxe" World's Fair Views.* [Chicago?: 1893?].

30x22½. 60 *l* of plates. C.t. ☺ .(BPL)

1655. *Portfolio of Midway types.* Chicago: The American Engraving Co. Publishers & Printers, °1893.

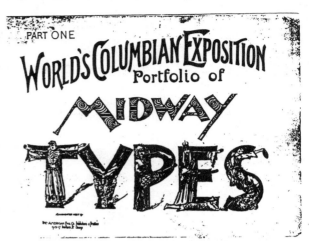

Subscription set: 20x27½. Tan wraps, black print with ethnic figures forming the letters in the word "types." Part One: (20) p. of ethnic ports. No text other than captions. Same as #1640.

---- Also issued as: *Chicago Times portfolio of the Midway types*; *Midway types*; and *World's Columbian exposition portfolio of Midway types.*

P→　☺ (GLD,LC)　　　　Each part: $5 - 10

1656. *Portfolio of photographs of the World's fair.* Chicago: The Werner Co., °1893; Chicago: The Werner Co., °1894.

Subscription set: 28x35. Wraps c.t.: "Portfolio of Photographs of the World's Fair" (see #1656). 16 numbers in "Household Art Series." Published weekly from Dec. 11, 1893 to March 26, 1894. Chicago: The Werner Co., °1893-94. 244 to 306 total pages (mostly unpaged illus). Bound numbers vary from 15 to 18?. The 306 p. version contains additional art illus from the Fine Arts Gallery. Note: 2 copyright years were found for issue no. 2 (Dec. 18, 1893) -- °1893 and °1894.

---- Probable subscription set for: *The Columbian gallery : a portfolio of photographs from the World's Fair* (#1599).

　☺ . (csuf,CHx,nwu,E,HL,NL,KyU,A,AIC,OhHx,WiHx,TD)　　　　Subscription set with covers: $40 - 70

1657. Ragan, H[arry] H[arger]. *Art Photographs of the World and the Columbian Exposition : An album of rare photographs of the Wonders of the Universe.* ... N.p.: Photograph Publishing co., 1893 [°1893 by Star Publishing Co.]; Chicago: Star Publishing Co., 1893 [°1893].

26½x32½. 7 *l*, 13-509 p. Gray embossed cloth hc with design and print in gold, light blue, and dark brown. Paged photos with captions on one side of each leaf. Frontis of H. H. Ragan.

　☺ . (GLD,csuf,PU,LC,S,UDe)　　　　$25 - 45

1658. *Rand, McNally & Co.'s pictorial Chicago and illustrated World's Columbian Exposition : Containing Views of Principal Buildings, Residences, Streets, Parks, Monuments, Etc.* Chicago: Rand, McNally & co., 1893 [°1893 by Rand, McNally & Co.]; Woodbridge, CT: RPI, 1989.

22½x30. 110 plates. Red cloth beveled hc, gold print.

---- 23½x28½. Maroon cloth beveled hc, gold print. C.t.: "Pictorial Chicago and the World's Columbian Exposition."

---- Also listed: 23x29 with 112 *l* (all illus); and 22½x28½ with 2 *l*, 110 plates.

　☺ . (csuf,LC,SI,NYPL,S,nwu,RML,SLP,NYSt,BPL,A,AIC,WiHx)　　　　$15 - 35

1659. *Rand, McNally & Co.'s Sketch Book : illustrating and describing the principal buildings, with their locations, dimensions, cost, etc. and Indexed Bird's-Eye View of the Grounds.* Chicago and New York: Rand, McNally & Co., Publishers, [°1892 by Rand, McNally & Co .].

16x21½. (48) p. illus and text. Red (or green) cloth embossed hc, gilt and black print and design. At head of title: "World's Columbian Exposition." C.t.: "World's Columbian Exposition Chicago 1893."

P↓　☺ . (GLD,KU,NYPL,OSU,SLP,A,BPL,S,TD,L)　　　　$10 - 25

1660. *Reminiscences of the fair : a portfolio of photographs of the World's Columbian Exposition : comprising its marvelous architectural, sculptural, artistic ... and scenic attractions.* Also presenting and describing The Magnificent Vistas, Water-Ways, Natural Scenery and Landscape Effects ... St. Louis: Lester, Lawrence & Miller, [°1894 by N. D. Thompson Publishing Co.].

29x35. 1 unpaged vol (chiefly illus). ☺ . (RPB)

1661. *Reproductions of water color paintings by American artists at the Columbian exposition held in Chicago, Ill., 1893.* [Chicago: 1893].

46x__. 23 colored plated, issued in portfolio. C.t. (UC)

1662. [Ropp, Silas]. *The World's fair souvenir album, containing general views of the Columbian exposition, grounds ...* Chicago: C. Ropp & sons, 1894.

20x27. (256) p., illus. (LC)

1663. *Round the world in midway plaisance : Albertype illustrations.* New York and Chicago: A. Wittemann (New York: The Albertype co.), °1893 by A. Wittemann.

22x14. (2) p., 16 *l* of plates. ☺ . (UDe)

1664. [Ryan, Carroll]. *Chicago the Magnificent.* New York and Montreal: John P. Williams, [°1893].

14x20. 64 p. (LC)

1665. *Scenes and Gems of art from every land.* With an introduction by General Lew Wallace, ... Springfield, OH: Mast, Crowell & Kirkpatrick, 1894, °1894.

26½x34½. 2 *l*, 5-20 p., 8 *l*, 1-16 p., followed by another t.p.: *The Photographic Panorama of the World's Fair being a magnificent collection of photographic views of the World's Columbian Exposition, Chicago, U.S.A., 1893 : forming a Pictorial history of the Greatest Achievement of the Age,* ... N.p.: n.p., n.d. This last section is 20 p. Thin tan wraps, burgundy print. ☺ . (LC)

1666. *Select photographic views of the World's Columbian exposition.* ... New York and St. Louis: N. D. Thompson publishing co., [°1893 by N. D. Thompson publishing co.].

28x34. (66) p. include 64 plates. Illus light maroon wraps. C.t.: "The Dream City" with illus much like that on the covers of the Dream City subscription set. ☺ . (OhHz,A)

1667. Shepp, James W., and Daniel B. Shepp. *Shepp's World's Fair Photographed. Being a Collection of Original Copyrighted Photographs Authorized and Permitted by the Management of the World's Columbian*

Exposition ... All described in Crisp and Beautiful Language. Chicago, Philadelphia: Globe Bible Publishing Co., [°1893 by D. B. Shepp]; New York: Hegger, [°1893].

23x28. 528, (1) p. Even pages are paged. Blue cloth hc, gilt and black print and design, t.p. printed in black. With the book open, the photo on the right is explained on the left facing page.
---- 21½x26½. Half leather over blue cloth hc, gold print.
---- Subscription set: 36 unbound issues. Pale blue-gray paper covers with red and black print -- hence, there are various bindings, e.g., half blue cloth over olive paper covered hc.
*   ◎ . (GLD,KU,csuf,KyU,CHx,NYPL,F,nwu,RML,LM,UDe,WyMus,LMi,OhHx,   Bound: \$15 - 30
       SLP,TU,UMi,NYSt,UoC,NL,A,BPL,AIC,OC,WiHx,TD,L)   Subscription set: \$25 - 60

1668. *Siegel, Cooper & Co.'s popular portfolio of the World's Columbian Exposition and Principle Places of Amusement. Chicago, 1893.* Chicago: Published by the Book Department of Siegel, Cooper & Co., n.d.

15½x23½. (32) p., color illus by C. Graham. Double page "The Official Birdseye [sic] View" at centerfold. Textured wraps, light olive green (or off-white) border surrounds Graham illus on front cover and Siegel's bldg illus on back cover. Format: illus on verso with ½ page text and ½ page ad on facing recto. Same illus and descriptive text in *Winters Art* #1697.
P→   ◎ . (CHx,OhHx,UDe,UoC,BPL)

1669. *Souvenir collection of views of the World's Columbian Exposition, Including a Lithographic Portrait of Christopher Columbus. ...* Springfield, OH: Mast, Crowell & Kirkpatrick, 1892.

27½x35½. Unpaged vol, illus. On t.p.: "Farm and Fireside Library. Published monthly ..." ◎ . (WiHx)

1670. *Souvenir of the World's Columbian Exposition : in photogravure.* New York and Chicago: A. Wittemann (New York: The Albertype Co.), °1893 by A. Wittemann.

13x18½. 1 *l* (t.p.), 40 *l* plates on one side. String tied rust brown cloth hc, gilt print. C.t.: "Souvenir of The World's Fair."
---- Decorative red (or blue) cloth hc with gilt print, black ornate border and pink rose flower.
P→   ◎ . (GLD,ALB,S,A)   \$15 - 25

1671. *Souvenir of World's Columbian Exposition.* ____: A. Wittemann, 18__.

16½x12. 72 p. Gray cloth hc decorated with flowers and vase. (cat)   \$20

1672. *Souvenir photographs of the World's fair.* [New York]: n.p., [°1893].

18x23. 20 photos. LC other name: Louis Clarence Bennett. (LC)

1673. *Souvenir : World's Columbian exposition. To be held from May until October, 1893, at Chicago, Illinois.* Chicago: Knight, Leonard & co., printers, [°1892 by Knight, Leonard & Co.].

12½x17½. 16 *l* color illus plus text. Pink wraps, gilt print.
---- 8x13. 16 *l*. Gray wraps, blue print.
⊚ (CHx)

1674. *The state buildings of the World's fair.* New York: Adolph Wittemann (New York: The Albertype co.), °1893.

11x18. 1 *l*, 12 plates. (CHx,LC)

1675. Stoddard, John L[awson]. *Famous parks and public buildings of America.* New York   Akron, OH   Chicago: The Werner Co., 1899.

ca. 24x33. 11 p., ca. 130 *l*. On t.p.: Stoddard, "The noted traveler and lecturer." ⊚ . (UMC,ncsu)

1676. Todd, F[rederick] Dundas. *World's Fair through a Camera. An interesting collection of views of grounds, exhibition buildings, foreign buildings, state buildings, interiors, and other views of general interest. From recent photographs by F. Dundas Todd.*   St. Louis: Woodward and Tiernan printing co., 1893.

Softbound: 12½x16½. 80 *l*, no frontis, illus. Gray-blue wraps with front cover photo montage which is same as frontis of hc version (#1677), cloth spine. C.t.: "World's Fair Through a Camera : Snap Shots By an Artist." Photos by Todd on <u>one</u> side of glossy paper. This version has many photos different from #1677.
P→   ⊚ (GLD,NYPL,UDe,UoC,L) $12 - 25

1677. Todd, F[rederick] Dundas. *World's Fair through a Camera. Snap shots by an artist. An interesting and unequalled collection of Views of Grounds, Exhibition Buildings, Foreign Buildings, State Buildings, Interiors, Midway Plaisance, Procession of all Nations, and other Views of Special and General Interest. From recent photographs by F. Dundas Todd. ...* Chicago: Wellington Publishing Co., 1893; St. Louis: Woodward and Tiernan Co., °1893; Woodbridge, CT: RPI, 1989.

Woodward (hardbound): 13x16½. 91 *l*. Brown (or sand, or gray, or hunter green, or red) embossed hc, gold print, decorated end papers. Photos by Todd on one side of glossy paper. Frontis is the same photo montage illus as on the cover of the paper bound version (#1676). C.t.: "World's fair Through a Camera. Snap shots By an Artist." Found with and without "The Union News Company, Agents, Chicago" on t.p.

---- Wellington. 91 *l* photos <u>both</u> sides. Embossed brown cloth hc.
---- Woodward (softbound): 12x16. On wraps: "New souvenir edition. 180 Original Views." C.t.: "'Snap shots,' or World's Fair through a Camera."

P↑   ◎ . (GLD,csuf,CHx,NYPL,HL,E,UDe,NL,A,BPL,AIC,WiHx,TD,L) $12 - 25

1678. *A trip through the Columbian exposition with a camera : a selection of instantaneous photographs of the principal building and general views. ...* Chicago: Globe lithographing and printing co., n.d.

Hardbound: 13½x18. 122 *l*. Maroon cloth hc, gold design. Photos one side on glossy paper. Below title: "From negatives made in August and September, 1893, by Thos. Harrison, photographer." [May be listed in a card catalog under Harrison as author.]
---- Softbound: 12½x17. 1 p., 71 plates. No copyright information anywhere. Camel wraps. Pale blue shield surrounded by gilt border design containing red accents. Found with maroon (or black) cloth spine. At bottom of cover: "Compliments of Bradner Smith & Co," or "Compliments of S. F. Leonard," etc.
---- Gray wraps with lettering on blue background. Except for color, the design is same as camel wraps. No advertiser name on cover.

◎ . (GLD,CPL,CHx,D,E,UoC,A,UDe,AIC,TD) $12 - 22

1679. *The Triumphs of the World's Fair and Scenes of the World : A Magnificent Showing of the Wonders of the World's Fair : The Marvelous Works of God and the Wonderful Accomplishments of Man : embracing a rare and elaborate collection of the most beautiful and noted buildings , statuary and lagoons of the Columbian exposition ...* Chicago: Zollmann & Hay Publishers, n.d.

28x33½. 240, (16) p. Gold on brown (or blue) cloth hc. C.t.: "Triumphs of the World's Fair and Scenes of the World."   ◎ . (A)

1680. *The Vanished City : The World's Columbian Exposition in pen and picture. An elaborate collection of photo-engravings of the buildings, grounds and exhibits, of the World's fair ...* Chicago, New York, London, Paris, Berlin: Werner Co., n.d.

28x35½. (270) p. Light brown cloth hc, design and print in red and black. Cover depicts a portion of fairground engulfed in fire; red flames shoot from the bldgs. Photos and captions both sides of pages. Post Fair reissue after many bldgs were burned by striking railway union workers on the night of July 5, 1894; other fires followed.

P→   ◎ (GLD,CHx,TD) $20 - 40

☞ J. C. Rogers bought several of the remaining smaller bldgs and had them set up in Kansas City.

1681. *The Vanishing City : A Photographic Encyclopedia of the World's Columbian Exposition : containing A Concise History and 224 Views - comprising All Main Buildings, All State and Territorial Buildings ...* Subscription ed. Chicago: Laird & Lee, publishers, 1893 °1893 by Laird & Lee.

16x23. (226) p. Orange-tan cloth hc, silver and black print and design, photos both sides with captions below each, t.p. in red and black. Similar plates with shorter captions are found in *Glimpses of the World's Fair*.

P→ ◎ (GLD,csuf,CHx,F,NYSt,BPL,UDe,WiHx) $20 - 35

1682. *The vanishing White City, a superb collection of photographic views of the great Columbian exposition.* Ed. Jessie Fawcett. Chicago: Peacock Publishing Co., 1894.

27x33. Unpaged. Half morocco over leather covered boards, gold design and lettering.
---- Columbian Art Series subscription ed. in 20 parts. Orange wraps, black print.
---- German ed. *Die verschwundene* (#1684).
(csuf,TD)

1683. *The Vendome club* ... [Chicago: Vendome Family Club], n.d.

15x20. 12 *l* text and lithos of WCE in sepia print. Lilac wraps with gilt print. At head of title: "The World's Columbian Exposition 1893." C.t. (CHx)

1684. *Die Verschwundene Weisse Stadt: Eine Sammlung Photographischer Aufnahmen auf der Columbischen Welt-Ausstellung: Umfassend die Herrlichen Gebäude, Bildhauerarbeiten, Kunstwerke...* Chicago: Peacock Publishing Co., 1893; Woodbridge, CT: RPI, 1989.

27x34½. 324 p. Leather hc with gilt lettering, angled view of German Bldg on cover. See English version #1682: *The vanishing White City.*
---- Subscription set: On covers: "Columbische Kunst Serie."
(csuf,SI,NYPL)

1685. *View album of Chicago.* Columbus, OH: Ward Bros. Pub., 1892.

16x25. (22) p. Dark blue cloth hc embossed with black print, decorated end papers. Bound view album of Chicago and WCE. Glossy b/w lithographs shown here are same type as found in many accordion fold out booklets from the Fair which were given away by various advertisers. Also on t.p.: "Reproduced from original photographs, from J. W. Taylor's American photographic series, Chicago, Ill."

P→ ◎ (GLD,SLP) $10 - 25

1686. *Views and description of the Columbian Exhibition Buildings; together with portraiture and biography of American Celebrities.* [New York: Moss Engraving Co.], 1893 [°1893].

15x23½. 46 *l* on stiff glossy stock, illus both sides. Tan stiff wraps with green design and brown print.
◎ . (LC)

1687. *Views of the World's Columbian Exposition : Chicago, 1893.* N.p.: n.p., n.d.

17½x17. (6) p. accordion fold. with black litho illus. Pale blue-gray pebble textured stiff wraps with scalloped edges. Tipped in color litho of shields of countries on front cover. C.t. On cover: "Compliments of [various advertisers]." (Examples: Decorah-Posten, Decorah, IA; M. M. Marks, Pottstown, PA.)
P→   ☺ . (GLD,A,TD) $12 - 20

1688. *Views of the World's Fair.* N.p.: n.p., n.d.

28x33. 1 unpaged vol, chiefly illus, ports. C.t.   (WiHx)

1689. *Views of the World's fair and midway plaisance.* Chicago: W. B. Conkey Co., 1894.

15x17. 1 *l*, (3) p. of port, (189) p. of plates. Decorative wraps in red and blue on yellow. On cover: "Franklin series, v. 1, no. 5, March 1904." For German version, see *Ansichten der Weltausstellung* (#1566).   (csuf,LC,S,UMi)

1690. *Vistas of the fair in color. A portfolio of familiar views of the World's Columbian Exposition : with a preface by Major Moses P. Handy, ...* Chicago: Poole Bros., ᶜ1894 by Poole Bros.

35x40. Subscription set of 20 parts. Each part has pulp tan wraps with chocolate print, glossy pages. Chiefly color plates. For example: No. 1: t.p. in chocolate print, (1) p. text, 4 color lithos with tissue guards; No. 2: 4 color lithos with tissue guards. On covers: "Art Color Series."
---- Also listed: 1 p., 80 *l* of colored plates.
---- Bound vol in leather.
    ☺ . (csuf,CHx,LC,S,nwu,UoC,AIC,WiHx,TD)

1691. *Water color souvenir of the World's fair, Chicago, 1893.* ____: ____, 18__.

7½x11½. 12 *l* color lithos on stiff smooth white stock. Sand wraps, dark blue print. C.t.   (CHx)

1692. *Waterman's illustrated album of the World's Columbian exposition, Chicago, Ill., 1893.* Chicago: C. E. Waterman, ᶜ1891.

10½x20. (23) p., illus. C.t.   (LC)

1693. *Welcome in* [sic] *Chicago, 1893.* [Germany?]: n.p., [ca. 189-].

13x10. 8 *l* of color plates. Cut in shape of bust of Columbus. Face on front wrap and back of head on back wrap.   (csuf)

1694. *The White City, beautifully illustrated.* [*Collection of views of the World's Fair.*] [Chicago, 1894].

    ob. 4°. 120 *l.* C.t.   (NYPL)

1695. *The white city by Lake Michigan : A Souvenir in Albertype.* New York and Chicago: A. Wittemann (New York: The Albertype Co.), °1893; Woodbridge, CT: RPI, 1989.

    22x14½. 17 *l.* Red (or ocher, or buff) stiff wraps, embossed gold letters and design of French's Republic Statue, string tied. Two albertype photo reproductions on one side of each leaf. Comes with manilla envelope for mailing at 2¢.
    ---- 22x14½. 16 *l.* Gray wraps, silver print.
    ---- 13x28. 14 *l* of plates. Alligator textured antique blue stiff wraps, string tied, silver print.
    ---- Blue cloth hc, silver print.
    P→   © (GLD,csuf,CHx,SI,UDe,SLP,BPL,OC,WiHx,TD) $15 - 25

1696. Wilde, Otto, and Albert Ganzlin. *Chicago weltausstellung 1893 : 32 blatt nach photographischen original-aufnahmen.* Berlin: Bendix & Krakau, 1893.

    Cover 25½x17. Plates 15½x23½. Red cloth hc with gilt and black print and design plus a bird's-eye of the grounds in blues and greens. Loose plates inside with decorative folding papers. (1) p. (t.p.) + 32 loose *l* of plates with brief captions in German. Cover orientation is different from plate orientation. ©. (UoC,nwu)

1697. *The Winters Art Lithographing Company's popular portfolios of the World's Columbian Exposition.* Chicago: The Winters Art Lithographing Co., [°1891 by Winters Art Litho Co.].

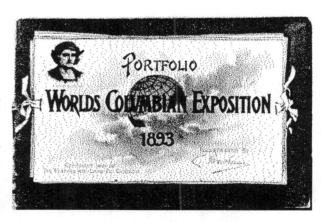

    16x24. (32) p., illus, plates, maps. White stiff wraps with green, red, black, and brown print and design, Giovio port of Columbus, string tied spine. 16 color lithographs of bldgs on stiff stock; written explanations on the other 16 pages. Four different booklets: 1) Main Bldgs, 2) States, 3) Foreign, 4) Lagoons and Oriental Bldgs. Illus by C. Graham. C.t.: "Portfolio : World's Columbian Exposition : 1893." Same as *Siegel, Cooper & Co.'s Popular* #1668.
    ---- Variant wraps found; different ports of Columbus -- e.g., gray wraps lettered in black and blue; gray wraps lettered in black and red.
    P→   ©. (GLD,KyU,csuf,CHx,PU,S,E,OhHx,D,UMi,A,BPL,TD)   Each: $15- 30

1698. ... *The wonders of the World's fair. A Portfolio of Views Presenting All Points of Interest About the Fair Proper and the Midway Plaisance.* Buffalo, NY: Barnes, Hengerer & Co., n.d.; Chicago: W. B. Conkey Co., 1894 [°1894].

    Conkey Subscription set: 27½x34½. "Acme Series." Weekly issues from Feb. 10, 1894. Sepia colored wraps, black print. Issued in 10 pts; (16) p. in each pt.

---- Barnes: 27x33½. (160) p., photos with captions both sides. Blue cloth beveled hc, gold print. Advertising book for Barnes, Hengerer Dept Store in Buffalo. Front end paper has hand written: "December 21, 1894, WF 1893."

---- Later editions were published in 1894 by different publishers and with varying titles: *Glories of the World's Fair*, by "The Fair" of Chicago (#1619); *The Great White City*, by the Syndicate Trading Company (#1622); and *City of Palaces* by the W. B. Conkey Co. (#1594).

P→ ⊚ . (GLD,CHx,LC,UDe,A,BPL,TD) Bound: $20 - 35
Subscription set: $30 - 50

1699. Wood, R. W. *Architectural details, from the buildings, at the World's Columbian Exposition, held in Chicago, 1893.* [Chicago?]: R. W. Wood, [1893?].

4°. 50 plates. C.t.　(NYPL)

1700. [Woolson Spice Company]. *Authentic World's Columbian Exposition album containing official designs and descriptions of the World's Columbian Exposition buildings.* Toledo, OH and Kansas City, MO: Woolson Spice Co., [1893].

13½x21. (36) p., colored illus. Wraps with port of Columbus.　. (BPL)

1701. [Woolson Spice Company]. *World's Columbian Exposition. 1492 1892.* [Toledo, OH: Woolson Spice Co., ᶜ1893.]

14½x23. 16 *l* pulp paper. Salmon wraps with black print and a lavender litho of the Administration Bldg centered between "1492" and "1892." C.t. Ad for Woolson which sold Lion Coffee.　⊚ . (LC)

1702. *World's Columbian Exposition.* Pawtucket, RI: Eastern Advertising co. (Printed in Germany), [ᶜ1892].

Souvenir ad for:
---- O.T. Brooks & Co., dealers in groceries, ... Athol, Mass. ...: 17½x9½. 12 *l* of plates (strip 100 cm. folded to form 12 *l*). Several plates open to reveal panoramic views. C.t.
---- John H. Higgins & Co. ... Woonsocket, R.I.: Purplish brown coated lithos. C.t. Light blue stiff coated wraps, dark blue design and print.
P→　⊚ . (GLD,UDe,csuf)　$8 - 18

1703. ... *World's Columbian Exposition art portfolio* ... [New York?: 1893?]

19½x27. 17 plates. String tied, beige wraps with red print. C.t. Advertisement stating: "With Compliments of the Fuchs & Lang Mfg. Co., New York." In envelope lettered: ... Reproductions of official water color paintings. Paintings by Childe Hassam and others.

---- "Compliments of G. L. Hergert." Light green wraps. 15 p.
⊜ . (CHx,PU,UDe,OhHx)

1704. *World's Columbian Exposition at Chicago : 1492 - 1893 - 1892.* [Portland, ME: Chisholm Brothers], n.d.

15½x24½. Accordion style fold out view book of WCE bldgs, etc. Green (or blue) hc, gilt print and design. C.t. On cover: "Published for the R.R. Trade." ⊜ . (D,MPL,HL) $8 - 18

1705. *World's Columbian Exposition, Chicago.* N.p.: n.p. (printed in Germany), n.d.

18x9½. 12 accordion folded leaves of grayish-brown coated lithos. Red paper covered boards, gilt border and lettering. C.t. Ads for Crystal Confectionery Co., Burlington, VT, on pastedown inside back cover and in gilt on back cover.
---- 18x9½. Variant plates and borders of plates. Red paper covered boards, black design and lettering.
---- 17½x9. Light green and cream lithos. Pink coated stiff wraps, red design and lettering. Compliments of Bush & Bull, Easton, PA. in blue on front wrap plus their ad on back wrap.
---- 17½x9. Purplish-gray lithos, no ads.
---- Also listed: 18x__. 10 plates.
---- Many advertisers and plate variations listed.
(csuf,Chx,UDe,KyU,HL) $8 - 18

1706. *World's Columbian Exposition : Chicago : 1893.* N.p.: Printed in Germany, n.d.

22½x14. 12 color lithos in continuous strip of textured paper; folded accordion style. Each litho surrounded by illus of branches with cherries. Beige hc, bold gilt lettering. C.t. On cover: "Printed in Germany." ⊜ (GLD) $8 - 18

1707. *World's Columbian Exposition : Chicago : North America.* N.p.: n.p., n.d.

23x14. 12 plates folded accordion style. Deep brown lithos, water tinted green. Brown hc, black cloth spine, gilt and black print and design. Two angels perched above world globe inscribed "North America."
---- Also listed: Plates on continuous strip to form 14 *l*. Ad piece for J. B. Williams Co., Glastonbury, CT, shaving soaps.
⊜ . (GLD,UDe,BPL,L) $8 - 18

1708. World's Columbian Exposition. Department of Photography. Arnold, C. D., and H. D. Higinbotham. *... Portfolio of Views : issued by the department of photography, ...* St. Louis: C. B. Woodward Co., 1893 [ᶜ1893 by C. D. Arnold]; Woodbridge, CT: RPI, 1989.

18x26. 1 *l* (t.p.) + 36 *l* of illus by the "official photographers." At head of title: "The World's Columbian exposition." C.t.: "World's Columbian Exposition : Chicago : 1492-1892." Same color illus and format as #1709 except this has 2 authors and different publisher.
(CHx,SI,OhHx,MPL,HL,UoC,BPL,RPB,AIC,WM,L)

☞ Do not confuse H[arlow] D[avidson] Higinbotham, manager of the photography department, with H[arlow] N[iles] Higinbotham, President of The World's Columbian Exposition 1892-93. H. D. H. was one of two sons of H. N. H.; Davidson was a maternal family surname.

1709. World's Columbian Exposition. Department of Photography. Arnold, C. D. ... *Portfolio of views : issued by the department of photography, ...* Chicago and St. Louis: National Chemigraph co., 1893 [°1893 by C. D. Arnold].

Unpaginated. String tied covers. At head of title: "Worlds' [sic] Columbian exposition."   C.t.: The World's Columbian Exposition : Chicago : 1492-1892." Photos on one side of each leaf. Photos in each book are different. This has the same cover illus and format as #1708.   Four separate books with identical cover illus and t.p. -- arbitrarily identified as follows:

---- GOLD: 19x25½. 37 *l*. Brown hc, black and gold lettering.
---- SILVER: 19x25½. 37 *l*. Brown hc, black and silver lettering.
---- SMALL GRAY: 19x25½. 19 *l*. Gray stiff wraps illus in gray half tone print and design.
---- LARGE GRAY: 25½x30½. Enlarged version, 13 *l*. Gray stiff wraps illus in gray half tone print and design.

P→   ⊚ . (GLD,csuf,CHx,NYPL,SI,S,OhHx,D,OSL,VaHx,E,NHSt,HL,A,BPL,UDe,RPB,AIC,WiHx,TD,L)   Each: $15 - 30

1710. World's Columbian Exposition. Department of Photography. Arnold, C. D., and H. D. Higinbotham. *Official Views of the World's Columbian Exposition.* Chicago: Published by the Department of Photography, World's Columbian Exposition Co., [°1893 by C. D. Arnold].

33x44. 2 *l*, (50) p. of plates. Dark blue cloth spine and hinge, light blue cloth remainder of hc, silver print, top edge dyed black. C.t.: "The World's Fair." Fifty large plates on 50 heavy paper leaves; each plate preceded by tissue guard with printed description. Fine quality.

⊚ (GLD,CHx,S,HL,UoC,nwu,AIC) $40 - 85

1711. World's Columbian Exposition. Department of Photography. Arnold, C. D., and H. D. Higinbotham. *Official views of the World's Columbian Exposition : issued by the department of photography.* [Chicago]: Press Chicago Photo-Gravure co., °1893 by C. D. Arnold; Woodbridge, CT: RPI, 1989.

18x26. 115 p., (1) p., plates one side on heavy paper; each plate preceded by tissue guards with printed description, the (1) p. is index. Black cloth hc, gold print. Issued by WCE, Dept of Photography.
---- 18½x28. Full leather hc, beveled edges. C.t.: "The World's Columbian Exposition" in script. Copyright information on verso of t.p.
---- 18x25. Maroon (or red) cloth hc, beveled edges. C.t.: "The World's Columbian Exposition" in gilt script. Copyright information is on t.p.; t.p. is in script. On verso of t.p.: "This volume is published by the World's Columbian Exposition." (facsimile script and signature of Higinbotham.)
---- Also listed: 1 *l*, 115 p., (1) p.

⊚ . (R,csuf,PU,SI,NYPL,S,OSL,UTn,HL,NYSt,UoC,NL,A,BPL,RPB,AIC,TD) $30 - 55

1712. World's Columbian Exposition. Department of Photography. Arnold, C. D., and H. D. Higinbotham. ... *State buildings : portfolio of views.* Chicago and St. Louis: National Chemigraph Co., 1893 [°1893 by C. D. Arnold]; Chicago: National Chemigraph Co., 1893.

17x25½. (38) p. Pale green cardboard wraps, blue-green cloth spine, printed cover design. Chemigraph reproductions of photos of State Bldgs as issued by the Dept of Photography. At head of title: "The World's Columbian exposition."
---- With black border around front cover design.
P→ Ⓢ (GLD,CHx,NYPL,F,BPL,TD,HL) $20 - 35

1713. World's Columbian Exposition. Department of Photography. [*Photographs of the Exposition*].

18x20½. 66 card mounted photographs. (UC)

1714. World's Columbian Exposition. Department of Photography. ... *Woman's building, issued by the Department of Photography.* Chicago: C. M. Hobart, 1893.

19x26. (13) plates. At head of title: "The World's Columbian Exposition."
---- Also listed: 18x25½. 15 p., 12 of which are plates. White wraps: black design of Womans' Bldg on gray background.
(CHx,S,L) $18 - 28

1715. *World's Columbian Exposition. Jackson Park, Chicago, Illinois, U.S.A. May 1st to October 31st, 1893.* Portland, ME: Chisholm Brothers, n.d.

Same caption title, pub info and size found with 2 cover titles. Accordion view books. Lithos vary.

C.t. 1: "World's Fair Album of Chicago 1893."
23x15. 11 purple-brown coated litho plates with bodies of water tinted green. Followed by (3) p. text, (1) p. Chisholm info. Folder precedes t.p. Finely textured red paper covered boards, red cloth spine, gilt print and design of the Administration Bldg.
---- Also listed: 10 plates.
---- Also listed by c.t. only: 12 *l.* Tan cloth, black spine, gilt design and lettering.

C.t. 2: "World's Columbian Exposition at Chicago. 1492 : 1892 : 1893."
23x15. 12 purple-brown coated litho plates, (3) p. text, (1) p. Chisholm info. Textured red paper covered boards, black cloth spine, gilt lettering and design of Machinery Hall. No plan tipped in on back cover.
---- Variant plates.
---- Plum cloth, black spine.
---- Also listed under c.t.: 12 plates, (8) p. followed by Jackson Park plan mounted on back cover.
Ⓢ (GLD,csuf,HL,UDe,RPB,CPL,BPL,OC,L) $8 - 18

1716. *World's Columbian Exposition : Jackson Park, Chicago, Illinois, U.S.A. May 1st to October 31st : 1893.* [Portland, ME: Chisholm Brothers], n.d.

16x24½. 16 plates accordion folded, 1 *l* (t.p.), (6) p. descriptive text + plan of Jackson Park mounted on inside back cover. Dark olive pebbled hc, black and gilt design, gilt lettering, green cloth spine. Purplish-brown and tan coated lithos. C.t.: "World's Fair Album of Chicago 1893."
---- Brown cloth hc, gilt and black lettering, gilt print, lighter brown spine.
Ⓢ (GLD,csuf,HL,WiHx) $8 - 18

1717. *The World's Columbian Exposition : photo-gravures.*
New York and Chicago: A. Wittemann (New
York: The Albertype Co.), ᶜ1893 by A.
Wittemann; Woodbridge, CT: RPI, 1989.

17½x22. 1 *l* (t.p.), 18 *l* of plates one side. String
tied tan wraps with gilt print and gray illus of
Court of Honor. Photos of exposition bldgs and
grounds.
---- 18x23. 1 *l* (t.p.), 18 *l* of plates one side. Solid
blue cloth spine, lighter blue cloth hc with gilt
print.
P→   ☺ . (GLD,SI,S,A,WiHx,TD) $15 - 25

1718. *World's Columbian exposition portfolio of Midway types.*

Subscription set: 19½x27½. Also issued as: *Chicago Times portfolio of the Midway types*; *Midway types*;
and *Portfolio of Midway types.*   (TD)

1719. *The World's Columbian Exposition Reproduced :
containing views of grounds, landscapes ... etc. ...
which had place at the World's fair, Chicago,
1893.*   Chicago: Rand, McNally & Co.
Publishers, 1894.

28x35. 120 *l*. Dark blue textured cloth on
beveled boards, gold print, red dyed edges.
Photos both sides with captions.
---- Also published as *Buildings and Art at the
World's Fair* #1580 (a later ed. by Rand,
McNally & Co., 1894), and *World's Fair Album*
#1722 (an earlier ed. by J. Waite, 1894).
---- Also listed: 28x34, 1 *l*, (222) p.
P→   ☺ . (GLD,CHx,LC,NYPL,RML,BPL,AIC) $25 - 45

1720. *World's Columbian Fair, Chicago.* N.p.: (printed in Germany), n.d.

18x13. Under this c.t. are found versions with 12 to 14 accordion folded plates (99 to 156 cm in total
length). Red paper covered boards, gilt print. Purplish-gray coated lithos. C.t.
---- As ad piece: e.g., Hales's California Stores.
    (csuf,UDe,HL,NL) $8 - 18

1721. *World's Columbian Fair : Chicago : 1893.* N.p.: n.p., n.d.

22½x14½. 14 plates on continuous strip folded accordion style. Tan hc, gilt print, gray and black
design, "1893" is in black print. Back cover: "Souvenir of Mitchell Bros. Union 10 per cent. Clothing
House." C.t.   ☺ (GLD,TD) $8 - 18

1722. *World's fair album ...* Chicago: J. Waite, 1894.

28x34. LC microfilm. Later editions published in 1894 by Rand, McNally & Co.: *The World's Columbian exposition reproduced* #1719, and *Buildings and art at the World's fair* #1580. (CHx,LC)

1723. *The World's fair album : containing photographic views of buildings, statuary, grounds ... at the World's Columbian exposition : Chicago, 1893.* Chicago and New York: Rand, McNally & co., Publishers, [ᶜ1893 by Rand, McNally & Co.].

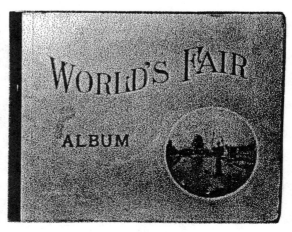

23x29. (100) p. Dark green cloth hc, gold print, red stained edges, decorated end papers. Glossy paper with photos front and back.
---- Blue-green paper covered boards, dark blue and white print, cloth spine.
---- Also listed: 24x29. (96) p.
---- Also listed: (7), 9-104 p.
---- Also listed: *The World's fair album, including photographic views of buildings, ...* 104 p.
P→   ⊚ . (GLD,csuf,LC,NYPL,UDe,A,CoU,WiHx,TD) $20 - 35

1724. *World's Fair Album of Chicago : 1893.* Portland, ME: Chisholm Bros., n.d.

23x15. 12 plates on continuous accordion folded strip. Dark blue paper covered boards, gilt print and design of Administration Bldg. C.t. Bottom of cover: "Published for the R.R. Trade." ⊚ (HL)

1725. *World's fair : Chicago : 1893.* [Chicago: Chas. D. Stone & Co., ᶜ1891].

27x36. 47 *l* with plates one side. Dark green pebbled cloth hc, gilt print, gilt edges. C.t.
⊚ (CHx)

1726. *The World's Fair : Chicago, 1893 : Photo-gravures.* New York: A. Wittemann, The Albertype Co., ᶜ1893.

18x23. 1 *l*, 54 *l* of illus. Dark blue hc, gold letters and design, gilt text edges, decorated end papers. Albertype photo reproductions are printed on one side of heavy tan paper.
P→   ⊚ (GLD,PU,NYPL) $20 - 35

1727. *World's Fair : Chicago 1893 : Souvenir : Illustrated : Being a complete and concise history of the principal World's Fairs, from the Crystal Palace, London, 1851, to the World's Columbian Exposition in Chicago, 1893. Full page Art-type illustrations and descriptions of the principal buildings ...* Chicago: The Anabogue Publishing Co., [ᶜ1891 by J. D. Jones].

17x25. 1 *l*, 9-263 (i.e., 259), (1) p. + fold out world map at end; numbers 141-44 are omitted in paging. Red cloth hc, gold lettering, lightly speckled edges. A history with two pages of text followed by a leaf with b/w lithograph on one side. May be listed under author: [Jones, John David].
P↓   ⊚ . (GLD,CHx,LC,NYPL,S,BPL,TD) $18 - 34

1728. *World's fair, 1893. Photographs.* Chicago?: H. W. Hine, 1894.

28½x35½. (256) p. C.t.   (UoC)

1730. ... *Worlds* [sic] *Masterpieces of Modern Painting : Selected From The World's Columbian Exposition At Chicago Etc.* Philadelphia: William Finley & Co. Publishers, °1893.

Subscription set: 1 issue: 44x31½. (55) p., 7 b/w mounted plates. Half maroon cloth (spine) over brown hc, gilt print. Elaborate navy blue litho and print on enclosed front wrap. Title given is from enclosed wrap. At head of (OhHx) title: "Section 1 : Edition de luxe. Copy No. ___." On binder's cover: "Edition de luxe, Japan proofs." Each illus accompanied by comment on painting and information about the painter." TD no. 477; OhHx no. 502. Only one issue ?

©. (OhHx,TD) $100

Chapter 11

SALESMEN'S SAMPLES

Selling books by subscription was a general practice in the 1890s. Representative salespersons canvased the neighborhood using an abbreviated "salesman's sample" to show potential customers. The sample showed examples of the print style, pictures or lithographs, and different bindings available. Although they were printed in relatively small numbers, they do not command "scarce" prices since they are incomplete. They fall more in the category of an interesting business variant.

1731. Bancroft, Hubert Howell. *The Book of the Fair : an Historical and Descriptive presentation of the World's Science, Art, and Industry, as Viewed through the Columbian Exposition at Chicago in 1893. ...* Chicago and San Francisco: The Bancroft Co., 1893.

40½x31. ca. 50 p. Describes the different editions printed. Uncommon.   (S) $75?

1732. Banks, Charles Eugene. *The artistic Guide to Chicago and the World's Columbian exposition. Illustrated.* Boston: John K. Hastings, [°1893 by R. S. Peale co.]; N.p.: R. S. Peale co., 1893 [°1893 by R. S. Peale co.].

23x16½. 1½ cm thick. Brown cloth hc, gilt and black print and design, decorative end papers. 4 fold frontis is bird's-eye Chicago shoreline.   (UoC,S) $20 - 35

1733. Blaine, James G[illespie], J[ames] W[illiam] Buel, John C[lark] Ridpath, and Benjamin Butterworth. *Columbus and Columbia : an authentic history of the man and the nation.* Philadelphia: Standard Publishing Co., n.d.

26½x20½. (4) p. illus description of book and agent's canvassing outfit. Caption title. At top of p. (1): "Prices and profits to agents for the Magnificent New Book." Describes 3 binding styles: cloth, half morocco, full morocco with gilt edges.

P→   ☻ . (S)

1734. Blaine, James G[illespie], J[ames] W[illiam] Buel, John C[lark] Ridpath, and Benjamin Butterworth. *Columbus and Columbia : A Pictorial History of the Man and the Nation ...* New York: Hunt & Eaton, 1892.

26½x20½. Cloth hc has same design as #752.   (S)

1735. Boyd, James P. *Columbia : from discovery in 1492 to the World's Columbian exposition, 1892. Columbus and his Discovery: ... World's fair and gathered nations.* Philadelphia and Chicago: J. H. Moore & co., n.d.

23½x17. Frontis is Genoa port of Columbus. Could be ordered in fine English silk cloth with sprinkled edges ($2.50) and in full morocco with gilt edges ($3.50).

☻ . (S) $70

1736. *California's monthly Worlds* [sic] *Fair Magazine. Devoted to advancing California's Interests at the Columbian Exposition.* [San Francisco]: B Fehnemann, n.d.

23x14½. Prospectus; subscription price $3 per annum. Tan wraps, black print and logo.   ☺ . (HL)

1737. Cameron, William Evelyn. *The World's Fair, being a pictorial history of the Columbian Exposition* ... Newark, OH: Allison Publishing Co., [1893].

A salesman's copy with sample bindings in leather and cloth.   (OhHs)

1738. Campbell, James B. *Campbell's Illustrated History of the World's Columbian exposition.* Chicago: J. B. Campbell, 1892.

39x28. ca. 132 p. Black border design on dark brown cloth hc, gold lettering.
(S)
$55 - 90

1739. *Campbell's prize history of the World's Columbian exposition.* ____: ____, 18__.

30x23. (1) p. ad for the 12 part 3rd vol. Salesmen's handout printed in purple.   (NL)

1740. *The Columbian Congress of the Universalist Church.* Boston and Chicago: Universalist publishing house, 1894.

21½x13½. (4) p. salesmen's handout. Caption title. At head of title: "Now ready."   (NL)

1741. *The Columbian decorative art.* Buffalo, NY: J. B. Young & co., ᶜ1893 by J. B. Young.

34½x26. p. 71-104 (probably sample book). Red hc, black design and lettering. C.t.= t.p. Contains art ideas from represented nations.   (S)

1742. Dean, C. *The World's fair city and her enterprising sons.* [Chicago]: United publishing co., 1892 [ᶜ1892 by C. Dean].

21½x16½. Green decorative cloth hc with gilt, silver, and black lettering and design. Sample spine imprint on back cover.   ☺ (HL)

1743. *The dream city : A Portfolio of Photographic Views of the World's Columbian Exposition.* ... St. Louis: N. D. Thompson Publishing co., 1893-94 [ᶜ1893 by N. D. Thompson Publishing co.].

Salesmen gave away a single glossy sheet sample of the first illus in the book: The Administration Bldg. Blank on the back side and measures 29x35.
(GLD)
$8 - 16

1744. Eagle, Mary Kavanaugh Oldham, ed. *The Congress of Women : Held in the woman's building, World's Columbian Exposition, Chicago, U.S.A., 1893.* ... Official ed. Chicago: John E. Hoham & Co., 1894 [ᶜ1894 by W. B. Conkey co.].

26½x19½. Frontis of the Woman's Bldg. Dark olive green cloth on beveled boards, gold lettering.
 ☻ (GLD) $25 - 50

1745. Flinn, John J[oseph], comp. "... *The best things to be seen at the World's fair.*" [Chicago: The Columbian Guide co., ᶜ by the World's Columbian exposition].

11½x17. (1) p. Pale blue gray (or buff) salemen's flyer. At top of flyer: "Now ready and for sale by uniformed agents on the grounds." ☻ (GLD,TD) $7 - 15

1746. *Gems of the World's fair and Midway Plaisance : With Accurate and Valuable Descriptions of Each ... The World's Fair in Picture and Story.* Philadelphia: Historical publishing co., 1894 [ᶜ1894].

28½x34½. Turquoise cloth front hc, silver print. C.t.: "Gems of the World's Fair and Midway Plaisance." Back cover and spine are red cloth, gold print: "Glimpses of America." Unusual double salesmen's sample. ☻ (GLD) $25 - 50

1747. [Holley, Marietta]. (Pseud. Josiah Allen's Wife). *Samantha at the World's fair.* New York: Funk & Wagnalls co., Publishers, n.d.

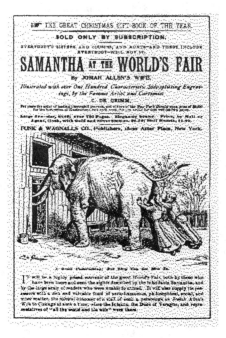

22x16. (1) p. illus salesmen's ad. Describes bindings: cloth and half leather. At top of ad: " ☞ The great Christmas gift-book of the year."
P→   ☻ . (S)

1748. [Jackson, William Henry]. *Jackson's Famous Pictures of the World's fair : Plan of Publication.* Chicago: The White City art co., n.d.

Single sheet describing the Educational Fine Art Series : Vol IV, serial no. 7-12. Published monthly. 12 pictures in each of the 7 "Artfolios;" last number (7) contains 8 pictures and 3 p. of descriptive text. Printed by The Lakeside Press, R. R. Donnelley & sons, co. ☻ . (RRD)

1749. [Jackson, William Henry]. *The White city (as it was) : Plan of Publication.* Chicago: The White City Art Co., n.d.

Single sheet describing the Educational Fine Art Series : Vol I, series 1-20. Published weekly. Single folios (parts) could be purchased at 50 cents. Printed by The Lakeside Press, R. R. Donnelley & sons, co. ☻ . (RRD)

1750. Johnson, Willis Fletcher, and John Habberton. "*My Country, 'Tis of Thee!*" : or, the United States of America; Past, Present and Future. A Philosophic View of American History and of Our Present Status, to be Seen in the Columbian exhibition. ... Philadelphia [and] Chicago: International publishing co., 1892 [ᶜ1892 by B. W. Urian].

21½x15. Incomplete paging. Brown cloth hc, gilt and black lettering and design, decorative floral end papers. Styles: 1) cloth, silk face, stamped in gilt and ink, sprinkled edges ($2.00); 2) half Russia, gold edges ($2.75). ☻ (TD,L) $20 - 35

1751. Kurtz, Charles M., ed. *Official : illustrations (three hundred and thirty-six engravings) from the art gallery of the World's Columbian exposition.* Philadelphia: George Barrie, 1893.

21½x15. White smooth cloth hc with gold embossed lettering and design both sides, red stained edges.
(F) $20 - 40

1752. Mabie, H., and M. Bright. *The Memorial Story of America.* Chicago: ____, 1892.
(cat) Worn: $18

1753. Melville, Geo. W., ed. *Proceedings of the Division of Marine and Naval Engineering ...* ____: ____, 18__.

24½x15. (4) p. salesmen's handout. List of papers included; price was $10. (NL)

1754. Mercer, L[ewis] P[yle]. *Review of the World's Religious Congresses of the World's Congress Auxiliary of the World's Columbian Exposition, Chicago, 1893.* Chicago and New York: Rand, McNally & Co., 1893.

20x14. (4) p. salesmen's handout. C.t. Buff paper with black print. (NL)

1755. Moses, John, and Paul Selby. *The white city. The Historical, Biographical and Philanthropical Record of Illinois, to which is added a sketch of the District of Columbia, the presidents of the United States, and Illinois at the World's Columbian exposition. Classified and illustrated.* Chicago: Chicago World Book Co., 1893.

21½x15. (4) p. prospectus. (csuf)

1756. Northrop, Henry Davenport. *Pictorial history of the World's Columbian Exposition : being a complete account of the great celebration of the four-hundredth anniversary of the discovery of America by Columbus. Containing a complete history of the World's fair: ... Embellished with Hundreds of Beautiful Engravings.* Des Moines, IA: M. L. Dudley & co., n.d.

23½x17. Bindings: blue-green cloth hc, gilt print and design; full morocco, gilt print and edges. ☺ . (S)

1757. Northrop, Henry Davenport. *Story of the new world. Being a complete History of the United States from the Discovery of the American Continent to the Present Time, ...* Magnificent Columbian ed. Philadelphia: National Publishing Co., [°1892 by J. R. Jones]; Philadelphia [and] Chicago: Elliott & Beezley, [°1892 by J. R. Jones].

National: 26½x19. Blue cloth front hc; black, red, and gold print; full embossed leather back cover, marbled edges. T.p. in red and black. A U.S. history expanded to include the WCE.

P→ ☺ . (GLD,S) $25 - 50

1758. *Official history of the World's fair : Being a Complete Description of the World's Columbian exposition From its inception, by Thos. W. Palmer, President ... Major Ben C. Truman, Department Chief of Floriculture and many others prominent in authority.* ____: Mammoth Publishing Co., n.d.

27x20½. To be available in 1) fine silk cloth, gull gold side and back; 2) half morocco, mottled edges, full gold side and back; 3) full morocco, gold edges and back, silk headbands. See also #1769. ⊚.(S)

1759. *The Official Memorial of the World's Columbian Exposition.* Chicago: The Henry O. Shepard Co. Printers and Publishers, n.d.

27½x19½. Green cloth hc, gilt print. Prospectus and sample pages. C.t.: "Memorial of the World's Columbian Exposition : by the Joint Committee on Ceremonies." ⊚.(A)

1760. *The Photographic World's Fair and Midway Plaisance : the main buildings, the entrances, the foreign, state and territorial buildings ...* Chicago, Philadelphia: Monarch Book Co., 1894; Philadelphia: Mammoth Publishing Co., 1894 [°1894 by W. B Conkey Co.].

16x24. 226 p. Green cloth beveled hc; silver, gold, and black embossed cover design. T.p. in red and black print. From W. B. Conkey photos. Unusual salesmen's sample since the sample is complete.
P→   ⊚ (GLD,S) $20 - 40

1761. Pierce, James Wilson. ... *Photographic history of the World's fair and sketch of the city of Chicago. Also, a guide to the World's fair and Chicago.* Baltimore: R. H. Woodward & co. overprinted with D. B. DePuy, Jr., 1893.

24x16. Notice: to be available in fine English cloth with plain edges ($2.00) and full morocco with gold edges ($3.50). At head of title: "Authentic edition." ⊚.(S)

1762. *Proceedings of the International Congresses of Education.* ____: ____, 18__.

35x22. (4) p. Salesman's handout lists congresses, papers presented, etc. "$2 per copy." (NL)

1763. Shepp, James W., and Daniel B. Shepp. *Shepp's World's Fair Photographed. Being a Collection of Original Copyrighted Photographs Authorized and Permitted by the Management of the World's Columbian Exposition,...* Chicago [and] Philadelphia: Globe Bible Publishing Co., 1893 [°1893 by D. B. Shepp].

23x28. Full leather blind-stamped front hc, blue cloth back cover, gold lettering, decorated end papers. Gilt, marbled, and plain edges respectively on the head, fore, and foot edges. T.p. printed in dark blue ink, text in black. ⊚ (GLD,S) $25 - 50

1764. *Shepp's World's Fair Photographed. A tornado of orders! The whole country swept as by a Prairie Fire! A tremendous avalanche of business! ...* Chicago [and] Philadelphia: Globe Bible Publishing Co., [1893].

30x61½. Yellow leaf with black print both sides. Full sized litho of Shepp's book cover in prospective. Solicits potential salesmen.   ⊚ (GLD) $15 - 36

1765. Shuman, Carrie V., comp. *Favorite dishes : a Columbian autograph souvenir cookery book : over three hundred autograph recipes, ...* Second ed. Chicago: Carrie V. Shuman, n.d.

20½x12½. (4) p. Prospectus. Buff smooth stock with black print. Book to be available in cloth ($1.50) and silk ($3.00).   ⊚ (GLD) $10 - 20

1766. *Special Instructions for the "World's Columbian Exposition, 1893." For agents* [sic] *use only.* N.p.: n.p., n.d.

15x9. 11 p., (1) p. Buff paper instruction pamphlet for the White and Igleheart sample book, this chapter. At the end, (1) p., is printed "The Publisher." It describes the door-to-door sales pitch and tactics to use. No cover; caption title.
  ⊚ (GLD) $15 - 30

1767. *Specimen Pages from "The Graphic History of the Fair".* Chicago: The Graphic Co., 1894.

41x28. (4) p., illus. Caption title. Below title: "Consists of 240 pages this size, printed on this quality paper, with nearly one thousand (1,000) illustrations ..."   ⊚ . (BPL)

1768. Sylvestre, Henri, Jr. ... *The Special Edition of Marvels in Art of the Fin de Siècle.* ____ : ____, 18__.

24½x15½. (4) p. salesmen's handout. Brown ink. C.t. Price was $50 for all 25 parts.   (NL)

1769. Truman, Ben[jamin] C[ummings]. *History of the World's Fair : being A Complete and Authentic Description of the Columbian Exposition from Its Inception.* Philadelphia [and] Chicago: John C. Winston & Co., 1893 [ᶜ1893 by Ben. C. Truman]; Philadelphia [and] Chicago: Mammoth Publishing Co., 1893.

Winston: 26½x21. Handsome morocco front cover and light blue cloth back cover decorated with brown, gold, and black print.
---- Providence, RI: W. W. Thompson and Co., [ᶜ1893 by Ben C. Truman]; Chicago: E. C. Morse and Co., [ᶜ1893 by Ben C. Truman]: T.p variants: ... *being A Complete and Official Description of* ... and Geo. R. Davis' name appears as first author.
  ⊚ . (GLD,S) $20 - 45
---- Large b/w broadside prospectus printed both sides.   (TD)

1770. Voris, Emma Frances. *The New Columbian White House Cookery : containing toilet, medical, and cooking receipts, comprehending economical and practical information ... superbly illustrated.* Chicago, Philadelphia, and Stockton, CA: Monarch Book Co. (Formerly L. P. Miller & Co.), [1893].

25½x19. Deep slate blue hc, black lettering and design. See #1041 for what appears to be the same publication by a different author.   ⊚ . (S)

1771. White, Trumbull, and Wm. Igleheart. *The World's Columbian Exposition, Chicago, 1893. A Complete History of the Enterprise; a Full Description of the Buildings and Exhibits in all Departments; and a Short*

Account of Previous Expositions, with an Introduction By ... Philadelphia: W. W. Houston & Co., 1893 [°1893 by J. W. Ziegler]; Philadelphia, Chicago: International Publishing, [°1893].

24x18. Textured full leather front hc, gold print; blue cloth back hc printed with design in blue, brown, gold, and black. 3 binding styles and 2 qualities of paper displayed.

⊜ (GLD,csuf) $20 - 40

1772. *World's Columbian Exposition Illustrated.* Chicago: J. B. Campbell, 1892.

39x28. 132 p.   (S)

1773. *World's Columbian Exposition souvenir, containing a Story of Christopher Columbus and his discoveries, a treatise on Illinois, Chicago and the Columbian exposition. Personal memoirs of leading citizens of Illinois.* Chicago: North American Engraving and Publishing Co., 1894.

30x16½. T.p. and first 78 p. of text with plates. Green cloth hc, black print.   (csuf)

1774. *The World's congress of representative women.* N.p.: n.p., n.d

17½x12½. (3)-30 p., ports (sample ports of women). Buff wraps. Plan of Women's Congress and 2 vol work of M. W. Sewall. The 2 vol in 1 price was $ 3.50; the 2 vol set price was $5.00. Salesmen's handout.   (NL)

1775. *The World's Fair in Water Colors : and the Prize Paintings of the Art Gallery.* N.p.: The Logansport Pharos, n.d.

28x21½. 1 antique blue leaf with black print one side. Announces 8 part portfolio of 64 p. text and 40 watercolors (titles listed).

⊜ (GLD) $7 - 15

1776. *... Yankee doodle at the fair : The Best of Everything.* Philadelphia: Printed and published by George Barrie, [°1893 by G. B.].

45x31½. glossy text. Flexible black pebbled cloth cover, no printing or design. Color and b/w illus. Sample articles. Three sample covers; each a beautiful multicolor litho. Bottom of each cover: "Copyrighted 1893 [or 1894] by G. B." Terms of subscription: $1.00 each monthly no. for a complete set of 12 numbers.   ⊜ (TD) $175

Chapter 12

STATES AND CITIES

The various states issued a tremendous amount of advertising literature and reports. The list here is surely incomplete. Prices will vary greatly, especially if the book is found in the state in which it was printed; local history can often command a premium price in its own region.

There were 50 states and territories in 1893. Thirty nine states and territories had buildings. Wyoming, Oregon, North and South Carolina, Alabama, Georgia, Mississippi, Tennessee, Nevada, Hawaii (Sandwich Islands), and Alaska did not. Unless designated otherwise in the publishing information, all publishers are located in the state cited.

Items from cities and states prior to U.S. Congressional selection of Chicago as the WCE site, are listed by the state from which they were issued.

All items are listed by the state of primary interest; brackets denote an item was issued in the state, not by the state. Hence, this chapter is, of itself, a state index, and the state name is not found in the index at the back of the book.

-Alabama-

1777. Alabama. *Acts of the General Assembly of Alabama, passed by the Session of 1892-93, held in the city of Montgomery, ...* Montgomery: Brown Printing Co., State Printers and Binders, 1893.

22x__. No WCE activity found. Also nothing in the 1890-91 Acts of Alabama. ☺ . (SamL)

-Alaska-

1778. Alaska. *Compilation of the acts of Congress and treaties relating to Alaska from March 30, 1867, to March 3, 1905, with ...* 59th Cong. 1st Sess. Senate. Doc. No. 142. Washington: GPO, 1906.

No WCE activity found. ☺ . (AkLRL)

-Arizona-

1779. Arizona (Territory). *Arizona. World's Columbian Exposition. Chicago, Ill. 1893.* Tuscon: Sunshine and Silver by authority of the World's Columbian exposition managers of Arizona, 1893.

40½x28. 2 (or 4?) issues. (4) p. each; promotional (no covers) of the Arizona Exhibit in the Mines and Mining Hall. Caption title. Facts, figures, land sales, sights, etc., in the Territory, in an illus newspaper format. [AZ, NM, and OK shared the Capitol Territories Bldg. The flat roof was used as a garden to display native plants of the region.]
☺ . (GLD,BM,UDe,AzHx) $20 - 40

1780. Arizona (Territory). *Session laws of the fifteenth, [sixteenth, seventeenth, eighteenth, nineteenth] legislative assembly of the territory of Arizona. ...* N.p.: n.p., n.d.

23x16. Bound together but separately paginated. 15th (1889): 74 p., 16th (1891): 165 p., 17th (1893): 142 p., 18th (1895): 118 p., 19th (1897) 140 p. Also 19 p. index at back of book. Tan leather hc, gilt print on red and black spine labels. 1897 Act provided for printing and binding together the 5 sessions. On March 19, 1891, (Act No. 103) the Territorial Legislature provided for a 4 citizen "Board of World's Fair Managers of Arizona" to act in conjunction with the two Territorial members the

President had appointed to the World's Columbian Commission. The Board was charged with securing "a complete and creditable display of the interests of the Territory." No compensation except actual expenses and $4/day subsistence for days of Board business. $30,000 was appropriated and made available by the sale of bonds; monies to pay bond interest was raised through increased real and personal property taxes. ☻ . (UMKC)

☞ June 1890, Governor Wolfley appointed George F. Coast, former mayor of Phoenix, and William Zeckendorf of Tuscon as members of the World's Columbian Exposition Commission. *Arizona Republican.* 6 June, 1890: 1. (AzHx)

☞ A brief reference to the WCE is made in *Legislative History, Arizona 1864-1912.* Compiled by George H. Kelly, State Historian, it was published in 1926. (AzHx)

-Arkansas-

1781. Arkansas. *Acts and resolutions of the General Assembly of the state of Arkansas, Passed at the Session, Held at the Capitol, in the City of Little Rock, Arkansas, which began on Monday, January 12th, and adjourned on Saturday, April 4th, 1891.* By authority. Morrilton: Pilot printing co., state printers, 1891.

House Concurrent Resolution No. 10: Action on bill to appropriate $100,000 for WCE exhibit was postponed. Approved Feb. 4, 1891. ☻ . (ArkHx)

1782. Arkansas. *Acts and resolutions of the general assembly of the state of Arkansas. Passed at the Session, held ... 1893.* By authority. Morrilton: Pilot printing co., state printers, 1893.

Act 48: Authorized a governor appointed 5 member board of directors for the "Arkansas World's Fair Association." Board to take charge of the AK WCE bldg and exhibits already collected so that the "great state of Arkansas may be advertised in the best manner possible." $15,000 was appropriated from the direct tax fund which had been paid to AK by the United States government. Of this, as salary, $1,000 was to be divided between the manager, lady assistant and janitor; $1,200 between the president and secretary. Approved Mar. 6, 1893. Act 69: authorized an educational exhibit; printing and binding of handouts not to exceed $300. Approved Mar. 17, 1893. ☻ . (ArkHx)

1783. Arkansas. *Arkansas. Eine genaue und zuverlässige Schilderung des Staates Arkansas zur Information für den farmer, den eine Heimstätte Suchenden und den, der sein Geld anlegen will.* N.p.: St. Louis Iron Mountain & Southern Ry Co [and] Little Rock & Fort Smith Ry Co, n.d.

23x15. 40 p. Faded green/beige wraps, black print and seals. C.t. In German. At bottom of cover: "G. A. A. Deane, land commissioner." Subject: Prospectus for potential farmers and homeowners -- people willing to immigrate to Arkansas. ☻ . (WM)

1784. Arkansas. Arkansas World's Fair Association. *Arkansas at the World's fair.* Little Rock: Arkansas Democrat Co. for the Arkansas World's Fair Association, 1893.

14 p. (UC)

1785. Arkansas. Arkansas World's Fair Directory. *Arkansas in 1892-1893. Prepared from data obtained from the census returns of 1890, and other authoritative sources. For the World's Columbian exposition.* Little Rock: "Diploma Press" Arkansas Democrat Co., 1893.

24x18. 132 p., frontis of State Capitol at Little Rock, many illus. Tan wraps, navy blue print and design. C.t.: "Arkansas. Illustrated." C.t., modest design along the upper and left borders, and back cover litho of Ourchita College, Arkadelphia are all in navy blue.   ⊚ . (LC,NYPL,NL)

1786. Arkansas. Cutter, Charles. *Cutter's guide to the hot springs of Arkansas. Illustrated.* St. Louis: Slawson printing co., 1893 ᶜ1876 by Charles Cutter.

19½x13½. 66 p. Light blue-green wraps with black print. 35th Edition. At top of cover: "Compliments of Arlington Hotel, Hot Springs, Ark."   ⊚ . (WM)

1787. Arkansas. *Fort Smith, Ark. Its History. Its Commerce. Its Location. Itself.* ____: ____, 189_.

22½x15½. 25 p. Yellow wraps, black print. C.t.: "Fort Smith, Ark. What it is. What it has. What it offers."   . (WM)

1788. Arkansas. *Welcher Staat ist's?* ____: ____, 189_.

16½x9½. Unpaged. Yellow-green wraps, black print and state seal. C.t. In German. First p. caption title: "Natürlich ist es Arkansas. Das Land des Sonnenscheines und Reichthums."   . (WM)

-California-

1789. [California]. *Afro-American Ostrich Farm from Fall Brook : San Diego Co. Cal. : Visit the Ostrich Farm, Midway Plaisance ... Admission 10 cents.* N.p.: Searle, n.d.

11½x13½. 1 *l* b/w ad with litho of ostriches and chicks.
P→   ⊚ (GLD) $12 - 26

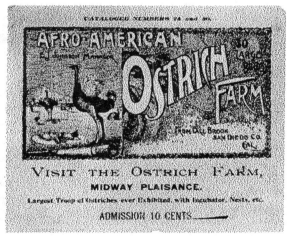

1790. [California]. Alameda County World's Fair Association. *Columbian Exposition Souvenir of Alameda County, California ...* Oakland: Tribune publishing co., n.d.; Woodbridge, CT: RPI, 1989.

15x22. 48 p., illus, maps. Gray wraps, red print, CA Bldg in brown on front cover. C.t.: "Alameda County, Central Garden Spot of California ..." WCE handout. On cover: Rand, McNally & co., Printers and Engravers, Chicago.
⊚ . (GLD,csuf,SI,F) $20 - 40

1791. California. Brook, Harry Ellington. *The County and city of Los Angeles in southern California : issued for distribution at the World's Columbian exposition by the county Board of Supervisors.* N.p.: Times-Mirror co., 1893.

22½x14½. 32 p. Teal wraps, black print, brown line design. Frontis is Los Angeles map. Cover illus of large globe covered with fresh oranges. Upper right cover: "World's Fair Edition."   ⊚ . (CHx)

1792. [California]. Brook, [Harry] Ellington, comp. *The Land of Sunshine : southern California : an authentic description of its natural features, resources and prospects. ...* Los Angeles: Southern California World's Fair Association Bureau of Information, 1893.

23x15. 2 *l*, 112 p. Glossy wraps with color tinted front and rear (CA Pavilion at WCE) illus. Tipped in pulp fold out land prospectus. Two page color map frontis on the 2 *l*.
P→   ⊚ (GLD,S,NL) $25 - 45

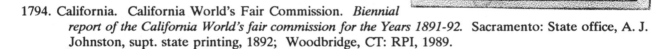

1793. California. *California café wine list : California Building, Jackson Park, Chicago, Illinois.* Chicago: Pettibone, Wells & co. printers, n.d.

22½x15. 24 p. Buff text paper. Tab indexed pamphlet of many wines for sale in the CA Bldg. C.t. Cover names L. D. Teal, Caterer.   ⊚ . (CHx)

1794. California. California World's Fair Commission. *Biennial report of the California World's fair commission for the Years 1891-92.* Sacramento: State office, A. J. Johnston, supt. state printing, 1892; Woodbridge, CT: RPI, 1989.

23x15. 19 p., plate, fold. frontis of CA Bldg. Black cloth hc, gilt lettering.
---- Also listed: 24 p.
        ⊚ . (csuf,SL,NYPL,CSA,NHSt,WiHx,HL)

1795. California. California World's Fair Commission. Cummins, Ella Sterling. *The story of the files : a review of Californian writers and literature.* [San Francisco: Co-operative printing co.], ᶜ1893 by Ella Sterling Cummins.

22½x15. 4 *l*, 460, (3) p. ads. Frontis of Indian maiden peering at ship on the horizon. Illus (including ports), plates. Tan paper covered beveled boards, chocolate print and floral design, speckled edges, decorative end papers. Errata slip at p. (439). "Issued under the auspices of the World's Fair commission of California, Columbian exposition, 1893." Description of literary works and criticism by CA writers. Libraries list author as: Ella Sterling (Clark) Mighels.
        ⊚ . (JHU,NYPL,UNR,UDe,NL,RPB,HL)

1796. California. California World's Fair Commission. *Final report of the California World's fair commission, including a description of all exhibits from the state of California, collected and maintained under legislative enactments, at the World's Columbian exposition Chicago, 1893.* Sacramento: State office, A. J. Johnston, supt. state printing, 1894; Woodbridge, CT: RPI, 1989.

23x15½. 1 *l*, vii, fold map, 240 p. + 65 *l* photos interspersed. Shiny burnt sienna (or black, or maize, or dark tan, or green) cloth hc, embossed gilt print. Frontis of CA Bldg at WCE. C.t.: "California at the World's Columbian Exposition. 1893."
---- Also appears in: California. Legislature. Senate. *The journal ... 31st sess. 1895.*
P↓   ⊚ (GLD,csuf,CHx,SL,NYPL,UNLV,F,SDHx,TnSt,UDe,UWy,HL,NYSt,UoC,NL,BPL,RPB,AIC) $30 - 50

1797. California. Keeler, Ezra W. *California for worldly eyes in 1893. The climate, products and resources ...* San Francisco: [Schmidt label & lith. co.], 1890.

19½x11½. 24 p., illus (includes plans). Decorative wraps in colors. A plan for the "pictorial presentation" of the state. C.t.: "California will beat the world in '93 at the Columbian fair, Chicago." Ads: p. 15-24. (csuf)

1798. [California]. Kern County World's Fair Association. *Location, resources, attractions and development of the Kern delta, Kern County, California, and its exhibit at the World's Columbian exposition.* Bakersfield: n.p., 1893.

25x17½. 24 p., illus, maps. Decorative wraps. Kern County includes the rich San Jacquin river valley north and east of Los Angeles. (csuf,NL)

1799. California. *Literary and other exercises in : California State Building, World's Columbian exposition, Chicago, 1893.* Chicago: Rand, McNally & Co., 1893; Woodbridge, CT: RPI, 1989.

23x14½. 96 p. Peach wraps with woven grid pattern, black print and litho of bear. C.t.= t.p. Relates events in the CA Bldg from May 1-Nov. 3, 1893. Nov. 3rd was the final CA banquet and closing.
 ☺ . (SI,HL,NL)

1800. California. Markham, H. H. *Resources of California.* Sacramento: A. J. Johnston, State Printer, 1893.

23x14½. 1 *l* (frontis), 144 p. Frontis: CA State Capitol bldg. Light green wraps with green and black illus and print both covers. Markham was governor. Handout at CA exhibit.
P→   ☺ (GLD,csuf) $20 - 45

1801. [California]. San Francisco Chronicle. *California at the World's Fair.* San Francisco: San Francisco Chronicle, 1893.

20½x15. Folded pulp *l* making (4) p., black print. Illus of CA Bldg with state seal and county list. Replica of their May 2, 1893, WCE articles in tiny newsprint is quite readable.
 ☺ (GLD) $12 - 28

1802. [California]. San Francisco World's Fair Association. San Francisco Women's Literary Exhibit. *Catalogue of Californian Writers issued by The San Franciscan Women's Literary Exhibit. Columbian exposition, 1893.* [San Francisco: 1893?].

14½x22½. 1 *l*, 22 p. Title given is from cover. ☺ . (HL)

1803. [California]. San Francisco World's Fair Association. San Francisco Women's Literary Exhibit. *A list of books by California Writers. Issued by The San Francisco Women's Literary Exhibit. Columbian exposition, 1893 ... Under the Auspices of the San Francisco World's Fair Association.* San Francisco: Raveley Printing Co., 1893.

23½x15. iv, 52 p. Gray wraps, black print. C.t.= t.p.   ☻ . (HL)

1804. [California]. Shasta County World's Fair Committee, comp. *Resources of Shasta County : California.* [San Francisco: Estate of A. J. Leary, printers], n.d.

17½x10. (1) p., p. 10, p. 11, 2-8 p. (i.e., 10 p.). Pale blue (or salmon) wraps, black print, pale pink pages. C.t.   ☻ . (HL,NL)

1805. California. *State of California : board of State Viticultural Commissioners : to exhibitors in The Viticultural Department Columbian Exposition.* [San Francisco, 1892].

20½x13½. (3)-7 p. Wraps same stock as text, black print and CA seal. C.t.   ☻ . (HL)

1806. California. *The Statutes of California and amendments to the codes, passed at the twenty-ninth session of the legislature, 1891. ...* Sacramento: State office, A. J. Johnston, supt. state printing, 1891.

23x15½. lvi, 566 p., 36 p. Leather hc. Chap. 38: Governor to appoint 7 commissioners, at least 1 from each congressional district, to constitute the "California World's Fair Commission." No pay but actual traveling expenses, not to exceed $2,000 each. $300,000 appropriated out of General Fund to erect bldgs and collect and maintain an exhibit. Approved: March 6, 1891.   ☻ . (MarL)

1807. California. *The Statutes of California ... 1893.* Sacramento: State office, A. J. Johnson, supt. state printing, 1893.

23x16. lv, 688, 40 p. Leather hc. Chap. 133: $25,000 appropriated for a "volume expository of the resources of the State of California, for the purpose of distribution" at the WCE. Approved Mar. 11, 1893. Chap. 134: $25,000 appropriated to defray expenses of transporting, insuring, and installing articles comprising the exhibit known as the "California Reception Room" in the Woman's Bldg. Chap. 149: Authorized appropriations from counties by class. Chap. 234: Board of supervisors authorized to appropriate money from the general fund.   ☻ . (MarL)

☞ Appropriations from counties (Chap. 149) did not always go smoothly: two letters at SDHx describe an over-spending accusation against one San Diego commissioner by another and her response.

-Colorado-

1808. Colorado. Agricultural Department, Colorado Exhibit. *The Resources, Wealth and Industrial Development of Colorado. Published by the Agricultural Department, Colorado Exhibit, at the World's Columbian Exposition, June 1, 1893.* N.p.: Press of G. M. Collier for the Agricultural Department, [ᶜ1893 by C. S. Faurot].

22½x14½. 196 p. Fine vertical aqua blue lines printed on wraps; black, aqua, and white print and design. C.t.: "A report on the resources and industrial development of Colorado." Illus of State Capitol Bldg, Denver, on outside back cover. Prepared under the auspices of the Colorado World's Fair Board of Managers. Faurot was Superintendent, CO Agriculture Dept.

$30

1809. [Colorado]. *At the foot of Pike's Peak. Some glimpses of a world famous resort lying amid the ... Rocky Mountains. With a word of suggestion for the World's fair traveler.* ___: ___, 189_.

14x18. Wraps with mountain view illus. C.t.   .(WM)

1810. Colorado. Board of World's Fair Managers of Colorado. *Circular A [submitting a "General plan for Colorado's educational exhibit at the World's Columbian Exposition."]* N.p.: n.p., [1892].

4°. No t.p.   (NYPL)

1811. Colorado. Board of World's Fair Managers of Colorado. *Report of Board of World's Fair Managers of Colorado.* Denver: ___, 1894.

71 p.   (UC)

1812. [Colorado]. *Colorado Gold Mining, Midway Plaisance, World's Fair. ...* N.p.: n.p., n.d.

14x9. Folded pulp *l* making (4) p., black print. The Automatic Model of the Saratoga Mine was open for display. It was invented by William Keast. Mining terms listed on p. (4).
☯ (GLD) $9 - 20

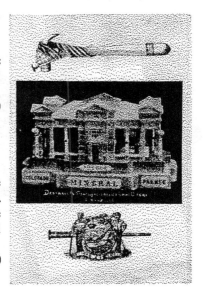

1813. [Colorado]. *The Colorado Mineral Palace casket.* N.p.: n.p., n.d.

14x9. (4) p. Illus of silver replica of Colorado Mineral Palace ("casket") on p. (1); illus and text in sepia (or navy blue) ink. Caption title from p. (2). From text description, the casket holds the Nebraska silver hammer and the gold "Montana Nail," also depicted on p. (1). All were displayed at the Woman's Bldg.
P→   ☯ (GLD,TD) $10 - 20

1814. Colorado. *Laws passed at the eighth session of the General Assembly of the state of Colorado, convened at Denver, on the seventh day of January, A.D. 1891.* Published by Authority. Colorado Springs: The Gazette Printing Co., State Printers, 1891.

23x16. 508 p. Rebound hc. WCE Act (S.B. 120): 6 citizen commission, including the governor, plus World's Columbian Commissioners and the CO Board of Lady Managers were designated "The Board of World's Fair Managers of Colorado." No pay except actual transportation expenses + $5/day when absent from home. Authorized counties to assess taxable property to make appropriations for county exhibits. $100,000 was appropriated from the state's general fund. Compelled the Board to call on all state-funded institutions for aid in developing the CO exhibit. Approved Apr. 18, 1891.   ☯ .(MarL)

1815. Colorado. *Laws passed at the ninth session ... Colorado ... 1893.* Published by authority. Denver: The Smith-Brooks Printing Co., State Printers, 1893.

23x16. 2 *l*, 654 p. Rebound hc. Chap. 167: $100,000 was appropriated. (Of the $100,000 appropriated in 1891, only $32,054 had been available in 1891 and 1892; by this 1893 amendment, the General Assembly appropriated more to carry out the original act and to erect the CO State Headquarter's Bldg.) Approved Feb. 1, 1893. ☻ . (MarL)

1816. Colorado. *World's Columbian Exposition, Department of Colorado. Act of Congress Creating World's Columbian Commission. Law Creating Board of World's Fair Managers of Colorado. Rules and regulations for government of board. Classification of exhibits. Names and addresses of Officers, Executive Committee and Members of Board.* Denver: Collier & Cleveland Lith. Co., ᶜ1891.

23x14½. 30 p. Gray wraps, black print. ☻ . (CPL,NYPL)

-Connecticut-

1817. Connecticut. Board of Lady Managers, World's Columbian Exposition. Knight, Kate Brannon. *History of the work of Connecticut women at the World's Columbian Exposition : Chicago, 1893 ...* Hartford: [The Hartford Press. Case, Lockwood & Brainard], 1898; New Haven, CT: RPI [n.p.], 1976.

27½x18½. vi, 171 p. and 25 *l* of interspersed plates. Frontis of the "Court of Honor," plates. Green cloth hc, gilt. Knight was president of the CT Board of Lady Managers.
☻ . (KU,KyU,csuf,CHx,SL,NYPL,UNLV,F,S,LMi,TnSt,UDe,SCSt,CtHx,NHSt,HL,NYSt,UoC,NL,RPB,WiHx) $30 - 50

☞ CT printed this report because Congress had postponed printing the report of the WCE Board of Lady Managers. This report was also published in the CT Managers' report #1819.

1818. Connecticut. Board of Lady Managers, World's Columbian Exposition. *Selections from the writings of Connecticut women.* Norwalk: Literary Committee, Connecticut Board of Lady Managers for the World's Columbian Exposition, 1893.

282 p.   (UC)

1819. Connecticut. Board of World's Fair Managers of Connecticut. *Connecticut at the World's Fair : Report of the commissioners from Connecticut of the Columbian Exhibition of 1893 at Chicago. Also Report of the Work of the Board of Lady Managers Of Connecticut.* Hartford: Press of The Case, Lockwood & Brainard Co., 1898; New Haven, CT: RPI, 1977.

24½x16½. x, 1 *l*, (9)-367 p., illus, plates, ports, plans, facsimiles. Dark maroon (or brown) hc, gilt. Photos of CT Bldg, Yale University exhibit, agriculture exhibit, etc. Report of the Lady Managers p. (199)-367 (also see #1817).
---- Also listed: 360 p. Black smooth hc.
---- Also listed: x, 10-360 p.
☻ . (KU,csuf,CHx,NYPL,UNLV,F,S,LMi,UDe,SCSt,CtHx,NHSt,UMi,NYSt,UoC,NL,BPL,RPB,WiHx,L) $40 - 65

1820. Connecticut. *History of music with methods employed in the New Haven public schools.* [New Haven: Press of Tuttle, Morehouse & Taylor], n.d.

17½x19½. 25, (3) p. White smooth wraps with blue print, glossy text pages. Text plus music tests administered. C.t.: Connecticut school document Number VIII : World's Columbian exposition 1893 : History of Music : New Haven Public Schools."
☻ . (GLD,NL) $15 - 32

1821. Connecticut. *Special Acts and Resolutions passed by the State of Connecticut, at the January Session, 1893.* Hartford: Press of the Case, Lockwood and Brainard Co., 1893.

23½x16. (3)-1228 p. Rebound hc. No. 18 authorized 16 named individuals to constitute the "Board of World's Fair Managers of Connecticut" and appropriated $65,000 to be paid out of the treasury. No. 179 appropriated $2,000 for the governor and staff to represent CT at the WCE opening. No. 483 appropriated an additional $5,000. No. 706 appropriated $600 for exposition of CT working oxen. (Yale,MarL)

-Delaware-

1822. Delaware. Harlan, C[aleb]. *Delaware's tribute to Columbus and the World's Columbian Exposition, Chicago, Illinois, U.S.A. : 1893.* [Delaware?]: n.p., ᶜ1892.

18x12½. 4 p. Wraps. Poem. C.t. Signed at end: C. Harlan. ☺. (UDe,RPB)

1823. Delaware. *World's Columbian exposition : department of Delaware : Names and residences of officers, committees, and members. Rules and regulations for the government of the board. Law constituting the board of World's fair managers of Delaware.* Dover: James Kirk & son, printers, 1891.

23x15. 12 p. Dark reddish brown (almost cordovan colored) wraps, gold printing. C.t.: "World's Columbian Exposition : department of Delaware" with state seal in center. ☺. (DelHx)

-District of Columbia-

1824. District of Columbia. *Annual Report of the commissioners of the District of Columbia ... 1892.* Washington: GPO, 1892.

23x16½. 1035 p. Rebound hc. Commissioners recommend that Congress appropriate $25,000 for an exhibit by the Nation's capitol. (HxDC)

☞ 1892 Annual report mentions earlier $ request -- probably in the 1891 report.

-Florida-

1825. Florida. *Fort Marion, St. Augustine, Fla. : Florida State Building, Jackson Park.* N.p.: n.p., n.d.

7x12. Pale green card, printed in black both sides. Souvenir of FL Bldg which was modeled after Fort Marion. (TD)

1826. Florida. Pio, Louis. *The East Coast of Florida. Its Climate, Soil and Products.* ____: ____, 189_.

20½x10½. Illus wraps of fruit and palm tree. Caption title. C.t.: "The East Coast of Florida." .(WM)

1827. Florida. *Regular session, 1893. Acts and resolutions adopted by the legislature of Florida at its fourth regular session, under the constitution of A.D. 1885, together with ...* Published by authority of law. Tallahassee: Printed at the Tallahasseean Book and Job Office, 1893.

23x15½. xxvi, 414 p., 64 p. Rebound hc. No. 54: Governor authorized to hold the Annual Encampment of the Florida State Troops at the city of Chicago, during the WCE. Approved June 2, 1893. [No WCE activity was found in the 1891 Acts.] ☺. (MarL,FSA)

-Georgia-

1828. Georgia. *Acts and Resolutions of the General Assembly of the State of Georgia. 1890-'91.* 2 vol. Atlanta: Geo. W. Harrison. State Printer. (Franklin Printing House), 1891.

No WCE statutes were found from 1890-93. Same publisher for 1892 (pub. 1893) and 1893 (pub. 1894). (MarL)

-Hawaii-

1829. [Hawaii]. *Hawaii : The burning crater of Kilauea : the greatest volcano on earth ... reproduced on the Midway Plaisance : World's fair 1893 : The palace of Pele-goddess of fire.* [St. Joseph, MI: A. B. Morse printing co.], n.d.

11x15½. (16) p. White wraps, green and red print, green litho of Pele rising above volcano. Describes construction, and operation of the model; b/w lithos of Kilauea.
P→   ☺ (GLD) $20 - 40

-Idaho-

1830. Idaho. *General laws of the state of Idaho passed at the first session of the state legislature, convened on the eighth day of December, A. D. 1890, and adjourned on the fourteenth day of March, A. D. 1891 at Boise City.* Published by authority. Boise City: Statesman printing co., 1891.

23x16. 280 p. Rebound hc. An act "creating a commissioner...": Authorized the governor to appoint one commissioner, the "Columbian Commissioner for Idaho," to serve without pay. He was given the power to employ as many assistants as he deemed necessary and was charged with sending as many articles for exposition as possible. Authorized erection of the Idaho Bldg, at a cost not to exceed $8,000. Approved March 1891. ☺ . (MarL,IdHx)

1831. Idaho. *General laws of the state of Idaho passed at the second session* [1893] *of the state legislature.* Boise City: Statesman printing co., 1893.

23x16. 253 p. Rebound hc. Appropriation Act: $30,000 out of any fund in the 1893 state treasury not otherwise appropriated. Approved Feb. 8, 1893. Act to secure fish: Made it legal for the World's Columbian commissioners to catch with a seine, net basket, etc. between March 1, 1893, and July 1, 1893, not to exceed 100 pounds of trout, bass, pike or any other species for exhibition at WCE and made it legal for any railroad company, express company or common carriers to transport fish during this time period. ☺ . (MarL,IdHx)

1832. Idaho. *Idaho at the Columbian exposition, 1893. Gem of the Mountains.* ____: ____, 189_.

13½x14½. Wraps with illus of ID Bldg. C.t. .(WM)

1833. Idaho. Idaho World's Fair Commissioner. Gregg, Herbert C. *Idaho : Gem of the Mountains. Official souvenir.* St. Paul, MN: Pioneer Press Co., 1893.

31x23½ (text). *35 l* including covers. Glossy paper cover and text. Illus, maps, port. C.t. Litho of Idaho log and field stone World's Fair Bldg on cover. ☺ . (PU,CPL,LC,WiHx)

1834. Idaho. Wells, James M. *Idaho at the World's Columbian Exposition. General instructions to all who are interested in our state. With sketch of the Idaho Building.* Boise: Statesman printing co., 1892.

20½x13. 24 p., plates. Wells was World's Columbian Commissioner for Idaho. ☺ . (WiHx)

-Illinois-

1835. [Illinois]. Burnham, Telford, and James F. Gookins. *Chicago the site of the World's fair of 1892 : the main exposition on the lake front, and Special Exhibitions at the Principal Parks, connected by a railroad circuit with all other lines of transportation, and the heart of the city.* ... Chicago: Rand, McNally, printers, 1889.

24x16. 28 p., 2 fold. maps. Early description and recommendation for joint WCE sites of Jackson Park <u>and</u> Grant Park (Michigan Ave.), connected by rail and steam ferry. [The final grounds included Jackson Park plus the Midway Plaisance. The steam ferry did subsequently exist -- the whaleback "Christopher Columbus."] (CHx,NL,AIC)

1836. [Illinois]. Chicago. *Chicago's last great day at the fair : Saturday, October 28, 1893.* N.p.: n.p., n.d.

28x21½. Unpaged. No wraps. Caption title. List of events at Music Hall starting at 10 a.m. includes address of welcome by Hon. Carter H. Harrison, Mayor of Chicago. ☺ . (WM)

☞ On October 28th, after the day's events, Mayor Harrison was mortally shot at his home by a disgruntled city employee. The murder modified the Closing Ceremonies. See booklet: *World's Columbian Exposition, Closing Ceremonies, October 30th 1893.* 20x15.--(WM call: T500 P96 no. 6)

1837. [Illinois]. Chicago. North Side Committee. *The North Shore Site.* [Chicago: n.p., 1890].

22½x15. (5) p. + trifold map of the proposed site tipped in at front cover. White wraps, black print and design. Dated Sept. 6, 1890. Arguments in favor of the North Shore Site for the WCE. Includes fold out plat showing railroad connections to the site. C.t. Site was on the lake front between Graceland Ave. and Lawrence. (CHx)

1838. [Illinois]. Chicago. *Official souvenir program of Chicago Day at the Fair : October 9th, 1893 : Twenty-Second Anniversary of the Great Fire.* Chicago: Thos. Knapp Printing and Binding Co., n.d.

26x17. (32) p. Buff wraps with red print, black Goes Co. litho on green background, "Chicago Day" on red background. All day celebration with parade and elaborate floats. Oct. 9th was the 22nd anniversary of the great Chicago fire. C.t.: Official Souvenir Programme : World's Columbian Carnival : Chicago Day : October 9th 1893." ☺ . (E,UDe,NL,F)

1839. [Illinois]. Chicago. The States' Association [of Chicago]. *Constitution, Roll of Members, Officers, and Committees.* [Chicago: J. C. Benedict, Printer for] The State's Association, n.d., [1890?].

14½x9. 12 p. Tan wraps, dark blue print. C.t. "The object of this Association shall be to enable the several State organizations of Chicago to co-operate for the purpose of promoting the success of the Columbian exposition..." The mayor was a member; dues $1 per annum. ☺ . (LC)

☞ This group was very important in gaining support for the Fair, and the Fair at Chicago. Residents living in Chicago and originally from other states formed "alumni" groups to get the word out across America. CHx has a series of one page ads soliciting aid, cooperation, etc.--(CHx call: qF38MZ 1893 D11 1889).

1840. Illinois. Chicago. *The World's fair. Where Shall it be Held? Points in favor of the west side.* [Chicago: Garfield Park Improvement Association], n.d.

21x13½. (4) p. plea for Garfield Park site; recognition it lacked the water view of the Jackson Park and North Side sites.   (CHx,UMi)

1841. Illinois. Horticultural Board of Control. Dunlap, Henry M., ed. *Report of the Illinois Horticultural Board of Control Having in Charge of the Fruit Exhibit of the State in the National Horticultural Building at the World's Columbian Exposition.* Bloomington: Pantagraph Printing and Stationery Co., n.d.

21½x14½. 75 p. Maroon textured heavy wraps, gold lettering.   (F) $20 - 35

1842. Illinois. Horticultural Board of Control. *Facts, not fiction : Illinois, A brief summary of its advantages as a Fruit Growing Section.* N.p.: n.p., 1893.

19½x13½. 30 p. Color lithographed wraps. Describes IL Fruit Exhibit in Horticulture Hall. C.t.: "A Horticultural State : Illinois Fruit Exhibit World's Columbian Exposition 1893."
P→   ⊚ (GLD,CHx,UDe) $15 - 30

1843. Illinois. Illinois Board of World's Fair Commissioners. *By-laws and rules of the Illinois Board of World's Fair Commissioners.* N.p.: n.p., n.d.

15x10½. 17, (1) p. Light green wraps, black print. C.t.
⊚ . (CPL)

1844. Illinois. Illinois Board of World's Fair Commissioners. *The Illinois building and exhibits therein : at the World's Columbian exposition : 1893.* Chicago: John Morris Co., n.d.; Woodbridge, CT: RPI, 1989.

23½x16. 152 p. includes illus and interspersed plates, glossy paper. Plates on one side only but verso counted in paging. Rust cloth hc, gilt print, decorative end papers. C.t.: "Illinois State Building 1893." ---- Autographed copies by John Virgin and W. D. Strykes, commissioners.
---- 156 p.
⊚ . (GLD,csuf,KyU,UWa,CHx,SI,F,S,UoC,NL,OC) $25 - 50

1845. Illinois. Illinois Board of World's Fair Commissioners. *Report of the Illinois Board of World's Fair Commissioners at the World's Columbian exposition. May 1 - October 30, 1893.* [Springfield: H. W. Rokker, Printer and Binder, 1895]; Woodbridge, CT: RPI, 1989.

23½x14½. xiii include a frontis of IL Bldg (on a recto), 757 p. includes plates. Red (or black or blue) cloth hc, gilt lettering on spine, decorative end papers.
⊚ . (GLD,csuf,CHx,SI,NYPL,F,S,SLP,NHSt,UMi,UoC,NL,A,nwu,WiHx) $35 - 65

1846. Illinois. The Illinois Conference of Charities and Corrections. *Hand-book of Chicago's Charities.* Chicago: Printed and illustrated by Edwin M. Colvin, [°1892 by John Visher].

20x14. 173, (1) p., 3 *l*, + unpaged color fold. map of Chicago and WCE grounds which follows the t.p., illus. Burnt sienna cloth hc, gold print. Includes item on the Emergency Hospital in the Woman's Bldg. ☉.(LC)

☞ The WCE Hospital handled 18,500 cases in 6 months; many cases were due to overheating, crowding, fainting, etc. 23 people died at the hospital. The hospital had an ambulance system.

1847. Illinois. Illinois Woman's Exposition Board. *History of the Illinois Woman's Exposition Board. (1891-94).* N.p.: n.p., n.d.

33½x20½. 27 mimeographed *l* (first 24 are paged). Mrs. Marcia Louise Gould, president. CHx call: qF38MZ 1893 F312W8. (CHx)

1848. Illinois. Illinois Woman's Exposition Board. *Illinois Women's Work : compiled by the Illinois Woman's Exposition Board as a tribute to the women of the county Columbian clubs. Mrs. Francine E. Patton ...* Springfield: Illinois State Register Print, 1893.

22x15. 104 p. Bound with the Board's *Official catalogue* (#1849). (CHx)

1849. Illinois. Illinois Woman's Exposition Board. *Official Catalogue of the Illinois Woman's Exposition Board.* Chicago: W. B. Conkey Co., Official Publishers to the Columbian Exposition, 1893; Woodbridge, CT: RPI, 1989.

22x15. 143 p. Frontis is a collage of Illinois Woman's Board members' ports. Bound with *Illinois Women's Work* (#1848). ☉.(CHx,SI,TU,NL)
---- 144 p. Presentation copy. Tissue guard protects frontis. Royal blue leather hc, gilt print title on spine, gilt print and design on front cover, beautiful royal blue and gilt end papers, all edges gilt. On cover: "Presented to Bertha Honoré Palmer President of the National Board of Lady Managers by The Illinois Woman's Exposition Board." CHx call: F38MZ 1893 F3 I2W7.

1850. Illinois. *Laws of the State of Illinois, passed by the thirty-seventh general assembly, at the regular biennial session which Convened at the Capitol, in Springfield, on the 7th day of January, A.D. 1891, and adjourned sine die on the 12 day of June, A.D., 1891.* Springfield: H. W. Rokker, State Printer and Binder, 1891.

21x14½. 239 p. Rebound hc. Appropriation Act: provided for IL participation in the WCE; created IL Board of World's Fair commissioners made up of the then present members of the State Board of Agriculture. Empowered the Board to properly install a collective departmental exhibit for the State; appropriated $800,000 from the state treasury; constituted the "Illinois Woman's Exposition Board" (4 member appointed by the Governor) which could control and expend 10% of the total appropriation. Approved June 17, 1891. (MarL)

1851. Illinois. *Laws of the State of Illinois, passed by the thirty-eighth general assembly at the regular biennial session which Convened at the Capitol; in Springfield, on the 4th day of January, A.D. 1893, and adjourned sine die on the 16th day of June, A.D. 1893.* Springfield: H. W. Rokker, State Printer and Binder, 1893.

21x14½. 205 p. Rebound hc. The 1891 $800,000 Appropriation Act was amended to provide: a board and $20,000 for a fruit display, a board and $15,000 for a dairy display, a board and $8,000 for a display of IL manufactured clay products, and a board and $3,500 for an apiary display. The amended act also empowered the board of commissioners to produce a collective departmental exhibit illustrating IL natural resources, $25,000 for the attendance and exhibit of the IL National Guard, a collection of natural history and archaeology, and architectural drawings of every IL public bldg erected and in use. By provision of the IL Constitution, appropriations ended with the expiration of the first fiscal quarter after adjournment of the next regular session of the General Assembly, therefore, any balance of the original $800,000 not paid out before Oct. 1, 1893, would be lost. The 1893 General Assembly reappropriated any balance unexpended as of Oct 1, 1893. Approved June 17, 1893.   (MarL)

---- *All the laws of the state of Illinois passed by the thirty-eighth general assembly, Convened January 4, 1893. Adjourned sine die June 16, 1893. With Head Notes and References to the Revised Statutes of 1891. By Myra Bradwell.* [Chicago]: Chicago Legal News Co., 1893.

25½x17½. >148 p. (some index missing). Tan leather hc, gilt lettered red and black spine labels.
☺ . (UMKC)

1852. Illinois. *Souvenir of the Illinois Dairy Exhibit, World's Columbian Exposition, 1893.* Chicago: J. F. Leaming & Co., n.d.

17x12. 31 p. Red stiff cloth covered paper wraps, gold print. Contains b/w drawings and photos of details of the exhibit.   (F) $15 - 30

1853. Illinois. State Bureau of Labor Statistics. "Coal Mining Exhibits at the World's Columbian Exposition." In *Statistics of coal in Illinois, 1893...* Springfield: H. W. Rokker, State Printer and Binder, 1894.

22½x15. (i)-(ix), x, 162 p. Black cloth hc, gilt print on spine. Article on p. 135-56.   (CHx)

1854. Illinois. 37th General Assembly. Senate. *A Bill for an act to provide for the participation of the State of Illinois in the World's Columbian exposition, authorized by act of Congress of the U.S.* N.p.: n.p., n.d.

Caption title is the same for both of the following: Feb. 1891: No. 129, and Apr. 1891: No. 374. CHx call: F37EB 1891.   ☺ (CHx)

-Indiana-

1855. Indiana. ... *Address to Governor Alvin P. Hovey and the General Assembly of Indiana, by the Commissioners and Lady Managers and Their Alternates for Indiana.* Indianapolis: William B. Burford, printer and binder, 1890.

22½x15. (4) p. Light green wraps, black print. C.t. Address given on Dec. 10, 1890, at Indianapolis was a plea to the governor to advertise Indiana resources through state representation at the WCE. 3 newspaper editorials printed inside back cover. At head of title: "Department of Indiana. The World's Columbian Exposition."   ☺ . (CPL)

1856. Indiana. Board of World's Fair Managers of Indiana. Committee on Education. ... *General exhibit of the Educational Work, of the state of Indiana, U. S. A. : prepared by committee on education.* La Porte: La Porte printing co., n.d.

23½x15½. 20 p. At head of title: "World's Columbian Exposition, 1893." ☺. (CPL,NL)

1857. Indiana. Board of World's Fair Managers of Indiana. Committee on Women's Work. ... *Committee on women's work. ... Department G.* Indianapolis: Wm. B. Burford, lithographer, printer and binder, 1892.

21x13. 14 p. At head of title: "Board of World's Fair Managers of Indiana." May Wright Sewall of Indianapolis was chairman (see #2268 for another Sewall item). Describes aims to be attained by the committee and exhibit types for women. [IN uses "women," not woman.] ☺. (NYPL)

1858. Indiana. Board of World's Fair Managers of Indiana. Havens, B. F. *Indiana at the World's Columbian Exposition. 1893. Report of B. F. Havens, Executive Commissioner. Board of World's Fair Managers of Indiana. June 14, 1893.* Chicago: Rand, McNally & Co., Printers, 1893.

23x15½. 32 p. includes covers, black print. C.t. IN State Bldg illus on p. 32 (back cover). ☺. (CPL,LC)

1859. Indiana. Board of World's Fair Managers of Indiana. Havens, B. F. *Indiana : World's Columbian Exposition, 1893. Final report of B. F. Havens, Executive Commissioner, Board of World's Fair Managers, Indiana. Terre Haute, Indiana, April, 1894.* Terre Haute: Globe Printing House, n.d.

22x15. 32 p. Sandstone wraps, black print. C.t.= t.p. ☺. (CPL,NYPL,WiHx)

1860. Indiana. Harper, Ida A. ... *The Associated Work of the Women of Indiana.* Indianapolis: Wm B. Burford, printer and binder, 1893.

22½x15. 52 p. Pale gray-blue wraps, black print. C.t.= t.p. At head of title: "Indiana World's fair monographs." ☺. (CPL)

1861. Indiana. *Laws of the state of Indiana, passed at the Fifty-Seventh Regular Session of the general assembly, Begun on the Eighth Day of January, A. D., 1891.* By authority. Indianapolis: Wm. B. Burford, contractor for state printing and binding, 1891.

23x16. 592 p. Rebound hc. Chap. 165: A 26 member commission appointed by the governor; known as "Board of World's Fair Managers of Indiana." Also many named *ex officio* members. No compensation except actual expenses. Board to appoint a salaried Executive Commissioner. Appropriation: $75,000 from any money in the Treasury not otherwise appropriated. Approved March 9, 1891. ☺. (MarL)

☞ IN had one of the largest state board of World's Fair managers. The size must have proved unwieldy as evidenced by the language of the 1893 statute below.

1862. Indiana. *Laws of the State of Indiana, passed at the fifty-eighth regular session ... 1893.* By authority. Indianapolis: Wm. B. Burford, contractor for state printing and binding, 1893.

23½x15½. 478 p. Rebound hc. Chap. 153: Whereas, the successful management of funds was found to be best secured by a small rather than a large number of persons, it was made the duty of the Executive Committee of the Board to close out the IN exhibit at the close of the WCE, including the sale of the IN Bldg and property distribution. Appropriation: $50,000 to complete, equip, and maintain the IN Bldg during the WCE. Of the $50,000, $1,000 was to be set aside to aid in exhibition and sale of women's work. Secretary of the Board's position abolished; all salaries to cease except those enumerated. Approved March 4, 1893. ☺. (MarL)

1863. Indiana. *Souvenir of the Dedicatory Ceremonies of the Indiana State Building, at Jackson Park, Chicago, Illinois, June 15, A. D. 1893.* N.p.: n.p., n.d.

22½x30½. 15 *l* + frontis litho, each *l* is numbered and printed on one side only. Cover is buff-colored laid paper, lettering in medium green. String tied with medium blue twisted cord, threaded through 3 holes. C.t. ☺. (InHx,NL)

1864. Indiana. *World's Columbian Exposition. Department of Indiana. Law constituting the Board of World's Fair Managers of Indiana. Rules and Regulation for the Government of the Board. Names and residences of Officers, Committees and Members of Board.* Indianapolis: Wm. B. Bufford, [1891?].

22x14½. 19 p. Light green wraps, black print. C.t. Clem Studebaker was President of IN Board. ☺. (SFe,CPL)

-Iowa-

1865. Iowa. *Acts and resolutions passed at the regular session of the Twenty-Third General Assembly of the state of Iowa, begun January 13, and ended April 15, 1890.* Published under authority of the state. Des Moines: G. H. Ragsdale, state printer, 1890.

25x16. 1 *l*, iv-xvi, 1 *l*, (iii)-xxiv, 213 p. Rebound hc. The earliest mention of the WCE was S. Res. (Jan. 16, 1890), favoring Chicago as the location for the WF. On Apr. 15, 1890, while Congress was still considering the bill providing for a World's Fair, the IA General Assembly authorized (Chap. 126) an 11 member "Iowa Columbian Commission" and appropriated $50,000 out of the state treasury (no appointments were to be made nor money drawn until it was known when the WF would be held). ☺. (KU,IaHx)

1866. Iowa. *Acts and resolutions passed at the regular session of the twenty-fourth general assembly of the state of Iowa, ... 1892.* Published under authority of the state. Des Moines: Geo. H. Ragsdale, state printer, 1892.

25x16. 216 p. Rebound hc. Chap. 81: $125,000 appropriated from the state treasury for carrying out the intent of Chap. 126 of 1890 (the $50,000 1890 appropriation was voided). Not more than 12.5% was to be used for salaries and expenses of employees. Effective after publication in the *Iowa State Register* and *Des Moines Leader* (Des Moines newspapers). ☺. (KU,IaHx)

1867. Iowa. Iowa Columbian Commission. Committee on Archæological, Historical and Statistical Information. *A hand book of Iowa, or the discovery, settlement, geographical location, topography ... of the State of Iowa. The Brightest Star in the American Constellation.* [Dubuque]: Published by the Commission [Telegraph Print], 1893.

23x15. 4 *l*, 154 p., (2) p. Light green (or tan) wraps, black print. Color map (2 *l*) between p. 52 & 53. Frontis (1st *l*) is a lithograph of the Iowa State Capitol. Yellow errata slip inserted before front end paper. C.t.= t.p. Handout at the Fair. Committee member authors were Charles Ashton, James O. Crosby, and J. W. Jarnagin. Contained in: *Report of the Iowa Commission* (#1870). P↑   ☉ (GLD,UMKC,CHx,OSU,SLP,NL,OC,WiHx) $15 - 27

1868. Iowa. Iowa Columbian Commission. ... *Minutes of meetings of the Iowa Columbian Commission.* Cedar Falls: Globe printing house, n.d.

22½x15½. 30 p. At head of title: "World's Columbian Exposition, Chicago, U.S.A., 1893." The Iowa Columbian Commission organized early (Sept. 2, 1890). F. N. Chase, Secretary.   ☉ .(CPL)

1869. Iowa. Iowa Columbian Commission. *The official directory of the Iowa Columbian Commission : containing the act of the Iowa general assembly creating the Iowa commission, also the act of Congress inaugurating the World's Columbian Exposition.* Cedar Falls: Gazette book and [sic] job printing house, 1890.

15½x9. 28, (1) p. Light blue-gray wraps, black print. C.t.= t.p. Early definition of Iowa at the WCE, commissioners, etc.   ☉ .(CPL)

1870. Iowa. Iowa Columbian Commission. *Report of the Iowa Columbian Commission, containing a full statement of its proceedings, including a list of all disbursements, accompanied by complete vouchers therefor : Chicago, A.D., 1893.* Cedar Rapids: Republican Printing Co., printers and binders, 1895; Woodbridge, CT: RPI, 1989.

23½x16. 421 p., (1) p. roster of employees at the IA Bldg. Dark blue (or brown) cloth hc, gold printed seal and c.t.: "Iowa at the World's Columbian Exposition Chicago 1893." A 2 p. color map is tipped in between p. 280-81. Frontis of Iowa State Bldg. Contains: *Hand Book of Iowa* at p. 223-377.
P→   ☉ (GLD,UMKC,csuf,CHx,SLF,OhHx,OSU,UoC,WiHx) $30 - 50

1871. Iowa. Iowa Columbian Commission. *Souvenir of the Dedicatory Ceremonies of the Iowa State Building, at Jackson Park, Chicago, Illinois, October 22, A. D. 1892.* [Chicago: Press of Pettibone, Wells & Co., ᶜ1892 by the Iowa Columbian Commission].

23x30. 1 *l* glossy frontis of IA Bldg, 15 *l* of text on fine tracing paper. Tan stiff wraps, sepia print. C.t.   ☉ .(NL,S,WiHx)

1872. Iowa. Iowa Columbian Commission. *Souvenir Program. Iowa State Days. September 20 and 21. World's Columbian Exposition, Chicago, 1893.* New York: The Albertype co., ᶜ1893 by Iowa Columbian Commission, Des Moines; Woodbridge, CT: RPI, 1989.

11x18. (15) p. Striking mustard yellow (or blood red) smooth heavy wraps tied with yellow ribbon, bold embossed gilt lettering.
---- Also listed: 32 p.
        ☉ . (GLD,KyU,SLF,WiHx) $20 - 35

1873. Iowa. McFarland, W. M. *Address of Hon. W. M. McFarland at the Columbian exposition, Chicago, formal opening of the Iowa building : May 1, 1893.* N.p.: n.p., n.d.

> 15x12. (16) p. including t.p. Maize wraps, illus of IA Bldg on outside back wrap. Black print c.t.: "Opening of the Iowa building, Columbian Exposition, Chicago, May 1, 1893." [McFarland was Iowa Secretary of State 1890-96.] ☻ (GLD) $20 - 35

-Kansas-

1874. Kansas. Board of Directors for the Kansas Educational Exhibit. *Report of the Board of Directors for the Kansas Education Exhibit at the World's Fair, Chicago, 1893.* Emporia: The Rowland Printing Office, 1894.

> 21½x14½. 29 p. Light lime green (or gray) textured wraps, black print. C.t.= t.p. KS superintendent, C. M. Light, reported that the entire (i.e., more than just KS) educational exhibit "surpassed anything in the educational line the world has ever seen." ☻ . (KU,KsHx,UMi,WiHx)

1875. Kansas. Board of World's Fair Managers of Kansas. ... *The board of managers, Kansas Exhibit. Proceedings of the Board. Financial statement showing receipts and expenditures; reports of superintendents in charge of departments. Topeka, Kansas, January 18, 1893.* Topeka: Crane & Co., 1893.

> 23x__. 21 p. At head of title: "World's Columbian Exposition, Chicago, Ill. 1893." (KsHx,WiHx)

1876. Kansas. Board of World's Fair Managers of Kansas. *The Board of World's Fair Managers of Kansas invites you to participate in the ceremonies incident to Kansas Week at the World's Columbian Exposition,* ... N.p.: n.p., n.d.

> 18x11. Folded *l* forming (3) p. including front cover. C.t. Light purple ink. Program of events for the week of Sept. 11th to 16th, 1893. See also #1884.
>
> ☻ . (GLD,KsHx) $14 - 28

1877. Kansas. Board of World's Fair Managers of Kansas. *Report of the Kansas Board of World's Fair Managers, Containing report of the Board of Fair Managers, Kansas exhibit from April 1892, to March 1893, and transactions of the Kansas Board of World's Fair Managers from March 1893 to Dec. 1893,* ... Topeka: Press of the Hamilton Printing Co., Edwin H. Snow, State Printer, 1894.

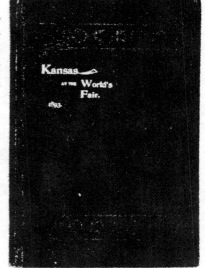

> 1st ed: 23½x16. 1 *l*, viii, 115 p. + many unpaginated photo illus. Knobby textured Prussian blue (or black) cloth hc, cloth spine, spine and cover with gilt print. C.t.: "Kansas at the World's Fair." Tipped in label before front end paper: "Compliments of T. D. Coburn, Secretary."
> ---- 2nd ed.: viii, 138 p. Black hc, gold print. A. H. Horton's address dedicating the KS Bldg on Oct. 22, 1892 is found at page 101. Program for "Kansas Week," Sept. 11-16, 1893, is found at p. 111-112. C.t.: "Kansas at the World's Fair. 1893."
> ---- 2nd ed.: 133 p. Dark red hc.

P→   ☻ . (GLD,KU,csuf,SI,NYPL,UMi,F,S,KsHx,USD,WiHx) $25 - 45

1878. Kansas. *Kansas educational exhibit At the World's Fair, Chicago, 1893.* Emporia: Rowland Printer, n.d.

13x17. (4) p. Caption title. 4 b/w vignettes. Lists exhibit locations, KS student/teacher population table and text. ☺ . (KsHx,NL)

1879. [Kansas]. Kansas Salt Company. *Souvenir of Hutchinson, Kansas.* [Hutchinson: Ewing Strumm, ᶜ1893].

15½x23. 36 *l* with photos on one side. Navy blue cloth hc, gilt stamped. Caption title. C.t.: "World's Columbian Exposition Souvenir : Kansas Salt Co. : Hutchinson, Kansas." Many of the photos depict aspects of the salt refining industry in Hutchinson. ☺ . (CPL)

1880. Kansas. *Kansas schools and Columbian exposition. Programme of exercises for Columbian Day, in the schools of Kansas. Proposed Time, March 25th and April 22d, 1892.* Topeka: Geo. W. Crane & co., printers and binders, 1892.

23x15. 16 p. Tan wraps. ☺ . (KsHx)

1881. Kansas. Kansas State Historical Society. Adams, F. G., ed. *Transactions of the Kansas State Historical Society 1889-'96; Together with ... Minutes.* Vol. V. Topeka: Press of the Kansas State Printing Co., J. D. Hudson, State Printer, 1896.

23½x16½. 695 p. Burgundy hc, gold print on spine. Of $500 appropriated for the Society's exhibit in the KS Bldg, $51.02 remained after placing, caring for, and returning the exhibit. Spine title: "Kansas Historical Collections : Vol. 5 : 1891-1896." (KU)

1882. Kansas. Kansas State Historical Society. *A Directory of the Kansas Historical Exhibit in the Kansas State Building, at the World's Columbian Exposition, 1893. Exhibited by the State Historical Society.* Topeka: [Press of the Hamilton Printing Co. (E. H. Snow, State Printer)], 1893; Woodbridge, CT: RPI, 1989.

23x15½. 36 p. Tan wraps, black print. C.t.= t.p. Exhibit contained KS pictures, books and newspaper files. ☺ . (KU,SI,NYPL,KsHx,NYSt,UoC,WM,WiHx)

1883. Kansas. Kansas State Historical Society. Kansas Educators, comp. *Columbian History of Education in Kansas. An account of the public-school system, ...* Topeka: Press of the Hamilton printing co., Edwin H. Snow, State Printer, 1893; Woodbridge, CT: RPI, 1989.

23½x16. 1 *l* (t.p.), (iii)-viii, (1), 2-231 p. Maroon shiny cloth hc with gilt print. C.t.: "Columbian History of Education in Kansas. 1893." Many b/w photos on one side of plates which are not included in pagination. ☺ . (UND,SI,NYPL,S,UoC,NL)

1884. Kansas. *Kansas Week at the World's Columbian Exposition, Jackson Park, Chicago, September 11th to 16th, 1893.* N.p.: n.p., n.d.

16x15. (2) p. not including cover. C.t. Times and program of events for the week. Also see #1876. ☺ . (KsHx)

1885. Kansas. *Kansas Week at the World's Fair.* N.p.: n.p., n.d.

22x14. (1) p. ad leaflet for State sponsored special train trip from Topeka and Kansas City to Chicago for Kansas Week at the WCE. ⊚ . (KsHx)

1886. Kansas. Lewelling, L. D. *An Address by Gov. L. D. Lewelling, Of Kansas. Delivered at the Kansas Building, World's Columbian Exposition, Chicago, September 12, 1893, the occasion being "Kansas Week" at the World's Fair.* N.p.: n.p., n.d.

23x15. 8 p. Beige tan wraps, black print. Title from cover. ⊚ . (CHx)

1887. Kansas. *Mineral Resources of Kansas.* N.p.: n.p., n.d.

22½x14½. 23 p. Buff wraps same as text, black print. C.t. Handout to demonstrate KS "great mineral wealth." KU catalog lists pub info: [Topeka: State Printer, 1893].

⊚ (GLD,KU) $12 - 26

1888. Kansas. *Programme of exercises for Columbian day in the schools of Kansas.* Topeka: Crane, 1892.

Oversize. 29 p. (KsHx)

1889. Kansas. State Board of Agriculture. Hay, Robert. ... *Geology and mineral Resources of Kansas. From the Eighth Biennial Report of the State Board of Agriculture, 1891-92.* Topeka: Hamilton Printing Co., 1893.

24x15½. Map, 66 p., (1 *l*), illus. Light green wraps, black print. Frontis is folding map by Hay. C.t.= t.p. At head of title: "World's Fair Edition."
---- Without "World's Fair Edition."
---- In Kansas U Geological survey. ... *Annual bulletin on mineral resources of Kansas.*
⊚ . (KU,UoC)

1890. Kansas. State Board of Agriculture. *World's Fair Report, Containing Statistics showing the growth of the state and the development of her resources. Also, papers showing the difference in climate conditions, crops adapted to different sections, horticulture, schools, churches, etc.* Topeka: Press of the Hamilton Printing Co., 1893; Woodbridge, CT: RPI, 1989.

23x15. 60 p. Orange wraps, black print. 1892: KS was 5th in corn, 4th in Oats, 1st in wheat. C.t.: "Kansas : Board of Agriculture. World's Fair Report. 1893." M. Mohler, Secretary.
(KU,SI,NYPL,F,UMi,WM) $20 - 30

1891. Kansas. *State of Kansas. Session laws of 1893, Passed at the Twenty-fifth Regular, the same being the Eighth Biennial Session of the Legislature of the State of Kansas.* Topeka: Press of the Hamilton printing co., Edwin H. Snow, State Printer, 1893.

24x16½. xvi, 308 p. Tan leather hc, black spine label with gilt print. On Spine: "Laws of Kansas. 1893." Chap. 3: Constituted a 7 member commission designated the "Board of World's Fair Managers of Kansas." Salary and expenses of $4/day for time actually employed; secretary to receive an additional $1/day. $65,000 was appropriated. Approved Mar. 4, 1893. Appropriated "[t]o Mrs. Hester Hanback and to Mrs. Robert B. Mitchell, for 16 month's service, each, as world's fair commissioners, each $500.00" (p. 21). ⊚ . (KU)

1892. Kansas. *The University of Kansas. Columbian Anniversary Year. 1893.* ____: ____, 189_.

    22½x14½. Unpaged. Slick white wraps with black print. C.t. (WM)

1893. Kansas. Walters, J. D. *Columbian history of the Kansas state agricultural college, located at Manhattan, Kansas.* Topeka: Press of the Hamilton printing co.: Edwin H. Snow, State Printer, 1893.

    23x15. 76 p. Pebble texture gold cover, black print. ☺ (WM)

1894. [Kansas]. [Woolger, Alice C.]. *Exposition study classes.* [Topeka?, KS]: n.p., ᶜ1892.

    24x__. 15 *l.* C.t. (LC)

1895. Kansas. Wooster, L. C. "Letter issued to potential exhibitors of the Kansas educational exhibit. 12 Oct. 1892." Kansas Historical Society Library, R 606 Pam V., Topeka.

    28x21½. 2 sheets. Suggestions and regulations for the Kansas educational exhibit. Wooster was Superintendent of Public Instruction. ☺ (KsHx)

1896. Kansas. ... *You are most cordially welcomed by Kansas : we would be pleased to have you visit all exhibits from our state.* N.p.: n.p., n.d.

    14x9. Stiff card printed in black both sides. At head of title: "1492. 1893. World's Columbian Exposition." List of Kansas exhibits and locations on back of card.
    P→ ☺ (GLD,TD) $10 - 18

-Kentucky-

1897. Kentucky. *Acts of the general assembly of the commonwealth Kentucky : passed at the regular session of the general assembly, which was begun and held on Wednesday the thirtieth day of December, one thousand eight hundred and ninety one.* ____: ____, 18__.

    23x16½. xx, 1,603 p. Rebound hc. Caption title given. On spine: "Acts 1891-92-93 Kentucky." Act of 1892 (Chap. 23): Appropriated $100,000 from the state treasury; created a 5 member board -- "The Kentucky Board of Managers of the World's Columbian Exposition." Board members to receive $5/day + actual expenses with limits. Directed no liquor be served on grounds set apart for KY and KY headquarters to be closed Sundays. Approved Apr. 14, 1892.

    Subsequent to this Act, the Board brought action against the KY State Auditor to compel him by mandamus to issue his warrant for money claimed to have been appropriated. KY highest court held the bill did not pass the Senate in the way required by the KY Constitution. <u>Norman, Auditor v. The Kentucky Board of Managers of World's Columbian Exposition</u>, 93 Ky. 537, (Ky. Ct. App. 1892), *rev'd*, 20 S.W. 901 (1893).

    The Act of 1893 (Chap. 132) again appropriated $100,000 from monies in the treasury, created the Board, and legislated the same provisions as the 1892 Act regarding liquor and Sunday closing. Approved Jan. 19, 1893. Chap. 158 added 2 additional Board members. Chap. 163: appropriated $10,935.64 out of the $100,000 to cover expenditures made by the Board in good faith before the

Court of Appeals declared the Act unconstitutional. Resolution No. 64, which became law on July 8, 1893, states that in view of the press and visitors' general dissatisfaction with the KY exhibit and its managers, KY would not assume any further payment after the expenditure of the appropriation.
. (KU)

1898. Kentucky. *Acts of the general assembly of the commonwealth of Kentucky : passed at the regular session of the general assembly, which was begun and held on Tuesday, the second day of January, one thousand eight hundred and ninety four.* Property of the state of Kentucky. Frankfort: Printed by the Capital Printing Co., 1894.

24x16. xi, 384 p. Quarter leather tan hc with marbled boards, black spine label: "Acts 1894." Chap. 12: Directed the payment of $1,008.15 to the "Columbian Clubs of Kentucky" which had expended the monies on the Kentucky Parlor in the Women's Bldg. The governor approved payment because he did "not regard it as an appropriation, but a legislative direction for the application of money already appropriated." Approved Feb. 22, 1894. ☺. (UMKC)

1899. Kentucky. [Kentucky Board of Managers]. *Kentucky Columbian Exhibit.* Chicago: Corbitt-Skidmore co. printers and engravers, n.d.

17½x9 (folded); (6) p. unfolds to 17½x27½. Brochure. C.t. At top of cover: "World's fair, Chicago, 1893." Text, table, illus in black print. Illus of coal arch entrance to KY Exhibit, Forestry Exhibit, and map of KY.
P→   ☺. (GLD,BPL,TD) $15 - 30

1900. Kentucky. Kentucky Board of Managers. *Report of the Kentucky board of managers of the World's Columbian exposition of 1893, to Governor John Young Brown.* Frankfort: Printed by the Capital Printing Co., 1894.

24x15½. 68 p. Gray wraps with black print. C.t.= t.p. ☺. (UoC)

-Louisiana-

1901. Louisiana. *Acts passed by the general assembly of the state of Louisiana at the regular session : Begun and Held at the City of Baton Rouge, on the Ninth Day of May, 1892.* Published by Authority. Baton Rouge: Printed by the Advocate, Official Journal of La, 1892.

23x14½. 184 p. Tan buckram. Act 37: Appropriated $18,000 for 1892 and $18,000 for 1892 [sic: i.e., 1893] from the general fund, through such agencies as the governor may select, for the purpose of making an LA exhibit at the WCE. ☺. (StLa,SSLa,HNO)

-Maine-

1902. Maine. Board of World's Fair Managers of Maine. *Report of the Board of World's Fair Managers of Maine With Accompanying Statement of Receipts and Expenditures. 1895.* Augusta: Burleigh & Flint, printers to the state, 1895.

23½x15. 36 p. + unpaginated photos. Dark maroon textured cloth hc, gold print. Frontis of ME State Bldg. [For more on the Maine Board, see "Maine's Exposition Officials." In *World's Columbian Exposition Illustrated.* 1 (July 1892): 108-13.]

⊕ . (UMe,F,E)

$25 - 45

☞ The Maine State Bldg, designed by Charles S. Frost, was moved from Chicago to Poland Spring, ME. It was reassembled there in 1895 by Hiram Ricker. Today it is the office of the Poland Spring Preservation Society. See #2351 for a centennial vol on the bldg. Article on the bldg: "A Maine showcase : Old Poland Spring resort revisited in 1893 building" by Jim Emple. *Bangor Daily News*, 1-2 Sept. 1990, Style [section]: 8. P↓,P↓

1903. Maine. Burleigh, Edwin C. *Inaugural address of Edwin C. Burleigh to the Legislature of the State of Maine, January 8, 1891.* Augusta: Burleigh & Flynt, printers to the state, 1891.

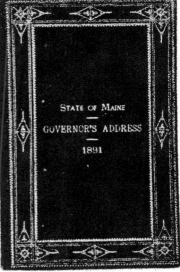

23½x15. 27 p. Dark blue texture hc, gold lettering and design. Tipped in label at front end paper: "Compliments of Edwin C. Burleigh." Call for funding for a ME state exhibit at WCE. [Mrs. Burleigh was second vice president of the Board of Lady Managers.] P→ ⊕ . (GLD)

$5 - 15

1904. Maine. Haynes, George H. *The State of Maine in 1893.* New York: Moss Engraving Co., 1893 [°1893 by George H. Haynes].

ca. 17½x26. 98 p. Title from cover. This was the state's book for distribution at the WCE. Also on cover: "Issued by authority of the World's fair managers of Maine." Very scarce. ⊕ . (E)

1905. Maine. *Journal of the House of Representatives of the state of Maine. 1891 : Sixty-fifth legislature.* Augusta: Burleigh & Flynt, printers to the state, 1891.

22½x15½. 821 p. Half leather with marbled paper covered boards. Contains several items regarding the state exhibit, appropriation of $2,000 for governor and staff at installation at WCE, appointments, etc.   ⊚ (GLD) $5 - 25

1906. Maine. *Private and special laws of the state of Maine. 1891. ____: ____, 18__.*

24½x15 (text). 574 p. Half t.p. Chap. 336: Allowed $40,000 for the ME exhibit; designated 4 men and 4 women were to comprise the "Board of World's Fair Managers of Maine (the men to be chosen two each from the two leading political parties); salaried executive commissioner but the remaining Board only to receive subsistence of $5/day + actual expenses. Approved Apr. 3, 1891.   . (UMe)

1907. Maine. State Board of Health. *Eighth report of the state board of health of the state of Maine for the Two Years Ending December 31, 1893 : 1892-1893.* Augusta: Burleigh & Flynt, printers to the state, 1895.

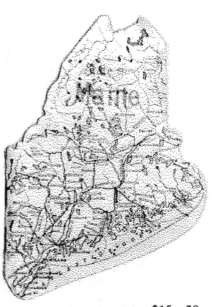

23½x15½. xi, 244 p. Black cloth blind-stamped hc, gilt printed spine. Contains brief description of the ME exhibit at Chicago. The exhibit was not installed until Sept. yet received a diploma.
    ⊚ (GLD) $5 - 20

1908. [Maine]. Waldron, Holman D. *The Summer State of Maine.* N.p.: Harriet B. Coe, n.d.

16½x10. 24 p. Glossy cardboard covers and text cut out in shape of State of ME, map as front cover design in blue, black, and red. ME bldg at WCE depicted on back cover in black. Handout at ME Bldg. T.p. is back side of front cover.
P→   ⊚ (GLD,E) $15 - 30

-Maryland-

1909. Maryland.   Board of World's Fair Managers of Maryland. *Maryland : its resources, industries and institutions : prepared for the board of World's fair managers of Maryland by members of Johns Hopkins university and others.* Baltimore: [The Sun job printing office], 1893.

25½x22. 3 *l*, vi, 504, (2) p. + 2 fold maps, no frontis. Dark blue cloth beveled hc, gilt print and design.
---- NL copy: laid in label before t.p.: "Compliments of [signed] Frank Brown Governor of Maryland."
        ⊚ . (NYPL,USD,NL)

1910. Maryland. Board of World's Fair Managers of Maryland. *Report of the board of World's Fair Managers of Maryland.* N.p.: n.p., n.d.; Woodbridge, CT: RPI, 1989.

ca. 23½x15. 82 p., microfilm. C.t. Cover litho of the MD State Bldg and a list of MD Managers, including Frank Brown, governor.   ⊚ . (JHU,SI)

1911. Maryland. *Laws of the State of Maryland, made and passed at a session of the general assembly begun and held at the city of Annapolis on the sixth day of January, 1892 and ended on the fourth day of April, 1892.* Published by authority. Annapolis: C. H Baughman & Co., State Printers, 1892.

23x16. 1186 p. Calf hc, red spine label. Chap. 212: Established the "Board of World's Fair Managers of Maryland" to consist of 11 MD residents appointed by the governor with senate approval; governor an *ex-officio* member. No pay other than expenses when absent from home on board business. Board to appoint salaried executive commissioner and clerical staff. $50,000 appropriated. An additional $10,000 contingent fund was placed under the governor's control and was to be used only in case of emergency. Approved March 30, 1892.   ☻ . (JHU,MarL)

-Massachusetts-

1912. Massachusetts. *Acts and resolves passed by the General Court of Massachusetts, in the year 1891, together with the constitution, the messages of the governor, list of the civil government, tables showing changes in the statutes changes of names of persons, etc., etc.* Boston: Published by the secretary of the commonwealth, Wright & Potter printing co., state printers, 1891.

25x17. 67 p. MA constitution + text p. 647-1365. Rebound hc, spine title: "Acts and Resolves of Massachusetts 1891." Chap. 98: Governor authorized to appoint a 5 member (3 men, 2 women) "Board of World's Fair Managers of Massachusetts;" $75,000 appropriated of which not less than $10,000 to be devoted to an educational exhibit.   ☻ . (KU)

1913. Massachusetts. *Acts and resolves passed by the General Court of Massachusetts, in the year 1892, ...* Boston: Published by the secretary of the commonwealth, Wright & Potter printing co., state printers, 1892.

25x17. 67 p. MA constitution + text from p. 1-825. Rebound hc, spine title: "Acts and Resolves of Massachusetts 1892." Chap. 79: Appropriated $12,000 for numerous dignitaries (more than 46) to attend the WCE opening ceremonies. Chap. 97: Instructed the Board to urge upon the director-general the importance of a road exhibit.   ☻ . (KU)

1914. Massachusetts. *Acts and resolves passed by the General Court of Massachusetts, in the year 1893, ...* Boston: Published by the secretary of the commonwealth, Wright & Potter printing co., state printers, 1893.

25x17. 67 p. MA constitution + text p. 675-1731. Light blue hc, black spine. Chap. 39: Appropriated an additional $25,000 for the MA exhibit. Chap. 88: Appropriated $12,000 to be used for dignitary representation (more than 46 citizens) and governor's banquet on MA Day, June 17th. Chap. 111: Resolved that the sergeant-at-arms be included among the dignitaries on June 17th.   ☻ . (KU)

☞ A total of $50,000 was appropriated for the MA State Bldg; to meet deadlines for clearing Jackson Park after the Fair, it was sold to scrap for $300.

1915. Massachusetts. *Acts and resolves passed by the General Court of Massachusetts, in the year 1895,...* Boston: Published by the secretary of the commonwealth, Wright & Potter printing co., state printers, 1895.

25x17. 67 p. MA constitution + text from p. 1-969. Light blue hc, black cloth spine. Chap. 16: Appropriated $200 for expenses of supplying the Board of Managers' report to MA exhibitors. Chap. 20: Authorized printing an additional 2,000 copies of the Board's report.   ☻ . (KU)

1916. Massachusetts. Board of World's Fair Managers of Massachusetts. *Comparative statistics concerning the agriculture of Massachusetts.* Chicago: Rand, McNally & Co., Printers, 1893.

21½x13. 22 p. Gray-green wraps, black print. Each page shows a comparison bar chart. C.t.: "Comparative Statistics of Massachusetts Agriculture." ⊚ . (LC,WM)

1917. Massachusetts. Board of World's Fair Managers of Massachusetts. Joyce, George Frederick. *Outdoor relief in the town of Brookline, Mass.* Boston: Massachusetts Board of Managers World's Fair, 1893.

24x__. 13, (1) p., folding map. (UC)

1918. Massachusetts. Board of World's Fair Managers of Massachusetts. *Massachusetts' care of Dependent and Delinquent Children : April, 1893 ...* Boston: Geo. H. Ellis, 1893.

23½x15. 3 *l*, (5)-68 p. + unpaged glossy illus. Light blue textured wraps, black print. C.t.= t.p. Compilation of articles by several people. (NL)

1919. Massachusetts. Board of World's Fair Managers of Massachusetts. *Origin and system of the Workingmen's Loan Association.* Boston: n.p., 1893.

23x__. 18 p. (UC)

1920. Massachusetts. Board of World's Fair Managers of Massachusetts. *Programme of grand Display of Fire Works, to be given at the World's Columbian Exposition, on the evening of "Massachusetts Day," Saturday, June 17, The Anniversary of Bunker Hill, by the Commonwealth of Massachusetts.* Chicago: Cameron, Amberg & Co., n.d.

21½x14. (4) p. Glossy paper, black print. Folded once. No covers.
⊚ (GLD,WM) $12 - 26

☞ H. J. Paine was manager of fireworks at the WCE. There were approximately 3 displays per week for the run of the Fair. He had a staff of 20 plus 100 part time helpers.

1921. Massachusetts. Board of World's Fair Managers of Massachusetts. *Report of the Massachusetts board of World's Fair Managers.* Francis A. Walker, Chairman. Boston: Wright & Potter printing co., state printers, 1894.

25½x18. 1 *l* (frontis of MA State Bldg), 246 p., 26 *l* of plates, maps. Tan (or slate) cloth embossed hc, gold print, tissue guard for each plate.
⊚ (GLD,csuf,MaHx,CHx,NYPL,F,UDe,BU,NHSt,HL,NYSt,UoC,BPL,L) $30 - 55

1922. Massachusetts. Board of World's Fair Managers of Massachusetts. *World's Columbian Exposition. Office of the advisory committee on fine arts for the state of Massachusetts.* Boston: Office of the Massachusetts board of managers, World's Columbian exposition, n.d.

20½x13. C.t. On cover: Frederic P. Vinton, Secretary. ⊚ . (WM)

1923. Massachusetts. *Catalogue of the Educational Exhibit of the Commonwealth of Massachusetts. World's Columbian exposition, Chicago, 1893.* Chicago: Kindergarten Literature Co., [1893].

19½x13½. 1 *l*, (4), (3)-68 p. Gray wraps, black print. C.t.= t.p. With this is bound: J. W. Dickinson's brief descriptive sketch of... school system; G. H. Martin's brief historical sketch of... school system; A. G. Goyden's brief historical sketch of... normal schools; G. A. Walton's brief descriptive sketch of teacher's training schools and classes of MA; and other articles.　☺. (PU,NYSt,NL)

1924. Massachusetts. Executive Department. [*Itinerary of the Massachusetts delegation at the dedication ceremonies of the World's Columbian Exposition, Jackson Park, Chicago, October...1892*]. [Boston: 1892].

8½x14. 32 p., (1) p. On back cover: "Massachusetts delegation to the World's Columbian Exposition, Chicago, 1892.　(MaHx)

1925. Massachusetts. Executive Department. [*Massachusetts Day, World's Columbian Exposition, Jackson Park, Chicago, June 17, 1893. Itinerary of the state delegation, etc.*]. [Boston: 1893].

8½x13. 24 p., 2 fold. tables.　(MaHx)

1926. Massachusetts. Massachusetts Horticultural Society. *To the farmers and horticulturists of Massachusetts. The Massachusetts Board of Managers of the exhibit at the World's Columbian Exposition at Chicago, has requested the...Society to...maintain on exhibition...resources of the "Old Bay State..."* Boston: n.p., 1892.

27½x21. Broadside. Call to citizens to provide display material.　(MaHx)

1927. [Massachusetts]. Massachusetts Institute of Technology. *Massachusetts Institute of Technology : Boston. A brief account of its foundation, character, and equipment prepared in connection with The World's Columbian Exposition.* Boston: Published by the Institute, 1893; Woodbridge, CT: RPI, 1989.

ca. 23x15. 39 p. Microfilm.　☺. (SI)

1928. [Massachusetts]. *Salem at the World's Columbian Exposition : Chicago, 1893.* Salem: Published by the Essex Institute (Printed at the Salem Press), 1893.

21½x14. 1 *l*, 56 p. Tan stiff wraps, light brown print and design.　☺. (CPL,CHx)

1929. Massachusetts. State Department of Health. *A guide to its exhibit at the World's Columbian Exposition, Department of Hygiene and Sanitation, Anthropological Building, 1893.* [Chicago: 1893].

23½x14½. 7 p. Cover same stock as text pages, black print and State seal. C.t.
---- Also listed: 8 p.
(CHx,NYPL,WiHx)

1930. Massachusetts. State Department of Inspection of Factories and Public Buildings. ... *School-houses and public buildings. How they may be safely constructed and properly heated and ventilated. Drawings on exhibition at the World's Columbian Exposition illustrating and describing methods of heating and ventilation and protection from fire, as approved and adopted by the... department...* Rufus R. Wade, Chief Inspector. [Boston: Wright & Potter Printing Co., 1893?].

26x__. 9 p., 1 *l*, 11-35 p., 1 *l*.　(OC,UoC)

1931. Massachusetts. Toomey, Daniel P. *Massachusetts of to-day; a memorial of the state : historical and biographical : issued for the World's Columbian exposition at Chicago.* Ed. Thomas C. Quinn. Boston: Columbia Pub. co., 1892 [°1892 Columbia publishing co.].

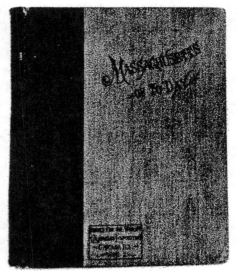

30½x25½. (2)-619 p., illus. Frontis of Plymouth Monument is p. (2). Brown and brown stippled cloth hc, top edge gilt. Describes Massachusetts areas and personalities.

P→   ⊜ (GLD,UMC,PU,NYPL,S,SLP,NYSt,BU,UoC,NL,BPL,RPB) $25 - 45

-Michigan-

1932. Michigan. Board of World's Fair Managers for the State of Michigan. Weston, I. M., ed. *Report of the board of World's fair managers for the state of Michigan.* Lansing: Board of State Auditors, under authority of the State Legislature (Robert Smith printing co.), 1899.

24x17. 204 p., 22 *l* of plates, illus, ports, tables. Black pebbled cloth hc with silver print.
⊜ . (LMi,UMi,UoC,NL,WiHx)

1933. Michigan. *Catalogues of some of the leading high schools of Michigan ... Columbian exposition, 1893.* 2 vol. N.p.: n.p., [1893?].

22x__. Illus, plates, plans, tables.   (LMi,UMi)

1934. Michigan. *Catalogues of the state educational institutions of Michigan, including the University, Normal school, Agricultural college, Mining school, School for blind, School for deaf, School for dependent children, Reform school for boys, Industrial home for girls, Columbian exposition, 1893.* N.p.: n.p., [1893?].

24x__. Various paging includes plans, forms, plates (1 fold.), tables (part fold.). Binder's title: Michigan public schools ...   (LMi,UMi)

1935. Michigan. Committee on Pomology, Arboriculture and Viticulture. *World's Fair Trees. Directions for Transplanting and Caring for Fruit Trees to be shown at the World's Columbian Exposition At Chicago in 1893.* Allegan: Edwy C. Reid, printer, 1892.

22½x15. 8 p., illus. Green wraps, black print. C.t. Caption title (running title): "Michigan pomology at the World's Columbian exposition." C.t. is for apparent series.   ⊜ . (csuf)

1936. Michigan. Fitch, Ferris S., comp. *Catalogue of the Public School Exhibit of the state of Michigan : showing the work of the public schools arranged alphabetically by cities and villages. ...* Pontiac: Oakland County Post, 1893.

24x__. 49 p., illus, maps.   (CPL)

1937. [Michigan]. *Illustrated atlas and Columbian Souvenir of Branch County, Michigan, Including a directory of free holders of the County, compiled, and published from official records and personal examination.*

Fort Wayne, IN: Atlas Publishing Co. (Engraved and printed by S. Wangertheim, Chicago), 1894 [ᶜ1894 by Atlas Publishing Co.].

45x38. 87, (27) p., 53 *l* of plates. Versos of many p. blank; p. 71-72 omitted in numbering. Black grained leather-like hc.   ☺. (LMi)

1938. Michigan. M'Cracken, S. B. *The migration of the gods: A metrical offering at the dedicatory exercises of the Michigan World's fair building : Chicago, April 29, 1893.* Lansing: Robert Smith & Co., printers and binders, 1893.

23½x15½. 12 p. Gray wraps, black print. C.t.: "The Migration of the Gods." Laid in label before t.p.: "With Compliments of S. B. McCracken." (printed).   ☺. (NYPL)

1939. Michigan. *Michigan and its resources, sketches of the growth of the state ...* 4th ed. Lansing: Robert Smith & co., state printers and binders, 1893.

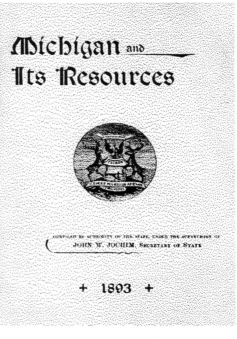

23x16. Folding colored map, 1 *l*, 287 p. Light green wraps, black print. Compiler, John W. Jachim was Secretary of State. 8,000 copies were handouts at the WF. ---- Same except wraps over bound with tan paper covered boards, tan cloth spine. Inscribed: "With Compliments of the Michigan Board of Worlds [sic] Managers from Samuel Roady M.E., Supt. Michigan Mineral Exhibit."
P→   ☺ (GLD) $18 - 36

1940. Michigan. Michigan State Board of Health. *Relative to the Michigan state board of health exhibit in the anthropological building at the World's Columbian exposition at Chicago in 1893.* By Authority. Lansing: Robert Smith & Co., State printers and binders, 1893; Lansing: R. Smith & Co., state printers, 1894; Woodbridge, CT: RPI, 1989.

23½x16. 18 *l*, 21 charts. On t.p.: "Published by the Michigan State Board of Health, for free distribution to persons interested in any of the subjects treated." (Diarrhea, cholera morbus, and intermittent fever all related to atmospheric temperature; remittent fever and influenza related to atmospheric ozone, etc.). "Tonsillitis follows temperature; rheumatism follows tonsillitis." [How true -- a half century before penicillin -- when patients with streptococcal infections often ended up with rheumatic diseases.] Health seal on t.p.
---- Also listed: 1894 "Third edition." (24) p., includes tables, diagrams.
     ☺. (LC,SI,LMi,UMi,UoC,WiHx)

1941. [Michigan]. Michigan Woman's Press Club. *Leaves from our lives : Columbian souvenir.* Grand Rapids: Dean Printing and Publishing Co., 1894.

23x19½. 63 p. Rebound. Contains ports and biographical sketches of members, with poetry and prose selections by them. Michigan women taxpayers and wage earners at p. 62-63.   ☺. (LMi)

1942. Michigan. *Public acts and joint and concurrent resolutions of the legislature of the state of Michigan, passed at the regular session of 1891. ...* By authority. Lansing: Robert Smith & co., state printers and binders, 1891.

24x17. xxix, 444 p. Rebound hc. No. 188: Established the "Board of World's Fair Managers for the State of Michigan." Board of 6 residents (2 women) and a salaried secretary, appointed by the governor; governor to act in an *ex officio* capacity. Compensation while performing duties: $3/day + actual and necessary transportation expense + $3/day subsistence when away from home. $100,000 appropriated; amount raised from assessment of taxable property in the years 1891 and 1892. Neither the State nor board to be held liable for any sum in excess of the amount appropriated nor held liable for damages to persons or property sustained by exhibitors or others. Approved July 2, 1891.
⊜ . (MarL,LMi)

1943. Michigan. *Public acts and joint and concurrent resolutions of the legislature of the state of Michigan, ... 1893, ...* By authority. Lansing: Robert Smith & co., state printers and binders, 1893.0

24x16½. xxxii, 595, (1) p. Rebound hc. No. 50: Appropriated an additional $25,000 for the MI exhibit; to be paid out of 1893 tax assessments. Approved Apr. 27, 1893. No. 57: $2,000 appropriated for a public school exhibit. Approved May 4, 1893. ⊜ . (MarL,LMi)

1944. Michigan. *World's Columbian exposition. State of Michigan. The Act of the Legislature Creating the Board of World's Fair Managers for the State of Michigan. Rules and Regulations of the Board : And General Information Concerning the Exposition. First edition. Issued by the State Board, April, 1892.* Flint: W. H. Werkheiser & sons, 1892.

21x14½. 65 p. + tipped in folding map of grounds + 14 *l* each with a lithograph one side and explanation of a major bldg at the Fair. Olive green (or pale blue) wraps, black print, frontis of MI Bldg at the WCE. ⊜ . (SFe,CHx,LMi,UMi)

-Minnesota-

1945. Minnesota. Board of World's Fair Managers of Minnesota. Barrett, J. O. *Minnesota and its flora.* Mankato: Free Press print, 1893.

23x15. 32 p. Green (or tan) wraps, black print. Handout at Minnesota Forestry Exhibit. J. O. Barrett was Secretary, State Forestry Association. C.t.
P→ ⊜ . (GLD,CHx) $15 - 25

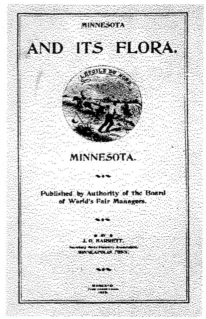

1946. Minnesota. Board of World's Fair Managers of Minnesota. *Final report of the Minnesota board of World's Fair managers, containing a complete review of the work of the board, together with tabulated statements of receipts and disbursements.* [St. Paul: n.p., 1894].

141 p. (UC,WiHx)

1947. Minnesota. Board of World's Fair Managers of Minnesota. *Minnesota: a brief sketch of its history, resources and advantages.* Published by authority of the State board of World's fair managers. St. Paul: The Pioneer Press Co., 1893.

22x14½. 123, (1) p. includes frontis of Minnehaha Falls, illus, fold. color map. Wraps with Pioneer Press color litho of Indian maiden in wheat field. C.t.: "Minnesota." ☺ . (csuf,UDe,SDSHx,USD,SLP,WiHx)

1948. Minnesota. Board of World's Fair Managers of Minnesota. *Minnesota Day at the World's Columbian Exposition : Friday, October Thirteenth, 1893.* [Minneapolis: Miller Printing Co., 1893?].

24½x17. 50 p., illus, frontis of the MN Bldg. Buff (or teal blue) wraps, black print. T.p. lists Board members. Oct. 13th was the occasion of the 36th anniversary of the adoption of the MN State constitution. ☺ . (UoC)

1949. Minnesota. Board of World's Fair Managers of Minnesota. *Souvenir manual of the Minnesota Educational Exhibit for the World's Columbian exposition : at Chicago : 1893.* [Minneapolis: Moffett, Thurston & Plank Printing Co.], n.d.; Woodbridge, CT: RPI, 1989.

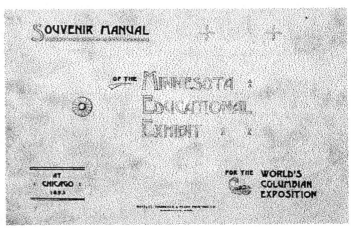

15x23. 112 p., plates. Light green wraps, brown print. Illustrated MN handout of exhibit, MN schools, statistics, etc. C.t.= t.p. P→ ☺ (GLD,csuf,SI,NYPL,F,USD,UMi,NL,TD) $20 - 35

1950. Minnesota. *General laws of the state of Minnesota passed during the twenty-seventh session of the state legislature commencing January eighth, one thousand eight hundred and ninety-one.* St. Paul: The Pioneer Press Co., 1891.

23½x17. 462, 75, 81, 1138 p. Rebound hc. Joint Res. No. 1: A joint committee of senate (3) and house (6) to consider and report upon the advisability of MN making an exhibit at the WF of 1893. Approved Feb. 3, 1891. Chap. 157: Established a 6 member commission appointed by the governor and designated the "Board of World's Fair Managers of Minnesota." No pay, no compensation for service, expenses, or transportation. Board authorized to appoint a paid superintendent. Governor and MN World's Columbian commissioners: *ex-officio.* At close of WCE, all exhibits not disposable at a profit to go to U of MN or MN Agriculture Society. Appropriated: $50,000; no part for erection of any bldg; not more than $5,000 of the appropriation for state headquarter rooms. Approved Apr. 20, 1891. ☺ . (MarL,MnStL)

1951. Minnesota. *General laws of the state of Minnesota passed during the twenty-eighth session ...* [1893]. St. Paul: The Pioneer Press Co., 1893.

22½x16. 468 p. Rebound hc. Chap. 217: Appropriated $100,000 to aid in securing a more complete and effective display and for erecting a state bldg. Board members to be reimbursed for necessary and actual expenses. Approved Feb. 17, 1893. ☺ . (MarL,MnStL)

-Mississippi-

1952. Mississippi. [*Laws of Mississippi*]. ____: ____, 18__.

No WCE statute found in the Laws of Mississippi for 1888, 1890, 1892 or 1894. Mississippi had an exhibit, however. See *Clarion-Ledger* (#1274) for a descriptive article. Miniature bales of cotton were sold as souvenirs. (MariL,MsA)

-Missouri-

1953. Missouri. Board of World's Fair Managers of Missouri. Gwynn, J. K., executive commissioner. *Full-term report of the World's fair board of the state of Missouri.* Jefferson City: Tribune printing co., state printers and binders, 1895.

23½x15½. 63 p. includes tables. Rebound hc. Bound in: *Appendix to senate and house journals of the thirty-eighth general assembly of the State of Missouri, (regular and extra sessions) 1895.* Reports are separately paginated. The report tracks the $150,000 appropriation. After interest, rebate of insurance, and proceeds of sale, the board returned $1,421.64 to the MO treasury. [N. H. Gentry was president of the Missouri board which was headquartered in Kansas City, Missouri.] ☯ (LC)

1954. Missouri. *A description of the Ozark Plateau in Southern Central Missouri.* ____: ____, 189_.

14x11½. Stapled wraps with illus of 2 flowers lower right corner. C.t.: "Southern Central Missouri. Ozark Plateau : The Land of Fruits and Flowers." . (WM)

1955. Missouri. Jones, Chas. H., and E[dwin] O[bed] Stanard. *Reasons why The World's Fair of 1892 should be located at St. Louis. Arguments made before the senate World's fair committee, January 8, 1890, ...* Washington, DC: R. H. Darby, 1890; Washington: GPO, 1890.

GPO: 23x15. 1 *l*, 20 p. On t.p.: "With introductory remarks by Gov. D. R. Francis." Same as #250. ---- Darby: 24x__. 36 p.
☯ . (LC,NL)

1956. Missouri. *Laws of Missouri, passed at the session of the thirty-sixth general asembly* [sic] *begun and held at the city of Jefferson, Wednesday, January 7, 1891. (Regular session.)* By authority. Jefferson City: Tribune printing co., state printers and binders, 1891.

23x16. 226 p., (2) p., xxxi. Rebound hc. An appropriations act (p. 33) created a 7 member "Board of World's Fair Managers of Missouri" of which at least 3 represented the agricultural interests of MO; no pay but $5/day + actual expenses. $150,000 appropriated from the revenue fund. At WCE termination, all mineral specimens, or peculiar specimens of wood and engravings, to be turned into the state bureau of geology; proceeds of all property sold which was built or made by reason of this appropriation was to be turned into the state revenue. Approved Mar. 27, 1891. ☯ . (KU)

1957. Missouri. *Laws of Missouri, passed at the session of the thirty-seventh general assembly, ... 1893. (Regular session.)* By authority. Jefferson City: Tribune printing co., state printers and binders, 1893.

23x16. 275 p., (3) p., xxxix. Rebound hc. Disposition of State Exhibit (p. 266): At the termination of the WCE, those specimens and exhibits in the collection of MO which were state property were to be turned over to the state university museum at Columbia, except minerals which were to be donated to the school of mines and metallurgy at Rolla. (Inconsistent portion of 1891 Act was repealed; the legislature felt the educational value of preservation was greater than small revenues these items would yield if sold.) Approved Mar. 27, 1893. ☯ . (KU)

1958. [Missouri]. St. Louis Congressional Committee on the World's Fair. *An Appeal by Professor S. Waterhouse, of Washington University to the People of His Native State, in behalf of St. Louis as the Site of the World's Fair, in 1892.* St. Louis: St. Louis Congressional Committee on the World's Fair, 1889.

21½x15. 16 p. pamphlet; no wraps. Sylvester Waterhouse's native state was NH. St. Louis committee chairman was E. S. Rouse. Waterhouse's arguments: 1) next year (1890), "the streets of St. Louis will be wholly lighted by electricity;" 2) greater than 500 miles of improved streets; 3) central location; etc. Written Dec. 1, 1889 from Washington U., St. Louis. (UMKC,NYPL,BPL)

1959. Missouri. Winslow, Arthur. *The Geology and Mineral Products of Missouri.* St. Louis: Woodward & Tiernan printing co., 1893.

26½x19. Stapled wraps. C.t. On cover: "From 'Missouri at the World's Fair.' (Official Publication of the World's Fair Commission of Missouri)." Winslow was State Geologist. ☻.(WM)

1960. Missouri. World's Fair Commission of Missouri. Cox, James, ed. *Missouri at the World's Fair : An Official Catalogue of the Resources of the State, with Special Reference to the Exhibits at the World's Columbian Exposition. ...* [St. Louis]: Press of Woodward & Tiernan printing co., 1893.

26½x20. 175 p., illus, maps. Buff (or yellow) wraps, black print. Cox was Secretary of the Bureau of Information of the St. Louis Autumnal Festivities Association. C.t.: "Missouri at the World's Fair. Official Publication of the World's Fair Commission of Missouri." Contains a brief history of the state, the situation of the state 1893, and the work of the Commission. Also contains "The Educational System of Missouri" which was reprinted separately (#1961). ☻. (UMKC,csuf,NYPL,NL,WiHx)

1961. Missouri. World's Fair Commission of Missouri. *The Educational System of Missouri. From "Missouri at the World's Fair." (Official publication of the World's fair commission of Missouri).* St. Louis: Woodward & Tiernan printing co., 1893.

26½x19. Frontis + (12) p. Frontis is b/w photo of the "University of the State of Missouri." Page (12) is a b/w illus of a St. Louis school. C.t. ☻ (NL)

-Montana-

1962. Montana. Board of World's Fair Managers of the State of Montana. *Montana : Exhibit at the World's Fair and a Description of the various Resources of the State, Mining, Agricultural and Stock Growing. ...* Butte: Butte Inter Mountain print, 1893.

17½x11½. 64 p., tables. Glossy white stiff wraps, dark blue and brown print and design. C.t: "Montana : History Resources Possibilities."

P→ ☻ (GLD,PU,CHx,NYPL,LMi,E,UDe,UMi,UoC,TD) $15 - 30

1963. Montana. *Laws, resolutions and memorials of the state of Montana passed at the second regular session of the legislative assembly. Held at Helena, the Seat of Government of said State, Commencing January 5th, 1891, and Ending March 5th, 1891. ...* Published by authority. Helena: Journal Publishing Co. Public Printers and Binders, 1891.

23½x15½. 388 p. Rebound hc. Act: Established a governor appointed 16 male resident board designated the "Board of World's Fair Managers of the State of Montana." MT members of the World's Columbian Commission and Board of Lady Managers to be *ex-officio* members. Board members (not officers): $5/day compensation for actual attendance. Board-appointed salaried executive commissioner. Board charged with task of inducing immigration to MT. Appropriated: $50,000 from the general fund. Approved Mar. 9, 1891. ☯ . (MarL)

-Nebraska-

1964. Nebraska. *Consolidated statutes of Nebraska, 1891, Being a Compilation of All the Laws of a General Nature in Force August 1, 1891. Based upon the Revised Statutes of 1866. Embracing ... The codes, state and federal constitutions, Magna Carta, etc.* Prepared Under Authority of the Legislature by J. E. Cobbey, Esq. Lincoln: State Journal co., printers, 1891.

23x15. (i-ix), x-xxiii, 1 *l*, (3)-506 p. Calf hc. Chap. 56, sec. 4536: $50,000 appropriated from the NE treasury; authorized the governor to appoint a 6 member "Nebraska Columbian Commission." $5/day for each day devoted to official service + actual traveling expenses. "[T]he location of said exposition is so near Nebraska's door, and all environments so remarkably auspicious to presenting to the best possible advantage, and advertise to the world in substantial manner, her products, ..." Approved Mar. 27, 1891. ☯ . (NeHx)

1965. Nebraska Dairymen's Association. *Nebraska's Dairy Resources.* Chicago: Rand, McNally & Co., Printers and Engravers, [1893].

15½x34 folds to 15½x8½. 7, (1) p., includes color litho front cover. C.t. At end of text and tables: "D. P. Ashburn, Superintendent : Nebraska Dairy Exhibit at Columbian Exposition."

    ☯ (GLD) $12 - 25

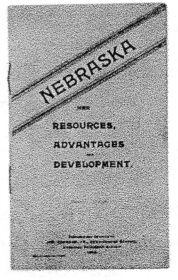

1966. Nebraska. Garneau, Jos. Jr., comp. *Nebraska : Her Resources, Advantages and Development.* [Omaha: Rees Printing Co., 1893].

18x10. 24 p. Blue (or light gray) glossy wraps, black print. "Nebraska Columbian Exhibit" on front cover. Garneau was NE Commissioner General.

P→   ☯ (GLD,TD,S) $10 - 20

1967. Nebraska. *Laws, Joint Resolutions, and Memorials, passed by the legislative assembly of the state of Nebraska at the twenty-third session, Begun and Held at the City of Lincoln, January 3, 1893.* Published by authority. Lincoln: State Journal Co., Printers, 1893.

22x15. xxii, 502 p. Rebound hc, section of red leather cover attached to spine reads: "Laws of Nebraska: 1893." Chap. 41: Repealed the Act of 1891 (sec. 4536) and appropriated $35,000 for the NE exhibit and expenses; authorized the governor to appoint a commissioner general. Approved Apr. 8, 1893. ☯ . (KU)

1968. Nebraska. State Board of Agriculture. *Nebraska. Products and Resources.* [Lincoln: State Journal Co., 1893].

Single *l* 22x30½ folded twice to make (6) p. 22x10. Printed in black and red both sides. Handout.
P↓   ☯ (GLD) $10 - 18

-Nevada-

1969. Nevada. *Nevada At the World's Fair. Accompanied by Illustrations of its Home Interests.* Carson City: J. A. Yerington (Printed in New York by The Albertype Co.), °1893 by J. A. Yerington.

11½x17½. 13 *l* on stiff stock, photos one side. String tied stiff red wraps. Photo of State Capitol bldg on front cover.   ☺ . (CPL,CHx,NvSt,UNR)

1970. Nevada. *Statutes of the state of Nevada passed at the sixteenth session of the legislature, 1893. Begun on Monday, the sixteenth day of January, and ended on Monday, the sixth day of March.* Carson City: State printing office, J. E. Eckley, superintendent, 1893.

22½x14½ (text). Chap. 109: Created "World's Fair Managers of Nevada" composed of 3 members. The 2 members of the National Commission to be *ex-officio* and serve without pay; one other appointed by the Governor to receive actual expenses + $5/day when away from home on board business. Members of the Board of Lady Managers and their alternates to be *ex officio* members. Appropriated $10,000 from the general fund to a WCE fund. Board given power to sell and deposit proceeds in the general fund at WCE termination. Approved Mar. 10, 1893.   ☺ . (NvSt)

1971. Nevada. World's Fair Managers of Nevada. *Report of Nevada State Board : World's fair commissioners, 1894.* J. A. Yerington, Chairman. Carson City: State Printing Office, J. G. McCarthy, Superintendent, 1895.

23x15. 29 p. Light brown wraps, black print and State seal. C.t. "Compliments State Board World's Fair Commissioners" label laid in before half title.
---- In *Appendix to Journals of Senate and Assembly of the seventeenth session of the legislature of the state of Nevada, 1895.* Same pub info.
    ☺ . (CPL,CHx,NvSt)

-New Hampshire-

1972. New Hampshire. *Laws of the state of New Hampshire : passed January session, 1891. Legislature Convened January 7, Adjourned April 11, 1891. With an appendix, containing the laws passed at a special session, December 1890.* Manchester: John B. Clarke, public printer, 1891.

ca. 24½x16. Chap. 61: Authorized a governor appointed 4 citizen commission designated the "Board of World's Fair Managers of New Hampshire." Commissioners to receive no pay; actual expenses + $3/day when necessarily absent from home. Board to appoint a paid executive commissioner. Authorized to erect a NH Bldg at a cost not to exceed $10,000. Total appropriation: $25,000. Approved April 11, 1891.   ☺ . (MarL,NHSt)

-New Jersey-

1973. New Jersey. *Acts of the One Hundred and Fifteenth Legislature of the state of New Jersey, and Forty Seventh Under the New Constitution.* [1891]. Trenton: MacCrellish & Quigley, State Printers, 1891.

24x15½. Chap. 140: Authorized an uncompensated 8 member board designated "The New Jersey Commission." Appropriated: $20,000 to pay necessary expenses and to enable the governor to have state depts prepare agricultural, mineral, and educational exhibits. Approved Mar. 18, 1891.   (☺ . NJSt)

1974. New Jersey. *Acts of the One Hundred and Sixteenth Legislature of the state of New Jersey, and Forty-Eighth Under the New Constitution.* [1892]. Trenton: MacCrellish & Quigley, State Printers, 1892.

24x15½. 597 p. Rebound hc. Chap. 102: Appropriated an additional $50,000 to further the work of the board and to build a proper bldg. Approved Mar. 23, 1892.
---- "Forth-Eighth" [sic] in title.
    © . (MarL,NJSt)

1975. New Jersey. *Acts of the One Hundred and Seventeenth Legislature of the state of New Jersey, and Forty-Ninth Under the New Constitution.* [1893]. Trenton: MacCrellish & Quigley, State Printers, 1893.

24x15½. 638 p. Rebound hc. Chap. 133: Appropriated an additional $60,000 to further work of the board, maintain the NJ Bldg, and for exhibits of agriculture, education, and geology. Authorized payment of expenses of the joint committee which had been directed to visit Chicago and to employ a secretary. Prohibited compensation for board members other than the secretary. Approved March 13, 1893.   © . (MarL,NJSt)

1976. New Jersey. Board of Women Managers of the Exhibit of the State of New Jersey. *Official Descriptive Catalogue of Colonial and Revolutionary Relics now in possession of the citizens of New Jersey.* Trenton: Naar, Day & Naar, book and job printers, 1893.

25½x18. 294 p. Compiled by Mary Sherrerd Clark by authority of the Board. C.t.: "Colonial and Revolutionary Relics in Possession of Citizens of New Jersey." A list of exhibit contributors and their individual contributions by county. Mrs. Edwin A. Stevens, Board Chairman.   © . (PU,LC)

1977. New Jersey. Department of Public Instruction. Committee on the Educational Exhibit at the World's Columbian Exposition. *Catalogue and Report of special committee of the New Jersey School Exhibit : at the World's Columbian exposition, At Chicago, 1893.* Trenton: The John L. Murphy Publishing Co., Printers, 1894.

23x15. 2 *l*, vi, 146 p., frontis of NJ school exhibit, plates, fold. map. Dark maroon embossed cloth hc, silver print, decorative end papers. 29 folded and stapled leaves in envelope. On back cover: educational statistics 1880-1890.   © . (PU,F,UoC,NJSt,WiHx) $30 - 45

☞   Garret A. Hobart, listed as a member of the New Jersey Commission, later became Vice President of the United States. Nicholas Murray Butler, listed as a member of the Paterson, NJ, Board of Education was President of Columbia University and winner of a Nobel Peace Prize. (NJSt)

1978. New Jersey. Fitzgerald, T. F., comp. *State of New Jersey. Manual of the Legislature of New Jersey : one hundred and sixteenth session, 1892. By authority of the legislature. Copyright secured.* Trenton: T. F. Fitzgerald, legislative reporter, n.d.

25½x16½. NJ Commissioners to the WCE are listed at p. 288. 7 listed members; 1 vacancy.   © . (NJSt)

1979. New Jersey. *New Jersey Building.* N.p.: n.p., n.d.

15½x11½. Folding white *l* making (4) p., black print. Directory of the NJ exhibits. Small illus of the NJ Bldg at head of title. Caption title.
    © (GLD,CHx) $9 - 18

1980. New Jersey. State Board of Agriculture. Dye, Franklin, ed. *New Jersey Hand-Book : World's Columbian Exposition -1893-.* [Trenton: John L. Murphy Publishing Co., 1893.]

15½x10. 70 p. Light green heavy wraps, black print and NJ state seal. Hand out at the NJ exhibit. ---- 63 p. Pale green wraps. ---- *New Jersey Hand-Book. World's Columbian exposition. Published by the State Board of Agriculture,* ... Trenton: The John L. Murphy Pub. Co., Printers, 1893. C.t. No seal.

                           ◉ . (KyU,F,UMi,NJSt) $20 - 35

1981. New Jersey. VanMeter, Anna Hunter. *Relics of ye Olden Days in Salem County, New Jersey, U.S.A. Reported for the Board of Lady Managers, World's Columbian Commission.* Salem: Printed by Robert Gwynne, 1892, copyright applied for.

22½x14½. 4 *l* + 5-100 numbered *l* printed on one side only, illus. Off-white stiff textured wraps, bold copper letters with gilt shadowing. All text print and illus in sepia. Pretty presentation. Bound at the top edge (14½ cm) "note-book style." C.t.= t.p. VanMeter was chairman, Salem County's Committee on Antiques.   ◉ . (PU,LC,NL)

1982. New Jersey. Yardley, Margaret Tufts. *The New Jersey Scrap Book of Women Writers : Published by The Board of Lady Managers for New Jersey to Represent the Many Writers who are not Bookmakers at the World's Columbian Exposition.* 2 vol. Newark: Advertiser printing house, 1893.

22x15. Frontis (ports), plates.   ◉ . (UDe,NJSt)

-New Mexico-

1983. New Mexico (Territory). ... *Acts of the legislative assembly, of the Territory of New Mexico, Twenty-Ninth Session. Convened at the Capitol, at the City of Santa Fe, on Monday, the 29th day of December, 1890, and Adjourned on Thursday, the 26th day of February 1891. Prepared for Publication by Benjamin M. Thomas, Secretary of the Territory.* By authority. Santa Fe: New Mexican Printing Co., 1891.

23x16. 317 p. Leather hc. At head of title: "Public property.--Any Public Officer in possession of this Book will deliver it to his successor. 1891." Act to provide for the collection, arrangement and display of the products of the Territory of New Mexico and appropriations: 9 sections (no. 11-20, p. 232-35) defining NM participation at the WCE. The 4 members of the Board to receive $4/day + actual expenses while away from home. Formed the "Territorial Board of World's Columbian Exposition Managers of New Mexico" consisting of 4 men appointed by the governor (2 from each of the 2 principal political parties). $25,000 appropriated. Empowered county commissioners to appropriate for county exhibits.   ◉ . (UNM)

1984. New Mexico (Territory). *New Mexico Day.* Chicago: Thayer & Jackson Stationery, Co., [1893].

19½x14½. Single card with black print one side. Program for NM Day: Sat., Sept. 16, 1893. At noon, the (New?) Liberty Bell was rung 13 times in honor of New Mexico. Gov. Thornton gave a reception at 4 p.m.   ◉ . (SFe)

1985. New Mexico (Territory). *San Juan County, New Mexico. Published by the Woman's Auxiliary Committee, W.C.E., of San Juan County. New Mexico, 1893.* Chicago: Rand, McNally & Co., 1893.

20½x15. 14 p. Orange wraps. C.t.   ◉ . (CPL)

1986. New Mexico (Territory).   Sierra County World's Columbian
Exposition Committee. Robin, Geo. E. *Mineral and other resources
of Sierra County, New Mexico. April 30, 1893.* St. Louis: Great
Western printing co., 1893.

22x15. 2 *l*, (5)-21, (2) p. Blue wraps, black print. T.p.: "First
edition of 10,000 copies." ☺ . (HL)

1987. New Mexico (Territory). The Woman's Columbian Committee of
Colfax County, comp. *Colfax County New Mexico : its resources and
opportunities.* Denver, CO: Press of M. A. Tully, n.d.

22½x14½. 15 p. Green wraps, black print. C.t. On cover: "For
Distribution at World's Fair." ☺ . (CPL)

1988. New Mexico (Territory). *World's Columbian Exposition department of
New Mexico.   Act of Congress Creating World's Columbian
Commission. Law Creating Territorial Board of World's Columbian
Exposition Managers of New Mexico.   Rules and Regulations for
Government of Board. Classification of exhibits.* Albuquerque: Citizen Print, 1891.

20½x12. 24 p. Pink (or dark gray) glossy wraps, black print. W. H. H. Llewellyn was secretary for
the NM Board.
P↑   ☺ . (SFe)

-New York-

1989. New York. Board of Education. ... *Free Lectures to the People.* ... N.p.: n.p., n.d.

12½x8. 23 p. includes front cover. Buff wraps, black print.   (CHx)

1990. New York. Board of General Managers and Judicial District Commissioners. *Executive session of
delegates from the Board of General Managers and the Judicial District Commissioners of the Exhibit of
the State of New York at the World's Columbian Exposition, held at the Rooms of the Exposition at
Chicago, Ill., May 12, 1892.* N.p.: n.p., n.d.

24x15. 59 p. Green paper spine. Caption title. Cover consists of 2 paragraphs of italics print
explaining that the Managers and Commissioners traveled to Chicago to learn exhibitor and space
information. ☺ . (CPL)

1991. New York. Board of General Managers. *Report of the board of general managers of the exhibit of the
State of New York at the World's Columbian Exposition: transmitted to the legislature April 18, 1894.*
Albany: James B. Lyon, State Printer, 1894.

26½x20½. 1 *l*, 647 p. Navy blue (or green) cloth hc with gold lettering and seal on spine and front
cover, fold. map in pocket inside back cover. Chauncey Depew (see #826) was President of the
Board. Very useful state report. Fairly common.
P↓   ☺ . (GLD,csuf,LC,NYPL,S,UDe,NHSt,HL,UMi,NYSt,UoC,A,BPL,RPB,WM,AIC,WiHx) $15 - 30

1992. New York. Board of General Managers. *Report to the Governor by the Board of General Managers of the Exhibit of the State of New York at the World's Columbian Exposition : December 31, 1892.* Albany: The Argus co., printers, 1893.

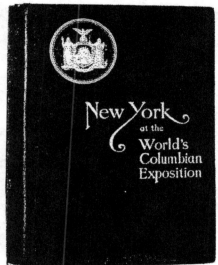

23½x15. 36 p. Light brown wraps, black print. C.t.= t.p. Submitted by Chauncey Depew.
⊚ . (CPL,NYPL,NL)

1993. New York. Board of Women Managers [of the State of New York]. *Board of Women Managers of the State of New York at the World's Columbian Exposition.* Albany: n.p., 1892-94, New Haven, CT: RPI, 1977.

1 vol. Meeting minutes from June 7, 1892, to May 22, 1894, each paginated separately. (KU,UNLV)

1994. New York. Board of Women Managers [of the State of New York]. *List of books and articles by Women, natives or residents of New York State.* Proof under revision. N.p.: n.p., n.d.

15x10. 76 p., t.p. Wrap same paper type as text. Same format as "List of Books" (#1995), only shorter. On cover: "Please send early notice of errors or omissions to Mrs Florence C. Ives, Assembly parlors, Albany, N.Y." LC has author as State Library, Albany. ⊚ . (LC,NYSt)

1995. New York. Board of Women Managers [of the State of New York]. *List of books by Women, natives or residents of the State of New York.* N.p.: n.p., [°1893 by Mrs. Frederick Putnam Bellamy].

16x11. 218 p. Gray wraps, black print, marbled edges. C.t.= t.p. ⊚ . (LC,NL,OC)

1996. New York. Board of Women Managers [of the State of New York]. Music Sub-committee. *Report of the Sub-committee on music for the state of New York for the Columbian exposition.* [New York: 1893].

20x__. 56 p. "Record of operatic performances in New York city and of the visits of some of the most distinguished musicians," p. 5-28. Directory of orchestras and other organizations, p. 29-56. (NYPL)

1997. New York. Board of Women Managers [of the State of New York]. *Report of the Board of Women Managers for the Exhibit of the State of New York at World's Columbian Exposition 1893.* By ____. New York: J. J. Little & Co., [1893].

23x15. 108 p., 15 plates. (cat,NYPL)

$25

1998. New York. Board of Women Managers [of the State of New York]. *Statistical Report of the women of the state of New York : (On Record in the Woman's Building) : Columbian Exposition Chicago 1893.* [New York: Trow Directory printing and bookbinding co.], n.d.

23x14½. 63 p. Dark beige wraps, black print and small design. From the Committee on Statistics. The volunteer editorial staff produced a literary patchwork quilt of information. Statistics are mixed into a section on NY statutes which relate to women.
⊚ . (F,NL)

$20 - 35

1999. New York. ... *Catalogue of New York State loan exhibit : of embroideries, miniatures, watches, snuff-boxes, fans, and laces.* New York: The Knickerbocker Press, n.d.; Woodbridge, CT: RPI, 1989.

18x13. 41 p. Light blue wraps, black print. C.t. At head of title: "World's Columbian Exhibition." Other author: Loan Exhibit.

⊗ . (GLD,CPL,SI) $15 -34

2000. New York. ... *The Chautauqua System of Education.* Buffalo: Wenberne-Sumner Co., printers, [1893?].

13x8. 37 p. Buff wraps, black print. (CHx)

2001. New York. *Chicago World : the Historical, Biographical and Philanthropical Record of New York and New York's state exhibits at the World's Columbian exposition : classified and illustrated.* [Chicago]: Chicago World Book, 1892 [°1892 by Chicago World Book co.].

27x17. 72 p. ?, illus.
---- Also listed: 1 vol. Various paging, illus plates, map.

⊗ . (CHx,SLP,RPB)

2002. New York. Davis, Katherine Bement. *Report on the exhibit of the workingman's model home : as exhibited by the State of New York at the World's Columbian exposition.* Albany: James B. Lyon, printer, 1895.

25x18½. Wraps. C.t.= t.p. ⊗ . (WM)

2003. New York. Department of Public Instruction. New York State Educational Exhibit. *The Schools of New York. A glance at the common school system of the Empire State. Prepared by the Department of Public Instruction.* Albany: James B. Lyons, State Printer, 1893.

24x15. 73 p. Brown cloth hc, black and gilt print and design. P→ ⊗ . (NYPL,UoC)

2004. New York. *Exhibit of the Woman's hospital in the state of New York, New York City.* ____: ____, [1893?]. (NYSt)

2005. New York. *Exhibits of the state of New York at the World's Columbian Exposition, Chicago, 1893.* [Chicago: A. C. McClurg and Co.], n.d.; Woodbridge, CT: RPI, 1989.

23x14½. (7) p. Cover has black print and small illus of NY Bldg; same stock as text. C.t. ⊗ . (SI,NL,TD)

2006. [New York]. The Italian Chamber of Commerce of New York. *Proceedings of a meeting of the board of directors, May 28th, 1891.* New York: Press of John Polhemus Printing Co., 1891.

23x14½. 8 p. including buff wraps. Above title: "The Italian chamber of commerce of New York and The World's Columbian exposition." ⊚ . (SFe,NYPL)

2007. New York. *Laws of the state of New York. Vol. I, passed at the One Hundred and Fifteenth Session of the legislature, begun January fifth, 1892, and ended April twenty-first, 1892, in the city of Albany; ...* Albany: Banks & Brothers, publishers, 1892.

23½x17. viii, 1484, 98, 47 p. Calf hc. Chap. 236: Constituted the "General Managers of the Exhibit of the State of New York": Chauncey M. Depew, John Boyd Thacher, Gorton W. Allen (all member of the World's Columbian Commission appointed by the President of the U.S.), and three other persons appointed by the governor. Declared the NY exhibit closed on Sunday. Set up a "Board of District Commissioners" for each NY judicial district; 3 members each. Authorized governor appointed and salaried secretary and chief executive officer of the Board of General Managers. Board of General Manager directed to appoint a Board of Women Managers. No paid board members; actual and necessary expenses paid. Board members not personally liable for debts. Board of General Managers empowered to prepare for NY's participation in the naval review in New York harbor, April, 1893. $300,000 appropriated from the state treasury. Approved April 6, 1892. ⊚ . (MarL)

2008. New York. *Laws of the state of New York, passed at the One Hundred and Sixteenth Session of the legislature, begun January third, 1893, and ended April twentieth, 1893, in the city of Albany. Vol. I.* Albany: James B. Lyon, printer, 1893.

23½x16. Chap. 188: Appropriated an additional $300,000. Approved Mar. 23, 1893. Chap. 497: Authorized the Board of General Managers to sell and dispose of property purchased from state appropriated monies and use proceeds to defray expenses incurred by them in carrying out the provisions of WCE legislation. Approved Apr. 29, 1893. ⊚ .(SUL)

2009. ---. ---. *Vol. II.* Albany: James B. Lyon, printer, 1893.

23½x16. viii, (1087)-1896, 114 p. index. Calf hc. Chap. 726: Provided $10,000 for the Board of Women Managers in addition to the $50,000 they had received through the Board of General Managers. ⊚ . (MarL)

2010. [New York]. *New York and the World's fair. 1892.* New York: [for] The Dry-goods committee, 1892.

23x15. 63, (1) p. Beige wraps, black and red print. On cover: "With the Compliments of the Dry-Goods Trade Of New-York City." C.t. ⊚ . (CHx)

2011. [New York]. New York City. Committee for the International Exposition of 1892. *Address to the Senate and House of Representatives of the United States of America.* New York: [Douglas Taylor], 1890.

38x__. 53 p., fold. plates (part color). C.t. (CHx)

2012. [New York]. New York City. Committee for the International Exposition of 1892. *Letter of William E. D. Stokes ... on the question of the location of the international exposition* [and] *letters of Mr. Stokes read at the meeting of the Board of Trade of Providence, R.I.* New York: D. Taylor, print., [1889].

27x__. 32 p. Includes: NY's candidacy for the World's Fair of 1892, by William Waldorf Astor. For another Stokes item, see #2022. (WiHx-missing)

2013. [New York]. New York City. Committee for the International Exposition of 1892. *Names of the Members of the committees for the International Exposition of 1892, and Minutes of the Meetings of July 25th and October 10th, 1889.* N.p.: n.p., °1889.

23½x15. 37 p. Tan wraps, black print. C.t.= t.p.   ☻ . (LC)

2014. [New York]. New York City. Committee for the International Exposition of 1892. *Official List of Committees and Committeemen for the International exposition of 1892.* [New York: Douglas Taylor, Printer], °1889.

20x12½. 15 p. Plain wraps (we assume these are the covers), black print. "Committee reports and financial plan" are not part of the title (differs from #2015).   ☻ . (LC)

2015. [New York]. New York City. Committee for the International Exposition of 1892. *Official List of Committees and Committeemen for the International exposition of 1892. Committee reports and financial plan.* [New York: Douglas Taylor, Printer], °1889.

22½x15. 32 p. Early description of New York's plan to host the Fair. First meeting was July 25, 1889. Contains long list of people signed up for various organizations.   ☻ . (LC)

2016. [New York]. New York City. Committee for the International Exposition of 1892. ... *Statement of the City of New York to the Special Committees of the Senate and of the House of Representatives on the Quadri-Centennial celebration of the discovery of America.* New York: n.p., 1890.

37x__. 53 p., frontis, illus (part folding). C.t.: "Address to the Senate and House of Representatives of the United States of America."   (MaHx)

2017. [New York]. New York City. Committee for the International Exposition of 1892. Towne, Henry R. *Financial project, for the International Exhibition, Columbus quadri-centennial, New York, 1892.* N.p.: n.p., [1889].

20x13½. 21 p. No printed cover. Caption title. Early definition of NY hosting WCE. "September 12, 1889" at end of article.   ☻ . (NYPL)

2018. [New York]. New York City. Committee for the International Exposition of 1892. Towne, Henry R. "To Hon. Hugh J. Grant: Mayor, and Chairman Committee on World's Fair." 26 Sept. 1889. Letter in ____ .

21x14. 13 p. + 4 fold out plans. Early description of where NYC would have placed the WCE had it hosted the Fair. In NYC, the Fair would have been across from the southeast corner of Central Park and eastward. The 4 plans are 4 proposals for the layout of the grounds.   ☻ . (NYPL)

2019. [New York]. New York City. Committee for the International Exposition of 1892. Towne, Henry R. "To Hon. Hugh J. Grant: Mayor, and Chairman of World's Fair Committee." 2 Oct. 1889. Letter in ____ .

21x14. 5 p. Plea by Towne for improved organization so New York City could gain the right to hold the WCE.   ☻ . (NYPL)

2020. [New York]. *Official Souvenir Programme of the New York Columbian Celebration: October 8 to 15, 1892 : In commemoration of the discovery of America.* New York: Rogers & Sherwood, 1892.

25½x18½. 64 p. Tan wraps, beautiful color lithograph on front cover, black printing. The New York celebration of 1892 preceded the Chicago WCE dedication of Oct. 21, 1892.

*P→   ☺ (GLD,E,TD) $20 - 40

☞ President Harrison declared a Columbus holiday for Oct. 21, the new calendar date of Columbus' landing. Casimiro Barela, senator from Colorado and a Hispanic, is the father of our Columbus Day holiday; at his initiation, Colorado had the first permanent Columbus Day in 1907. Other states followed. In 1934, the U.S. set Oct. 12 (old calendar) as Columbus Day. Further legislation in 1968 and 1971 made the second Monday in October the federal holiday.   (SHM).

2021. New York. *Souvenir of the dedicatory ceremonies of the New York State Building, at Jackson Park, Chicago, Illinois, October 22, 1892.* [New York: Lehmairer & Bro., °1892].

23x30. 8 *l*, 1 plate. C.t.   (NYPL,RPB)

2022. [New York]. Stokes, W[illiam] E[arl] D[odge]. "How New York lost the World's fair. Platt and Fassett did it!" New York, 10 Oct. 1891.

23x__. 22 p. Caption title. Address by Stokes. For another Stokes item see #2012.   (NYPL)

2023. [New York]. Wiman, E[rastus]. *An argument for Staten Island as the most desirable site for the World's Fair of 1892 ...* New York: E. Wiman, 1889.

16°. 16 p., 1 fold. map. C.t.   (NYPL)

-North Carolina-

2024. North Carolina. *Laws and resolutions of the state of North Carolina passed by the general assembly at its session of 1891, begun and held in the city of Raleigh on Wednesday, the eighth day of January, A.D. 1891. ...* Published by authority. Raleigh: Josephus Daniels, State Printer and Binder, 1891.

23½x17. xlii, 1543 p. Calf hc, red and black spine labels. Chap. 590: Established "The Board of World's Fair Managers of North Carolina" consisting of the governor *ex officio* and the board of agriculture. Non-officer members not entitled to compensation except actual expenses for transportation and $3/day when absent from home. Board to appoint salaried executive commissioner. World's Columbian Commissioners and the Board of Lady Managers to be *ex officio* members. Appropriation: $25,000 to be paid from money covered into the NC treasury from the U.S. treasury by act of Congress entitled "An act to refund direct land taxes." Ratified Mar. 9, 1891.   ☺ . (MarL)

2025. North Carolina. *Public laws and resolutions of the state of North Carolina passed by the general assembly at its session of 1893, ...* Published by authority. Raleigh: Josephus Daniels, State Printer and Binder, 1893.

23½x16½. xxx, 555 p. Calf hc. Chap. 110: Amended 1891 law to pay for appropriation out of any moneys not otherwise appropriated if the direct tax fund was insufficient. Ratified Feb. 11, 1893. Chap. 187: Authorized superior court clerks to be absent from office for 30 days to attend WCE; to leave competent deputy in office. Ratified Feb. 28, 1893.   ☻ . (MarL)

2026. North Carolina. State Board of Agriculture [of North Carolina]. *Hand-book of North Carolina, with illustrations and map. State board of agriculture.* Raleigh: Presses of Edwards & Broughton, 1893.

23½x15½. 1 *l*, viii, 1 *l*, 333 p. + fold. map laid in back. Striking glossy litho wraps in black with red print. First *l* is frontis: a series of ports of State Board of Agriculture members and officers.   ☻ . (NL)

-North Dakota-

2027. North Dakota. *Laws passed at the second session of the legislative assembly of the state of North Dakota. Begun and Held at Bismarck, the Capital [sic] of said State, on Tuesday, the Sixth Day of January, A. D. 1891, and Concluded March Sixth, A. D. 1891.* Bismarck: Tribune, printers and binders, 1891.

23x15 (text). 350 p. Calf hc. Chap. 30: $25,000 appropriated out of ND treasury. Approved Mar. 9, 1891. Chap. 128: authorized the governor to appoint 5 member "Board of World's Fair Managers of North Dakota" and allowed actual travel expenses + $5/day when absent from home.   ☻ . (UND,MarL)

2028. North Dakota. *Laws passed at the third session of the legislative assembly of the state of North Dakota. ... 1893.* Bismarck: Tribune, state printers and binders, 1893.

23x15 (text). 313 p. Calf hc. Chap. 136: Appropriated an additional $15,000 to insure a proper exhibit of ND resources, complete and maintain the ND Bldg, etc. Approved Mar. 2, 1893. Chap. 137: Declared the Act immediately effective because of limited time to prepare the exhibit. Approved Mar. 6, 1893.   ☻ . (UND)

☞ Emergency measures were common as the states attempted to ready their exhibits in time for opening.

2029. North Dakota. State Board of World's Fair Managers for North Dakota. *North Dakota at the World's Columbian Exposition : Chicago, 1893.* N.p.: Published by Authority, [1894].

23x15. 116 p., illus. Light green wraps, black print and ND seal. C.t. [ND Bldg architecture by J. J. Silsbee, Chicago, is very much like the President's Home at the UND designed by Joseph Bell Deremer, 1902-03. The restored home now houses the UND Alumni Association.]   ☻ . (UND,UoC)

-Ohio-

2030. Ohio. Board of World's Fair Managers of Ohio. Committee on Forestry. ... *The Ohio Forestry Exhibit consists of All the native Forest Trees ...* N.p.: n.p., [1893?].

8½x13½. 1 *l* ad card with brown print. Exhibit prepared by W. A. Kellerman, Ohio State U. "Compliments of" Thos. Van Horn (autographed). At head of title: "Chicago World's Columbian Exposition 1893."

P↓   ☻ (GLD) $12 - 25

2031. Ohio. Board of World's Fair Managers of Ohio. Executive Commissioner. *First quarterly report of the Executive Commissioner : to the board of World's Fair managers of Ohio.* Columbus: [Journal-Gazette Printing House], 1892.

22½x15. 32 p. Light gray wraps, black print. Front cover litho shows the OH Bldg. C.t.= t.p. Apr.-July 1892.
---- In *Speeches and papers by Ohio men.* Columbus: Office of the executive commissioner, 1892. Vol 5, no. 19. 22x16. Dark green hc with gold lettering.
☺ . (CPL,OSU,OhHx)

2032. Ohio. Board of World's Fair Managers of Ohio. *Ohio in the Columbian Exposition. Regulations of Board of Managers of Ohio. Ohio State Law. National Law. National Regulations as to States. Directory of Ohio Board of Managers.* First ed. Ashland: Ohio Board of World's Fair Managers, 1891.

20½x14. 31 p. Yellow-green wraps with black lettering. Dated August, 1891. ☺ . (OhHx)

2033. Ohio. *The State of Ohio. General and Local Acts passed and joint resolutions adopted by the sixty-ninth general assembly, at its Extraordinary and Adjourned Sessions, Begun and Held in the City of Columbus, October 14th, 1890, and January 6th, 1891, respectively.* Vol. LXXXVIII. Published by State Authority. Columbus: The Westbote co., state printers, 1891.

25x18. 1010 p. Half calf and marbled hc. WCE Act (p. 234): Governor to appoint a 15 member commission designated "Board of World's Fair managers of Ohio;" *ex-officio* members were also enumerated. Board authorized to appoint an executive commissioner and fix his pay. No compensation but actual travel expenses + $4/day when necessarily absent from home. $100,000 appropriated from the state treasury general fund. Passed Mar. 26, 1891. There is a small amendment the following year printed at p. 203-204 of vol 89. ☺ . (KU)

-Oklahoma-

2034. Oklahoma (Territory). *Report of Governor William C. Renfrow, to the third Legislative Assembly of World's Columbian Exposition. Exhibit M. Governor's message 1895.* [Guthrie: Daily Leader Press, 1895].

8°. 11 p. (NYPL)

2035. [Oklahoma Territory]. Santa Fe Rail Road. ... *Cherokee strip and Oklahoma : Opening of Cherokee Strip; Kickapoo, Pawnee and Tonkawa Reservations.* Chicago: Poole bros., [1893].

38x94½ sheet folds to 19x10½. 28, (2) p. + (6) panel map (i.e., 36 total panels each 19x10½). Map is red and black Oklahoma Territory map. C.t. Title printed twice [on (2) p.] in red and black. At head of each title: "Columbian edition. Santa Fé Route." Paged text of Oklahoma and Cherokee strip attributes with b/w litho illus. ☺ (GLD,WM) $20 - 50

2036. Oklahoma (Territory). *The Statutes of Oklahoma, 1893. Being a Compilation of all the Laws now in force in the Territory of Oklahoma. Compiled Under the Direction and Supervision of Robert Martin, Secretary of the Territory by W. A. McCartney, John H. Beatty and J. Malcolm Johnston, a Committee Elected by the Legislative Assembly.* Guthrie: State Capital [sic] printing co., 1893.

26x16. Appropriations. Chap. 4. § 15: $15,000 for the purpose of making an exhibit of Territorial products "advertising to the world the resources of the Territory and inducing immigration." Exhibit under the direction of the governor. ☉ . (UOL)

-Oregon-

2037. Oregon. *The Journal of the house of the legislative assembly of the state of Oregon for the eighteenth regular session. 1895.* Published by authority. Salem: W. H. Leeds, state printer, 1895.

22x16. (3)-689 p. Rebound hc. Concurrent H. Res. No. 25: legislature to look into the "acts and doings" of the OR WF Commission. Joint H. Res. No. 13: Legislature spoke with high praise of Commission's completed task, and noted by "strict economy" the Commission had saved $18,280.69 out of the $60,000 appropriated. Joint H. Res. No. 19: Authorized publishing 20,000 of the revised ed. of Oregon's World's Fair Commission report to replace the 1st and 2nd ed. of a pamphlet entitled "The Resources of Oregon" which "were entirely exhausted, having been distributed abroad for the purpose of inducing immigration" to OR. There was a great demand for literature from persons contemplating relocating west. [The original typescript legal size pages of the resolution are located at OSL.] ☉ . (OrHx)

2038. Oregon. Oregon World's Fair Commission. *Report of the Oregon World's fair commission to the Legislative Assembly, Eighteenth Regular Session. 1895.* Salem: Frank C. Baker, state printer, 1894.

22x15. 74 p., illus. Pink wraps, black print. C.t.= t.p. George T. Myers was President of the Oregon WF Commission. ☉ . (LC)

2039. Oregon. *The State of Oregon. General and special laws and joint resolutions and memorials passed and adopted by the seventeenth regular session, 1893. Begun on the ninth day of January, A. D. 1893, and ended on the eighteenth day of February thereof.* Salem: Frank C. Baker, state printer, 1893.

22x16. 962 p. Rebound hc, red leather spine label: "Oregon 1893." Act to Create a Commission (p. 7): Enumerated *ex-officio* members plus the governor to appoint 6 members to the "Oregon World's Fair Commission." No pay but traveling expense reimbursement allowed. Members (one each) to represent: agriculture, horticulture, mining, packers' association, and OR resident member of Board of Lady Managers. $60,000 appropriated from the general fund; no part be used in the construction of a state bldg or clubhouse. Nothing in the Act to prevent the commission from soliciting or receiving private contributions. Passed notwithstanding the objections and veto of the Governor. Filed Feb. 13, 1893. ☉ . (OSL,MarL)

2040. Oregon. *The State of Oregon. General and special laws and joint resolutions and memorials enacted and adopted by the eighteenth regular session of the legislative assembly 1895. ...* Salem: W. H. Leeds, state printer, 1895.

22x16. (3)-689 p. Rebound hc. General Laws: "An Act [H.B. 382] to pay for ... appropriations" authorized payment of $2,000 in claims against the Commission. ☉ . (OrHx)

-Pennsylvania-

2041. Pennsylvania. Board of World's Fair Managers of Pennsylvania. Brownfield, Robert L., comp. *Pennsylvania Art Contributions : State Building, Art Gallery and Woman's Building : World's Columbian exposition.* Harrisburg: Edwin K. Meyers, State Printer, 1893; Woodbridge, CT: RPI, 1989.

20½x13½. 61 p. catalog on glossy paper. Light green pulp wraps, black print. Gives WCE location of PA art. C.t.= t.p.
P→　　⊚ (GLD,CHx,SLS)　　　　　　　　　　$10 - 30

2042. Pennsylvania. Board of World's Fair Managers of Pennsylvania. Farquhar, A. B., comp. *Pennsylvania and the World's Columbian Exposition: rules regulations and classifications with an introductory chapter on the resources of the commonwealth.* Harrisburg: E. K. Meyers State Printer, n.d.; Woodbridge, CT: RPI, 1989.

23½x16. 1 *l* frontis of State Capitol, 191 p. Gray wraps, black print and design.
---- Label after front cover: "Compliments of C. M. Kishpaugh, Department of Internal Affairs."
---- Also listed: 186 p.
---- Black cloth hc.
P↓　　(GLD,csuf,CHx,SL,NYPL,F,SLP,BPL,RPB)　　$25 - 36

2043. Pennsylvania. Board of World's Fair Managers of Pennsylvania. Farquhar, A[rthur] B., Executive Commissioner. *Catalogue of the Exhibits of the State of Pennsylvania and of Pennsylvanians at the World's Columbian exposition.* N.p.: Clarence M. Busch, State Printer of Pennsylvania, 1893; Woodbridge, CT: RPI, 1989.

24x16. Folding map, 3 *l*, 218 p. + unpaginated photos. Light gray wraps. Frontis of Liberty Bell displayed inside the PA Bldg at the WCE. Guards were constantly at the Bell -- as they are today.
P↓　　⊚ . (GLD,KyU,SL,NYPL,SLP,UMi,UoC,NL,BPL)　$25 - 45

2044. ---. ---. ---. ---. N.p.: Clarence M. Busch, State Printer of Pennsylvania, 1893.

23½x16. Folding map, 3 *l*, 284 p. + unpaginated photos. Half leather marbled paper covered boards, marbled end papers, red dyed edges. Frontis of Liberty Bell displayed inside the PA Bldg. This is the same text to p. 218 as #2043; the photographs are different and a 66 p. appendix added.
⊚ (GLD,CHx,LC,LMi)　　　　　　　　　　　$25 - 45

2045. Pennsylvania. Board of World's Fair Managers of Pennsylvania. *Minutes of the Board of World's Fair Managers and of the Executive Committee; July 1, 1891 - Feb. 27, 1894.* Harrisburg: n.p., 1894?; Woodbridge, CT: RPI, 1989.

23½x16. Variously paged throughout. Red dyed edges. Caption titles.　. (SL,NYSt,UoC)

2046. Pennsylvania. *Laws of the general assembly of the commonwealth of Pennsylvania, passed at the session of 1891, in the one hundred and fifteenth year of independence, together with A Proclamation by the Governor, declaring ... and the Supplements thereto.* By authority. Harrisburg: Edwin K. Meyers, state printer, 1891.

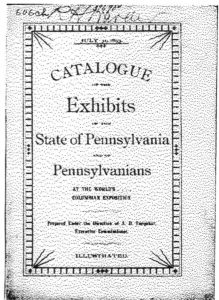

23x16½. 511 p. + al to a201 p. Rebound hc, red and black spine labels with gilt print: "Laws of Pennsylvania. 1891." No. 316: Set out a 30 citizen-member-Governor-appointed Board to act in conjunction with the Governor, Lieutenant Governor, President *pro tempore* of the Senate and Speaker of the House. The Board was designated "The Board of World's Fair Managers of Pennsylvania." No compensation but necessary expenses paid. Appropriated $300,000 from the general fund. Approved June 22, 1891.   ☻ . (UMKC,SLP)

2047. Pennsylvania. *Laws of the general assembly of the commonwealth of Pennsylvania, passed at the session of 1893,...* By authority. Harrisburg: Edwin K. Meyers, state printer, 1893.

23x16. 519 p. + al to a301 p. Rebound hc, red and black spine labels with gilt print: "Laws of Pennsylvania. 1893." No. 15: Request from the state legislature that PA members of the U.S. Senate and House vote against the repeal of Sunday closing. Approved Feb 11, 1893.   ☻ . (UMKC,SLP)

2048. Pennsylvania. Pennsylvania Advisory Committee on Art. ... *Department of fine arts. General Information For the Artists of Pennsylvania and Others.* N.p.: n.p., n.d.

23x17½. 25 p. Beige smooth wraps with green lettering except "D" and "A" in red. At head of title: "Issued by the Pennsylvania Advisory Committee on Art. World's Columbian Exposition, 1893. Chicago, Ill., U. S. A."   ☻ . (WM)

2049. [Pennsylvania]. Philadelphia. Beck, James M. *The City of Philadelphia. An address delivered at the World's Columbian exposition, Jackson Park, Chicago, Ill., on Pennsylvania Day, September 7th, 1893.* Philadelphia: Press of Allen, Lane & Scott, 1893.

23½x15. 9 p. Gray smooth wraps, black print. C.t.= t.p.   ☻ (GLD) $16 - 34

2050. [Pennsylvania]. Philadelphia. Joint Special Committee of Councils on World's Columbian Exposition. Vickers, George Edward. *Philadelphia : the story of an American city.* Philadelphia: Dunlap printing co., 1893; Woodbridge, CT: RPI, 1989.

22½x16½. 10 *l*, 235 + (45) p. photos. Half leather with black cloth boards, decorated end papers.

---- Gray wraps, black print and design.
---- Also listed: 3 *l*, 5-235, (1) p. plates, ports.
P↓   (GLD,SI,UDe,USD,SLP,UMi,OC)   Either binding: $20 - 45

2051. [Pennsylvania]. Philadelphia. Williams, Talcott. *Philadelphia, A City of Homes.* Philadelphia: [Avil ptg. co.], n.d.

18x12½. 12 p. Extract from March 1893 *St. Nicholas.* Sand wraps, black print. Below title on cover: "The Workingman's Model House, Columbian World's Fair, Chicago, 1893." Essentially a description of row homes; illustrated inside front cover.

@ (GLD) $15 - 30

2052. [Pennsylvania]. *Pittsburgh : Pennsylvania : U.S.A.* N.p.: The Eichbaum press, n.d.

9½x16. 47 p. text, (1) p. map. Tan wraps, bold black print and leaf design. "'1898" on poem p. (1) is printer's error; latest date mentioned in text is March 1893. Exhibit location south of Machinery Hall, WCE, is hand stamped on back wrap. @ (GLD) $14 - 26

2053. Pennsylvania. State Committee on Woman's Work. *A condensed statement of the work done by women in Instruction, Reform, Philanthropy and Missions, during one fiscal year in the state of Pennsylvania. To which is added a Statement on the Industrial Work of Women in the State, with Statistics.* Harrisburg: Edwin K. Meyers, state printer, 1893.

23½x16½. 138 p., frontis, illus. Harriet Anne Lucas, Chairman. @ . (CHx,LC,USD,SLP,NL)

2054. Pennsylvania. State Fish Commissioners. Meehan, William E[dward], comp. ... *Fish, fishing and fisheries of Pennsylvania.* Harrisburg, E. K. Meyers, state printer, 1893; Woodbridge, CT: RPI, 1989.

24x16. 106 p., frontis, plates, illus. At head of title: "Pennsylvania's Fish Exhibit at the World's Columbian Exposition, Chicago, 1893." T.p. states Meehan was Associate Editor of *Philadelphia Public Ledger.* @ . (PU,SI,SLP,Yale,TU)

-Rhode Island-

2055. Rhode Island. ... *Acts, resolves and reports of the General Assembly of the State of Rhode Island and the Providence Plantations. Part I.--May session. 1891... Part II.--January session. 1892.* Providence: E. L. Freeman & son, printers to the state, 1892.

23½x15. At head of title: "1891-92." Chap. 991: Created "The Board of World's Fair Managers of Rhode Island." Board consisted of: 1) members and their alternates of World's Columbian Commission, Board of Lady Managers, and World's Columbian Commissioner-at-large; 2) eight citizens appointed by the governor, in equal number from the two leading political parties. No compensation, actual transportation expenses only. Board authorized to appoint an executive commissioner and fix his salary. Appropriation: $10,000 from the general fund. Passed May 29, 1891. Chap. 1027: Set compensation at $5/day when necessarily absent on Board business; mandated Board elect an executive commissioner with offices in Providence; increased the appropriation to $25,000. Passed Aug. 4, 1891. @ . (RILaw)

2056. Rhode Island. ... *Acts and resolves passed by the General Assembly of the State of Rhode Island and Providence Plantations.* ... Providence: E. L. Freeman & son, state printers, 1893.

23½x15. At head of title: "1892-93." Resolution No. 14: Appropriated $7,000 to enable the Governor and specified others to represent RI at the opening ceremonies. Passed June 3, 1892. ☺ . (RILaw)

2057. Rhode Island. Board of Rhode Island Women Commissioners. Palmer, Fanny Purdy. *A list of Rhode Island literary women, (1726-1892,) with some account of their work.* Providence: E. L. Freeman & Son, 1893.

4°. 24 p., frontis (port). (NYPL)

2058. Rhode Island. Board of World's Fair Managers of Rhode Island. *Catalogue of the educational exhibit of the state of Rhode Island : World's Columbian exposition : Chicago, 1893.* Chicago: Kindergarten Literature Co., [1893].

20x13½. 29 p. Gray wraps printed in black. Exhibit was in the Liberal Arts Bldg, Section K, Columns P, Q. ☺ . (CPL,WM)

2059. Rhode Island. Board of World's Fair Managers of Rhode Island. *Report of the Rhode Island board of World's Columbian commissioners, to his excellency D. Russell Brown, Governor.* Providence: E. L. Freeman & son, state printers, 1894.

23½x15½. 63 p. Hc. At top of t.p.: "Public Document] [no. 2." ☺ . (NHSt,BPL,RPB)

2060. Rhode Island. Board of World's Fair Managers of Rhode Island. ... *Rhode Island Day at World's Columbian Exposition : Itinerary of the Special Party, consisting of the Official Representatives of the State and their friends.* [Providence: Livermore and Knight Co., 1893?].

11x8½. 16 p. Embossed light yellow felt covers, string tied, gilt print. Opens like a note pad, hinge at top (8½ cm). At head of title: "October 5th, 1893." Dr. E. Benjamin Andrews was president of the World's Fair Managers of Rhode Island.
P→ ☺ (GLD) $15 - 35

2061. Rhode Island. Board of World's Fair Managers of Rhode Island. Williams, Alonzo, ed. *Rhode Island Day at The World's Columbian Exposition : Chicago, Illinois : October the fifth : eighteen hundred and ninety-three.* [Providence: E. L. Freeman & son, printers], n.d.

26½x19½. 4 *l*, (7)-80 p., frontis (port of Gov. Brown), plate. Morocco.
---- 27½x19½. Wraps.
☺ . (CHx,LC,NYPL,S,NYSt,NL,BPL,E,RPB)

2062. Rhode Island. Dailey, Charlotte Field, ed. *Rhode Island Woman's Directory : for the Columbian Year : 1892.* Providence: Rhode Island Woman's World's Fair Advisory Board, 1893.

21½x14½. 121 p. ☺ . (RPB)

2063. Rhode Island. *World's Columbian exposition, Department of Rhode Island. Act of Congress creating World's Columbian commission; law creating board of World's fair managers of Rhode Island; rules and regulations of government of board. Names and addresses of ...* Providence: E. L. Freeman & son, state printers, 1891.

23½x14½. 48 p. Wraps.   ☺ . (CPL,RPB)

2064. [Rhode Island]. Wyman, J. C. *Rhode Island at the World's fair.* [Boston: 1894].

(14) p., illus. Extracted from the *New England magazine*, June 1894, vol 19, p. 427-40.   (RPB)

-South Carolina-

2065. South Carolina. [*Laws of South Carolina*]. ____: ____, 189_.

No WCE activity found in the laws for the years 1890-93.   (SCAG).

-South Dakota-

2066. South Dakota. *Circular letter of the Board of Woman's Commissioners of South Dakota, to Superintendents, Teachers and Pupils of the Public Schools.* Pierre: Daily Capital co. printers and bookbinders, n.d.

ca. 21½x12½. 4 p. C.t. Dated January 11, 1892.   ☺ . (USD)

2067. South Dakota. *Common school examination. For the World's Fair Educational Exhibit, South Dakota.* N.p.: n.p., 1892?.

22½x12. (4) p. Printed. Caption title. Dated December 16, 1892.   ☺ . (USD)

2068. South Dakota. *Laws passed at the third session of the legislature of the State of South Dakota, Begun and Held at Pierre, the Capital* [sic] *of said State, on Tuesday, the Third Day of January, A.D. 1893, and Concluded March 3, A.D. 1893.* Pierre: Carter Publishing Co., 1893.

23½x16. xciii, 1 *l*, 329 p. Rebound hc. Chap. 176: Established the governor appointed 9 member (plus state treasurer) "South Dakota World's Fair Commission." No compensation but actual transportation expenses + $5/day when on commission business. Commission authorized to purchase or lease the SD Bldg already erected at the WCE after appraisal by 5 persons appointed by the governor. Empowered the commission at close of WCE to sell and dispose of the SD Bldg and exhibition objects at the best price. Also, the act created the "South Dakota Womans' World's Fair Commission" consisting of 9 women appointed by the governor and given exclusive charge of the educational dept, fine arts and womens' work. They also received actual transportation expenses and $5/day subsistence. Appropriated from the general fund: $50,000 for the SD World's Fair Commission and $10,000 for the SD Womans' World's Fair Commission. Approved Feb. 24, 1893, and immediately in force because the Fair was only two months away.   ☺ . (MarL)

2069. South Dakota. ... *List of Awards for South Dakota.* [Sioux Falls: Executive Committee on Awards, 1894].

21½x14. 7 p. Printed. At head of title: "First edition." Dated March 14, 1894.   (USD)

2070. South Dakota. *Minutes of the Second Meeting of the Woman's World's Fair Commissioners of South Dakota.* N.p.: n.p., 1892?

22½x15. 3 p. Printed. Dated May, 1892. (USD)

2071. South Dakota. *Report of the Committee of the Woman's World's Fair Commission in Regard to the Educational Exhibit.* Yankton: n.p., 1892?

21½x14. 3 p. Printed. Dated January 14, 1892. (USD)

2072. South Dakota. *Report of the Woman's World's Fair Commission of South Dakota to the Honorable Charles H. Sheldon, Governor of the State of South Dakota.* N.p.: n.p., n.d.

22½x13. 10 p. Printed. (USD)

2073. South Dakota. *... South Dakota Educational Exhibit. Inventory of Exhibit. Notes and Explanations.* N.p.: n.p., n.d.

21½x13. (4) p. At head of title: "World's Columbian Exposition. Chicago, 1893." Caption title. ⊚ (NL,WM)

2074. South Dakota. South Dakota World's Fair Commission. *South Dakota at the World's Fair : Illustrated. Report by Executive Commissioner.* [Pierre]: n.p., [1894].

24x15. (6), 42 p. + 25 *l* of plates. Frontis of SD Bldg at the WCE. The SD Bldg was dedicated July 12, 1893, Gov. C. H. Sheldon in attendance. Report includes appendix of finances of the commissioners of the State. ⊚ . (SDSHx,USD)

2075. South Dakota. South Dakota World's Fair Commission. *Souvenir : of the Dedicatory Ceremonies of the State of South Dakota Building, at Jackson Park, Chicago, Illinois, July 12th, A. D. 1893.* [Sioux Falls: Brown & Saenger, Printers], n.d.

21½x27½. (15) p. String tied wraps. WiHx copy signed by Wm. B. Sterling. C.t. (WiHx)

2076. South Dakota. *Souvenir of South Dakota.* Sioux Falls: Brown & Saenger printers, n.d.

10x18½. (32) p. + fold. map before back wrap. Tan wraps, black print and great seal of the state. C.t. Litho of SD Bldg on back wrap.
P→ ⊚ (GLD)

$18 - 36

-Tennessee-

2077. Tennessee. *Acts of the state of Tennessee passed by the forty-seventh general assembly 1891.* Published by authority. Nashville: Albert B. Tavel, Printer to the State, 1891.

21½x15½. 611 p. Rebound hc. Chap. 182: County courts of Tennessee counties authorized and empowered to make appropriations of money to provide for an exhibit of their county resources at the WCE. Passed Mar. 25, 1891. ⊚ . (MarL,TnSt)

-Texas-

2078. Texas. *General laws of the state of Texas passed at the twenty-second legislature convened at the city of Austin, March 14, 1892, and adjourned April 12, 1892.* Austin: Ben C. Jones & Co., state printers, 1892.

22x15½. No reference to the WCE in laws passed during 1889, 1891, 1892, 1893, and 1895. (MarL,SMU)

2079. Texas. Houston. *The City of Houston and Harris County Texas. World's Columbian Exposition souvenir.* Houston: Charles F. Morse, under the auspices of The Post Engraving Co. (Cummings & sons, printers), 1893.

17x18½. ca. 80 p. String tied illus wraps. On back wrap: "Compliments of the new Hutchins house, ..." ⊚ . (A)

2080. Texas. *San Antonio.* ____: San Antonio Bureau of Information, n.d.

9½x15. Wraps. C.t. On cover: "Texas Building, Jackson Park, Chicago." Text explains that ignorant legislation and unaccountable prejudice were responsible for Texas having "absolutely nothing in the way of an exhibit." Contains Texas statistics. . (WM)

-Utah-

2081. Utah (Territory). *Exhibit of Utah at the World's Columbian Exposition. Report: [To accompany H.R. 7827.].* 52d Cong. 1st Sess. H. Rept. 993. Apr. 5, 1892.

2 p. Committee on the Territories recommended passage of the bill enabling Utah to participate in the WCE. Also see #274.l. (csuf,NYPL)

2082. Utah (Territory). *Laws of the Territory of Utah, passed at the Twenty-ninth Session of the Legislative Assembly, held at The City of Salt Lake, the Capital [sic] of said Territory, Commencing January 13, A. D. 1890, and Ending March 13, A. D. 1890.* Published by authority. Salt Lake City: The Deseret News Co., 1890.

24x16. viii, 171 p. Rebound hc. Chap. 58: Empowered the governor to appoint 3 "suitable persons to represent the Territory" as commissioners at the next World's Fair ("1892 or thereafter.") Commissioners empowered to collect money and objects for exhibition and to secure sufficient exhibit space. No salary; actual expenses paid. Appropriation: $3,000. Approved Mar. 13, 1890. ⊚ . (MarL)

2083. Utah (Territory). Utah Board of Lady Managers. *World's fair Ecclesiastical History of Utah. Compiled by representatives of the religious denominations.* Salt Lake City: George Q. Cannon & sons co., printers, 1893.

22½x15½. 2 l, (vi)-vii, (9)-318 p., illus, ports. No frontis. Burgundy cloth over beveled boards, gilt print, decorative gold end papers. Preface by Sarah M. Kimball, Chairman. ⊚ . (NYPL,HL,nwu)

2084. Utah (Territory). Utah World's Fair Commission. *Utah at the Worlds* [sic] *Columbian Exposition.* [Salt Lake City?: Salt Lake Lithographing Co., °1894 by E. A. McDaniel]; Woodbridge, CT: RPI, 1989.

26½x18. 172, L (i.e., 50) p., illus. Frontis of the UT Bldg. Dark gray embossed binding with gold lettering and black design. PU preface signed "E. A. McDaniel." ☉. (PU,SI,LMi,SLP,HL,WiHx)

2085. Utah (Territory). Utah World's Fair Commission. *The Utah World's Fair Advocate.* 1 (1892).

No. 1 (June 1892): 22½x15. 44 p., 1 *l* ads. Gray wraps, black print. On cover: "Authorized official organ Utah World's Fair Commission." Contains county organization, by-laws and rules, etc. See same at #1420. ☉. (CPL)

-Vermont-

2086. Vermont. *Acts and resolves passed by the general assembly of the state of Vermont, at the eleventh biennial session, 1890.* Published by authority. Burlington: The Free Press Association, printers, n.d.

22x15½. 1 *l*, (3)-350 p. 3 sessions in 1 vol, separately paginated. Calf hc, red and black spine labels, gilt print: "Laws of Vermont" and "1886-'88,'90." Act No. 173: Created the "Columbian Commission of Vermont" made up of the Governor, the 2 commissioners appointed by the President of the U.S., the 2 lady managers appointed by the President of the Exposition. No compensation but any actual necessary expenses not paid by the U.S. Government. $5,000 appropriated from the VT treasury. Approved Nov. 26, 1890. The appropriation was increased to $15,000 by Act No. 16 of the 1891 Special Session. Approved Aug. 27, 1891. ☉. (VtSSt,MarL)

2087. Vermont. *Acts and resolves passed by the general assembly of the state of Vermont, at the twelfth biennial session, 1892.* Published by authority. Burlington: The Free Press Association, printers and binders, 1892.

22x15½. 1 *l*, (3)-504 p. but bound together with special sess. 1891, 13th sess, and 14th sess. Act No. 236: Appropriated $14,750 to erect a VT Bldg; Bldg to be sold at the close of the WF, proceeds to pay claims, remainder to be returned to VT treasury. Approved Nov. 12, 1892. Res. No. 320: Governor to appoint 10 or more commissioners; no pay and no expenses except that of printing reports. ☉. (VtSSt,MarL)

2088. Vermont. Columbian Commission of Vermont. *Report of the World's Columbian Commission of the state of Vermont.* Rutland: The Tuttle co., official printers, 1894.

23½x15. 16 p., frontis: "Vermont State Building at World's Fair." Wraps. ☉. (NHSt)

2089. Vermont. State Board of Agriculture. Spear, Victor I. *Vermont, A Glimpse of its Scenery and Industries.* Montpelier: Argus and Patriot Print, 1893.

14½x23. 64 p. Light green heavy wraps, raised gold lettering and design. Publicity hand out from the state organization at the Fair. B/w photos. (F) $20 - 40

-Virginia-

2090. Virginia. *Acts and joint resolutions passed by the general assembly of the state of Virginia, during the session of 1891-92.* Richmond: J. H. O'Bannon, superintendent of public printing, 1892.

23x16. (3)-1236 p. Chap. 704: Commission of 10 residents, one from each congressional district, and designated "The Board of World's Fair Managers of Virginia." 7 of the male members constituted a quorum. No pay except actual necessary expenses for members who were not officers. Displays and handouts were to attract "public attention to the state and its superior advantages." This Act made it lawful for counties, cities and towns to make appropriations and expenditures and to levy and collect such amounts as deemed necessary. Approved March 4, 1892. [The VA Bldg at the WCE was a replica of Mount Vernon.]   ☺. (UVa,MarL,VaHx)

2091. Virginia. Board of World's Fair Managers of Virginia. *Organization, by-laws, plan of work, local and general, of the Board of World's Fair Managers of Virginia, including an official directory of the board of managers, officers or the board and auxiliary board, and of the officers of the Columbian exposition at Chicago.* N.p.: n.p., 1892.

17½x12. 54 p. Green wraps, black print. C.t. Also listed at 55 p.
☺. (CPL,F,VaHx) $20 - 35

2092. Virginia. "... Communication from the governor inclosing the report of the World's fair commissioners." *Journal of the senate of the commonwealth of Virginia: ... 1893.* Richmond: J. H. O'Bannon, superintendent public printing, 1893.

22½x14. VA senate documents variously paged. At head of title: "Senate doc. No. XVI." 39 p. Dated 7 Nov., 1893.   ☺. (UVa)

2093. Virginia. State Board of Agriculture. Lyman, H. L. "Report on the World's Fair." *Report of the state board of agriculture of Virginia. 1893.* Richmond: J. H. O'Bannon, Superintendent of Public Printing, 1893.

24x15½. Wraps. Lyman's report from p. 115.   ☺. (UVa)

2094. Virginia. *Works of Edward V. Valentine, sculptor, of Richmond, Virginia, in the Mount Vernon (Virginia State) Building, at the World's Columbian exposition, Chicago, Ill.* [Chicago?: 1893?].

19½x12½. (4) p.   ☺. (VaHx)

-Washington-

2095. Washington. Hestwood, J[ames] O. *The Evergreen State Souvenir : containing A Review of the Resources, Wealth, Varied Industries and Commercial Advantages of the state of Washington. Published for Distribution at the World's Columbian Exposition.* 1st ed. Chicago: W. B. Conkey Co., 1893 ᶜ1893.

25½x17. 72 p., map, illus. Green wraps, black fancy litho design and print. T.p.: "First edition, 100,000 copies."   ☺. (csuf,CHx,S,NL)

2096. Washington. Meany, Edmond S. *Washington World's Fair Commission.* [Seattle, Chicago, etc.: 1891-1893].

27 *l.* Press releases by the Commission, May 1891-Oct. 1893. Mounted press releases with typewritten t.p. and table of contents. (Located: UWa).   (UWa)

2097. Washington. *Session laws of the state of Washington session of 1891. Compiled in chapters, with marginal notes by Allen Weir, secretary of state.* Published by authority. Olympia: O. C. White, state printer, 1891.

> 24x16. 1 *l*, 485 p. Rebound hc. Chap. 108: Established the "Washington World's Fair Commission" made up of named individuals from the various counties. WA World's Columbian Commissioners and Board of Lady Managers to be *ex officio* members. Commission charged with electing officers, an executive committee of 9, and appointing a salaried executive commissioner. No pay but expenses up to $100/year. State mining bureau to send all the mineral collections and cabinets belonging to WA. Appropriation: $50,000 for 1891 and $50,000 for 1892 out of any money in the state treasury not otherwise appropriated. Approved Mar. 7, 1891. ☺ . (MarL)

2098. Washington. Washington (State) World's Fair Commission. *Biennial Report of the Washington World's Fair Commission for the Years 1891 and 1892...* Olympia: O. C. White, State Printer, 1893.

> 28x16½. 36 p. Reported that a commission called "Washington World's Fair Commission" had been constituted of 33 named members, one each from the various counties. No pay but allowed $100/year each for expenses. Noted the appropriation from the state treasury had been $50,000 for 1891 and $50,000 for 1892. With this is bound their "Final report 1894" (#2100). (UWa)

2099. Washington. Washington (State) World's Fair Commission. Evans, Elwood, ed. *The State of Washington : a brief history of the discovery, settlement and Organization of Washington, the "Evergreen state" as well as ...* [Tacoma: World's Fair Commission of the State of Washington, Tacoma Daily News, 1893].

> 21½x14½. 224 p. Light green wraps, black print and design. Illus cover and t.p. are identical. Story of history, data, production, etc. for the State. Washington was admitted as a state in Nov. 1889. Printed for handout at the WA Bldg.
> P→   ☺ (GLD,csuf,LC,USD,NL,OC,WiHx) $25 - 50

2100. Washington. Washington (State) World's Fair Commission. ... *Final report* [of the Washington World's Fair Commission, ?] *1894 ...* Olympia: O. C. White, State Printer, 1894.

> 49 p. With their Biennial report, 1892 (#2098). (UWa)

-West Virginia-

2101. West Virginia. [*Acts of the legislature of West Virginia, ... 1891*]. ____: ____, 189_.

> Chap. 115: Authorized the Board of World's Fair Managers for West Virginia. Approved Mar. 16, 1891.

2102. West Virginia. *Acts of the legislature of West Virginia, at its twenty-first regular and extra sessions commencing January 11, and February 25, 1893.* Charleston: Moses W. Donnally, Public Printer, 1893.

23x15½. 232 p., 286 p. corporations, xcii p. index. Rebound hc. General Appropriations, Chap. 1: $20,000 appropriated for 1893 from 1893 revenues to carry out the provisions of the 1891 Act. ☉ . (MarL)

2103. West Virginia. Board of World's Fair Managers for West Virginia. Morgan, Benj[amin] S[tephen], and J[acob] F. Cork. *Columbian History of Education in West Virginia.* Charleston: Moses W. Donnally, Printer, 1893.

23x15. 4, iv, 1 *l*, 204 p. + many unpaged glossy illus, plates, ports, frontis of 5 bldgs on WV University campus. "Bibliography of history of education in West Virginia, including a list of Virginia statutes relating thereto." Also published separately and in West Virginia. Dept of free schools. Biennial report of the state superintendent of free schools ... 1890/92, with the title *History of education in West Virginia.* ☉ . (PU,USF,NL,WiHx)

2104. West Virginia. Board of World's Managers for West Virginia. Summers, Geo[rge] W. *The Mountain State. A description of the natural resources of West Virginia. Prepared for Distribution at the World's Columbian exposition.* Charleston: Moses W. Donnally, Printer, 1893.

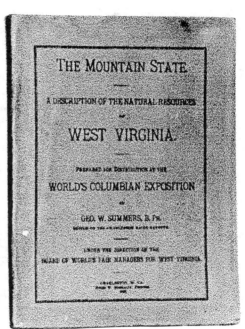

21x15. Fold. map, 259 p., (3) p. of county information with fold out. Tan wraps, black print. Color fold out map frontis. C.t.= t.p.
P→   ☉ (GLD) $20 - 38

2105. West Virginia. Elkins, S. B. *Speech of Hon. S. B. Elkins, Of West Virginia, delivered on West Virginia State Day, at the Columbian exposition, Chicago, August 23, 1893.* Wheeling: Daily Intelligencer steam book and job press, 1893.

23½x15. Wraps. C.t. Caption title: "West Virginia : Its Resources and Development." ☉ . (WM)

2106. West Virginia. Harris, John W. *Address of John W. Harris at the World's Columbian Exposition, Chicago, on "West Virginia Day." August 23, 1893.* [Wheeling]: Press of the Wheeling Register, 1893.

23x15. Stapled wraps. C.t.= t.p. ☉ . (WM)

2107. West Virginia. MacCorkle, Wm. A. *Address of Gov. Wm. A. MacCorkle : at the World's Columbian Exposition, Chicago, on "West Virginia Day." August 23, 1893.* Wheeling: West Va. Printing Co., Printers, 1893.

23x15. Stapled wraps. C.t.= t.p. ☉ . (WM)

-Wisconsin-

2108. Wisconsin. *At The Head Of The Lakes.* ____: ____, 189_.

17x13. Two ports and illus of machine on t.p. C.t.: "At The Head Of The Lakes : Superior : The New Flour City." Cover illus of industrial site, windmill, etc. . (WM)

2109. Wisconsin. *The Laws of Wisconsin, except city charters and their amendments, passed at the biennial session of the legislature of 1891, together with the joint resolutions and memorials. Also post-office address of the circuit judges, and times and places for holding circuit courts. With index of session laws since 1878.* Vol. I. Published by authority. Madison: Democrat printing co., state printers, 1891.

Chap. 433: Authorized governor appointed 6 man, 1 woman commission to be designated the "State Board of World's Fair Managers, of Wisconsin." No pay but actual transportation expenses + $5/day when absent from home. WI World's Columbian Commissioners and WI members of the Board of Lady Managers to be *ex-officio* members. Board to appoint a salaried executive commissioner responsible for securing WA's exhibit and objects therein. Appropriation: $65,000 from the state treasury. No member of the board to be personally liable for debts contracted by board. Approved Apr. 24, 1891. ☺. (MarL,WiHx)

2110. Wisconsin. *The Laws of Wisconsin passed at the biennial session of the legislature of 1893. Together with the joint resolutions and memorials.* ... Published by authority. Madison: Democrat printing co., state printers, 1893.

23x16. 434 p. Rebound hc, spine: "Laws of Wisconsin: 1893." Chap. 140: Amends the law of 1891. Appropriated $100,000: agriculture, $32,144; mines and mining, $18,450; fisheries, $13,967; forestry and timber, $11,000; educational, $3,738; floricultural, $500; finishing and maintaining the WI Bldg, $17,000; miscellaneous $3,201. Approved Apr. 11, 1893. ☺. (KU)

☞ At the close of the WCE, the Wisconsin Bldg was purchased by J. C. Rogers, a Wamego, KS, banker, and removed to Kansas City, MO, where it was rebuilt at 7th and Grand. It was first operated as a club, then leased to a hotel as an annex, and finally became the home of the B.P.O.E. lodge No. 26 in 1898. About 1959, the [Kansas] City Mission moved into the bldg; about 1969, it was demolished and the site became a parking lot. P→

ELKS' CLUB

2111. Wisconsin. Peck, George W., Jr. *"Ousconsin." The badger state's Columbian souvenir.* [Milwaukee: Letter Press by King, Fowle & Co.], 1893.

13x20. 1 *l*, 28 p., 63 *l*. Pebble-textured ivory stiff wraps, sepia print, frontis of WI Bldg. 63 *l* are gravure plates on one side. ☺. (CPLA)

2112. [Wisconsin]. *Pen and sunlight sketches of the principal cites in Wisconsin (omitting Milwaukee). Their growth, resources, manufactures, financial institutions and prospects. Also views of the Nation's pride, the World's Columbian exposition.* Chicago: Phoenix publishing co., n.d.

26½x21½. (21)-269, (11) p. Dark maroon cloth beveled hc, gilt print. "Wisconsin at the World's Columbian Exposition" at p. 269. (11) p. are bldgs and text about the grounds. ☺. (UoC)

2113. Wisconsin. State Board of World's Fair Managers, of Wisconsin. *Report of the State Board of World's Fair Managers of Wisconsin. With accompanying documents.* Madison: Democrat printing co., state printers, 1893.

22½x14. 41 p. ⊚ . (WiHx)

2114. Wisconsin. State Committee on Education Exhibit for Wisconsin. Stearns, J[ohn] W[illiam], ed. *The Columbus History of Education in Wisconsin.* [Milwaukee]: State Committee on Education Exhibit for Wisconsin, 1893.

23½x__. viii, 720 p., illus, ports. Each port followed by biographical sketch (sketches prepared by Miss E. Hellen Blair). (UC)

2115. Wisconsin. State Historical Society Library. *List of books by Wisconsin authors exhibited by the state historical society of Wisconsin in the Wisconsin state building : World's Columbian exposition : 1893 : Published by Authority of Law.* Madison: Democrat printing co., state printers, 1893.

23x14½. 14 p. Gray wraps, black print. C.t.= t.p. Books listed by subject categories.
⊚ . (LC,NYPL,BCM,NYSt,UoC,NL,OC)

2116. Wisconsin. *World's Columbian Exposition. Department of Wisconsin. Containing Act of Congress Creating World's Columbian Commission. Law Creating State Board of World's Fair Managers. By-laws of the board. Rules governing exhibits. Names and addresses of Officers, Committees, and Members of the Board.* N.p.: n.p., 1891.

22x15. 22 p. Green wraps. C.t. On cover: "Issued August, 1891." Map on back wrap. ⊚ . (CPL,WiHx)

-Wyoming-

2117. Wyoming. *Session laws of the State of Wyoming enacted by the first state legislature convened at Cheyenne on the twelfth day of November, 1890. Also act of Congress admitting state of Wyoming, state constitution and rules of supreme court.* Published by authority. Cheyenne: The Daily Sun publishing house, 1891.

25½x16½. (7)-447 p. Chap. 94: Created the "World's Fair Managers of Wyoming," a 5 member board (one the state engineer and the others appointed by the governor). Authorized the erection the WY Bldg at a cost not to exceed $10,000 and gave the Managers the authority to unite with a neighboring state in the erection of a bldg if deemed advisable. Appropriation: $30,000. Approved Jan. 10, 1891.
⊚ . (WYMus,MarL,WYLaw)

Chapter 13

WORLD'S CONGRESSES

210 Congresses, totaling over 1200 sessions, were held during the World's Fair. The idea of a series of congresses with representatives from all parts of the earth originated with Charles Carroll Bonney. He went to H. N. Higinbotham (WCE) with his plan and came out President of the World's Congress Auxiliary. The Auxiliary organized all of the Congresses. (See Wiring Diagram foldout.)

Mrs. Potter Palmer, president of the Board of Lady Managers of the World's Columbian Commission, suggested to Bonney there be a Woman's Branch of the World's Congress Auxiliary; her idea was accepted and she became President of the Woman's Branch.

Rules: 1) "World's Congress Auxiliary" is cited as an author only for items it directly issued (i.e., was primary author -- see organizational diagram.) It is understood to be the author of every citation in this chapter. 2) The preliminary publications, scopes, and organization lists are located by department or division; proceedings, transactions, and reports are listed by the Congress from which they were generated.

The Congresses evolved over a period of time; therefore, many items are printed with dates. Also, the organization changed, so some items may be found under different departments; e.g., Religion was originally under the Department of Science and Philosophy. As the Religious Congresses grew in size, the Department of Religion was formed to handle them all.

2118. Congress of Evolutionists. ... *Programme of The Congress of Evolutionists : to be held in the memorial art palace ... September 27th, 28th, and 29th, 1893.* N.p.: n.p., n.d.

21½x15. 8 p. Wraps same stock as text. At head of title: Auxiliary information. C.t. ⊚.(WM)

2119. Congress of Photographers. *Congress of Photographers.* N.p.: n.p., [1893?]; Woodbridge, CT: RPI, 1981.

23x14½. ca. 60 *l*, talks are paged separately. Black pebbled cloth hc, gold print. .(CH₃,AIC)

2120. Congress on Africa. ... *Official programme of the congress on Africa, Commencing August 14, 1893, in the memorial art palace, ...* N.p.: n.p., n.d.

21x15. 12 p. Caption title. Auxiliary information at head of title. Program prepared for the Committee by Frederic Perry Noble, Secretary, and employee of NL. For another Noble item, see #2164. ⊚ (NL)

2121. Congress on Mathematics and Astronomy. ... *Programme of congress on mathematics and astronomy, to be held in the Memorial Art Palace, ... week of August 21st, 1893.* N.p.: n.p., n.d.

20½x15½. Unpaged. Wraps same stock as text, black print. At head of title: Auxiliary information. C.t. ⊚.(WM)

2122. Department of Agriculture. General Division of Forestry. ... *Preliminary address of the committee of the World's congress auxiliary on forestry.* N.p.: n.p., n.d.

20½x15. 5 p. Wraps same stock as text, black print. At head of title: Auxiliary information. ⊚.(WM)

2123. Department of Agriculture. ... *The Scope of this* [Agriculture] *department.* N.p.: n.p., n.d.

    20x14. (6) p. Caption title.   (NL,WM)

2124. Department of Art. General Division of Photographic Art. ... *Committee of the Congress of Photographers.* N.p.: n.p., n.d.

    20x14. Auxiliary information at head of title.   ☞.(CHx)

2125. Department of Art. *[Preliminary publication.]* ... *The Scope of This* [Art] *Department.* N.p.: n.p., n.d.

    20½x15. Unpaged. Wraps same stock as text, black print. Ellipse: Auxiliary information and list of divisions: "Architecture, Painting, Sculpture, Engraving, Decorative Art, Photographic Art, Etc." Caption title. ☞.(WM)

2126. Department of Commerce and Finance. Division of Insurance. *Address of the committee of the World's Congress Auxiliary on a fire insurance congress...* B. J. Smith, Chairman. [Chicago?: 1892?].

    21x__. 3 p.   (MaHx)

2127. Department of Commerce and Finance. ... *Official programme of The Department of Commerce and Finance commencing June 19, 1893, in the Memorial Art Palace,* ... N.p.: n.p., n.d.

    21½x15. Auxiliary information at head of title. C.t. ☞.(CHx)

2128. Department of Commerce and Finance. ... *Preliminary address of the committee on arrangements for the congress of this division. Among the chief objects of the World's Congress Auxiliary is the promotion of cordial international commercial arrangements...* [Chicago?: 1892?]

    21x__. 4 p.   (MaHx)

2129. Department of Commerce and Finance. *[Preliminary publication.]* ... *The Scope of this* [Commerce and Finance] *Department.* N.p.: n.p., n.d.

    21x15. (10) p. Wraps same stock as text, black print. Caption title. Ellipse: Auxiliary information and topics "Including Transportation, Exchange and Distribution, with Divisions of Banking, Stock Exchange, Boards of Trade, Water Commerce, Railway Commerce, and Insurance." ☞.(CHx,NL,WM)

2130. Department of Education. ... *Department of Education. General Division of University Extension.* N.p.: n.p., n.d.

    21x15. 7 p. glossy text. Auxiliary information at head of title. General ideas in the evolution of plans for the Congress. George Henderson, Chairman. Contains partial list of the advisory council and preliminary program. ☞(NL)

2131. Department of Education. ... *Official programme of The Department of Education, commencing July 17, 1893, in the memorial art palace,...* N.p.: n.p., n.d.

20½x15½. 40 p. Wraps same stock as text pages, black print. At head of title: Auxiliary information. At top of front wrap in bold print: "Third edition of July 20." and "Education." C.t.   ☺.(WM)

2132. Department of Education. ... *The Scope of this* [Education] *Department.* N.p.: n.p., n.d.

20x15. (10) p. Wraps same stock as text pages, black print. Ellipse: Auxiliary information and subject list including common, blind, musical, high, academic, and chautauquan schools. Caption title.
☺.(NL,WM)

2133. Department of Education. The World's General Educational Congress. *Preliminary address of the Commissioner of Education of the United States (W. T. Harris)* ... ____: ___, [1893].

8°.   (BM)

2134. Department of Engineering. ... *Official programme of The Department of Engineering, commencing July 31st, 1893, in the memorial art palace* ... N.p.: n.p., n.d.

21½x15½. 32 p. Wraps same stock as text pages, black print. At head of title: Auxiliary information.
C.t.   ☺.(WM)

2135. Department of Engineering. *[Preliminary publication.]* ... *The scope of this* [Engineering] *department.* N.p.: n.p., n.d.

20½x15. (8) p. Wraps same stock as text pages, black print. Caption title. Ellipse: Auxiliary info and a list of engineering subjects covered: civil, electrical, military, roads, bridges, sewerage.   ☺.(NL,WM)

2136. Department of Government. General division of Political and Economic Reform. *Preliminary address of the Committee of the World's Congress auxiliary on a suffrage congress.* ____: ___, 18__.

4 p. pamphlet.   (InHx)

2137. Department of Government. General division of Political and Economic Reform. ... *Programme of the suffrage congress, commencing August 7, 1893, in the Memorial Hall Art Palace, Michigan Avenue and Adams Street, Chicago.* N.p.: n.p., n.d.

21x15. Auxiliary information at head of title. Caption title.   ☺.(CHx)

2138. Department of Government. ... *General Opening of the Congresses of this Department, including Jurisprudence and Law Reform; Civil Service Reform; Suffrage in Republic, Kingdom and Empire; and the Government of Cities : Monday Morning, August 7, 1893--10 a.m. Hall of Columbus.* ... N.p.: n.p., n.d.

21x15. Auxiliary information at head of title. Caption title.   ☺.(CHx)

2139. Department of Government. *[Preliminary publication.]* ... *The Scope of this* [Government] *Department.* ... N.p.: n.p., n.d.

21x15. (12) p. Wraps same as text pages, black print. Caption title. Ellipse: Auxiliary information and list of topics: i.e., law reform, international law, administration of justice, political and economic reform, government of cities, executive administration, protection of intellectual property, arbitration and peace. ⊚ . (CHx,NL,WM)

2140. Department of Labor. *[Preliminary publication.]* ... *The Scope of this* [Labor] *Department.* N.p.: n.p., n.d.

20½x15. Unpaged. Wraps same stock as text pages, black print. Caption title. Ellipse: Auxiliary information and a list of areas covered by the Department which includes industrial and economic problems, labor organization, mutual benefit societies, cooperative arrangements, profit sharing schemes, building associations, household economics, etc. ⊚ . (WM)

2141. Department of Labor. ... *Programme of the labor congress to be held in the Memorial Art Palace ... week of August,* [sic] *28th 1893.* N.p.: n.p., n.d.

20½x15. 6 p. C.t. Ahead of program on p. (1): "Department of labor." ⊚ (NL)

2142. Department of Literature. General Division [Congress] of Authors. ... *Programme of the Congress of Authors. To Convene in the Art Institute, Chicago, During the Week beginning July 10, 1893.* ...

20½x15. 4 *l.* Auxiliary information at head of title. C.t. Naturalist John Burroughs spoke in the Hall of Columbus on Thursday, July 13, 1893; Charles Dudley Warner presiding. ⊚ . (CHx)

2143. Department of Literature. General Division of Libraries. ... *Preliminary address of the committee on a congress of librarians, to be held at Chicago, July 10-15, 1893.* [Chicago: 1893].

Trifold to 20½x15. (5) p. No wraps. Caption title. Auxiliary information at head of title. Contents: list of advisory council for the congress. Women's committee chairman was Elizabeth A. Young; general committee chairman was Frederick H. Hild. ⊚ (NL)

2144. Department of Literature. General Division of Philology. ... *Programme of a congress of philologists.* ... *July 11-15, 1893, under the auspices of the World's Congress Auxiliary* ... N.p.: n.p., n.d.

20½x15. 7 p. includes cover. C.t. At top of p. 2: "Preliminary programme." (NL)

2145. Department of Literature. *[Preliminary publication.]* ... *The Scope of This* [Literature] *Department.*

20x15. (12) p. Wraps same stock as text, black print. Ellipse: Auxiliary info. Caption title. (NL,HL)

2146. Department of Literature. ... *Programme of the congress of librarians, July 12-15, 1893.* N.p.: n.p., n.d.

21x15. (3) p. not including front cover. Auxiliary information at head of title. C.t. List of speakers and topics for each session. ⊚ (NL)

2147. Department of Literature. ... *Programme of the World's congress of historians and historical students convened in Chicago during the week beginning July 10, 1893.* N.p.: n.p., n.d.

20½x15. (5) p. At head of title: Auxiliary information. C.t. William F. Poole was chairman. Contents: topic and speaker program for July 11-13. Congress rules, papers, etc. at #2150. ☉.(NL,WM)

2148. Department of Literature. ... *Programme of the World's folk-lore congress, to convene in Chicago during the week commencing July 10, 1893.* ... N.p.: n.p., n.d.

23x15. (6) p. not including wrap. Wraps same stock as text. Auxiliary information at head of title. C.t. Committee members of the Folk-Lore Congress listed on front wrap. ☉.(NYPL,NL,WM)

2149. Department of Literature. ... *Programme of the World's folk-lore congress, to convene in Chicago during the week commencing July 10, 1893* ... N.p.: n.p., n.d.

23x15. 12 p. including cover. "Concert of folk songs and national music given ... July 14, 1893 ... under the direction of Frederic W. Root, ..." (NL)

2150. Department of Literature. *The World's Congress of historians and historical students, to Convene in Chicago during the Week commencing July 10, 1893.* N.p.: n.p., n.d.

20½x15. 4 p., glossy text. Caption title. Contains rules, organization, and papers, debates, procedures. For the program, see #2147. ☉ (NL)

2151. Department of Medicine. *Official Programme of the World's Congress of Homoeopathic Physicians and Surgeons* ... Chicago: Thayer & Jackson Stationery Co., n.d.

18x11½. 23 p. Light orange wraps, black print. (CHx)

2152. Department of Medicine. *The Scope of This* [Medicine] *Department.*

20x15. (8) p. Caption title. (NL)

2153. Department of Moral and Social Reform. *[Preliminary publication.]* ... *To facilitate the holding of Conferences and Conventions, ... Preliminary divisions.* N.p.: n.p., n.d.

20½x15. Caption title. First ellipse: Auxiliary information. ☉.(WM)

2154. Department of Music. ... *Official programme of the department of music, commencing July 3, 1893, in the Memorial Art Palace,* ... 3rd ed. N.p.: n.p., n.d.

21x15. 16 p. Auxiliary information at head of title. C.t. Theodore Thomas was chairman. On July 7th, Mrs. Theodore Thomas gave paper entitled: "The work of Woman's Amateur Musical Clubs in America."
---- 19½x15. 16 p.
☉.(CHx,NL)

2155. Department of Music. *[Preliminary publication.]* ... *The Scope of This* [Music] *Department.* N.p.: n.p., n.d.

21x15. (8) p. Caption title. At ellipse: Auxiliary information. ⊜.(CHx,NL,WM)

2156. Department of the Public Press. *[Preliminary publication.]* ... *The Scope of This* [Public Press] *Department.* N.p.: n.p., n.d.

21x15. (7) p. Caption title. At ellipse: Auxiliary information. Scope, organization, and objects of the dept. ⊜.(CHx,NL,WM)

2157. Department of the Public Press. *Programme of the Public Press Congresses. May 22 to 28, inclusive, 1893. Memorial Art Palace* ... Chicago: Knight, Leonard & Co., printers, n.d.

23x15½. 20 p. C.t. ⊜.(CHx)

2158. Department of Religion. Woman's Branch. ... *Preliminary address of the woman's general committee on religious congresses in connection with the exposition of 1893.* N.p.: n.p., n.d.

20½x15. At head of title: Auxiliary information. Caption title. ⊜.(WM)

2159. Department of Religion. Woman's Branch. ... *Preliminary outline of programme for the woman's congress of missions, to be held October second, third and fourth, 1893.* N.p.: n.p., n.d.

20½x15. At head of title: Auxiliary information. Caption title. ⊜.(WM)

2160. Department of Religion. *[Preliminary publication.]* ... *Department of Religion.* ... *To unite all Religion against all Irreligion;* ... N.p.: n.p., n.d.

20½x15. Caption title. First ellipse: Auxiliary information. ⊜.(WM)

2161. Department of Religion. ... *Programme of The World's Religious Congresses of 1893. Including Churches, Missions, Sunday Schools, and other Religious Organizations.* [Chicago: Rand McNally & Co.], n.d.

21½x15. 162 p. Pale green wraps, black print. Auxiliary information at head of title. C.t.: "The World's Religious Congresses of 1893. General Programme." Complete listing of dates for each religious congress. Text of selected hymns for use in the Congresses and Parliament of Religions held in connection with the World's Columbian Exposition at p. 145-62.
---- Preliminary ed. Same except 20½x14.
          ⊜.(CHx,NYPL,UoC)

2162. Department of Religion. *World's Congress Auxiliary of the World's Columbian Exposition of 1893. Department of Religion.* N.p.: n.p., n.d.

21x13½. 8 p. pamphlet addressed to Dʳ Joseph Toner, Washington DC (1ˢᵗ page); hand signed in ink "John Henry Barrows" (bottom p. 8). This format was a "form letter" to those appointed members of the Advisory Council on Religious Congresses, WCE. Includes a long list of those already appointed from various countries. Unique or rare. (LC)

2163. Department of Science and Philosophy. General Division of African Ethnology. ... *Preliminary address of the Auxiliary committee on an African ethnological congress, at Chicago, in 1893.* N.p.: n.p., n.d.

20½x14½. 3 *l*. Caption title. At head of title: "The World's Congress Auxiliary of the World's Columbian Exposition. Department of science and philosophy. General division of African ethnology." Joseph E. Roy, D. D., Chairman General Committee Congress of African Ethnology. Written in Chicago, April, 1892. (NYPL,BM)

2164. Department of Science and Philosophy. General Division of African Ethnology. ... *Report in Behalf of the General Committee, by its Chairman, Joseph E. Roy, D. D.* N.p.: n.p., n.d.

19½x14½. 28 p. Caption title. At head of title: "The World's congress auxiliary of the World's Columbian exposition. Department of science and philosophy. General division of African ethnology." Genesis of the Congress on Africa and a report on progress of preparation for the Congress on Africa. F. P. Noble, Newberry Library, was secretary. (For other Noble items see #949 and #2120.) ⊚ . (NYPL,NL)

2165. Department of Science and Philosophy. ... *Preliminary Address of the General Committee on Zoölogical Congresses in Connection with the Exposition.* N.p.: n.p., n.d.

20½x15. At head of title: Auxiliary information. Caption title. ⊚ . (WM)

2166. Department of Science and Philosophy. ... *Programme of The World's Congress on Geology, to be held in the Memorial Art Palace, ... August 21-26, 1893.* N.p.: n.p., n.d.

21x15. Auxiliary information at head of title. Caption title. ⊚ . (CHx)

2167. Department of Science and Philosophy. *[Revised preliminary publication.]* ... *The Scope of This* [Science and Philosophy] *Department.* N.p.: n.p., 1891?.

21x15. Caption title. Scope, organization, etc. of the dept which included: Editors, Leading Writers, and Publishers of Daily and other Periodical Publication. Includes the organization of the Woman's Branch. Printed date at end of pamphlet: "September, 1891." ⊚ . (CHx,WM)

2168. Department of Temperance. *[Preliminary publication.]* *The Scope of This* [Temperance] *Department.* N.p.: n.p., n.d.

21½x15. Ellipse: Auxiliary information and temperance quotes. Caption title. ⊚ . (WM)

2169. Department of Woman's Progress. ... *The Department of Woman's Progress.* N.p.: n.p., n.d.

19½x14½. 1 *l* (t.p.), 3-26, (1) p. Wraps are same stock as text paper, white with black print. Auxiliary information ahead of title.
Contents: Three publications with the same format as those World's Congress Auxiliary items published separately. 1) "Special announcement in relation to the congress of representative women to be held during the week commencing May 15, 1893." p. (5-6). 2) "Preliminary address of the committee of a World's congress of representative women at Chicago in 1893." p. (7-12) (same as #2170). 3) "Report of the progress to date, made by the committee of arrangements for a World's congress of representative women." p. 12-26. ⊚ (NL,WM)

2170. Department of Woman's Progress. ... *Preliminary address of the committee on a World's congress of representative women at Chicago in 1893.* [Chicago: 1892].

Trifold to 21x15. (5) p. Auxiliary information ahead of title. Caption title. Preliminary work for the congress; also includes the constitution for The International Council of Women.   ⊚ (NL)

2171. Department of Woman's Progress. ... *Program to date for a World's congress of representative women to be held in Chicago, May 15-22.* N.p.: n.p., n.d.

19½x14½. 6 p. Caption title. Contents: extracts of preliminary address and day by day program of events. Chairman was May Wright Sewall.   ⊚ (NL)

2172. Historical Congress. Newton, Mary Mann Page. *Colonial Virginia: a paper read before the historical congress at Chicago, July 13th, 1893, together with a series of World's Fair Letters.* Richmond, VA: West, Johnston & Co. Publishers, 1893.

17½x13½. 71 p. Pale blue wraps with dark blue print and design. C.t.: "Colonial Virginia and World's Fair Letters." Also catalogued under: Mary Mann Page Newton Stanard.   ⊚ . (NYPL,VaHx,UVa,NL)

2173. International Christian Conference. *Christianity practically applied. The discussions of the International Christian Conference : held in Chicago, October 8-14, 1893 ... and under the auspices and direction of the Evangelical Alliance for the United States. The general conferences.* New York: The Baker & Taylor co., [°1894 by The Evangelical Alliance for the United States].

22½x15½. 1 *l*, vii, 517 p., 1 *l*. Brown cloth hc, gilt design and spine lettering.   ⊚ . (NL)

2174. International Christian Conference. *Christianity practically applied. The discussions of the International Christian Conference : held in Chicago, October 8-14, 1893 ... and under the auspices and direction of the Evangelical Alliance for the United States. The section conferences.* New York: The Baker & Taylor co., [°1894 by The Evangelical Alliance for the United States].

22½x15½. x, 509 p., 2 *l*. Brown cloth hc, gilt design and spine lettering.   ⊚ . (NL,OC)

2175. International Congress of Anthropology. Hale, Horatio. *The Fall of Hochelaga: a study of popular tradition.* Cambridge, MA: [The American Folk-Lore Society], 1894.

25x15. 14 p. Wraps. Rpt. from *The Journal of American Folk-Lore* 7(Jan.-Mar. 1894): 1-14 (see #1334). At end of article: "prepared for the World's Congress of Anthropology." Presentation copy from the author at McGill U. The River of Hochelaga was renamed the St. Lawrence by explorer, Jacques Cartier.   ⊚ . (mcg,NLC)

2176. International Congress of Anthropology. ... *Programme of The International Congress of Anthropology, to be held in the memorial art palace, ... during the week August 28 to September 2, 1893.* N.p.: n.p., n.d.

21x15. Unpaged. Wraps same stock as text pages, black print. At head of title: Auxiliary information. C.t. Local committee and executive committee members listed on front wrap.   ⊚ . (WM)

2177. International Congress of Anthropology. Wake, C. Staniland, ed. on behalf of the publication committee. *Memoirs of the International Congress of Anthropology.* Chicago: The Schulte publishing co., 1894; Woodbridge, CT: RPI, 1989.

    25x17. 1 *l*, v-xix, 19-375 p., illus, 6 pl. Maroon cloth hc, gold print on covers and spine.   © . (Sl,NYPL,BM)

2178. International Congress of Charities, Correction and Philanthropy. *Circular, no. 1* [to no. 4]. Chicago: 1892-93.

    8°. Four circulars published individually.   (NYPL)

2179. International Congress of Charities, Correction and Philanthropy. *Programme, rules officers and members for their general exercises of June 1893,...* Baltimore: Johns Hopkins Press, 1894.

    8°. 47 p.   (UC,NYPL)

2180. International Congress of Charities, Correction and Philanthropy. *Report of the proceedings.* Baltimore: Johns Hopkins Press, 1894.

    1st section. John Huston Finley, ed. *The public treatment of pauperism... report of the 1 section of the ... congress.* 8°. 2 *l*, 319 p.
    2nd section. Anna Garlin Spencer and Charles Wesley Birtwell, eds. 163 p.
    3rd section. John S. Billings and Henry M. Hurd, eds. 719 p.
    4th section. G. Alder Blumer and A. B. Richardson, eds. 193 p.
    5th section. Frederick H. Wines in section 4. 107 p.
    6th section. Daniel C. Gilman, ed. *The organization of charities... report of the 6 section of the ... congress.* 8°. xxxii, 400 p.
    7th section. Amos G. Warner in section 2. 127 p.
    8th section. George H. Knight in section 4. 22 p.
        (UC,NYPL)

2181. International Congress of Education. Bardeen, C[harles] W[illiam]. *The history of the educational journalism in the state of New York : a paper read July 28th, 1893, before the department of educational publications of the international congresses of education of the World's Columbian exposition.* Syracuse, NY: C. W. Bardeen, publisher, 1893.

    22½x14½. 45, (1) p. Printed wraps. NYSt copy: front cover autographed by Bardeen.   © . (NYSt)

2182. [International Congress of Education]. Harris, William T[orrey]. *The World's Educational Congress. A paper read before the department of superintendence of the National Education Association, at Brooklyn, N.Y., February 16, 1892.* Rpt. from Journal of Education, Boston.

    18½x12½. 1 *l*, (3)-11 p. C.t. Harris was U.S. Commissioner of Education. Contents: ground work and planning for WCE. © (NL,RPB)

2183. International Congress of Education. National Educational Association. ... *Official programme of The International Congress of Education of the World's Columbian exposition. July 25-28, 1893. Under charge of the National Educational Association, United States of America. All meetings to be held in the Memorial Art Palace ...* N.p.: n.p., n.d.

20½x15½. 32 p. Bold print at top of cover: "N.E.A." and "July 25-28." At head of title: Auxiliary information. C.t. Wraps same stock as text, black print. ⊚ . (WM)

2184. International Congress of Education. National Educational Association. *Proceedings of the International Congress of Education of the World's Columbian Exposition : Chicago, July 25-28, 1893.* New York: Press of J. J. Little & Co. for National Educational Association, 1894; 2nd ed. New York: Press of J. J. Little & Co. for National Education Association, 1895.

1894: 23½x16½. xviii, 1005 p. Black hc, gold lettering on spine. W. T. Harris chaired the Education Congress as requested by Charles C. Bonney. This vol takes the place of the National Educational Association's "Journal" for 1893.
---- Also listed: 1894. xviii, (2), 7-1005, (1) p.
---- 2nd ed. 1895: 23x15½. xviii, (3)-1005, (1) p.
⊚ . (KU,CPL,NYPL,NL)

2185. International Congress of Education. *Questions for Discussion at the World's Educational Congress, Chicago, U.S.A., July 25th to 28th, inclusive, 1893. Supplementary to former list printed in the Announcement.* [Chicago: 1892?].

8°. Single sheet. (BM)

2186. International Congress of Education. *World's Educational Congress, Chicago, U.S.A. July 25th to 28th, inclusive, 1893. Preliminary announcement ...* [Chicago?: 1893?].

8°. 8 p. (MaHx,BM)

2187. International Congress on Sunday Rest. 7th, Chicago, 1893. *The Sunday problem; its day aspects, physiological, industrial, social, political, and religious papers presented at the International congress on Sunday rest, Chicago, Sept. 28-30, 1893.* Boston: J. H. Earle, 1894.

19x__. 5, 9-338 p. (UC)

2188. International Congress on Sunday Rest. 7th. Chicago, 1893. *The Sunday problem ... Papers presented ... Sept. 28-30, 1893.* New York: Baker & Taylor co., [°1894].

19x__. 334 p. (UC)

2189. International Congress on Water Transportation. *Water Commerce Congress, Chicago, 1893* 21 pamphlets. Boston: Damrell & Upham, n.d.

25½x17½. Black print on blue cloth hc folder, holds all 21 pamphlets. String tied edges. Each pamphlet a talk at the Congress. Above each talk title: "Water Commerce Congress, Chicago, 1893." First pamphlet lists papers, members, organization, etc. (CHx,RPB)

2190. International Eisteddfod Congress. *... Eisteddfod Gydgenedlaethol Ffair y Byd. Medi 5ed, 6ed, 7ed, 8ed, 1893. Dan Nawdd y Cymrodorion Cenedlaethol, Chicago.* \ *... International Eisteddfod of the World's Fair. September 5th, 6th, 7th, 8th, 1893. Under the auspices of The National Cymrodorion of Chicago. Souvenir Program.* Chicago: The Cambro Printing Co., 1892; N.p.: n.p., n.d.

Cambro: 25x17. 93 p. Brown stiff wraps, black print. No border around title on t.p. Program for meetings and music. At head of Welsh title: "'Y Gwir yn Erbyn y Byd.' ... 'Dan Nawdd Duw a'i Dangnef." At head of English title: "The truth Against the World."
---- N.p.: 66 p. Beige wraps. Border around title on t.p. At head of Welsh title: "'Y Gwir yn Erbyn y Byd.' ... 'Faith ac Ysbryd Cymru Wen.'" At head of English title: "The truth Against the World."
    ⊚ . (NL,S)

2191. International Eisteddfod Congress. ... *Welshmen as Factors. The successful prize essay at the International Eisteddfod of the World's Columbia* [sic] *exposition, Chicago, 1893. By "William Penn."* [___: Press of Thomas Griffiths, 1899].

19x14. 429 p. At head of title: "Facts about Welsh factors. 'Y gwir yn erbyn y byd.'"   ⊚ . (S)

2192. International Eisteddfod Congress. ... *The World's Columbian Exposition : international eisteddvod, Chicago, 1893. Cais a gwahoddiad cenedlaethol ac eisteddfodol. A National and Eisteddvodic Call and Invitation.* Chicago: Rand, McNally & Co., Printers, 1891; Woodbridge, CT: RPI, 1989.

23x15. 16 p. Drab green wraps, black print. C.t.= t.p. At head of title: "'Y Gwir yn Erbyn y Byd.' 'Duw, a Pyhob Daioni.' 'Calon wrth Galon.'" The gathering of Welsh bards and minstrels in the old Druid custom commenced Sept. 5, 1893. [The authors ask: Do they still gather?]   ⊚ . (Sl,NHSt,UoC,NL)

2193. International Electrical Congress. *Proceedings ... Aug. 21-25, 1893.* New York: 1894.

8°.   (NYPL)

2194. International Engineering Congress. Division of Marine and Naval Engineering and Naval Architecture. Melville, George W[allace], ed. *Proceedings of the International Engineering Congress, division of marine and naval engineering and naval architecture. Held in connection with the World's Columbian Exposition at Chicago, July 31 - August 5, 1893.* 1st ed. 2 vol. New York: John Wiley & sons, 1894.

22½x12½. Vol I: xxv, 43 p. (25 papers). Vol II: 42 p. (20 papers). Melville was Engineer-in-Chief, U.S. Navy.   ⊚ . (BM,UMi,NYSt)

2195. International Engineering Congress. Division of Military Engineering. Comly, Clifton. *Operations of the Division of military engineering of the International congress of engineers, held in Chicago last August, under the auspices of the World's Congress Auxiliary of the World's Columbian Exposition.* Washington: GPO, 1894.

23½x__. 982 p., illus, 55 plates (part fold.), 42 diagrams (part fold.). Contains bibliographies. Comly was Major of Ordinance.
---- Also: S. Doc., 53d Cong., 2d Sess. (1894).
    ⊚ (NA,NYPL,UMi,NYSt)

2196. International Engineering Congress. Divisions C. and D. Mining and Metallurgy. *Proceedings, papers and discussions.* 2 vol. New York: Amer. Inst. Min. Eng., 1894.

8°. In *Amer. Inst. Min. Eng. Trans.* vol. 22, 23.   (NYPL)

2197. International Folk-Lore Congress. Bassett, Helen Wheeler, and Frederick Starr, eds. *The International Folk-Lore Congress of the World's Columbian Exposition, Chicago, July, 1893.* Chicago: Charles H. Sergel co., 1898.

25x__. 3 *l*, 3-512 p., plates, ports, facsimiles. *Archives of the International Folk-Lore Association.* Vol I. Contains papers read at the congress. (BM,UDe,UMi,OC)

Rpt.: New York: Arno Press, 1980. 23x__. 512 p. Series: International Folk-lore Association. Archives, vol 1. Folklore of the world. (OC)

2198. International Folk-Lore Congress. Culin, Stewart. *Retrospect of the folk-lore of the Columbian Exposition.* [Boston: 1894].

8°. Caption title. Rpt: *Journal of American folk-lore* 7(1894): 51-59 (see #1334.) (NYPL)

2199. International Folk-Lore Congress. [*Papers and Transactions ...*] Chicago: C. H. Sergel Co., 1898.

2 *l*, 3-512 p. From the Archives of the International folklore association. Vol 1. (UWa)

2200. International Geographic Conference. National Geographic Society. *Proceedings of the International Geographic Conference in Chicago, July 27-28, 1893.* Washington, D.C.: National Geographic Society, 1893.

8°. *The National Geographic Magazine,* vol 5. (BM)

2201. International Mathematical Congress. ... *Mathematical papers read at the international mathematical congress : held in connection with the World's Columbian exposition Chicago 1893.* Ed. by the Committee of the Congress. New York: Macmillan and co. for the American mathematical society, 1896.

23½x15½. xvi, 411, (3) p. Dark olive cloth hc, gilt print on spine. At head of title: "Papers Published by the American Mathematical Society.-- Vol. I." Committee: E. Hastings Moore, Oskar Bolza, Heinrich Maschke, Henry S. White. ☺ . (csuf,BM,NYSt,OC)

2202. International Meteorological Congress. Fassig, Oliver L., ed. *Report of the International Meteorological Congress, held at Chicago, Ill., August 21-24, 1893, under the auspices of the Congress Auxiliary of the World's Columbian Exposition.* 3 part in 1. Washington: Weather Bureau, 1894-96.

8°. xxi, 772 p. include partially colored maps and 43 plates. U.S. Dept of Agriculture. Weather Bureau. Bulletin no. 11. (UC,BM)

2203. International Pharmaceutical Congress. *The International Pharmaceutical Congress : Art Palace, Chicago, 1893. Programme.* N.p.: n.p., n.d.

20½x16. Caption title. Program beginning Aug. 21, 1893 at 10 a.m. ☺ . (WM)

2204. International Pharmaceutical Congress. *Report of the proceedings of the seventh International pharmaceutical congress, held at Chicago, August 21, 22, 23, 1893.* Chicago: R. R. Donnelley and sons co., for American Pharmaceutical Association, 1897.

23½x__. (1), xxx, 102 p.   (UC)

2205. Latin Historical Society, Chicago. *The religions of the world. World's fair, Parliament of religions. The World's great religions, clearly defined by their greatest living exponents.* Chicago: Latin Historical Society, [1893].

12°. 16 p.
---- Also listed: 1 *l*, 64 p.
       (UC)

2206. Philosophical Congress. ... *Programme of the philosophical congress : to be held in the Memorial Art Palace, ... during the week of August 21st, 1893.* N.p.: n.p., n.d.

21½x15½. Unpaged. Wraps same stock as text, black print. C.t. At head of title: Auxiliary information. List of committee members on front wrap. R. N. Foster, Chairman.   ☻ . (WM)

2207. Public Press Congress. Smith, William Henry. *The Public Press as the Advocate of Human Rights and the Champion of the Interests of the Common People : An address ... before the Press Congress, May 23.* N.p.: n.p., n.d.

19½x13. 16 p. Entire booklet, including cover, is of cream-colored stock. At head of title: "The World's Congress Auxiliary of the World's Columbian exposition of 1893." C.t.   ☻ . (InHx)

2208. Theosophical Congress. *The Theosophical Congress : held by the Theosophical Society at the parliament of religions, World's fair of 1893, at Chicago, Ill., September 15, 16, 17. Report of proceedings and documents.* New York: American section headquarters T. S., 1893.

23x15. 195 p.   ☻ . (OC)

2209. Universal Peace Congress. Butterworth, [H.]. *White city by the inland sea. Ode read at the opening of the Chicago Peace Congress, Aug. 14, 1893.* Boston: Am. Peace Society, 1893.

12°. 18 p., 1 plate, 2 port. Poem.   (NYPL)

2210. Universal Peace Congress. *Official report of the fifth universal peace congress held at Chicago, United States of America, August 14 to 20, 1893, under the auspices of the World's Congress Auxiliary of the World's Columbian Exposition.* Boston: The American Peace Society, n.d.

24x15½. 332 p. Black cloth hc, gilt print. The World's Congress Auxiliary, Dept of Government organization for this congress, followed by the program are found on the first pages of the book. Speakers included E. Everett Hale and William E. Curtis, Bureau of American Republics.
       ☻ (GLD,csuf,BM,BPL,OC) $20 - 35

2211. Woman's Branch. *The Columbian Association of Housekeepers and Bureau of Information...* Mrs. John Wilkinson, et al. [Chicago?]: n.p., n.d.

21x__. 4 p. (MaHx)

2212. Woman's Branch. Committee on Christian Missions. ... *Preliminary Address of the Woman's Committee of the World's Congress Auxiliary on Christian Missions.* N.p.: n.p., n.d.

20½x15. At head of title: Auxiliary information. Caption title. ☺.(WM)

2213. Woman's Branch. Committee on Household Economics. *The preliminary address of the Woman's Committee on Household Economics...* Mrs. John Wilkinson, Chairman. [Chicago?: 1892?].

21x__. 4 p. (MaHx,WM)

2214. Woman's Branch. Committee on Labor Congress. *Preliminary Address of the Woman's Committee of the World's Congress Auxiliary on Labor Congresses.* N.p.: n.p., n.d.

20x15. (4) p. Caption title. (NL)

2215. Woman's Branch. *Programme of the World's Congress of Representative Women : May 15-21, inclusive, 1893. Memorial Art Palace Chicago.* Chi[cago]: Knight, Leonard & Co., Press, [1893].

23x15. 55 p. Tan wraps printed in black. C.t. A complete listing of representatives and events. 3rd and 6th ed. Each edition listed as 5,000 copies apiece. Sessions included those found at #2265, #2266, #2267, the Dept Congress of the Women's National Indian Association, and the National-American Woman Suffrage Association of May 18th (#2307).

☺ (GLD,NL) $25 - 50

2216. Woman's Branch. World's Committee of Women's Missionary Societies. *Program of Conference : under the auspices of the World's Committee of Women's Missionary Societies : to be held in hall number 6 of the art palace, Chicago. Friday and Saturday. September 29 and 30, 1893.* N.p.: n.p., n.d.

23x15. Unpaged. Wraps same stock as text, black print. C.t. ☺.(WM)

2217. Woman's Christian Temperance Union. ... *Program of the second World's and twentieth national conventions ... Memorial Art Palace, October 16, 17, 18, 19, 20, and 21, 1893.* [Chicago: 1893].

21x__. 28 p. C.t. At head of title: "The World's Congress Auxiliary of the World's Columbian Exposition of 1893." (CHx)

2218. World's Columbian Dental Congress. *Transactions of the World's Columbian Dental Congress : Chicago, August 14, 15, 16, 17, 18 and 19, 1893.* Ed. A. W. Harlan and Louis Ottofy for the general executive committee. 2 vols. Chicago: Press of Knight, Leonard & Co., 1894.

23x14½. Vol 1: xliv, 511 p. Vol 2: x, (2), (513)-1068 p. Frontis (vol 2), illus, plates (4 of the plates have illus both sides), fold. tables, diagrams (part fold.). Contributions in English, a few in French and German. ☺. (CPL,NYPL,UMi,UoC)

2219. World's Congress Auxiliary. Bonney, Charles C[arroll]. "Letter to Governor Prince." 5 Mar. 1891. State Records Center & Archives, Santa Fe, NM.

21½x14½ folded. (4) p., letterhead reads: "Not Things, but Men: The World's Congress Auxiliary of the World's Columbian Exposition." Prince was asked to participate in the Congress of Governors, a Committee of the Auxiliary. ☺. (SFe)

2220. World's Congress Auxiliary. Bonney, Charles Carroll. *World's Congress Addresses : Delivered by the President, the Hon. Charles Carroll Bonney, LL.D., to the World's Parliament of Religions and the Religious Denominational Congresses of 1893 : with the Closing Addresses at the Final Session of the World's Congress Auxiliary.* Chicago: The Open Court publishing co., 1900.

18½x12. iv, 1 *l*, 88 p. Tan stiff wraps, black print. At head of title: "The Religion of Science Library. No. 42." C.t.: "World's Congress Addresses."
---- Also listed: iv, 83 p.
---- Chicago: The Open Court publishing co. [and] London: Kegan Paul, Trench, Trübner & co (Limited), 1900. 19½x13½.
☺. (CHx,LC,UoC)

2221. World's Congress Auxiliary. Bonney, Charles C[arroll]. *The World's Congresses of 1893. Opening Address by the president, Charles C. Bonney. Delivered in the permanent Memorial Art Palace, in Chicago, on Monday morning, May 15, 1893.* Chicago: Knight, Leonard & Co., printers, n.d.

21x15½. 20 numbered leaves. C.t. ☺. (CHx,NL)

2222. World's Congress Auxiliary. ... *Final session of The World's Congresses of 1893, Memorial Art Palace, Saturday, Oct. 28th. President's Closing Address, and Proclamation of the World's Congress Fraternity.* N.p.: n.p., n.d.

21x16. (10) p. Pamphlet of folded glossy paper with sewn binding. Caption title. At head of title: "Not things, but men. The World's Congress Auxiliary of the World's Columbian Exposition of 1893. President: Charles C. Bonney. ..." ☺. (nwu)

2223. World's Congress Auxiliary. ... *First Report of the Auxiliary to the directory of the exposition.* [Chicago: 1891].

20x15. 39 p. White glossy wraps, black print. At head of title: "Not Things, But Men. Not Matter, But Mind. The World's Congress Auxiliary of the World's Columbian Exposition." C.t.= t.p.
☺. (SFe,NYPL,NL)

2224. World's Congress Auxiliary. ... *General programme of the series of World's congresses to be held at Chicago in connection with the World's Columbian exposition of 1893.* N.p.: n.p., n.d.

15x11. 16 p. Caption title. On p. (1): General Officers and purpose. Auxiliary motto: Not things, but men. Not matter, but mind. At top of page: "[corrected to January 1, 1893]."
---- "[Issued October, 1892.]": 21x15½. (15) p. Caption title. Auxiliary motto: "Not things, but men." On p. (1): The organization of the Auxiliary.
☺. (SFe,KyU,CHx,NYPL,WM,HL) $12 - 24

2225. World's Congress Auxiliary. ... *The general programme of The World's Congresses of 1893.* N.p.: n.p., n.d.

20½x15½. (18) p. including wraps. Wraps same stock as text. C.t. At head of title: "Not things, but men." Following title: "[Edition of April 1, 1893.]"
---- 15x11. 16 p. including front wrap. C.t. At head of title: "Not things, but men." Following title: "[Edition of May 1, 1893.]"
⊚ (GLD,NL) $12 - 24

2226. [World's Congress Auxiliary]. Ireland, John. *Discourse. Inauguration of the work of the Congress Auxiliary of the World's Columbian Exposition.* N.p.: n.p., [1892].

4°. 9 *l.* Advance copy.--(NYPL call VC p.v. 27)   (NYPL)

2227. World's Congress Auxiliary. ... *List of World's Congress Departments, Divisions and Chairmen of Committees as contained in the Preliminary Publications of the Auxiliary, to January, 1892.* N.p.: n.p., n.d.

19x14 (text). (10) p. At head of title: "The World's Congress Auxiliary of the World's Columbian Exposition of 1893." This is the first pamphlet in a bound vol (LC call AS 3 1893a) listed as *The world's congresses of the Columbian exposition. Preliminary publications* (see #2233). That vol contains many dept circulars and is an excellent source for learning the organization of the Auxiliary.
---- 2 vol containing 32 pamphlets.
---- 26 p.
*   ⊚ . (LC,ICRL,UoC,NL,RPB,WM)

2228. World's Congress Auxiliary. ... *The Object of This* [World's Congress Auxiliary] *Organization.* N.p.: n.p., n.d.

17½x15. 2 *l* folded glossy manila paper. Dated October 30, 1890. Caption title. At head of title: "The World's Congress Auxiliary of the World's Columbian Exposition." Early definition of the World's Congress Auxiliary by Bonney and Lyman Gage.   ⊚ . (CHx)

2229. World's Congress Auxiliary. *Original announcement.* [Chicago?: 1890?]

20x14. (4) p. of glossy text. Caption title. On last p., nice litho of Memorial Art Palace on Michigan Ave. [now The Art Institute]. Bonney's list of themes which the Congresses were expected to consider. Dated Oct. 30, 1890.   ⊚ . (NL,WM)

2230. World's Congress Auxiliary. [*Programs, addresses, etc.,*] 3 vols. Chicago, 1893.   (UoC)

2231. World's Congress Auxiliary. *Proposal of a Congress of World's Congresses, in Connection with the World's Columbian Exposition of 1892.* N.p.: n.p., n.d.

20½x17. (1065) p. (hand counted but variously paged and unpaged), 7 cm thick. A compilation of the early papers from the Auxiliary, C. Bonney, chairman. (LC one-of-a-kind: AS3 1893b) .
*   (LC)

2232. World's Congress Auxiliary. *Reasons why the government of the United States should print and distribute the proceedings of the World's congresses, held in connection with the World's Columbian exposition.* N.p.: n.p., n.d.

21x15. (3) p. Single folded sheet of paper without cover or binding. At head of title: "Not things, but men. The World's Congress Auxiliary of the World's Columbian exposition of 1893. President, Charles C. Bonney. ..." ☻ . (nwu)

2233. World's Congress Auxiliary. *The world's congresses of the Columbian exposition. Preliminary publications...* N.p.: n.p., n.d.

188 p. Contains many dept circulars. (LC call: AS3 1893a). (LC)

2234. World's Congress Auxiliary. Young, Clarence E. *[List of congresses to convene in the permanent memorial art palace, foot of Adams street, during the week commencing Monday, August 14, 1893.]* Chicago: n.p., 1893.

20½x15. (4) p. including cover. Title from top p. (2). ☻ (NL)

2235. World's Congress Auxiliary. Young, Clarence E. *The World's Congress Auxiliary of the World's Columbian exposition of 1893.* [Chicago]: n.p., n.d.

20x15. 3 p. No wraps. Caption title. Young was secretary along with Benj. Butterworth. General information for those who anticipated attending Congresses. ☻ (NL)

2236. World's Congress of Architects. American Institute of Architects. Stone, Alfred, ed. *Proceedings of the twenty-seventh annual convention : American institute of architects : Held at Chicago, July 31 and August 1, 1893.* Chicago: Inland Architect Press for The Board of Directors, A.I.A., 1893.

23½x18½ (text). 399 p., 4 *l.* Charcoal wraps, gold print, marbled edges. The A.I.A. annual meeting was held in Chicago as part of the World's Congress. ☻ . (LC,NYPL)

2237. World's Congress of Architects. Guastavino, Rafael. *Lecture written for the Congress of Architects, in connection with the Columbian exposition, on Cohesive Construction, its past, its present; its future?* Chicago: 1893.

ca. 25x16½. 16 p. C.t. Micropublished in "American Architectural Books," based on the Henry-Russell Hitchcock bibliography by the same title. New Haven, CT: RPI, 1972. ☻ . (AIC,NYSt)

2238. World's Congress of Bankers and Financiers. *World's Congress of Bankers and Financiers : comprising addresses upon selected financial subjects, and also a series of papers on banking in the several states and territories, prepared by delegates specially appointed by the governors. Presented at its meeting in Chicago, June 19 to 24, 1893, ...* Chicago: Rand, McNally & Co., publishers, 1893.

24x17. 2 *l,* (9)-615 p. Red-brown cloth hc, beveled boards, gilt print spine.
---- n.d. but [°1893]: 24x16. half morocco, gilt edges.
☻ . (CHx,LC,NYPL,RML,SLP,UMi,UoC)

2239. World's Congress of Disciples of Christ. *Addresses delivered at the World's congress and general missionary conventions of the Church of Christ held at Chicago, in September, 1893.* Chicago: S. J. Clarke, 1893.

8°. 248 p., frontis, plates, ports. On cover: "Twelve masterly addresses." (NYPL,OC)

2240. World's Congress of Eclectic Physicians and Surgeons. *Programme of the World's congress of Eclectic Physicians and Surgeons, May 29 to June 3, inclusive, 1893. ...* N.p.: n.p., n.d.

20½x15. 6 *l.* C.t. ☺.(CHx)

2241. World's Congress of Eclectic Physicians and Surgeons. *Report ... May 29 to June 3, 1893; together with the journal of the several divisions, the scientific and professional papers.* Orange, N.J.: Chronicle Pub. Co., 1894.

8°. In: *National Eclectic Medical Association Trans.*; vol 21 (Columbian memorial vol). (NYPL)

2242. World's Congress of Homoeopathic Physicians. Dudley, Pemberton, ed. *Transactions of the World's Congress of homoeopathic physicians and surgeons ... Chicago, Ill., May 29 to June 3, 1893.* Philadelphia: Sherman & Co., printers for the American Institute of Homoeopathy, 1894.

23½x16. xv, (1) + 17-1109 p., diagrams. Black cloth hc, gilt spine print. ☺.(LC,UMi,UoC)

2243. World's Congress of Instructors of the Deaf. *Proceedings of the thirteenth convention of American Instructors of the deaf and dumb.* (UC,NYPL)

2244. World's Congress of Medico-Climatology. McKay, A[ugustus] F., ed. *American Climates and Resorts : a reprint from July, 1893 to July, 1895 : comprising proceedings of the World's Congress of Medico-Climatology held in Chicago, May 29 to June 3, 1893. ...* N.p.: n.p., [°1895].

30½x23. 4 *l*, 208 p., 4 *l*, illus. ☺.(LC)

2245. World's Congress of Missions. Wherry, E. M., comp. *Missions at home and abroad.* New York: American Tract Soc., [°1895].

19½x__. 486 p. (NYPL)

2246. World's Congress of Religions. Columbian Catholic Congress. *The Columbian Catholic Congress of the United States : to be convened at Chicago in the "hall of Columbus" : memorial art palace ... September 4, 1893 : preliminary program : order of proceedings : papers, etc. ...* [Chicago: Cameron, Amberg & co. printers], n.d.

23x15. (4) p. not including wraps. Wraps same stock as text pages, black print. C.t. (NL)

2247. World's Congress of Religions. Columbian Catholic Congress. *The Columbian Catholic Congress of the United States : to be convened in the memorial art palace ... : commencing : Monday, September 4, 1893 : daily programme : order of proceedings : papers, etc. ...* [Chicago: Cameron, Amberg & co., printers], n.d.

23x15. 11 p. including front cover. Wraps same stock as text papers, black print. C.t.   ☺ (NL)

2248. World's Congress of Religions. Columbian Catholic Congress. Douglas, Ro[bert] M. *Trade combinations and strikes. An Address by Ro. M. Douglas, before the Columbian Catholic Congress of the World's Columbian Exposition, Delivered at Chicago, Ill., September 6th, 1893.* ____: ____, 1893.

22½x13½. 15 p. Brown wraps. Caption title. Discussion of labor and management.   ☺ . (S)

2249. World's Congress of Religions. Columbian Catholic Congress. *Progress of the Catholic Church in America and the great Columbian Catholic Congress of 1893 : a magnificent work of two volumes in one book ...* 5th ed. Chicago: J. S. Hyland & Co., [°1897].

25½x18½. 2 vol in 1. Vol I: 471 p. + vol II: 202 p. Black cloth hc with gold print, quarter leather, marbled edges.   ☺ . (UND)

2250. World's Congress of Religions. Columbian Catholic Congress. *Souvenir and official programme, of the Catholic Congress, held at the World's Columbian Exposition, Chicago, Ill. : September 4, 5, 6, 7, 8 and 9, 1893.* [New York: Isaac H. Blanchard, 1893].

24x16½. 71 p., (1) p. ad plus ads on insides of both wraps. Ports, illus. White slick wraps with dark royal blue print and border design. C.t.= t.p. except for Sept. dates.   ☺ (NL)

2251. World's Congress of Religions. Columbian Catholic Congress. *The World's Columbian Catholic Congresses and educational exhibit : containing three volumes in one : embracing Official Proceedings ... Catholic Education Day ... An Epitome of Catholic ...* Chicago: J. S. Hyland & Co., [1893 °1892].

25x19. 202, 467, (1), 42, (5) p., illus, ports. Maroon cloth hc, gold lettering, silver and black design, gilt edges. Frontis of O'Connell, Satolli and Maurelian. Contents: The World's Columbian Catholic congresses (vol 2); Epitome of church progress in the U.S. (vol 3); Catholic Education Day and educational exhibit.
---- Chicago: J. S. Hyland & Co., °1893. 2 vol in 1. The mix of separately paginated "volume" and "part" is confusing. 25x18½. Frontis is port of Leo III, same maroon cover. Vol II: World's Columbian Catholic Congress: 1 *l*, 9-202 p. Part II: Catholic Education Day: 48 p., 1 *l*. Part II is referred to as "volume" in the index at back of book.
     ☺ . (csuf,CPL,CHx,RPB)

2252. World's Congress of Religions. Columbian Catholic Congress. *The World's Columbian Catholic congresses and educational exhibit. To which is added an epitome of Catholic Church progress in the United States.* Chicago: J. S. Hyland, [1893, °1892].

25x__. 3 vol in 1.   (RPB)

2253. World's Congress of Religions. Columbian Catholic Congress. *The World's Columbian Catholic Congresses : with an epitome of church progress : containing three volumes in one ...* Chicago: J. S. Hyland & Co., [°1893 by J. S. Hyland & Co.].

25x19. 3 vol in 1. 202, 467, 47 p. Dark maroon with gilt lettering on cover and spine. Frontis of O'Connell, Satolli, and Maurelian. The whole consists of 3 units: a) Official Proceedings of the

Chicago Catholic Congresses; b) Epitome of Catholic church progress in the United States; c) Catholic Education Day. ⊜ . (TnSt)

2254. World's Congress of Religions. *The Columbian Congress of the Universalist Church : papers and addresses at the congress held as a section of the World's Congress Auxiliary of the Columbian Exposition 1893.* Boston and Chicago: Universalist publishing house, 1894, [ᶜ1893 by Universalist Publishing House].

20½x14½. xiii, 361 p. Dark green cloth hc, gold lettering. Frontis of Art Institute with tissue guard. John W. Hanson spoke. Also see Hanson #2256.
P→   ⊜ (GLD,CHx,BM,UoC,RPB,OC) $15 - 30

2255. World's Congress of Religions. Hanson, J[ohn] W[esley], ed. *The Religions of the World : The Doctrines and Creeds of Mankind stated in Official Documents by Eminent Representative Expounders.* N.p.: n.p., [ᶜ1896].

24x18. 720 p. including frontis, illus, ports. T.p. in red and black. ⊜ . (LC)

2256. World's Congress of Religions. Hanson, J[ohn] W[esley], ed. *The World's Congress of religions; the addresses and papers delivered before the Parliament, and an abstract of the congresses held in the Art Institute, Chicago, Illinois, U.S.A., August 25 to October 15, 1893, Under the Auspices of The World's Columbian Exposition. ... with marginal notes.*
[Chicago: W. B. Conkey Co., 1893]; Chicago: W. B. Conkey Co., 1894 [ᶜ1893]; Chicago: The Monarch Book Co., 1894; Chicago: Webb, 1894; Chicago and Philadelphia: International, 1894 [ᶜ1893]; New York and Providence: Langan & Bro., 1894; Philadelphia: W. W. Houston & Co., 1894 [ᶜ1893 by W. B. Conkey Co.]; Springfield, MA: Willey, 1894;   Syracuse, NY: Goodrich Pub. Co., 1894; Woodbridge, CT: RPI [International], 1989.

24x18½. 1196 p. includes frontis, illus, plates, ports. Frontis of the newly constructed Art Institute on Michigan Avenue. An eclectic assembly of papers delivered at the Parliament of Religions and list of World Congresses on Religion.
---- Houston: Olive green cloth hc, gilt and black embossed lettering and design, decorated end papers.
---- International: Full leather with elaborate floral blind-stamp and gilt print, gilt edges.
P→   ⊜ . (GLD,CHx,LC,SI,NYPL,F,S,E,CoU,NL,BPL) $25 - 45

2257. World's Congress of Religions. McClure, J[ames] B., ed. *World's Fair Sermons by Eminent Divines at Home and Abroad.* Chicago: Rhodes and McClure, 1893 ᶜ1893.

19½x13½. (4)-(8), 9-307 p., 2 *l* ads. Black cloth hc, speckled edges. "Vol. I" on t.p.   (CHx)

2258. World's Congress of Religions. Mercer, Lewis Pyle. *Emanuel Swedenborg and The New Christian Church.* ... World's Congress Series. Chicago: Western New-church Union, 1893.

13½x8½. 109 pulp p. White wraps with red print and spine. P→   ☻ (GLD) $8 - 16

☞ Mercer (1847-1906) was committee chairman for the New Jerusalem Church Congress and a prolific writer on religious subjects, especially the teachings of Swedenborg.

2259. World's Congress of Religions. Mercer, Lewis Pyle, ed. *The New Jerusalem in the World's Religious Congresses of 1893.* Chicago: Western New-church Union, 1894.

21x__. xii, 454 p., frontis. Discussion of the World's Parliament of Religions and New Jerusalem Congress at the WCE. (UC)

2260. World's Congress of Religions. Mercer, L[ewis] P[yle]. *Review of the World's Religious Congresses of The World's Congress Auxiliary of the World's Columbian Exposition. Chicago, 1893.* Chicago and New York: Rand, McNally & Co., 1893 [°1893].

19½x14. 334 p., 1 *l*, illus. Yellow glossy wraps, black print and design. Frontis is port of Rev. Mercer. Describes the Congresses and the Parliament "religious symposium." Many quotes from the speakers.
---- 20½x14½. Half calf, gilt edges.
---- Same: *The World's religions in a nutshell.* (New Title). Globe Library No. 295. 19x13½. Wraps.
      ☻ . (LC,RML,UMi,OC)

2261. World's Congress of Religions. *Programme of the Unitarian Church Congress.* N.p.: n.p., n.d.

21½x15. 4 *l*, program listing meetings from Sept. 16-23, 1893. C.t. Many addresses including one by Rev. E[dward] E[verett] Hale, Unitarian pastor and prolific author (*The Man Without a Country*, etc.). [Hale was instrumental in sending emigrants to KS Territory to make it a "Free State" when it voted for statehood before the Civil War.]
      ☻ (GLD) $10 - 18

2262. World's Congress of Religions. Savage, Minot J[udson], introduction. *The World's congress of religions.* Boston: Arena publishing co., 1893.

20x14. vii, 1 *l*, 428 p., 6 *l* ads. Green cloth hc, silver and gold print, small emblem lower right corner. Briefly describes a variety of religions at the WCE. 3 p. introduction by Savage. C.t.= t.p.
      ☻ . (CHx,LC,NYPL,OC)

2263. World's Congress of Religions. Stevans, C[harles] M[cClellan], ed. *The World's Congress of Religions : being a complete and concise history of the most inspiring convocation of civilization, wherein was given full expression to the irrefutable evidence establishing the independence of mind and the supremacy of human conscience.* Chicago: Laird & Lee, publishers, 1894 [°1894].

19½x13½. 4 *l*, 9-363 p., frontis shows the Archbishop of Zante. Heavy stock gray slick wraps, red and black print, black design. On outside of back cover is an ad for Laird & Lee's *Glimpses of the World's Fair* (192 photo reproductions). ☻ . (LC,BM,OC)

2264. World's Congress of Religions. Zehender, Wilhelm von. *Die welt-religionen auf dem Columbia-Congress von Chicago im September 1893. Mit einigen Zusätzen und Erläuterungen.* München: Druck der Buchdruckerei der "Allgem. Zeitung," 1897; Gotha: Friedrich Andreas Perthes, 1900.

"Allgem. Zeitung": 21x14. viii, 252.
---- Perthes: (Zweite neubearbeitete auflage): 21x14. viii, 261, (1) p. Gray wraps, black print. C.t.= t.p.
     ☻ . (LC,NYPL)

2265. World's Congress of Representative Women. ... *Department Congress of the National Alliance of Unitarian and Other Liberal Christian Women...* N.p.: n.p., n.d.

20½x15. (4) p. folded program. At head of title: "World's Congress of Representative Women ..." C.t. ☻ GLD $10 - 16

2266. World's Congress of Representative Women. ... *Department Congress of the National Columbian Household Economic Association.* ... N.p.: n.p., n.d

20½x15. (4) p. folded program. At head of title: "World's Congress of Representative Women." ☻ (GLD) $10 - 16

2267. World's Congress of Representative Women. ... *Department Congress of the Young Ladies National Mutual Improvement Association ... Friday, May 19, 1893.* N.p.: n.p., n.d.

21½x14. (4) p. folded program for one of the sessions. At head of title: "World's Congress of Representative Women." C.t. ☻ (GLD) $10 - 16

2268. World's Congress of Representative Women. Sewall, May Wright, ed. *World's Congress of Representative Women : A historical résumé for popular circulation of the World's congress of representative women, convened in Chicago on May 15, and adjourned on May 22, 1893, under the auspices of the woman's branch of the World's congress auxiliary.* 2 vols. Chicago and New York: Rand, McNally Co., 1894 [°1894].

23½x16½. 952 p. (2 vol paged continuously), plates. Dark blue hc, gilt design, gilt print on spine. Frontis of the New Art Institute. Sewall was chairman of Committee on Organization.
---- 2 vol in 1. 22½x15. 1 *l*, xxiv, 1 *l*, 952 p. paged continuously. Speckled edges.
     ☻ . (csuf,CPL,CHx,LC,NYPL,RML,BM,UoC)

2269. World's Congress of Representative Women. *World's Congress of Representative Women.* [Chicago: 1893].

18x__. 30 p. CHx call: F38MZ 1893 N1W6.   (CHx)

2270. World's Congress of Stenographers. "Official Report of the Proceedings of the World's Congress of Stenographers." In *The National Stenographer.* 4 (1893): 239+.

24½x17. Gray wraps, black print. See #1366 for periodical listing. ☺.(NYPL)

2271. World's Congress of the Deaf. *Proceedings of the World's Congress of the Deaf and the Report of the Fourth Convention of the National Association of the Deaf...* ____ : ____, [1895?].

22½x__. vii, (9)-282 p. (BM,UoC)

2272. World's Congress on Jurisprudence and Law Reform. Field, David Dudley. *American Progress in Jurisprudence : a paper prepared by request for the world's congress on jurisprudence and law reform, in connection with the Columbian Exposition in Chicago.* New York: Martin B. Brown, printer, 1893.

23x14½. 16 p. Light gray smooth wraps, black print. ☺.(CPL)

2273. World's Congress on Ornithology. *Papers Presented to the World's Congress on Ornithology ...* Chicago: Charles H. Sergal Co., 1896.

25x16½. 208 p. Quarter leather hc, decorated end papers. Edited by Mrs. E. Irene Rood, chairman of the Woman's Committee of the Congress under the direction of Dr. Elliott Coues, President of the Congress. Congress held Oct. 18-21, 1893. The 26 papers read before the Congress are included. Title continues: "Birds must and shall be protected." (KU,NYPL)

2274. World's Fisheries Congress. Kunz, George Frederick. *... On pearls, and the utilization and application of the shells in which they are found in the ornamental arts, as shown at the World's Columbian exposition.* Washington: GPO, 1894.

29½x__. 1 *l*, p. 439-57, plates 18-41 (include color frontis). At head of title: "The World's fisheries congress, Chicago, 1893." "Article 46.-- Extracted from the Bulletin of the U.S. Fish commission for 1893." (UC)

2275. World's Fisheries Congress. [*Report and papers of the World's Fisheries Congress, held at Chicago, October 16-19, 1893.* Washington: G.P.O., 1894].

1 *l*, iii-vii, 462 p., 41 plates. Bulletin of the U.S. Fish Commission, vol XIII, 1893. Papers also published separately as U.S. Commission of Fish and Fisheries. Doc. 237-278. (UC)

2276. World's Horticultural Congress. *Selection in seed growing, comprising papers read before the seedsmen's session of the World's auxiliary horticultural congress, Chicago, August 16, 1893. With discussion on same by William Meggat, ... and others. The seedsman's trial grounds, by W. Atlee Burpee, to which are appended several newspaper articles ...* Philadelphia: W. Atlee Burpee & co., 1894 [°1893 by W. Atlee Burpee & Co.].

19x13. 98 p., 7 *l*, illus. Yellow wraps, black (or green) print and design showing Horticultural Hall from the Wooded Island. The 7 *l* are ads for Burpee books on gardening.

---- 1896 variant entitled *Selection in seed growing; comprising papers read before the Seedsmen's Session of the World's Auxiliary Congress, Chicago, Aug. 16, 1893.*

P↑   ☉ . (GLD,LC) $15 - 32

☞ Burpee lived on a large farm in Bucks County, PA, and experimented with all the seed types his company sold.

2277. World's Library Congress. American Library Association. Dewey, Melvil, ed. ... *Papers Prepared for the World's Library Congress Held at the Columbian Exposition.* Washington: GPO, 1896.

23x14½. 329 p. Wraps.

---- In U.S. Bureau of Education. "Reprint of chapter IX of pt. II of the report of the commissioners of education for 1892-93." Whole number 224. Same title and pub info. 2 *l*, p. 691-1014.

☉ . (CHx,NYSt,E,TD)

2278. World's Parliament of Religions. Barrows, John Henry. ... *Christianity, the world-religion* ... Madras: Christian literature society for India, 1897.

1st ed., 5000 copies. xvii, 176 p. World's parliament of religions p. (140)-59. Errata slip at end. (OC)

---. ---. 7 vol. Barrows' lectures 1896-97. No. 7: The World's parliament of religions [Chicago, 1893].
(OC)

2279. World's Parliament of Religions. Barrows, John Henry. ... *Christianity the world-religion : lectures delivered in India and Japan.* Chicago: A. C. McClurg and co., 1897.

20x__. 412 p. Barrows' lectures, 1896-97. "The World's parliament of religions" [Chicago, 1893]: p. 293-328. (OC)

2280. World's Parliament of Religions. Barrows, John Henry. *Echoes of the Parliament of Religions.* N.p.: n.p., n.d.

(11) p. No t.p. In OC Parliamentary pamphlets, vol 5. [Barrows was Chairman of the general committee on religious congresses in the Dept of Religion, World's Congress Auxiliary.] (OC)

2281. World's Parliament of Religions. Barrows, John Henry, ed. *The World's parliament of religions : An illustrated and popular story of the World's first parliament of religions, held in Chicago in connection with the Columbian exposition of 1893.* 2 vols. Chicago: Parliament Publishing Co., 1893 [°1893]; London: "Review of Reviews" Office, 1893; Toronto: n.p., [1893]; Woodbridge, CT: RPI [Parliament], 1989.

Parliament: 23x16½. Vol I: xxiv (include frontis photo from a session of Parliament), 800 p. Vol II: 2 *l* (include frontis photo of Higinbotham), 805-1600 p. Navy blue (or black) cloth beveled hc, gilt and silver print, charcoal dyed top edge.

---- Parliament. Listed as brown calf, gilt and blind stamped.

---- Review of Reviews: Khaki cloth hc, gilt print.

☉ (GLD,CHx,SI,NYPL,F,mcg,BM,UDe,USD,UTn,SLP,CoU,NYSt,HL,BPL,OC) $35 - 65

2282. World's Parliament of Religions. Barrows, John Henry. ... *First report ... The World's First Parliament of Religions.* N.p.: n.p., [1892].

20½x14. 10 *l.* Caption title. At head of title: "The World's Congress Auxiliary of the World's Columbian Exposition. Department of Religion." (NYPL)

2283. World's Parliament of Religions. Barrows, John Henry. *Parliament of Religions and the propaganda of peace.* N.p.: n.p., n.d.

20 p., mss. No t.p. In OC Parliamentary pamphlets, vol 6. (OC)

2284. World's Parliament of Religions. Barrows, John Henry. *The Parliament of Religions at the World's Fair.* New York, London and Toronto: Funk & Wagnalls, Co., [1892].

C.t. Black print. Pages 451-456 are reprinted here from *The Missionary Review of the World* (June 1892). With this is bound Barrows' "Results of the Parliament of Religions" (New York: 1894). In OC Parliamentary pamphlets vol 6. (NYPL,OC)

2285. World's Parliament of Religions. Barrows, John Henry. *The Religious possibilities of the World's Fair. Address.* N.p.: n.p., [1892].

21½x14. 8 p. Caption title. Address given at the 11th International Convention of the Young People's Society of Christian Endeavor, July 10, 1892, at Madison Square Garden. In OC Parliamentary pamphlets, vol 5. [Barrows (1847-1902) was the President of Oberlin College. Late in life (1901) he ruled out the use of tobacco there.] (NYPL,OC)

2286. World's Parliament of Religions. Barrows, John Henry. *Results of the Parliament of Religions.* New York: 1894.

24x__. 14 p. C.t. Reprinted from the September, 1894, issue of the *Forum.* Bound with Barrows' *The Parliament of Religions at the World's Fair* (New York: 1892). (OC)

2287. World's Parliament of Religions. Barrows, John Henry. *The World's first Parliament of Religions; its Christian spirit, historic greatness and manifold results.* Ed. George S. Goodspeed. Chicago: Hill & Shuman, [°1895].

62 p., port. (OC)

2288. World's Parliament of Religions. Barrows, John Henry. *World's first parliament of religions.* Rpt. New York: Funk, n.d.

(9) p. Rpt. from "the Homiletic Review" May, 1893. In OC Parliamentary pamphlets, vol 5. (OC)

2289. World's Parliament of Religions. Boardman, George Dana. *The Parliament of Religions : an address before the Philadelphia Conference of Baptist Ministers : October 23, 1893.* 2nd ed. Philadelphia: The National Baptist Print, 1893 °1893.

23x15. 16 p. Pale blue wraps. On t.p.: "Copyrighted December, 1893." UoC copy autographed by Boardman.   ☺ . (HL,UoC)

2290. World's Parliament of Religions. *A chorus of faith as heard in the parliament of religions : held in Chicago, Sept. 10-27, 1893.* Introduction by Jenkin Lloyd Jones.   Chicago: The Unity Publishing Co., 1893 [°1893].

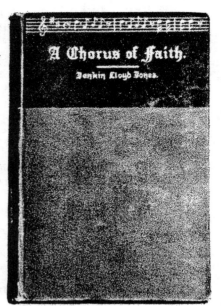

20x13½. 333 p. Sepia and maroon cloth hc, gilt print.
P→   ☺ . (LC,UoC)

2291. World's Parliament of Religions. *The Gospel in pagan religions : some thoughts suggested by the World's Parliament of Religions to an orthodox Christian.* Boston: Arena Pub. Co., 1894.

20x__. xi, 150 p.   (OC)

2292. World's Parliament of Religions. Higginson, Thomas Wentworth. *... The Sympathy of Religions.* Chicago: Unity Mission office, n.d. [prior to Sept. 1893].

19x13½. 1 *l*, (5)-38 p. Greenish-tan pulp wraps, red and black print. At head of title: "Freedom, Fellowship and Character in Religion. Parliament of Religions Edition : World's Fair, Chicago." C.t. Essay originally written in 1855-56, subsequently printed as a tract in the "Unity Mission" series. Special ed. for the World's Parliament of Religions "to be held."   ☺ . (NL)

2293. World's Parliament of Religions. Houghton, Walter R., ed. *Neely's history of The Parliament of Religions and religious congresses at the World's Columbian Exposition ...* [?1st ed]. Chicago: n.p., 1893 [°1893 by Frank Tennyson Neely].

17x11½. 2 vol in 1. Organization for the Congress began in 1890; it was carried out by the committees until the WCE opened in May, 1893.
---- 2nd ed.: Chicago: F. T. Neely, °1893.
---- 3rd ed.: Chicago: F. T. Neely, °1893. 2 vol in 1. Dark blue hc, gold print.
---- 4th ed.: Chicago and New York: F. Tennyson Neely, Publisher, 1893. 22½x16½. 1001 p. 2 vol in l. Black hc with silver print.
---- 4th ed.: Issued in 5 parts, bound in 2 vol.
---- Also listed: 4th ed.: Chicago: F. T. Neely, 1894.
---- Also listed: 5th ed.
        ☺ . (CHx,NYPL,UNLV,S,CoU,UMi,NYSt,UoC,BPL,OC)

2294. World's Parliament of Religions. Jewish Denominational Congress. *Judaism at the World's Parliament of Religions : Comprising the papers on Judaism read at the parliament, at the Jewish denominational congress, and at the Jewish presentation.* Cincinnati: Robert Clarke & Co. for the Union of American Hebrew Congregations, 1894 [°1894].

24x16½. xxii, 1 *l*, 418 p. Green pebble cloth hc, red leather spine label, gold print.   ☺ . (LC,BM,RPB,OC)

2295. World's Parliament of Religions. Jewish Women's Congress. *Papers of the Jewish women's congress. Held at Chicago, September 4, 5, 6 and 7, 1893.* Philadelphia: The Jewish publications society of America, 1894 [°1894].

23½x15½. 268, (2) p. "Contents" + (8) p. book ads. Green cloth hc, gilt print and design. ☉ . (csuf,CHx)

2296. World's Parliament of Religions. Kuroda, S. *Outlines of the Mahâyâna as taught by Buddha.* Tokyo: Printed by "Shueisha," (1893).

19x12½. 2 *l*, vii, 27, (l) p. Decorative green glossy wraps, string tied. "[F]or circulation at the World's Parliament of Religions." ☉ . (CPL)

2297. World's Parliament of Religions. Lorimer, George C[laude]. *The Baptists in history : with an introduction on the parliament of religions.* Boston: Silver, Burdett & Co., [°1893].

19x12 (text). 117 p. According to t.p., Lorimer was "Minister at the Temple." ☉ . (LC,OC)

2298. World's Parliament of Religions. Mansfield, E[lvira] S., ed. *Adventual essays delivered at the congress of the Parliament of religions, a branch of the World's congress auxiliary of the great Columbian exposition, Chicago, Ill., Sept. 14, 1893.* Boston: Advent Christian publication society, 1893.

19x__. iv, 1 *l*, (7)-151 p., frontis, ports. (NYPL,OC)

2299. World's Parliament of Religions. Moxom, Philip S. *The Argument for Immortality : a paper read before the Parliament of Religions, Chicago, September 13, 1893.* N.p.: Houghton Mifflin Co., [°1894 by John Henry Barrows].

23x14½. 15 p. Pale green-tan wraps, black print. C.t.= t.p. ☉ .(NYPL)

2300. World's Parliament of Religions. Religious Congress for Friends. *Friend's presentation of their faith, works and hopes in the World's parliament of religions, and proceedings in their denominational congress, ninth mo., 19th, 20th, 21st and 23d.* [Chicago: W. B. Conkey Co., printers and binders], 1893.

22½x14½. 147 p. Tan wraps, black print. C.t.: "Proceedings of the Religious Congress for Friends in the World's Parliament of Religions Chicago, 1893." (NYPL)

2301. World's Parliament of Religions. *The Religious event of the nineteenth century; a ... report of the addresses ... before the World's Parliament of Religions ... Chicago ... under the auspices of the World's Columbian Exposition of 1893 ... The whole comprising an elaborate exposition of the religious thought of the world.* Chicago: The Werner Co., [°1893].

Folio. 144 p. NYPL film reproduction. (NYPL)

2302. World's Parliament of Religions. Sutcliffe, Eben Malcolm. [Pseudo. for: Souvielle, Eliza Madelina]. *Sequel to the Parliament of Religions.* Chicago: American Authors' Protective Publishing Co., 1894 [°1894].

28x19. 5 *l*, (1), 14-187 p. Beautiful dark green cloth hc, beveled boards, gold and red print and design. Eben Malcolm Sutcliffe printed on cover and t.p. The Parliament was so popular it was extended past the scheduled closing. ☺ . (LC,OC)

2303. World's Parliament of Religions. United Brethren. *The church of the United Brethren in Christ : represented at the World's Columbian exposition : Chicago, Illinois 1893.* Dayton, OH: United Brethren publishing house, W. J. Shuey, Publisher, 1893; Woodbridge, CT: RPI, 1989.

15½x10. 47 p. Gray wraps with black print. Gives doctrine of the denomination and listing of church hierarchy.
---- 14½x9½. 47 p. Tan wraps with red print. Lists of church books inside front wrap and both sides of back wrap.
  ☺ . (GLD,SLF,WiHx) $12 - 25

2304. World's Railway Commerce Congress. *Addresses delivered before the World's railway commerce congress, held in Chicago, Ill., June 19-23, 1893. Under the auspices of the World's Columbian auxiliary of the World's Columbian exposition. Official report.* Chicago: The Railway Age and Northwestern Railroader, 1893.

22x14½. v, 265 p., 1 *l* of book ads, tables. Rebound. ☺ . (NYPL,UMi,NYSt,UoC)

2305. World's Religious Parliament Extension. *The World's parliament of religions and the religious parliament extension.* Chicago: The Open Court publishing co. [R. R. Donnelley & Sons Co. printers], 1896.

31½x23½. 5 *l*, 45 p., 1 *l*. Blue-gray paper covered boards, black print. Ornate t.p. in red and black. T.p. verso: "Five Hundred copies of the book have been printed from type on Dutch hand made paper for private distribution. No copies are for sale." C.t.= t.p. Contains: The World's parliament of religions by Bonney, and extension and progress of the movement by Dr. Paul Carus. Fine quality.
  ☺ . (CHx)

2306. World's Religious Parliament Extension. *The World's Parliament of Religions and the Religious Parliament Extension, a memorial published by the Religious Parliament Extension Committee.* Popular ed. Chicago: The Open Court Publishing Co., 1899.

23½x__. 1 *l*, 56 p. "Popular Edition, Enlarged by the Publication of the Main Responses Received in Acknowledgment of the Memorial." (UC)

2307. World's Suffrage Congress. *... Department Congress of the National-American Woman Suffrage Association ...* N.p.: n.p., n.d.

25½x18. Glossy *l* folded twice to make (6) p., ports of suffragettes. Congress held August 8-12, 1893 at the Memorial Art Palace (Art Institute). Program of speakers which included the important suffragettes and Clarence Darrow as well.
P→ ☺ (GLD)

                      $16 - 23

2308. World's Temperance Congress. Stearns, J[ohn] N[ewton], ed. *Temperance in all nations. History of the cause in all countries of the globe. Together with the papers, essays, addresses, and discussions of the World's Temperance Congress, held by the National Temperance Society, in Chicago, Ill., June, 1893.* 2 vol. New York: The National Temperance Society and Publication House, [°1893].

24x__.   (UC)

☞ Stearns' pseudonym was "Uncle Robert Merry." He wrote a number of songs, games, puzzle books for children under the pseudonym in his early days. He was a prolific temperance speaker and an early advocate of prohibition by Constitutional amendment.

2309. World's Temperance Congress. *The World's Temperance Congress. Under the auspices of the "World's Congress Auxiliary" of the World's Columbian Exposition. National Temperance Society. Memorial Art Institute, ... June 5, 6, and 7, 1893.* N.p.: n.p., n.d.

23x15. Caption title. Lists committee members for the Congress.   ☺ . (CHx)

As an aid to finding further publications in this category, consult:

1) Bonney, Charles C. "Bibliography of World's Congress Publications." *The Dial.* 20 (No. 229. 1896): 7-10. New York: Kraus Reprint Corp., 1968.

Chapter 14

RECENT BOOKS ABOUT THE WORLD'S COLUMBIAN EXPOSITION

World's Columbian Exposition items written primarily after 1901 are included here. Reviews, analyses, critiques in book and thesis form are included, as well as personal accounts of Fair visits, biographies, anniversary celebrations. Modern reprints of original publications are located with the original's citation.

2310. Addams, Jane. *Twenty Years at Hull-House with Autobiographical Notes.* New York: The Macmillan Co., 1923 [°1910].

19½x14. xvii, 462 p. Cinnamon cloth hc, gilt print spine. Addams was active at the Congresses. CHx copy autographed.   (CHx)

2311. Allen, Robert V. *Russia looks at America : the view to 1917.* Washington: Library of Congress : For sale by the Supt. of Docs., U.S. GPO, 1988.

24x__. vi, 322 p. "Forty commissars in Chicago [1893]," p. 183-228.   (CHx)

2312. American Secular Union and Freethought Federation. *Pan-American exposition. Some reasons why it should be open on Sundays. Mistakes made by directors of the World's Fair in 1893 a warning to officers of this Exposition.* [Chicago?: 1901?].

12°. 15 p. Caption title. NYPL film reproduction.   (NYPL)

2313. Andersen, Magnus. *70 års tilbakeblikk på mitt virke på sjø og i land.* Oslo: Magnus Andersens forlag, 1932.

23x16. 368 p., illus, ports. Red and black print and design dust jacket over brown cloth hc, black and gilt print and design. At p. 129-71: "Vikingeferden til Chicago utstillingen 1893" [The Viking expedition to Chicago for the 1893 exposition]. For Andersen's 1895 book on his WCE travels, see #622; for other Andersen entries, see #1024, #1542, and #2415. Title translates: 70 years in retrospect on my work on sea and land.   ☺ . (CHx)

2314. Anderson, Norman D., and Walter R. Brown. *Ferris wheels.* New York: Pantheon Books, [°1983].

20½x22. 53, (3) p., illus. Red paper covered hc with off-white spine, gilt print on spine, colorful dust jacket. The wheel at WCE p. 16-28. Traces the history and influence of the Ferris wheel since 1893. Young adult book.   ☺ (csuf,UNLV,GPL)

2315. Applebaum, Stanley. *The Chicago World's fair of 1893 : a photographic record.* ... New York: Dover, publications, inc.,[°1980 by Dover Publications' Inc.].

28x21½. Frontis of a corner of the Agriculture Bldg + 5 *l*, 116 p. Gray-brown or sepia wraps. B/w photographic record of WCE from concept to wrecking ball including bldg interiors and exteriors, sculpture, paintings, bird's-eye views of the grounds, Ferris wheel, etc. "Dover Architectural Series."
*   ☺ . (GLD,csuf,UNe,CHx,USF,F,TnSt,BCM,StLa,nwu,LM,E,BU,ncsu,UMi,NYSt,UoC,LSU,A,AIC,BM,WiHx)

2316. Badger, [Rodney] Reid. *The Great American Fair : The World's Columbian exposition & American culture.* Chicago: Nelson Hall, [°1979 by Reid Badger].

Hardbound: 26½x21. xvi, 266 p. Red-brown paper covered hc, copper lettering, dust jacket. Softbound: 20½x25½. xvi, 177 p. + 25 *l* of plates. Brown glossy wraps, black print and illus. Contemporary perspective of the WCE. Presents background, planning, organization, financing, construction, operations, and subsequent impact.
* ☺ . GLD,UND,UMKC,UMC,csuf,CHx,TnSt,BCM,OSU,nwu,UNR,USD,SCSt,SLP,NHSt,HL,TU,UMi,NYSt,UoC,NL,LSU,A,E,RPB,AIC,WiHx,TD)

2317. Badger, Rodney Reid. *The World's Columbian Exposition: patterns of change and control in the 1890s.* PhD diss. Syracuse U, 1975. Ann Arbor: UMI, 1976. 7618490.

UMI: 21½x16½. vi, 314 *l*, illus. PhD in Social Science. (csuf,CPL)

2318. Baker, Charles H[inckley]. *Life and character of William Taylor Baker : President of the World's Columbian exposition and of the Chicago board of trade, by his son.* New York: The Premier Press, 1908.

25x16½. 293 p., plates, frontis (port of Wm. T. Baker). Blue cloth hc, gilt print. 300 copies printed; csuf has presentation copy signed by the author. William Taylor Baker was WCE president in 1891 after Gage retired. ☺ . (csuf,UMi,AIC)

2319. Barnes, Joseph W. *Katharine B. Davis and the workingman's model home of 1893.* Rochester, NY: Rochester Public Library, 1981.

21x__. 20 p. Rochester history; vol 43, no. 1. (WiHx)

2320. Beachboard, J. H., ed. *United States Postal Card Catalog.* Heyworth, IL: United Postal Stationery Society, 1990.

23½x16. 371 p. Dark red vinyl over cardboard. WCE cards are featured on p. 283-96, 300-01.

2321. Beer, Thomas. *The mauve decade : American Life at the End of the Nineteenth Century.* Garden City, NY: Garden City publishing co., inc., [1926].

21x14. 268 p. Mauve paper covered boards, tan cloth spine. Description of the "Gay 90s" as style turned to Art Nouveau. (TD)

2322. Bigler, Brian. *The Norway Building of the Great Chicago World's Fair of 1893.* [pending mid-1992 publication]. See Norway, #624.

2323. Bloom, Sol. *The Autobiography of Sol Bloom.* New York: G. P. Putnam's Sons, [1948].

22x__. 345 p., port. Chapters 9-16. Bloom is credited with turning the Midway into a major attraction. For Bloom's guide see #1083. (CHx)

2324. Bolton, Charles E[dward]. *A model village of homes : and other papers.* Boston: L. C. Page & co., Publishers, 1901.

19½x12½. 308 p., frontis (port). Includes a visit to the WCE. ☻. (OC)

2325. *The Books of the fairs : a microfilm collection drawn from the holdings of the Smithsonian Institution libraries.* Woodbridge, CT and Reading, England: RPI, 1989.

28x21½. 5 units. ? Lists microfilm holdings on World's Fairs: 1834-1916. [A new edition is planned for 1992, the 500th anniversary of Columbus in the New World.] ☻. (UMKC)

2326. Braun, Judith Elise. "The North American Indian Exhibits at the 1876 & 1893 World Exposition: The Influence of Scientific Thought on Popular Attitudes." MA diss. George Washington U, 1975.

iv, 118 *l*, illus. (csuf)

2327. Broun, Elizabeth. *American Painting and Sculpture in the Fine Arts Building of the World's Columbian Exposition, Chicago, 1893.* PhD diss. U of Kansas, 1976. Ann Arbor: UMI, 1976. 772197.

28x22. xxiii, 303 *l*, ciii *l* of photos. Black cloth hc. PhD in Fine Arts.
---- UMI: 20½x15.
☻ (KU,csuf,CHx,AIC)

2328. Brown, Waldo R. *Altgeld of Illinois.* New York: B. W. Huebsch, Inc., 1924.

21x15. 342 p. Navy blue cloth hc, gold print. Altgeld was governor of Illinois during the Fair and participated in many official events. (CHx)

2329. Burg, David F. *Chicago's white city of 1893.* [Lexington]: U Press of Kentucky, [°1976 by the U Press of Kentucky].

23½x16. xv, (1), 381, (1) p. Silver cloth hc, gray embossed spine. Blue dust jacket, white print. Some b/w illus. Touches upon the industrial exhibits, arts, architecture, landscaping, lighting system, Ferris wheel, contributions by women, congresses, etc. Readable.
---- 23x15. Softbound. Same paging.
* ☻. GLD,UND,UMKC,UMC,UMSL,KU,KyU,CHx,nwu,UNLV,UNR,E,BU,SCSt,ncsu,OSU,SLP,TU,UMi,UoC,NL,LSU,RPB,AIC,OC,WiHx,TD)

2330. Burnham, Daniel H. *The Final Official Report of the Director of Works of the World's Columbian Exposition.* 2 parts. Rpt. Introduction by Joan E. Draper, preface by Thomas Hines. New York & London: Garland Publishing, 1989.

23x31. Illus. White and blue hc. On cover: "Part One" or "Part Two." Part One (Vols 1-3): xix, 3 *l*, 98 p.; 85 p.; 68 p. Part Two (Vols 4-8): xix, 1 *l*, 118 p.,1 *l*; 73 p., 1 *l*; 99 p., (1) p., Il-I38 index. For the original report, see #152. ☻. (CHx,USF,nwu,ncsu,TU,UMi,AIC,BM)

2331. *The Burnham index to architectural literature.* 10 vol. New York: Garland Publishing, 1989-

35x___. Preface by Jack Perry Brown; Ryerson and Burnham Libraries of The Art Institute of Chicago. Index includes WCE architecture publications. (AIC)

2332. [Butler, Rush C., Jr.] comp. and ed. *Chicago : the World's youngest great city.* N.p.: Halsey, Stuart & co. incorporated, [°1929 by American Publishers Corporation, Chicago].

30½x23. 5 *l*, 15-196 p. Chocolate and tan paper covered boards with deco bust illus. C.t.: "Chicago." Description and illus of WCE p. 155-60. Also, early plans for the 1933 Fair. ☉ (GLD)

2333. Chappell, Sally Anderson. *The Chicago World's Fair, 1893.* Filmstrip. De Paul U. Chappell, 1976. (LC)

2334. *Chicago and its two fairs, 1893-1933.* Chicago: Geographical publishing co., [°1933].

19x27½. 50 *l* are primarily 1893 and 1933 photos. Flexible burgundy (or red) stiff textured wraps, bird's-eye photo inside front cover spans two pages. Colorful Century of Progress card glued to front cover. ☉ (GLD,CHx,nwu,WiHx,TD)

2335. Columbian Catholic Congress. *The World's Columbian Congresses and Educational Exhibit.* Rpt. Vols I and III. 1893. New York: Arno Press, 1978 [°1893].

23½x16. 7 *l*, 9-107 p., 1 *l*, 42 p., 4 *l*, illus. Burgundy embossed vinyl covers, gilt print. Rpt. of vol I (*The World's Columbian Catholic Congresses*, and vol III (*Catholic Education Day and Educational Exhibit*) of the 1893 ed. (PU,UoC)

2336. Cooley, George S., and Arthur P. Traczyk. *Ho-o Den.* Chicago: Department of Planning, City and Community Development, City of Chicago, 1978.

28x44. 17 p. includes illus, maps, plans. Subject: Tea houses--U.S.--Illinois--Chicago. (AIC)

2337. Cordato, Mary F. *Representing the expansion of women's sphere: women's work and culture at the World's Fairs of 1876, 1893, and 1904.* PhD diss. New York U, 1989. Ann Arbor: UMI, 1990.

v, 519 p. (CPL)

2338. Crook, David H[eathcote]. "Louis Sullivan, The World's Columbian Exposition, and American Life." PhD diss. Harvard U, 1963; Cambridge, MA: Harvard U Microreproductions Dept., [1963?].

(6), 465 *l*, includes bibliography. Sullivan, an important architect at WCE, was also the promoter and "father" of the skyscraper for efficient, regional business consolidation. (CHx,AIC)

2339. Cummins, Cedric. *The university of South Dakota : 1862-1966.* Vermillion: Dakota Press, U of South Dakota, 1975.

21½x14. v, 334 p., 12 *l* of plates. Pages 53-57 describe the Oct. 15, 1893, burning of University Hall, the institution's only academic structure, and its subsequent replacement in part with an assortment of materials from the WCE SD Bldg and other exhibits. ☉ . (USD)

☞ Although the unused bldg shows disrepair, recent interior and exterior photographs received from Librarian K. Zimmerman, USD, show some parts of the SD Bldg used in the reconstruction of Old Main. The rounded balcony, a conspicuous feature of the interior of the SD Bldg, is still in place in Old Main. Original photographs of the SD Bldg are found in *South Dakota at the World's Fair* (see #2074). P↓,P↓

2340. Cunningham, Michael James. *The image of the artist in Chicago fiction following the World's Columbian Exposition.* PhD diss. Bowling Green State U, 1978. Ann Arbor: UMI, 1979. 7907985.

20½x16. (1), iv, 297 *l* includes bibliography. Microfilm of typescript. ⊚ (csuf,CPL,CHx)

2341. Darnall, Margaretta Jean. *From the Chicago fair to Walter Gropius : changing ideals in American architecture.* PhD diss. Cornell U, 1975; Ann Arbor: UMI, 1975?. 765922.

21x16. viii, 175 *l*, includes vita and bibliography, illus. Fine Arts thesis. ⊚ (csuf,CHx)

2342. Darney, Virginia Grant. *Women and World's Fairs : American International Expositions, 1876-1904.* PhD diss. Emory U, 1982. Ann Arbor: UMI, 1983.

(8), 252 *l*, includes bibliographic essay. ⊚ (CHx)

2343. Docherty, Linda Jones. *A Search for identity : American art criticism and the concept of the "Native School," 1876-1893.* Diss. U of N. Carolina - Chapel Hill, 1985. Ann Arbor: UMI, 1986. (CPL)

2344. Doolin, James P. *1893 Columbian Exposition Admissions and Concessions Tickets.* Dallas, TX: Doolco, Inc., [°1981 by Doolco, inc.].

28x21½. (4), 22, (1) p. catalogue of over 159 tickets. Glossy wraps, illus of the six admission tickets. C.t.= t.p. Last (1) p. is for "Collector's notes."
* ⊚ . (GLD,CHx,F,E,UoC,A,AIC,L)

☞ A collection of tickets and concession applications-- (CHx call: qF38M2 W1893 H1); a ticket collection--(CHx call: qF38M2 1893 Z, box 3).

2345. Dowling, Elizabeth Meredith. *Ornament and the Machine in American Architecture in the Late Nineteenth and Early Twentieth Centuries.* PhD diss. ____ U?, °1981. Ann Arbor: UMI, ____.

21x17. xii, 186 p.   (CPL)

2346. Downey, Dennis B[ernard]. *Rite of passage; the World's Columbian Exposition and American life.* 2 vol. PhD diss. Marquette U, 1981 °1982. Ann Arbor: UMI, 1982?.

28x__. (5, i, 420 *l*)
---- UMI: 22x16½. (3), i, 420 p.
(csuf,CPL)

2347. Druyvesteyn, Kenten. "The World's Parliament of Religions." PhD diss. U of Chicago, 1976.

ii, 294 *l*. [The U of Chicago, bordering the Midway Plaisance on the north, had its opening on October 1, 1892, just before the dedication of the Fair. D. Burnham helped design the first bldgs on campus and led the effort in establishing the architecture at the Fair.]   ☉ (csuf,OC)

2348. Duis, Perry [R]. *Chicago : Creating New Traditions.* Chicago: Chicago Historical Society, 1976.

28x21½. 144 p. Multicolor wraps. Chicago illus history includes the WCE.   (TD,HL)

2349. Eglit, Nathan N. *Columbiana : The Medallic History of Christopher Columbus and the Columbian Exposition of 1893.* [Chicago]: Published by the Author, [1965]; [Chicago]: Published by the Author, 1987.

[1965]: 19½x13½. 144 p. White stiff wraps, black print and design. CPL copy is signed "Nathan N. Eglit, 1965."
---- 1987: 160 p.
(CPL,CHx,E,L)

2350. *The Ellsworth family : In Two Volumes.* New York: National Americana Society, 1930.

35½x__. Vol 1 (James William Ellsworth): 99 p. Vol 2: (Lincoln Ellsworth). Color coat of arms frontis, plates, ports. Blue cloth hc in slip case. James William Ellsworth was a member of the Board of Directors and Chairman of the Committee on Liberal Arts of the WCE.   ☉ . (AIC)

2351. Emple, Jim. *The Maine State Building from Chicago to Poland Springs [Maine].* Provisional title for centennial volume.

2352. English, Maurice. *The Testament of Stone.* N.p.: Northwestern U Press, 1963.

23½x16. 4 *l*, (ix)-xxvii, 227 p. Black cloth hc. WCE at p. 79.   (CHx)

2353. Field, Cynthia. *The city planning of Daniel Hudson Burnham.* PhD diss. Columbia U, 1974. Ann Arbor: UMI, °1975.

ix, 544 *l*, includes bibliography.   ⊜ (CHx)

2354. Field, Marshall & Co. *Catalogue autumn exposition, 1923 Marshall Field & Company. Chicago celebration of the 30th anniversary World's Columbian exposition under auspices of the Chicago Historical Society.* N.p.: n.p., n.d.

20x13½. 31 p. Plain paper wraps with black print and design. C.t.   ⊜ (CHx,AIC)

2355. Findling, John E., and Kimberly D. Pelle, eds. *Historical Dictionary of World's Fairs and Expositions, 1851-1988.* New York Westport, CT London: Greenwood press, [°1980].

24x16. 3 *l*, (vii)-xix, 443 p. Red cloth hc, black front and spine plates with gilt lettering and border. Definition descriptions of each WF from the first to 1988. It lists sources for each of these fairs.
*   (SDHx,E,HL)

2356. French, Mrs. Daniel Chester. *Memories of a sculptor's wife.* Boston and New York: Houghton Mifflin co., 1928 [°1928 by Mary French].

22½x15½. Frontis of Daniel Chester French and his statue of Lincoln [on the Mall, Washington, D.C.], tissue guard, 3 *l*, (ix)-x, 1 *l*, 294 p. Many illus are not included in pagination. Navy blue cloth hc, gilt print. [French was the sculptor of the great statue of the "Republic" in the "Court of Honor," WCE.]   (csuf)

2357. Friebe, Wolfgang. *Buildings of the World Exhibitions.* Leipzig: ____, 1985.

28x25. 226 p. Cloth hc.

2358. Friz, Richard. *The Official Price Guide to World's Fair memorabilia.* New York: House of Collectibles, 1989.

20½x13½. 354 p., illus. Color glossy wraps. Contains short list of common WCE books.   (TD)

2359. Gilbert, James [Burkhart]. *Perfect Cities : Chicago's Utopias of 1893.* Chicago and London: U of Chicago Press, 1991.

24x16. xiv, 279 p., illus, maps. Bibliographical references at p. 229-64 and index. The experiments of the Fair: Pullman's labor, and Dwight Moody's evangelical crusades.   (csuf,F,CHx)

2360. Goldstein, Leslie S. "Art in Chicago and the World's Columbian Exposition of 1893." MA thesis. U of Iowa, 1970.

28x22. vi, 170 *l*, photos.   ⊜ (CHx,AIC)

2361. Greenhalgh, Paul. *Ephemeral Vistas: The Expositions Universallas, Great Expectations and World's Fairs, 1851-1939.* ____: St. Martin's Press, 1988.

24x16. 258 p. Cloth hc.   (ref)

2362. Harris, Neil, ed. *The land of contrasts: 1880-1901.* New York: G. Braziller, [1970].

> 24x__. xii, 365 p. includes illus, facsimiles. Series: The American Culture, 5. Contains: "Letters of an Altrurian Traveller" (see #2372). Errata slip inserted. (AIC)

2363. Harrison, Edith (Ogden) (Mrs. Carter H.). *"Strange to say---" : recollections of persons and events in New Orleans and Chicago.* Chicago: A. Kroch, 1949.

> 24x__. 188 p., illus, ports. p. 66-73. (CHx)

2364. Hartman, Donald K. *Fairground fiction : Detective Stories of the World's Columbian Exposition. ...* N.p.: Motif Press, 1992 [°1992 by Epoch Books, Inc.].

> 20½x13½. xiv, 450 p., (1) p. (ad), paged illus. Glossy antique blue wraps, black print and illus of Ferris wheel. Introduction, reprints of two detective novels, and excellent bibliography of WCE related fiction. ☉ (GLD)

2365. Hilton, Suzanne. *Here today and gone tomorrow : the story of world's fairs and expositions.* 1st ed. Philadelphia: Westminster Press, °1978.

> 24x__. 191 p., illus. Presents accounts of 8 large expositions held in U.S. including the WCE. The premise is that WFs stimulate technical progress. (CHx)

2366. Hines, Thomas S. *Burnham of Chicago : Architect & Planner.* Chicago and London: U of Chicago Press, °1974.

> 23x15. v-xxiii, 1 *l*, 3-445. Burnt orange wraps ("paperback"), illus of Burnham on cover. (CHx)

2367. Hobbs, Franklyn. *The World's Fair of 1893 Made Chicago.* Chicago: Chicago World's fair centennial celebration, 1933.

> 19x12½. 1 *l*, 3-8 p. Lime green wraps, darker green design, black print. Short sections on the Fair, building, bank clearing, gain in bank deposits, and poor crops. ☉ (CHx)

2368. Hoffman, Donald. *The Architecture of John Wellborn Root.* Baltimore and London: The Johns Hopkins U Press, °1973.

> 17½x24. 4 *l*, ix-xviii, 1 *l*, 263 p., 1 *l*. Silver hc, copper foil print. Root and the WCE p. 220. (CHx)

2369. Holt, Elizabeth G., ed. "The Expanding World of Art 1874-1902." In *Universal Expositions and State-sponsored Fine Arts Expositions,* vol 1. ____: Yale U Press, 19__.

> 26x18. 406 p. Cloth hc.

2370. Horowitz, Helen Lefkowitz. *Culture & The City : Cultural Philanthropy in Chicago from the 1880s to 1917.* [Lexington]: The U Press of Kentucky, [°1976].

22½x14½. xv, 288 p. Gray cloth hc, lime green foil spine title. WCE scattered p. 1-172. ⊚ (csuf)

2371. Howells, William Dean. *The Altrurian Romances.* A selected ed. of W. D. Howell. Vol. 20. Bloomington and London: Indiana U Press, 1968 [ᶜ1968].

24x16½. xxxiv, 1 *l*, 494 p. Blue cloth hc, gilt print, blue-gray dust jacket with black print. Intro. and notes by Clara Kirk and Rudolf Kirk include comments about the WF and Howell's "Altrurian Traveler." ⊚ (GLD)

2372. Howells, William Dean. *Letters of an Altrurian Traveller (1893-94).* Facsimile reproduction. Gainsville, FL: Scholars' Facsimiles & Reprints, 1961; Gainsville, FL: Scholars' Facsimiles & Reprints, 1979.

22x14½. 127 p. Teal blue hc, gold print on spine. From Nov. 1892-Sept. 1894, Howells wrote 23 Altrurian essays for *The Cosmopolitan*: the first 12 are contained in *A Traveller From Altruria*; the other 11 are reprinted here. Intro. by Clara M. Kirk and Rudolf Kirk. Howells describes (his) visit to the WCE p. 20-34.
---- Also listed: 23x__. xii, 127 p.
⊚ (UMKC,UMC,CHx,USF,NLC,OSU,BU,SLP,HL,TU,UMi,NYSt,UoC,LSU,nwu,RPB,OC)

2373. *Impressions by great journalists of The Most Unique and Original Concern in America.* Chicago: Chicago House Wrecking co., [ca. 1906].

13x8. 32 p. Wraps, litho of 40 acre Chicago House Wrecking Co. plant on back wrap. Article by William E[leroy] Curtis: "Laying the St. Louis fair in ruins!" Describes the demolition of the 1904 St. Louis fair. Four Harris brothers, owners of the wrecking co., purchased the Ferris Wheel for $9,000. They spent $175,000 to take it down in Chicago and set it up again in St. Louis. [Collector L. John Harris inherited this booklet from his grandfather who was an owner of the wrecking co.] ⊚ . (H)

2374. Jackson, George, comp. *History of all Centennials, Expositions and World Fairs ever held also The Fundamental Principles of Successful County and State Fairs.* [Lincoln, NE: Wekesser-Brinkman Co.,] 1937.

26½x18. 145 p., plates, ports, tables. Jackson was secretary Nebraska State Fair. WCE p. 73. (KU)

2375. Japan. [*Fukushima-ken kangyō rinji hōkoku*]. 3 vol. ____: ____, [1973].

22x__. 3 vol: 70, 14, 832 p. In Japanese; Romanized title. Subject: Temporary report of developing the financial business. One topic is the WCE. Series: Meiji zenki sangyō hattatsu shi shiryō : Kangyō hakuran shiryō ; 3-5. Translates: History of development of industry for the first period of Meiji. (LC)

2376. Johnson, Diane Chalmers. *American art nouveau.* New York: H. N. Abrams, 1979.

33x__. 311 p., illus (some color). Bibliography: p. 299-304. Index. (CHx)

2377. Jones, Lois Stodieck, comp. *The Ferris wheel.* [Reno, NV]: The Grace Dangberg Foundation, Inc., ᶜ1984.

26x18½. iv, 28, (1) p. Color illustrated glossy paper covered boards. Limited to 500 copies. Compiled for the Carson Valley Historical Society; part of the Dangberg Historical Series. Original Ferris Wheel material and photographs were collected by Eva K. Dangberg Greenfield, a niece of Ferris and daughter of H. F. Dangberg of Carson Valley.   ⊚ . (GLD,GDF,NVSt,GPL)

2378. Karlowicz, Titus Marion. *The architecture of the World's Columbian Exposition.* PhD diss. Northwestern U, 1965. Ann Arbor: UMI, 1966. 662721.

20½x15½. 355 *l* + plates, fold. maps. Includes lists of architects and structures designed, engineers and works, artists, and sculptors.   ⊚ (csuf,CPL,CHx,nwu,RPB,AIC)

2379. Kirkland, Caroline, ed. *Chicago yesterdays : a sheaf of reminiscences.* Chicago: Daughaday and co., 1919 [ᶜ1919 by Daughaday and co.].

24x17. 310 p. (text to p. 297, followed by index). Frontis: Wm Butler Ogden, Chicago's first mayor. T.p. in red and black. Gray cloth hc with black cloth spine, gilt print, gilt top edge. Chapter on WF by Lucy M. Calhoun at p. 283-97.   ⊚ . (CHx,HL)

2380. Kitagawa, Joseph M. *The 1893 World's Parliament of Religions and its Legacy : Eleventh John Nuveen Lecture : Sponsored by The Divinity School and the Baptist Theological Union.* N.p.: n.p., [1983].

27½x15½. 2 *l*, 15 p. Beige wraps, dark brown print. C.t. ⊚ . (UoC)

2381. Knutson, Robert. *The White City - The World's Columbian Exposition of 1893.* PhD diss. Columbia U, 1956. Ann Arbor: UMI, 1956. 17062.

i, (2), ii-iii, 289 *l*, includes bibliography. Microfilm of typescript. UMI: 20x15.   ⊚ . (csuf,CHx,UFl,WiHx)

2382. Kogan, Herman. *A continuing marvel : The Story of The Museum of Science and Industry.* Garden City, NY: Doubleday & co., inc., 1973.

21½x14½. 233 p. Blue dust jacket with black print over blue cloth hc. Fine Arts Bldg described. (TD)

2383. Lancaster, Clay. *The incredible World's parliament of religions at the Chicago Columbian exposition of 1893 : A Comparative and Critical Study.* Fontwell, Sussex: Centaur Press, 1987.

22½x14½. 264 p. includes illus, ports. No frontis. Burnt sienna cloth hc, gilt print on spine only. ⊚ . (nwu,AIC,BM)

2384. Larson, Everette E., ed. *Christopher Columbus Collection of The Library of Congress.* Bethesda, MD: U Publications of America, 199_.

Microfilm of the LC Columbus collection in two parts, with printed guides. Available late 1991 and early 1992, respectively. This is just one of <u>many</u> Columbus offerings which appeared in commemoration of the Quincentennial.   ⊚ . (LC)   Complete: $5,335

2385. Lauzon, A[ugust] A[drian]. *The United States Columbian issue : 1893.* Kalamazoo, MI: Chambers publishing co., [1942]; Rpt. Southfield, MI: Postilion Publications, [ca. 198-].

Chambers: 22½x16. 69 p., illus. Blue wraps, black print. "Chambers handbook series." Postage stamps issued to commemorate the WCE. They were the 1st U.S. postal commemoration stamps issued.
---- Postilion: 27x21½. Tan wraps with black print.
           ☺ . (csuf,LC,TD)   [1942]: $100

2386. Lawson, Robert. *The Great Wheel.* New York: Viking Press [and] Canada: MacMillan Co. of Canada Limited, 1957.

24x16. 188 p., illus by Lawson. Blue and yellow dust jacket over green cloth hc, black print, silhouette of Ferris wheel on front cover. Narrative of Mr. Ferris and his wheel.
---- Heavy duty blue cloth (school type) cover.
        (KU,UMC,USF,NvSt,UMi,LSU,GPL,TD)

2387. Lederer, Francis L. "The Genesis of the World's Columbian Exposition." MA diss. U of Chicago, 1967.

28x__. 82 *l.*
---- Xerox of rpt. 22x16. 82 p.
        (csuf,CHx,UoC)

2388. Lewis, Dudley Arnold. *Evaluations of American architecture by European critics, 1875-1900.* PhD diss. U of Wisconsin, 1962; Ann Arbor, MI: UMI, 1984?.

UMI: 21x__. xiv, 515 *l* including illus. Architecture includes WCE.   (AIC)

2389. Lewis, Julius. "Henry Ives Cobb and the Chicago School." MA diss. U of Chicago, 1954; Chicago: Library Dept of Photographic Reproduction, U of Chicago, [1954?].

ii, 91 *l* includes bibliography. Microfilm of typescript.   (CHx)

2390. Lipkowski, Kristin. "An abbreviated guide to Columbian guide books." Library science 301, Dr. Krummel. Fall, 1979.

28x21½. viii, (1) p., 24 *l.* Bibliography, leaf viii.   (CHx)

2391. Luckhurst, Kenneth W. *The Story of Exhibitions.* London & New York: The Studio Publications, 1951.

25½x16. 221, (3) p. index, b/w illus. Gray hc with gold print. WCE information is scattered from p. 143 to 221.   ☺ (KU)

2392. Marshall, W[illiam] L[ouis], comp. *Notes on Talcott's method of determining terrestrial latitudes, including Horrebow's claim thereto, in connection with Engineer department exhibit, World's Columbian exposition, 1893.* [Richmond?: 1919].

24x__. 61 p., illus, 4 plates, 2 ports (including frontis). C.t.: "The Talcott method of determining latitude, originated by Capt. Andrew Talcott ... and the zenith telescope developed by him." LMi: "Marshall's compilation apparently a reprint of the notes published in 1893." (LMi,UMi,NYSt)

2393. Mazzola, Sandy Raymond. *When music is labor : Chicago bands and orchestras and the origins of the Chicago Federation of Musicians, 1889-1902.* PhD diss. Northern Illinois U, 1984; Ann Arbor, MI: UMI, 1984.

(5), 362 *l* include bibliography. Microfilm of typescript. (CHx)

2394. McCullough, Edo. *World's fair midways : An Affectionate Account of American Amusement Areas : from the crystal palace to the crystal ball.* [1st ed.] New York: Exposition Press, [°1966 by Carnivaland Enterprises, Inc.].

21½x14. 190 p., illus. Red, black, and white dust jacket over red cloth hc, gilt print. Chapter III on WCE. ☻. (CHx)

2395. McGlothlin, Chris A. *World's fair spoons : volume 1 : The World's Columbian Exposition.* Tallahassee: Florida Rare Coin Galleries, Inc., [°1985].

31x24. ix, 170 p., glossy paper. Excellent b/w illus. Dust jacket over red leatherette hc, gold print. 334 spoons listed as well as variants. Color frontis of enamel spoon. Chapter 3 is history of the WCE.
P→ ☻. (GLD,csuf,R,CHx,E,L)

2396. Meites, Hyman L., ed. *History of the Jews of Chicago.* Member's Numbered Ed. Chicago: Jewish Historical Society of Illinois, °1924.

30½x23. xxxiv, (35)-854. Gilt edges. Chap. 8 concerns Jewish presence at the WF; other articles throughout. (CHx)

2397. Monroe, Harriet. *The difference, and other poems (including the Columbian ode).* 1st ed. Chicago: Covici-McGee co., 1924.

19x__. 5 *l*, 123 p., ports. Poem. (CPL,UoC)

2398. Monroe, Harriet. *Harlow Niles Higinbotham : a memoir : with Brief Autobiography and Extracts from Speeches and Letters.* Chicago: n.p., 1920.

24½x18½. 5 *l*, 9-59 p. Sepia tone frontis port of Higinbotham. Dark gray paper covered boards, tan cloth spine, gilt print cover and spine. Pages are of heavy rag stock; ragged edges. ☻. (CHx)

2399. Moore, Charles. *Daniel H. Burnham: Architect, Planner of Cities.* 2 vols. Boston and New York: Houghton Mifflin Co., 1921; rpt. New York: Da Capo Press, 1968.

1921: 28½x20. Vol I: (i-vii), viii-xviii, 1 *l*, (1)-260 p.; Vol II: (i-v), vi-ix, (1)-238 p., 1 *l*. Dark green cloth hc, gilt print and design front cover and spine. C.t.: "Daniel H. Burnham." Frontis of Vol I: color photo of Burnham with tissue guard. Frontis of Vol II: b/w photo of Burnham. Burnham was Chicago architect whose leadership and promotion of WCE was indefatigable.   (CHx)

2400. Morrison, Hugh. *Louis Sullivan, prophet of modern architecture.* New York: Peter Smith, 1952.

23½x16. 4 *l*, vii-xxi, 23-391 p. Burnt orange cloth hc, black print on spine. Frontis of Sullivan. WCE scattered p. 133 to 206. Sullivan was architect of the Transportation Bldg.   (CHx)

2401. Neufeld, Maurice F[rank]. "The Contribution of the World's Columbian Exposition of 1893 to the idea of a planned society in the United States : a study of administrative, financial, esthetic, sociological, and intellectual planning." PhD diss. U of Wisconsin-Madison, 1935.

28x21½. v, 442 *l*, 1 plate. Includes bibliography.   ☺ (UMC,csuf,CHx)

2402. Olson, Frederick I., and Virginia A. Palmer. *A guide to Wisconsin survivals from Chicago's Columbian Exposition of 1893.* [Milwaukee, WI: F. I. Olson and V. A. Palmer, 198_].

28x21½. 23 *l*. Typescript. Caption title. List and description of WCE artifacts found in Wisconsin. Written before Chicago gave up the 1992 fair.
---- Appended photos of the items.--(A)
     ☺ . (A,WiHx)

2403. Otis, Philo Adams. *The Chicago Symphony Orchestra: Its Organization Growth and Development.* Chicago: Clayton F Summy Co. Publishers, °1924.

24½x17½. 1 *l*, 466 p. Dark blue cloth hc, gold print. C.t.= t.p. Dedicated to memory of Theodore Thomas; describes the music halls and programs at the WF.   (CHx)

2404. Pace, Barney. *An experimental novel about the Columbian exposition of 1893 : The fame and fortune of Jimmie Dawson.* PhD diss. U of Michigan, 1982 °1982. Ann Arbor: UMI, 1982. 8215062.

22x17. 1 *l*, xix, 326 *l* include bibliography. Microfilm of typescript. A study of America's Gilded Age with a focus on the era's centerpiece, the WCE. The author's research taught him the tenacity of the American rags to riches dream in the face of the contradictory reality of America sliding into the depression of 1893.
---- Also listed: 349 p.
     ☺ . (CPL,CHx,LMi,UMi)

2405. Packer, E. E. *The White City : Being an Account of a Trip to the World's Columbian Exposition at Chicago in 1893.* San Diego: ____, 1933.

2406. Paper Mountain. *Columbian Exposition : Costumers' designs for procession of the centuries.* [Platteville, WI: n.p., 1977].

28x22. 13 typewritten *l*. CHx list no. 43. Describes float contract and plans which were abandoned prior to WCE Dedication Day.   (CHx)

2407. Peterson, Harold F. *Diplomat of the Americas : a biography of William I. Buchanan (1852-1909).* Albany: State University of New York Press, 1977.

24x__. 458 p., illus, ports. Partial contents: Homage to America's discoverer, Chicago, 1890-1894, p. 46-72.   (CHx)

2408. Peterson, Jon Alvah. "The origins of the comprehensive city planning ideal in the United States, 1840-1911." PhD diss. Harvard U, 1967; Harvard U Library, Microreproduction Dept., [1967?].

(1), 5, ii-xii, 472 *l.* Includes bibliography.   (CHx)

2409. Pockrandt, Florence D. "Lotus ware: A ceramic product of the nineties. (A problem in museum education)..." MA diss. [Columbus]: Ohio State U, 1942.

54 p., typewritten. The materials collected and used in the writing of this thesis are deposited in OhHx library vault.   (OhHx)

2410. *Poetisas Mexicanas: Siglos XVI, XVII, XVIII y XIX.* Edición facsimilar. [Rpt]. México: Universidad Nacional Autónoma de México, 1977.

22½x14½. lxxviii, 1 *l*, xxxiii, 362 p., 1 *l.* Multicolor litho stiff wraps. On t.p.: "Estudio preliminar: Ana Elena Díaz Alejo y Ernesto Prado Velázquez." Preface of original book is by José María Vigil. This analyzes the original publication which is appended in the back in its entirety. For original publication see #592. ☺. (LC)

2411. Press Veterans of '93. *The day's doing of the Press Veterans of '93 as guests of A Century of Progress, August 12, 1933.* [Chicago: 1933].

23x__. (16) p., illus. Who's who: p. (9)-(15).   (CHx)

2412. Press Veterans of '93. [Miscellaneous pamphlets]. N.p.: n.p., n.d.

27x20½. Typed mss of Aug. 12, 1933. The members of the press who covered the 1893 Fair met in Chicago for the 1933 Fair (40th anniversary). Banquet has cable from Pres. F. D. Roosevelt stating he had been at the WCE at the age of 11.--(CHx call: qF38SP P85z). [These 30 and 40 year reunions and displays attest to the strong influence the WCE 1893 Fair had on Chicago and people.]   (CHx)

2413. *The Quest for Unity : American Art Between World's Fairs, 1876-1893.* [Detroit, MI]: The Detroit Institute of Arts, 1983 [°1983 by Founders Society Detroit Institute of Arts].

30x23. 286 p. includes 20 p. of plates, illus (some color), ports. Frontis plate depicts Louis Comfort Tiffany, Pedcock Mosaic. Gray wraps, black lettering, Whistler color illus in gray and green. Published in conjunction with the exhibition organized by the Detroit Institute of Arts, Aug. 22 - Oct. 30, 1983. ☺. (nwu,RPB,AIC)

2414. *Rand McNally & Company's souvenir Guide to Chicago : a compendium of reliable information for shoppers and sightseers desiring to visit the stores and manufacturing districts, and the points of special interest in the city and its immediate suburbs.* Chicago [and] New York: Rand McNally & co., [ᶜ1912 by Rand, McNally & Co.].

21½x15. Red cloth cover with white print. WCE text and photos published at this late date -- 1912. Coincident with the 20th anniversary of the WCE. ? ☻ . (UoC)

2415. Rasmussen, Rasmus Elias. *Viking : from Norway to America.* Trans. Helen Fletre. Ed. Rolf H. Erickson ... [et al]. Chicago: Treptow & Johnson, 1984.

28½x22. 95 p. Black cloth hc, gilt print. Translation of *"Viking" fra Norge til Amerika.* Bergen: 1894. Rasmussen was a crew member on Andersen's "Viking." For more on the Viking, see #622, #1024, #1542, and #2313. ☻ . (CHx)

2416. Roesch, Roberta Fleming. *World's Fairs : Yesterday, Today, Tomorrow.* New York: John Day Co., [ᶜ1962].

21x16. 96 p. Gold hc with black print, b/w design (library binding), dust jacket in black, peach, and yellow. Book for young people. Describes world's fairs including the WCE. (UNM,CPL,CHx,SDHx)

2417. Ross, Ishbel. *Silhouette in diamonds : The Life of Mrs. Potter Palmer : illustrated.* New York: Harper & Brothers, publishers, [ᶜ1960 by Ishbel Ross].

22x15. xi, 276 p. Rust hc, gilt print spine and logo lower right front cover. WCE p. 82-99. ☻ . (A)

2418. Rossen, Howard M., and John M. Kaduck. *Columbian World's Fair Collectibles : Chicago (1892-1893).* Des Moines, IA: Wallace-Holmestead Book Co., [ᶜ1976 by Howard M. Rossen and John M. Kaduck].

28x21½. xi, 149 p. Cover illus, stiff wraps. (GLD) copy signed by Kaduck; (A) copy signed by Rossen. A standard color illus price guide of WCE collectibles of all types including a few books.
* ☻ . (GLD,csuf,CHx,E,A,AIC,L)

2419. Rydell, Robert William II. *All the world's a fair : America's international expositions, 1876-1916.* PhD diss. U of California - Los Angeles, 1980; Ann Arbor, MI: UMI, 1980.

xi, 505 *l.* Includes vita and bibliography. (CHx)

2420. Rydell, Robert W[illiam II]. *All the World's a Fair : Visions of Empire at American International Expositions, 1876-1916.* Chicago: The U of Chicago Press, 1984; Chicago: The U of Chicago Press, 1987.

Hardbound: 1984. 23½x16. x, 328 p. Blue cloth hc, red lettering on spine. Bibliography of new and old books of U.S. Fairs; hypothesizes racist underpinnings at U.S. World's Fairs.
---- Softbound: 1987. 23x15. x, 328 p. Colored illus glossy wraps.
☻ (GLD,CHx,BCM)

2421. Saint-Gaudens, Homer, ed. *The Reminiscences of Augustus Saint-Gaudens.* 2 vol. New York: The Century Co., 1913.

23x16. Vol 1: 393 p. Vol 2: 381 p. Beige cloth hc, olive green spine, gold embossed lettering. Details of life of Augustus Saint-Gaudens who was the chief sculptor at the Fair and designer of the award medal. Details of award medal design.   (F)   2 volume set: $125 - 175

2422. Scudder, Janet. *Modeling my life, ... with illustrations from photographs.* New York: Harcourt, Brace and co., °1925.

22½x15. 4 *l*, vii-viii, 297 p., frontis port of Scudder. Dusty blue cloth hc, gold design, bold black print on covers and spine. Art work for WCE bldgs under the direction of Burnham.   (CHx)

2423. Seager, Richard Hughes. *The World's Parliament of Religions, Chicago, Illinois, 1893 : America's religious coming of age.* PhD diss. Harvard U, 1986 °1986; Ann Arbor, MI: UMI, 1987.

vi, 286 *l* includes abstract, bibliography at (278)-86. Microfilm of typescript.   (CHx)

2424. Shaw, Marian. *World's Fair Notes.* St. Paul, MN: Pogo Press, Inc., [to be published and copyrighted by Pogo Press in 1992].

25x18. Manuscript with *Argus* magazine articles; manuscript written in 1893 and not previously published. Shaw was a teacher in the Minnesota school system. She wrote 20 articles describing various bldgs and exhibits during her stay at the Fair.   (H)

2425. Shaw, William Provan. "The World's Columbian Exposition: its revelations and influences." MA diss. Clark U, 1935.

184 *l*.   (csuf)

2426. Shepard, George Brooks, ed. *Untrodden fields in history and literature : and other essays by Franklin Harvey Head.* 2 vol. Cleveland: The Rowfant Club, 1923 [°1923 by the Rowfant Club].

20½x15. Vol 1 makes no reference to the WCE. Vol 2: 6 *l*, (15)-270 p., Chicago and WCE are scattered from 15-74. Coincident with 30th anniversary activities. Brown hc (heavy cardboard), cloth spines with gilt print, gilt top edge, boxed in slip-in brown cloth hc boxes. CHx copy states: "One hundred fifty and fifteen copies, of which this number thirteenth of the fifteen printed for the Head family and for special distribution."
---- 2 vol. Same size and paging. Non presentation hc, fine quality.
        ☻ . (CHx)

2427. Siegal, Arthur S. *Chicago's Famous Buildings; a photographic guide to the city's architectural landmarks and other notable buildings.* 2nd ed. Chicago: The U of Chicago Press, 1969.

This is one of a large number of Chicago architecture books which contains pictures and accounts of the WF bldgs.   (UNM)

2428. Simkin, Colin. *Fairs : Past & Present.* Hartford: n.p., n.d. [copyright by The Travelers].

35½x28. 3-30, (1) p. ad which is the inside back wrap. Includes some WCE photos and text. Probably issued around the time of the NY 1939 World's Fair.   (NL)

2429. Sparks, George R[obert]. *The Dream City : A story of the World's fair.* Chicago: n.p., 1923.

> 16x12½. 5 *l*, 121 p., frontis of "The Wonderful MacMonnies Fountain," plates. Blue cloth hc. T.p. states the original dust jacket was designed by J. Allen St. John. Illus from photos loaned by CHx. For children. Publication coincided with 30th anniversary events.   ⊚ (LC,CHx,NYPL,F,HL,nwu,L)

2430. Spear, Allan H. *Black Chicago : the making of a Negro ghetto.* Chicago & London: The U of Chicago Press, [°1967].

> 23x15. Brief description of Colored American Day at the WCE and Black speaker Fannie Barrier Williams at the Congress of Representative Women.   (CHx)

2431. Spillman, Jane Shadel. *Glass from World's fairs : 1851-1904.* Corning, NY: The Corning Museum of Glass, 1986 [°1986 by The Corning Museum of Glass].

> 23½x21. 59 p., illus (some color). Glossy paper color illus hc. Bibliography p. 55-56.   ⊚ . (CHx,A,TD)

2432. Swift, Harold H[iggins]. ... *The World's Columbian Exposition and the University of Chicago : Radio Talks by Harold H. Swift and Nathaniel Butler : Broadcasted by the Daily News Station, Hotel LaSalle : Chicago, October 2 and 3, 1923.* [Chicago: U of Chicago Press], 1923.

> 23x15. 11, (1) p. White wrap printed in black. C.t. At head of title: "The University of Chicago." Coincident with the 30th anniversary festivities.   ⊚ . (OSU,OC)

2433. Tallmadge, Thomas Eddy. *The Story of architecture in America.* New enlarged and rev. ed. New York: W. W. Norton & co., inc., [°1936].

> 22½x__. xi p., 1 *l*, 332 p., frontis, illus (plans), plates. "The World's Fair, 1893," p. 195-213.   (CHx)

2434. Taylor, Earl R., comp. *A Checklist of the Robert A. Feer collection of world fairs of North America.* Boston: Boston Public Library, 1976 °1976 by the Trustees of the Public Library of the City of Boston.

> 28x21½. 2 *l*, iv, 107 p. Tan wraps, black print and illus. A bibliography of WF holdings which includes the WCE a p. 23-40.   (BPL)

2435. Thompson, Mildred I. *Ida B. Wells-Barnett : An Exploratory Study of an American Black Woman, 1893-1930.* Black Women in United States History (Series). Ed. Dorlene Hines. Brooklyn: Carlson Publishing Inc., 1990.

> 23½x16. xiv, 1 *l*, 289 p., 17 p. Red cloth hc, red end papers, black and white design and print. Well's pamphlet *The Reason Why the Colored American is Not in the World's Fair* (#1053) was distributed at the Haiti Pavilion where Frederick Douglass was in charge. August 25, 1893, was "Colored American Day" at the WCE.   (CHx)

2436. Tozer, Lowell. *American attitudes toward machine technology, 1893-1933.* PhD Diss. U of Minnesota. 1953. Ann Arbor, MI: UMI, 1988.

> 22½x14½. xv, 1 *l*, 261 p.   ⊚ (csuf,PU)

2437. Treseder, Mable L. *A visitor's trip to Chicago in 1893.* Ed. for publication by Sheldon T. Gardner. N.p.: n.p., 1943.

> 29x23. 2-32 p. Orange 3-hole binder with title typed on front white label. Typewritten mss. Mable Treseder married Harry L. Gardner; Sheldon was their ?son. She died in 1934. This manuscript was handwritten when Mable was 18 years old; it describes the WCE as seen through her eyes.--(CHx call: qF38H T72 1893).   ⊚ (CHx)

2438. Upton, George P., ed. *Theodore Thomas, a musical autobiography.* 2 vol. Chicago: A. C. McClurg & Co., 1905.

> 23½x15½. Vol I: 2 *l*, 327 p. Vol II: 2 *l*, 327 p. Dark brown cloth hc, gold and black print, gilt top edge.   (CPL)

2439. Vignocchi, Bernice Elizabeth Gallagher. *Fair to look upon: An analysis and annotated bibliography of Illinois women's fiction at the 1893 World's Columbian Exposition in Chicago.* 2 vol. PhD diss. Northwestern U, 1990. Ann Arbor: UMI, 1990. 9032008.

> 21x16½. vii, 511 p.   ⊚ . (CPL)

2440. Waters, H. M. *A History of Fairs & Expositions.* London: Reid Bros., 1939.

2441. Weimann, Jeanne Madeline. *The Fair Women.* [Chicago]: Academy Chicago, [ᶜ1981 by Jeanne Madeline Weimann].

> 24x20½. ix, 611 p., illus. Blue cloth hc, gilt print spine. 2 period women by the Woman's Bldg are depicted on the dust jacket. Detailed account of the struggle, controversy, setbacks, and triumphs that produced the Woman's Bldg and its exhibits. Led by Mrs. Potter Palmer, such notable women as Mary Cassatt, Susan B. Anthony, and Julia Ward were involved.
> ---- 25½x20½. Wraps with same illus as dust jacket above.
> ---- Issues with errors in paging.
> ⊚ . (UND,UMKC,UMC,csuf,BCM,nwu,UNR,USD,ncsu,SLP,CoU,NHSt,TU,UMi,LSU,UoC,A,RPB,AIC,BM,OC,WiHx,TD)

2442. *The Woman's Building Chicago 1893 : the Woman's Building Los Angeles 1973.*   ____: A Women's Community Press edition, ᶜ1975 by Maria Karras.

> 27x21. (14) p. B/w photo montage on front wrap, black lettering and brown lettering. Text and photos from 1973 fair are in black; text and photos from WCE are in brown.   ⊚ . (nwu)

2443. *The World's Columbian Exposition: Centennial Bibliographic Guide.* Greenwood Series. Westport, CT: Greenwood Publishing Co., to be published 1992.

> 23x15½. ca. 450 p. A part of the Greenwood Series: Bibliographies and indexes in American History. Compiled by D. J. Bertuca, et. al., University of Buffalo, Buffalo, NY.

2444. Ziff, Larzer. *The American 1890s: The Life & Times of a Lost Generation.* New York: Viking Press, 1966.

Chapter 15

UNPUBLISHED UNIQUE WORKS

Although our intention in writing this book is to describe published works as completely as possible, we found many personal and unique items. What follows is an eclectic sample of works and collections available to the student and researcher. Similar items are occasionally available for sale and tend to be expensive because of their uniqueness.

With minor exceptions, this chapter is not indexed.
Organized alphabetically by source locator.

2445.　DIARIES:

a.　GLD: 1) Chase, Mary E. Diary: May 11-31, 1893. 8½x15. (79) of (92) p. with text. Brown pebbled leather flexible covers. An account of visits to numerous WCE bldgs prior to opening of the WF; many reported unfinished.　$50 - 100
2) Fogels, Tilghman. *Excelsior Diary.* 9½x6½. ca. (400) p. Red flexible leather cover , marbled edges. Back cover flap extension folds over the fore edge and slips into a slot in the front cover to hold the diary covers closed. Flap has a pencil pocket and pencil. First p. of diary section has original date crossed out (January, Friday 1, 1886) and "June 10, 1893" written in. Below date reads "Tilghman Fogels [Hecktown, PA] Exspence [sic] on Trip to Worlds [sic] Fair." This diary has many hand written pages describing bldgs visited, facts about the Fair that interested him, and expenses until June 14th: e.g., supper, 20¢, alavated [sic] 25¢.　$50 - 100

b.　IaHx: 1) Hinton, Eugene M. 1891-95 diary. Photocopy of p. 88-105 describing WCE exhibits and bldgs; illus booklet "Souvenir of the World's Columbian Exposition," admission tickets, etc.--(Clara Hinton Papers, Box 22, Folder 3); 2) Miller, Margaret Spragg. Hazelton, IA. Diary, 1880-95. Family went to the World's Fair in 1893. They may have had some kind of display; account is not clear.--(D 27).

c.　InHx: 1) Brooks, John and Jesse. Journal 1852-99, wherein he mentions details of a trip to the WCE.--(M316, BV 1777-9); 2) Churchman, Mrs. F. M. Diary of her trip to WCE, May and July, 1893. Description of IN Bldg, p. 8.--(M54, OM13); 3) Holloway, William R. 7 pages of notes about the WCE.--(M145, BV 1478-95, BV 1865-69, F227-9n).

d.　UMi: 1) Patterson, Frances Todd. 3 vol of diaries, 1892-94, including a record of participation in the WCE.--(Bentley Historical Library); 2) Peck, Edwin Spencer. Notebooks/diary 1891-1896. Notes on WCE.--(Bentley Historical Library).

e.　Yale: Douglass, Frederick. Diary, 1886-94. [Douglas was a commissioner in charge of WCE exhibits.]--(Frederick Douglass Papers. Microfilm. Manuscripts and Archives).

2446.　MISCELLANEOUS

a.　AIC: 1) Bertha Honoré Palmer correspondence (1891-1899). 8 linear ft. Collection of letters to Palmer, Sara Hallowell and others concerning art for the WCE. Arranged by subject and correspondent's name.--(00.7); 2) Daniel H. Burnham Collection. 17 linear ft. Business and personal correspondence, photographs, scrapbooks, diaries, and memorabilia. The WCE is particularly well documented.--(724.81 B96L, 1985:3., 1989:18); 3) Peter J. Weber Collection. 1 linear ft. Largely photos; documents Weber's early architectural career with the WCE, then with Burnham; 4) C. D. Arnold's

WCE photographs. 3 linear ft., 4 oversize portfolios. 1029 platinum prints; 5) Copy book of letters concerning the WCE by the firm of McKim, Mead and White, Feb. 11, 1890 to Apr. 4, 1893. 30½x__. 500 sheets.--(224.81 M15c); 6) Architectural details of WCE bldgs. 27x__. 41 plates.--(725.91 C53Wa); 7) The jubilee banquet, Oct. 11, 1893. 29½x__. Newspaper clippings mounted on 7 *l.*--(725.91 C53wj).

b.   CHx: 1) Ferris Wheel: Misc. pamphlets including carbon typescript subscriptions for bonds to re-erect the wheel at a permanent site; complementary tickets, press pass, press release; typescript statement of receipts week by week; 9 p. legal size typescript story of Ferris from the time the wheel idea originated through the results; 4 p. report of weights of material furnished by Detroit Bridge & Iron Works; 2) Children's Bldg: "Applications for Exhibits and Concessions." 36x22. 153 p. ledger book with handwritten record of applications. Cover is half red leather over black cloth hc. In gilt: "Children's building. World's Columbian exposition."--(qF38MZ W1893 H1C); 3) Engineering: "Report of the Electrical Engineering Department of the World's Columbian Exposition." 33x21. 3 cm thick carbon typescript hinged at 21 cm edge. Half leather over maroon cloth hc, gilt print. Includes early schemes and problems encountered.--(qF38MZ 1893 D3E5); 4) World's Fair Anniversary Exhibit (1923).--(qF38MZ W1923 P1T folio).

c.   CSA: California World's Fair Commission: payroll 1891-94; requisition book, 1892; alphabetical register of visitors; register of visitors; Ledger (expenditures) 1891-93; Disbursement Ledger, 1891-94. Handwritten, unpublished minutes of the CA World's Fair Commission, 1891-94 and the Education Committee, 1891.

d.   csuf: California. "List of applicants for California World's Fair Commission, Chicago 1893." 26½x20½. 152 p. black half leather over black cloth hc of which 108 p. contain a list of applicants with comments regarding job desired, references, etc. Applicants were signing up at the WCE CA Bldg for work at the CA mid-winter fair.

e.   CU: Miscellaneous grouping. Syracuse, NY, WCE commissioners' minute and letter books; correspondence. *The Morning Advertiser's Souvenir of the World's Fair* photograph album published by Rand McNally, Chicago & New York, 1893, and *World's Fair art portfolio*, 1894.

f.   CVHx: Souvenirs, photos, certificates, clippings, articles, and memorabilia surrounding George W. G. Ferris and the Ferris Wheel.--(CVHx no. 5-G-62 to -74, 136-G-47 to 51, 137-H-402, 195-G-36.

g.   DelHx: List of WCE prizes won by Delawareans; print of award presented to the State of Delaware for its colonial exhibit.--(Print Collection, Oversize 2.4).

h.   DelHx: Charles T. R. Bates, memorabilia from his service as a WCE guide; WCE newspaper articles he wrote.--(Bates collection).

i.   FSA: Files of Governors Fleming and Mitchell. Correspondence, majority relating to the WCE.

j.   GLD: 1) Clem Studebaker's signed Indiana WCE papers; 2) Cabinet photos.

k.   GPL: Files.--(Ephemera file: G. W. G. Ferris; Ephemera file: Ferris Wheel).

l.   HL: File containing tickets, souvenir postal cards, 2 booklets illustrating bldgs, programs, clippings, promotional items.

m.   IaHx: WCE records (correspondence, reports, vouchers, etc) from offices of the Governor, Secretary of State, Auditor, Treasurer, and Executive Council.--(Archives Collection - Des Moines).

n.   IdHx: 1) Folders of material on the WCE in the papers of Governors Norman B. Willey (AR 2/2) and William McConnell--(AR 2/3); 2) Collection of Calvin C. Clawson, assistant commissioner from Idaho, and Czarina Fuller Llewellyn Clawson, assistant commissioner from Blain County.--(MS 165); 3) Cornerstone contents from the Columbian Club: Boise Womens' Association Bldg. The Club, founded in 1892, was commissioned by Governor Willey to help prepare the state for the WCE.--(MS 356); 4) Invoices submitted for payment by James M. Wells, Columbian Commission, for work and materials for the ID Bldg.--(AR 55x).

o.   InHx: 1) Meredith, Virginia C. Letter to Frances M. Goodwin,with a diploma of honorable mention.--(Frances M. and Helen M. Goodwin Collection -- M332); 2) Papers as Chairman, Committee on Awards.--(Meredith, Solomon Papers -- M203, F589-91n); 3) Appointment to Board of Lady Managers, April 25, 1890.--(OM222).

p.   InHx: 1) Benjamin Harrison correspondence with George F. Lasher.--(Harrison Papers -- M132); 2) Correspondence regarding Samantha West Miller's attempt to get appointed to Jury of Awards, 1891-92.--(Elizabeth Jane Miller Hack Collection -- M123, OM29, BV 1369-71); 3) Letter of B. F. Havens, executive commissioner, to S. M. Reynolds.--(Stephen Marion Reynolds Papers -- M235).

q.   KsHx: 1) "Kansas educational exhibit at the Columbian exposition, 1893." File containing pamphlets, letters. 2) Preparations for the Exposition. (National Fairs Clipping Volume, Number 1).

r.   KU: Louis Singleton Curtiss, architect who designed the MO Bldg at the WCE. A collection of items mentioning Curtiss and his bldgs -- theses, newspapers, booklets, books.--(Spencer Research Kansas Collection: RH MS 35).

s.   LaMus: Invitation, ticket to dedication ceremonies; ribbons awarded, etc.--(Record Group 68 - not completely catalogued).

t.   MaHx: "Tickets, cards, circulars from the Columbian Exhibition, Chicago, 1893 ..." 30½x__. 245 p.

u.   MPA: File of contracts with companies constructing the building for the Manitoba exhibit, and letters.

v.   MPL: "Christopher Columbus" whaleback. Ship information and data record.--(The Herman G. Runge Collection).

w.   NAC: Extensive files of Canadian exhibit correspondence, letter books, photographs and advertising. 1) General correspondence. 168 p. (includes #336).--(RG 72, vol 105); 2) Canadian Pavilion. 285 p.

Correspondence from April 1893, through 1894 regarding the dismantling and disposal of the pavilion.--(RG 72, vol 76).

x. NeHx: 1) Collection consisting of archival material arranged as WCE printed matter (exhibits, awards), and guest registers.--(RG41); 2) Manuscript Record: John Gregory Bourke correspondence, etc. Bourke was on special duty as translator and interpreter at the Spanish mission of La Rabida.--(MS28); 3) "Catalogue of Nebraska Exhibits at the World's Columbian Exposition." 28x20½. 41 p. Typescript. Also, "List of Awards for Nebraska." 26½x19. 45 p. Handwritten; facsimile of John Boyd Thacher signature.--(RG 41 Box 1 F.1).

y. NHSt: 1) Certificates of awards to New Hampshire.--(FVT 606 P3nh); 2) Register book (4 vol): Sons and daughters of New Hampshire.--(BVT 929.4 W929).

z. NL: 1) Ackerman, William K. (WCE Auditor). Typewritten carbon copy of auditor's report to Nov. 12, 1893 and statement of collections. Cover letter addressed to H. N. Higinbotham. 32x20½. 21 p. + 9 p. concession receipts. Gift of Ackerman to NL.--(R1832.0057); 2) Architectural quality lithos (11) of side views of major bldgs, also grounds, mounted on linen sheets.--(W3725.16); 3) Board of Lady Managers. a) Pamphlets: "Statistics on Woman's work in the States" (broadside); call by Industrial Dept supt, Helen M. Barker, for States to send their statistics (1) p.; call for list, aims, etc. of organizations for inclusion in an encyclopedia (1) p.; "Exhibits by women. How They Will Be Installed, Etc." 8 p.--(R1832.018). b) "Lady Managers Circulars." Single sheet stationery and notices.--(fR1832.013); 4) Illinois Woman's Exposition Board Register. 43x__. 1002 p.--(MS R1832.4312); 5) Phelan Bibliography. "Catalogue of World's fair publications, procured by Mr. Phelan." 30x20½. 6 p. typescript on tracing tissue. Short title bibliography of WCE items purchased for CPL.--(R1832.15).

aa. OC: A vol containing John Henry Barrows "Parliament of religions at the World's fair" rpt., also contains: general programs, letters written to Dr. Boardman, and newspaper clippings.--(091.2 B279). Large collection of the writings, lectures, etc. of John Henry Barrows, who became president of Oberlin College.

ab. OhHx: Pamphlets on WFs including Chicago, 1893.--(PA Box 9,9a; 2) Also WCE microfilm.--(reel 842 of the Washington Gladden Collection).

ac. PI: Visitor books record group, 1888-1896.

ad. PU: 1) "Visitors to the exhibit of the College of New Jersey, World's Columbian Exposition, Chicago, 1893." Guest book.--(P03.73 .12f); 2) "Princeton U Alumni Register, World's Columbian Exposition, Chicago, 1893."--(P03.73 .13f).

ae. RPB: Brown University. Registry book for visitors to the Brown University exhibit at the World's fair, Chicago, 1893.--(1-E-B81W0).

af. SDHx: Correspondence between San Diego commissioners.

ag. SDSHx: 1) South Dakota state bldg Visitors' Register.--weighing several hundred pounds; 2x3 feet or larger. Made by Brown & Saenger Co. of Sioux Falls and illustrated in plate 24 of *South Dakota at the ...* (see #2074).--(K.928); 2) A miniature reproduction of the register measuring 1x2 inches, blank inside, made by Eugene Saenger in 1892.--(1982.059).

ah. SFe (New Mexico): 1) "Executive Commissioner's Final Report. To The World's Columbian Managera. [sic] of New Mexico." 34½x20½. 23 *l* carbon copy of typed legal sized manuscript. Signed by "T. B. Mills, Ex[ecutive] Com[missioner]" who was in charge of collection and arrangement for the NM exhibit; salary $150/month and necessary expenses. This Report details the individual exhibits, contributors, county of origin, etc.; 2) Correspondence, financial accounts, check book receipt stubs, and other unpublished items from the WCE.

ai. TD: WCE invitations, calling cards, tickets, philatelic items.

aj. UFl: WCE book articles; photos. (Manuscript collection box 86).

ak. UMi: 1) List of U Michigan exhibits at the WCE-- (Bentley Historical Library); 2) Correspondence of Raymond Cazallis Davis, Librarian of U Michigan, regarding the U Michigan exhibition of professors' books at the WCE; correspondence with George Davis.--(Bentley Historical Library).

al. USD: 1) "Bulletins, Circulars, etc., of the South Dakota Educational. World's Columbian Exposition, 1893." 35x__. 1 bound vol containing 38 numbered items: letters, handwritten inventories, typewritten Commission minutes and exhibit floor plans; 2) SD Educational exhibit, register for visitors. 36x__. 152 p. With comments; 3) 9 bound vol of USD student papers for educational exhibit at the WCE; 4) 22 bound vol of SD city school student papers for exhibit at the WF; 5) 12 bound vol of SD common school student papers for exhibit at the WF; 6) J. W. Mauck, USD president and superintendent of the SD educational exhibit: 3 post-WCE letters concerning purchase of the SD Bldg for use in reconstructing Old Main on the USD campus. (All located at Richardson Archives, I. D. Weeks Library). [Old Main currently (1992) stands unused at USD.]

am. UVa: Virginia. Letters, photographs listed under Stephens and Townsend.

an. UWy: Small WCE clipping file.--(American Heritage Center).

ao. VaHx: Register of Visitors to Virgina's Mount Vernon Bldg. May 15 - Sept. 29, 1893.--(Board of World's Fair Managers - Record Group 61).

ap. WaSt: Washington World's Fair Commission, Records: 1891-94. Correspondence, vouchers, ledgers, bills, receipts, court papers, documents, and minutes.

aq. WiHx: Wisconsin Board of World's Fair Manager's minutes and proceedings, treasurer's cash book, disbursement book, contracts let by the Board, specifications for contractors in building the WI Bldg, insurance policies on the bldg and contents, and a detailed listing of WI exhibits. 4 archives boxes, 2 vol.--(MAD 3/9/G6).

ar. WM: Over 200 ad, catalog, and descriptive booklets. Several under a single call number in general categories by topic and country; e.g., American agricultural machinery, 28 booklets.-- (T500 A2 A27).

as. Yale: WCE collection is part of Exhibition collection, 1867-1904.--(Exhibition collection. Manuscripts and Archives).

2447. SCRAPBOOKS:

Although not published, their unique and personal character in describing the WCE is special and can provide insights that published material does not. Because of this, they are some of the more expensive WF paper collectibles. The following are examples of the scrapbooks that may be found:

a. A: "Columbian Exposition 1893 : Cartoons." Cartoon and newspaper editorial page photos in a marble board scrapbook.

b. BPL: Photographs, a personal photographic album with family pictures and pictures of the Columbian Exposition.--(SCH.F893 (145f)).

c. CHx: 1) Harpel, Charles. "Scrapbook of newspaper clippings, etc., relating to Chicago and Illinois, compiled by Charles Harpel, during the World's fair, 1893." 23x16. ca. 501 p. of clippings glued into a published book (some pages clipped out to make room for added material), black cloth hc, marbled edges.--(F38A S4-2); 2) "History of the World's Columbian exposition: a scrapbook."--(qF38MZ W1893 S4H); 3) Kerfoot, John Barrett. "Scrapbooks on the World's Columbian Exposition of 1893." 35 vol, 5 boxes, 1 pkg.--(qF38MZ 1893 L1K5); 4) [Longley, W. E.]. "Scrapbook of pictorial views of the World's Columbian Exposition, 1893." [Oak Park, IL: 1893]. 38x__. 2 vol, illus.--(qF38MZ 1893 C1L6 folio); 5) Mulligan, Marian (Nugent). "Scrapbook of clippings, photographs, etc., relating to Col. James A. Mulligan and his family and their activities." 5 vol. 30-38 cm. Vols 4 and 5 have much material on the WCE. Compiled by Mrs. Mulligan and her grandson John C. Carroll, Jr.--(qF38DA M954); 6) Peabody, Selim Hobart. "Social invitations to Selim Hobart Peabody, chief of the department of Liberal Arts of the World's Columbian Exposition, Chicago, 1893." 2 vol. 29½x__. Leather hc, gilt decoration on covers and spine, gilt print on spine: "Record of Entomology Vol I (Vol II) Lepidoptera" (having nothing to do with the scrapbooks themselves). Peabody's collection of invitation to various functions including the individual State's dinners.--(CHx call ?); 7) "Picture cards distributed for advertising products displayed at the World's Columbian Exposition, 1893." ca. 36x28. 28 p., 30 sheets. Picture cards mounted on scrapbook pages. Loose scrapbook cardboard pages. Ad cards mounted one side.--(qF38MZ W1893 K1P); 8) Rice, Wallace de Groot. "Scrapbook of clippings of the Chicago Journal relating to Lincoln, World's Columbian, politics, education and professions." N.p.: n.p., n.d. 25x18. Black cloth spine, black paper covered loose leaf binder.--(F38T R37-7); 9) Roewade, Alfred Jensen. Scrapbook. 37x__. Scrapbook compiled by Roewade, an architect and civil engineer. Chiefly about the WCE, where Roewade worked in the Engineering Dept.--(qF38JR D2R7); 10) "A scrapbook."--(F38MZ W1893 L1S4); 11) "Scrapbook."--(qF38MZ W1893 S4A); 12) "Scrapbook of clippings on the World's Columbian exposition." 40x26½. Cloth spine with marbled boards intended for storing "Invoices" (spine).--(qF38MZ S4-7 folio); 13) "Scrapbook of clippings relating to fine arts exhibits of the World's Fair exposition."--(CHx call ?); 14) "Scrapbook of newspaper clippings on the conclusion, destruction, and final statistics of the World's Columbian Exposition, 1893." 52x42. Quarter leather and black textured cloth. Clippings from Chicago newspapers.--(qF38MZ 1893 L1S45 folio); 15) "Scrapbook of newspaper clippings on the World's Fair, compiled from newspapers dated 1893." 3 vol. 33½x43½. Illus, half leather with marbled boards. Spine reads "Chicago."--(1F38MZ 1893 B1); 16) "Sculptors of the World's fair." Clippings.--(F38MZ W1893 B9); 17) [Stuart, Albert C.], comp. "'93' we were there..." [Chicago: n.p., n.d.]. 30x22½. 34 hand numbered pages, 1 l, cover and pages of heavy stock. C.t.: "Association of 93'rs." A scrapbook of clippings, tickets, programs, etc. Albert Stuart's personal scrapbook.--(qF38MZ 1893 B1T2).

d. F: Hanson, John A. Bound scrapbook. 25½x18. 382 p. of clipping, articles, tickets, and handwritten entries. $175 - 300

e. GLD: 1) Lane, S. A. Photo-scrapbook. 18x23½ and 5 cm thick. 84 p. of heavy stock. 1st 12 p. have disbound and mounted Chisholm plates with hand printed captions. One mounted and captioned photo on each remaining page. Memo at back of book: "Mr. S. A. Lane had this Album made at the Beacon Bindery and he mounted and lettered the Photos, made by Mr. J. W. Bickwell of Oak Park Ill. and furnished by J. S. Lane." Black leather hc with gilt c.t.: "The white city." $200 - 400.
2) Scrapbook from Massachusetts. 38x30. 103 *l*, olive cloth thick hc. Professional quality assembly of materials including Columbus, Columbus Day 1892, WCE and destruction thereof. High quality assembly of various materials on the WCE from 1891 to 1897. $200 - 600

f. GPL: Scrapbook. Events regarding Galesburg, IL, including clippings related to George Washington Gale Ferris.--(Historical Events: Vol 1, Pt. 2).

g. HL: Scrapbook. 28½x22. Contains ports of employees of the Wellington Catering Company at the WCE, and daily gate pass booklets.--("Ephemera: Chicago's World Columbian Exposition, 1893").

h. InHx: Butler, Amos W. Scrapbook. Includes poem written by Mrs. S. S. Harrell (in *Madison Courier*) "Indiana in the World's Fair."--(M34).

i. KsHx: Humphrey, Adele Alice. "Attractions at the World's Fair: [the Kansas Bldg, etc.]."--(Biog. Scrapbook. H. v.14. p. 134-135).

j. NL: 1) DeLong, Heber. "Memories of the World's Columbian exposition, Chicago, 1893." 57x__. Contains numerous autographs.--(Case+R1832.222); 2) Walker, E. R. "World's Fair 1893 Album." 20½x25½ b/w photos (43) each mounted on heavy cardboard. 30½x27. Brown cloth hc album. Back of each page stamped: "E. R. Walker : Photographer : 195 Wabash Avenue : Chicago."--(R1832.951); 3) Wilson, George H. "Correspondence, clippings, pictures, etc., relating to the Bureau of Music." 35x57.--("Thomas 400").

k. NYPL: NYPL Janvier Collection. "Collection of pamphlets, badges and tickets, relating to the Chicago Exhibition of 1893." 8°. 14 pieces.--(VC(Chicago 1893) p.v.6, no.8a3).

l. PU: Scrap-book, 1893. Unpaged. 32x__. Souvenirs and programs of the WCE.--(Ex 9011.25 .25q).

m. S: 1) Audubon, Florence. 28½x23. Prints of the U.S. and photos of the WF ($25); 2) "Columbian Souvenir." 43x36. 60 *l* with ad pieces laid in both sides. Beautiful embossed bust of Columbus on cover. Carefully assembled.--(no. 6198) ($350); 3) Rice, Elizabeth. 23½x14½. Hc book with glued in newspaper accounts of WCE. 130 p.--(no. 4774) ($90); 4) Scrapbook. 32x26. 100 p. 1893. Newspaper article clippings about the WF.--(no. 3525) ($80).

n.   SI: 1) [*The Daily Inter Ocean*]. Chicago: Inter Ocean, 1891. Scrapbook of 208 leaves with clippings, some illus.--(RPI temp. reel 106, no. 8); 2) [Newspaper clippings]. Various publishers, 1893-94. 28 p. of newspaper clippings, some with illus.--(RPI temp. reel 112, No. 13).

o.   SStU: Grunendike, Edward Booth. Scrapbook (80) p. of WCE engravings, pictures, and other illus, inscribed to Ed and Ulamie Grunendike from Mary E. Haworth, 1903.--(Archives).

p.   UMi: Weston, Isaac M[ellen]. Scrapbook and papers concerning the Michigan exhibit at the WCE. Weston was president of the Michigan Board of World's Fair Managers.--(Bentley Historical Library).

q.   UoC: 1) [Sanders, Edgar], comp. ["World's Fair Clippings, Chicago, 1893."] Scrapbook. 37x__. Also other papers. [Sanders was a horticulturist].--(Crerar Library); 2) "Scrapbook on the World's Columbian exposition, Chicago, 1893."--(T500 f.LiS4); 3) *Standard*. "Clippings from the *Standard* on the World's Columbian exposition, Chicago, 1893." 19 p.--(?).

Chapter 16

BEFORE AND AFTER THE WCE

THE MADRID EXPOSITION OF 1892

The Madrid Exposition ran for three months starting in November 1892. Cooperation with Spain was shattered just five years after the Exposition during the short Spanish-American War of 1898. The Acting Commissioner-General for the Madrid Exposition was G. Brown Goode, who was also an important figure at the World's Columbian Exposition. The Columbus relics from Madrid were transported to the Columbian Exposition and housed in the replica of La Rabida. The following items are useful precursors to the World's Columbian Exposition.

2448. *Exposición Histórico-Americana de Madrid, Catálogo de la Sección de México.* 2 vol. Madrid: Est. Tip. "Sucesores de Rivadeneyra," 1892-1893.

Introduction by Francisco de Paso y Troncoso regarding the work of the Columbian Board of Mexico at the Madrid Exposition. (ref)

2449. *Exposición Histórico-Americana de Madrid para 1892. Sección de México. Catálogo de la colección del señor presbitero don Francisco Plancarte.* México: Imp. de Ignacio Escalante, 1892.

Written in collaboration with Francisco del Paso y Troncoso, director of the National Museum of Mexico. Mexico at the Madrid Exposition in late 1892. (ref)

2450. Galindo y Villa, Jesús. *Exposición Histórico-Americana de Madrid de 1892.* México: Imp. del Gobierno Federal en el ex-arzobispado, 1893.

Data relative to the section of the Republic, of the "Alzate" society at the Madrid Exposition. (ref)

2451. Hough, Walter. *The Columbian Historical exposition in Madrid.* N.p.: n.p., n.d.

24x15½. (271)-277 p. Tan wraps, black print. Rpt. on heavy stock from the *American Anthropologist*, July, 1893. Caption title. Signed by author.
      ⊛ (GLD) $16 - 32

2452. U.S. Commission to the Madrid Exposition. ... *Catálogo de los objetos expuestos por la Comisión de los Estados Unidos de América en la Exposición histórico-americana de Madrid, 1892.* Madrid: Est. tip. "Sucesores de Rivadeneyra," 1892.

24½x__. ix, 120, 48, 35, 13, 29, 10, (1) p., plan. At head of title: "Cuarto centenario del descubrimiento de América." Last p. incorrectly numbered 149. The "Inconografia colombina" (see #2455) has special t.p. (UC)

2453. U.S. Commission to the Madrid Exposition. *Commemoration of the fourth centenary of the discovery of America.* Washington, D.C.: Press of W. F. Roberts, [1892].

24x15. 22 p. Buff wraps with black print. Caption title. C.t. same and adds: "Madrid, 1892." The U.S. Commission from the Smithsonian Institution included George Brown Goode.

$15 - 30

2454. U.S. Commission to the Madrid Exposition. [Fewkes, Jesse Walter]. *Catálogo de los objetos etnológicos y arqueológicos exhibidos por la expedición Hemenway.* Madrid: Jaramillo, impresor, 1892. (UC)

2455. U.S. Commission to the Madrid Exposition. *Iconografia colombina. Catálogo de las salas de Colón.* Madrid: Est. tip. "Succesores de Rivadeneyra," 1892.

24½x__. 29 p. Found in #2452. (LC)

2456. U.S. Commission to the Madrid Exposition. *Report of the United States Commission to the Columbian Historical exposition at Madrid. 1892-93. With special papers.* Washington: GPO, 1895.

23x16. 411 p. Dark olive cloth hc, gold print spine. Numerous b/w illus, many plates which are not included in paging, 1 color litho with tissue guard between p. 330-31. Contains: "Message from the President of the United States, transmitting : The report, with accompanying papers, of the Commission of the United States for the Columbian Historical Exposition at Madrid in 1892 and 1893." William Eleroy Curtis' report starts at p. 215.
---- U.S. 53d Cong. 3d sess. House. Ex. doc. 100. 24½x15½. 411 p. Speckled gray wraps. C.t.= t.p.
☉ . (GLD,F,NYSt,UMi)

$35 - 65

2457. U.S. Commission to the Madrid Exposition. U.S. National Museum. ... *Catálogo de la colección arqueológica del Museo nacional de los Estados Unidos, por el profesor Thomas Wilson.* Madrid: Est. tip. "Sucesores de Rivadeneyra," 1892. (UC)

THE CALIFORNIA MID-WINTER EXPOSITION

An extension of the Columbian Exposition, the California Mid-Winter Exposition held in San Francisco's Golden Gate Park in early 1894 has post-WCE interest. Many people felt the World's Columbian Exposition (May 1 - Oct. 30, 1893) should have had a longer design life. The Mid-Winter Exposition did show the vigor and suitable year around climate of California.

THE PROPOSED CHICAGO WORLD'S FAIR OF 1992

Chicago won and relinquished the bid for the 1992 World's Fair which will now be held in Seville, Spain, Apr. 20 - Oct. 12, 1992. The following were early planning publications for a Chicago 1992 fair.

2458. *1992 World's Fair Forum papers.* Evanston, IL: Center for Urban Affairs and Policy Research, Northwestern U, 1984-[1986].

28x22. 7 vol. "... a series of papers, arranged thematically, that grew out of seven public forums presented by the Center for Urban Affairs and Policy Research in Chicago during 1984. The programs were developed with partial funding from the Illinois Humanities Council ..."-- Acknowledgments. (AIC)

Vol I: *Legacies from Chicago's World's fairs : a background for fair planning.* April, 1984.

28x22. 27, 20, 5, (52) p. Contents: Harris, Neil. "Great American Fairs and American Cities: The Role of Chicago's Columbian Exposition."-- 27 p. Smith, Carl S. "Insight and Irony: The Literary Heritage of the White City."-- 20 p. Condit, Carl. "The Century of Progress Exposition: An Outline of Its Contributions to the Building Arts."-- 5 p. ☺ . (nwu)

Vol IV: *Neighborhood development and citizen participation in Chicago's World's fairs.* February, 1895.

28x22. 10, 18, 14, 5 (comments) p. Contents: Binford, Henry C. "The 1893 World's Fair: A Force for Neighborhood Change."--10 p. Peterman, William A. "The World's Fair, Urban Development and Neighborhood Impacts."-- 18 p. Bernstein, Scott, and Kathryn Tholin. "Neighborhood Development and Citizen Participation: Reflections on the Proposed 1992 World's Fair."-- 14 p. ☺ . (nwu)

2459. Chicago. World's Fair Advisory Committee. *Executive summary : a report to Mayor Harold Washington.* Chicago: World's Fair Advisory Committee, 1983.

28x21½. 14 *l*. Blue wraps, black print. C.t. Marcus Alexis was chairman of the WF Advisory Committee.
---- Also contained in a bound vol, variously paged.
☺ (CHx)

☞ This summary and the following 4 items from the World's Fair Advisory Committee describe the debate whether Chicago should host the 1992 WF. Recommendations included Chicago not using any city money for the Fair and bear no financial liability, neighborhoods be on boards, equal opportunity for Chicagoans, and the Fair be environmentally sound. The decision was to not hold the Fair in Chicago.

2460. Chicago. World's Fair Advisory Committee. *World's Fair Advisory Committee : written material from hearing : Jones Commercial High School : October 1, 1983.* Chicago: World's Fair Advisory Committee, 1983.

28x__. ca. 130 *l* in various foliations, maps, plans. (CHx)

2461. Chicago. World's Fair Advisory Committee. *World's Fair Advisory Committee : written material from public hearing : Department of Human Services Center, 10 South Kedzie, October 5, 1983.* Chicago: World's Fair Advisory Committee, 1983.

28x__. ca. 170 *l* in various foliations, maps, plan. Includes written material submitted to the Committee in response to other public hearings. (CHx)

2462. Chicago. World's Fair Advisory Committee. *World's Fair Advisory Committee : written material from public hearing : Northeastern Illinois University : October 4, 1983.* Chicago: World's Fair Advisory Committee, 1983.

28x__. ca. 170 *l*. Includes written material from Oct. 4, 1983 hearing at the Illinois Institute of Technology. (CHx)

2463. Chicago. World's Fair Advisory Committee. *World's Fair Advisory Committee : written material from public hearings : Olive-Harvey College : October 11, 1983.* Chicago: World's Fair Advisory Committee, 1983.

28x__. ca. 125 *l* in various foliations, map, plans. Includes summaries of all six hearings.   (CHx)

2464. *Chicago World's Fair - 1992 Authority : for Transportation Element of 1992 World's Fair Plan : Revised June 1985.* Chicago: De Leuw, Cather & Co., [1985?].

28x21. Variously paged per the 3 chapters. White glossy stiff wraps with blue design and black print. Flow of traffic for the 1992 Chicago World's Fair.   ☉ . (UoC)

2465. Friends of the Parks (Chicago). *World's Fair alternate site configuration.* [Chicago]: The Friends, [1984].

28x__. 1 portfolio, illus, maps. Caption title. Accompanied by: 1992 World's Fair fact sheet (4 *l*), cover letter (1 *l*), press release (2 *l*), and maps (3 *l*). Includes 3 photos.   (CHx)

2466. McClory, Robert. *The Fall of the Fair : Communities Struggle for Fairness.* N.p.: Chicago Center for Neighborhood Technology for the Chicago 1992 Committee, 1986.

21½x13½. 46 p. Light yellow wraps printed in black. C.t.= t.p. Describes Chicago debating its bid for the 500th Columbian Anniversary from the International Bureau of Expositions (BIE). Chicago and Illinois ultimately rejected hosting the 1992 World's Columbian Fair.   ☉ (GLD)

2467. Nagro, C[ostagnole] F[ortunato]. *Columbian Odysseys : Linking the Old World With the New : historical edition for the commemoration of the 500th anniversary of the first voyage to the New World : a salute to the Chicago World's fair, 1992.* [Roselle, Ill.: Columbian Society], [°1984 by C. F. Nagro].

21x13½. 44 p. plus red tone illus of U.S. Capitol on inside back wrap. White wraps with red print and illus. Compilation of material relating to Columbus.   ☉ . (UoC)

Index

Titles and authors are intermixed and arranged alphabetically. There are at least two index entries for those books which have both title and author. Authors' names are complete. Titles are short but include at least the first unique word. Official authors: "WCA" (World's Congress Auxiliary), "WCC" (World's Columbian Commission), and "WCE" (World's Columbian Exposition) are given where this information is deemed helpful -- as are country names and state abbreviations.

Titles which begin with English or foreign definite articles are alphabetized by the word following this initial article; e.g., English "A, An, The"; French "L', La, Le, Les"; German "Die, Der, Das, Ein"; and Spanish "El, La." In this index accents over letters have no effect alphabetically.

Hyphenated words are alphabetized as though the hyphen is not present and the words are separate. Numbers in titles are entered as though the number is written out (e.g., 1893 is indexed under eighteen).

-A-

-O-

Memoranda

Memoranda